CURIOUS LAND

CURIOUS LAND

JESUIT ACCOMMODATION AND
THE ORIGINS OF SINOLOGY

D. E. MUNGELLO

UNIVERSITY OF HAWAII PRESS

HONOLULU

Paperback edition published by University of Hawaii Press
Printed in the United States of America

94 93 92 91 89   4 3 2 1

Curious Land: Jesuit Accommodation and the Origins of Sinology
was first published as Studia Leibnitiana, Supplementa 25 (1985)
by Fritz Steiner Verlag Wiesbaden GmbH

Library of Congress Cataloging-in-Publication Data

Mungello, David., E. 1943–
  Curious Land.

  Bibliography: p.
    Includes index.
    1. Jesuits—Missions—China—History—17th century.
  2. China—Study and teaching—Europe—History—17th
  century.   I. Title.
  [BV3417.M86   1989]   951'.007'04   88–27874
  ISBN 0–8248–1219–0 (pbk.)

TABLE OF CONTENTS

PLATES

TABLE

To the meaning of life

— my daughter Lisa Anne & son Michael Campbell

INTRODUCTION

The history of the seventeenth-century Jesuit mission in China is very much like a plant which developed from a common stem of aims into various branches. In this work I trace the development of one branch of that organic growth and its relationship to the early European study of China which I call "proto-sinology". I focus on the branch of the Jesuit mission which built on the foundations laid by Fr. Matteo Ricci and which developed and evolved in the works of Frs. Semedo, Magalhaes, Martini, Couplet and Bouvet. Because of the flexibility and empathy manifested toward China in this line of Jesuit missionary development, I refer to it as "accommodative" or as "Jesuit accommodation".

Although the fundamental aim of the Jesuit mission was directed at proselytizing and converting the Chinese to Christianity, the Jesuits' intellectual inclinations led them to work for this aim through the European dissemination of information about China in order to secure broad-based support for their missionary effort among European savants and princes. This dissemination combined with a high degree of interest among European savants in this "curious land" called China.

The blending of a vast range of interests with amateur boldness of investigation was so characteristic of seventeenth-century Europe that we find these attitudes reflected in a word which appeared throughout the literature of this time — "curious"[1]. For Europeans of that age, the word "curious" had little of

---

1 Recent scholarly work on the seventeenth-century meaning of the words *curiosus* and *curiositas* is limited and tends to emphasize the notion of *curiositas* (curiosity) in its broad historical and theological contexts rather than *curiosus* (curious) in its more specific application to serious works on China, as used in this study. On the difference between the ancient and modern meanings of the notion *curiositas* and on the theological objections to *curiositas* as voiced by St. Augustine, see Henri-Irénée Marrou, *Saint Augustin et la fin de la culture antique* (Paris, 1938) pp. 148–157, 277–280, 350–352 & 473f. On the evolution in meaning of *curiositas,* see André Labhardt, "Curiositas. Notes sur l'histoire d'un mot et d'une notion," in *Museum Helveticum* 17 (1969): 206–224. On the significance of the word to the travel literature of the seventeenth century and how the notion of *curiositas* absorbed changes in the intellectual climate to acquire a new and more important significance in the economic, theological and scholarly realms and how travel literature served to accommodate new discoveries with the knowledge of Antiquity, e.g. the geography of the Ancients, see Dieter Lohmeier, "Von Nutzbarkeit der frembden Reysen. Rechtfertigungen des Reisens in Zeitalter der Entdeckungen," in *Trier Beitrage* 1979, Sonderheft 3, pp. 3–8. On the seventeenth-century evolution of the meaning of *curieus* from an object of human

the sense of merely attention-arousing or prying associated with the word in twentieth-century usage. Rather, the word was used in a sense closer to the Latin adjective *curiosus* which referred to painstaking accuracy, attention to detail and skillful inquiry. For seventeenth-century savants, China was a remote land which demanded the most "curious" investigation in the sense of being detailed, skilled and accurate. This sense of "curious" is crucial to this study because it provides the historical link between the intellectually-minded Jesuit proponents of accommodation in China and the European proto-sinologists.

The history of the seventeenth-century Jesuit mission in China is insepa-rably connected to the early study of China in Europe or proto-sinology. Al-though the missionary preoccupation of the Jesuits distinguished them from these proto-sinologists, the Jesuits' work as the primary seventeenth-century disseminators and interpreters of information about China — its geography, language, government, philosophy, history and society — provided the intel-lectual foundations for those European savants who became proto-sinologists. The Jesuit missionaries to China often had direct and close contact with these savants — both while on return visits to Europe and through correspondence from China. These proto-sinologists are distinguished from later sinologists by their lesser degree of knowledge and focus in their study of China. Breadth of learning, so prized by seventeenth-century minds, fostered the inclusion of (sometimes exotic) interest in China within their range of interest without disrupting the non-sinological thrust of their work.

Whether Jesuit accommodation was wise from a missionary point of view can still be debated. But it is clear that the attempt to synthesize the two cul-tures led to a selective understanding of China which made the Jesuits the primary suppliers of information about China to Europe in the seventeenth century. There was a great deal of innate curiosity among Europeans about China and it was to the Jesuits' advantage to stimulate this curiosity and thereby foster support for the China Mission. Not surprisingly, the framework of the Jesuits' Confucian-Christian blending became the intellectual funnel through which most information from the Jesuits about China flowed. This framework influenced the selection of information which the Jesuits presented to Europe as well as their interpretation of it. There were other interpretations of this ma-terial made by a minority group of Jesuit dissenters as well as most of the non-Jesuit missionaries to China, but the impact of Jesuit accommodation was so influential in the seventeenth-century flow of information about China to

---

interest to a remarkable thing, especially in its political context, see Gotthardt Früh-sorge, "Exkurs: Curieus und curieuse Methode," in *Der politische Körper. Zum Begriff des Politischen im 17. Jahrhundert und in den Romanen Christian Weises* (Stuttgart, 1974) pp. 193–205. On the intellectual and historical development of *curiositas*, see Hans Blumenberg, *Der Prozeß der theoretischen Neugierde* (Frankfurt am Main, zweite Auflage, 1980).

Europe, that those with conflicting views were merely able to criticize and lacked the power to fully establish a competing interpretive framework of their own.

The term "accommodation" applies to the setting in China where Jesuit missionaries accommodated Western learning to the Chinese cultural scene and attempted to achieve the acceptance of Chinese literati through the Confucian-Christian synthesis. The term "proto-sinology" applies to Europe where the assimilation of knowledge about China took place. The flow of information about China to Europe took place primarily through the Jesuit channels of letters, official reports, personal visits and published works. This book emphasizes the latter category, though it also includes unpublished material. As this information reached Europe, it aroused enormous enthusiasm among certain circles of savants who were stimulated to publish a wide variety of proto-sinological works about the Chinese language and its culture. From this rich body of seventeenth-century European literature on China, I have chosen to concentrate on several of the most widely read and influential books published during that time. For the proto-sinological side of the movement of ideas from China to Europe, I have focused on certain important topics in the intellectual life of that century in Europe in which China played an important role. Although I am concerned with culture as a broad category, I give particular emphasis to the areas of history, language, philosophy and religion.

The works under consideration which were written by Jesuit missionaries were for the most part knowledgeable and based upon extended experience in China. By contrast, the proto-sinological works were written by European savants whose enthusiasm far exceeded their knowledge. The Confucian-Christian synthesis of the Jesuit father Ricci was based upon a profound accommodative insight into contemporary Chinese culture, while the Jesuit father Kircher's proto-sinological interpretation of the Chinese language and culture was based upon a superficial understanding of China which was subsumed to his monumental non-sinological research. The search of the German proto-sinologists Müller and Mentzel for a *Clavis Sinica* was founded on amateur enthusiasms, while the translation of the Confucian Classics by the China Jesuits in *Confucius Sinarum philosophus* was based upon a long and sustained effort of studying the Chinese classical language.

In spite of the differences in the intellectual depth of these works on China, each of them reflect the flow and assimilation of information about China to Europe by way of Jesuit accommodative channels. Once this information about China reached Europe, its assimilation tended to focus on those ideas which were of the greatest current importance and interest to Europeans. (Unlike later sinologists, whose interests were geared primarily toward China, the proto-sinologists geared their interests in China toward Europe.) In the seventeenth century, these ideas involved the reconciliation of China's long history with Biblical chronology, the assimilation of Chinese notions of "Middle Kingdom'' geography with newly expanded European geographical knowledge of the world, integrating the new information about China into established Hermetic theories, reconciling the "noble pagan" status of the Chinese with Christianity, assimilating information on the Chinese language into the European search for a universal language and the related search for a *Clavis Sinica* (Key to deciphering the Chinese language), and, finally, reconciling traditional Chinese numerological notions with some of the most advanced European arithmetical theory.

The seventeenth-century search for a universal language fostered a European fascination with the Chinese language. Francis Bacon and other distinguished intellects perceived Chinese as a model language whose ideographic principles transcended regional and dialectical variations. This perception made Chinese a much-discussed candidate in the search for a universal language which would recapture the simplicity and clarity thought to have been lost with the Biblical Primitive Language of Adam. With certain exceptions, informed missionaries did not encourage this viewpoint, nor did many encourage the somewhat related, but less distinguished search for a *Clavis Sinica* which would simplify the learning of the difficult Chinese language and which was conducted by the proto-sinologists Müller and Mentzel at Berlin. Nevertheless, the account of China's role in the search for a universal language and the related German search for a *Clavis Sinica* showed how the information supplied mainly by Jesuit proponents of accommodation in the China Mission was assimilated by European scholars. The belief in the possibility of a universal language included the acceptance of the premises that all languages shared an underlying structure which, once discerned, would allow not only for the creation of an ideal, universally understood language, but also the construction of keys for deciphering unknown languages, such as Chinese.

The information about Chinese history which was carried to Europe by the Jesuit fathers Martini and Couplet made claims for a high antiquity among European savants and resulted in the promotion of a chronology based on the Septuagint rather than the Vulgate version of the Bible. This activity also produced a number of inventive, but bizarre theories. The responses of seventeenth-century proto-sinology to China were made by enthusiastic, somewhat eccentric and sometimes brilliant savants, but nearly all were sadly unprepared to undertake such study and some were publicity-conscious. The borrowing of ideas about China from one another took place on a round-robin scale which would by today's standards be scandalously plagiaristic. There were also instances of direct and sophisticated intellectual exchanges between China and Europe, such as that conducted by the Jesuit Bouvet and the eminent scholar Leibniz which led to their discovery of the striking resemblances between the numerological diagrams of the ancient Chinese Classic, the *I ching* (Book of changes), and Leibniz' newly developed binary system of arithmetic.

Ricci's formulation of accommodation defined the lines of debate among Christian missionaries over how the Christian mission in China should be conducted. This debate eventually grew into the Chinese Rites Controversy and involved questions of whether the Chinese possessed an indigenous name for the Christian God and whether traditional Chinese ancestral and Confucian rites were permissible for Chinese Christians. Fostered by inter-missionary rivalries in China, the Rites Controversy carried to Europe where it became entangled with differing theological positions on grace held by the Jansenists and Jesuits and with the rising political tide of anti-Jesuitism.

For most Jesuit proponents of accommodation during the seventeenth century, the Chinese figure par excellence was Confucius. Confucius' significance was early perceived by Ricci who saw him as a key to his Chinese-Christian synthesis. Eminently rational but only implicitly religious, Confucius and his philosophy were admirably blendable with the explicitly religious Christianity. The continuity of Ricci's accommodation policy throughout much of the seventeenth century was reflected in the continued exaltation of Confucius in the appearance at Paris in 1687 of the Jesuits' long-underway translation project of three of the Four Books in *Confucius Sinarum philosophus.* Like Ricci, the editor Couplet and the Jesuit translators rejected the Sung Neo-Confucian interpretations and turned instead to the commentary of a prominent Ming official, Chang Chü-cheng, who was an orthodox Confucian, but unsympathetic to the metaphysical tendencies of the school of Sung Neo-Confucians. Also, like Ricci, the editor and translators of *Confucius Sinarum Philosophus* laid great emphasis upon the Four Books. During the seventeenth century, the Four Books served as primary language texts for newly arrived Jesuits in China. As the most fundamental texts of official Chinese culture, the Four Books constituted one of the foundations of Ricci's Confucian-Christian synthesis.

Confucius Sinarum philosophus represented not only a culmination of that part of Ricci's accommodation which promoted Confucius as the synthesizing medium, but also the conclusion to a phase of Jesuit accommodation. Changing dynasties in China and the quickening of the Rites Controversy in Europe caused a small and — from the European perspective — obscure group of Jesuit proponents of accommodation led by Bouvet to displace Confucius with the K'ang-hsi emperor as the model of exaltation. For Bouvet, this substitution also admirably fulfilled his European agenda at the court of Louis XIV. Whereas Confucius has provided philosophical support and social prestige for a Chinese-Christian synthesis, the K'ang-hsi emperor could provide political support, which had become crucial to the survival of Jesuit accommodation. Bouvet and the Figurists shifted the formula of accommodation away from the Confucian Four Books and toward the Hermetically-fraught numerology of the ancient Chinese Classic, the *I ching.* However, it must be emphasized that Ricci's formula of accommodation had been evolving throughout the seventeenth century and the intellectual leap to Figurism was a rather small one. The immediate political gains which the Jesuits obtained in moving in this direction and which were so helpful in dealing with Jesuit opponents in China were cancelled out by leading accommodation into an intellectual dead end.

The evolution of accommodation in China was powerfully shaped by internal Chinese developments. When Ricci began formulating his strategy around 1600, Chinese culture was marked by an openness and creativity which saw the recombination of formerly distinct teachings into new syncretisms. In this atmosphere, Ricci and other missionaries, such as Semedo, Magalhaes and Martini, attempted in their written works on China to forge a Jesuit syncretism by appropriating the most commanding Chinese cultural medium — the Confucian tradition — as a moral complement to Christian religiosity. This appropriation was achieved by separating modern Confucians from ancient Confucians on the grounds that while the moderns engaged in practices which were polytheistic, pantheistic or even atheistic, the ancient Chinese sages, whom Confucians revered as their masters, had worshipped a monotheistic God. This strategy rested on a brilliant insight which not only accorded with contemporary reality, but also melded with what little was known of high Chinese antiquity and appealed to the Chinese reverence of antiquity.

In 1644 the native Chinese dynasty of the Ming was officially concluded by the ascent of Manchu overlordship in the Ch'ing dynasty. In the aftermath of disaster, reflective Chinese literati blamed this loss not only on the proliferation of eunuchs, but also on the syncretic cultural atmosphere of the late Ming. Chinese faulted other Chinese for straying too far from the orthodox fount of Confucius. When the Manchu rulers embraced the most orthodox form of Confucianism then available — the Sung Neo-Confucian interpretations of the Confucian Classics — the dominance of this orthodoxy in late seventeenth-century China was guaranteed. The parameters of allowable creativity in interpreting the Confucian Tao (Way; Truth) were severely contracted from what had been allowable in the early part of the seventeenth century and new and foreign teachings became less welcome in China.

Where did this change in the Chinese cultural climate leave the Jesuits' accommodation policy? It left it in need of modification. Parts of Ricci's program, such as the grounding of an indigenous Chinese Christianity upon Chinese high antiquity remained sound. But Ricci's cultivation of Chinese literati as an element of accommodation was made less possible by a change in cultural atmosphere and by shifts in those who were patrons of the Jesuits. By the end of the seventeenth century, the missionaries were no longer converting literati of the Grand Secretary status of Hsü Kuang-ch'i. Therefore the plan to incorporate Confucianism — that is, a form of Confucianism which pre-dated Sung Neo-Confucianism — into a Confucian-Christian synthesis became less feasible. The new political and cultural realities had a manifest influence on a Figurist like Bouvet who had far less contact with Chinese literati than had Ricci. The elevated position of Bouvet and of many other Jesuits in China depended totally upon the Manchu court at Peking and specifically on the K'ang-hsi emperor. By contrast, Ricci's contacts with the court and the throne had been limited by the recluse tendencies of the Ming Wan-li emperor.

The altered Jesuit situation contributed to the shift in Jesuit accommodation: Ricci had appealed to the literati, but Bouvet appealed to the throne. Like Ricci, Bouvet still focused on Chinese antiquity, but unlike Ricci, Bouvet no longer spoke of Confucius. Instead, he focused on the *I ching*, which though claimed by the Confucian tradition as one of their own, chronologically predated Confucius. It was not any Manchu imperial opposition to the Four Books and to Confucianism which led Bouvet to relinquish Confucius. However, in the Manchu sponsorship of a revived Confucian orthodoxy based upon the interpretations of the Four Books by the abhorrent Sung Neo-Confucians, the more creative options for a Confucian-Christian syncretism which had been open to Ricci in the freer atmosphere of the late Ming were now closed.

If Bouvet had continued to promote a Confucian-Christian synthesis based on the Four Books, then given his isolation in the Manchu court, it was almost inevitable that he would have used the Sung Neo-Confucian interpretations. But since seventeenth-century missionaries had consistently rejected Sung Neo-Confucianism on the grounds that the materialism and atheism in their commentaries on the Classics excluded the possibility of deriving a Creator and all-powerful God from the Classical texts, Bouvet felt compelled to build a Chinese-Christian synthesis on another aspect of Confucian culture. This he did by using the *I-ching*, a work from the Five Classics which commanded the respect not only of the Confucian literati, but more importantly, of the K'ang-hsi emperor.

But by drawing from the Hermetic tradition and pushing Chinese antiquity farther into the past in an attempt to make it more reconcilable with a new Chinese-Christian synthesis, the Figurists came into conflict with traditional Biblical claims of high antiquity for the Jews. Figurism was regarded as theologically heterodox at Rome and the radicalness of Figurism tended to discredit Jesuit accommodation as a whole. Its heterodox implications prohibited its exponents from communicating their ideas in published works and so the implications of Figurism were understood and appreciated by few Europeans, with notable exceptions like Leibniz. Furthermore, it is doubtful that Figurism provided a sufficiently wide Chinese social base for an effective accommodation. Bouvet's focusing exclusively on the court made Jesuit policy more subject to imperial whim and changes of succession than Ricci's literati-based accommodation had been. The polemicized atmosphere produced by anti-Jesuit criticism, the Sorbonne censure of 1700 and the propaganda effects of the Missions Étrangères began to alter the nature of the works on China being published in Europe by Jesuit proponents of accommodation. The situation fostered propaganda at the expense of content. By the end of the seventeenth century, the most substantive information on China being provided by the Figurists tended to be found in less public mediums, such as the correspondence between Bouvet and Leibniz. Although Figurism continued to be developed privately during the early eighteenth century, it fell victim to the Rites Controversy and to its own heterodox implications. In short, the Figurists never constituted more than an obscure minority whose ideas were more potentially threatening than actually damaging. There was another attempt to preserve the framework of the Confucian-Christian synthesis by once again laying emphasis on the Four Books. The aim was to reinterpret the Neo-Confucian commentaries on the Four Books in a way which made them reconcilable with Christianity, but this attempt lies beyond the time frame of this work and is only briefly treated.

The structure of this work follows the pattern of seventeenth-century history in interweaving the works of the proto-sinologists with those of the Jesuit proponents of accommodation. After an opening chapter in which the primary themes are placed in their historical setting, the second chapter presents Ricci's formulation of Jesuit accommodation in China followed by the third chapter which shows how Ricci's formulation was continued by Semedo and Magalhaes in the mid-seventeenth century. The fourth chapter presents how Martini's works on Chinese geography and history stimulated proto-sinology. The fifth chapter deals with the eminent polyhistor Kircher and shows how the proto-sinologists integrated and subsumed their study of China into their other research and theories. The sixth chapter on the seventeenth-century search for a universal language shows that even if knowledge of the Chinese language disseminated by proto-sinologists in Europe was superficial, it nevertheless was pervasive among savants of that time. Chapter seven presents the puzzling and frustrating search of German proto-sinologists for an expedited method of learning Chinese – the so-called *Clavis Sinica*. The last three chapters return to the evolution and ultimate public censure of Jesuit accommodation which occurred in the last years of the seventeenth century.

This book grew out of a plan to investigate a single European collection of books and manuscripts which the aim of reconstructing the seventeenth-century European conception of China. During a research visit made in 1974 to the Leibniz-Archiv in Hannover, Germany as part of the research for *Leibniz & Confucianism*, I was struck by the potential of the old Regia Bibliotheca Hannoverana collection as a source for reconstructing how Europeans conceived of China in the seventeenth century. It is not the uniqueness of the collection at Hannover, but the fact that it is representative of collections throughout Europe which make it valuable as a source for this sort of study. Since my aim was to focus on several of the most widely read and influential books on China published during that time, this representative quality served me well. Later, when lacunae occurred, I was able to supplement my sources with visits to the Staats- und Universitätsbibliothek in Göttingen, the Staatsbibliothek Preussischer Kulturbesitz in West Berlin, the Deutsche Staatsbibliothek in East Berlin, the Biblioteca

Apostolica Vaticana in Rome and the Herzog August Bibliothek in Wolfenbüttel. In addition to published works, the Hannover collection contains the Leibniz correspondence and papers, many of which have not yet been published. Leibniz' sustained fascination with China flowed through his vast correspondence which he conducted with some of the most brilliant savants of his time. Also, as court librarian of Hannover during the years 1676–1716, Leibniz' interest in China shaped the collection there.

In the summer of 1977 I was able to return to Hannover through the support of the Deutschen Akademischen Austauschdienst (DAAD) to compile a list of primarily seventeenth-century European-language works on China which had been collected in the ducal library. Unfortunately, I found no Chinese-language works and the sixteen volumes which Fr. Bouvet sent to Leibniz ca. 1700 had disappeared with barely a trace. Nevertheless, the 78 titles which I located were remarkable not only in their importance, but also in their accessibility. Nearly all of the works listed in the Systematischem Bandkatalog compiled by the librarian Daniel Baring in 1720 had survived the passage of time and war and were carefully preserved in the efficient new facility of the Niedersächsische Landesbibliothek Hannover. Armed with this list, I was able to obtain support from the Alexander von Humboldt-Stiftung (AvH) for two years of research (1978–1980) at Hannover.

Although I have endeavored to explore seventeenth-century Sino-European relations in new ways, this book nevertheless builds upon the work of a number of scholarly predecessors or contemporaries who have written works in this area. This list is too long to acknowledge individual contributions here, but my indebtedness to their works is expressed in some detail at appropriate points in the book.

Although the essential research for this book had been completed and the approximate configuration of the chapters established at the conclusion of my Humboldt grant in June of 1980, the ideas in the work had not yet been brought into full articulation. Consequently, the manuscript required an additional four years of revisions and refinements. This was a difficult and frustrating period, and yet a necessary and rewarding struggle. It was a period which I could not have worked through alone and it would be thoroughly ungrateful of me not to acknowledge the assistance of those who most contributed to this process.

To Ms. T. Korai Kitao, Professor of Art History at Swarthmore College, I am indebted for evaluating certain illustrations from the seventeenth-century European literature on China in terms of possible parallels to the broader stream of seventeenth-century European art. To Mr. Wing-tsit Chan, Professor Emeritus at Dartmouth University and Professor at Chatham College and certainly the doyen among English-language translators of Confucian texts, I am indebted for clarifying the relationship between the *Tao-hsüeh* and *Li-hsüeh* branches of Neo-Confucianism. I am indebted to Fr. John W. Witek, S.J., Associate Professor of History at Georgetown University, for carefully going through the entire manuscript. I am deeply indebted to Mr. John E. Wills, Jr., Associate Professor of History at the University of Southern California, for helping me to clarify the major themes of the work. To my closest professional colleague, Mr. Knud Lundbaek, Professor Emeritus of Aarhus Universitet, I am indebted for countless suggestions toward improving the manuscript and for his steadfast encouragement.

Without the support of the Alexander von Humboldt-Stiftung (Bonn) and the Deutscher Akademischen Austauschdienst (Bonn), this book could not have been written. The Humboldt-Stiftung, in particular, was instrumental not only in supporting the research, but also in facilitating publication of the book through a printing subsidy. The dedication of these institutions to sponsoring the research of foreign scholars in the Bundesrepublik Deutschland is a wonderful monument to a venerable and, thankfully, lasting German tradition in scholarship.

I stand very much in debt to Frau Dr. Eva S. Kraft, staff librarian of the Ostasienabteilung, Staatsbibliothek Preußischer Kulturbesitz in West Berlin, for her generosity in sharing her research and materials on the German proto-sinologists Andreas Müller and Christian Mentzel. I vividly recall several chats in her office with its window-panorama of the Berlin Wall and East Berlin. The individual to whom I am most indebted for assistance in both the research and finding of a publisher is my *Betreuer*, Herr Dr. Albert Heinekamp, Leiter of the Leibniz-Archiv, Niedersächsische Landesbibliothek Hannover. For his helpfulness and kindness, I owe a debt which can never be repaid. Finally, for enduring and encouraging me throughout the seven years that this book was in preparation, I am deeply indebted to my wife, Christine.

D.E.M.   Wolfenbüttel, October 1984

CHAPTER I
THE SEVENTEENTH-CENTURY EUROPEAN BACKGROUND TO THE ACCOMMODATION OF CHINA

1. EUROPEAN EXPANSION AND MISSIONARIES

The seventeenth century was a time of European expansion. Although the Iberian states of Spain and Portugal were in decline and central Europe went through the process of being exhausted by a long war, the states of western Europe — England, Holland and France — were in vigorous ascent. This century saw the conclusions to a number of wars whose roots were in the Reformation, but the religious issues of these wars seemed increasingly to be absorbed by political concerns. The Thirty Years War (1618–1648) in central Europe thoroughly blurred sectarian lines, but was nonetheless economically and politically devastating to German territories. In England, the conflict between Puritans, Anglicans and Catholics evolved into a civil war (1642–1649), then Cromwell's Republic (1649–1660), followed by the Restoration (1660–1688) and ultimately the Glorious Revolution (1688). These events produced the death of a king and the historical triumph of Parliament.

If the elevated conception of the divine right of kings was not matched by the abilities of the Stuart kings in England, it certainly was matched across the Channel in the person of Louis XIV (r. 1661–1715) of France. Louis the Great's talents were reinforced by the foundations laid by a succession of brilliant royal advisers — Cardinal Armand-Jean du Plessis Richelieu (1585–1642), Cardinal Jules Mazarin (1602–1661) and the arch mercantilist Jean Baptiste Colbert (1619–1683). In carrying kingship to a high art, Louis XIV created a model both of a monarch and a palace (Versailles) which would be imitated for many years throughout Europe[1]. Although the last years of the Sun King's reign were less successful than his earlier years, this time of turmoil is omitted from our study because it lies beyond 1700. Nevertheless, both the British and French experiences in the seventeenth century had produced two powerful historical models for the development of the modern nation-state.

Seventeenth-century European expansion had a significant religious dimension. Throughout the period of the discovery voyages in the sixteenth century, the kings of Spain and Portugal had taken the initiative in promoting Christian missions with financial aid as well as passage for missionaries aboard Spanish and Portuguese ships. During this time, the Jesuits played the leading role,

---

1 See Pierre Goubert, *Louis XIV and twenty million Frenchmen* Anne Carter, trans. (New York, 1972).

followed by the Franciscans and Dominicans. While these missionary programs were very successful in establishing mission bases throughout the world, they were hindered by the political connection with the Spanish and Portuguese authorities which entangled them in secular concerns, including trade[2]. In addition, there were intense rivalries between the religious orders which had their roots in fundamental differences over missionary methods.

When Columbus sailed to America in 1492 under the patronage of the Spanish crown, a question of world jurisdiction between Portugal and Spain was raised. In 1493 Pope Alexander VI attempted to resolve matters by drawing a line on a north-south meridian 100 leagues to the west of the Cape Verde Islands[3]. The territory to the west of this line was to be the Spanish sphere while the territory to the east was to be the Portuguese sphere and all rights and privileges within these spheres were to be enjoyed by their respective monarchs. This division was the basis of the system of the *padroado* which entailed Spanish and Portuguese jurisdictional control over the Church, including the appointment of bishops in their spheres. While the system of the *padroado* had worked reasonably well during the sixteenth century, by 1600 the growth of the missions had created a burden on Spain and Portugal which they were less and less able to handle. As the seventeenth century progressed and Iberian fortunes declined, this situation intensified. Portugal, in particular, with its population of barely one million could no longer fulfill its duties and, as a result, many bishoprics remained vacant for years[4].

Because of the damage these vacant bishoprics were creating in the missionary effort, Rome acted to bring all missionary activity under the direction of a central authority in Rome. Consequently, in 1622 the Sacred Congregation for the Propagation of the Faith was created. Propaganda attempted to free missionary activity from the Spanish and Portuguese restrictions. In 1659 Propaganda instructed missionaries that they should adapt Christianity to the indigenous cultures of foreign people rather than imposing European manners and customs. Native cultures were to be changed only when they contradicted the Christian religion and morality[5]. (Controversy would later arise not over the principle, but over its application). Propaganda laid great emphasis upon developing indigenous clergy as well as introducing more secular clergy to balance off the members of religious orders.

2 Stephen Neill, *A History of Christian missions* (Harmondsworth, Middlesex, England, 1964), p. 177.
3 This division between Spain and Portugal was formally established in the Papal bull *Inter caetera* of May 4th 1493. See Neill, pp. 141–142 & G. F. Hudson, *Europe and China: a survey of their relations from the earliest times to 1800* (Boston, 1961) p. 191.
4 Neill, p. 178.
5 Neill, p. 179.

Propaganda's effort to diminish the influence of Spain and Portugal was furthered with the founding of the Société des Missions Étrangères seminary at Paris in 1663. Now French influence in the missions increased at the expense of the Iberian powers. Finally, Propaganda brought the conflict with Portugal and Spain to a head with an increase in the number of overseas bishoprics. Propaganda circumvented the Spanish and Portuguese prerogatives of appointing bishops in their respective world spheres through the legal device of vicars apostolic who acted as direct representatives of the Pope. Since the vicars apostolic lacked any territorial title for the area in which they worked, this device circumvented the Spanish and Portuguese territorial prerogative on legal and canonical grounds. Nevertheless, the Spanish and Portuguese regarded these vicars apostolic as an invasion of their privileges. The antagonism between Portugal and Rome persisted until 1950 when an agreement between the Vatican and Portugal was concluded which finally resolved the controversy over the *padroado*[6].

2. ARISTOTELIANISM, COPERNICANISM AND HUMANISM

The accommodation of China by seventeenth-century Europeans reflected the primary intellectual movements of that period. This was true both of the formative phase of the Confucian-Christian synthesis in China and of the assimilation of information about China in Europe. Seventeenth-century Europe was marked by the vigorous competition between advocates of learning. On one hand there was the tradition of Aristotle embodied in the Middle Scholasticism which dominated the universities. On the other hand there were the mathematical and experimental approaches to knowledge embodied in the new societies of learning which stood, for the most part, outside of the established institutions of learning. The Aristotelian tradition was by no means so sterile nor so anti-experimental as it has been portrayed by its opponents. Furthermore, the organic branch of this tradition made a significant contribution to the Scientific Revolution through the medical faculty at the university of Padua[7]. Other branches of Middle Scholasticism were less revolutionary and their resistance to Copernican heliocentrism is well known, though not so simple-minded as portrayed by Galileo Galilei through the mouth of "Simplicio" in the polemical and influential work, *Dialogo . . . sopra i due Massimi Sistemi del Mondo; Tolemaico, e Copernicano* (1632)[8].

6 Neill, pp. 180–182.
7 Hugh Kearney, *Science and change 1500–1700* (New York, 1971) pp. 77–88.
8 Galileo Galilei, *Dialogue concerning the two chief world systems – Ptolemaic and Copernican* Stillman Drake, trans. (Berkeley, 1953).

The struggle between the Aristotelian-Ptolemaic worldview containing geocentrism and crystalline spheres and the Copernican worldview with its heliocentrism and orbiting planets is one of the most famous intellectual controversies of the seventeenth century. Throughout that century, the Jesuits in China were forced to assume a mediating position in which they attempted to accept the discoveries of Galileo and other heliocentrists while clinging to the Aristotelian-Ptolemaic interpretation of them. The formulator of accommodation in China, Fr. Ricci, was not a professional astronomer, but he had studied at the famous Collegium Romanum under one of the most eminent mathematicians in Europe, Christoph Clavius (Klau), S.J. (1537–1612), a man who had established his reputation by overseeing the final computations of the Gregorian calendar reform[9]. At the time of Galileo's invention and use of the telescope to make his famous planetary discoveries, Galileo and Clavius had been friends for over twenty years. When Galileo sent word to Clavius in 1610 about these discoveries, Clavius together with his successor in the Chair of Mathematics at the Collegium Romanum, Christoph Grienberger, S.J. (1561–1636), verified Galileo's discovery[10].

With his discoveries supported by Clavius' unquestioned authority in the field, Galileo was officially received at the Collegium Romanum in 1611 where a meeting of Church dignitaries was arranged in his honor[11]. Clavius welcomed Galileo's discoveries and was shaken by them, but he was not yet ready to abandon geocentrism[12]. Still, there is evidence that Clavius' geocentric convictions were wavering during his last days[13]. When Galileo began publicly attacking the Aristotelian-Ptolemaic view and promoting Copernicanism, he became deeply implicated in a cosmological and theological controversy which he had insufficient expertise to handle. When Clavius died in 1612, Galileo lost his primary supporter in the Church. There followed in 1616 a decree that Galileo's proposal of heliocentrism was erroneous. A trial and public condemnation followed in 1633.

The situation became increasingly difficult for Jesuit mathematicians who had been at the forefront of European astronomy in terms of being aware of new discoveries. The Church's rulings of 1616 and 1633 restricted the Jesuits in China and elsewhere from using the heliocentric theory to explain astronomical phenomena which, however, increasingly demanded heliocentrism in order to make sense. As a compromise measure, the Jesuits introduced to the Chinese the theory of Tycho Brahe (1546–1601) which maintained the Aristotelian-

9 Marie Boas, *The Scientific Renaissance 1450–1630* (New York, 1962) p. 323.
10 Pasquale d'Elia, S.I., "The Spread of Galileo's discoveries in the Far East (1610–1640)," *East & West* (Rome) 1 (1950): 156–157.
11 d'Elia, "The Spread of Galileo's discoveries," p. 157.
12 Giorgio de Santillana, *The Crime of Galileo* (Chicago, 1955) pp. 23–24.
13 Santillana, p. 30. The story of the decree of 1616 and the formal condemnation of 1633 is described in detail in Santillana's *The Crime of Galileo*.

Ptolemaic feature of the earth at the center of the universe with the sun circling it while having the remaining planets circle around the sun rather than the earth. The Tychonic system was less than fully satisfactory and Copernicus' name and ideas occasionally crept into Jesuit writings in China, though the Copernican theory was not fully explained by a Jesuit in China until 1670[14]. As a result, the Jesuit presentation of astronomy in China in the seventeenth century was slowly transformed from a conservative, but relatively open presentation into an obsolete and illogical account[15].

The Jesuit astronomers brought to China superior techniques in predicting eclipses — a crucially important activity at the Chinese court. Furthermore, they brought a clear explanation of Euclidean geometry and how it applied to an analysis of planetary motion; the notion of a spherical earth divided into meridians and parallels; and skills of precision instrument-making, including the technique for constructing a telescope[16]. But along with these positive contributions, the Jesuits also brought a closed geocentric conception of the universe with its solid concentric crystalline spheres which conflicted with the more fluid features of the native Chinese *hsüan yeh* cosmological conception of heavenly bodies floating in empty space. So while the Jesuits brought superior skills, they also brought a cosmological theory which Europeans were then beginning to reject for the more fluid Copernican heliocentrism with its planets orbiting in empty space, and which was in certain ways strikingly similar to the *hsüan yeh* theory.

Regardless of what the Jesuits were compelled by Papal rulings to do in the area of cosmology, the theories about the physical world which they presented to China in the first half of the seventeenth century have been analyzed as consistently Aristotelian[17]. In their systematic and logical argumentation, in their appeal to traditional authority, in the absence of empirical inquiry and

---

14 The first explanation of Copernicanism in China appears to have been made by the Jesuit Michel Benoist (Chiang Yu-jen, 1715–1774) on the occasion of the 50th birthday celebration of the Ch'ien-lung emperor. Copernicus' *De revolutionibus* (1543) had just been removed from the Index in 1757, thus permitting discussion of the Copernican theory. See Nathan Sivin, "Copernicus in China," *Studia Copernicana* 6 (1973): 94.

15 The description of this degeneration of Jesuit astronomy in China in the seventeenth and eighteenth centuries is described in the above cited article by Mr. Sivin. He states (p. 69n) it is well known that Ricci's *Ch'ien k'un t'i i* (Explication of the material heaven and of the earth) (ca. 1608) was based upon the work of his teacher Clavius, *In sphaeram Joannis de Sacro Bosco commentarius* (1585). However, Mr. Sivin notes that Ricci did not include Clavius' reservations about the Ptolemaic system and the potential role of Copernicanism.

16 The observations in this paragraph are drawn from Joseph Needham's *Science and civilisation in China* 7 vols. in progress (Cambridge, 1954–) III, 437–438.

17 See Williard J. Peterson, "Western natural philosophy published in late Ming China," *Proceedings of the American Philosophical Society* 117 (1973): 295–322.

lack of application of mathematics to the understanding of nature, the Jesuit writings presented a view of natural philosophy which was quite close to the approach still dominating European academic life, though it was increasingly coming under criticism from the proponents of the new experimental and mathematical learning.

In certain areas apart from natural philosophy, the Jesuits were leaders among Christian orders of the seventeenth century in breaking away from the teachings of Aristotle. The Humanist tradition of the Renaissance was very evident in Ricci's work. His very popular treatise on friendship, *Chiao yu lun (De amicitia)* (1601) was written in imitation of the Latin style of Cicero[18]. The Chinese literati responded very favorably to the Renaissance Humanist adherence to literary elegance and persuasive rhetoric and these dual principles pervaded Ricci's works. The dialogue was a favorite classical model of composition dating from Plato, the philosopher whom many Renaissance Humanists had championed against Aristotle. Ricci's very significant work, *T'ien-chu shih-i* (The true meaning of the Lord of Heaven), consists of a dialogue between a Chinese literatus and a Christian philosopher. The dialogue was a favored literary form for argumentative presentations and one notes that Galileo's great *Dialogo* advocating Copernicanism and attacking Aristotelianism was written in the form of a dialogue some 30 years after Ricci's work.

Alongside of these Renaissance Humanist elements, a good deal of Scholastic reasoning can be found in Ricci's *T'ien-chu shih-i*. Furthermore, the Scholastic tendency toward rationally based, all-encompassing systems might be seen in Ricci's proposal to create a Confucian-Christian synthesis as well as in the project which symbolized that synthesis – the Jesuit translation of the Confucian Four Books. In the *Analects*, Confucius expressed his reluctance to discuss spirits, though he did not deny their existence. Such an attitude appeared to wonderfully complement Christianity. Unlike the bewildering array of competing deities which Buddhism and Taoism offered, Confucianism respected spirits, but from a distance. Confucianism complemented Christianity by offering it plenty of room to introduce spiritual elements. On the other hand, the thinking in the Four Books as a whole appears to be more complementary to the Humanist emphasis on compositional structure and rhetorical persuasion than to Scholastic deductive logic. In sum, I think it clearly arguable that Ricci's tendency toward a breadth of learning and skills in the literary arts, mnemonics, geography, geometry and arithmetic, conversation and diplomacy rather than an

---

18 Aloys [Louis] Pfister, S.J., *Notices biographiques et bibliographiques sur les Jésuites de l'ancienne mission de Chine, 1552–1773* (Shanghai, 1932–1934) p. 35. For a lively exchange over Ricci's treatise on friendship, see Marius Fang Hao, "Notes on Matteo Ricci's *De Amicitia*," *Monumenta Serica* 14 (1949–1955): 574–583 & Pasquale M. d'Elia, S.J., "Further notes on Matteo Ricci's *De Amicitia*," *Monumenta Serica* 15 (1956): 356–377.

expertise in any one area brings him very close to embodying the ideal of the Renaissance Man[19].

3. HERMETISM

In studying the role which European intellectual movements played in the accommodation of China by seventeenth-century Europeans, one must distinguish between two different aspects of this accommodation. In the above, we have been speaking of the attempt of Jesuits working in China to find a synthesis embracing Chinese and European cultures which would win intellectual acceptance among the Chinese and facilitate their conversion to Christianity. But the second aspect of accommodation in which European intellectual traditions played a role was in the assimilation into European culture of information about China which was supplied mainly by Jesuit missionaries to China.

There was one intellectual tradition which bridged both the formulation of accommodation in China and the assimilation of information about China in Europe. This was Hermetism. Although Hermetic documents had been used since the time of Augustine, the tradition really was not formulated until the Renaissance. In 1460 a monk from Macedonia arrived in Florence and presented a Greek manuscript to Duke Cosimo de' Medici[20]. The Duke turned the manuscript over to Marsilio Ficino for translation into Latin and the result was presented in 1471 and eventually became known as the *Corpus Hermeticum.* Other major Hermetic documents appeared shortly thereafter. The *Corpus Hermeticum* captured the imagination not only of Ficino, but also of Renaissance Europe and, as a result, Spanish, French and Dutch translations soon followed.

Ficino and others believed that the manuscript he translated belonged to high antiquity and dealt with Mercury Trismegistus, an Egyptian priest who was said to have lived several generations after Moses. He was known as Thoth among the Egyptians and Trismegistus among the Greeks. "Trismegistus" meant "thrice great", i.e. greatest philosopher, priest and king. According to Ficino, Plato said it was customary among the Egyptians to choose a priest from among a group of philosophers and then to select a king from a group of priests. Ficino further claimed that Pythagoras and ultimately Plato descended from Hermes Trismegistus. In effect, Ficino saw the philosophy of Neoplatonism, then being revived

19 After formulating this view on the Humanist elements in Ricci, I was delighted to see it confirmed and further developed by the Italian scholar, Piero Corradini, in a paper, "Actuality and modernity of Matteo Ricci, a man of the Renaissance in the framework of cultural relations between East and West," published in the *International Symposium on Chinese-Western Cultural Interchange* (Taipei, 1983) pp. 173–180.

20 The monk's name was Leonardo da Pistoria. See Wayne Shumaker, *The Occult sciences in the Renaissance* (Berkeley, 1972) p. 201.

in Renaissance Florence, to be based upon highest antiquity. For the Renaissance, antiquity was as much a mark of validity and truth as was logic.

The significance of Hermetism lay in its blending of a pagan philosophy with Christianity. In his drive to syncretize Neoplatonism with Christianity, Ficino was symptomatic of a Renaissance passion for synthesis[21]. This syncretic passion was fed by the Renaissance belief that the ancients had not only been physically larger and mentally brighter, but that they had lived in a more harmonious setting than later men whose diversity was a mark of degeneration. (One is reminded of the Biblically-based Tower of Babel story with its belief that the ancients spoke only one language). This same syncretic drive led the Renaissance thinkers to believe that Eastern religions must have been reducible in antiquity to a single pattern which approximated Christianity. Although the Renaissance thinkers had to admit that the ancients would have lacked Revelation which came historically only with Christ, they implied that the ancients maintained some sort of contact with God and therefore possessed divine insight. In short, Hermes Trismegistus became a quasi-Christian who was capable of solving the perennially perplexing problem of how to bridge pagan philosophy and Christianity.

The belief that the *Corpus Hermeticum* dated from remote antiquity persisted until it was disproved through textual analysis by the scholar Isaac Casaubon in 1614[22]. The *Hermetica* were charged by Casaubon to be the product of the early Christian era and not written by the legendary Hermes. Rather than being an Egyptian doctrine, Casaubon claimed that the *Hermetica* reflected a Greek teaching drawn from a blend of Platonism and Christianity[23].

In ancient Egyptian history, Thoth (Theut) was a local god of Middle Egypt who was later associated with the god Osiris, a god of agriculture, as his secretary-scribe. Through this association, Thoth was regarded as the inventor of writing in the form of the hieroglyphs and of all sciences connected with writing[24]. Through this association, Hermes Trismegistus was linked by the Hermetists with language. This link was of fundamental importance in shaping the assimilation of information about China made by the Jesuit Athanasius Kircher (1601–1680) of Rome. Fr. Kircher was a polyhistor whose intellectual interests paralleled the breadth of intellect cultivated among savants at that time. His extensive research and experimentation in medicine, mathematics, physics, music, archeology, volcanoes and his development of a famous ethnological museum in Rome show him to have participated in the experimental spirit which animated the work of the seventeenth-century learned societies. His interest in languages also led him to be part of the search for a universal language.

21 Shumaker, p. 205.
22 Casaubon's dating of the *Corpus Hermeticum* is described by Frances Yates in her *Giordano Bruno and the Hermetic tradition* (New York, 1964) pp. 398–402.
23 Yates, *Giordano Bruno*, p. 400.
24 Shumaker, p. 208.

Kircher's Hermetism was expressed in his fascination with the Egyptian hieroglyphs[25]. In his ponderous *Oedipus Aegyptiacus* (1652), Kircher carried on the Renaissance tradition of interpreting the Egyptian hieroglyphs as containing hidden truths about both God and the world. Kircher's fascination with Egypt dovetailed with his archeological research as he searched for the Egyptian city of Heliopolis (City of the Sun) in which light carried Neoplatonic connotations of divine truth[26]. Among the hieroglyphs on the obelisk of Heliopolis, Kircher found several forms of what he called the Egyptian cross, which he compared to the Christian cross[27].

The Hermetic syncretic passion carried over in Kircher to his treatment of China in his monumental work *China illustrata* (1667). Since all cultures were reduced by Kircher to a harmonious unity and since Egyptian culture was primary, Chinese culture was seen as derivative of Egypt. *China illustrata* was a collection of information about China whose importance derived from the excellence of Kircher's sources. Kircher's location at the Collegium Romanum and his status as an eminent Jesuit brought him into contact with missionaries returned from China and he included large amounts of information on China which had been received directly from these missionaries. But Kircher's intellectual Hermetic outlook as an Egyptian disseminationist led him to insert interpretations into this work which contradicted the outlook of the China Jesuits. Whereas the missionaries admired China as a model of rationality, Kircher disparaged it as a degenerated Egyptian colony. Whereas the missionaries praised the literary culture of China, Kircher disparaged the Chinese characters as pale imitations of the Egyptian hieroglyphs.

The Hermetic tradition continued to play a role in the seventeenth-century European accommodation of China after Kircher's passing in 1680. At the end of the century, the Figurist theory of the French Jesuit and China missionary Joachim Bouvet made claims for the legendary Chinese inventor of language, Fu Hsi, which were similar to the claims made for Hermes Trismegistus as inventor of the hieroglyphs. But whereas Kircher viewed the Egyptian hieroglyphs as the oldest language in the world, Fr. Bouvet judged the Chinese Classic *I ching* (Book of changes) of Fu Hsi to be the oldest written work. Just as Kircher saw the hieroglyphs as containing a secret, divine significance, Bouvet saw the diagrams of the *I ching* as containing a key to reducing all phenomena of the world into quantitative elements of number, weight and measure. Just as Hermes Trismegistus had preceded Christ's Revelation and yet obtained anticipatory knowledge of the divine mysteries, so did Bouvet claim that the Christian mysteries were contained in a prophetic manner in this most ancient Chinese text.

25 Yates, *Giordano Bruno,* p. 416.
26 Yates, *Giordano Bruno,* p. 418.
27 Athanasius Kircher, *Oedipus Aegyptiacus* 3 vols. (Rome, 1652–1655) III, 332f.

4. SOCIETIES OF LEARNING

Ricci's image and reputation were so powerful that they reverberated down through the seventeenth century among Jesuits in China and we continue to find individual Jesuits capable of a wide variety of skills in handling the Chinese language, teaching mathematics and forging cannon. However, new intellectual traditions quite different from Scholasticism, Humanism and Hermetism played a significant role in the seventeenth-century European accommodation of China. One of the most significant of these was the new interest in experimental knowledge which was, of course, part of the Scientific Revolution. The prophet of this movement was Francis Bacon (1561–1626), the prominent English statesman of late Elizabethan and early Stuart England. Bacon criticized the Aristotelians for their excessive reliance on rationalism and their neglect of experimentation and designed a grand scheme for the advancement of knowledge. His work was very influential, though he neglected mathematics and his own creative contribution to the Scientific Revolution is subject to debate. Nevertheless, his call for experimental knowledge was fulfilled in the founding of societies of learning.

The forerunner of these societies was the Accademia dei Lincei of Rome (1600–1630) of which Galileo was a member[28]. The first organized society was the Accademia del Cimento of Florence which lasted only ten years from 1657 to 1667. Of longer lasting significance were the Royal Society of London founded in 1662, the Académie des Sciences of Paris founded in 1666 and the Akademie der Wissenschaften of Berlin founded in 1700. A direct link between these scientific societies and the Jesuits in China came with the sponsorship of a mission of six French Jesuits (including Bouvet) to China in 1685. Louis XIV used the scientific research of the Académie as a pretext for circumventing the opposition of the Portuguese king to this expedition. Four of the six Jesuits in this mission were inducted into the Académie and made astronomical observations with instruments supplied by the Académie.

As far-fetched as some of Bouvet's notions seemed, they were supported by one of the leading advocates of societies of learning in Europe, Leibniz, who became convinced that the mystical qualities of his binary system of arithmetic were confirmed by Bouvet's discoveries in the ancient Chinese texts. Leibniz was the outstanding polymath in a century where polymaths were the intellectual model. In his youth, he had studied Aristotelianism at Leipzig under one of the

---

28 Martha Ornstein, *The Role of scientific societies in the seventeenth century* (Chicago, 1928) p. 74. Ornstein's work is still the standard comprehensive survey of early scientific societies. It has been reprinted several times, most recently in 1975. A useful survey of more recent work in the field is found in Robert E. Schofield, "Histories of scientific societies: needs and opportunities for research," *History of Science* (Cambridge) 2 (1963): 70–83.

most distinguished Scholastic philosophers of the seventeenth century, Jakob
Thomasius (1622—1684). Though Leibniz maintained a lifelong interest in
Scholastic problems, his mind refused to be confined to any one intellectual
tradition and we find him also studying in his youth at Jena under the mathematical and anti-Scholastic tutorship of Erhard Weigel (d. 1699). Leibniz corresponded with Thomasius over the possibility of reconciling Aristotelianism
with the new mechanistic philosophy of Cartesianism[29]. Although Leibniz
eventually transferred from the conservative academic atmosphere of Leipzig
to the most progressive of German universities at Altdorf where he took a
doctoral degree in law, he found the academic atmosphere stifling and so rejected
the offer of a professorship at Altdorf to depart forever from the academic
setting[30].

During the years 1672—1676 the youthful Leibniz lived in Paris where he
met some of the most eminent savants of the time, including one of Colbert's
first apointees to the Académie des Sciences, the mathematician and physicist
Christian Huygens (1629—1695)[31]. With an introduction from Huygens, Leibniz
visited London in early 1673 where he met Henry Oldenberg, a first secretary
of the Royal Society and the editor of the proceedings of the Society, the
Philosophical Transactions. Leibniz also met the chemist Robert Boyle. In
February he formally presented a model of his calculating machine to the Royal
Society, which appears to have inspired the jealousy of the mathematician Robert
Hooke (1635—1703)[32]. Leibniz applied for membership in the Royal Society
and was admitted in 1673[33]. Back in Paris, Leibniz continued to work on his
calculating machine with the help of a mechanic and in January 1675 presented
it to the Académie des Sciences[34]. Among the many eminent literary figures
whom Leibniz met in Paris was the royal librarian, Melchisedec Thévenot (1620—
1692) whose famous collection of travel literature included important information on China[35]. When Leibniz departed from Paris in 1676, he had laid the
foundations of personal contacts with many of the most eminent figures of the
experimental science movement. Though he returned neither to London nor
Paris, his prolific correspondence maintained these contacts until the end of his
life. Leibniz was to be based permanently at the court of Hannover and during
the last quarter of the seventeenth century, he devoted himself to the establishment of a learned society in Germany. Berlin turned out to be the most pro-

29 Kurt Müller & Gisela Krönert, *Leben und Werk von Gottfried Wilhelm Leibniz. Eine
   Chronik* (Frankfurt am Main, 1969) pp. 7 & 16.
30 Ornstein, p. 179.
31 Müller, p. 29 & Ornstein, p. 147.
32 Müller, p. 32.
33 Müller, p. 34 & Ornstein, pp. 107 & 186.
34 Müller, pp. 36—37.
35 Müller, p. 44.

mising setting. Unlike the Royal Society and the Académie des Sciences which were established by groups of enthusiastic amateurs, the founding of the Akademie der Wissenschaften in Berlin was essentially the work of one man — Leibniz[36].

5. THE SEARCH FOR A UNIVERSAL LANGUAGE

Although Leibniz' inspiration for a learned society in Germany came from the London and Paris societies, his proposals for the Berlin society included a much broader range of activities, including science, history, art, police, medicine, archives, schools, machines, commerce and trade[37]. Not only did his prospects for a learned society reveal his interest in experimental knowledge, but they also revealed his concern for practical knowledge and utilitarian consequences, including mechanical application and the development of a more efficient language of communication[38]. Leibniz' dissatisfaction with Latin as the language of instruction led him to propose the greater use of the German vernacular[39]. However, Leibniz' logical and mathematical inclinations were so powerful that he shared the feeling of many savants of his age that a truly universal language should replace Latin.

The seventeenth-century European search for a universal language had Biblical roots in the widespread assumption that the Primitive Language — a language of utter simplicity, clarity and uniformity — given by God directly to the first man, Adam, had been lost with the dispersion of tongues which occurred at the Tower of Babel. According to Scriptures, man was guilty of the sin of pride in attempting to compete with God by building a Tower of Babel and God punished mankind by replacing the Primitive Language with a proliferation of different tongues. Consequently, much of the search for a universal language involved an attempt to restore the Primitive Language, and Biblical scholars devoted a great deal of effort to reconstructing this lost language. Although many felt that the lost Primitive Language had been ancient Hebrew, others felt that a more exotic language, such as Chinese, because of its great antiquity, most closely approximated the Primitive Language.

The search for a universal language was joined by the advocates of the new mathematical and experimental learning, except that the experimentalists did not seek to revive the Primitive Language, but to reconstruct a wholly new language on the basis of mathematical and mechanical principles. The prophet

36 Ornstein, p. 177.
37 Ornstein, p. 185.
38 Leibniz' concern for practical application of learning is shown in Philip P. Wiener, "Leibniz's project of a public exhibition of scientific inventions," in Philip P. Wiener & Aaron Noland, eds., *Roots of scientific thought* (New York, 1957) pp. 460–468.
39 Ornstein, pp. 181–182.

of experimental science, Francis Bacon, enunciated the aim of this Universal Language – to create "Real Characters" which would be capable of communicating their meaning to all nationalities in a clear, logically self-evident manner rather than in the usual arbitrarily agreed-upon manner of languages. This search also drew upon the medieval *Ars Combinatoria* of Ramon Lull (ca. 1232–1316) which used a combinatory wheel and tables for finding truth. This mechanical means of apprehending truth had a tremendous appeal not only to the experimentalists, but also to mathematicians. The two intellectual inclinations were sometimes combined in one mentality, as in the case of Galileo, Leibniz and Newton, but they were just as often isolated. Bacon and Boyle emphasized experiment while having very little appreciation for mathematics whereas Copernicus and Johannis Kepler were essentially mathematicians who either did very little observing or relied upon the observations of others.

Bacon's suggestions that the Chinese language might satisfy the criteria of Real Characters was taken up in the universal language schemes of the Englishmen George Dalgarno and John Wilkins. Bishop Wilkins was a prime mover in the formation of the Royal Society and was appointed as secretary, along with Oldenburg. But whereas Oldenburg performed an enormous amount of work, Wilkins' appointment appears to have been largely honorary and in recognition of the many services he had performed for the Society[40]. The minutes of the Royal Society indicate that Wilkins was working on a universal language scheme in 1662 – actually he had discussed the constitution of a Real Character in 1641 – and by 1668 submitted to the Society *An essay toward a Real Character and a philosophical language*[41]. A committee of fifteen members of the Society, including such eminent figures as Boyle, Hooke, Christopher Wren and John Wallis, were named to examine Wilkins' book and to discuss it at a meeting in the fall of 1668, but no further reference to the book appears in the minutes[42]. Wilkins derived his notion of a universal language from the universally understood symbols used in chemistry, mathematics and music. He conceived of producing a language capable of communicating in 3,000 symbols. Furthermore, this was to be a "philosophical language" in the sense that all the symbols would be logically reducible to distinct classifications. Although Wilkins is credited as being the author of the *Essay*, it is indicative of the collaborative way in which work in the Royal Society was done that this was a joint production[43].

40 See Dorothy Stimson, "Dr Wilkins and the Royal Society," *The Journal of Modern History* 3 (1931): 551; *The Mathematical and philosophical works of the Right Rev. John Wilkins* (reprinted London, 1707) p. 247; & Jonathan Cohen, "On the project of a universal language," *Mind* 63 (1954): 59.

41 Stimson, p. 557.

42 Stimson, pp. 557–558.

43 Wilkins credited Seth Ward with the idea of a "philosophical language," Ray and Willughby for drawing up the tables of planets, animals and insects, and William Lloyd for composing the dictionary and tables in it. See Stimson, p. 559.

The seventeenth-century search for a universal language was just as actively pursued on the continent as in England. A very different approach to the construction of a universal language is found in Kircher's *Polygraphia nova et universalis ex combinatoria arte detecta* (A new and universal writing in many languages revealed from the combinatory art) (1663)[44]. Kircher's approach made no attempt to construct a "philosophical" (i.e. classifiable) language, but was organized around the somewhat mechanical structure of a "pentagloss" in which each basic word was rendered in equivalents in five European languages (Latin, Italian, French, Spanish and German). With Kircher, the emphasis was upon the combinatory principle derived from Lull, but the systems of both Wilkins and Kircher reflect a common interest in cryptography[45]. In continental Europe, Kircher was joined in the search for a universal language by many other savants, including Leibniz.

One interesting offshoot of this search for a universal language was the attempt to construct a *Clavis Sinica* (Key to Chinese) or a key which would expedite the learning of the Chinese language. Although the attempt to develop such a key was confined entirely to Berlin, it aroused the interest and elicited inquiries from scholars throughout Europe, including the Royal Society in London. The principal force behind this attempt was not so much the growing knowledge of Chinese in Europe as the belief that languages were reducible to a readily comprehensible structure. This key was essentially a logical rather than linguistic device and it emphasized classification. The scholar who first proposed the idea of a *Clavis Sinica* was an eccentric German cleric and proto-sinologist named Andreas Müller. The fascinating record of his attempt and failure to construct such a key is a complex and painful story. With Müller's death, the *Clavis Sinica* was taken up by his sinological successor in the Berlin court, but already in the hands of Christian Mentzel the *Clavis Sinica* was evolving into what the term would eventually signify for late eighteenth- and early nineteenth-century Europeans, namely, a Chinese grammar.

6. MERCANTILISM

The interest of the seventeenth-century scientific societies in practical affairs was very strong. With the Académie des Sciences, this interest was dominated by Louis XIV and his ministers, especially Colbert. The astronomical observations which the 1685 mission of French Jesuits to China made were not intended solely for the sake of pure science, but were to be used to improve French

44 In translating "polygraphia" as "writing in many languages," I follow the rendering of George E. McCracken in "Athanasius Kircher's universal polygraphy," *Isis* 39 (1948): 216.

45 Ornstein, p. 94 & McCracken, p. 218.

navigational charts and maps[46]. In England, the more distant relationship of the monarch to the Royal Society gave the wishes of the individual members freer play. The leading lights of the Royal Society were not professional academics or scientists, but enthusiastic amateurs whose backgrounds were often commercial. Furthermore, in the early seventeenth century, mathematics was considered a mechanical subject, more apt for tradesmen than for academics[47]. In addition to laboratory experiments, a second important line of investigation of the Royal Society was directed at gathering information on the natural history and physical conditions of foreign countries. To this end, Sir W. Petty, who possessed a background in commerce, was assigned the task of composing a history of shipping, clothing and dyeing[48]. There was a tremendous thirst for travel literature among seventeenth-century Europeans, but there was also a conjunction here between the intellectual interests of the Royal Society and commerce. This conjunction was reflected in the assigning to a British East India Company agent a set of queries based on a list of 22 questions about foreign lands which the Royal Society had composed[49].

The seventeenth century was the age of mercantilism in Europe in which governments saw trade as an extension of the national treasury. The conduct of trade was to be carefully controlled and monitored because the increase of national wealth was thought to be contingent upon the draining of wealth from other lands. In 1600 the preeminent model of mercantilist success was Spain which had drained gold and silver from its colonial empire in the Americas and used this wealth to hire a professional army. The emerging governments of seventeenth-century Europe which aspired to displace the Iberian powers believed that trade was the key to power and they fostered the development of trade by issuing government monopolies to private traders. This created joint stock companies chartered by a monarch in the name of the state. As these activities carried the emerging nations of England, Holland and France into the Americas and Asia, Spain and Portugal felt that their colonial spheres were being invaded.

One year after the Papal division of the world between Spain and Portugal, these two powers renegotiated their spheres of division in the Treaty of Tordesillas (1494). The meridian dividing their respective spheres was moved from 100 leagues to 370 leagues (approximately 1,480 miles) west of the prime meridian at the Cape Verde Islands with the Portuguese controlling the zone east of this meridian and the Spanish controlling the zone to the west[50]. This me-

46 Guy Tachard, *Voyage de Siam des pères Jésuites envoyéz par le Roy aux Indes et à la Chine* (Paris, 1686) pp. 16–18 & John W. Witek, S.J., *Controversial ideas in China and Europe: a biography of Jean-François Foucquet, S.J. (1665–1741).* (Rome, 1982) p. 38.
47 Ornstein, p. 93.
48 Ornstein, p. 104.
49 Ornstein, p. 104.
50 Hudson, pp. 190–191.

ridian was located in the mid-North Atlantic Ocean, but intersected the eastern
tip of South America, thus allowing the Portuguese to lay claim to Brazil as well
as to most, but not all, of Asia. In 1517 Magellan claimed the Moluccas in the
East Indies for Spain because it was assumed that the meridian 370 leagues west
of the Cape Verde Islands continued around the Earth, dividing the world into
Spanish and Portuguese hemispheres. The Moluccas were claimed to lie just
within the western extremity of the Spanish hemisphere[51]. By these lines of
demarcation, which were by no means precise, Spain and Portugal divided the
world between themselves. But by the mid-seventeenth century, Spain and
Portugal were in such decline that they could no longer exclude the newly
emerging European powers from invading their colonial spheres. However, they
could and did continue to claim their prior monopolies. The Portuguese claim to
the *padroado* hampered missionaries of all nationalities traveling to Asia by
requiring that they depart from Europe by way of Lisbon and only with the
specific approval of the Portuguese crown.

The most important seventeenth-century joint stock companies trading in
China were the British East India Company chartered in 1600, the Dutch East
India Company (Vereenigde Ost-Indische Compagnie) chartered in 1602 and the
French East India Company (Compagnie Française des Indes Orientales) chartered
in 1664. These companies grew to an enormous size and the Dutch East India
Company, for one, directly employed 12,000 men at the end of the century[52].
During this century, the Dutch company surpassed its English and French
counterparts in East Asia both in establishing territorial bases and in achieving
financial success. It was also the Dutch company which had the most substantial
contact with the Chinese during this time[53]. Sino-Dutch trade in the early

51 Hudson, p. 231. The demarcation line of the Treaty of Tordesillas was not precise and
   it was necessary to establish officially the location of a Spanish-Portuguese line of demarcation in East Asia in the Treaty of Zaragosa (1529). Nevertheless, this line had
   only approximate significance because the Spanish bases in the Philippines lay to the
   west of it and technically within the Portuguese sphere.

52 Carlo M. Cipolla, *Before the Industrial Revolution: European society and economy,
   1000–1700* second edition (New York, 1980) p. 116. For a brief description of the
   structure of the East Indian companies, see Wolfgang Reinhard, *Geschichte der europäischen Expansion* vol. 1: Die alte Welt bis 1818. (Stuttgard, 1983) pp. 156–183.

53 The contact between the Dutch company and the Chinese is the subject of a study by
   John E. Wills, Jr., entitled *Pepper, guns & parleys: the Dutch East India Company and
   China, 1662–1681* (Cambridge, Massachusetts, 1974). Mr. Wills' book focuses on relations between the Dutch trading company and the new Manchu government in China
   in the aftermath of the expulsion of the Dutch from Taiwan by the forces of the pirate
   and Ming Loyalist, Cheng Ch'eng-kung (Koxinga) in 1661. Wills treats in detail the
   cooperative Sino-Dutch effort to defeat the Cheng forces aimed at establishing Manchu
   control of Taiwan and restoring Dutch trade on the southeast China coast. His study
   is based largely upon the archives of the Dutch East India Company housed in the
   General State Archives (Algemeen Rijksarchief) in The Hague. In contrast to the
   thorough and careful preservation of these records by the Dutch, Wills found the
   Chinese records on these relations to be sparse, lost or inaccessible (pp. 3–4).

seventeenth century was profitable from both sides. The Chinese exported raw silk, silk fabrics, sugar, gold, tutenag (an alloy of copper, zinc and nickel) and manufactured goods such as lacquerware and pottery. The Chinese imported dye, incense woods, jewels, and large quantities of pepper[54]. The Dutch operated out of their main Asian base at Batavia to oversee a widespread circuit of trade between Japan, China, Southeast Asia, India, Yemen and Holland. Taiwanese sugar was sold in Persia and Europe, while white silk from China was sold in Japan and Europe. The Dutch carried pepper and sandalwood to China and bought gold, tutenag, raw silk and silk fabrics from the Chinese. The Dutch carried the Chinese raw silk and silk fabrics to Japan where they sold them for silver, taking this silver plus the Chinese gold and tutenag to India to buy cotton fabrics which were exchanged for spices for Indonesia. The profits from the inter-Asia trade were used to purchase cargoes for Europe, in addition to maintaining the Company's facilities and fleets in Asia[55].

In spite of the religious differences between the Dutch of the East India Company and the Jesuit missionaries to China, there were numerous contacts. Dutch ships were used not only to carry the Jesuits' mail between China and Europe, but Jesuits sometimes traveled on Dutch ships. On his voyage as procurator from China to Europe in 1682, the Jesuit Philippe Couplet made a layover in Batavia and met Andreas Cleyer, a German who was serving as the physician of the Dutch East India Company[56]. Couplet and Cleyer shared a common interest in Chinese medicine and they were joined in this interest by a correspondent, Christian Mentzel who was a physician at the court of the Elector in Berlin[57]. A serious illness of the Great Elector's first brought Mentzel and Cleyer into contact and Cleyer was able to provide Mentzel with Chinese texts and materials to answer his queries about Chinese medicine[58]. Over the years a correspondence developed in which books and materials on Chinese and European medicine and natural sciences were exchanged.

7. GALENIC VERSUS PARACELSIAN MEDICINE

Although Mentzel served in a relatively backwater court of Europe, he had obtained his medical degree from the leading medical center in Europe – Padua.

---

54 Wills, *Pepper, guns & parleys*, pp. 9–10.

55 Wills, *Pepper, guns & parleys*, p. 20.

56 See John E. Wills, Jr., "Some Dutch sources on the Jesuit China Mission, 1662–1687," *Archivum Historicum Societatis Iesu*, forthcoming.

57 The common interest of Cleyer, Couplet and Mentzel in Chinese medicine is treated in an article by Eva S. Kraft entitled "Christian Mentzel, Philippe Couplet, Andreas Cleyer und die chinesische Medizin," in *Festschrift für Wolf Haenisde* (Marburg, 1975) pp. 158–196. Also see Walter Artelt, *Christian Mentzel, Leibarzt des Grossen Kurfursten, Botaniker und Sinologe* (Leipzig, 1940) pp. 21–25.

58 Kraft, "Mentzel, Couplet, Cleyer und chinesische Medizin," p. 175.

Padua remained a center of Aristotelianism where a tradition of scientific
Scholasticism survived long after it had died out in the medieval universities
at Oxford and Paris[59]. There was a broad range of interest in nature among the
philosophical faculty at Padua, but it was the medical faculty which was most
famous for its contribution during this time. In addition to Aristotelian empiri-
cism, a major intellectual influence upon the medical faculty there was the
anatomical and medical work of the Hellenistic Greek, Galen (129–199), whose
theories had been revived in the Renaissance. With the discovery of new treatises by Galen in the sixteenth and early seventeenth centuries, the Galenist
school at Padua continued to flourish[60]. The eminent physician Andreas Vesalius (1514–1564) – the "father of modern anatomy" – was professor there
in the years 1537–1544. His pupil, Gabriele Fallopio (1523–1563), the dis-
coverer of Fallopian tubes, took over Vesalius' position in 1551. The Galenic
tradition was carried on by Fabricus of Acquapendente (1537–1619) who was
a professor at Padua for many years and who taught William Harvey (1578–
1657). It was during this time that the famous anatomy theatre was built there
in 1595. Harvey returned to England and between 1616 and 1625, staying
largely within the medical methodology learned at Padua, made the fundamental
discovery that the blood circulated through the heart[61].

Whereas the Galenic tradition dominated the established medical teaching
institutions during the seventeenth century, there was also an anti-establishment
movement in medicine which took its inspiration from Paracelsus (1493–1547),
a Swiss-born German physician. Paracelsus was not only anti-academic, but also
antagonistic toward the social elite which used the establishment medical facilities. Whereas university-trained physicians tended to serve the medical needs
of the landowners and the bourgeoisie, the peasantry and laborers could only
afford the medical advice of the self-taught pharmacists. The academic physicians based their treatment on the ancient Greek traditional belief that disease
resulted from an imbalance in the four basic humours – phlegm, choler, mel-
ancholy and blood[62]. Since this imbalance was thought to affect the whole
body, treatment was applied in a wholistic sense through such techniques as
bleeding and induced sweating and vomiting. By contrast, Paracelsian medicine
stressed localized centers of disease and the use of chemical medicines in treatment. Paracelsus derived his ideas from a variety of anti-Aristotelian ideas,
including Neoplatonism and the Jewish Kabbala.

Although Paracelsian medicine was enormously influential, especially among
pharmacists, the most significant Paracelsian of the seventeenth century was an
aristocrat of the Spanish Netherlands named Juan Baptista van Helmont (1577–

59 Kearney, p. 77.
60 Kearney, pp. 78–79.
61 Kearney, p. 80.
62 Kearney, pp. 115–116.
63 Kearney, pp. 126–129.

1644) who rejected his social origins to become an intellectual radical. Van Helmont rejected Scholasticism to study the Kabbala and developed a mysticism which aroused the concern of Church officials[63]. He obtained his degree in medicine at Louvain in 1609 and became rabidly critical of academic medicine and specifically of the Galenic doctrine of humours. In spite of the lifelong accusations of heresy made against him by the Inquisition, one of Van Helmont's grounds for rejecting Galenic medicine was its pagan rather than Christian foundations. Van Helmont's interest in fermentation, gases and seeds in bodily organs led him to conceive of chemical processes which foreshadowed the modern notion of the enzyme. Also, he seems to have been the first to have described the role of acid in stomach digestion.

8. GEOGRAPHY

In seventeenth-century Europe, geography was a relatively new discipline in its own right. In medieval times, the theoretical study of geography had been part of cosmology and theology while practical geography had been linked to navigation and astronomy. Only under the impetus of the sixteenth-century discovery voyages had geography detached itself from these other fields to form an independent discipline and to be accepted as such in the European universities[64].

There arose among seventeenth-century Europeans a tremendous interest in far-distant and exotic lands as well as a practical interest among the joint stock trading companies in geographical information to aid their navigation. The Jesuits played an important part in the expansion of geographical knowledge in Europe, especially with regard to Asia. The precise geographical location of Cathay had perplexed cartographers since the fourteenth century. Marco Polo's Asian place names were incorporated into the Ptolemaic atlas and remained in use in that form until by the late sixteenth century, new information from recent voyages to Asia showed that Ptolemy's presentation of Asia was largely imaginary[65]. The Jesuits began introducing European geography to China with Matteo Ricci's map of the world[66]. Ricci also was able to solve the old cartographical problem of Cathay by identifying it with China. However, the most significant achievement of the Jesuit geographers in China was to inaugurate an interpolation of European and Chinese geographical and cartographical knowledge.

64 Donald F. Lach, *Asia in the making of Europe* 5 volumes in progress (Chicago, 1965–)
    II, 3; 488.
65 Lach, *Asia in the making of Europe* II, 3; 487.
66 The third edition of Ricci's map of the world, published at Peking in 1603, is reproduced in detail in Pasquale M. d'Elia, *Il mappamondo cinese del P. Matteo Ricci.* (Vatican, 1938).

Throughout the seventeenth-century, China Jesuits joined such Europeans as Richard Hakluyt (1552?–1616) and Samuel Purchas (1575–1626) in providing information about Chinese geography and cartography. These Jesuits included, in addition to Ricci, Michele Ruggieri, Martino Martini, Michael Boym, Alvaro Semedo and Philippe Couplet[67]. European interest in maps of China was so great that it generated commercial competition between Joannis Bleau in Amsterdam and the Royal French cartographer, Nicholas d'Abbeville Sanson (1600–1667) at Paris. When Martini's *Novus atlas Sinensis* (1655) was published as part of Bleau's twelve-volume atlas of the world, Sanson was dissatisfied with Martini's map of China. Consequently, he supplemented the material in Martini's map with three other maps of China by Ricci-Ruggieri, Boym and Semedo, respectively, and published the results in the second edition of his textbook of Asian geography, *L'Asie* (Paris, 1658)[68].

9. HISTORY

The challenge to the intellectual authority of Aristotle and Ptolemy carried over to the study of ancient history in Europe. In the second half of the seventeenth century, Roman, Greek and Biblical history all began to be reevaluated with a skeptical eye and past historians were frequently denounced as mythmakers. This situation was aggravated by Renaissance and Reformation traditions in which historians had not viewed themselves as objective scholars. The Humanist historians followed the classical Greek and Roman model of writing history for the edification of their readers. Their goal was twofold: to produce a work of literary grace and to pass judgment on the past. Reformation historians had been so affected by religious warfare that many historians became apologists for a particular religious or political viewpoint and organized extensive documentation solely to support their argument.

With the rise of broad cultural skepticism in the seventeenth century, the precise dating of the Biblical chronologists began to come under questioning. Not only was the tendency toward extremely precise dating of Biblical events criticized, but the entire chronological outline of the events in the Bible was brought into question by increasing knowledge of ancient Egypt, Assyria and China. New information about these foreign cultures caused Europeans to expand their chronological framework. Even the defender of the Faith, Bishop Jacques-Bénigne Bossuet, was reluctantly forced to respond to this new information. In 1770 when he produced the revised third edition of his *Discours sur l'histoire universelle* (1681), he adopted the Septuagint version of the Old

67 Boleslaw Szcześniak, "The Seventeenth century maps of China – an inquiry into the compilations of European cartographers," *Imago Mundi* 13 (1956): 116–136.
68 Szcześniak, "Seventeenth century maps of China," pp. 116–118.

Testament over the Vulgate in order to lengthen the Biblical chronology by five centuries[69].

A new objective approach to the study of history emerged. In Antwerp, a group of Jesuits called Bollandists under the leadership of Fr. Daniel Papebroch (d. 1714) attempted to sort out the mythological from the true information about the saints in editing the massive *Acta Sanctorum*. This new approach to history attracted the interest of polymaths such as Leibniz who undertook the compilation of a history of the House of Braunschweig. Leibniz consulted with Fr. Papebroch over techniques[70]. But while Leibniz applied newly developed objective methods of gathering and selecting documents, he lacked the tools to fully understand the historical significance of this mass of material.

In summation, the background to the first great intellectual encounter between Europe and China shows that this was an age in which Europeans reached out acquisitively, spiritually and intellectually into the world. And yet, as Europeans came into contact with foreign lands, such as China, the content of the foreign culture had to be interpreted and assimilated in ways which created complex syntheses and sometimes naive and contradictory reconciliations. This is the subject matter of this book.

---

69 Paul Hazard, *The European mind (1680–1715)* J. Lewis May, trans. (Cleveland, 1963) pp. 210–211.
70 Müller, p. 78.

CHAPTER 2

RICCI'S FORMULATION OF JESUIT ACCOMMODATION IN CHINA: THE STRUGGLE FOR LITERATI ACCEPTANCE

1. FR. RICCI'S BACKGROUND

The primary formulator of Jesuit accommodation in China was a monumental figure. Born in Macerata on October 16th 1552 of a wealthy family, Matteo Ricci is described by Chinese sources as possessing a curly beard, blue eyes, a voice like a great bell and a powerful memory[1]. He excelled in languages, was a charming and tactful conversationalist, an excellent mathematician and a quite competent astronomer[2]. Fr. Ricci possessed a remarkable flexibility of intellect and character which enabled him to absorb enormous amounts of Chinese culture and to formulate a policy of accommodation which was both a daring mission strategy and a profound formula for the meeting of Chinese and European cultures.

Morally, Ricci was more complex than many historians have described him. He appeared to have scrupulously subscribed to the Mosaic commandments dealing with killing, adultery, stealing, lying and envy. He did less well in honoring his parents and he showed some highly human equivocation in that most fundamental of Christian commandments – love. His intolerance and dislike of the Buddhist monks in China was surprising in its intensity. The tendency has been to treat this dislike as part of a quite orthodox Christian opposition to idolatry and it was true that Ricci's dislike of Buddhists as idolaters pales to only moderate dimensions when compared with the standard of his times. Nevertheless, his dislike of Buddhists sharply contrasted with a normally sympathetic attitude toward the Chinese. In his journals, even the notorious eunuchs of Ming times were less severely criticized than the monks.

Ricci's attitude toward his parents was ambiguous and this is surprising when one considers his great success and affinity with the parental-worshipping Chinese literati. According to Fr. Trigault, Ricci entered the Society of Jesus

---

1 This description of Matteo Ricci appeared in a Chinese local history, *Jen-ho hsien chih* ch. 22, fol. 21–22, and was translated by A. C. Moule in "The First arrival of the Jesuits at the capital of China," *The New China Review* 4: 455. In his article, Moule also made a tentative translation of the most widely disseminated Chinese account of the arrival of the Jesuits in Peking, namely, the four-page passage in the *Ming shih* (Annals of the Ming dynasty). See Chang T'ing-yü *et al, Ming shih* 28 vols. (Peking, 1678–1739); reprinted 1974) XXVIII (*chüan* 326), 8458–8462.

2 Ricci was a good student of the eminent Jesuit astronomer, Christopher Clavius, but not a creative astronomer in his own right.

without his father's permission[3]. After the fact, the eighteen-year-old Matteo wrote to his father requesting approval. This letter so enraged his father, who had planned a legal career for his son, that he began a trip to Rome with the intention of removing his son from the Jesuit novitiate. While enroute − and with echoes of Saul traveling to Damascus − the father fell ill and appears to have taken the illness as a divine sign. Consequently, he sent his blessings to his son. Also according to Trigault, after receiving permission to join the India Mission, Ricci traveled from Rome to Genoa and could not be persuaded to detour to visit his family at Macerata. Trigault treated this as a positive sign of Ricci's intense devotion to his vocation and possibly he was implying a parallel to St. Ignatius' avoidance of visiting his family while traveling through Spain[4]. Nevertheless, these events raise questions about the degree of Ricci's devotion to his parents.

The Christian faith, unlike that of Confucianism, places God above family in the sense that God's claim on one's life takes precedence over parental claims. Parental devotion is one of the Ten Commandments, as the missionaries stressed to the Chinese, however devotion to one's parents was secondary to devotion to God. The order of the Biblical Commandments is significant: the first four deal with honoring God while not until the fifth do we find the command to honor one's parents. Practically speaking, familial ties have competed with God for the attention of Christians and celibacy was one means used by the Jesuits to insure that devotion to God would have priority. Jesus himself spoke of the priority of God over family by saying: "If any one comes to me and does not hate his father and mother, his wife and children, his brothers and sisters − yes, even his own life − he cannot be my disciple" (*Luke* 14: 26 of New International Version). In his choice of death on the cross, Jesus served mankind while abandoning his mother. Yet Jesus did honor his mother by appointing his favored disciple as a surrogate son even while dying on the cross (*John* 19: 26−27) and one doubts that this fact went unnoticed in filial-minded China.

These flaws in Ricci were real, but they were mild and do not appreciably diminish the glory of a man who has been praised by an eminent contemporary scholar as "one of the most remarkable and brilliant men in history"[5]. Nor is praise of Ricci limited to the West − he has been honored recently by favorable treatment in mainland Chinese periodicals, and no less by those Hong Kong children whose school T-shirts bear his name[6].

3 Matthaei Ricci & Nicolao Trigautio, *De Christiana expeditione apud Sinas* (Augsburg, 1615) pp. 1 & 2 of Trigault's unnumbered preface.
4 I am indebted to Fr. John W. Witek, S.J. for suggesting this analogy between Ricci and St. Ignatius.
5 Joseph Needham, *Science & civilisation in China* 7 vols. in progress (Cambridge, 1954−) I, 148.
6 Ricci recently has received favorable treatment in mainland Chinese periodicals. These

2. THE RICCI-TRIGAULT PRODUCTION OF
DE CHRISTIANA EXPEDITIONE APUD SINAS

De Christiana expeditione apud Sinas was the work which first conveyed
Ricci's accommodation policy to a wide European audience. It was the fruit
of two collaborators who never met — Ricci and the Belgian Jesuit Nicholas
Trigault (1577–1628). Fr. Trigault arrived in Macao in 1610, but Ricci died at
Peking on May 11th 1610 and Trigault did not reach the capital until December
of 1611. In response to a request from the General of the Society of Jesus,
Claude Acquaviva, Ricci had begun to write in Italian a history of Christianity
in China relatively late during his residence in China — that is, in the years
1608–1610 — though whether he intended the work to be published is uncertain. The manuscript was found in Ricci's desk after his death[7]. In order to
insure its survival, a copy in Italian was made as well as a translation into Portuguese. Late in 1612, the new mission superior, Fr. Longobardi, appointed Trigault as procurator whose task was to return to Europe in order to promote
Jesuit mission interests[8]. Trigault stated that his first thought upon being
selected for this office was of translating and publishing Ricci's manuscript[9].
Trigault was regarded as a skilled Latinist whereas Ricci's literary Italian had
become rusty from limited use in the nearly thirty years since leaving Italy. So
it appears that part of Trigault's contribution to this work was to improve its
literary quality[10].

Trigault embarked for Europe from Macao on February 9th 1613. During the
sea voyage to India, he worked on translating the manuscript into Latin and
inserting material either where there was an editorial need or where Ricci had
left lacunae[11]. The project was interrupted between India and Rome where
instead of continuing on by sea around the Cape of Good Hope to Portugal,
Trigault sailed to the Persian Gulf and then traveled overland through Persia
and Egypt and finally on to Rome where he arrived on October 11th 1614.
After arriving in Rome, Trigault was pressed by the more urgent duties to which

include (1) Lü T'ung-liu, "K'ou-tung Chung Hsi wen-hua te hsien ch'ü che — Li Ma-
t'ou" (The first stimulator of mutual understanding between Chinese and Western
cultures — Matteo Ricci), *Renmin Ribao* (Beijing) November 4th 1979; (2) "Matteo
Ricci, pioneer of East-West cultural exchange," *China Pictorial* (Beijing) 7 (July 1982):
32–33; (3) a cartoon-illustrated biography of Ricci by Wu, the first chapter of which
appeared in *Hua kan* 3 (1982): 16–20; (4) Lin Jin Shui, "Li Ma-t'ou tsai Chung-kuo
huo-tung yü ying-hsiang," *Lishi yangjiu* 1 (1983).

7 Ricci-Trigault, p. 4 of Trigault's preface.

8 Edmond Lamalle, S.I., "La propagande du P. Nicolas Trigault en faveur des missions
de Chine (1616)." *Archivum historicum Societatis Iesu* 9 (1940): 53.

9 Ricci-Trigault, p. 4 of Trigault's preface.

10 See page 23 of the new introduction by Fr. Joseph Shih, S.J. in the reprinting of the
French translation of Ricci-Trigault's work entitled *Histoire de l'expedition chrétienne
au royaume de la Chine 1582–1610* (Lille, 1617; reprinted Paris, 1978).

11 Ricci-Trigault, p. 4 of Trigault's preface.

Longobardi had assigned him as procurator, namely, to secure the independence of the China Mission from the Japan Mission[12]. Trigault succeeded in achieving this independence from the Fr. General Acquaviva before the end of 1614[13]. With his primary objective achieved, Trigault now turned to seeking silver, new recruits, books for a mission library in Peking and valuable gifts for the Chinese emperor and literati[14]. An important part of this task involved a propaganda effort of which the translation and publication of Ricci's commentaries were crucial. Consequently, in the midst of other activities at Rome, Trigault spoke of finding isolated hours to bring the effort to completion[15]. In the process, he added two concluding chapters dealing with Ricci's death and the securing of a burial grounds and temple from the Wan-li emperor (r. 1573–1620) through an imperial decree. Trigault also inserted brief sections, probably in the spirit of improving the text, such as the opening lines of chapter 4:5[16]. Trigault's style tends to be a bit more pompous than Ricci's. Other than these additions by Trigault and nearly four chapters in books four and five which derive from reports on activities in other missions, the entire work was written by Ricci. The result was published in Augsburg in some 645 pages, plus prefatory and index material, in 1615.

The respective contributions of Ricci and Trigault to this book were not clarified until the twentieth century. The Italian manuscript of Ricci's original text was first published by Fr. Pietro Tacchi Venturi in 1911–1913[17]. The text was later published with extensive annotation, indices and Chinese characters by Fr. Pasquale M. d'Elia, S.J. in *Fonti Ricciani* (1942–1949). Any student of Ricci must make the original text his focus of attention. However, since the purpose here is to study the seventeenth-century European conception of China and since the respective Ricci and Trigault contributions were inseparably

---

12 Lamalle, p. 55.

13 Lamalle, pp. 58–59.

14 Lamalle, p. 60. The books that Trigault obtained became the nucleus of the Jesuit library in the Nan-t'ang (South Church) of Peking. For a discussion of Trigault's important contribution to the building of the Jesuit library of Peking, see H. Verhaeren, C.M., *Catalogue de la bibliothèque du Pé-t'ang* (Peking, 1949; reprinted Paris, 1969) pp. vii-xii.

15 *De Christiana expeditione*, p. 4 of Trigault's preface.

16 Trigault also inserted brief sections to Ricci's manuscript which he probably added in the spirit of editorial improvements, such as the opening lines of chapter 4; 5. Compare *De Christiana expeditione* (ch. 4; 5) pp. 355–356 & Pasquale d'Elia, S.I., *Fonti Ricciane* 3 vols. (Rome, 1942–1949) II, 49. In the above and following citations from *De Christian expeditione apud Sinas* and in the translation of this work by Louis J. Gallagher, S.J., *China in the Sixteenth Century: the Journals of Matthew Ricci 1583–1610* (New York, 1953) (referred to hereafter as *Journals*), chapter and section citations are included in parentheses in order to facilitate comparison of the two works.

17 Pietro Tacchi Venturi, *Opere storiche del P. Matteo Ricci* 2 vols. (Macerata, 1911–1913).

meshed in the seventeenth-century reader's eyes, the focus of this study will be on the published *De Christiana expeditione*. Finally, my limited examination has found that the differences between the original manuscript and the published version derive more from Trigault's deletions of manuscript material than from changes in translation[18].

The history of the consecutive editions and translations of the Ricci-Trigault work confirms the books's enormous influence upon the seventeenth-century European conception of China. The original Latin edition was republished in 1616, 1617, 1623 and 1684. A French translation was published at Lyon in 1616, 1617 and 1618, and republished in 1978. A German translation appeared at Augsburg in 1617. A Spanish translation was published at Seville and Lima in 1621. An Italian translation was published at Naples in 1622 and, finally, an English translation appeared in Purchas' *His pilgrims* (London 1625). Therefore merely ten years after its appearance, the Ricci-Trigault *De Christiana expeditione* was available in six languages. Consequently, in terms of numbers of readers, this work was probably the most influential book on China published in seventeenth-century Europe. Trigault concluded his European trip in April of 1618 and returned to China, but his literary product continued to promote the Jesuit mission and to disseminate information about China long after his departure.

Trigault divided the work into five books, the first of which contained introductory observations on topics such as China's geography, fertility, products, mechanical arts, arts and sciences, customs, rites, superstitions and religious sects which included Islam, Judaism and Christianity. Books 2–5 were a history of the Jesuit mission in China from Fr. Francis Xavier's unsuccessful attempt in 1551–1552 to enter the Chinese mainland from Shang-ch'uan island until the spring of 1611 or one year after Ricci's death. Ricci's attitude and approach, which shaped the dominating — though not always unanimous — approach of Jesuits in China, stressed the study of Chinese literature and culture and integration into Chinese literati society. Ricci-Trigault wrote:

> We [i.e. the Jesuits] have been living here in China for well-nigh thirty years and have traveled through its most important provinces. Moreover, we have lived in friendly intercourse with the nobles, the supreme magistrates, and the most distinguished men of letters in the kingdom. We speak the native language of the country, have set ourselves to the study of their customs and laws and finally, which is of the highest importance, we have devoted ourselves day and night to the perusal of their literature[19].

Ricci clearly distinguished this approach from that of writers — primarily missionaries of other religious orders — who had never penetrated into mainland

18 However, I note that M. Gernet regards the Trigault translation of Ricci's diaries as often unfaithful to the original text. See Jacques Gernet, "La politique de conversion de Matteo Ricci et l'evolution de la vie politique et intellectuelle en Chine aux environs de 1600," in *Sviluppi scientifici, prospettive religiose, movimenti rivoluzionare in Cina* (Florence, 1975) p. 117n.

19 Ricci-Trigault, (ch. 1; 1) p. 3.

China from their bases in Macao and the Philippines. They were said to speak "not as eyewitnesses but from hearsay". To a certain extent, Portuguese and Spanish cultural factors converged with the outlooks of the Franciscan, Dominican and Augustinian orders to foster somewhat rigid and Europocentric attitudes and approaches among their missionaries[20]. Distinguishing himself from them, Ricci stressed flexibility and sympathy in his approach to the Chinese people and culture and therefore his method is referred to as one of "accommodation".

To comprehend Ricci's method, it is not enough to think only in terms of Europeans studying the Chinese language and culture and living among Chinese. The Jesuits in China were not missionaries on short-term service of three or even ten years who viewed China as a place which they would eventually leave. Ricci-Trigault repeatedly emphasized that they entered China with the intention of spending the remainder of their lives there. Those Jesuits who returned to Europe — either temporarily or permanently — were ordered to do so on behalf of mission needs. This attitude not only reflected Jesuit missionary policy, but it reflected the only terms on which Chinese would admit foreigners as long-term residents in China[21]. The Jesuits were well aware of this and stressed it in their petitions seeking official permission to reside in Chinese towns and cities. This attitude of permanent residence had another effect and this involved China changing the missionaries. The power of Chinese culture to sinify foreigners has been frequently noted by historians. However, given the post-1500 political, military and technological decline of China vis-à-vis Europe, China's sinifying powers had begun to diminish when Europeans appeared in China after 1550. While it is true that most Westerners of the nineteenth and twentieth centuries who resided in China were little sinified, some — certainly not all — of the Jesuits during the time of and immediately following Ricci were significantly changed by their experiences in China. This was eminently true of Ricci who entered China at thirty years of age and never left during the remaining 27 years of his life[22].

3. RICCI'S UNDERSTANDING OF CHINESE GEOGRAPHY, TECHNOLOGY AND CULTURE

Fundamental to Ricci's accommodation policy was an understanding of basic information on the geography, technology and culture of China. The

20 A dissenting viewpoint which defends the Franciscan missionaries in China against charges of rigidity is found in J. S. Cummins, "Two missionary methods in China: mendicants and Jesuits," *Archivo Ibero-Americano* 38 (149–162) (1978): 33–108.
21 Ricci-Trigault, (ch. 1; 6) p. 62.
22 The Jesuit proponents of accommodation continue to be plagued by misunderstanding by scholars. For example, it is misleading to say, as James T. C. Liu does, that the Je-

degree of ignorance and misinformation about China found in Europe at that time was revealed by the confusion over Cathay. Since the time of Marco Polo (1254–1324) and his book dealing with Cathay, there had been ambiguity among Europeans about the precise location of this land. The ambiguity was increased by the tendency to see Cathay as a fabled land of the imagination rather than real. During the years following the publication of Polo's *Il Milione*, writers added fictitious elaborations to the work which they felt were fully in the spirit of the original and these additions were published as indistinguishable parts of the work. Ricci's geographical and mathematical skills combined with his residence in China to clarify the location of Cathay (Ch'i-tan). Until Ricci's time, Cathay and China were generally thought to be distinct places. In the second chapter of *De Christiana expeditione*, Ricci identified both Marco Polo's Cathay and the *Serica regio* (land of silk) with China[23]. He explained that the Chinese were unaware of such designations as *Serica regio*, Cathay or China and referred to their country as *Chung-kuo* or kingdom at the center of the world[24].

Ricci's readings of longitude and latitude for China are said to have been derived from maps found in the 1579 edition of the Chinese atlas *Kuang yü t'u*, originally composed by Chu Ssu-pen (1273–1335/40) and later edited by Lo Hung-hsien (1504–1564)[25]. Ricci placed China, including the island of Hainan, between 19° and 42° north latitude, which was quite close to today's reading. His computation of China's longitude appears to have been less accurate, but any evaluation of seventeenth-century longitudinal readings is complicated by the arbitrary and previously moveable character of the prime meridian. Ricci based the prime meridian in the Canary (i.e. Fortunate) Islands, which means that it was somewhere between 16.35° and 18° west longitude, using today's reckoning

suit accommodative approach "tolerated many elements of Chinese culture, insofar as they did not infringe upon Christian doctrines." (James T. C. Liu, "What Can Be Done with China?" *China Notes* 12 (spring 1979): 66) Many seventeenth century Europeans opposed Jesuit accommodation precisely because they felt it *did* infringe upon Christian doctrine and so the evidence of history itself, quite apart from theoretical considerations, does not sustain Mr. Liu's charge. Mr. Liu also makes the criticism that the Jesuit approach was "primarily applied to upper-class, conservative Chinese . . . rather than to poor Chinese." Such an observation is true, and yet surely as a criticism it is possible only with the hindsight of history. Not only could similar criticism be applied to a broad spectrum of the Chinese philosophies and religions seriously studied today, but the fact is that those missionaries who appealed to poor Chinese tended to be far more culturally chauvinistic and scornful of Chinese culture than were the proponents of accommodation. Finally, in regard to Mr. Liu's criticism that although Jesuit accommodationism was "seemingly openminded, the rock-bottom was also paternalistic," I contend throughout this book that a close study of certain Jesuits and the degree to which China changed them reveals that the charge of "paternalism" is at least diminished, though concededly not banished.

23 Ricci-Trigault, (ch. 1; 2) pp. 3–4.
24 Ricci-Trigault, (ch. 1; 2) p. 5.
25 Pasquale d'Elia, S.I., *Il Mappemondo Cinese del P. Matteo Ricci* (Vatican, 1938)

of the prime meridian from Greenwich, England[26]. Ricci-Trigault placed China's eastern shore at 132° east longitude – actually Ricci wrote 131° and Trigault changed it to 132°[27]. If one adjusts this figure to today's prime meridian, Ricci's figure for the eastern shore of China was approximately 115° east longitude which compares to contemporary readings of 122°.

In addition to basic geographical information, Ricci offered information on the population of China. Apparently drawing again from the *Kuang yü t'u*[28], Ricci stated that in 1579 there were 58,550,801 males on the tax rolls – a probable reference to the *ting* (labor tax toll of able-bodied adult males). To compute a total population figure, the reader must add women, children and those males exempt from taxation. The exempt categories included soldiers – whom Ricci estimated at one million – eunuchs, the emperor's relatives, magistrates, scholars and unspecified others. The Jesuit Martino Martini used a very similar tax roll figure of 58,914,284 in his *Novus atlas Sinensis* of 1655 to project a total population estimate of approximately 200 million[29]. However, in *China illustrata* (1667), the Jesuit Athanasius Kircher spoke of the population of China as 150 million[30]. Even though the latter figure appears somewhat low, given a projection based upon Ricci-Trigault's figure and excluded categories, it is probable that Fr. Kircher drew his demographic information from Ricci-Trigault's *De Christiana expeditione* as well as from Martini's atlas and confirmed this information in personal conversation with Martini in Rome[31]. How accurate were these population estimates? Ho Ping-t'i's study of the popu-

---

p. 207, n. 112 & p. 132; Henri Bernard, S.J., "Les sources mongoles et chinoises de l'atlas Martini (1655)," *Monumenta Serica* 7 (1945): 131; & Boleslaw Szcześniak, "Matteo Ricci's Maps of China," *Imago Mundi* 11 (1954): 127.

26 d'Elia, *Fonti Ricciane*, I, 13. The various islands to which the prime meridian was assigned in the seventeenth century include the Tenerife Island (28.15 N 16.35 W) in the Canary Islands; La Palma Island (28.40 N 17.50 W) in the Canary Islands; Ferro (Hierro) Island (27.45 N 18 W) in the Canary Islands; S. Nicolau Island (16 N 24 W) in the Cape Verde Islands off Cape Verde, West Africa; Corvo Island (39.41 N 31.08 W) in the Azores Islands; and an island called St. Jacob (or Saint-Jacques) which I have been unable to locate. These alternate sites for the prime meridian are found in Zedlar, *Grosses vollständiges Universal-Lexicon aller Wissenschaften und Künste* (Leipzig & Halle, 1739) XXI, 560 and *Encyclopédie ou dictionnaire raissone des sciences, des arts et des métiers* (Aneufchastel, 1765) X, 383.

27 Ricci-Trigault, (ch. 1; 2) p. 6 and *Fonti Ricciani* I, 13. The English translator, Fr. Gallagher, implies that Trigault mistakenly wrote *centesimo duodecimo* instead of *centesimo secundo* for the western frontier of Hunan province, but according to Fr. d'Elia, Ricci's manuscript states 112° (95° east longitude adjusted to the Greenwich prime meridian).

28 Ricci-Trigault, (ch. 1; 2) p. 7. Fr. d'Elia in *Fonti Ricciane* I, 14–15, suggests that Ricci is referring to the 1679 edition of the *Kuang-yü t'u.*

29 Martino Martini, *Novus atlas Sinensis* (Amsterdam, 1655) p. 5.

30 Athanasius Kircher, *China illustrata* (Amsterdam, 1667) p. 166.

31 Martini, *Novus atlas Sinensis,* p. 5.

lation of China from 1368 to 1953 finds the demographic sources on China during the period of Ricci's estimate to be fragmentary and frequently inaccurate. However, Mr. Ho's population estimate of 150 million for the year 1600 coincides with Kircher's figure[32]. On the other hand, and in support of drawing a higher population estimate from Ricci's figures, Mark Elvin refers to a Chinese population of "over 200 millions in 1580"[33].

Ricci's attitude toward China was sufficiently balanced to make objective comparisons between Europe and China. For example, he stated that in no other kingdom in the world could such variety of plant and animal life be found[34]. He described China as self-sufficient in food and materials. Vegetables, which were said to be consumed in far greater amounts than in Europe, were able to be harvested two or three times a year because of favorable climate, fertile soil and the industry of the people. While olives and almonds were not grown there, China and its southern regions in particular grew fruits unknown in Europe, such as the litchi and longan. Chinese horses and other beasts of burden were described as smaller than their European counterparts, but more numerous, cheaper in price and superior in carrying power. Ricci stated that the Chinese network of

32 See Ho Ping-t'i, *Studies on the Population of China, 1368–1953* (Cambridge, Massachusetts, 1959). According to Mr. Ho, the fragmentary and inaccurate nature of the demographic records of China between the reign of the first Ming monarch, the T'ai-tsu emperor (1368–1398), and 1741 make a population estimate for a year such as 1579 extremely difficult to reconstruct. In lieu of definite population figures, which Mr. Ho thinks impossible, given the presently available information, he offers certain ranges or limits in population of China for the period between the end of the fourteenth century and the mid-eighteenth century (p. 157). He states that during the late fourteenth century, the Chinese population "probably exceeded 65,000,000 to an unknown degree" (p. 22). The population is said to have grown in a more or less linear fashion from 1368 to 1600, contrary to the stationary population figures of the Ming (p. 23). By 1600, Ho estimates that the population of China was in the neighborhood of 150,000,000 (p. 264). In conjunction with the upheavals of the Manchu conquest during the second quarter of the seventeenth century, there were severe population losses, followed by slow recovery until by 1700, the population had again climbed to 150,000,000 (pp. 277–278). In ·1700, which is the concluding year of this study, the population of China stood on the verge of a tremendous period of growth in which it more than doubled to approximately 313,000,000 by 1794 (p. 278). One notes, incidentally, that Ho's study (p. 175) includes one reference to Ricci's *De Christiana expeditione apud Sinas*. The passage cited – Ho mistakenly cites it as page 12 instead of page 11 of the Gallagher translation – is only two pages beyond Ricci's population estimate on which Ho is, unfortunately, silent. Mark Elvin's *The Pattern of the Chinese Past* (Stanford, 1973) pp. 310–311, confirms the general demographic pattern outlined by Ho, but Mr. Elvin, drawing from the work of the Japanese scholar, Miura Kōzen, stresses the role of epidemic disease, especially the outbreaks of 1588 and 1641, in reducing the population in late traditional China. Ricci's journals are conspicuously silent on the great epidemic of 1588.

33 Elvin, p. 255.

34 Ricci-Trigault, (ch. 1; 3) pp. 9–10.

rivers and canals was so extensive than one could travel almost anywhere on them[35]. As for ocean-going vessels, the Chinese ships were said to be few in number and inferior to their Western counterparts[36]. On the negative side, Ricci judged Chinese glass-blowing and paper to be inferior to those of Europe, though he noted that paper was far more common in China than elsewhere[37]. Tea and lacquer were presented as novelties unknown to Europe[38]. Finally, saltpeter was extensive, but confined largely to the fireworks which were said to be quite lavish. Unlike in Europe, saltpeter was little used in preparing gunpowder and the Chinese state of weapon technology was described as deficient[39].

Ricci's evaluation of Chinese technology was mixed. He regarded Chinese architecture as completely inferior to that of Europe, both in style and durability. The latter defect was explained partially by the lack of substantial foundations in China[40]. However, Chinese printing was said to excel that of Europe. Ricci placed its origin at least five centuries before the origin of printing in Europe, which he dated from 1405. The use of a large number of characters rather than an alphabet had given rise to a unique type of printing, which Ricci described with fascination and admiration. A text was first written with ink and brush on a sheet of paper which was then inverted and pasted onto a wooden tablet. After drying, the surface was carefully scraped until only the outline of the characters remained. These were then carved in low relief. Using this block, a skilled printer could produce 1,500 copies in one day. Additions and alterations could quite easily be made on the tablets through patching. Ricci was clearly impressed with the efficiency of this method and had found it serviceable in mission work. For example, he described how this wood block method enabled one to produce small amounts of a pamphlet or a book on religious or scientific subjects which the fathers had done using the domestic servants in their mission houses. The simplicity of printing with wood blocks explained the very large number of books sold at very low prices in China[41].

In the matter of appreciating Chinese fine arts, the Jesuits were bound to European styles of pictorial art and Ricci was no exception. Chinese landscapes,

35 In this passage, Ricci appears to betray his limited geographical knowledge of China. It is mainly the terrain of eastern China which is suitable for canals and it is primarily here that Ricci traveled. However, this vast number of boats — which Ricci estimated to exceed those in all other parts of the world — would have been mainly limited to fresh water.

36 Ricci-Trigault, (ch. 1; 3) p. 11.

37 Ricci-Trigault, (ch. 1; 3) pp. 14—15.

38 Ricci-Trigault, (ch. 1; 3) pp. 16—17.

39 Ricci-Trigault, (ch. 1; 3) p. 18.

40 Ricci-Trigault, (ch. 1; 4) p. 19.

41 Ricci-Trigault, (ch. 1; 4) pp. 20—21. The standard twentieth-century study of printing in China expresses an admiration for wood-block printing similar to that of Ricci. See Thomas Francis Carter, *The Invention of Printing in China and its Spread Westward* (New York, 1925) pp. 26—27.

with the emphasis on pale washes and brushstroke rather than on color and perspective, were barely mentioned. Rather, Ricci fixed on the minimally developed Chinese tradition of portraiture, defects in statuary and lack of use of oil paints. According to Ricci: "The Chinese, who in other respects are so ingenious, and by nature in no way inferior to any other people on earth, are very primitive in the use of these latter arts, because they have never come into intimate contact with the nations beyond their borders"[42]. Ricci described Chinese music as "producing a monotonous rhythmic beat as they know nothing of the variations and harmony that can be produced by combining different musical notes". Finally, Ricci frowned on the Chinese love of dramatic shows and the large number of youths involved in trooping across the land in traveling dramatic groups. Ricci noted that these dramatic groups were employed at Chinese banquets and, along with the eating and drinking, could lead to a banquet lasting for ten hours[43]! One imagines Ricci's negative comment born of many hours of sitting captive at such banquets by the demands of etiquette, while other mission needs awaited action. When fine art converged with literary art, Ricci was more appreciative, as with Chinese calligraphy. Here no critical words pass from him in his description of the Chinese preoccupation with the elegance of their script[44].

Ricci began his discussion of Chinese liberal arts and sciences by stating that educated Chinese stressed the written language far more than the spoken language[45]. He noted that even friends living close together in the same city would communicate by writing rather than by meeting and talking. Ricci stated that the Jesuits had concentrated on learning *kuan-hua* (literally, official's language)[46] of which the term "mandarin", which means both "official" and official language", is a fairly close equivalent. Later, Ricci explained the Portuguese origin of the term "mandarin" as possibly from mandando (ordering; commanding) and noted that the use of the term "mandarin" to designate Chinese scholar-officials was already widespread in Europe[47]. Ricci stated that the Jesuits did not learn regional dialects and that *kuan-hua* was so widespread that even women and children understood it. However, this surely was an exaggeration as the general populace would have been able to understand *kuan-hua* only where it was a regional dialect, which is primarily in northern China but also in certain parts of the Yangtze River valley. Elsewhere in China, the official dialect would have been comprehensible only to scholar-officials and this was precisely the group that Ricci wished to cultivate and identify with. A sign of sinification

42 *Journals* (ch. 1; 4) p. 22.
43 Ricci-Trigault, (ch. 1; 4) p. 23.
44 Ricci-Trigault, (ch. 1; 4) pp. 23–24.
45 Ricci-Trigault, (ch. 1; 5) p. 27.
46 Ricci-Trigault, (ch. 1; 5) p. 28.
47 Ricci-Trigault, (ch. 1; 6) p. 47.

in Ricci was his remark about the conciseness of written Chinese. He stated: "This method of writing by drawing symbols instead of forming letters gives rise to a distinct mode of expression by which one is able, not only with a few phrases but with a few words, to set forth ideas with great clearness, which in our writing would have to be expressed in roundabout circumlocutions and perhaps with far less clarity"[48]. From the above description of Chinese geography, technology and culture, we can judge that Ricci had an understanding of China which though weak in certain areas, was on the whole a deep and solid basis on which to ground his accommodation.

4. RICCI'S CONFUCIAN-CHRISTIAN SYNTHESIS

The history of imperial China was a series of digressions, returns and regenerations at the fount of Confucius. During this 2,100 year period, the Sage was the primary point of reference for defining philosophical perspectives[49]. Certainly there were influential non-Confucian teachings in the history of imperial China, such as Taoism in the Six Dynasties period (221–581) and Buddhism in the T'ang Dynasty (618–906) and certainly there were popular and court pressures which could not be characterized as Confucian. But non-Confucian teachings only briefly broke out of the heterodox classification imposed by Confucians and when they did, it was usually only to be blended in some degree with Confucianism. The blending sometimes took the form of a syncretizing of systems, but more often it constituted separate parts of an individual's life. A scholar-official might be impeccably Confucian in his public life, practice Taoist longevity techniques in his private life and bury his parents with Buddhist rites. The Chinese religions were not so demanding in their claims upon the loyalty of their adherents as was the Judeo-Christian tradition.

There was a great deal of creativity in Chinese intellectual history, though the parameters of this creativity were less broad than the European tradition is accustomed to having them. The range of allowable Chinese creativity tended to lie between orthodox Confucianism on one hand and syncretisms of Confucianism, Buddhism and Taoism on the other, but these parameters were not nearly so sterile as they appear. (Many minds were indeed stifled, but the stifling was associated more with the limitations of the curriculum and forms of the fateful examination system than with the content of these three traditions).

48 *Journals* (ch. 1; 5) p. 29.
49 The major exception to this claim is the Six Dynasties period (220–581) when Confucianism lost influence and Taoism and Buddhism were ascendant as independent cultural forces. But even this exception is tempered by the fundamental breakdown of the imperial system during this time, particularly in the area of administration, the traditional source of Confucianism's motivation and power.

Chinese creativity cultivated subtlety and depth rather than diversity and originality, and this may be seen in the intensity of the debate over what constituted orthodox Confucianism.

Anti-Confucians during this period were normally perceived as rebels in the sense of challenging the established intellectual and moral order. Doubtless, this long-lasting influence of Confucianism was due not only to the power and flexibility of the Sage's ideas, but to the merging of Confucianism with the administrative system of China. The Classics became the standard educational curriculum through providing the content of the literati examinations. As an egalitarian path to wealth and power, the Confucian examination system functioned imperfectly, but with remarkable resilience. The emphasis upon following precedents found in the Classics provided both a stabilizing and stifling influence in the areas of literature and government. These Classics fostered a great deal of lip-service and a significant amount of actual service toward attending to the needs of the people. The emphasis on moral and spiritual cultivation in Confucianism produced a number of moral ideas which were perenially mouthed and in many instances followed.

Ricci arrived in China during a very creative period in her cultural history. But "creative" in late traditional China did not normally mean anti-Confucian. Even the most severe critics of Confucianism during the late Ming period, such as Li Chih (1527–1602), were more critical of a type of sterile, stifling and insincere Confucianism than of Confucianism as a whole[50]. For example, Li was far more critical of Chu Hsi's interpretation of Confucianism, which had become an intellectually oppressive orthodoxy, than of Confucius himself.

But if Li Chih was extreme, this does not mean that the more tempered forms of his ideas were not shared by many Chinese of the late Ming. During this time, many creative currents were syncretistic and stressed a belief that the teachings of Confucianism, Buddhism and Taoism were in essential agreement. Other creative forces were only implicitly syncretistic, such as the Neo-Confucian school of Wang Yang-ming (1472–1529). Wang and most of his followers had believed themselves to be firmly in the Confucian tradition and its truest expositors. However, Wang's emphasis on subjective and meditative elements introduced strains into Confucianism which had strong affinities to Buddhism and Taoism. The frequently harsh Confucian criticism of Buddhism as a heterodoxy, a criticism which flourished during periods dominated by the return to the fount of Confucius, abated somewhat in the Ming and was a telling sign

---

50 The most comprehensive recent study on Li Chih is that of Jean-François Billeter, *Li Zhi philosophe maudit (1527–1602)* (Geneva, 1979). Also see Hok-lam Chan, *Li Chih 1527–1602 in contemporary Chinese historiography* (White Plains, New York, 1980). Also see Wm. Theodore de Bary's discussion of Li Chih in the context of Ming individualism in his article "Individualism and humanitarianism," in Wm. Theodore de Bary, ed. *Self and society in Ming thought* (New York, 1970) pp. 188–225.

of the age's openness to syncretism. The creativity of the late Ming was not all channeled into one syncretic movement. It is a recurring feature of the history of Confucianism that individuals will arise to dispute the claims to orthodoxy of a currently dominant type of Confucianism. Such individuals will propose a return to a more genuine form of Confucius' teachings. Since all Confucians based their views on a particular commentarial interpretation of the Classics, each claim to orthodoxy almost always involved a rejection of the currently dominant commentaries and a reexamination of the texts of the Classics themselves. Most major claimants to reinterpretation would offer their own commentaries and draw from other earlier commentaries that supported their viewpoint. However, the most fundamental claim in each reinterpretation was not to a novel vision – which would have been abhorrent! – but to having perceived the *original* and *true* meaning of the Classics. Since the Classics were themselves claimed as records of the legendary sages – Confucius himself insisted that he was merely a transmitter (*Lun yü* 7:1) – the attempt was to revive the outlook of the revered sages themselves.

Ricci's accommodation method combined such a perception of the nature of the Confucian tradition with a tactical approach for introducing Christianity into China. Both factors are necessary to understand his policy of accommodation. Ricci presented Confucius, whom he dated in accordance with the best sources as being born in 551 B.C. and living more than seventy years, in laudatory terms. Ricci stated: "This great and learned man . . . spurred on his people to the pursuit of virtue not less by his own example than by his writings and conferences. His self-mastery and abstemious ways of life have led his countrymen to assert that he surpassed in holiness all those who in times past, in the various parts of the world, were considered to have excelled in virtue"[51].

However, for a Christian the fact remains that Confucius was a pagan, even if a virtuous one. Consequently, we find Ricci handling this delicate situation by choosing his words carefully: "Indeed, if we critically examine [Confucius'] actions and sayings as they are recorded in history, we shall be forced to admit that he was the equal of the pagan philosophers and superior to most of them." The "pagan philosophers" included Plato and Aristotle, who were enormously esteemed by Christians of Ricci's time. So while Ricci noted that the learned Chinese revered Confucius as their common master and dared not question any of his statements, he did not treat Confucius as a competitor to Jesus. Ricci explained that this was because the Chinese philosophers and rulers of past ages had honored Confucius as a mortal, but not revered him as a god. In a claim which would become hotly debated during the Rites Controversy, Ricci flatly denied that the Confucians revered Confucius with religious rites[52].

51 *Journals* (ch. 1; 5) p. 30.
52 Ricci-Trigault, (ch. 1; 5) p. 29, (ch. 4; 6) p. 368 & (ch. 1; 10) p. 108.

Ricci was far less flattering of the type of learning that he associated with Confucius' name, that is, "moral philosophy"[53]. Here Ricci betrayed vast amounts of European chauvinism and cultural myopia in his discussion. He claimed that moral philosophy was the only one of the higher philosophical sciences with which the Chinese were acquainted. He regarded their treatment of moral philosophy as defective mainly because they had no understanding of logic, by which he apparently meant the formal methodology associated with Aristotelian deductive logic. Consequently, Ricci stated that their science of ethics was confused, though he conceded that it was aided by the light of reason. Ricci's training in ethics was doubtless done in the Aristotelian mold, and this was the standard with which he measured Chinese moral theory.

Of the nine Chinese Classics, Ricci stated that Confucius compiled four (i.e. the Four Books) and personally wrote the Five Classics. Though this viewpoint is questioned today, Ricci was probably following the New Text viewpoint which since the Han Dynasty (206 B.C.-A.D. 220) had claimed that Confucius had composed the Six Classics[54]. The classic of *Music (Yüeh)* was lost sometime before the Han Dynasty, thus leaving five – the *Changes (I)*, *Odes (Shih)*, *History (Shu)*, *Rites (Li)*, and *Spring & Autumn (Ch'un-ch'iu)*. In contrast, the Old Text school claimed that the Duke of Chou (d. 1094 B.C.) had written the Six Classics and that Confucius was essentially a transmitter of the teachings of the Duke[55]. Contemporary scholars incline toward the view that most of the Five Classics were written before Confucius' time, but that he wrote the *Spring & Autumn*, the appendixes to the *Changes* and edited the other Five Classics[56].

Ricci's claim that Confucius compiled the Four Books is somewhat confusing. Of the four – the *Analects (Lun yü)*, *Great learning (Ta hsüeh)*, *Doctrine of the Mean (Chung yung)* and *Mencius (Meng-tzu)* – the *Analects* is a collection of the sayings of Confucius compiled by his disciples after his death. The *Mencius* was the work of the philosopher of the same name who was a follower of Confucius and whose lifespan (371–289 B.C.?) chronologically followed that of Confucius. The *Great learning* and *Doctrine of the Mean* were originally chapters in the *Rites*, or one of the Five Classics which Ricci claimed that Confucius wrote. These two chapters were not extracted and re-edited as separate works until the time of Chu Hsi (1130–1200), whose editing and commentaries actually created the category of the Four Books and elevated it to its pre-eminent status in the Ming and Ch'ing dynasties. From the time of the Yung-lo emperor (r. 1402–1424) until 1905 when the examination system was abolished,

53 Ricci-Trigault, (ch. 1; 5) p. 29.
54 Fung Yu-lan, *A history of Chinese philosophy* Derk Bodde, trans. 2 vols. (Princeton, 1953) I, 46 & II, 133–136.
55 Fung, *History* I, 56.
56 Fung, *History* I, 65–66 & Wing-tsit Chan, *A Source book in Chinese philosophy* (Princeton, 1963) p. 18.

the Four Books and Five Classics with Chu Hsi's commentaries constituted the curricular content of the examination system[57].

An examination of the original Italian manuscript confirms that Ricci was the author of this confusing claim regarding Confucius' authorship of the Four Books[58]. The Jesuits became preoccupied with the Confucian Four Books soon after they began arriving in China. Ricci's predecessor by two years. Michele Ruggieri (1543–1607), was perhaps the first to attempt to translate the Four Books into a European language[59]. Ricci followed almost simultaneously and there is evidence that Ricci's Latin paraphrase and commentary on the Four Books was used in teaching Chinese to newly arrived Jesuits[60]. Fr. d'Elia was probably correct in his claim that Ricci's work eventually became the basis of the translations of three of the Four Books – the *Great Learning, Doctrine of the Mean* and *Analects* – found in *Confucius Sinarum philosophus* (Paris 1687)[61]. However, Ricci's attitude toward Chu Hsi's commentaries on the Four Books, one of the foundations on which Neo-Confucianism was built, was very negative and was based upon both intellectual and strategic grounds. In Ricci's view, Neo-Confucianism contradicted Christianity too much to allow for an intellectual reconciliation between the two teachings. Furthermore, Chu Hsi's Neo-Confucianism was not sufficiently syncretic in spirit to allow room for a strategy of accommodation between it and Christianity.

The term "Neo-Confucian" is of European origin and has no Chinese equivalent. It is derived from a phase of regeneration at the fount of Confucius referred to in the term *Tao-t'ung* (Transmission of the True Way). The notion

---

57 See Ichisada Miyazaki, *China's examination hell* Conrad Schirokauer, trans. (New Haven, 1981) pp. 14–17.

58 d'Elia, *Fonti Ricciane* I, 42–44 & Ricci-Trigault, (ch. 1; 5) p. 32. The confusion over Ricci's supposed authorship of the Four Books was increased by Fr. Gallagher in his translation of Ricci-Trigault with this misleading sentence: "This volume, being a summary in excerpts from the four books mentioned, is called the Tetrabiblion." A more informed rendering of the Latin original would be "This volume is composed of the four books which they called the Four Books (*Ssu-shu*)." (*Id volumen, quia libris quatuor continetur Tetrabiblion appellarunt.*)

59 Ruggieri's effort to translate the Four Books is discussed by Knud Lundbaek in "The First Translation from a Confucian Classic in Europe," *China Mission Studies (1550–1800) Bulletin* 1 (1979): 1–11.

60 Trigault included reference to Ricci's Latin paraphrase and commentary on the Four Books [*De Christiana expeditions* (ch. 4; 3) p. 344], but deleted other references to the Four Books found in Ricci's diaries. See d'Elia, *Fonti Ricciane* I, 330 (3; 18) and I, 380 (3; 13). Evidence that the Four Books was used as part of the early language training of newly arrived Jesuits in seventeenth century China is found in the writings of Frs. Ricci-Trigault, Longobardi and Magalhaes. See *De Christiana expeditione* (ch. 4; 3). p. 344; Nichola Longobardi, *Traité sur quelques points de la religion des chinois* (Paris, 1701) in Christian Kortholt, ed., *Vivi illustris Godefridi Guil Leibnitii epistolae ad diversos* 4 vols. (Leipzig, 1735) II, 165; and Gabriel de Magaillans (Magalhaes), *Nouvelle relation de la Chine* (Paris, 1690) p. 102.

61 d'Elia, *Fonti Ricciane* II, 33n.

of *Tao-t'ung* may be traced to the T'ang dynasty precursor Han Yü (768–824) who attacked Buddhism by emphasizing that the transmission of the true teaching from the ancients and through Confucius had lapsed with Mencius[62]. However, the complete theory of *Tao-t'ung* was not formulated until Chu Hsi who argued that the *Tao* (True Way) which had lapsed with Mencius had not been revived until the early Sung dynasty philosophers Chou Tun-i and the Ch'eng brothers[63]. Chu Hsi expanded the theory of *Tao-t'ung* into a philosophical teaching known as *tao-hsüeh* (the True Way School). This school went from being banned in 1195–1202 to being pronounced the official state philosophy in 1240 and, in the process, its name was changed from *tao-hsüeh* to *li-hsüeh* (School of Principle)[64].

Neo-Confucianism has traditionally been divided into two branches. The first branch stressed the notion of *li* (principle) and is often described as rationalistic. This *li-hsüeh* (School of Principle) is also called "Ch'eng-Chu Neo-Confucianism" after its leading spirits – Ch'eng I (1033–1107) and Chu Hsi. The second branch of Neo-Confucianism – *hsin-hsüeh* (School of Mind) – stressed inner development and is said, somewhat vaguely, to be a form of philosophical idealism. It is also called "Lu-Wang Neo-Confucianism" after its two leading representatives – Lu Hsiang-shan (1139–1193) and Wang Yang-ming (Wang Shou-jen, 1472–1529). Contemporary Chinese scholars, such as Ch'ien Mu, have challenged this division of the Neo-Confucian tradition into School of Principle and School of Mind branches as misleading[65]. But whatever the degree of philosophical differences, there were historical tensions between the two branches and different attitudes toward the notion of *Tao-t'ung*[66]. Ricci was familiar with the Ch'eng-Chu school and referred by name to Chu Hsi and to one of the Ch'eng brothers – probably Ch'eng I – in his *T'ien-chu shih-i* (The true meaning of the Lord of Heaven)[67]. But Ricci showed little awareness of the Lu-Wang branch of Neo-Confucianism. He was opposed to Neo-Confu-

---

62 Wing-tsit Chan, *A source book in Chinese philosophy*. (Princeton, 1963) p. 450.

63 Wing-tsit Chan, "The *Hsing-li ching-i* and the Ch'eng-Chu School of the Seventeenth Century," in Wm. Theodore de Bary, ed., *The unfolding of Neo-Confucianism*. (New York, 1975) pp. 567–569.

64 The transition from *tao-hsüeh* to *li-hsüeh* is described in the following articles: James T. C. Liu, "How did a Neo-Confucian school become the state orthodoxy?" *Philosophy East & West* 23 (1973): 483–505 and John Winthrop Haeger, "The intellectual context of Neo-Confucian syncretism," *Journal of Asian Studies* 31 (1972): 499–513.

65 See Tu Wei-ming, "Reconstructing the Confucian tradition," *Journal of Asian Studies* 33 (1974): 445–449.

66 See Chan, "The *Hsing-li ching-i* and the Ch'eng-Chu School of the Seventeenth Century," p. 568 and Julia Ching, "Truth and ideology: the Confucian Way (*Tao*) and its transmission (*Tao-t'ung*), *Journal of the History of Ideas* 35 (1974): 371–388.

67 Li Ma-t'ou [Matteo Ricci], *T'ien-chu shih-i* (1603) book 1, pp. 20a–21a.

cianism on the grounds that it had deviated from the original content of Confucianism and had led away from the original theism into pantheism and atheism.

Ricci claimed that although the ancient Chinese believed in the immortality of the soul, many modern literati taught that the soul ceased to exist along with or shortly after the death of the body[68]. He stated that the doctrine most widely held by the literati of his time was borrowed from the Buddhists ca. 1100 and that this doctrine taught that the entire universe was composed of one substance continuous with its creator. The doctrine which Ricci was referring to was Neo-Confucianism, essentially of the Ch'eng-Chu branch, and the early cosmological borrowing of Neo-Confucianism was as much, if not more, Taoist than Buddhist. For example, the fundamental Neo-Confucian diagram dealing with the *T'ai-chi* (Supreme Ultimate) probably was derived by Chou Tun-i (1017–1073) indirectly from the Taoist master Ch'en T'uan (ca. 906–989). More specifically, Ricci was referring to *ch'i* (matter-energy), though the emphasis upon *ch'i* and the lack of complementary reference to *li* (principle) was more akin to the philosophy of another formative figure in Neo-Confucianism, Chang Tsai (1020–1077), than to Ch'eng-Chu Neo-Confucianism as a whole. However, Ricci accurately captured the sense of unity and harmony of substance pervading the Neo-Confucian cosmology which emerged in the Sung period. Ricci's claim that God was considered as part of the cosmos (i.e. pantheism) rather than being transcendent of the world, as in Christian theism, was less accurate. The Ch'eng-Chu Neo-Confucians said that *T'ai-chi* their supreme cosmological concept, was part of the world. However, the degree to which the Neo-Confucians saw *T'ai-chi* as a divine figure equivalent to the Chinese equivalents for God — *Shang-ti* or *T'ien* — is debatable. The interpretations of the Classics by Chu Hsi and his school had developed a cosmology which competed with Christian conceptions of God and Creation. Consequently, we find Ricci in his *T'ien-chu shih-i* directly criticizing the Neo-Confucian concept, *T'ai-chi*[69].

In his *T'ien-chu shih-i*, Ricci clearly distinguished the teachings of the ancient Classics from the Neo-Confucian re-interpretations[70]. He wrote: "The Western scholar states that although he has respectfully studied the ancient Classics and books and has heard of the earliest *chün-tzu* (superior man) honoring and revering *Shang-ti* (the Lord-on-high) of Heaven and Earth, he has not yet heard of them elevating *T'ai-chi* (the Supreme Ultimate), as if *T'ai-chi* were *Shang-ti* and the father-creator of the myriad things"[71]. While Ricci had argued that the use of *Shang-ti* in the ancient Chinese Classics was close to the Christian sense

68 Ricci-Trigault, (ch. 1; 10) pp. 105–106.
69 The Neo-Confucian usage of *T'ai-chi* dates from the *T'ai-chi t'u-shuo* (Explanation of the diagram of the Supreme Ultimate) by Chou Tun-i.
70 Cf. John D. Young's discussion of Ricci's formulation of "original Confucianism" (*hsien-ju*) in his *Confucianism and Christianity: the first encounter* (Hong Kong, 1983) pp. 28f.
71 Li, *T'ien-chu shih-i* bk. 1, p. 14b.

of God, he clearly rejected any equivalence between the Neo-Confucian *T'ai-chi* and God. In elaboration of a statement by Confucius, Ricci wrote: "You say that *li* (principle) encompasses the spirit of the myriad things and transforms and generates the myriad things. This is really *T'ien-chu* (Lord of Heaven; God). How can you refer to this *li* as merely *T'ai-chi*"[72]?

In the late Ming, Ch'eng-Chu Neo-Confucianism was firmly established as the official orthodoxy and the syncretic blending of Confucianism, Buddhism and Taoism into one teaching was one of the most creative and powerful intellectual currents of late Ming intellectual life. In one sense, Ricci's rejection of both the orthodox and creative forces appears as a rather indiscriminate rejection of the mainstream currents of Chinese culture in order to insert Europeanized Christianity in their place[73]. But if one looks closer, I believe one will see that Ricci's rejection of these two powerful currents was made *because of* his absorption of and participation in the syncretic and creative spirit of the late Ming. Ricci's sinification drew him into this mainstream spirit and the elements which Ricci rejected were certainly mild in comparison with what Li Chih rejected. What Ricci rejected was well within the limits of the acceptable for that time. A hundred years later, Chinese culture became far less creative and open, and there was a widespread return to the fount of Confucius. Consequently, one finds Jesuits of Ricci's accommodative mental-set in the following century harmonizing Ch'eng-Chu Neo-Confucianism with Christianity. One notable example of this is found in the translation of the Classics by Fr. François Noël (1657–1729) entitled *Sinensis imperii libri classici sex* (1711)[74]. Also, Fr. Joseph de Prémare (1666–1736) in his *Lettre sur le monotheisme des chinois* (composed ca. 1728) attempted to reconcile Neo-Confucian cosmology with Christianity[75].

But the most telling evidence of Ricci's sinification into late Ming cultural life was not the negative grounds of what he rejected, but the positive grounds of what he created. Ricci created a Confucian-Christian synthesis which was fully within the spirit of late Ming syncretism. Instead of a syncretism blending Confucianism of the Wang Yang-ming school with Buddhism and Taoism, Ricci proposed a Confucian-Christian synthesis. Ricci noted that the Confucian scholar-officials even denied that they belonged to a religious sect, but rather

---

72 The statement by Confucius is from the *Lun yü* 15.28: "a man is able to enlarge the *Tao*, but the *Tao* is not able to enlarge man."

73 For Ricci's criticism of the Ming syncretic teaching "the three teachings (Confucianism, Buddhism and Taoism) are one teaching," see Ricci-Trigault, (ch. 1; 10) p. 116.

74 See David E. Mungello, "The first complete translation of the Confucian Four Books in the West," in *International Symposium on Chinese-Western Cultural Interchange* (Taipei, 1983) pp. 515–541.

75 See David E. Mungello, "The Reconciliation of Neo-Confucianism with Christianity in the writings of Joseph de Prémare, S.J.," *Philosophy East & West* 26 (1976): 389–410.

constituted an academy devoted to good government and the welfare of the empire, with an emphasis upon keeping an ordered and peaceful society[76]. The scholar-officials were said also to have sought to foster the moral cultivation of the individual and the economic stability of the family, though the specific gentrylike context of this economic fostering was not noted. Ricci described the Five Relationships (*wu lun*) of Confucianism as the relationships between father and son, husband and wife, master and follower, elder and younger brothers, and between comrades or equals. Ricci stated that the Confucian precepts were in conformity with the innate light of reason and Christian truth. He further stated that the Confucians taught that one should not do to others what one did not wish done to oneself, which is a negative formulation of the Golden Rule expressed by Jesus in *Matthew* 7:12 and *Luke* 6:31. Ricci noted that, unlike Christianity, Confucianism permitted polygamy, frowned upon celibacy and was tolerant of other religions.

Ricci prepared the ground for his Confucian-Christian synthesis by stating: "The teachings of the academy, save in some few instances, are so far from being contrary to Christian principles, that such an institution could derive great benefit from Christianity and might be developed and perfected by it"[77]. It is interesting to compare how this statement in Ricci's commentaries was confirmed by a more private expression made in a letter in 1609 to the vice-provincial of Japan, Fr. Francesco Pasio. There Ricci wrote: "The sect of the literati has little to say about the supernatural, but its moral [ideals] are almost entirely in accord with our own. Accordingly, I have undertaken in the books I have written to laud [Confucian ethical teachings] and to use them to confute the other [two sects]. I have avoided criticizing [basic Confucian doctrine] but have sought to interpret it where it appears to conflict with our holy faith ... I have not failed, however, to dispute those new opinions of the literati in which they depart from the ancients"[78].

The Confucianism in Ricci's synthesis was to be drawn from a re-interpretation of the Classics based upon a study of the ancient texts. Ricci maintained that this study would reveal the affinities between ancient Confucianism and Christianity in the areas of theism and morality and confirm that the Chinese at one time had revered a monotheistic God. Ricci's own words were quite clear on this point: "Of all the pagan sects known to Europe, I know of no people who fell into fewer errors in early stages of their antiquity than did the Chinese. From the very beginning of their history it is recorded in their writings that they recognized and worshipped one supreme being whom they called the King

76 Ricci-Trigault, (ch. 1; 10) p. 109.
77 *Journals* (ch. 1; 10) p. 98.
78 Translated and quoted by George L. Harris, "The Mission of Matteo Ricci, S.J.," *Monumenta Serica* 25 (1966): 127. The original Italian text is found in Tacchi Venturi, *Opere storiche* II, 386.

of Heaven, or designated by some other name indicating his rule over heaven and earth ... [the ancient Chinese] also taught that the light of reason came from heaven and that the dictates of reason should be hearkened to in every human action"[79]. In regard to the always thorny problem of pagan status and salvation, Ricci was flexible and did not deny salvation to the ancient Chinese. He wrote: "One can confidently hope that in the mercy of God, many of the ancient Chinese found salvation in the natural law, assisted as they must have been by that special help which, as the theologians teach, is denied to no one who does what he can toward salvation, according to the light of his conscience." Ricci believed the evidence that the Chinese did indeed seek salvation through the natural law was found in their 4,000 year history of moral service for the common good and in their books filled with teachings on virtue[80].

In the traditional Chinese context, Ricci realized that a mere demonstration of the antiquity of an idea would establish the *authority* for acceptance by contemporary Chinese of a reinterpretation of the Classics. In his synthesis, Confucianism was to contribute primarily social and moral ingredients and Christianity mainly spiritual ingredients. One should note that Ricci's view of social elements was quite encompassing and included ancestral rites as well as rites honoring Confucius. In Ricci's viewpoint, the annual rites performed by the literati to departed ancestors, which included the placing of food on the graves, was intended mainly for the purpose of teaching the living, particularly children and young adults, to honor their parents[81]. Such an interpretation would bring the ancestral rites nicely into line with Christian love of one's parents. Yet Ricci realized that he was on tenuous theological grounds here and added that those Chinese who converted to Christianity should replace the custom of placing food on the graves of ancestors with giving alms to the poor or toward the cause of saving souls. Finally, Ricci stated that the Chinese clearly did not consider their departed ancestors to be gods and therefore did not petition them with requests. Ricci felt that in his synthesis, only the later and Neo-Confucian accretions to pristine Confucianism were being displaced. Most of the Confucian elements would remain intact — if one accepted Ricci's reinterpretation of Confucianism — and ease the entry of literati converts into the Christian faith.

Ricci counted on the commanding role of the literati as model-builders in Chinese society to bring along the less educated masses. To a large extent, Ricci's Confucian-Christian synthesis was an attempt to displace Buddhist and Taoist spiritual elements in Chinese society with Christian spiritual elements. The synthesis was clearly created with an educated and cultured elite in mind and the question of the degree to which it might have succeeded with the

79 Journals (ch. 1; 10) p. 93.
80 Ricci-Trigault, (ch. 1; 10) p. 104.
81 Ricci-Trigault, (ch. 1; 10) pp. 107–108.

people at large remains even more problematic than with the literati. Another potential stumbling block to realizing the synthesis was Ricci's apparent unfamiliarity with the complexity and deep-seated controversies on textual questions dealing with the Confucian Classics. Ricci's synthesis was of a depth and profundity which transcended its use as mere mission strategy. He saw the fate of Christianity in China hang on the encompassing issue of Chinese acceptance of the Confucian-Christian synthesis[82]. After Ricci's death in 1610, the cultural and political milieu in China continued to evolve during the transition from one dynasty to another, but his synthesis was sufficiently well-grounded to continue to serve as a framework for the meeting of Chinese and European cultures. Throughout the seventeenth century other Jesuits, with assistance from sympathetic Chinese literati, continued to develop and evolve Ricci's accommodationism into new forms while maintaining the basic formula which Ricci had first developed.

Ricci's choice of Confucianism rather than Buddhism or Taoism for the indigenous element in the synthesis with Christianity was the result of a careful consideration not merely of the circumstances of a given time and place, but also of the inner dynamics of the respective Chinese teachings. Although Buddhism originated in India, Ricci was dealing with its Chinese form. His harsh criticism of Buddhism was due largely to his perception of it as a competitor to Christianity. By contrast, our own age has seen daring attempts to synthesize Buddhism and Christianity into Christian Zen, though whether this blending has broad spiritual potential remains to be seen[83]. Ricci was aware of certain similarities between Christianity and Buddhism, but he was unwilling to concede to the Buddhists what he had conceded to the ancient Confucians, namely, that Buddhism had developed through natural law a morality similar to Christianity. Instead, Ricci argued that Buddhism had borrowed those elements from Western philosophers and from Christianity, and had then distorted them[84]. In spite of Ricci's lapse in perception, the similarities between Buddhism and Christianity are quite strong in the areas of ethics and spiritual practice, though far less so in matters of ontology and theology. The fundamental notion of Buddhist compassion bears a strong similarity to the equally fundamental Christian love.

82 Several scholars have recently published works which explore the seventeenth-century Chinese response to the teachings which the Jesuits presented. These works include two articles by Willard J. Peterson, "Fang I-chih: Western Learning and the 'Investigation of Things.'" in The Unfolding of Neo-Confucianism (New York, 1975) Wm. Theodore de Bary, ed. (New York, 1975) pp. 369–411 and "From interest to indifference: Fang I-chih and Western Learning," Ch'ing-shih wen-t'i (1976), 60–80. More recently, two monographs have appeared: Jacques Gernet, Chine et christianisme. Action et réaction (Paris, 1982) and John D. Young, Confucianism and Christianity: the first encounter.

83 See William Johnston, The still point (New York, 1971) & by the same author, Christian Zen (New York, 1971).

84 Ricci-Trigault, (ch. 1; 10) pp. 110–111.

Both religions have strongly pacifist strains and highly developed traditions of celibacy. Both share certain highly developed meditative traditions, including chanting, prayer beads and contemplation. But the similarity of Buddhism to Christianity proved less crucial to Ricci's search for a synthesis than did the complementarity of Confucianism to Christianity.

Ricci's accommodation method, his Confucian-Christian synthesis and particularly his negative attitude toward Buddhism have received criticism from certain modern sinologists. Otto Franke argued that Ricci would have been wiser had he synthesized Christianity with the views of Li Chih than with an orthodox body of Confucians because later, in the eighteenth century, these Confucians would turn against the China Mission[85]. Herr Franke argued that Li Chih could have enlightened Ricci that ancient China — in which Ricci perceived similarities with Christianity — had not been Confucian, but pre-Confucian. Furthermore, according to Franke, Ricci's narrow-minded perception of Li Chih as a Buddhist and therefore a heretic, eliminated him from serious consideration in Ricci's mind. Franke's treatment was insightful, but ignored the Jesuit pattern of working through the intelligentsia and the established scholar-officials.

More recently, Jacques Gernet has argued that Ricci's rejection of Buddhism and identification with a highly rationalistic strain in late Ming China was a mistake. M. Gernet claimed that Christianity had too much in common with Buddhism to effectively oppose it and that the surfacing of the similarities was only delayed by Jesuit tactics. Gernet emphasized that in spite of some superior techniques in mathematical and geographical sciences, Ricci's European cosmology was pre-Copernican and medieval. His Aristotelian-Ptolemaic vision of a closed, finite universe, locked into its crystalline spheres, ran contrary to the more fluid cosmologies shared by the entire spectrum of Chinese thinkers. Consequently, Ricci's identification with the Tunglin movement on the grounds that its literati and the Jesuits shared an opposition to eunuchs, to Buddhist influence among the literati and to speculative philosophy was doomed to failure[86]. Gernet aptly analyzed the aspects of Ricci's accommodation method working against success, but he neglected the positive elements which, in my view, outweigh the negative.

Ricci concluded his description of the Chinese system of government with some comparisons unfavorable to Europe. First, Ricci was struck by the Chinese lack of military aggression, though when he spoke of the complete lack of ag-

85 Otto Franke, "Li Tschi und Matteo Ricci," *Abhandlungen der preussischen Akademie der Wissenschaften* (Berlin) (1937) Philosophisch-historische Klasse nr. 10, pp. 1–62.

86 See Jacques Gernet, "La politique de conversion de Matteo Ricci," & "A propos des contacts entre la Chine et l'Europe aus XVIIe et XVIIIe siècles," *Acta Asiatica* (Tokyo) 23 (1972): 78–92. Also see M. Gernet's treatment of Ricci in his "Philosophie chinoise et christianisme de la fin du XVIe au milieu du XVIIe siècle," *Actes du colloque international de Sinologie* (Paris, 1976) pp. 13–25 & *Chine et christianisme* p. 25f.

gression in Chinese history, he was exaggerating[87]. The lessened degree of both military and individual physical aggressiveness in Chinese society is a phenomenon which Western observers have often found notable, thought not always, as in Ricci's case, praiseworthy. A second point on which Ricci praised the Chinese was their government by "philosophers", that is, by the scholar-officials. The administration of the realm was said to be totally in their hands. Ricci was particularly struck by the elevation of the literati over the military class in advising the emperor. So low was the status of military leaders that very few were even admitted to councils of war! Ricci claimed that in the eyes of aspiring leaders of the populace, the lowest literatus rank was more esteemed than the highest military ranking. Ricci was so impressed by this situation that he failed to perceive the extent to which China's defenses had been weakened by military laxity. Less than forty years after Ricci wrote these words, China succumbed to conquest by an aggressive and far less civilized northern people known as the Manchus (Tartars). But such was the power of Chinese culture that sinification gradually sapped the Manchu military outlook and prowess while the Manchus eventually became the staunchest defenders of a rigidified Neo-Confucian orthodoxy.

The perception of Chinese government as run by philosophers, which was made by Ricci and other writers after him, had an enormous effect upon idealizing China in the eyes of European learned society. An idea is often more powerful than reality and the realities of late Ming China did not live up to the ideal of government by philosophers. Although Ricci was extremely critical of the avarice of the powerful eunuch Ma T'ang[88], he was on the whole not very critical of the eunuchs and he praised the Wan-li emperor in moderate tones. He seems to have lacked the historical perspective and familiarity with the internal workings of the Chinese government — which later Jesuits would acquire — to comprehend the degree to which the Wan-li emperor had dissolved most of his contacts with the scholar-officials and how he communicated with them almost exclusively through his palace eunuchs. The severity of the emperor's actions is revealed in the fact that between 1589 and 1615, he never appeared in a general audience. In 1590, he ended his contacts with the Hanlin scholars, an academy of preeminent scholars who normally advised the emperor. Finally, between 1591 and his death in 1620, the Wan-li emperor held only six interviews with his grand secretary — the major official in the government[89]! Not only did the Wan-li emperor use the eunuchs to communicate his wishes to the literati, but increasingly, he appointed eunuchs to administrative duties, which effectively displaced the scholar-officials' authority. Since the eunuchs were

---

87 Ricci-Trigault, (ch. 1; 6) pp. 58–59.
88 Ricci-Trigault, (ch. 4; 11) pp. 394–405.
89 Goodrich & Fang, pp. 326–327. A slightly more sympathetic view of the young Wan-li emperor is found in Ray Huang, *1587, a year of no significance* (New Haven, 1981).

generally less educated than the literati and had less independent claim to status, they owed their loyalty totally to the emperor. By contrast, the prime loyalties of the scholar-officials were to the Confucian teachings by which they had achieved rank and to the social class which embodied these teachings. The literati owed loyalty to the emperor as the theoretical head of the Confucian ideological system. The eunuchs were particularly subject to corruption and many historians have regarded the proliferation of their numbers and powers in late Ming China as a negative sign of the times as well as a contributing cause to the fall of the Ming.

5. RICCI'S TREATMENT OF BUDDHISM

In the section of *De Christiana expeditione apud Sinas* devoted to religious sects, Ricci gave a brief description of Buddhism which he referred to as "Sciequia" (*Shih-chia*, i.e. Sakyamuni Buddha) or "Omitose" (*A-mi-ta-fo*, i.e. Amitabha Buddha)[90]. Amitabha Buddha was the Buddha of the Western Paradise and the prayerful repetition of his name was widely believed to lead to rebirth in this paradise. This was initially a cult of a popular, devotional nature which by the time of the Ming period had blended with other forms of Chinese Buddhism. Ricci's other name for Buddhism, "Sakyamuni", referred to the historical Buddha, Gautama, who is usually regarded as the earthly founder of Buddhism. However, Ricci's description lacked any reference to the Buddha as a man or religious founder, though he did note that the "founders" of Buddhism died before it came to China. Ricci probably fused the account of Sakyamuni's death in the fifth century B.C. with the claim that there were many Buddhas and concluded that these founders of Buddhism had died before the religion reached China. Ricci was aware that Buddhism came to China from India and that it was carried by the Chinese to Japan. He reproduced the story of the dream of a new religion by the Han emperor Ming (r. A.D. 58–75) which led to a Chinese embassy being sent to the west to investigate. Contemporary students of Buddhism doubt the historical veracity of this widely propagated story about Emperor Ming's dream and consequent embassy to India as the basis for the introduction of Buddhism into China. Studies by both Kenneth K. S. Ch'en and E. Zürcher cite conflicting details as to the dates of the expedition, destination, names of envoys and foreign monks said to have returned with the embassy[91]. However, their ultimate grounds for rejecting the authenticity of the account is that Buddhism was already introduced into China at the time of the purported dream.

---

90 Ricci-Trigault, (ch. 1; 10) pp. 109–112.
91 See Kenneth K. S. Ch'en, *Buddhism in China* (Princeton, 1964) pp. 29–31 & E. Zürcher, *The Buddhist conquest of China* (Leiden, 1959) pp. 21–22.

In repeating the basic details of this legend surrounding Emperor Ming's dream, Ricci was approximately accurate. However, his Europocentric outlook led him to make some outrageous claims. He suggested that the dream was really about Christianity, which was at the time said to be preached in India by the Apostle Thomas. Thus, Ricci claimed that the Chinese embassy sent by the Emperor Ming to investigate Christianity mistook Buddhist teaching for the Christian one. Secondly, Ricci suggested that Buddhism borrowed certain ideas from Western philosophers, including the Four Element theory. Buddhism was said to have borrowed the notion of a multiplicity of worlds from the school of Democritus and the transmigration of souls from Pythagoras. Ricci vaguely suggested Buddhist borrowings from Christianity of a modified Trinity, notions of rewards in heaven and punishments in hell, celibacy and a chant that closely resembled the Gregorian chant. But in Ricci's view, whatever elements of truth might have been found in Buddhist doctrine had been thoroughly confused and overlaid with error.

Ricci's description of the historical development of Buddhism in China showed how thoroughly he had absorbed the viewpoint of the Confucian literati. He noted that initially Buddhism flourished because its teachings on the immortality of the soul and future happiness had a popular appeal. (Although much confusion has traditionally surrounded the Buddhist doctrine of the self or soul, it is quite clear that Buddhism took its goal to be the extirpation of self or soul on the grounds that it is the troublesome source of endless desires and suffering.) Ricci voiced typically Confucian anti-Buddhist rhetoric when he stated that Buddhism's growth was paralleled by the "unconscious spread of its vile pest of impostures"[92]. As with most rhetoric, Ricci stated that nothing undermined the growth of Buddhism more than the negative reputation which the Confucians gave it. Underlying the Confucian viewpoint was the historical fact that during its early development in China (ca. A.D. 200–845), Buddhism competed with Confucianism and Taoism in a frequently hostile atmosphere. The anti-Buddhist persecution of 845, which did irreversible damage to Chinese Buddhism, was largely the result of Confucian maneuvering and resurgence of Confucian strength. Although Ricci noted a fluctuation in the fortunes of Buddhism in China, he stated that the enormous output of writings on Buddhism had been responsible for its continued vitality. To a Christian – or a Confucian – with a strong sense of the difference between orthodoxy and heterodoxy, the variety of Buddhist doctrine and its apparent inability to be reduced to a single system was appalling.

Ricci was highly critical of the "osciami" (*ho-shang*), which translates as "bonzes" or monks. As a man of learning and culture, Ricci was repelled by the gross and unlettered habits of the monks of that time, which stood in such contrast to the fastidiously refined literati. He was particularly repulsed by the

92 *Journals* (ch. 1; 10) p. 100.

monks' moral laxity which made a mockery of their celibacy. Nor was Ricci impressed by the Buddhist monasteries which he described as "large and noisy hotels"[93]. Nevertheless, he noted that Buddhism was undergoing a revival. In his estimates of two or three million Buddhist monks in late Ming China, Ricci vastly exceeded recent estimates by scholars[94].

6. RICCI'S TREATMENT OF TAOISM

Ricci's references to Buddhists and Taoists blurred the two together. This was partly due to the general tendency found among Christian missionaries toward reducing all non-Judeo-Christian religions to a single pagan category[95]. It was also due to the syncretic blending of Buddhist and Taoist notions, doctrines and practices which had occurred by the time of the Ming. However, in his description of the three major religious teachings of the Chinese, Ricci showed that he was aware of fundamental distinctions between Buddhism and Taoism. He reproduced the widely held account that Taoism originated with Lao-tzu, a legendary contemporary of Confucius[96]. But Ricci departed from this account by saying that Lao-tzu left no writings. Actually, the small, but famous *Tao-te-ching* (the Way of power-virtue classic) has been widely ascribed to Lao-tzu and carries the distinction of being the single Chinese work most-translated into Western languages. Ricci appeared to have been unfamiliar with this work as well as with the magnificently subtle *Chuang-tzu*, attributed to the fourth century B.C. philosopher of the same name. In fact, in a surprising lapse of literary knowledge, Ricci seemed to have been entirely unaware of the philosophical stream of Taoism and identified Taoism totally with the priests and practices associated with the more obviously religious forms of Taoism.

Actually, Taoism consisted of a large number of schools with beliefs and practices which hung together by only tenuous threads. One of the most fundamental of these threads was the "reversal of the Tao", i.e. the reversal of the aging process in Nature. In addition to a philosophical current associated with Lao-tzu and Chuang-tzu and a religious current, there was a Taoist alchemy

93 *Journals* (ch. 1; 10) p. 101.
94 According to Mr. Ch'en (*Buddhism in China*, p. 452), a census made approximately 100 years after Ricci's time and during the reign of the K'ang-hsi emperor (1662–1721) revealed that the Buddhist sangha (i.e. monastic community) consisted of 110,292 monks and 8,615 nuns. These numbers were far below Ricci's estimate of two or three million monks.
95 Johannes Beckmann, S.M.B. attempts to show that in spite of the tendency of missionaries to reduce other religions to a single pagan category, Christian missionaries in China had a number of contacts with Taoism. See Fr. Beckmann's article, "Die katholischen Missionare und der Taoismus vom 16. Jahrhundert bis Gegenwart," *Neue Zeitschrift für Missionswissenschaft* 26 (1970): 1–17.
96 Ricci-Trigault, (ch. 1; 10) p. 112.

centered about the search for an elixir of immortality. Ricci mentioned this alchemy in a negative light several times in his commentaries, but associated it only vaguely with Taoism[97]. Ricci had little interest in Chinese alchemy, perhaps because he saw alchemy as an obstacle to the Confucian-Christian synthesis. He treated the alchemical pursuit in Chinese society as an incurable obsession, equivalent to a mental and spiritual imbalance. He may have perceived the Taoist quest for immortality as a competitor to the type of immortality which Christianity offered. This possibility is strengthened by the fact that Ricci noted that the Taoist alchemical quest for immortality most appealed to the same sort of intellectual Chinese as did the Confucian-Christian synthesis. He realized that the quest for immortality was intellectually demanding and that the literati was particularly attracted to its pursuit[98]. Ricci stated that just as many wealthy Chinese seeking to transmute base metals into silver were reduced to poverty through spending vast sums on alchemical experiments, so did the seekers of immortality go beyond the limits of reason. (On the other hand, he felt that Confucianism and Christianity fully harmonized with reason.) Ricci noted that in Peking, most of the high-ranking scholar-officials and eunuchs were "addicted to this foolish pursuit"[99].

The rumor that the Jesuits possessed a secret alchemical formula for converting base metals into silver plagued them in their relations with the Chinese. The latter sometimes felt that the fathers were withholding this secret from them or, in the case of a eunuch in Peking, lost interest in the fathers after discovering that they possessed no such secret[100]. Sometimes the quest for an

97 Ricci-Trigault, (ch. 1; 10) p. 115.
98 Ricci-Trigault, (ch. 1; 9) p. 102.
99 *Journals* (ch. 1; 9) p. 91. Ricci acquired first-hand awareness of several literati absorbed in alchemy. One of these was Ch'ü Ju-k'uei (Ch'ü T'ai-su), one of the first literati-followers of Ricci, who was baptized in 1605. (See Arthur W. Hummel, ed., *Eminent Chinese of the Ch'ing Period (1644–1912)* (Washington, 1943) p. 199.) Ch'ü was the son of an eminent literati family of Kiangsu who, according to Ricci, had received a literati education, but instead of pursuing the standard examination quest, became diverted in bad company and practices, including a mania for alchemy. (See Ricci-Trigault, (ch. 3; 3) pp. 252–253.) Ricci's description makes this fascination for alchemy appear similar to contemporary addictions to gambling.
100 Ricci-Trigault, (ch. 3; 5) pp. 267–268, (ch. 3; 13) p. 311 & (ch. 4; 3) p. 342. Ch'ü Ju-k'uei was only one of a number of literati attracted to the Jesuits because of a widespread belief that along with their knowledge of mathematics and astronomy, the fathers possessed the secret of converting base metals into silver. Ricci's chagrin over this source of attraction doubtless contributed to his sharp words on Chinese alchemy. According to Ricci, this rumor was fed by the belief that the Portuguese were thought to buy huge amounts of mercury from the Chinese at very high prices and to carry the mercury on their ships to Japan from which they returned laden with silver coins. The Portuguese were thought to apply a mysterious foreign herb in Japan in order to convert the mercury into silver. (See Ricci-Trigault, (ch. 2; 10) pp. 204–205.)

elixir of immortality proved a stubborn personal obstacle to Christian conversion in the same manner as a belief in lucky and unlucky days[101]. Contemporary scholars do not share Ricci's low regard for Taoist alchemy and take it rather to be a singular achievement in the historical development in the Chinese understanding of nature. But in fairness to Ricci and his situation in late Ming China, to criticize him for failing to develop a comprehensive and objective understanding of Chinese alchemy would involve an unrealistic expectation and one prompted by the benefit of nearly four centuries of sinological research and hindsight.

7. SOME CONCLUDING REMARKS ON RICCI'S POLICY OF ACCOMMODATION

Ricci portrayed the Chinese as flexible rather than closed-minded. This portrayal was interesting because it contrasted with many descriptions of the Chinese of this time as smug in their sense of cultural superiority. In order to appeal to the traditional Chinese view of their nation as the "Middle Kingdom", Ricci composed a map of the world in Chinese (*Shan-hai yü-ti ch'uan-t'u*) with China in the central position[102]. However, Ricci noted that after being presented with the geographical fact, "the Chinese, for the most part, acknowledge their former error and make it a source of no little mirth"[103].

The intellectual emphasis in Ricci's accommodation method derived not merely from his own intellectual inclinations, but also from what he perceived in the Chinese[104]. In *De Christiana expeditione*, Trigault inserted the statement

101 Ricci-Trigault, (ch. 5; 1) p. 595.
102 There were at least three editions of Ricci's map of the world: (1) 1584 at Shaoching (2) 1601 published in the *Yüeh lin kuang i* by Feng Mu-kang and (3) 1602 at Peking. The 1602 edition of the map is preserved in the Bibliotheca Vaticana. Both the 1584 and 1602 editions of this map are reproduced by Fr. d'Elia in *Fonti Ricciane* II, plates viii & 11, respectively. For further information on Ricci's map, see Boleslaw Szcześniak, "Matteo Ricci's Maps of China," *Imago Mundi* 11 (1954); 126–136. Also see the following: Lionel Giles, "Translations from the Chinese Map of Father Ricci," *The Geographical Journal of the Royal Geographical Society* 52 (1918): 367–385 & 53 (1919): 19–30; J. F. Baddeley, "Father Matteo Ricci's Chinese World-Maps, 1584–1608," *The Geographical Journal of the Royal Geographical Society* 53 (1919): 254–270; E. Heawood, "The Relationships of the Ricci Maps," *The Geographical Journal of the Royal Geographical Society* 53 (1919): 271–276; & L. Carrington Goodrich, "China's First Knowledge of the Americas," *Geographical Review* 28 (1938): 400–411.
103 *Journals* (ch. 1; 2) p. 7.
104 One of the most penetrating studies of the Jesuits' perception of seventeenth-century China and the Chinese response to these Jesuits is written by Paul A. Rule. Unfortunately, his doctoral dissertation "K'ung-tzu or Confucius? the Jesuit interpretation of Confucianism" (Australian National University) remained in a state of revision at the time of this writing. However, an article by Mr. Rule has been published whose con-

very much in accord with Ricci's position that the Chinese "are slow to take a salutary spiritual potion, unless it be seasoned with an intellectual flavoring"[105]. Ricci's accommodation method may be aptly described as "intellectually flavored Christianity". Clearly, part of this flavoring must be seen as Confucianism. In the view of Ricci-Trigault, the flavoring also took the form of those aspects of European science which would appeal to the Chinese. Much of what the Jesuits taught was new in China and this novelty was greatly appreciated by many, though not all, literati in the open intellectual climate of the late Ming. However, this European science was also useful and fifty years after Ricci's death, when the intellectual climate of China had turned conservative, the missionaries would be stressing the practical rather than the novel aspects of European science. The particular form in which Jesuit accommodation was expressed stemmed from the Chinese stress upon the written language. Ricci saw that it was not merely a Socratic-type of verbal dialectic which would persuade the Chinese of the validity of Christianity, but books written in a Chinese of a high literary standard[106]. This was not merely the aim that Ricci set for himself in his Chinese compositions, of which *T'ien-chu shih-i* was the most eminent example. This perception was acceded to by his superior, Fr. Valignano, and provided the establishment of a training program for new Jesuit missionaries while setting the direction of the entire Jesuit program in China for the next century.

tents are drawn from his longer study. See Paul A. Rule, "The Confucian interpretation of the Jesuits," in *Papers on Far Eastern History* (Canberra) 6 (1972): 1–61. Another useful interpretation of the Jesuits' approach in China, from the point of view of a non-sinologist, is found in Donald W. Treadgold, *The West in Russia and China* vol. 2. *China, 1582–1949* (Cambridge, 1973) pp. 1–34.

105 *Journals* (ch. 4; 5) p. 325. For a closer examination of what Ricci wrote and what Trigault added, compare d'Elia, *Fonti Ricciane* II, 49 with Ricci-Trigault, (ch. 4; 5) pp. 355–356.

106 Ricci-Trigault, (ch. 5; 17) p. 595.

CHAPTER 3
THE CONTINUATION OF JESUIT ACCOMMODATION IN THE
WORKS OF SEMEDO AND MAGALHAES

1. INTRODUCTION

After the initial formulation of Jesuit accommodation by Ricci, the enormous task remained of carrying the project forward. Among those Jesuits in the China Mission who inherited this project after Ricci's death were Frs. Semedo and Magalhaes. They continued to develop and implement Ricci's program of accommodation in the middle years of the seventeenth century. Neither were seminal thinkers of the level of Frs. Ricci or Bouvet, but they were highly capable Jesuits who achieved a high degree of proficiency in the Chinese language and a sophisticated understanding of Chinese culture and society. Both conveyed the mature fruits of their knowledge to Europe through literary works. Although Magalhaes was an individualistic personality who often resists generalization, both Semedo and Magalhaes were admirers of Chinese culture. Both accepted the basic accommodative premises that the ancient Chinese had worshipped a Supreme Being akin to the Old Testament God and both believed that the Confucian Classics contained vestiges of this worship.

Both Semedo and Magalhaes devoted considerable attention to describing the Chinese language. Not only did this interest in Chinese reflect the practical demands of Jesuit accommodation, but it also was part of the fascination of seventeenth-century Europeans with foreign and exotic languages and the search for a universal language. Such a search was fraught with religious implications. While Semedo made few changes in Ricci's original formula for accommodation, Magalhaes contributed to its evolution in the joint composition of the radical treatise *T'ien-hsüeh ch'uan-kai* (A summary of the spread of the Heavenly Teaching). The latter introduced the claim that both the Chinese and Europeans were descended from a common Biblical source and that the similarity of the morality of the ancient Chinese to Christianity was due to the Chinese receiving their Old Testament morality directly rather than indirectly through natural theology.

2. THE BACKGROUND OF FR. SEMEDO'S *IMPERIO DE LA CHINA*

Alvaro Semedo (1586–1658) was a Portuguese Jesuit who arrived in China in 1613[1]. Unlike other Jesuits, including his more famous contemporary, Fr.

---

1 Alvaro Semedo was born in Niza, diocese of Portalêgre, Portugal in 1586. He entered

Adam Schall von Bell who was stationed at Peking, Fr. Semedo remained in the south of China throughout his many years of residence. In perhaps his only trip to northern China, he visited Sian in 1625 and was the first European to examine the newly recovered Nestorian Tablet. In 1636, he was sent to Europe to secure further assistance and to procure new recruits. Between 1640 and 1644, he visited Lisbon, Madrid and Rome, where he furthered the aims of his mission by publishing a long report on China, known most commonly under the Spanish title of *Imperio de la China*. Upon his return to China, he occupied the important post of vice-provincial of the China Mission and in 1649 spent several months in captivity in Canton. He is said to have been freed through the influence of Fr. Schall. Semedo remained in Canton until his death in 1658 or 1659.

In the tradition of Fr. Trigault before him and many Jesuits afterwards, Semedo's visit to Europe was also intended to secure support for the Jesuit mission by the publication of reports from China geared to European interests. Semedo wrote such a report in 1640 in Portuguese entitled "Relaçao de propagaçao de fé regno da China e outros adjacentes". He apparently handed the manuscript over to a printer while passing through Lisbon and Madrid in 1642 and the work was published in Portuguese in Madrid in 1641 and in Lisbon in 1642[2]. It was translated into Spanish, then rearranged and given an historical style by Manuel de Faria i Sousa and republished under the title *Imperio de la China* at Madrid in 1642. It was in this form that the text was translated and published in Italian (1643), French (1645) and English (1655). In terms of publicizing the Jesuit China mission throughout Europe, the work was very successful.

In addition to working within China to secure the success of the Confucian-Christian synthesis, Semedo wrote a work (*Imperio de la China*) which was part of the Jesuit funnel for conveying information about China back to Europe

---

the Jesuit novitiate in 1602 and in 1608 departed for Goa where he completed his studies. He arrived at Nanking in 1613 and, in the company of Fr. Alvonso Vagnoni (1568 [1569]–1640), endured prison and other privations during the anti-Christian persecution in 1616 in Nanking. He and most of the missionaries were exiled to Macao where he remained until 1621. In an attempt to avoid the past, he changed his Chinese name from Hsieh Wu-lu to Tseng Te-chao. With the easing of the persecution, he returned to Kiangsi and Kiangnan provinces where he enjoyed the patronage of the Christian literatus, Michael Yang T'ing-yün. For Semedo's birthdate, I follow P. Dehergne's 1586 rather than P. Pfister's 1585. Cf. Joseph Dehergne, S.J., *Répertoire des Jésuites de Chine de 1552 à 1800* (Rome, 1973) p. 245 with Aloys [Louis] Pfister, S.J., *Notices biographiques et bibliographiques sur les Jésuites de l'ancienne mission de Chine, 1552–1773* 2 vols. (Shanghai, 1932–1934) p. 143.

2 Carlos Sommervogel, S.J., *Bibliothèque de la Compagnie de Jésus* 12 vols. (Brussels & Paris, 1890–1932) VII, 1114 & Robert Streit, *Bibliotheca Missionum* vols. V & VII (Rome, 1929–1931) V, 778.

for its assimilation. The generally sympathetic manner in which Semedo presented China to European readers shows that this work was part of the Jesuit policy of accommodation in China. *Imperio de la China* consisted of 362 pages in quarto and was divided into two parts. The first part, which occupied two-thirds of the work, was described in the table of contents as dealing with the "temporal state of China" and included a great variety of topics. The second part treated the "spiritual state of China" and was really a history of the Jesuit mission in China since the arrival of St. Francis Xavier in 1552. Semedo's exclusion of other Christian orders from his account of this period is explained in part by the tendency of non-Jesuit missionaries to work against Ricci's formula for accommodation. Semedo presented his accommodative outlook within a broad context of topics which included the geography of China, the Chinese people and their habits, the language, education and examination system, degrees, books and sciences, banquets, games, marriage, funerals and sepulchres, relisions, superstitions and sacrifices, military weapons, nobility, government, prisons and punishment, the Moslems, Jews and other nationalities resident in China and the history of Christianity in China until the arrival of the Jesuits.

3. SEMEDO'S PRESENTATION OF THE CHINESE LANGUAGE

Although Fr. Juan Mendoza's *Historia . . . de la China* (1596) and the Ricci-Trigault *De Christiana expeditione apud Sinas* (1615) had contained brief descriptions of the Chinese language, Semedo's description expanded these to present new material. His 23-year residence in China had given him considerable fluency in Chinese, though this appears to have been limited to speaking and reading as there is no record of any compositions in Chinese. Even his reading seems to have been limited for in regard to the Chinese Classics, he displayed only a general knowledge in *Imperio de la China.* His detailed descriptions of such things as the literati examinations, degrees, Buddhists, Taoists, Confucians and eunuchs reflected a broad range of contact with Chinese society. Consequently, I would judge Semedo to have been less of a scholar than Jesuit missionaries like Frs. Ricci, Martini, Schall, Boym, Couplet or Bouvet. His descriptions have a ring of authority and his attitude was markedly sympathetic to the Chinese. In contrast to such Jesuits as Frs. Kircher or Grueber, Semedo was far less critical of Chinese religions. He manifested that fondness and respect for the Chinese which came to mark the attitudes of so many Jesuits of long-time residence in China.

Semedo began his discussion of the Chinese language by stressing its great antiquity. He stated that many consider it to be one of the 71 languages created at the destruction of the Tower of Babel (*Genesis* 11: 1—9). Semedo argued that the antiquity of Chinese books proved the language to be more than 3,600 years old, that is, dating from about 2000 B.C. . (Two pages later, Semedo gave a 100-year older estimate of the Chinese language, that is, more than 3,700 years old.)[3] The twentieth-century archeological recoveries and study of Shang dynasty oracle bone inscriptions have shown Semedo's dating to have been quite realistic. In describing the Chinese language, Semedo correctly noted the function of "Quonthoa [i.e. *kuan-hua*, literally, official language] of the language of the Mandarins"[4] in unifying the far-flung territories of the Chinese empire, some of which, particularly in the far north and south were inhabited by non-Chinese barbarian races. Semedo, like Ricci[5], insisted that the Chinese written language was monosyllabic. It is true that written characters are monosyllabic, and that literary Chinese preserved this increasingly archaic usage into Semedo's day and down into the twentieth century. However, spoken Chinese combined these monosyllabic characters into polysyllabic words. Consequently, Semedo gave a misleading impression when he stated that Mandarin consisted of only "326 words" which when compounded by the changing of aspirations and accents yielded 1,228 terms. He was really speaking only of the possible range of sounds in Chinese and these were given further variation by polysyllabic usage in speaking.

Like Ricci, Semedo appreciated the lack of grammatical complexity in Chinese and noted that the words were indeclinable and the parts of speech such as nouns, verbs and adverbs were often interchangeable. He contrasted this grammatical simplicity of Chinese with the grammatical complexity of Latin, which required years of study. Semedo's point on the grammatical simplicity of Chinese was echoed by European writers on China throughout the seventeenth century. This supposed simplicity combined with the ability of Chinese writing to communicate among different East Asian tongues – a point made by Semedo as well as by Mendoza and Ricci-Trigault before him – would foster the belief in Chinese as a model for a universal language[6]. While Semedo stressed that Chinese did not have the inflectional and tense complexities of Latin and European vernacular languages, he neglected to clarify for his European reader that the use of particles and word order gave a grammatical complexity, particularly to written Chinese. It is interesting to note that those who later in the century used this perception of grammatical simplicity and universality in Chinese to stress its credentials as a model for constructing a universal language were, on the whole, amateur sinologists. While Semedo may have been a primary source for inspiring such thinking, he did not himself speak of Chinese as a universal model. On the contrary, he included some negative remarks about Chinese, for example, he noted that the conciseness of Chinese yielded an

---

3 Alvaro Semedo, *Histoire universelle de la Chine* (Lyon & Paris, 1667) pp. 48 & 50. (All page citations, unless otherwise noted, are to this French edition.)

4 Semedo, p. 49.

5 Ricci-Trigault, (ch. 1; 5) pp. 25–26.

6 See chapter six which deals with the seventeenth-century European search for a universal language.

ambiguity or lack of precision[7]. Ricci-Trigault had discussed how the confusion of spoken Chinese was resolved by recourse to the written character. Like Ricci-Trigault, Semedo noted the distinction between style of writing and speaking[8]. In an observation which the vernacular literary movement of early twentieth-century China would attempt to reverse, Semedo stated that any Chinese who attempted to write as he spoke would be an object of ridicule.

Semedo attributed the invention of Chinese characters to "Fu Hsi, one of the first kings" of China. No doubt drawing from the traditional association of the trigrams with the invention of writing, Semedo stated that the characters were initially much more simple than in his time, but that they evolved and in the process created four types of script[9]. (See plate 1.) The first and most ancient type of script was preserved in old books, understood only by the literati and used only in such things as decorative writing of the sort found in seals and emblems. This was a reference to the *chuan-shu* (seal script) which of the four styles most clearly preserves the pictographic origins of Chinese writing. The second script, called *"Chincu"*, was said to be the type most used in writing and printing. This was a reference to the *chen-shu*, also called *chiao-shu*, which was the most common printed style from ca. 200 B.C. until a simplified script was promulgated in mainland China beginning in the 1950s. The third type, *"Taipre"*, was said to be used only in legal documents and notices and referred to the *li-shu* which have a very square and precise shape. The fourth type of script, *"Sie"*, is described as an abbreviated form of writing which is so diverse that it demands a special study for comprehension. This referred to the *tsao-shu* (running-grass or full cursive style) which was a calligraphic art form practiced by the literati. Semedo has described the *ssu-t'i* or four traditional styles of Chinese script, but his transliterations are unrecognizable by this writer. It may be that he was using a regional Chinese dialect. Certainly it is puzzling how his demonstrated command of the Chinese spoken language could have so consistently failed him in transliterating these characters and perhaps a more linguistically trained eye will yet explain these apparent contradictions.

Semedo stated that the number of characters extended to 60,000 — Ricci-Trigault placed the maximal number at 70–80,000[10] — which were arranged in order in a dictionary called the *"Haipien"* or "great sea of letters"[11]. He also spoke of a shorter dictionary of 6–8,000 characters. These dictionaries were said to be consulted in the same manner as a contemporary European would consult a Latin dictionary whenever encountering an unknown word.

---

7 Semedo, p. 49. Cf. the Italian translation of Semedo's *Imperio de la China* entitled *Relatione della grande monarchia della Cina* (Rome, 1643) p. 44.
8 Ricci-Trigault, (ch. 1; 5) pp. 26–27 & Semedo, p. 50.
9 Semedo, pp. 50–51.
10 Ricci-Trigault, (ch. 1; 5) p. 26.
11 The following section summarizes page 51 of Semedo's *Histoire universelle de la Chine*.

Semedo then gave a brief description of the composition of Chinese characters. In contradistinction to the three famous "characters" published by Mendoza in 1586, here we have probably the first occurrence of an illustrated example which so intrigued Europeans that it was repeated in book after book on China. (See plate 10 and the discussion of this illustrated example in chapter five.) Semedo began the example with a horizontal line, meaning "one" (*i*), to which he added an intersecting vertical line to form a cross meaning "ten" (*shih*). He then added another horizontal line at the bottom to yield "earth" (*tu*), then added another horizontal line at the top to yield "king" (*wang*) and finally added a dot at the right side to yield "precious stone" (*yü*)[12]. The printer mistakenly placed this dot at the upper right instead of the lower right side of the character, though surely Semedo knew the correct form. In a somewhat amusing manner, this error was duplicated in book after book and reveals the strong parroting dimension in seventeenth century European proto-sinology.

Semedo went on to note that the character form of "precious stone" (*yü*) usually formed part of the various characters designating precious stones and gems. Words designating species of trees and types of metals similarly had the radical forms *mu* (tree) and *chin* (metal), respectively, in their composition. On the other hand, he noted that this type of character formation was not always employed. Here Semedo has presented a very simplified, but basically accurate account of the use of radicals in the formation of Chinese characters. He went on to speak of the role of "simple letters" (i.e. radicals) in the formation of "composite" letters. For example, the radicals for "sun" (*jih*) and "moon" (*yüeh*) combined to form "light" (*ming*). Additionally, the radicals for "heart" (*hsin*) and "gate" (*men*) were combined with the sense of a heart pressed within the passage of a gate to yield the meaning of "sadness, affliction" (*men*)[13].

Semedo spoke of the Chinese reverence for characters which prohibited them from allowing even a scrap of paper with writing to lie on the ground and which led them to spend a great deal of money in acquiring a page of old characters. He was aware of the ancient evolution of writing materials from a stylus to brush and spoke highly of the quality and variety of Chinese paper. But when he dated the invention of paper from 800 years prior to his own time (ca. 1640) and the invention of printing to 1,600 years prior to his own time, Semedo appears to have inadvertently switched these two dates[14]. The wide interval which separated the inventions of paper and printing was widely recognized in China and it is unlikely that Semedo misunderstood their order of invention[15]. Semedo saw the greatest advantage of the Chinese over other nations in the art of printing. He traced the primary distinction between Chinese and European printing to the use of carved wooden blocks versus smelted metal founts.

12 Semedo, pp. 51–52.
13 The above section summarizes page 52 of Semedo's *Histoire*.
14 Semedo, pp. 52–54. Cf. Semedo, *Relatione della grande monarchia della Cina* p. 47.
15 See Carter, *The invention of printing in China* pp. 1–6 & 28–39.

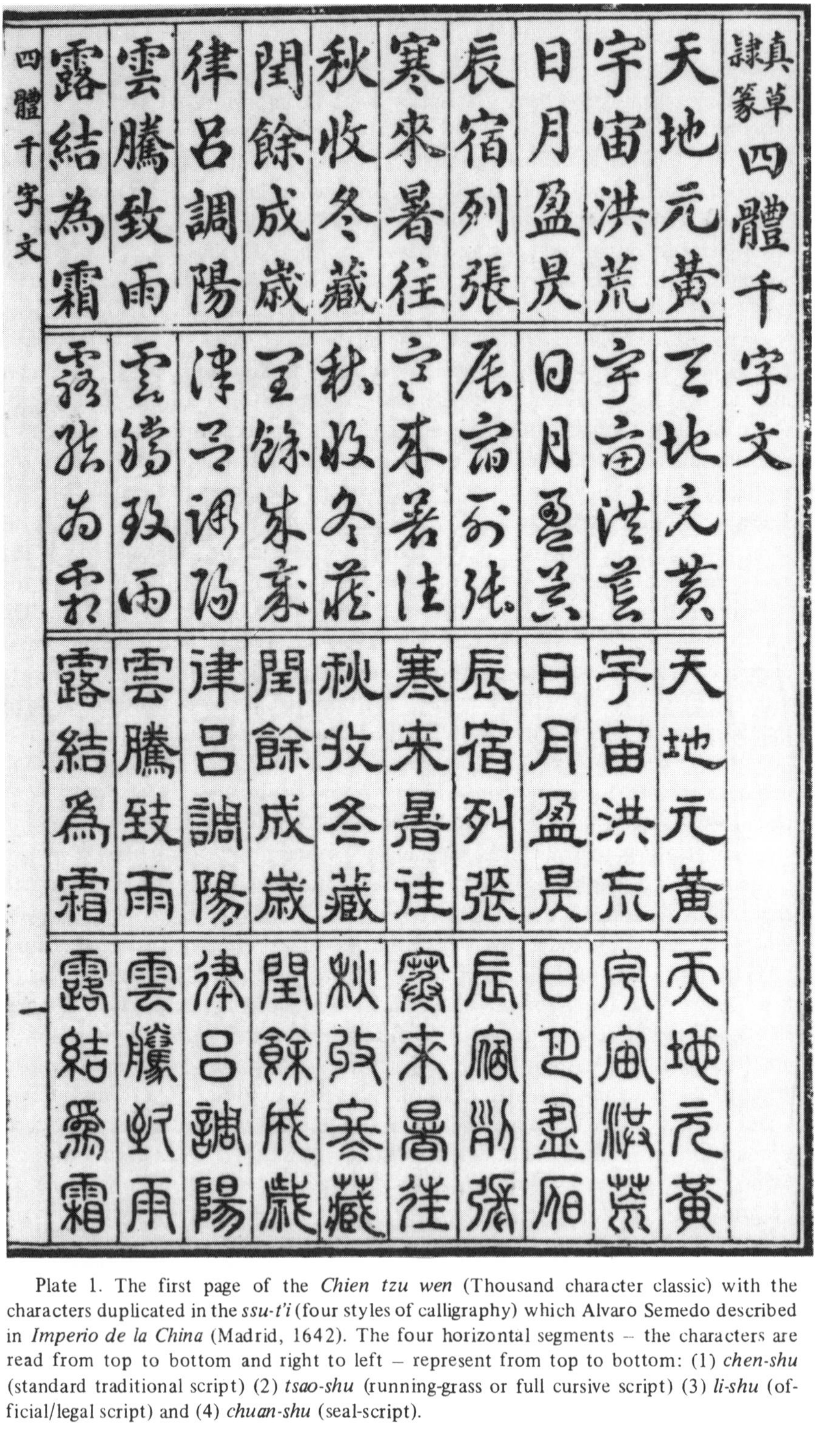

四體千字文

真草隸篆

天地元黃
宇宙洪荒
日月盈昃
辰宿列張
寒來暑往
秋收冬藏
閏餘成歲
律呂調陽
雲騰致雨
露結為霜

天地元黃
宇宙洪荒
日月盈昃
辰宿列張
寒來暑往
秋收冬藏
閏餘成歲
律呂調陽
雲騰致雨
露結為霜

天地元黃
宇宙洪荒
日月盈昃
辰宿列張
寒來暑往
秋收冬藏
閏餘成歲
律呂調陽
雲騰致雨
露結爲霜

天地元黃
宇宙洪荒
日月盈昃
辰宿列張
寒來暑往
秋收冬藏
閏餘成歲
律呂調陽
雲騰致雨
露結爲霜

四體千字文 一

Plate 1. The first page of the *Chien tzu wen* (Thousand character classic) with the characters duplicated in the *ssu-t'i* (four styles of calligraphy) which Alvaro Semedo described in *Imperio de la China* (Madrid, 1642). The four horizontal segments – the characters are read from top to bottom and right to left – represent from top to bottom: (1) *chen-shu* (standard traditional script) (2) *tsao-shu* (running-grass or full cursive script) (3) *li-shu* (official/legal script) and (4) *chuan-shu* (seal-script).

4. SEMEDO'S PRESENTATION OF CHINESE LEARNING
AND EDUCATION

Fr. Semedo presented a very sympathetic, almost idealized portrait of Chinese education. He noted the early role of moral teachings in such areas as virtue, good manners and filial obedience. He accurately emphasized the role of memorization, calligraphy and composition in the traditional Chinese curriculum[16]. He wrote that the medium of education in China was not schools and universities. Rather, the wealthiest families took into their homes a private tutor who established a very close relationship with his pupils and taught them good manners and conduct, as well as matters of government, the arts and sciences. Semedo praised this manner of instruction, particularly for its moral cultivation, which was crucial since those with immoral reputations were not permitted to take the examinations. Semedo clearly perceived the idealized importance of moral cultivation in the traditional training of Confucian literati.

Middle income families were said by Semedo to send their children to teachers who "never receive any more than they can instruct"[17]. In this respect, he compared the tendency of European schools to overload teachers with pupils, but surely he exaggerated Chinese virtue here. In China, as Semedo noted[18], teachers were almost entirely drawn from the ranks of aspiring or failed degree candidates. In spite of the moral cultivation, their frequently destitute situations must have contributed to breakdowns in pedagogical standards. When these middle income students advanced beyond this level of schooling, then a certain number of parents or neighbors might share a teacher in common and pay him largely through providing meals or perhaps both bed and board. Although Semedo did not specifically mention clans, it was primarily clan-sponsorship of a teacher to which he was referring. This means of providing bright but poor students with access to the examination ladder of success apparently impressed him.

In describing Chinese education, Semedo failed to note the tyranny which rote memorization of sterile composition forms, such as the prescribed *pa-ku* (eight-legged) essay, imposed upon creative Chinese minds. But then, such criticism was then voiced more quietly than in later times. He was aware of the intense competition among examination candidates for degrees[19], but did not impress upon the reader that by far the majority of degree aspirants never achieved their goal. On the other hand, the Ming period was a time in which the examination system provided an increased social mobility. But on the whole, China of Semedo's time accepted the examination system with all its

16 Semedo, pp. 55–56 Cf. Miyazaki, pp. 15–16.
17 Semedo, p. 57.
18 This paragraph summarizes p. 58 of Semedo's *Histoire*.
19 Semedo, p. 58.

frustrations and Semedo accurately reflected this wide degree of acceptance, even if he was not fully sensitive to the murmurs of complaint.

Semedo presented a very colorful account of the examination process in what was apparently a provincial examination. The cubicles in which each candidate sat were described in detail as 4 1/2 feet long, 3 1/2 feet wide, of the height of a man and with dirt-covered floors. Within each cubicle was a table for writing and eating and a chair. During the examination, under each table sat a guard-servant with his mouth gagged in order to prevent him from speaking[20]! Semedo stressed the small dimensions of the cubicles and of the passageways leading to and from them. He included an extended description of the examination and the conferral of the degree of bachelor (*hsiu-ts'ai*), licentiate (*chü-jen*) and doctor (*chin-shih*)[21].

Equally colorful and detailed was Semedo's description of the eunuchs in China, whom he numbered at 12,000 as of 1626[22]. While his estimate of their numbers was probably conservative, he accurately described the unusually broad distribution of eunuchs in Ming society. He mentioned them in palaces, colleges, classes, tribunals, posts and occupations. Normally, eunuchs in China were mainly confined to the palace where their primary task was the overseeing of the imperial concubines. Here their tendencies toward corruption were somewhat checked by the close proximity of the emperor. Unlike the literati, whose status derived from their achievement in the examinations and a frequently gentry background, eunuchs tended to come from poor families and be less educated and as a result were totally dependent on the favor of the emperor. So in the best of times the eunuchs helped on the emperor's side to maintain a balance between the authority of the emperor and that of the administering mandarinate[23].

In the late Ming this system began to break down as a series of weak-minded and eccentric emperors withdrew into their palaces and placed the government increasingly in eunuch hands. The most prominent example of this type of ruler was the Wan-li emperor who combined extravagant expenditure with extreme withdrawal. He alienated the scholar-officials by cutting off contact with them and by dispensing in irrational outbursts severe punishments on those officials who displeased him. He ruined the peasantry by taxing them to such a degree

20 Semedo, p. 59. Semedo's description of a gagged guard-servant under the table of each candidate's cubicle is at odds with the account in Miyazaki's *China's examination hell*, pp. 44–45. Mr. Miyazaki claims that the servants were forbidden to accompany the candidates into the examination compound. One soldier was assigned as an attendant for every twenty candidates, but far from being gagged, these soldiers shouted their commands and appeared to enjoy intimidating the candidates.
21 Semedo, pp. 61–71.
22 Semedo, p. 167.
23 Cf. Joseph R. Levenson, *Confucian China and its modern fate* 3 vols. Berkeley, (1964) II, 26–27.

that many deserted the land and turned to banditry for survival. In this power vacuum, eunuch influence grew and eunuch corruption and tyranny proliferated on a grand scale. This fostered a partisan spirit among the literati and caused many to withdraw from government service[24].

Yet Semedo showed little awareness of these unfortunate events. This lack of awareness was partly because of his distance from Peking. On the other hand, he was in contact with Jesuits resident at the capital. We have noted in the preceding chapter that Fr. Ricci, who resided in Peking from 1601 until 1610, was surprisingly mute on this deteriorating climate. A more fundamental cause of the general Jesuit lack of awareness was their lack of sufficient historical knowledge of China. This lack of a long range perspective prevented them from perceiving the present as a decline from different and better times. Nevertheless, some perceptions are made unconsciously and one does note that Semedo discussed Chinese emperors historically and in terms of their office rather than as distinct personalities[25]. This contrasts strongly with late seventeenth century Jesuit portrayals of early Ch'ing dynasty emperors, including most particularly, the K'ang-hsi emperor.

While Semedo's description of Chinese society was filled with detail that rings with authenticity, his presentation of Chinese arts and sciences was far sketchier. Yet he accurately wrote that the Chinese of that time devoted themselves mainly to the study of good government among the ancients while neglecting the other ancient arts and sciences[26]. Historians of Chinese science have confirmed a regression of knowledge of the natural sciences which occurred in China during the Ming (1368–1644) and Ch'ing (1644–1911) dynasties. By the time of Semedo's arrival, this regression was well underway and it is to Semedo's credit that unlike most other Western observers, he did not deny, but recognized that more developed forms of Chinese science had existed in earlier times.

Semedo's interpretation of the early intellectual development of China was seen basically through Confucian eyes and stressed good government. Fu Hsi, Shen Nung and Huang-ti were said to have been the early kings who initiated the development of moral and speculative sciences through the use of "even and uneven numbers, ... ciphers and characters"[27]. This was a reference to the *yang* (whole) and *yin* (divided) lines from which the *I ching* (Book of changes) diagrams were composed and to other numerical forms found on Shang dynasty (ca. 1500–1050) oracle bones and Chou dynasty (ca. 1050–221 B.C.) bronze and coin forms. These are called "counting-rod" forms, from the fact that they were rods used for calculating on a flat board[28]. The early kings developed

24 Goodrich & Fang, pp. 324–337.
25 Semedo, pp. 155–167.
26 Semedo, p. 71.
27 Semedo, p. 71.
28 Needham, III, 5–17.

laws which were said by Semedo to have been handed down to other kings in a direct line of transmission. This notion of direct transmission from the ancients was later formulated by Neo-Confucians of the Sung dynasty into a doctrine of *Tao-t'ung* (Transmission of the Way) by which they saw themselves as direct heirs to the learning of the ancients[29]. According to Semedo, this hand-to-hand transmission of the ancient learning ended at the beginning of the Chou dynasty, to which he gave the standard traditional dating of 1123 B.C., as opposed to the current historical dating of ca. 1050 B.C.. At this time, King Wen, the founder of the Chou dynasty, and the Duke of Chou, whom Semedo described as King Wen's grandson, explained these numbers and deciphered these characters in the form of the *Book of changes*.

The next key figure in Semedo's description of the development of Chinese arts and sciences was Confucius. The latter was said to have organized learning into the *Wu-ching* (Five Classics). In addition to this, Semedo claimed that Confucius wrote "other books, in addition to the sentences and witticisms which have been carefully collected and of which they have made several volumes"[30]. Semedo was clearly referring to Confucius' *Lun yü* (Analects) here, but appears to have bestowed too much authenticity on all of the statements attributed to Confucius.

Semedo gave a very favorable assessment of Confucius, though he misdated his life to ca. 150 B.C. instead of the more agreed-upon 551–479 B.C.[31]. Although Confucius' precise life-dates are still subject to some questioning, his approximate life-dates were well known in the seventeenth century and Semedo's mistake here represents an unusually wide lapse in accuracy. Confucius had a large number of disciples who roamed the realm as peripatetic philosophers in search of a prince willing to follow their program of good government. The antagonism which these Confucians aroused among the other philosophic schools and their reputation as meddlers were clearly captured in the anti-Confucian anecdote told by Semedo. The master, Confucius, was said to have been stranded in a coach in front of a stream and so sent out a disciple to seek information on how to ford a crossing. When questioned by the disciple, a lowly farmer asked how this philosopher who is said to know so much, did not know even how to ford a small stream[32]. Nevertheless, Semedo noted that Confucius appeared to have vanquished his opponents, for his reputation among contem-

29 For a discussion of the Sung Neo-Confucian conception of *Tao-t'ung* (Transmission of the Way), see Julia Ching, "The Confucian Way (Tao) and its Transmission (Tao-t'ung)," *Journal of the History of Ideas* 35 (1974): 371–389 & Wing Tsit-chan, "Chu Hsi's completion of Neo-Confucianism," in Francoise Aubin, ed. *Sung studies, memoriam Étienne Balazs* 2nd series, I (1973): 73–81.

30 Semedo, p. 72.

31 Semedo confirmed this misdating on the following page when he stated that Confucius had been dead for about 1,800 years, i.e. since about 160 B.C.. Semedo, pp. 72–73.

32 Semedo, p. 72.

porary Chinese was exceedingly high. He was regarded as a "saint, master and doctor of the realm" and his books and pronouncements were read as if divine in origin[33]. Furthermore, public temples were built in his honor and great ceremonies held in them, particularly at the time of the examinations when all newly successful candidates were made to revere Confucius and to recognize him as their master. Finally, of no small importance in ancestrally-minded traditional China, Confucius' living ancestors were said to be honored with titles and revenues.

Semedo then proceeded to describe the books that Confucius had "brought to light"[34]. These involved the two main categories of the Chinese Classics then current in China — the Five Classics and Four Books. He described the *Book of changes* as treating natural philosophy, generation and corruption, fate prognostication and judgment derived from principles of nature, all of which Semedo regarded as melding with morality and politics. The *Shu ching* (Book of documents) was presented as a type of history dealing with the period of good government associated with the first kings of China. The *Shih ching* (Book of odes) contained the poetry of the ancients and dealt with various customs of that time. Semedo gave no title for the fourth Classic, but clearly had in mind the *Li chi* (Book of rites), which he described as dealing with ceremonies and civil customs, including services to God and religion, of the ancients. The *Ch'un-ch'iu* (Spring and autumn annals) was described as annals which contained both good and evil examples of ancient kings presented for purposes of moral didacticism. The Four Books were not described in detail, but mention was made of those books which were partly from Confucius and partly from Mencius, dealing with the personal conduct of rulers. Here Semedo captured the Confucian stress on good government as being derived from and resting upon familial and personal morality[35].

Semedo's discussion of particular sciences and liberal arts in China was organized around the European medieval conception of the "seven liberal sciences" or "seven liberal arts". These are synonymous terms which consist of the *Trivium* (grammar, logic and rhetoric) and the *Quadrivium* (arithmetic, geometry, music and astronomy). Because this classification was so distinctly European, it is not surprising that Chinese learning fared rather badly in the discussion. In accordance with this traditional classification, Semedo treated grammar as the fundamental science. He felt that the monosyllabic and indeclinable nature of Chinese made it fairly easy to derive its rules of syntax, but he noted the existence of troublesome particles[36]. Chinese logic or dialectic was treated as nonexistent, except for common-sensical guidelines. Semedo

33 Semedo, p. 73.
34 Semedo, p. 73.
35 Semedo, pp. 75—76.
36 Semedo, p. 76.

was, not surprisingly, unaware of the Chinese School of Logicians or Dialecticians (*Pien che*), also known as the School of Forms and Names (*Hsing ming chia*), which included Hui Shih (380–305 B.C. ?) and Kung-sun Lung (b. 380 B.C. ?)[37]. On the other hand, his impressions reflected that the influence of this School of Logicians was minor and that the interest of the Chinese in formal logic was not great. Rhetoric was said to be taught more by example than by formal rules. This statement neglected the importance of highly structured verse or compositional forms in Chinese literature. Perhaps it also reflected Semedo's relative lack of experience in Chinese composition[38].

In terms of arithmetic, Semedo noted that although the Chinese had no knowledge of algebra, they practiced a basic mathematics for which they used a marvelous instrument – the abacus, which he described in some detail. Though the Chinese were said to be completely ignorant of algebra, they were "sufficiently instructed" in geometry, as confirmed by their ability to compose cartographic maps of the world[39]. Mr. Needham's research has shown Semedo to have been quite wrong here and has documented that Chinese mathematical development inclined in the direction of algebra rather than geometry[40]. A protean form of algebra seems to have been present from the earliest times in China, as in the use of a counting-board with numbers arranged in such a way that certain positions were occupied by quantities consisting of unknowns and powers[41]. The Chinese cartographic computations to which Semedo referred were normally done in Europe with geometry and so Semedo assumed that the Chinese would have done likewise. But Mr. Needham has shown that the Chinese computations were made using algebra[42].

Semedo stated that the nine Classical works (Four Books and Five Classics) together with the glosses and explanations of them constituted the material on which the literati examinations were based[45]. He added that there was only one universally accepted gloss and explication, and though the author was not mentioned, it is clear that the reference was to the commentary and interpretation of Chu Hsi. According to Semedo, those seeking to become bachelors (the lowest degree) were examined only on the Four Books, while those seeking the licentiate (the middle degree) were examined on all nine works. He stressed

37 See Fung, *History* I, 192–220 & Chan, *Source book* pp. 232–243.
38 Pfister, p. 146 credits only one work in Chinese to Semedo. This work, entitled *Tzu k'ao*, is said to consist of Chinese-Portuguese and Portuguese-Chinese vocabularies, which may or may not have been printed. Such a work would have demanded little in terms of Chinese compositional skills.
39 Semedo, p. 77.
40 Needham, III, 91 & 112.
41 Needham, III, 112.
42 Needham, III, 23–24 & 112–113.
43 Semedo, p. 74.

the rigorous training required to pass such examinations and stated that the candidates were permitted no memory aids, either in the form of a single book or even a sheet of notes during the examination.

5. SEMEDO'S TREATMENT OF CHINESE
PHILOSOPHY AND RELIGION

Jesuit accommodation was based upon a selective blending of Christianity with certain elements of Chinese culture, combined with a conscious rejection of other elements. The selection was based upon an interpretation of Chinese philosophy and religion which is clearly apparent in Semedo's *Imperio de la China*. Semedo described the tripartite division of Confucian cosmology into Heaven, Earth and Man and noted that while the natural sciences were dealt with in the first two divisions, morality was treated in the third division. However, he was not insensitive to the Confucian unity by which the social and political sphere associated with Man was to reflect and harmonize with the Heavenly and Earthly spheres[44]. Contained in the part dealing with Man were the "five moral virtues" which Semedo described as Piety, Justice, Law, Wisdom and Fidelity. These were translations of the Chinese *Jen* (Benevolence), *I* (Righteousness), *Li* (Ritual), *Chih* (Wisdom) and *Hsin* (Belief), respectively. Finally, there was a description of the "five orders of persons" (i.e. the five cardinal human relationships in Confucianism) as father-son, husband-wife, king-vassal, elder brother-younger brother and friend-friend. Semedo did not explain that most of these relationships involved a superior-inferior structure in which commands were supposed to be in moral harmony with the universe and responses were supposed to be obedient. Perhaps he considered this sort of hierarchical structure too natural to merit explanation. But later he specifically noted the crucial sense of the Confucian subordination of the individual to the family and of the family to the state. It would not be inconsistent with Semedo's presentation to add the Confucian qualification that the state must be subordinated to the universal harmony in the form of the "Mandate of Heaven" (*T'ien-ming*).

Semedo described the sects of China as three in number: (1) the sect of the literati founded by Confucius; (2) the sect of the Taoists which derived from the philosopher Lao-tzu; and (3) the cult of the pagodas which followed Shih-chia (Sakyamuni Buddha). The sect of the literati was presented as the oldest sect which recognized a Sovereign Lord who had the power to punish and reward humans[45]. Semedo confused the ancient Chinese chronology here. The worship of a Sovereign Lord named *Shang-ti* (Lord-on-high) and *T'ien* (Heaven)

44 Semedo, p. 75.
45 Semedo, p. 126.

dated from the Shang and Chou dynasties, respectively. Since both forms of worship preceded Confucius by several centuries, he could not have been their founder. Confucius saw himself essentially as a transmitter of ancient tradition, though he appears to have done some creative synthesizing in merging his own interpretation of the ancients with this ancient reverence of a Sovereign Lord.

According to Semedo, there were no temples for worshipping this Lord, no particular ceremonies or prayers to be used in this reverence, and no priests dedicated to this Lord's service. These statements, while not actually false, are misleading. Semedo failed to give enough emphasis to the fact that the worship of a Sovereign Lord had been absorbed into state ritual in certain annual acts traditionally performed by the "Son of Heaven" (i.e. emperor). The Chinese are said not to bestow incidental features on the Lord as did western peoples with their false gods. Nevertheless, Semedo argued that the lack of a "complete understanding of the true God" led the Chinese to superstitious worship of the *San-tsai* (Three Beginnings), namely, Heaven, Earth and Man[46]. At the courts of Peking and Nanking, sumptuous temples were said to have been built to honor these Three Beginnings and only ministers of high rank could perform the rites devoted to them.

Semedo conceded that there were other temples devoted to guardian spirits, to spirits of rivers and mountains, to famous men and to ancestors and that the literati sacrificed to all of these. The petitions involved in these reverences were directed toward the present life rather than involving the soul in the afterlife[47]. Unlike other later missionary interpreters, Semedo did not emphasize the idolatrous aspect of these literary devotions, but rather stressed their didactic function in society. He stated that the intent of the literati in sacrificing to Heaven and Earth and to universal fathers was to cultivate a reverence for these things in the people such that it would extend to their individual parents and to the fostering of a desire to emulate the ancients. In short, there was praise for the literati tendency of reducing everything to the good government of the state, to the harmony of families and to the practice of personal virtue.

Semedo presented Taoism as being founded by Lao-tzu, whom he mistakenly referred to as "Tausu" (Tao-tzu)[48]. The mistake is possibly explained by Semedo's erroneous belief that the name of the sect, *Tao*, was the same as the name of the founder, when in fact two different words were involved. *Tao* of Taoism means "the Way; Path" while *lao* of Lao-tzu means "old" in a reverent sense and together with *tzu* means "old master", an honorary title ascribed to the founder of Taoism. Semedo reproduced the traditional Chinese belief that Lao-tzu was a contemporary of Confucius. However, twentieth-century

---

46 Semedo, p. 126.
47 Semedo, p. 127.
48 Semedo, p. 127.

Chinese scholars have questioned this dating and many have placed Lao-tzu in the fourth or third centuries B.C.[49].

Semedo's account of Taoism reflected his inability to assimilate its multiplicity. He described some Taoists who lived together in a religious order, practiced celibacy, wore common clothing and left their hair and beards uncut. Aside from the manner of their hair, these Taoists closely resembled Buddhist monks. But Semedo seemed unaware that such Taoist monks constituted a very small percentage of Taoist followers. And, of course, celibacy was quite different from the Art of the Bedchamber which was practiced mainly by elderly Chinese men, including some with publicly impeccable Confucian credentials. Certainly the art of the bedchamber was practiced quietly and with restraint and it was also in decline at this point in Chinese history. Semedo gave no sign of any awareness of this Taoist tradition.

No doubt in accordance with Judaic, Christian and Islamic exclusiveness, Semedo treated the three Chinese sects as mutually exclusive paths. In fact, it was quite common for the Chinese teachings to intermingle in the same person, as in the case of the literatus who might practice Confucianism on a public level and Taoism and Buddhism on more private levels. Likewise was it typical for a Chinese peasant woman to shop around spiritually by spreading her petitions among various temples. Semedo mentioned the Taoist belief in a heaven and hell in another life though he omitted any reference to a belief in transmigration, which Taoism sometimes shared with Buddhism. He spoke of the attempt to regenerate youth through exercise and meditation, the cultivation of levitation and the ability to fly from place to place, and to a Taoist priesthood. These elements were treated as manifestations of the same religious sect when in fact they belonged to very different groups who shared only a minimal overlap of beliefs in regard to the Tao[50].

Semedo called Buddhism "the cult of pagodas"[51]. He was aware that it was founded in India by a man named "Xaca" (Shih-chia), i.e. Sakyamuni, and claimed that the death of Sakyamuni's mother during his birth motivated him to seek a new path to Truth. Actually, it was Sakyamuni's belated discovery of old age, sickness and death which so disturbed him that he abandoned his comfortable life and set off on a quest which ended in Enlightenment. Semedo, like Ricci, confused legend with fact when he stated that Buddhism entered China in A.D. 63 by order of Emperor Ming of the Han dynasty who had a dream about Buddhism. As noted in the previous chapter, it is probable that Buddhism entered China not by imperial command, but by the work of missionaries from Central Asia during the first five centuries of the Christian era. In his

---

49 Fung Yu-lan argues for dating Lao-tzu from the Warring States period (480–222 B.C.) in his *History* I, 170–172. Wing-tsit Chan presents a current summary of the debate over the dating of Lao-tzu in his *Source Book*, p. 138.

50 Semedo, p. 128.

51 Semedo, p. 129.

discussion of Buddhism, Semedo overemphasized the role of Buddhist monks and deemphasized the role of the Buddhist laity in China[52]. Of the three sects, it was only the Buddhists whom Semedo specifically claimed to have worshipped idols. But he was far less harsh on the Buddhists than was Ricci, and he certainly contradicted the chauvinistic stereotype often associated with Portuguese and Spanish missionaries in China. On the contrary, Semedo wrote that most of the sects of which he had spoken were "not at all scandalous, but on the contrary . . . patient, mild and deferential"[53].

Semedo also referred to the syncretic movement of the Ming which attempted to harmonize the three main teachings[54]. He quoted their famous phrase "*san chiao i ho*" which he faithfully rendered as "there are three types of doctrine, but there is only one truth". In this syncretism, the literati were thought to deal with the government of the state, the order of families and the conduct of people. The Taoists concerned themselves not with their families or government, but with their bodies. The followers of Sakyamuni Buddha neglected the body and concentrated on the soul, inner peace and the repose of the conscience. All this was said by Sakyamuni to be summarized in the phrase: *Ju chih kuo*; *Tao chih hsing*; *Shih chih hsin* ("the literati govern the state, the Taoists govern the body and the Bonzes govern the heart"). In conclusion, Semedo referred to a secret sect outlawed by the government which had acquired many followers and was regarded with horror by the governors. This sect was said to perform their ritual activities at night in secret and it was believed that its followers sought to overthrow the government. The reference here was to a quasi-religious secret society of the type of the White Lotus sect[55]. Semedo devoted a short chapter (chapter 30) to describing the Moslems and Jews whom he encountered in China[56]. However, according to recent joint research by Fr. Dehergne and Donald Daniel Leslie, what Semedo thought was a community of Jews at Nanking, were in fact Moslems[57].

52 Semedo, p. 130.

53 Semedo, p. 131.

54 Semedo, p. 134. For a general discussion of the *san-chiao* (Three Teachings) movement in the context of Sung and Ming dynasty syncretism, see Judith A. Berling, *The Syncretic Religion of Lin Chao-en* (New York, 1980) pp. 32–61.

55 These quasi-religious secret societies associated with Buddhism, such as the Maitreya Society, White Lotus Society and White Cloud Society, are briefly described by Kenneth Ch'en in *Buddhism in China,* pp. 426–433.

56 Semedo, pp. 220–224.

57 Joseph Dehergne and Donald Daniel Leslie, *Juifs de Chine* (Rome & Paris, 1980) p. 38.

6. THE BACKGROUND TO FR. MAGALHAES'
NOUVELLE RELATION DE LA CHINE

The Jesuit father Gabriel de Magalhaes (Magaillans) (1610–1677) is a delight to those appreciative of individuals who smudge historical stereotypes. Possessing all the ingredients of anti-accommodation, he did not adopt that outlook. Instead he displayed accommodative characteristics, such as an enormous sympathy and admiration for the Chinese and their culture as well as the belief that the ancient Chinese had worshipped the monotheistic God. However, he criticized Chinese isolationist and xenophobic tendencies and he drove the leader of the Peking Jesuits, Fr. Verbiest, nearly to distraction with his unceasing insistence that the Jesuit clerical vows be scrupulously followed in the Peking residence. (Meticulousness over observing the smaller details of religious vows has traditionally not been a Jesuit strongpoint.)

Fr. Magalhaes was a Portuguese Jesuit who arrived in Hangchow in 1640[58]. Soon after his arrival there, he was sent to Ch'engtu in the inland province of Szechwan. He arrived in late August 1642 and began a close association with the slightly senior Fr. Lodovico Buglio (1606–1682) which would continue throughout the remaining 35 years of his stay in China.

Under Fr. Buglio's guidance, Magalhaes applied himself to the study of Chinese. Based on the explanation of Chinese which later appeared in his *Nouvelle relation de la Chine*, Magalhaes had a good ear for languages but was far more sensitive to the oral aspects of Chinese than to the script[59]. When the Manchu invasion of China reached Szechwan, Frs. Buglio and Magalhaes were caught in the middle between the notorious Chinese bandit-leader, Chang Hsien-chung (1605–1647) and the Manchu forces. After being captured by the latter in 1647, Magalhaes and Buglio achieved safe treatment through their claimed association with the famous Fr. Schall of Peking. In response to a question from the Manchu commander, Magalhaes stated that Schall was their "elder brother" — a term which admirably blended the Jesuit religious and Chinese social contexts. The fathers were ordered to Peking which, after suffering considerable privations enroute, they reached in 1648.

58 Fr. Magalhaes was born at Pedrogão, Portugal into the family of the eminent explorer Magallen (1470–1521), who had died less than a century before Magalhaes' birth. Magalhaes was raised by a pious uncle and studied in the university at Coimbre. Whether the explorer's spirit still ran in his blood or whether he was influenced by social currents at that time in Portugal, Magalhaes was led to enter the Jesuit order and requested service in the east. He reached Goa in 1634 where he taught rhetoric and studied theology, which comes late in the Jesuit training. See Dehergne, *Répertoire* pp. 161–162 and Pfister, pp. 251-254. Also see the necrology by Magalhaes' close associate, Buglio, in Magaillans, *Nouvelle relation* p. 371f. I regret that I was unable to make use of a work which recently came to my attention: Irene Pih, *Le Pere Gabriel Magalhaes. Un Jesuite portugais en Chine au XVIIe siècle* (Paris, 1979).

59 Gabriel de Magaillans [Gabriel de Magalhaes], *Nouvelle relation de la Chine contenant la description des particularitez les plus considérables de ce grand empire* (Paris, 1690) pp. 84–97.

Happily for the fathers, the Jesuits were in good graces with the new rulers. In response to the Shun-chih emperor's gift of a church, house and income, the Jesuits served the new ruler in various technical capacities. Fr. Magalhaes employed his engineering skill to build several amusing mechanical pieces[60]. One of these was a carillon and turret-clock which Magalhaes arranged, using a spiked drum and trip-wires, to play Chinese tunes on the hour. This curiosity-piece became quite famous in Peking and later was the occasion for a visit to the Jesuit house by the K'ang-hsi emperor (r. 1662–1722)[61]. Magalhaes and Buglio were very active in apostolic work in and around the capital and in 1655 founded the famous Tung-t'ang (Eastern Church) of Peking[62]. Yet Magalhaes appears not to have mastered the delicate art of missionary diplomacy in the capital. His tendency toward contention surfaced in 1649 when he is said to have stirred up enough trouble to cause the Jesuit vice-provincial, Fr. Francisco Furtado (1587–1653), to petition for Schall's dismissal from the Bureau of Astronomy, though this was rejected by the throne[63].

The death of the Shun-chih emperor in 1661 led to a government by regency with the youthful K'ang-hsi emperor. In this atmosphere, the anti-Christian resentments among the literati were able to surface and early in the regency, Magalhaes was charged with bribing an official — a very serious crime at that time — and was indicted before a tribunal. In the imperial Chinese state, and still to a large degree in contemporary China, one attempted by all means to prevent a case from coming before a tribunal because indictment carried the presumption of guilt. But Jesuit influence was at such a low point at this time that the case could not be put off. So Magalhaes was tried and, not surprisingly, suffered severe torture of his feet during the proceedings. But the charges were not sustained and he was eventually released.

In 1664 there appeared a short treatise entitled T'ien-hsüeh ch'uan-kai (Summary of the spread of the Heavenly Teaching) which reflected the process of continual evolution and development which Ricci's accommodation underwent throughout the seventeenth century[64]. In a fashion typical of the Jesuits in China, this treatise was the work of a collaborative effort involving several

60 Pfister, p. 253.
61 Verbiest described the K'ang-hsi emperor's visit to the Jesuit house in Peking in a letter of May 11th 1684 which has been transcribed by Fr. Bernard-Maitre in "Ferdinand Verbiest, continuateur de l'oeuvre scientifique d'Adam Schall," *Monumenta Serica* 5 (1940): 103. Also see Needham, IV; 2, 437.
62 Pfister, p. 253 & Dehergne, *Répertoire* p. 162.
63 Goodrich, *Dictionary of Ming Biography* p. 471.
64 Li Tsu-po, *T'ien-hsüeh ch'uan-kai,* in Wu Hsiang-hsiang ed., *T'ien-chu-chiao tung-chuan wen-hsien hsü-pien* 3 vols. (Taipei, 1966) II, 1043–1068. A copy of this treatise may be found in the Bibliotheca Vaticana, Fond Raccolta Generale Oriente III. 213. int. 12 where it was among the volumes brought from China by Fr. Couplet and presented to Pope Innocent XI in 1685. This treatise is treated by the author in the arti-

Jesuits and a Chinese convert. The impetus for the work was provided by the anti-Christian official, Yang Kuang-hsien, who in 1660 published his *P'i-hsieh-lun* (An exposure of an heretical doctrine). Yang's work contained a harsh attack on Schall who then occupied the prominent position of head of the Bureau of Astronomy. Schall's devoted disciple in the Bureau was a Christian convert named Li Tsu-po (*tzu* Jan-chen, d. 1665). It appears that Li was the one who actually composed the *T'ien-hsüeh ch'uan-kai* as a defense of Schall. However, the close Jesuit associates, Buglio and Magalhaes, appear to have provided many of the ideas found in Li's treatise and in any case they certainly worked closely with Li in the composition of the work. But *T'ien-hsüeh ch'uan-kai* was not only a defense of Schall and Christianity – it was also a new formulation of Ricci's accommodation.

The attempt to adapt Christianity to Chinese culture began on the first page of *T'ien-hsüeh ch'uan-kai* in which Biblical Creation was described with traditional Chinese terminology. Ricci had used the traditional Chinese term for God, *Shang-ti*, which dated from at least the Shang dynasty, to describe Christian monotheism. But Li Tsu-po added a new dimension to Ricci's accommodation in that his cosmological elaboration of Heaven as a creative force was borrowed from Neo-Confucianism of the Sung dynasty. This drawing from a Neo-Confucian tradition is interesting because it contradicted the anti-Neo-Confucian attitudes of early Jesuit accommodation. But the really radical element which this treatise introduced to Jesuit accommodation was the claim that the Heavenly Learning (i.e. Biblical Teachings) came to China not after the death and resurrection of Jesus, but much earlier. In fact, Li claimed that Biblical teachings were carried to China by the first descendants of Adam and Eve. The founding Chinese sage, Fu Hsi, was claimed to have been one of these descendants of Adam! According to this treatise, Biblical teachings were established in China during the legendary reigns of Yao and Shun and lasted throughout the Hsia, Shang and Chou dynasties. Li cited passages from the *Book of documents, Book of odes, Chung yung* and *Mencius* as vestigial evidence of this prior existence of Biblical teachings in ancient China[65].

How then did the authors of the *T'ien-hsüeh ch'uan-kai* explain the disappearance of Biblical teachings from China? Their explanation was another sign of the accommodation method in practice in that it took an impeccably Confucian form. As in the explanations of so many other Confucian revivals in Chinese history, the cause of the difficulty was traced to the Ch'in dynasty when Chinese became enmeshed in factiousness and bitterness. Scholars relinquished morality for the sake of mere utility and profit. The rulers of the Ch'in dynasty embraced the philosophy of Law (i.e. *Fa-chia* or Legalism) rather than

cle, "Die Schrift T'ien-hsüeh ch'uan-kai als eine Zwischenformulierung der jesuitische Anpassungsmethode im 17. Jahrhundert," in *China Mission Studies (1550–1800) Bulletin* 4 (1982): 24–39.
65 Li Tsu-po, *T'ien-hsüeh ch'uan-kai,* II, 1058–1061.

Morality and spurned Classics such as the *Book of documents* and *Book of odes*. Later, according to Li, Biblical teachings — including the account of Jesus — were reintroduced to China through the apostle St. Thomas, the Nestorians and Matteo Ricci[66]. This claim of foreign origin of the Chinese via Fu Hsi from Adam so enraged Yang Kuang-hsien that he attacked the *T'ien-hsüeh ch'uan-kai* in the opening pages of his *Pu te i* (I cannot do otherwise) of 1665, one of the most influential anti-Christian works in pre-modern Chinese history[67]. The polemical exchange continued when Buglio, who was prolific in composing works in Chinese, undertook, with some help from his Peking colleagues who doubtless included Magalhaes, to write a rebuttal to Yang. This appeared as *Pu te i pien* (A refutation of 'I cannot do otherwise'), which was published in 1665.

On September 15th 1664, Yang Kuang-hsien filed a formal accusation with the Ministry of Rites against Schall and his associates. To his previous charges of erroneous astronomical calculations, sedition and indoctrinating the people with false doctrines, Yang added the new charge that in 1658 Schall had selected an inauspicious day for the burial of an imperial prince and that this had contributed to the early deaths of both the Shun-chih emperor and his empress. As a result of this charge, Magalhaes was again imprisoned, along with Schall, Verbiest, Buglio and several Chinese associates in the Bureau of Astronomy. Though condemned to death, the sentences were commuted and the fathers were eventually freed. However, five of the Chinese astronomers who also happened to be Christians, including Li Tsu-po, were executed[68]. Magalhaes, along with Buglio, Verbiest and the now ill and paralyzed Schall, were permitted to remain at the Peking court while the other missionaries were expelled from the inland regions to Macao and the churches were closed. But when Yang, who had become head of the Bureau of Astronomy, was unable to obtain satisfactory results, he was dishonored and Verbiest was appointed in 1669 as vice-director of the Bureau, which was to remain under the guidance of Europeans until early in the nineteenth century[69]. In January of 1669, Magalhaes wrote a

---

66 Li Tsu-po, *T'ien-hsüeh ch'uan-kai*, II, 1062–1066.
67 Yang Kuang-hsien, *Pu-te-i*, in Wu Hsiang-hsiang, ed., *T'ien-chu-chiao tung-chuan wen-hsien hsü-pien*, III, 1076 (second page of original un-numbered text). A sympathetic account of Yang's role in this anti-Christian movement is presented by John D. Young in "The Early Confucian Attack on Christianity: Yang Kuang-hsien and his *Pu-te-i*," *Journal of the Chinese University of Hong Kong* 3 (1975): 155–186. Also see Paul A. Cohen, *China and Christianity: the Missionary Movement and the Growth of Chinese Antiforeignism, 1860–1870* (Cambridge, Massachusetts, 1963) pp. 24–27.
68 Young, p. 169 and Hummel, p. 891.
69 Hummel, p. 892.

long letter dealing with this persecution since 1664. This letter was later translated by Fr. Intorcetta and published in 1672[70].

In his old age, Magalhaes became obsessed with seeing that the vows of the order were scrupulously followed and he was a thorn in the side of Verbiest, who in his duties as director of the Bureau of Astronomy and as superior of the Jesuit mission in Peking depended upon the flexibility inherent in Jesuit accommodation to keep the Christian cause alive and prospering. Three years before Magalhaes' death, the former torture wounds in his feet reopened and the swelling made a reclining position impossible. Consequently, he was forced to sit through the nights, which he is said to have endured with great patience[71]. This portrayal of patient suffering appears to represent more than a polite speaking well of the dead. Like many cantankerous individuals, Magalhaes seems to have been held in a certain affection by many of those around him. This seems to have been the case particularly among the ruling house where the Chinese reverence for age and long service – at the time of his death, Magalhaes had been residing in Peking for 28 years – had been adopted by the Manchus. Consequently, one finds that when Fr. Magalhaes died in May of 1677, he was honored by having his epitaph written by the young K'ang-hsi emperor.

Unlike his close companion Buglio, Magalhaes was not a prolific writer. He is credited with two works in Chinese – *Ch'ao-hsing-hsüeh yao* (The essentials of theology) and *Fu-huo-lun* (A treatise on the resurrection of bodies). Though each of these works are described as being two volumes in length, they are probably only *chüan*, that is, traditional Chinese textual units which are somewhat longer than Western-style chapters, but shorter than Western-style volumes. Magalhaes' major work derived from his *"Doze excellencias da China"*, a manuscript composed in 1668 in Portuguese. Magalhaes' manuscript must have been judged valuable by his confreres, for when Fr. Couplet traveled to Europe as procurator in 1681, he carried the manuscript of the deceased Magalhaes with him[72]. In Rome, Couplet turned the manuscript over to Cardinal d'Estrées, who conveyed it to Abbé Claude Bernou for translation[73]. Part of the fair copy of the manuscript had been burned and Bernou was forced to use the damaged manuscript[74]. It is not surprising that the end result reflected a significant number of editorial changes made by the translator's hand. These included an altering of Magalhaes' original structure of twelve sections to twenty-one chapters. Bernou was a sufficiently serious student of China to be capable of adding a section of notes at the end of each chapter. The abbé also made deletions and

---

70 Intorcetta's translation of Magalhaes' letter of January 1669 may be found in Francesco Tizzoni, ed., *Compendiosa relatione della stato della Missione Cinese* (Rome, 1672) pp. 77–114.

71 Pfister, p. 254.

72 Sommervogel, V, 308 & Pfister, p. 255.

73 Pfister, p. 255, gives a variant spelling of P. Bernou's name as "Bernon."

74 Henri Cordier, *Bibliotheca Sinica* 5 vols. (Paris, 1904–1922) 2nd ed., revised. I, 36.

composed a map of Peking on the basis of information supplied in the text by
Magalhaes[75]. (See plate 2.) Bernou's map of Peking had overtones of accommodating China to Europe in that it appears to have followed the orthogonal
plans of New World cities, such as Philadelphia. Finally, Bernou gave Magalhaes'
work the new title of *"Nouvelle relation de la China"*, under which it was
published at Paris in 1688 with the author's name gallicized to Gabriel Magaillans. Public demand for the work led to reprintings in 1689 and 1690. Couplet,
who had just left Paris late in 1687 for England, Portugal and Spain, was unable
to see the harvest of this joint effort, though perhaps he was still in England to
witness the appearance of the English translation of 1688[76]. While Couplet's
Confucius Sinarum philosophus was scholarly, Magalhaes' *Nouvelle relation de
la Chine* was light and popular in tone. The 21 chapters dealt with a wide range
of subject matter, including Chinese history, language, manners, navigation,
government with descriptions of the various tribunals in Peking, and the layout
of the streets and palace.

7. MAGALHAES' PRESENTATION OF THE CHINESE LANGUAGE

The continuing interest of Jesuits in the Chinese language is shown in Magalhaes' *Nouvelle relation de la Chine*, though his presentation of the Chinese
characters and language shared the oral perspective found in Semedo's *Imperio
de la China*. Magalhaes argued for the high antiquity of Chinese characters by
saying that they predated Egyptian hieroglyphs[77]. He claimed that unlike
other nations whose languages were based on an alphabet of 24 letters, the
Chinese had "54,409 letters". This claim was misleading in several ways. First
of all, Chinese characters do not bear the equivalent building-block role of
letters in an alphabet, though the radicals — as in the system of 214 radicals —
are somewhat more comparable in function. Secondly, the total number of
Chinese characters can be no more precisely measured than can the total number
of words in English or French or any other living language because the ancient
form of the language has lost archaic characters and the contemporary form
of the language is in the process of creating new words. Also, Magalhaes' estimate of the total number of characters was low. He was clearly impressed by

---

75 According to Sommervogel, V, 308, Bernou's map differed considerably from the
   maps of Peking later produced by Frs. Gaubil and Du Halde. Ricci-Trigault's *De
   Christiana expeditione* included a map of the royal palace of Peking on a leaf attached
   behind the title page of the 1615 edition.

76 Gabriel Magaillans, *A New History of China Containing a Description of the Most Considerable Particulars of that Vast Empire* John Ogilby, trans. (London, 1688).

77 Magaillans, p. 84. (This and following citations which use only the name Magaillans
   refer to the *Nouvelle relation de la Chine* (Paris, 1690) edition of Magalhaes' work.)

the power of the Chinese language to communicate and spoke of its "grace, vivacity and force".

Magalhaes believed that the key to the expressive power of the Chinese language lay in the pictographic nature of the characters or, as he put it, "figures and images which express and represent in life what they signify"[78]. He analyzed Chinese "letters" into simple and composite forms[79]. The simple form – which he illustrated with the characters *hsin* (heart-mind), *mu* (tree; wood), *ju* (like; similar) and *chu* (master; lord) – were said to be made from "lines, points and folds". Composite "letters" – such as *shu* (compassion), *chu* (pillar) and *lin* (forest) – were formed by joining simple "letters" together. Magalhaes argued that Chinese "letters" were hieroglyphs, that is, pictorial or symbolical representations of words, syllables or sounds. He gave several reasons to support his claim[80]. First, the ancient Chinese "letter[s]" of characters such as *jih* (sun), *yüeh* (moon) and *pen* (root) were simplified figures and images of the visible things which they represented. Secondly, modern Chinese "letters" retained several vestiges of a hieroglyphic principle of composition, e.g. *chia* (a married woman) was composed of *nü* (woman) and *chia* (house; family) and signified a woman who was in the house of her marriage and not the house of her parents. Thirdly, Magalhaes noted that the hieroglyphic nature included a representation not only by reproducing natural shapes, but also by signifying elements without shape, such as souls, beauty, virtue, vices and actions. Fourthly, unlike the letters of the alphabet of European languages, which by themselves signified nothing, each Chinese "letter" had a meaning that it preserved when joined with other diverse "letters". Here, Magalhaes went astray because of his neglect – a neglect common to seventeenth-century European interpreters of the Chinese language – of the phonetic aspect of Chinese. For example, Magalhaes cited the composite form *ling* (bell) which he interpreted to be composed of the simple forms *chin* (metal) and *ling* (command) because one commanded the sound of a bell. Whether Magalhaes' interpretation of the etymological origin of the character *ling* (bell) was correct or not, there were characters in Chinese which included an element essentially phonetic in function and this would contradict Magalhaes' thesis that Chinese was a purely hieroglyphic language.

Magalhaes' fifth reason for arguing that Chinese characters were hieroglyphs derived from his claim that the learning of Chinese was simplified by the hieroglyphic principle. By this principle he meant the organization of characters into series, each of which was identified by its respective radical element, such as the *huo* (fire) radical or the *shan* (mountain) radical – i.e. the principle of reducing characters to radicals. Magalhaes was very misleading here because he

---

78 In his presentation of the Chinese language (Magaillans, p. 84), Magalhaes spoke of drawing from a treatise on the Chinese language which he composed. This treatise, unfortunately, appears to be lost.

79 Magaillans, pp. 84–85.

80 Magaillans, pp. 86–89.

implied that this principle of organization using radical elements made Chinese easier to learn than the non-radical European languages. It was certainly justifiable for Magalhaes to praise the "beauty and subtlety of spirit of Chinese"[81]. But it was an exaggeration, which incidentally was shared by a number of Jesuit missionaries, for him to argue that Chinese was easier to learn than Greek, Latin or any other European language because of: (1) this hieroglyphic principle for organizing the script (2) the fewer number of phonetic sounds and (3) the simplicity which excluded the European infinity of words and grammatical elements dealing with time, number and person[82]. The apparently greater simplicity of Chinese was a perception made by many European observers of China and was absorbed into the seventeenth-century search for a universal language.

Magalhaes' presentation of Chinese phonetics stressed the "admirable artifice" with which Chinese "letters" had been invented[83]. He claimed that Chinese was monosyllabic − this, as has been noted, would be true only in regard to the classical literary script, not the spoken Chinese of that time − and contained only 320 different sounds, not counting tonal variations. Unlike many seventeenth-century European writers on China, Magalhaes displayed a keen appreciation of tonal variations and presented the word *po* with eleven variations which appear to have been the five tones of contemporary usage combined with aspirated-unaspirated distinctions[84]. Magalhaes spoke at some length on the eleven variations of pronunciation in his treatise on Chinese characters and language which he composed for newly arrived missionaries, and which has since been lost. Magalhaes' presentation of the phonetic variations of Chinese in *Nouvelle relation de la Chine* was one of and perhaps even the best among published works in seventeenth-century European literature and is certainly worthy of study by trained linguists for information it could give about Chinese pronunciation of that time.

Magalhaes' remarks on the relative simplicity of learning to speak and write Chinese are sometimes puzzling. For example, he claimed that all the Jesuit fathers, although fully matured adults, after only two years in the China Mission, were so knowledgeable in the language that they could "confess, preach and compose with as much facility as if it were their natural language"[85]. Magalhaes claimed that this could never happen with European languages! He attempted to prove his point by citing those Jesuits who had composed in Chinese. However, his exaggerated praise of the compositional powers of several Jesuits, including Ricci, diminishes the credibility of his argument. Ricci received considerable help from Christian literati in his compositions and, in the case of

81 Magaillans, p. 89.
82 Magaillans, pp. 96−87.
83 Magaillans, p. 89.
84 Magaillans, p. 91.
85 Magaillans, pp. 97−98.

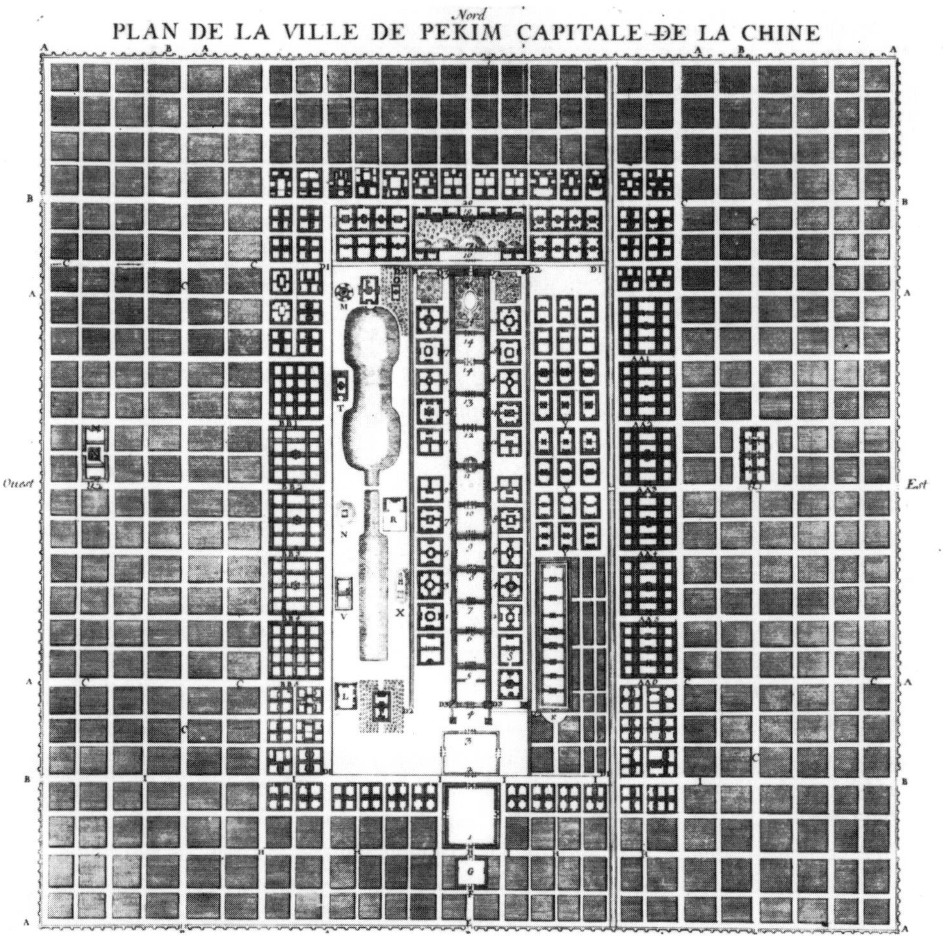

Plate 2. Abbé Bernou's map of Peking, constructed from information supplied in Gabriel de Magalhaes' *Nouvelle relation de la Chine* (Paris, 1690). Courtesy of the Niedersächsische Landesbibliothek Hannover.

his *T'ien-chu shih-i*, appeared to have spent several years revising it before publication[86]. It is difficult to believe that Magalhaes was unaware of this. It took years for the Chinese literati themselves to master the difficult art of Chinese composition with its many stylistic demands. Surely the Jesuit fathers could not have mastered this art without years of effort. So although Magalhaes' remarks on certain phonetic aspects of Chinese reflected a deep familiarity, his comments on written or literary Chinese revealed a probable combination of ignorance and exaggeration.

In his notes on Magalhaes' chapter on the Chinese language, the editor-translator Bernou referred the reader to the sixth chapter of Semedo's *Imperio de la China* for confirmation of Magalhaes' remarks on the Chinese language, but then curiously added that the presentations of Chinese by Frs. Semedo and Magalhaes were unlike those found elsewhere[87]. Bernou was aware of the similarities and uniqueness in Semedo's and Magalhaes' presentations, but he lacked the knowledge to detect errors in their explanations. Semedo's *Imperio de la China* was published in 1640 and probably was composed a full thirty years before Magalhaes composed his *Nouvelle relation de la Chine* in 1668. After his return from Europe, Semedo resided in Canton from 1649 until his death in 1658 or 1659. The only time Magalhaes appears possibly to have passed through Canton was enroute from Macao to Hangchow in 1640. Otherwise, Magalhaes was in Szechwan from 1642 until 1647 and then in Peking from 1648 until his death in 1677. Consequently, it appears that the paths of Semedo and Magalhaes did not cross, though given the limited number of Jesuits in China, they were doubtless aware of one another's existence.

In their presentations of the Chinese language, both Semedo and Magalhaes favorably compared the structural simplicity of Chinese to the complexity of European languages. Semedo stated that Mandarin consisted of only 326 words, i.e. sounds, which were compounded through variations in aspiration and accent to yield 1,228 phonetic elements[88]. Magalhaes spoke of Chinese (Mandarin dialect?) containing 320 different sounds which were compounded through aspiration and tonal variations[89]. Because of the close proximity in time and missionary occupation between Semedo and Magalhaes, some common influence seems likely. If influence through personal contact is excluded, could Magalhaes have received Semedo's explanation of Chinese through reading a manuscript of the latter's work? A clear answer to this question is complicated

---

86 Not only did Ricci have a great deal of help from Chinese literati in composing *T'ien-chu shih-i*, but he had the benefit of prior attempts among Jesuits in China to compose a catechism in Chinese. This first catechism is the subject of an article by Jacques Gernet entitled "Sur les different versions du premier catechisme en Chinois de 1584," in *Studia Sino-Mongolica* (Wiesbaden) 25 (1979): 407–416.

87 Magaillans, p. 107.

88 Semedo, p. 49.

89 Magaillans, p. 89.

by the differences found in the two presentations. Magalhaes' treatment of Chinese phonetics was more detailed than that of Semedo, but Semedo's appreciation of the Chinese script was superior and showed a greater awareness of the important distinction in seventeenth-century China between oral and written Chinese[90]. Magalhaes placed the number of characters at exactly 54,409[91], while Semedo more realistically spoke of the number exceeding 60,000[92]. These differences diminish the possibility of reducing the common features of their presentations to a direct influence of Semedo upon Magalhaes through the written word. More likely is the possibility that a common influence upon Semedo and Magalhaes was exerted through a interpretation of the Chinese script and language shared by a number of Jesuit confreres.

Magalhaes concluded his chapter on the Chinese script and language with what was probably the first presentation of a fragment of Chinese text to a European audience. The fragment consisted of sixteen characters taken from the opening lines of the *Ta hsüeh*, one of the Confucian Four Books. Magalhaes sought to illustrate "the beauty of this language, and the great intellect of this nation" by reproducing and translating these characters[93]. He noted the importance of the Four Books of Confucius in the Jesuit mission program by stating that these books were the focus of linguistic training and acculturation for newly arrived Jesuits in China. By drawing from the commentaries of Chu Hsi and Chang Chü-cheng (1525–1582) in presenting this text, Magalhaes showed that the Jesuits were using this commentary by Chang Chü-cheng at least as early as 1668. Chang's work was favored by mid-seventeenth-century Jesuits in China and would be the primary commentary on which Couplet and his confreres relied in the composition of *Confucius Sinarum philosophus.* But Magalhaes appeared poorly informed of Chang's life and he erred doubly when he wrote that 1610 was the year both of Chang's death and of Ricci's arrival at the court in Peking when actually Chang died in 1582 and Ricci established permanent residence at Peking in 1601[94].

Magalhaes rendered the opening *Ta hsüeh* passage as follows: "The method of learning of great men consists of three things. The first is to illumine the rational nature. The second is to renew the people. The third is to abide in the highest good"[95]. Following his translation, Magalhaes presented a two-page

90 Semedo, p. 50.
91 Magaillans, p. 84.
92 Semedo, p. 51.
93 Magaillans, p. 102.
94 Magaillans, p. 103. It is hard to believe that Magalhaes was uninformed of the fact that Ricci arrived in Peking in 1601 and died there in 1610. Possibly he had intended to write the year 1601 and an error – typographical or otherwise – transposed the 0 and 1 to yield 1610.
95 Magaillans, pp. 103–104.

"commentary and explication" of the *Ta-hsüeh* passage, which appears to be a very loose translation-paraphrase of Chang Chü-cheng's commentary[96].

Magalhaes regarded these words of Confucius in this *Ta hsüeh* passage to be eminently appropriate for explaining the task of the preacher of the Christian Gospel in China. The missionary's first obligation was to perfect himself after which, following through the progressive chain, he reached the highest good which was God[97]. Magalhaes argued from the premise that *chih shan* (the highest good) signified the "sovereign and supreme good which contains and comprehends all others", and can only be a designation for God[98]. Therefore, Magalhaes regarded this passage as testifying to the ancient Chinese belief in God. Not surprisingly, Magalhaes admitted of mixed success in attempting to convince Chinese literati of the validity of this argument. No less difficult was his attempt to convince Chinese that this statement confirmed that Confucius, whom Magalhaes took to be the speaker of the passage, believed in God. Nevertheless, in spite of weaknesses in logical rigor and persuasive power, Magalhaes' argument indicated that he, too, was a seeker after a formula of accommodation which would blend Christianity into Chinese culture by using the Confucian texts.

8: MAGALHAES' PRESENTATION OF CHINESE CHRONOLOGY

One of the distinguishing marks of Magalhaes' *Nouvelle relation de la Chine* is the clarity with which he presented the material on China. This clarity blended with a basic, though not necessarily detailed, understanding of the fundamental aspects of Chinese culture to make his work an excellent popular introduction to China for European readers. This clarity was evident in his brief chapter on the antiquity of China. By contrast, a lesser degree of clarity is found in Fr. Martini's *Sinicae historiae decas prima* (1658), one of the first works to outline the problem posed by Chinese history to the Biblically-based chronology of Europeans and especially to that based on the Vulgate. Though Magalhaes' account did not appear in print until after the publication of the detailed explication of Chinese chronology by Couplet in his *Tabula chronologica monarchiae Sinicae* (1686), the latter appears to have been limited to a learned readership, while Magalhaes' description of Chinese antiquity reached a far larger audience in its more popularly oriented French and English editions.

Magalhaes noted that the Chinese had preserved a continuous record of twenty-two "families", i.e. dynasties, and 236 kings over a period of 4,025 years, that is, from 2357 B.C. down to A.D. 1668 when Magalhaes was writing[99].

96 Chang Chü-cheng, *Ssu-shu chih-chieh* (1651 ed.) pp. 1a–1b.
97 Magaillans, pp. 105–106.
98 Magaillans, p. 106.
99 Magaillans, p. 73.

As to the origin of Chinese history, he spoke of three bodies of opinion[100]. The first was found in certain fables and myths which held that China began "several hundreds of thousands" of years ago. Magalhaes noted that these accounts were not taken seriously by the learned. The second opinion, which Magalhaes claimed that most literati subscribed to, dated China from Fu Hsi. The latter was said to have reigned in Shensi province from 2952 B.C. and meant that Chinese history would have involved a span of 4,620 years. The third opinion held that China began with the reign of Yao in 2357 B.C. and was therefore 4,025 years old. Magalhaes noted that every Chinese literatus subscribed, at a minimum, to the dating of China's origins from Yao in 2357 B.C.[101]. To dispute this date would have been equivalent to espousing heterodoxy and were the missionaries to have done so, he believed that the acceptance of Christianity in China would have been barred. It is exactly for this reason that the Jesuits sought and received, as Magalhaes noted, permission to use the Septuagint instead of the Vulgate chronology. The Vulgate dating of Creation at precisely 4004 B.C. and the Flood as 2349 B.C. conflicted with even the most conservative Chinese accounts of the origin of their nation, whereas the Septuagint dating of the Creation at approximately 5200 B.C. and the Flood at approximately 2957 B.C. allowed for greater reconciliation of Chinese chronology with the Biblical account of history. In short, it was possible to conceive of the Flood as occurring prior to Fu Hsi's reign and thereby preserve the universal patriarchy of Noah. By contrast, the Vulgate dating of the Flood at 2349 B.C. would have postdated the ascent to the throne of Yao in 2357 B.C. and could not have been reconciled with Noah's universal patriarchy. The existence of variations in the Septuagint dating — for example, Magalhaes referred to the Flood preceding Fu Hsi's reign by 200 years and therefore implied that the Flood would have occurred in 3152 B.C. instead of in the above cited 2957 B.C. — contrasted with the more rigid Vulgate datings and was a boon to the flexibility needed in order to reconcile the Chinese and European chronologies. [By way of comparison, one notes that Couplet's *Tabula chronologica* dated the origin of Chinese chronology from the reign of Huang-ti (the Yellow Emperor) in 2697 B.C. .]

9. CONCLUSION

Magalhaes was quite frank in his admiration for China's great antiquity and stated that no other nation in the world could claim a series of kings (i.e. history) so ancient, long and continuous[102]. But Magalhaes was no starry-eyed admirer and noted that this admirable history had fostered a pride among Chinese which

100 Magaillans, pp. 73–74.
101 Magaillans, p. 74.
102 Magaillans, p. 75.

led them automatically to prize what originated in China and to despise foreigners and all things foreign, although they had little or no understanding of foreign things and of the advantages which they could receive from them. What Magalhaes criticized was not exactly xenophobia or active hatred of foreigners and things foreign. The subject of Chinese xenophobia is a deep one and one might usefully ask how this cultural pride and insularity could have contributed to xenophobia and to what extent such attitudes represented the educated equivalent of the more violent, uneducated expressions of Chinese xenophobia[103].

Magalhaes cited several examples of how Chinese cultural pride affected their perception of foreign elements. The first was the distortion with which the Chinese represented foreign areas in their maps. According to Magalhaes, "they give a vast expanse to China, but they represent other realms without order, without position and without any sign of good geography"[104]. Since China had a distinguished tradition in cartography, Magalhaes' remarks could validly apply only to the deterioration of that tradition which took place in the Ming and, even then, his criticism may not have been entirely justified. In another example, Magalhaes referred to the response of the magistrate who headed a criminal tribunal in Szechwan province when Magalhaes was there with Fr. Buglio in 1642–1647. In response to charges brought against the fathers by a number of Buddhist monks, Magalhaes quoted the magistrate as saying that as long as the missionaries did not teach new doctines, the empire was large enough to contain foreigners. If however, the missionaries taught doctrines differing from what the Chinese sages had professed, then they should be punished and expelled[105]. Finally, Magalhaes wrote of the surprise that numerous literati had expressed when they discovered that the Chinese Classics were unfamiliar to Europeans. Magalhaes' feelings of frustration in introducing Christianity to China were clearly evident from his descriptions. If his understanding and sympathy for the Chinese and their culture did not reach the depth of certain other Jesuits, it was nonetheless genuine. His admiration for the Chinese helped to balance off his frustration such that his remarks on Chinese cultural pride and exclusiveness cannot be dismissed as mere bigotry.

The works by Frs. Semedo and Magalhaes reflect how the basic elements of Ricci's accommodation policy were accepted by Jesuits of the mid-seventeenth century in China. These elements included the continuation of the Jesuit study

103 For a survey and analysis of anti-Christian attitudes in seventeenth-century China, see Lu Shih-chiang, "*Yu Ming-Ch'ing chih chi Chung-kuo chih-shih fen-tzu Fan-Chiao yen-lun k'an Chung-Hsi wen-hua chiao-liu* (A survey of the Chinese intellectuals' Anti-Christian opinions as related to the cultural exchange between China and the West 1583–1723)," in *International Symposium on Chinese-Western Cultural Interchange* (Taipei, 1983) pp. 407–430. Reprinted in *China Mission Studies (1550–1800) Bulletin* 6 (1984): 1–42.
104 Magaillans, p. 75.
105 Magaillans, p. 75.

and translation of the Confucian Four Books, the positive evaluation of education and knowledge in China, and a sympathetic attitude toward the Confucian literati, though a slightly less critical treatment of Buddhism and Taoism than Ricci had expressed. Yet in spite of the continuities with Ricci's accommodation, the work of Semedo and Magalhaes did not represent a static continuation, but rather a gradual evolution of the accommodation policy in that slight modifications were made to Ricci's outlook and new ideas about the relation between Chinese and European cultures were introduced, such as the notion that Biblical teachings had been carried to China by descendants of Adam and Eve during China's earliest antiquity. Finally, both Semedo and Magalhaes had a strong interest in the Chinese language. Whereas Ricci-Trigault had conveyed only a bare sketch of the Chinese language in *De Christiana expeditione apud Sinas*, Semedo and Magalhaes both gave detailed presentations which dovetailed with one another in so many respects that it is likely they were drawing from a linguistic theory of Chinese commonly held by China Jesuits of that time. These presentations were assimilated by Europeans and contributed to the growing fascination with the Chinese language found in seventeenth-century Europe.

CHAPTER IV
THE PROTO-SINOLOGICAL ASSIMILATION OF CHINA'S HISTORY AND GEOGRAPHY IN THE WORKS OF MARTINI

I. THE BACKGROUND TO FR. MARTINI'S WORKS

Martino Martini (1614–1661) was a Jesuit whose chief contribution to the accommodation effort in China was in the areas of geography and history. Sometimes claimed as both German and Italian, Martini was born in Trento, the major city of the Tyrol. He entered the Society of Jesus in 1632 and studied at the Collegium Romanum where he was tutored in mathematics by the eminent polymath, Fr. Athanasius Kircher[1]. Fr. Martini arrived at Hangchow in 1643 at a time when China was wracked with the Manchu conquest and civil disorder. This disorder had the effect of easing the usual restrictions on travel in China and furthermore made mobility a prudent safety precaution. Martini claimed to have visited seven of fifteen Chinese provinces and though the exact extent of his travels are subject to debate, his personal observations were important to the composition of his famous atlas[2].

There is a story that Martini told about his first encounter with the Manchu invaders of Ming China which echoes other stories of Jesuit audacity and facility in dealing with shifting circumstances[3]. According to Martini's account, this encounter took place while he was in the city of Wenchou in Chekiang province

---

1 Athanasius Kircher, *China illustrata* (Amsterdam, 1667) preface, p. 1.

2 Martini made his claim of visiting seven Chinese provinces at the conclusion of the preface to his *Novus atlas Sinensis* (Amsterdam, 1655) p. 26. However, he did not identify these seven provinces by name. The Chinese scholar Ma Yong disputes the claim of Hsü Tsung-tse that during the years 1644–1645, Martini traveled widely in the northern provinces, visited Peking and the Great Wall. Mr. Ma claims that at this time, military conditions in north China would have been too chaotic for such an extensive itinerary. Though Fr. Hsü does not note this, the ultimate source of his information concerning Martini's travels was probably Martini's own words in his dedication to *Novus atlas Sinensis*. See Hsü Tsung-tse, *Ming-Ch'ing chien Yeh-su-hui shih-i ch'ü t'i-yao* (Taipei, 1958) p. 384 & Ma Yong, "*Chin-tai Ou-chou Han-hsüeh-chia te hsien-ch'ü Ma-erh-ti-ni,*" *Lishi yanjiu* 6 (1980): 157.

3 This story appeared in some later editions of Martini's *De bello tartarico,* including the Latin edition published at Amsterdam by Johannes Janssonius in 1665, pp. 126–128, and in the version of *De bello tartarico* appended to *Novus atlas Sinensis* (Amsterdam, 1655) pp. 18–19. The story is not found in the first edition of *De bello tartarico* published at Antwerp in 1654 nor in the French translation of that edition made in Paris by Jean Henault in 1654. The account also appeared in Pfister, p. 257, and in an abbreviated version in Abbé Huc's *Le Christianisme en Chine* (1857) II, 381.

on a mission for the Ming pretender, Chu Yü chien[4]. When the Manchus captured Wenchou, Fr. Martini was lodged a short distance away in a large house where several Chinese had taken refuge with him. As the Manchus approached, Martini had a large red poster hung over the door of the house inscribed with seven characters which said: "Here lives a doctor of the divine Law who has come from the Great West". Martini prepared tables under the poster and piled them with impressively bound European books and other eye-catching devices such as telescopes, mirrors and mathematical instruments. In the middle of all this he placed an altar with the image of Jesus. When the Manchus arrived, they were said to have been so impressed with this display that, far from harming Martini, their commander received him with honor and asked if he were willing to transfer his loyalty to new masters. When Martini agreed, his head was shaved in Manchu style and his Chinese clothes and hat were replaced with Manchu ones. He was permitted to return to his church in Hangchow and was given safeguards to protect him and his Christian followers from harm.

Martini was not alone among Jesuits in achieving a quick shift in allegiance from the Chinese to the Manchus. In Peking, the Jesuits, led by Fr. Adam Schall von Bell (1592–1666), made a far more difficult transfer of allegiance while maintaining and even improving on their high official status at court and in the Bureau of Astronomy. At the same time, Jesuits in the south of China, such as Michael Boym (1612–1659), continued to serve the cause of the last Ming pretender, Chu Yu-lang, who was called – with more optimism than realism – the Yung-li emperor (r. 1647–1661)[5].

In 1650 Martini was appointed procurator of the Jesuit mission of China and was charged with returning to Europe in order to secure aid for the mission and to present the Jesuit case in the rising controversy surrounding the Chinese rites issues. He disembarked from Fukien province and sailed via the

---

4 The Ming pretender Chu Yü-chien served a short-lived reign based in Fukien province as the Lung-wu emperor (July 1645–October 1646) which ended with his imprisonment and execution by the advancing Manchu forces. Weichou is referred to on the map of Chekiang, opposite pp. 108–109, on p. 120 and in the thirteenth page of the tables in Martini's *Atlas*. Pfister's confusion of Wenchou as a suburb of Hangchow possibly stemmed from the common reference of the time to Wenchou as a "small Hangchow" because of the similarity of its waterways and beautiful, large buildings to Hangchow. See Martini, *Atlas*, p. 120.

5 It is notable that Fr. Boym left Macao around January 1st 1651 – shortly after Martini left Hangchow for Europe – carrying written appeals for aid addressed separately to Pope Innocent X and the Jesuit General. Two of the appeals were written by the dowager empress Helena (née Wang) and two by the eunuch Achilles P'ang T'ienshou, both of whom were Christian converts. The Chinese original copies of the two letters to the Pope are preserved in the Vatican, though the letters to the Jesuit General are available only in Latin translation. See Goodrich, p. 20 & Hummel, p. 195. For partial translations of these letters, see E. H. Parker, "Letters from a Chinese Empress and a Chinese Eunuch to the Pope in the year 1650," *Contemporary Review* (January 1912): 79–83 and Nigel Cameron, *Barbarians and mandarins* (Tokyo, 1970) p. 233.

Philippines and Batavia, where after being temporarily imprisoned by the Dutch, reembarked – probably on the *Oliphant*[6]. Finally, after seven months at sea, he reached Bergen, Norway in August 1653[7]. Martini travelled to Hamburg and then on to Amsterdam where he arranged with the publisher Joannis Blaeu to print his *Novus atlas Sinensis* in Blaeu's well-known geographical series. In June 1654, he departed from Amsterdam enroute to Antwerp and, later, Brussels. Throughout his travels in northern Europe, he was enthusiastically received by a number of savants[8].

The segment of his journey between Amsterdam and Antwerp was the occasion for some fascinating meetings between Martini and a scholar of Middle Eastern languages, Jacobus Golius (Gool) of Leiden (1596–1667)[9]. Golius had long had a great interest in China and had collected a number of Chinese books, none of which he could read[10]. Golius's blend of enthusiasm and ignorance was typical of seventeenth-century European students of sinology and it led him to contact Martini and arrange for a meeting while Martini was passing through Leiden enroute to Antwerp. So pressed was Martini by his duties, that he was able to spare Golius only the brief interval between changing barges at Leiden. Golius came prepared with questions and was not disappointed in Martini's answers. In one of his questions, Golius sought to establish a connection between Cathay, whose influence had extended to the Middle East, and China. From Martini's response, Golius confirmed the connection and discovered that the Persian names of the Cathayan duodecenary cycle corresponded to the twelve Earthly Branches (*ti-chih*) of Chinese[11]. These twelve elements combined with the ten Heavenly Stems (*t'ien-kan*) to form the sexagenary cycle (i.e. cycle of sixty), popularly known as the "Cycle of Cathay". But Martini was soon off for an eight-day stay in Antwerp where he was to make arrangements for the publication of his *Sinicae historiae decas prima* (Antwerp 1655). Golius was so stimulated by this short meeting that he obtained a two-week leave from his duties at the university of Leiden to visit Antwerp. There in June of 1654 and in spite of other duties, Martini was said to have been both courteous and attentive to Golius' questions.

In Antwerp, Golius met the young Chinese whom Martini had brought with him to Europe and who was possibly the first educated Chinese to be brought to Europe by a Jesuit. This Cheng Ma-no (Emmanuel de Siqueira, 1633–1673)

6 Martini appears to have traveled from Batavia to Europe on the *Oliphant*, a vessel of the Dutch East India Company. See J. J. L. Duyvendak, "Early Chinese studies in Holland," *T'oung pao* 32 (1936): 311n.
7 *De bello tartarico*, preface.
8 Theophili Siegfridi Bayeri, *Museum Sinicum* 2 vols. (St. Petersburg, 1730) preface, p. 20.
9 The meetings between Golius and Martini are described in Duyvendak, pp. 298–305.
10 Golius' collection of Chinese books is described in Duyvendak, pp. 314–317.
11 Duyvendak, p. 300.

later entered the Society of Jesus, studied philosophy and theology at the Collegium Romanum and returned to China in 1671[12]. Before departing, Golius received from Martini several Chinese books and manuscripts[13]. Martini is also said to have presented Golius with the red character poster which secured his transfer from Ming to Manchu masters in Wenchou. Duyvendak speculated that since this account of Martini's first contact with the Manchus did not appear in the first edition of *De bello tartarico historia* (1654), it was Golius who persuaded Martini to include it in the next edition[14]. Presumably Martini made the insertion during his short stay at Brussels. After returning to Leiden, Golius wrote a piece on the discoveries he had made through his contact with Martini and this piece, entitled "De Regno Catayo Additamentum" was added as an appendix to Martini's atlas[15].

Urgent matters called Martini to Rome before the end of 1654. There he urged the establishment of an overland route to China, recommended the education of Chinese youth and defended the Jesuit position on the Chinese rites[16]. He was persuasive enough to secure the only pro-Jesuit papal decree of the Rites Controversy, issued by Pope Alexander VII on March 23rd 1656. But Martini — too busy to await the Pope's reply — had already left Rome in January for the sea voyage from Genoa to Lisbon and then in April of 1657 on from Lisbon to China. His sobriquet, "the Admiral", was established enroute when he and his ten mission recruits were attacked by pirates. Martini is said to have played a heroic part in a bloody battle[17].

Martini finally reached Hangchow in 1659. His final two years were spent there where he was active in evangelical work, oversaw the building of a new church and cultivated the literati. This was probably the period when he composed several theological treatises in Chinese as well as a Chinese translation of extracts on the theme of friendship, drawn from Cicero and Seneca. The latter work, entitled *Chiu yu pien,* was published in Hangchow in 1661, the year in

12 See Pfister, p. 381. Duyvendak (p. 301n) apparently overlooked Pfister's reference to Cheng Ma-no when he claimed that he found no mention anywhere of the Chinese who accompanied Martini. For more detail, see Francis A. Rouleau, S.I., "The first Chinese priest of the Society of Jesus. Emmanuel de Siqueira. Cheng Ma-no Wei-hsin. 1633–1673," *Archivum historicum Societatis Iesu* 28 (1959): 3–50.

13 An attempt to trace the Chinese books which Martini contributed to Golius' collection is found in Duyvendak, p. 314f.

14 Duyvendak, p. 328.

15 Martini, *Novus atlas Sinensis,* appendix, pp. i-xij. In this appendix, Golius included his discovery of the close association between Cathay and China, and specifically between the component elements of the sexagenary cycle. In perhaps the earliest graphic explanation of the Chinese sexagenary cycle to appear in Europe, Golius included the Chinese characters, Chinese romanization and a rendering of the Cathayan equivalents in Arabic script.

16 Francis Rouleau, "Martino Martini," in *New Catholic Encyclopedia* IX, 310.

17 Rouleau, p. 310.

which Martini died from an overdose of the cathartic form of rhubarb[18]. The choice of the accommodative theme of friendship by Martini, and before him by Ricci, signifies one path which the Jesuits cultivated to Chinese literati souls. The theme's recurrence would seem to indicate a certain effectiveness and the theme is characteristically Jesuit in its cosmopolitan and somewhat wordly nature. Both Ricci and Martini were highly talented men of extroverted personalities and this doubtless furthered their friendships with literati.

2. MARTINI'S *DE BELLO TARTARICO HISTORIA*

Fr. Martini wrote several books within a framework of accommodation which had a strong impact upon the European assimilation of information about China. His *De bello tartarico historia* presented detailed news on the major political event of seventeenth-century China — the Manchu conquest. The work's short length — most editions were under 200 pages — and journalistic content were aimed at popular appeal and, as such, the book was an enormous success. Between 1654 and 1706 the work was republished over twenty times, appearing in French, German, English, Italian, Dutch, Portuguese, Spanish, Swedish and Danish editions[19]. Some editions were illustrated, including the Latin edition of 1655 published in Amsterdam which contains eight engravings. But not all of the editions of *De bello tartarico* include these engravings, for example, the French translation published at Paris in 1654 does not. Therefore, it is quite possible that the illustrations were added by a printer without Martini's knowledge. The matter is complicated by the fact that the French edition of 1654, in addition to lacking the eight illustrations, also lacks the map of China which Martini specifically mentioned in the preface.

Among the illustrations in *De bello tartarico* is a particularly dramatic one which depicts a scene from the imperial palace at the time of the capture of Peking by the rebel leader Li Tzu-ch'eng in 1644. (See plate 3.) Martini's text stated that after the Ch'ung-chen emperor (r. 1628–1644) learned that all escape routes had been cut off, he decided to hang himself[20]. But before doing so, because of his fears over the imminent defilement of his young daughter, he took a sword and killed her with a stab between the breasts. This stabbing scene was dramatically depicted as the young heroine, portrayed with rather heavy European rather than Chinese physical features and wearing European

---

18 The titles and short descriptions of Martini's Chinese-language works are found in Pfister, p. 260.

19 For further discussion of Martini's *De bello tartarico historia,* see Edwin J. Van Kley, "News from China; Seventeenth Century Notices of the Manchu Conquest," *Journal of Modern History* 45 (1973): 563–568 & "An Alternative Muse; the Manchu Conquest in European Literature," *European Studies Review* 6 (1976): 21–24.

20 *De bello tartarico* pp. 89–90.

style clothing, lifted her eyes to Heaven with hands raised in supplication, while the blood spurted from the wound in her breasts. The emperor also was depicted with solid European features and European clothing, except for the exotic hat. To the left in the engraving we see through a doorway into a garden where a man hangs dead from a tree.

While the theme of this engraving is drawn from Chinese sources, its distinctly European form shows how information about China was being adapted for the European reader. The art historian T. Kaori Kitao notes some striking parallels between this portrayal of the slaying of the Ch'ung-chen emperor's daughter and Pietro da Cortona's fresco in Santa Bibiana, Rome, painted in the years 1624–1626 and which depicts a woman's martyrdom through her refusal to worship idols[21]. (See plate 4.) Ms. Kitao describes the engraving from the 1655 Amsterdam edition of Martini's *De bello tartarico* as unmistakably Roman Baroque in both conception and design. The derivation of this Martini engraving from Cortona's Santa Bibiana or its derivatives is suggested by the following elements in the engraving: the dominating female protagonist with full-proportioned anatomy, round head, upturned eyes and upraised arms – such a female martyr was a favorite artistic subject of seventeenth-century Europeans. The possibility of Martini's engraving having been derived from Pietro's work is further reinforced by the pedimented, draped wall canopy to the right behind the emperor's daughter, the niche with a conche containing an apparently female statue in the middle background, and, finally through the archway to the left, the distant landscape depicting a secondary episode which in some sense iconographically prefigures an event to come. In the latter case, the man hanging from a tree foretells the fate of the Ch'ung-chen emperor himself. The secondary episode is a representational device for producing a continuous narration in which the hanging follows as scene two from the primary scene in the foreground.

The saintly martyrdom of Bibiana is portrayed in her resignation, saintly pose, pious look as well as in the horror of the recoiling attendants. The parallels to the portrayal of the slaying of the Chinese princess are striking – too striking to be accidental, though Ms. Kitao notes that Cortona's own work need not have been the direct source of Martini's engraving since there were other representations in this style which were derived from Cortona. The widespread influence of Cortona's new and very personal style may be gauged from the fact that he has been judged by an eminent art historian as being – along with Bernini and Borromini – part of the great trio of Roman High Baroque artists[22]. Ms. Kitao adds that while this mode of representation portrays the woman as

---

21 Private correspondence of T. Korai Kitao to the author, dated January 8th 1982.
22 Rudolf Wittkower, *Art and Architecture in Italy 1600 to 1750* (Harmondsworth, Middlesex, England, 1958) pp. 152 & 163.

Plate 3. An imaginary depiction of the last Ming monarch, the Ch'ung-chen emperor, killing his daughter (Princess K'un-i?) to avoid her defilement by the approaching enemy in 1644 in Peking, from Martino Martini's *De bello tartarico* (Amsterdam, 1655). Courtesy of the Niedersächsische Landesbibliothek Hannover.

Plate 4. Pietro da Cortona's fresco depicting a saint's refusal to worship idols (1624–1626). Santa Bibiana, Rome. Courtesy of Santa Bibiana, Rome.

a saintly figure, the assassin is inevitably seen as a villain whose villainous character is reinforced in the prefiguration of his ultimate hanging. This iconographical
interpretation is interesting because while Martini's text describes the Ch'ung-
chen emperor acting out of honorable motives, other historians have been more
negative in their descriptions of his last hours.

The general outlines of Martini's account of the last days of the Ch'ung-chen
emperor are confirmed by the historical record, though it is probable that
Martini took liberties in dramatizing certain small details. According to recent
research by Frederic Wakeman, Jr., as the situation of the Ming throne became
desperate, the Ch'ung-chen emperor lapsed into a mood of despair and ineffectiveness[23]. The Emperor neglected matters associated with the practical survival
of the Dynasty, while sinking into self-righteous pity and shifting the blame for
the state of affairs onto his officials. His manner of suicide reflected and reinforced his attempt to absolve himself of all guilt for the fall of the Dynasty.
Unfortunately, the Ch'ung-chen emperor's performance of this rite of suicide
failed to match the dignity of his conception. As Li Tzu-ch'eng's troops entered
the outskirts of the capital on April 24th 1664, the emperor was drunk. It
was in this drunken state that he took a sword and went on a rampage of mutilation of at least two crown princesses and one consort. (The Empress Chou had
already committed suicide). In this rampage, the Emperor killed Princess K'un-i,
and this was apparently the incident on which the illustration in Martini's *De
bello tartarico* was based. Near midnight, the Emperor attempted to flee the
palace disguised as a eunuch, but was stopped. Consequently, on the morning
of April 25th, he mounted Coal Mountain, which lay within the palace compound, and strangled himself with his sash[24].

All three of the books published by Martini during his return to Europe —
De bello tartarico, *Novus atlas Sinensis* and *Sinicae historiae decas prima* — were
composed together and with the promotional and recruiting intention of a Jesuit
procurator in mind. Martini made this quite clear in his brief, but significant
preface to *De bello tartarico* where he gave the clear impression that this book
represented a mere appetizer to the other two works. Martini stated that the
many questions which he was asked by Europeans about the land, people and
culture of China prompted him "to give the public a small narration in which

23 Frederic Wakeman, Jr. "The Shun Interregnum of 1644," in *From Ming to Ch'ing:
   Conquest, Region and Continuity in Seventeenth Century China* Jonathan D. Spence
   & John E. Wills, Jr., eds. (New Haven, 1979) pp. 49–51.
24 Mr. Wakeman (p. 80) notes that his portrayal of the Ch'ung-chen emperor's unbalanced
   condition during his final hours is based upon the account of events by Ch'ien Hsing
   in *Chia-shen ch'uan-hsin lu* which is printed in *Chung-kuo nei-luan wai-huo li-shih
   ts'ung-shu* (Shanghai, 1940) ts'e 12. However, Wakeman cites the accounts of several
   other scholars (Chi Liu-ch'i, Chang Tai and T'an Ch'ien) who present the Emperor's
   final actions in a more favorable light. Since these more favorable accounts are relegat-
   ed to footnote status, one infers that Wakeman agrees with the past tendency of sinologists to regard the negative account by Ch'ien Hsing as more reliable.

I have summarized all the revolutions which happened in this great realm in the last 40 years" (ca. 1614–1654)[25]. This small narration was *De bello tartarico*. Consequently, while *Sinicae historiae decas prima* and the *Atlas* had been underway for sometime, *De bello tartarico* appears to have been rather quickly composed for immediate popular consumption – it appeared before either of the other two works – and with the aim of stimulating public interest in the other more substantive works. This would explain why Martini devoted most of the preface of *De bello tartarico* to the *Atlas* and *Sinicae historiae decas prima*.

Martini referred to his history to come, i.e. *Sinicae historiae decas prima,* as an attempt to describe all major events in China since the time of the Flood. By presenting a 4,000-year history of China – actually, Martini's history stopped just prior to the birth of Christ and therefore omitted 1,600 years from his intended span – Martini saw himself as fulfilling a promise which Trigault had made in 1615 in his preface to *De Christiana expeditione apud Sinas*. This reflected the continuity of Jesuit scholarly efforts, of which more will be said in following chapters. Based upon his study of the histories of the Chinese, Martini promised to reveal different "nations" which had populated China, its ancient lawgivers, its religion, imperial princes and wars which had changed its boundaries. Secondly, Martini offered a work of maps, i.e. *Novus atlas Sinensis,* as a necessary complement to the European understanding of China. These maps were said to reveal the extent of the provinces, course of rivers, location of towns, lakes, mountains and forests. He also promised to give in great exactitude what he had learned in his voyages to and throughout China.

Martini spoke of having been "destined for a long time" by his superiors to travel to Rome in order to deal with affairs of the new church in China[26]. By this he implied that he had been involved with *Sinicae historiae decas prima* and the *Atlas* as long-range tasks assigned to a potential procurator. Indeed, he worked for ten years in consulting people who had knowledge useful to these literary projects. He consulted those Chinese most learned in history, read the best writings in Chinese history and collected all the memoires he was able to find on these subjects. In regard to the *Atlas*, he corrected the general map of the empire and individual maps of each province. During the seven months at sea between Java and Norway, he finished reading nearly all of the histories he had begun in the Far East. During this time he was also able to compose the brief descriptive sections of the towns which accompanied each provincial map. Referring briefly to *De bello tartarico*, Martini spoke of including a small map of China. (See plate 5). Although this map was too small to contain detailed accuracy, its general accuracy was attested to by Martini by the fact that it was composed by "philosophers" [i.e. literati] of China". However, one notes that

25 *De bello tartarico*, preface.
26 *De bello tartarico*, preface.

this small map compares very poorly with the general map of China found in Martini's *Atlas*. (Compare plates 5 and 6.)

Toward the conclusion of the preface to *De bello tartarico*, Martini reminded the reader of his role as Jesuit procurator by saying that these maps and descriptions in the *Atlas* had been done in order to show the need for missionaries to instruct the Chinese in Christianity. Also, Martini spoke of his *Sinicae historiae decas prima* as comparing the chronology of the Chinese to that of the Bible. But the accommodation was tilted toward Europe in that Martini spoke of evaluating the Chinese chronology in terms of Biblical chronology.

3. MARTINI'S *NOVUS ATLAS SINENSIS*

Martini's *Novus atlas Sinensis* and *Sinicae historiae decas prima* had an impact upon Europeans which operated less through the large readership of *De bello tartarico* than through a thought-provoking stimulation of proto-sinological interest in China. His readers, in turn, wrote books which though usually amateurish and lacking Martini's first-hand experience of China, nevertheless disseminated Martini's information and ideas to a broad readership, and thereby greatly influenced the formation of European conceptions of China.

The first of these two works to be published was *Novus atlas Sinensis* which appeared in Amsterdam in 1655[27]. The *Atlas* was published as part six of Joannis Bleau's *Theatrum orbis terrarum sive novus atlas*. The first edition contained seventeen double-page maps with 171 pages of accompanying text, a nineteen-page catalogue of longitude and latitude markings of cities and forts, arranged by province and size of city, and the appendix by Golius. There is one general map of China and Japan (see plate 6.) and one map for each of the fifteen provinces of China plus one for Japan. Interspersed between these

---

27 The Niedersächsische Landesbibliothek Hannover possesses a copy of Martini's *Novus atlas Sinensis* (Amsterdam, 1655) 2° (32.5 cm. x 50 cm.) published by Johannis Blaeu. This library also possesses the French translation of Martini's *Atlas* entitled "Description geographique de l'empire de la Chine" and published in Melchisédec Thévenot's *Relations de divers voyages* III (1666) 216 pp. in-folio. Sommervogel, V, 650, claims that Martini's *Atlas* appears in volume II of Thévenot's work and that it contains no maps. But in the edition of Thévenot which I examined, the *Atlas* appears in volume III (1666) and contains a large fold-out general map of China and Japan which differs only slightly from its equivalent in the first (Bleau) edition of Martini's *Atlas*. The *Atlas* also appeared in a Latin edition in 1655, in French and Dutch editions in 1656 and in a Spanish edition in 1659. A facsimile edition of the *Atlas* in somewhat smaller than original dimensions was printed as part of an international symposium honoring Martini held in Trento in October 1981 and sponsored by the Museo Tridentino di Scienze Naturali. In addition, a polylingual translation of the preface to the *Atlas* in Italian, French, English and German was published as an accompanying volume.

maps were chapters in the text describing each province and these were subdivided in terms of major provincial cities. These provinces were, in the order of treatment and with Martini's romanizations: (1) Pecheli (Pei-chih-li) or Peking region, (2) Xansi (Shansi), (3) Xensi (Shensi), (4) Xantung (Shantung), (5) Honan, (6) Suchuen (Szechwan), (7) Huquang (Hukwang), (8) Kiangsi, (9) Nanking (Nanking district; Nan-chih-li) or Kiangnan, (10) Chekiang, (11) Fokien (Fukien), (12) Quangtung (Kwangtung), (13) Quangsi (Kwangsi), (14) Queicheu (Kweichow) and (15) Iunnan (Yunnan). The regions of Peichihli and Nanchihli were administrative regions centered around the northern and southern capitals of Peking and Nanking at the beginning of the Ming dynasty and reflected the Ming preservation of two capitals. The provincial designation "Kiangnan" appears to have become the exclusive designation for this region when the Manchus disestablished Nanking as the second capital. These provinces remain a part of the People's Republic of China today, except that Hukuang province has given way to Hupei province while Kiangnan has been divided to form Anhwei and Kiangsu provinces.

The maps in the *Atlas'* oversize folio edition (32.5 x 50 cm.) are impressive in their beauty[28]. Each map was tinted in shades of blue, red, pink, yellow, gold and green — a process which in seventeenth-century European printing was done by hand. The maps were profusely illustrated not only with mountains, forests and rivers, but also with presumably representative Chinese figures in the cartouches containing the map legends. These figures are much more distinctly Chinese in physical features and costume than are the Chinese depicted in the *De bello tartarico* Latin edition published at Amsterdam in 1655. Unlike the illustrations in certain editions of *De bello tartarico*, it appears likely that Martini supervised the illustrations in his *Atlas*.

In compiling the *Atlas*, Martini relied on Chinese written sources, the pooled geographical knowledge of his Jesuit confreres and his own travel experience. He stated in the preface to the *Atlas* that all his information had been drawn from Chinese books on geography and maps[29]. In his preface to *De bello tartarico*, he added that through knowledge gained from his own travels in China, he had been able to correct defects in the Chinese sources. On the basis of Martini's remark that he had begun gathering together over fifty Chinese books to take on the journey to Europe after he learned of his assignment there[30], Duyvendak implied that Martini had begun working on the *Atlas* rather late during his first stay in China[31]. But this implication is at odds with the impression which

---

28 Sommervogel, V, 649, clarifies that there are two Latin editions, of which the first is a more deluxe edition involving 171 instead of 134 pages of text. My access was to the first edition.

29 Martini, *Atlas* pp. 3–4.

30 Martini, *Atlas* p. 147.

31 Duyvendak, p. 311.

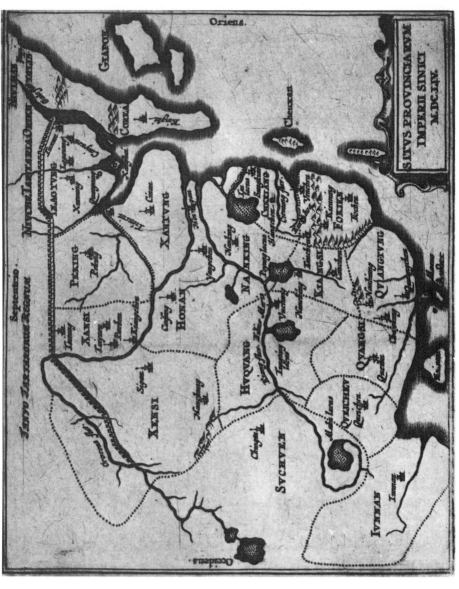

Plate 5. A map of China with provincial boundaries as of 1654, from Martino Martini's *De bello tartarico* (Amsterdam, 1655). Courtesy of the Niedersächsische Landesbibliothek Hannover.

Plate 6. A detailed map of China, from Martini Martino's *Novus atlas Sinensis* (Amsterdam, 1655). Courtesy of the Niedersächsische Landesbibliothek Hannover. →

Martini gave in the preface to *De bello tartarico* where he spoke of ten years of preparation for these literary works.

Although Martini implied that the preparation of the *Atlas* and *Sinicae historiae decas prima* occupied ten years, he clearly stated in the preface to *De bello tartarico* that he began the actual composing of these two works in the Philippines while waiting for ongoing passage to Europe. Later in the same preface, he stated that in addition to finishing nearly all of the Chinese histories that he had begun in East Asia and brought on board, he also advanced his *Atlas* a good deal by composing the descriptions of towns and provinces which were interspersed between the maps. In sum, a picture of the preparation and composition of the *Atlas* emerges as follows. Through his inherent talents and interests and his anticipated journey to Europe as procurator, Martini conceived of a work on geography soon after arriving in China. He began gathering information and started examining Chinese maps in the process of traveling about China. His gathering of information continued until his return voyage to Europe and one of the final acts of preparation was his gathering together of fifty-plus Chinese books, some of which must have dealt with the *Atlas*.

Jesuit accommodative interest in the cartography of China dated from the time of the pioneering missionaries Ruggieri and Ricci. The latter produced a map of China which was first published by the French royal geographer, Nicolas Sanson, in 1656[32]. Semedo's map of China appeared at London in 1655 in the English edition of his *Imperio de la China*[33]. Boym's map of China was reprinted by Sanson in 1670[34]. There was a great deal of interpolation of ideas and sharing of results among Jesuit missionaries in China. Clearly the seventeenth-century Jesuit translation of the Confucian Four Books which culminated in *Confucius Sinarum philosophus* was one such cooperative project. Possibly another was Martini's *Atlas*[35]. In spite of certain discrepancies between the maps of Ruggieri-Ricci, Semedo, Boym and Martini in regard to the size of China relative to Europe, it appears that all of these maps derived from Chu Ssu-pen's *Kuang yü t'u* (Enlarged terrestrial atlas) as edited by Lo Hung-hsien in the edition of 1579[36].

32 See Boleslaw Szcześniak, "The Seventeenth Century Maps of China: an Inquiry into the Compilations of European Cargographers," *Imago Mundi* 13 (1956): 119–120. The Ruggieri map is really ascribed to Matteo Neroni, whom Mr. Szcześniak identifies as Matteo Ricci, hence this writer's designation of the authorship as "Ruggieri-Ricci." Fr. Bernard speaks of Ricci in regard to a project of an atlas of China 50 years before Martini's *Atlas* appeared. See Henri Bernard, S.J., "Les sources mongoles et chinoises de l'atlas Martini," *Monumenta Serica* 7 (1945): 133.

33 Szcześniak, "The Seventeenth Century Maps of China," pp. 123–124.

34 Szcześniak, "The Seventeenth Century Maps of China," p. 122.

35 Mr. Szcześniak states that Martini's *Novus atlas Sinensis* "undoubtedly, was a compilation of researches by other missionaries." See Szcześniak, "The Seventeenth Century Maps of China," p. 131.

36 Szcześniak, "The Seventeenth Century Maps of China," p. 131.

The evidence indicates that the major Chinese source of Martini's *Atlas* was the *Kuang yü t'u*[37]. Working within the tradition of Chinese geography and supplemented with new geographical information through the Mongol conquest of Asia, Chu Ssu-pen (1273–1337) composed his map of China sometime between 1311 and 1320 under the title *Yü t'u* (Terrestrial atlas). The map existed only in manuscript or epigraphic form until it was revised and expanded by Lo Hung-hsien (1504–1564) and printed ca. 1555 as *Kuang yü t'u*. This work consisted of a general map of China, provincial maps and special maps, all drawn in measured squares. (The similarity of the arrangement of *Kuang yü t'u* to Martini's *Atlas* is immediately apparent.) This work apparently circulated widely as new editions appeared in 1558, 1561, 1572 and 1579, and until 1799[38]. As noted in an earlier chapter, Ricci appears to have made use of the 1579 edition. Copies of *Kuang yü t'u* in two *chüan* began finding their way to Europe by 1601[39]. Other Chinese sources for the Jesuit maps have been suggested, but without confirmation[40].

In his *Tratados historicos, politicos, ethicos, y religiosos de la Monarchia de China* (Madrid 1676), the Dominican missionary Domingo Navarrete criticized Martini's atlas for being filled with fantasies and errors, but the Jesuit Ferdinand Verbiest argued that such errors were due to Martini's Chinese sources rather than to Martini's own eyewitness accounts, which were relatively limited[41]. In fact, Martini's atlas has been praised as the most valuable European work of geographical information on China to appear in the seventeenth century and a work which dominated such information on China until 1735[42]. Although other Jesuits had drawn maps on China, Martini was the most talented and skillful geographer among the over two-hundred Jesuits sent to China in the seventeenth century.

As with Ricci-Trigault's *De Christiana expeditione apud Sinas*, Martini's atlas also contained a tax-roll figure. His figure of 58, 914, 284 excluded all women and children, as well as members of the imperial family, magistrates, eunuchs, soldiers and Buddhist and Taoist monks[43]. One notes that Martini's

37 Walter Fuchs, *The "Mongol Atlas" of China by Chu Ssu-pen and the Kuang-yü-t'u* Monumenta Serica monograph VIII. Peiping, 1946. p. 11.
38 Bernard, "Les sources de l'atlas Martini," p. 131.
39 Duyvendak, p. 311.
40 Duyvendak, p. 313, mentions two other possible sources of Martini's *Atlas*: (1) the anonymous Ming reprint of *Li-tai ti-li chih-chang t'u* with preface by Su Shih (1036–1101) and (2) the *Ti-t'u tsung-yao* by Wu Hsüeh-yen and Chu Shao-pen, first published in the Ming period.
41 Navarrete, *Tratados historicos . . . de la Monarchia de China* (Madrid, 1676) p. 24 & *Correspondence de Ferdinand Verbiest (1623–1688)* Frs. Josson & Willaert, eds. (1938) pp. 270, 273 & 314–315.
42 Ferdinand Freiherr von Richthofen, *China. Ergebnisse eigener Reisen* 5 vols. (Berlin, 1877) I, 674–677.
43 Martini, *Atlas* p. 5.

figure involved a slight increase over that of Ricci's partial population figure of 58,550,801 which, given the similarity of the exclusions, probably was drawn from a similar source — most likely from the roll of able-bodied males (*ting*). From this tax-roll figure, Martini projected a total population figure of approximately 200,000,000. However, given the fact that Martini was writing at mid-century rather than, like Ricci, early in the century and given the concensus among demographers that China suffered severe population losses in the second quarter of the seventeenth century, one wonders if Martini's tax-roll figure was considerably out of date by 1655[44].

As with most pioneering efforts, the *Novus atlas Sinensis* was far from faultless and one of the problem areas was Martini's longitudinal readings. A comparison of Martini's maps and tables of latitude and longitude with their counterparts in contemporary cartography shows general agreement in latitudinal readings, but discrepancies in longitudinal readings[45]. Actually, Martini used

44 See the discussion of Ho Ping-t'i population figures in conjunction with treatment of Ricci's population estimate for China in chapter I.

45 Unlike latitude which has consistently been computed from the equator, longitude has been based upon an arbitrarily assigned and shifting prime meridian from which one computes 180° east or west. A method of determining longitude was formulated in 1530 by Roger Gemma Frisius, a humanist scholar who taught medicine and mathematics at Louvain. However, this method required an accurate timepiece which was invulnerable to distorting conditions of the sea. Since such a timepiece was not developed until 1759 by the Englishman John Harrison, it is unlikely that Martini used Frisius' method. See Lloyd A. Brown, *The Story of Maps* (Boston, 1949) pp. 208–240. Also see George Kish, ed., *A Source Book in Geography* (Cambridge, Massachusetts, 1978) pp. 349–350.

Europeans in the seventeenth and eighteenth centuries pursued the secret of unraveling the computation of longitude with a passion. Large financial prizes were offered in Holland, France and England to the inventor of an accurate method of computing longitude. Bleau, the famous map publisher who published Martini's *Novus atlas Sinensis,* was one of those designated by the Dutch authorities to evaluate proposals for such a method. Frisius' method required the transporting of a timepiece, but it was not the only approach. Others believed in the possibility of determining longitude by observing the stars. In 1636, Galileo offered the Dutch his proposal for computing longitude through observing the movements of the four satellites of Jupiter with a telescope. Dutch interest in Galileo's proposal was discouraged by Roman Catholic authorities, but one wonders if the Jesuits at the Collegium Romanum could have learned of Galileo's proposal and taught it to Martini who was studying there prior to his departure for China in 1640? At any rate, Martini computed longitudinal readings for his maps of China with a limited measure of accuracy.

One cannot directly compare Martini's longitudinal readings to contemporary readings because the latter are based upon a prime meridian at Greenwich, England, and this placement was not widely accepted until 1888. In the early modern era in Europe, the prime meridian tended to be placed at islands in the Atlantic Ocean and relatively close to the western coast of Europe. This placement had the advantage of lying west of the Old World (Europe) and east of the New World (the Americas). It also simplified readings for Europe by making all of Europe lie east of the prime meridian. Apparent-

two prime meridians in computing longitude in the *Atlas*. In his tables, he placed only the readings based upon a prime meridian at Peking. In doing so, Martini was accommodating his European reader to the developed tradition of Chinese cartography which reflected the view of China as the "Middle Kingdom", that is, occupying the center of the world. By accepting the Chinese reckoning, he was not simply flattering a Chinese bias which did little harm to longitudinal fact, but was recognizing the sophisticated nature of Chinese geographical knowledge. But in his maps, Martini used both reckonings of longitude – one which placed the prime meridian at Peking and another which was intended for his European readers and which placed the prime meridian just west of Europe. If one assumes, for example, that Martini followed Ricci in placing the prime meridian at the Fortunate Islands (i.e. the Canaries), then his longitudinal readings might be compared to contemporary longitudinal readings if they are adjusted by subtracting approximately $17°$[46]. When this adjustment is made, one finds that the discrepancy between Martini's and contemporary longitudinal readings is considerably diminished, though not entirely removed. For example, Martini placed Xuntien (modern Peking city) at $40°$ north latitude and $145°$ east longitude[47]. Modern cartographers place the center of Peking at $39°55'$ north latitude and $116°25'$ east longitude. By contemporary standards, Martini was fairly accurate in determining latitude, but given the adjusted longitudinal figure of $128°$ (adjusted to the Greenwich prime meridian by subtracting $17°$ from $145°$), less accurate in computing longitude[48].

Though one can concede that by contemporary cartographic standards, Martini's maps were imprecise and lacking in detail, as a seventeenth-century pioneering effort, they were quite remarkable. They entranced curious Euro-

ly Martini used one of the Canary island sites for the prime meridian which is found in his *Atlas*.

46 Mr. Szcześniak emphasizes the collaborative nature of Jesuit map-making in regard to China and believes that the China maps of Frs. Ricci, Ruggieri, Martini, Boym and Couplet all placed the prime meridian at the Fortunate (Canary) Islands. See Boleslaw Szcześniak, "The Seventeenth Century Maps of China: An Inquiry into the Compilations of European Cartographers," *Imago Mundi* 13 (1956): 116, 123 & 131–132.

47 Martini, *Atlas*, map opposite p. 1 & pp. 26–27; catalogue on first page.

48 As an alternate reading, one notes that Martini placed Quangcheu (modern Canton city) at $23°15'$ N latitude or just below the Tropic of Cancer and $123°58'$ E longitude (adjusted to the Greenwich prime meridian by subtracting $17°$ from $140°58'$) (see Martini's *Atlas*, maps opposite p. 1 and pp. 132–133; tables on the 14th page.) By comparison, contemporary cartographers place the center of Canton at $23°6'$ N latitude and $113°16'$ E longitude. Again, the latitudinal figures are quite close, but the discrepancy with the adjusted longitudinal figure from Martini is $10-12°$. In addition to the above discrepancies, Ferdinand von Richthofen found differences measured in longitudinal minutes, i.e. fractions of degrees, between the latitudinal and longitudinal reckonings of Chinese cities found in Martini's *Atlas* and those made by other Jesuits in China. (See Richthofen, I, 676n–677n.)

peans with new information about this little known and remote land and in so doing carried forward the intellectual meeting of Europe and China.

4. MARTINI'S *SINICAE HISTORIAE DECAS PRIMA*

Martini's third major work was *Sinicae historiae decas prima res à gentis origine ad Christum natum in extrema Asia, sive Magno Sinarum Imperio gestas complexa* (The first ten divisions of Chinese history, affairs in far Asia from the beginning of the people to the birth of Christ, or surrounding the emerging great empire of the Chinese). Although its editions were limited to two in Latin – Munich (1658) and Amsterdam (1659) – and a French translation (Paris, 1962), the work appealed to erudite Europeans as an attempt to reconcile traditional Chinese and Biblical chronologies. The contents of this work of serious intellectual accommodation considerably surpassed the pocketbook-size and popular tone of *De bello tartarico*[49]. Although the primary topic of concern in *Sinicae historia decas prima* was history, Martini interspersed information on the Chinese classical literature into the historical narrative. His emphasis on and interpretation of the school of Confucius accorded with Ricci's model of accommodation[50].

Martini began his history of China with the reign of Fu Hsi in 2952 B.C., but he did not begin dating the first 60-year cycle until the supposed reign of the Yellow Emperor from 2697 B.C. . He concluded his history in the 58th year of the 45th cycle in 1 B.C. with the end of the reign of "Ngayus", i.e. the latinized name of Emperor Ai or Ai Ti (r. 6–1 B.C.). This represents 44 cycles of 60 years each, which equals 2,640. When 58 years of the 45th cycle were added, this yields a total of 2,698 years and brings one to the year A.D. 1. There is some question of whether Martini wrote a sequel or *decas secunda*. The Jesuit missionary, Fr. Johann Grueber, writing on March 14th 1665, expressed the belief that Martini's continuation of his history from the birth of Christ down to the fifteenth century had been printed in Munich[51]. Thévenot printed Grueber's letter in his *Relations de divers voyages curieux*. But Thévenot noted that Martini's *decas secunda* was lost and attempted to reconstruct it from a Persian manuscript[52].

---

49 While the Munich edition of 1658 of *Sinicae historiae decas prima* contained 362 pages in-quarto, the Amsterdam edition of 1659 contained 413 plus 7 pages in-octavo. All following page references will be to the Munich edition.

50 See Giorgio Melis, "Chinese Philosophy and Classics in the Works of Martino Martini, S.J. (1614–1661)." In *International Symposium on Chinese-Western Cultural Interchange* (Taipei, September 1983) pp. 473–513.

51 Fr. Grueber's letter of March 14th 1665 was reprinted in Thévenot, IV (1692), 22f.

52 *Catalogue général de livres imprimés de la Bibliothèque nationale* vol. 186 (1960), col. 144 & Sommervogel, V, 650.

Although *Sinicae historiae decas prima* limited itself to the period of history prior to the birth of Christ, i.e. prior to the mid-Han dynasty, it was the first genuine history of China to appear in a European language and it would remain the sole such work until Jean-Baptiste Du Halde's *Description géographique, historique, chronologique, politique et physique de l'Empire de la Chine* (Paris 1735) in four volumes. But Fr. Du Halde's work was essentially derivative of Martini's history, of Le Comte's *Nouveaux mémoires sur l'etat présent de la Chine* (Paris 1696) and particularly of the current reports sent to him by the Jesuits in Peking[53].

Seventeenth-century Europe had a passion for precise chronologies and that passion was inevitably tied to the Bible. Just a few years prior to the appearance of Martini's *Sinicae historiae decas prima*, James Ussher (1581–1656), archbishop of Armagh in Ireland, had published a chronology in his *Annales veteris et Novi Testamenti* (London 1650–1654). Drawing from the Hebrew Masoretic texts, Archbishop Ussher stated that the creation of Adam occurred in 4004 B.C. and that the Noadic flood occurred in 2349 B.C.[54]. The widespread acceptance of these dates is indicated by the fact that soon after their appearance, they were inserted into the margins of reference editions of the King James' version of the Bible, where they may still be found in certain editions today.

The Vulgate version of the Bible made by St. Jerome in the fourth century and based on Hebrew texts no longer extant, supported Ussher's chronology. But prior to Jerome's translation, there was a preference for the Septuagint-based chronology[55]. The "Septuagint" — literally "seventy", possibly in ap-

---

53 Sommervogel, V, 650, discusses Fr. Du Halde's derivations from Martini. Also see C. R. Boxer, "Some Aspects of Western Historical Writing on the Far East, 1500–1800," in *Historians of China & Japan* E. G. Pulleyblank & W. G. Beasley, eds. (London, 1961) p. 314. Quite a controversy arose over Du Halde's editing of these reports. It appears that Jean-Baptiste-Du Halde (1674–1743) was an editor with enormous talents for putting his finger on what the reading public wanted. In the eighteenth century, the French-reading public wanted a culture idol and China presented itself as a likely candidate. Consequently, Du Halde, in editing the Jesuit reports from China, initially for *Lettres édifiantes et curieuses* (34 volumes, 1702–1776) and secondarily for his *Description . . . de l'empire de la Chine,* removed material unsympathetic to the Chinese or to the Jesuits. The missionaries in the field complained over the omissions, but Fr. Du Halde had judged his reading public correctly. They were greatly influenced by Du Halde, and Voltaire honored him by placing him on the list of great men of his time (Boxer, pp. 312–315 & Arnold H. Rowbotham, *Missionary and Mandarin: the Jesuits at the Court of China* (Berkeley, 1942) pp. 256–257). In any case, Martini's history certainly was surpassed by the Jesuit Joseph de Moyriac de Mailla who translated and drew extensively upon Chinese sources in his *Historia générale de la Chine ou annales de cet empire* 13 vols. (Paris, 1777–1785) which included translations from Chu Hsi's *T'ung-chien kang-mu* (Boxer, pp. 314–315 & Rowbotham, p. 352).
54 Jack Finegan, *Handbook of Biblical Chronology* (Princeton, 1964) p. 191.
55 For instance, Eusebius (ca. 260 – ca. 340) expressed this preference in his *Chronicle*

proximate reference to seventy-two translators — refers to a Greek version of the Old Testament, the first part of which is said to have been translated at Alexandria under the reign of Ptolemy Philadelphus (285–246). According to the computation in Eusebius' *Chronicles*, the Septuagint supported dating the Creation at 5200 B.C. and the Noadic flood at 2957 B.C.[56]. Recognizing that there are slight variations in Septuagint-based chronologies[57], one may nevertheless note the considerable differences between these figures and Ussher's dating of the Creation and Flood at 4404 B.C. and 2349 B.C., respectively.

Into an intellectual climate which was increasingly accepting Ussher's dates came Martini's *Sinicae historiae decas prima*. The information which Martini presented on Chinese history challenged the dominant European trend. Martini was quite aware of the significance of this challenge and raised it in the opening pages of his book[58]. Martini had been greatly impressed by the antiquity of China and by the accuracy of the history which recorded this antiquity. He believed that the standard of Chinese historical records was unsurpassed by any other nation[59]. But unlike proto-sinologists like Athanasius Kircher, Andreas Müller and Christian Mentzel, Martini possessed a knowledge and critical faculty in dealing with Chinese civilization which set his work off from the naive tone of the others. He reproduced some of the Chinese legends merely as examples to which he gave little credence, such as the Chinese myth of creation of the universe from an egg in which a yolk was transformed into the earth, the albumen into the air and the shell into the sky[60]. Martini regarded P'an Ku, the supposed first Chinese, as less of an historical figure than Mentzel's *Zeit-Register* interpreted Martini to claim[61]. For Martini, the divide between legend and history was the reign of Fu Hsi (2952–2838 B.C.)[62]. In support of this divide, Martini noted that the Chinese themselves were skeptical of events described in the records which occurred before Fu Hsi's time. By comparison, contemporary sinology regards Fu Hsi as legendary and places the divide between legend and history in the Chinese records between the Hsia and Shang dynasties (ca. 1500 B.C.). But because twentieth-century archeological discoveries in China have confirmed as history what had formerly been regarded by most Western sinologists — though not Chinese scholars — as mere legend, the dividing line between Chinese legend and history must be regarded as fluid.

for the Septuagint over the Hebrew and Samaritan-based chronologies. Eusebius' views were translated by Jerome in the Vulgate, although Jerome himself inclined toward the Hebrew-based chronology. Finegan, p. 156.

56 Finegan, pp. 156 & 184.
57 See Edwin J. Van Kley, "Europe's 'Discovery' of China and the Writing of World History," *American Historical Review* 76 (1971): 360.
58 Martini, *Sinicae historiae* p. 3.
59 Martini, *Sinicae historiae* p. 10.
60 Martini, *Sinicae historiae* pp. 3–4.
61 Cf. Christian Mentzel, *Kurtze chinesische Chronologie oder Zeit-Register aller chinesischen Kayser* (Berlin, 1696) p. 6 and Martini, *Sinicae historiae*, pp. 3–4.
62 Martini, *Sinicae historiae* pp. 3, 11 & 13.

In the seventeenth-century Biblical view of human history, all mankind, except for Noah and his descendants, were thought to have been destroyed at the time of the Flood. Consequently, Noah was regarded as the father of all mankind. But if any other people had a continuous history dating from before the Flood, then Noah's universal patriarchy was destroyed. This was exactly the threat which Martini's account of Chinese history posed. According to Martini, the reign of the first Chinese emperor, Fu Hsi, was dated from 2952 B.C. . But according to the Ussher chronology, the Flood did not occur until 2349 B.C. . Either Noah was not the father of mankind or one of the chronologies was wrong.

The Jesuits of the China Mission had long been aware of the conflict in chronologies and had received permission in 1637 to use a chronology based on the Septuagint, rather than the Vulgate[63]. If the Flood had occurred in 2957 B.C., as the Septuagint supported, then it was possible to reconcile the Chinese chronology with the reign of Fu Hsi or the beginning of Chinese civilization and thereby preserve Noah's universal patriarchy. But there were problems with this solution. The Chinese records included an account of a flood, but according to Martini's *Sinicae historiae decas prima*, this flood was dated by the Chinese as occuring during the reign of Yao (2357–2257 B.C.). While such a date would be chronologically reconcilable with the Ussher dating of the Noadic flood at 2349 B.C., it would threaten the universal patriarchy of Noah since a separate line of descent, this line from Yao, would claim to have survived the Flood to propagate the Chinese race.

Martini offered no clear solution to this problem. He recognized that two dates were proposed for a flood in China – one before 3000 B.C. and the other during the reign of Yao. He noted that there were European chronologists, i.e. followers of Ussher and the Vulgate-based chronology, who placed the Noadic flood in the reign of Yao (2357–2257 B.C.)[64]. However, he preferred using the Septuagint-based chronology to place a flood in China before 3000 B.C.[65]. With a skepticism much more characteristic of modern than seventeenth-century sinology, Martini cast some doubt on whether the flood described in the Chinese accounts was identical with the Noadic flood. He noted that the Chinese records said nothing of the origin and cause of this flood and it was not clear whether it was part of a universal flood or a local phenomenon. At any rate, Martini was convinced that eastern Asia was inhabited before the time of the Noadic flood[66]. Unlike John Webb, who drew from Martini's account to argue that Yao was in fact Noah, Martini was willing to leave the problem unresolved. Yet his book was a powerful stimulus on those more creative, if less knowledgeable, minds such as

---

63 Antoine Gaubil, *Traité de la chronologie chinoise* (Paris, 1814) pp. 283–285.
64 Martini, *Sinicae historiae* p. 27.
65 Martini, *Sinicae historiae* p. 3.
66 Martini, *Sinicae historiae* pp. 3 & 10.

Isaac Vossius, Georg Horn and John Webb, who were prompted to debate various solutions to the chronological and related issues[67].

For Martini, Fu Hsi and his invention of the trigrams were historical facts. In his belief that the *I ching* was the most ancient Chinese book, Martini came close to the conclusions of modern sinologists in regard to the core of the *I ching* text[68]. On the other hand, while many sinologists base their claims for the antiquity of the core of the *I ching* on its archaic language, Martini's reasons derived from Chinese historical records and from his belief that the first science among the Chinese was mathematical[69]. By contrast, the Jesuit authors of the preface to *Confucius Sinarum philosophus* (1687) disparaged the tradition of Chinese commentators which exalted the *I ching*. These Jesuits conceded the *I ching's* highest antiquity with great reluctance[70].

Like so many later Europeans, Martini was fascinated by the 64 hexagrams of the *I ching*. In his view, the mathematical knowledge associated with the *I ching* diagrams had been transmitted from generation to generation in China since the time of Noah. Martini shared the widely held Chinese view, claimed in the famous commentary on the *I ching* by Wang Pi (A.D. 226–249), that Fu Hsi had invented the hexagrams. (Others have ascribed their invention to King Wen (fl. ca. 1050 B.C.) and the modern tendency is to see the hexagrams as an invention of early Chou times.) Martini stated that the ancient Chinese philosophers regarded chaos as the beginning of all things from which proceeded spiritual phenomena followed by material things[71]. Martini treated the diagrams of the *I ching* as exemplifying this process. Most fundamentally, *yin* represented the hidden and incomplete while *yang* represented the open and complete. Following the principles of generation and corruption, *yin* and *yang* expanded to the eight trigrams which represented heaven, earth, lightning, mountains, fire, clouds, water and wind, respectively. From these eight trigrams the 64 hexagrams were generated and these were portrayed in Martini's *Sinicae historiae decas prima* in one of the earliest, if not the earliest, illustrations of the 64 hexagrams to appear in a European book[72]. (See plate 18.)

67 For a brief account of these solutions, see Van Kley's "Europe's 'Discovery' of China," pp. 363–366. John Webb's theories are treated in the chapter on the seventeenth-century European search for a universal language.
68 Martini, *Sinicae historiae* p. 6. Among those sinologists who regard the *I ching* to be the oldest extant Chinese work is Wolfgang Bauer, *China und die Hoffnung auf Glück* (Munich, 1974) pp. 38 & 579 and the late Peter Boodberg. However, there is no firm agreement among modern scholars as to when the *I ching* was composed. It was probably a composite work composed over a long period of time from the sixth century to the third century B.C.. See Wing-tsit Chan, *Source book* p. 262.
69 Martini, *Sinicae historiae* p. 7.
70 See Couplet, Pröemialis Declaratio in *Confucius Sinarum philosophus* (Paris, 1687) pp. xv & xviii.
71 Martini, *Sinicae historiae* p. 5.
72 Martini, *Sinicae historiae* p. 6.

Martini connected Fu Hsi's invention of the *I ching* diagrams with the latter's great interest in determining the mathematical patterns extending from the heavens to man[73]. The association of Fu Hsi's trigrams (*kua*) with the cosmic dimensions of heaven and earth is clearly implied in the Great Appendix of the *I ching*, surely one of the most fertile, but ambiguous, passages in Chinese literature. Martini referred to Fu Hsi's interest as "astrology", but it would have been the more mathematical form of astrology prevalent in the seventeenth century rather than the modern degenerated vestige. Martini repeated the legend that Fu Hsi was said to have first observed the 64 hexagrams on the back of a dragon emerging from a lake. (Actually, Chinese tradition speaks of the dragon as emerging from a river and refers to this river diagram as *Ho-t'u lo-shu*.) By this means, Fu Hsi bestowed a significance on the dragon which made it a most auspicious omen in China as well as the imperial symbol. However, one detects a certain discomfort in Martini's reproducing of this legend and he concluded his discussion of the dragon by saying that the Chinese view of dragons was filled with superstition[74].

Martini also credited Fu Hsi with the invention of Chinese characters[75]. His presentation is a little misleading since according to the traditional Chinese account, Fu Hsi was regarded as the inventor of writing through his creation of the trigrams. But these trigrams were not thought to have developed into full-blown characters until after Fu Hsi's time, whereas Martini implied that Fu Hsi created them as fully developed characters. Martini was more accurate in reproducing Chinese legend when he stated that Fu Hsi created the written forms in order to replace the more cumbersome use of knots, although he did not specify that the Chinese regarded the knots as having been used for counting. Modern scholars such as Marcel Granet and Joseph Needham have raised doubts over whether the diagrams of the *I ching* were consciously used in their early forms for quantitative purposes, though Mr. Needham concedes that single binary arithmetical generations may have been performed as an unintentional by-product[76].

Martini stated matter of factly that the "letters" invented by Fu Hsi resembled the Egyptian hieroglyphs in that the shape of the sign signified the meaning. By this, he meant that the principle of ancient Chinese writing was pictographic in the manner of Egyptian writing. Martini demonstrated this with a chart of six sample Chinese characters[77]. (See plate 7.) On one side of the chart a simple

73 Martini, *Sinicae historiae* p. 11.
74 Martini, *Sinicae historiae* pp. 11–12.
75 Martini, *Sinicae historiae* p. 12.
76 See Marcel Granet, *La pensée chinoise* (Paris, 1934) p. 176f & Needham, II, 342–343.
77 Martini, *Sinicae historiae* p. 12.

Plate 7. An illustration of the pictographic development of Chinese writing, from Martino Martini's *Sinicae Historiae decas prima* (Munich, 1658) p. 12. Courtesy of the Niedersächsische Landesbibliothek Hannover.

picture was drawn and on the other side the Chinese character which supposedly evolved from the picture was presented as follows: three humps depicting mountains evolved into *shan* (mountain); a circle with a dot in the middle evolved into *jih* (sun); a picture of a creature-form evolved into *lung* (dragon); a picture of a sceptre with an eye became *chu* (lord, master, king); a picture of a bird evolved into *niao* (bird) and a picture of a chicken evolved into *chi* (hen, rooster).

Martini spoke of having a Chinese book which recorded six different styles of ancient writing and which reminded him of writing he had seen on the obelisks (?) of Rome. Martini was referring here to a book containing ancient etymologies of characters which the Chinese cultivated as a sophisticated body of knowledge. It was a recognized fact that the more ancient character forms were frequently pictographic. (See Semedo's description of the ancient seal script in chapter three and plate 1.) But Martini and other seventeenth-century European students of the Chinese language overemphasized this pictographic element at the expense of the phonetic element which played a significant role in the expansion and evolution of Chinese characters into their modern forms.

Although Martini's treatment of the Chinese language was brief, it had a strong influence upon Europeans with proto-sinological interests. But one might ask if Martini's interpretation of the Chinese language was not in turn influenced by someone else. Although Martini's statements on the pictographic element in the development of Chinese characters seem to have been sufficiently grounded in his own work with the language, his references to similarities between Chinese characters and Egyptian hieroglyphs were superficial. Martini was a former student of Athanasius Kircher and had visited Fr. Kircher for extensive discussions on China during his stay in Rome in 1654–1655. Kircher gathered a great deal of information on the Chinese language and culture from these talks, but one wonders if the influence was all one way. Could Kircher's preoccupation with the Egyptian hieroglyphs have predisposed Martini to perceive a similarity? At any rate, by the end of the seventeenth century, the proposed underlying similarity between the characters and hieroglyphs had become widely accepted as fact and it is clear that Martini's *Sinicae historiae decas prima* and Kircher's *China illustrata* both contributed to this ungrounded belief.

One of the most valuable achievements of Martini's history was the presentation of a full list of Chinese rulers and reign dates from the origins of Chinese history until 6 B.C. . The accuracy of Martini's work is seen by comparing his chronology with a standard contemporary Chinese chronology[78]. The only significant differences are that the Chinese chronology: (1) omitted the first two emperors in Martini's list — Fu Hsi and Shen Nung — on the grounds that

---

78 For a representative modern Chinese chronology, I have used the chronology found in the appendix of the general Chinese dictionary, *Tzu hai* (Shanghai, 1938; reprinted Taipei, 1968). This chronology is widely reproduced, with little variation.

they were too legendary to include (2) inserted Ti Chang (r. 2366–2356) between Ti K'u Kao and Yao and (3) varied some of the earlier reign dates 1–3 years. Aside from these differences, Martini's chronology was almost an exact replica of the modern Chinese chronology. Key dates from Martini's chronology are presented in the accompanying table. Differences with a modern Chinese chronology are noted specifically or by including the variant date in brackets.

Table
Key Royal Ascension Dates from Martino Martini's Sinicae historiae decas prima

p 11	Fu Hsi	2952 B.C.	omitted in
			modern Chinese
p 13	Shen Nung	2837	chronology

p 14	Huang Ti	2697 [2698]	
p 20	Shao	2597 [2598]	
p 21	Chen Hsü	2513 [2514]	
p 23	Ti K'u Kao	2435 [2436]	
[	Ti Chang]	[2366]	added in modern
			Chinese chronology
p 24	Yao	2357	
p 30	Shun	2258 [2255]	
p 34	Yü (first ruler of the Hsia dynasty)	2207 [2205]	
p 54	Chieh (last ruler of the Hsia)	1818	
p 58	T'ang (first ruler of the Shang)	1766	
p 77	Chou (last ruler of the Shang)	1154	
p 86	Wu (first ruler of the Chou dynasty)	1122	
p 195	Shih Huang-ti (sole ruler of the Ch'in dynasty)	246	
p 230	Liu Pang; Kao Ti (First ruler of the Han dynasty)	206	
p 301	Wu Ti (famous ruler of the Han)	140	
p 360	Ai Ti	6 B.C.	

Since Chinese history was so closely linked to reign periods, Martini's list represented a significant achievement. By 1658 then, Europeans had an accurate outline of how the Chinese viewed the first 3,000 years of their chronological record. However, an ancient chronology may derive from legendary as well as historical sources. The Chinese appear to have been more aware of this than Martini. We have seen in the above that Martini was not an uncritical believer of Chinese legends, but he was greatly impressed with the pains that the Chinese took to guarantee objectivity in their records. For example, he noted that the official record of an emperor was made after the emperor's death so that "deceit and flattery" might be eliminated from the account[79]. Consequently, whenever

79 Martini, *Sinicae historiae* p. 10. Possibly Martini was referring to the *Shih-lu* (Veritable record) of each emperor's reign which was composed at the end of a reign. See Han Yu-shan, *Elements of Chinese historiography* (Hollywood, 1955) pp. 9 & 44.

he found a date attached to an event, Martini tended to regard such an event as historical, as in the case of the royal ascension dates for Fu Hsi and Shen Nung.

Martini's errors, which were compounded by less knowledgeable Europeans, derived from the failure to realize that chronological precision, particularly in a nation with the antiquity and historical consciousness of the Chinese, was not always a sign of historical accuracy, but sometimes precisely the reverse. The situation was exacerbated by the seventeenth-century rage for precise dating of Biblical and other ancient events. This obsession with dating dominated the thinking of the age to such an extent, that when the Chinese chronology was first discovered, Europeans did not question the historical veracity of the chronology so much as whether the dating of events was reconcilable with European records. This concern for reconciling traditional Chinese chronology with Biblical chronology was one of the predominating European interests which Jesuit accommodation served.

5. CONCLUSION

Martini's contribution to Jesuit accommodation was made within two significant areas of seventeenth-century concern — geography and ancient history. The voracious European thirst for travel literature as well as the mercantile interest in trading with foreign countries created a demand for geographical information which Joannis Bleau responded to in his famous series of atlases on the entire world. By investigating Chinese geography and cartography, Martini was able to produce an atlas in the Bleau series. His *Novus atlas Sinensis* reconciled Chinese and European geographical knowledge, allowing the traditional Chinese notion of a "middle kingdom" which occupied the center of the world to remain intact, and yet demonstrating its relativity by showing that the prime meridian could be placed just as readily at the Canary Islands as at Peking. In the area of ancient history, Martini addressed the intensely debated seventeenth-century issue of the precise dating of the Creation and the Noadic Flood. By introducing the traditional dates of ancient Chinese history, Martini caused Europeans to reconcile Biblical chronology not merely with Western history, but with world history. In this way, Jesuit accommodation contributed to expanding the European historical horizon.

CHAPTER V
THE PROTO-SINOLOGIST KIRCHER AND THE HERMETIC
CONNECTION IN THE EUROPEAN ASSIMILATION OF CHINA

1. THE CONTENT, COMPOSITION AND THE CONTRIBUTORS OF
CHINA ILLUSTRATA

One of the most influential books in shaping the European conception of
China in the late 1660s and 1670s was Athanasius Kircher's *China monumentis
qua sacris profanis, nec non variis naturae & artis spectaculis, aliarumque rerum
memorabilium argumentis illustrata* (China elucidated through its sacred, profane
[literary] monuments, natural elements, arts and other arguments). The wide
range of subject matter and many illustrations made *China illustrata* the "Chinese
encyclopedia of the seventeenth century"[1]. The work relied heavily upon accommodative missionary sources, but Fr. Kircher's work as a proto-sinologist
was dominated by European Hermetism rather than Jesuit accommodation.

China illustrata first appeared in Amsterdam in 1667 in a Latin edition,
followed in 1668 by a Dutch edition, in 1669 by an abridged English edition
and in 1670 by an expanded French edition[2]. Because of the emergence of
French as a dominant European language in the late seventeenth century, the
French edition has been widely cited. However, the translation by F. S. Dalquié
is marred by minor errors which have given rise to misunderstandings[3].

---

1 Adolf Reichwein, *China and Europe: intellectual and artistic contacts in the eighteenth
  century* J. C. Powell, trans. (London, 1925) p. 20.
2 There were two nearly identical Latin editions of *China illustrata* published at Amsterdam in 1667. According to Sommervogel, IV, 1064, the edition by Jacobum à Meurs
  (Jacobus van Meurs) was a counterfeit edition of the original edition by Joannem
  Janssonium à Waesberge (Johannes Janssonius van Waesberge; Jean Jansson à Waesberge). One notes changes and omissions in the text of the Meurs edition (e.g. pp. 132
  & 133) which support Sommervogel's claim. Waesberge also published at Amsterdam
  the French edition, the Dutch edition (*Tonneel van China*) and the abridged English
  edition (*An Embassy from the East India Company of the United Provinces to China*).
  For further detail, see Cordier, I, 26–27; Sommervogel, IV, 1063–1064; and Boleslaw
  Szcześniak, "Athanasius Kircher's *China illustrata*," *Osiris* 10 (1952): 388–389. Unless
  otherwise indicated, the following citations of *China illustrata* are to the Amsterdam
  edition of 1667 printed by Waesberge.
3 According to Henri Havret, *Le stèle chrétienne de Si-ngan-fou* Variétés Sinologiques
  no. VII (1895), XII (1897) & XX (1902), XII, 54, Dalquié mistranslated a statement
  by Boym, thus contributing to the mistaken belief expressed by Kircher and others
  that a facsimile tablet of the Nestorian Monument was made at the time of the stone's
  recovery ca. 1625. Also, Pelliot points out that Dalquié erred in translating the name of
  Boym's Chinese collaborator on the Nestorian inscription. The "Andreae Don Sin" of
  China illustrata p. 7, was rendered by Dalquié as "le P. André don Dion Sin," (*La*

Both the Latin and French editions were divided into six parts, the first of which dealt with an interpretation of the famous Syrian-Chinese monument, more familiarly known as the Nestorian Monument, dating from A.D. 781. The second part dealt with the various missionary routes to China from the time of St. Thomas the Apostle down to the most recent overland journey of Fr. Johann Grueber. The third part dealt with the "idolatry" said to have been introduced from Egypt and Greece into the religions of Persia, India, Tartary, China and Japan. Kircher felt that this theory of origins sufficed to explain the three major sects of China — Confucianism, Buddhism and Taoism. While the fourth part of *China illustrata* dealt with natural and man-made elements of particular fascination found in China, the fifth part treated the architecture and mechanical arts of the Chinese. The sixth part attempted to explain the Chinese written language. Only the French edition contained two supplements. The first of these was a response by the Jesuit missionary Jean Grubere (Johann Grueber) to a set of questions by the Grand Duke of Tuscany. The second was a Chinese-French dictionary, perhaps the first published Chinese-European language dictionary, although it is more accurately described as a 44 folio-page vocabulary.

The dimensions and scope of *China illustrata* were ambitious, particularly given the extent of European knowledge of China in 1667. There has been a great deal of confusion about authorship, even though Fr. Kircher did mention a number of people, primarily Jesuits, as sources. Late seventeenth-century scholarship would be considered careless by today's standards of crediting authors. We can best begin to sort out the authorship question by noting that Fr. Kircher, like so many of the proto-sinologists of Europe, knew very little about China. Yet the works which authors such as Kircher, Andreas Müller, Christian Mentzel and others wrote contain material whose accuracy far exceeded their level of knowledge. This is because these proto-sinologists had knowledgeable sources who can be identified as China missionaries — primarily, but not exclusively, of the Society of Jesus. (The proto-sinologists can be distinguished from the missionaries most simply by the fact that almost none of the former set foot in China while nearly all of the latter did.)

What this situation amounted to is that the proto-sinologists were primarily compilers and editors of reports — both oral and written — which originated with the China missionaries. The essentially editorial and journalistic nature of much of proto-sinology led to some contradictory results which, in the case of Kircher, are particularly apparent. *China illustrata* consisted of some very high praise of China combined with some very severe criticism. In the first section of part three, Kircher referred to China as the "richest and most powerful" nation in the world[4]. Nature and art had been so well disposed to China that it seemed like a realm "apart from the world". The Chinese state was said to be

---

Chine illustrée p. 11), thus falsely rendering the Chinese as a priest. See Paul Pelliot, "Michael Boym," *T'oung pao* 31 (1935): 112n.

4 *China illustrata* pp. 164–166.

governed by a king who was a philosopher or who, at least, permitted rule by doctors in the style of Platonists (i.e. rule by "philosopher kings") and in accordance with the wishes of the "divine philosopher" (Plato?). Kircher asked rhetorically who could doubt the happiness of this state where the emperor had no more difficulty ruling over 150,000,000 people than a father had in directing a household. The towns, people, bridges, roads, boats and architecture were all said to be magnificent. Furthermore, the peasants were diligent and the soldiers vigilant. The state was well policed and criminals were justly punished. The annual tax load was not fixed, but fluctuated according to the vicissitudes of the times. In short, Kircher portrayed a utopia, but his portrayal was filled with inaccuracies.

Though I have accentuated the utopian features in the above, I do not mean to neglect the fact that Kircher's description of China also included a number of accurate details, including facts of geography, royal descent, administration by a "Mandarin" (scholar-official) class and even the estimate of the population of mid-seventeenth century China as 150 million. For most of the above, Kircher was drawing his information from Martini's *Atlas*. However, in part three of *China illustrata*, Kircher portrayed Chinese religions as ridden with abominable falsehoods borrowed from the pagan religions of the West. By contrast, the Jesuit proponents of accommodation, several of whom were acquaintances of Kircher's, very carefully distinguished ancient Chinese religion, with its modern vestiges in Confucianism, from the pagan religions of Egypt, Greece and Rome[5]. These Jesuits shared Kircher's negative assessment of Chinese religions by criticizing Buddhism and, to a less extent, Taoism, but they did not limit themselves to defining Chinese religions solely in terms of Confucianism, Buddhism and Taoism. The accommodative approach was to stress the possibilities of elements shared between Christianity and Chinese religions, such as in the form of universal natural religion, i.e. religious truth accessible through reason, or in the form of a common descent through the Biblical patriarchs. Secondly, the accommodative approach sought elements from Christianity and Chinese religions which would meld in a complementary manner.

Kircher granted nothing to the Chinese in terms of indigenous natural religion, nor did he recognize the ancient *Shang-ti* (Lord-on-high) or *T'ien* (Heaven) to be early monotheistic forms which had since degenerated, as proponents of accommodation like Ricci had maintained. At most, Kircher saw certain vestiges of Christianity in China, such as the cross of the Trinity, left from missionary work by earlier apostles like St. Thomas[6]. For Kircher, the strongest religious influences on China were the Egyptian and Greek pagan religions. Kircher's position is understandable only in terms of his groundings in the Hermetic

---

5 E.g., Ricci-Trigault, *Journals* p. 93.
6 Kircher, *China illustrata* pp. 131–133.

tradition of Christian apologetics which argued that certain pagan texts contained vestiges of Christianity. The primary texts of this tradition were ascribed to Hermes Trismegistus, Orpheus and Pythagoras and the tradition is referred to variously as Hermetism or *prisca theologia* (Ancient Theology)[7].

Kircher followed the Renaissance revival of this tradition led by Marsilio Ficino which read into the Egyptian hieroglyphs esoteric truths about the world and God. Along with the hieroglyphs, the Egyptian cross was said to anticipate the Christian cross and Trinity[8]. Through Kircher's Hermetic views, one can better understand how the culture, hieroglyphs and religion of Egypt occupied a certain primacy in his interpretation of pagan cultures. Consequently, according to Kircher, the similarities of Chinese religions to the Egyptian and Greek religions must have been due to borrowing. The irony here was that the missionaries on whom Kircher relied for information about China, such as Frs. Martini and Ricci, were proponents of accommodation who believed that Chinese culture should be blended with Christianity on a more equal basis than Hermetism dictated. Their accommodative premises were so formative in the composition of their written works, that one wonders if it was possible to separate their descriptions from their premises and interpretations. Yet this is exactly what Kircher attempted. He not only broke with the accommodative interpretations, but in blending their information into his Hermetically dominated perspective, it was Hermetism and not accommodation which took priority. Not until the end of the seventeenth century would Hermetism and accommodation be more harmoniously blended by certain Jesuits of the China Mission called Figurists.

The sources whom Kircher cited in his preface were more like contributors than sources and Kircher's role in composing *China illustrata* was more comparable to that of a very active editor than author[9]. But the seventeenth century was not so sensitive to plagiarism as we are today and Kircher's style of writing was such that to the casual reader, he appears to be more of an author than he actually was. If contemporary editing style had applied, *China illustrata* probably would have been presented as a collection of separately authored articles on China. As a result of this confusion over authorship, Kircher has been credited with a great deal more knowledge of China than he possessed or even claimed. For example, a reputable monograph on seventeenth- and eighteenth-century European languages quite erroneously refers to Kircher as the apparent "foremost authority on the subject [of Chinese characters] in the seventeenth century"[10].

7 D. P. Walker, *The Ancient Theology* (London, 1972) p. 1f.

8 Frances Yates, *Giordano Bruno and the Hermetic Tradition* (New York, 1964) pp. 416–420.

9 Kircher's preface to *China illustrata* consists of three un-numbered pages.

10 Paul Cornelius, *Languages in Seventeenth- and Early Eighteenth-Century Imaginary Voyages* (Geneva, 1965) p. 72.

The first source-contributor Kircher mentioned was Martini. Kircher showed a certain paternal pride in his former mathematics pupil. The teacher-student context had probably been the Collegium Romanum before 1640 when Martini embarked for China. Martini returned to Rome in the fall of 1654 and stayed until January 1656, for the specific purpose of presenting to the Roman authorities the Jesuit position of accommodation on the Chinese rites concerning ancestors and Confucius. During that time, Martini must have met with his old teacher, Fr. Kircher, and it is difficult to believe that as a fellow-Jesuit, Kircher would not have been aware of the struggle in which Martini was engaged. Opponents of Jesuit mission policy were numerous in Rome and Martini's mission must have involved some intense lobbying. Yet we also know that Kircher was absorbed in a tremendous variety of research projects and possibly he sought to avoid political controversy. At any rate, Kircher omitted reference in *China illustrata* to differences between himself and Jesuit proponents of accommodation. Clearly, he was no such proponent, and yet he must have been aware of the dominant Jesuit policy in the China Mission[11]. It is possible that Kircher chose silence in a controversial matter as an expedient means of maintaining his good ties with accommodative Jesuits, while not antagonizing those enemies of accommodation in Rome who sponsored his multifarious and expensive research projects. In further regard to Martini's contributions to Kircher's work, the first section of part four of *China illustrata* dealt with the geography and political structure of China, which was taken from Martini's *Atlas*[12]. Also, Kircher repeatedly cited and quoted from the *Atlas* throughout a section on rocks and minerals as well as on architecture and other mechanical arts[13]. But the borrowing was not all one way. Martini's *Atlas* borrowed most of what it said on the Nestorian Monument from Kircher's *Prodromus Coptus sive Aegyptiacus* (Rome 1636)[14]!

The second contributor whom Kircher mentioned was the Jesuit, Michał Piotr Boym (1612–1659). In spite of this second-place mention, Fr. Boym seems to have been the most significant contributor to *China illustrata*. Boym was a missionary who accomplished enormous amounts, given the relatively brief period of time (1645–1651 and 1658–1659) that he spent within the sphere of Chinese culture. He might have accomplished a great deal more if his involvement with a fascinating, but fruitless diplomatic mission had not cut short his life.

---

11 Mr. Szeześniak in his article, "Athanasius Kircher's *China illustrata*, p. 392, is quite wrong to characterize *China illustrata* as representing "not only Kircher's own religious philosophy, but that also of the whole Western missionary venture in the Far Orient." Kircher's views were mainly non-accommodative and although they were shared by a number of missionaries, very few of the latter were fellow-Jesuits.

12 Kircher, *China illustrata*, pp. 164–175.

13 Kircher, *China illustrata*, pp. 205–219.

14 Havret, no. 12, p. 60.

Fr. Boym was a Polish Jesuit who, after spending some time in Rome, arrived in the south China region in 1645[15]. Fr. Semedo, in his capacity as Jesuit vice-provincial of the China Mission, assigned Boym to the court of the last Ming pretender, the Yung-li emperor (Chu Yu-lang, r. 1647–1661)[16]. When Boym first arrived at the Ming court late in 1649 or early 1650, the cause there was not yet desperate and he was assigned to assist Andreas Wolfgang Koffler (1603–1651) in ministering to the high-ranking Christian converts. Fr. Koffler had arrived at the court in 1645 and was aided in his proselytizing efforts by a number of Christian converts, including the high-ranking eunuch Achilles P'ang T'ien-shou (d. 1657)[17] and the governor of Kwangsi province, Ch'ü Shih-ssu (1590–161)[18]. With the aid of these converts, Fr. Koffler succeeded in converting the dowager empress Wang Lieh-na (Helena), i.e. official wife of the Yung-li emperor's father; the dowager empress Ma Ma-li-ya (Maria), i.e. the mother of the emperor; and the heir Chu Ts'u-hsüan, Tang-ting (Constantine)[19]. With the probable encouragement of Fr. Koffler, the dowager empress Helena and the eunuch P'ang addressed written pleas for the Ming cause to Pope Innocent X and to the Jesuit general, Fr. Goswin Nickel[20].

Boym appears to have been with the Ming court for less than one year when he was delegated the task of carrying these letters to Rome. He departed from Chao-ch'ing in November of 1650 with two Chinese Christian companions assigned by the eunuch P'ang. These were Cheng An-te-lo (Andreas) and Kuo Jo-hsi (Joseph)[21]. In January of 1651 Boym left Macao, but Kuo fell ill and returned to China. The nineteen-year old Cheng — who was apparently from a

---

15 Fr. Boym was born in Lwow, Poland as the son of a royal physician of Hungarian origin to King Sigismond III. He entered the Jesuit novitiate in Krakow in 1631 and, after spending some time in Rome, embarked for China from Lisbon in 1643. Details are somewhat sketchy for the following years, but in 1645 he was in Tongking and in 1646 on Hainan Island. When the Manchu invasion threatened the island, he returned to Tongking and then went to Macao in late 1649 or early 1650.

16 Fang Hao, *Chung-kuo T'ien-chu-chiao shih jen-wu ch'uan* 3 vols. (Hong Kong, 1970) I, 306. At the time of Boym's arrival, the court of the last Ming pretender was at Chao-ch'ing in Kwantung province. Manchu military pressure forced it into a series of wanderings, criss-crossing Kwangtung and Kwangsi provinces. The pursued court later fled into Yunnan province and ultimately crossed the border into Burma, where the Yung-li emperor's heir and many of his court met death at the hands of the Burmese in April of 1662 (Hummel, p. 194 & Goodrich & Fang, p. 723).

17 Pelliot, "Michael Boym," p. 98.

18 Ch'ü Shih-ssu was a distant nephew of Ignatius Ch'ü Ju-k'uei; T'ai-su, one of the first literati followers of Ricci. See Hummel, p. 199 & Ricci-Trigault, *Journals*, pp. 230–233 *et passim.*

19 Fang, I, 305.

20 A popular treatment and translation into English of the letters to the Pope are found in E. H. Parker, "Letters from a Chinese Empress and a Chinese Eunuch to the Pope in the Year 1650," *Contemporary Review* (January 1912): 79–83.

21 Goodrich, p. 20. Fang, I 307 – possibly following Pelliot, "Michael Boym" p. 112 – suggests the alternate surnames of Chen for Cheng and Lo for Kuo.

high-ranking family and bore the military title of *yu-chi*[22] – remained with Boym throughout the entire journey and would later bury him on the south China border in 1659. On their journey to Europe, they traveled by sea to Goa, then overland through Persia and Smyrna to the Mediterranean. They arrived at Venice in November of December of 1652. Before proceeding on to Rome, Boym met with the Doge and the Senate at Venice and shared a letter from the eunuch P'ang[23]. Boym's tendency to dress in Chinese clothing must have further increased his curious aura in the eyes of the Venetians.

Boym's stay in Rome was extended by the death of Innocent X in January of 1655 and the election of Pope Alexander VII in April. Boym's letters from China, which probably had been on the agenda of the ailing Innocent X, were brought to the new Pope's attention. But during his three years in Rome, Boym did not obtain a personal audience with either Pope[24]. This cannot be attributed to anti-Jesuit feeling on the new Pope's part because Alexander VII (d. 1667) was friendly to the Jesuits and it was at this time that Fr. Martini secured the pro-accommodation pronouncement from the Holy Father. It was almost inevitable at that time in Rome that a Jesuit of the China Mission would be drawn into the Rites Controversy debate and it was not surprising to find Boym defending accommodation against Dominican critics from the universities at Louvain, Douvai, Ingolstadt and Gratz[25]. It was also during his stay in Rome that Boym made the contact with Fr. Kircher that was to figure so prominently in *China illustrata.*

Responses from the Pope to both the dowager empress Helena and to the imperial eunuch P'ang were finally forthcoming in December of 1655[26]. Boym left Rome soon afterwards and departed from Lisbon in March of 1656. His return voyage was marked by difficulties and delays throughout. He was delayed in Goa for one year, attacked by the Dutch, refused entry into China at Macao by the Portuguese and later blocked by the Manchus from entering China through the Kwangsi border[27]. The outlook for the Ming cause was bleak and possibly Boym learned that the dowager empress Helena had died in 1651[28]. Boym's frustration must have been intense. At only forty-seven years of age, he succumbed to an unspecified illness and died at the border between Kwangsi and Tongking in August of 1659.

22 Pelliot, "Michael Boym," p. 112.
23 Pelliot, "Michael Boym," p. 115 & Girard de Rialle, "Une mission chinoise à Venise au XVIIe siècle," *T'oung pao* 1 (1890): 99–117.
24 Dehergne, *Répertoire,* p. 34.
25 Fang, I, 308.
26 Although most sources refer only to the replies of Pope Alexander VII, Fang Hao, I, 311, quotes a communication signed by the Jesuit General Goswin Nickel and dated December 25th 1655.
27 Goodrich, pp. 20–21.
28 Hummel, p. 195.

The writings of Fr. Boym have been little studied and several questions of authorship have arisen over them[29]. The reasons for these questions are undoubtedly due more to the collaborative nature of the production of many missionary works than to any attempted plagiarism. Frequently there were uncompleted manuscripts left in China by a deceased author which were carried back to Europe by later missionaries. Oftentimes these manuscripts passed through many hands and ended with a European unfamiliar with the Chinese language or culture. Boym's wide range of talents and interests corresponded to the seventeenth-century polyhistor model. His linguistic talent was demonstrated in the degree of knowledge of Chinese that he achieved in such a relatively short stay in the Chinese-speaking regions. His botanical interests were reflected in his *Flora Sinensis* (Vienna 1656), a remarkable work of drawings and descriptions of mainly south China plants for which he probably made arrangements to publish while in Europe during 1652–1656[30]. His medical concerns were reflected in *Clavis medica ad Chinarum doctrinam de pulsibus* which included Boym's translation of the treatise on the pulse, *Mo ching,* by the famous physician Wang Shu-ho (265–317). Boym also contributed to the *Clavis medica,* a description of 289 Chinese drugs with romanized Chinese names[31]. The physician Andreas Cleyer edited this work and Fr. Couplet appears to have been responsible for publishing it in Belgium in 1686[32]. Boym's interest in cartography was reflected in several maps he made of China, the best known of which is the atlas preserved in the Vatican library and entitled *Magni Catay, quod olim Serica, et modo Sinarum est monarchia,* said to be based on the *Ti-t'u tsung-yao* (1643) compiled by Wu Hsüeh-yen *et al*[33]. But one should note that Boym's cartographic efforts were not the equal of Martini's.

In terms of contributions to Kircher's *China illustrata,* Boym must be given priority in the segment on the Nestorian Monument. Also, several sections in part four of *China illustrata* which deal with Chinese plants, animals, birds and snakes[34] are said to be drawn from Boym's *Flora Sinensis*[35]. The bilingual

---

29 See Szcześniak, "The Writings of Michael Boym," *Monumenta Serica* 14 (1949–1955): 481–538.

30 See Harmut Walravens, "Eine Anmerkung zu Michael Boyms *Flora Sinensis* (1656) – einer wichtigen naturhistorischen Quelle," *China Mission Studies (1550–1800) Bulletin* 1 (1979): 16–20.

31 Goodrich, p. 21.

32 Sommervogel, II, 70–71, lists an earlier publication of an approximate form of this work entitled *Specimen medicinae sinicae, sive opuscula medica ad mentem Sinensium* (Frankfurt, 1682). According to the article on Boym by L. Carrington Goodrich and Szcześniak in the *Dictionary of Ming Biography,* p. 21, Boym's Chinese medical books with his marginal notes are preserved in the "Prussian Library in Berlin" (Staatsbibliothek Preussischer Kulturbesitz, West Berlin?).

33 Goodrich, p. 21. A copy of the *Ti-t'u tsung-yao* in three *chüan* with Boym's marginalia is found in the Borgia Cinese collection of the Biblioteca Vaticana.

34 Kircher, *China illustrata,* pp. 176–205.

35 Szcześniak, "Kircher's *China illustrata,*" p. 501.

"Divinae legis compendium" (*T'ien-chu chiao-sheng yüeh-yen*) or catechism of *China illustrata* has been the source of some much-debated questions of origin[36]. By contrast, little doubt has been expressed over the claim that Boym was the main source for the information in the sixth part of *China illustrata* which attempted to analyze and explain the Chinese written language. The core of this section is claimed by Boleslaw Szcześniak to have come from a short treatise by Boym with illustrations of *chuan* (sealscript) writing[37]. Mr. Szcześniak also believes that Kircher altered Boym's original meaning by adding the remarks on Chinese characters and Egyptian hieroglyphs[38]. Another disputed contribution involving Boym is the Chinese-French dictionary which appeared in the French edition of *China illustrata*[39].

The third source of *China illustrata* whom Kircher cited in his preface was Fr. Phillipo Marino [Philippus Marinus] of Genoa, the procurator of Japan, whose contribution was made orally to Kircher. The fourth source cited was Johann Grueber (1623–1680) who had made a remarkable return voyage in 1661–1664 from China using an overland route through Asia. Fr. Grueber's return to Rome in 1664 and conversations with Kircher provided much of the material found in parts two and three of *China illustrata* where a great deal of information is found on Tibet, India and Mongolia. Fr. Roth, whom Kircher claimed in his preface to have a considerable knowledge of Persian, Indostanic and Brahmanic (i.e. Sanskrit) languages, probably wrote much of the material on Hindu doctrine and Sanskrit found in part three of *China illustrata*. Grueber also wrote a response to a series of questions by the grand duke of Tuscany which appeared in the French edition. In the course of composing *China illustrata*, Kircher drew on other sources such as Fr. Semedo on the Nestorian

---

36 Kircher, *China illustrata,* pp. 121–129. The Catechism in *China illustrata* consists of forty-six numbered paragraphs followed by the Ten Commandments and a concluding passage presented in parallel columns of Chinese romanization and Latin translation. Boym himself included a *"Sinicus catechismus"* in his list of works published in his *Briefse relation* (Paris, 1654). (See Sommervogel, II, 72–73.) Pelliot followed Pfister in attributing the original Chinese Catechism to João Soerio, S.J. (1566–1607) although he regarded it as probable that Boym romanized and translated the work. (See Pelliot, "Michael Boym," pp. 135–136 & Pfister, p. 57.) Duyvendak stated that Boym neither romanized nor translated the Catechism and suggested that the text was brought to Europe by Martini, who probably did not himself do the romanizing and translating. (See Duyvendak, pp. 324–326.) There is also a debate over whether the Chinese text of the Catechism was written in 1602 or 1606–1607. (See Szcześniak, "The Writings of Michael Boym," pp. 497–498.")

37 Szcześniak, "The writings of Michael Boym," p. 449.

38 Kircher, *China illustrata* pp. 233–235.

39 Kircher, *La Chine illustrée*, pp. 324–367. Mr. Szcześniak in "The Writings of Michael Boym," pp. 501–502, claims that this Chinese-French dictionary was Boym's work, while Walter Simon denies that it was authored by Boym. See Walter Simon, "The Attribution to Michael Boym of Two Early Achievements of Western Sinology," *Asia Major* new series 7 (1959): 165–169.

Monument[40], but to a much slighter degree than with the previously mentioned contributors[41].

China illustrata, like the Ricci-Trigault work of a half-century earlier, was intended to be interesting reading to a public stimulated by the reports of missionaries and Portuguese, Spanish and Dutch traders returned from East Asia. The fifty pages of illustrations are generally of a good quality and are certainly entertaining depictions of what must have been extreme exotica to the mid-seventeenth-century reader. The presence in this and other works by Kircher of what that age called "curious" phenomena has led certain scholars to conclude that interest in such phenomena was primarily responsible for Kircher's study of orientology[42]. Yet if one looks closely at the Chinese people depicted in the illustrations of *China illustrata*, the European cast to their physical features will be readily apparent. The fact is that the illustrations as well as the descriptions of China could have been made far more "curious", exotic and foreign than they were. But for Kircher, the basic elements of Chinese culture, such as its religions, were not new beliefs developed on the other side of the world. They were rather derivations from Egyptian and Greek religions. And the Chinese language was not a unique development of China because the Chinese characters were said to demonstrate the same principles of development found in and therefore derived from the Egyptian hieroglyphs. A simple explanation of Kircher's one-world attitude involves European provincialism and Christian chauvinism. But a deeper explanation would involve Kircher's belief in universal principles, such as the possibility of a universal language, which is treated in the following chapter.

2. KIRCHER AND THE CHINESE LANGUAGE

Kircher's interest in China was inspired in part by his fascination with deciphering exotic languages, specifically with what he identified as the hieroglyphic languages of the Chinese, Brahmans and Mexicans as derived from the Egyptian hieroglyphs[43]. He demonstrated this interest in his examination of the Chinese script in the sixth and last part of *China illustrata*. At the beginning of this examination, he expressed his debt to Fr. Boym who, according to Kircher, taught him "to read and to write in Chinese" during Boym's visit to Rome in 1653–1656[44]. Surely Kircher exaggerated here for his knowledge of Chinese was extremely limited. Furthermore, one might question the degree of Boym's expertise in Chinese, not only because of the limited number of

40 Kircher, *China illustrata*, p. 6.
41 Szcześniak, "Kircher's *China illustrata*," p. 405.
42 Hans Kangro, "Athanasius Kircher," in *Dictionary of Scientific Biography* (New York, 1973) VII, 375.
43 Kircher, *China illustrata*, p. 225.
44 Kircher, *China illustrata*, p. 225.

years he had been exposed to the language in China, but also on the lack of Chinese-language works ascribed to his name[45] . By contrast, a number of Boym's missionary contemporaries acquired the ability to compose in Chinese and authored a considerable number of works. Nevertheless, Boym's translations from Chinese and his use of characters in *Flora Sinensis* indicated a basic facility in Chinese. Also, Boym's Chinese traveling companion, Cheng An-te-lo, was available to give further linguistic assistance and it is probable that Boym's knowledge of Chinese continued to develop throughout his journey to and from Europe.

Kircher dated the invention of the Chinese language from 300 years after the flood associated with Noah in *Genesis* 6–9[46] . Kircher described this period as one when the descendants of Noah ruled in all regions of the world (*Genesis* 9:18 and 10:1–32). According to Kircher, the "Emperor Fu Hsi" was the inventor of this "Art" of writing and he taught it to his successors who were the descendants of Noah[47] . Here Kircher saw Chinese history dovetailing with Biblical history. Explicating from the tenth chapter of *Genesis*, he spoke of Ham, one of the three sons of Noah, transferring his people eastward from Egypt into Persia and thence into Bactria. Kircher identified "Zoroaster, King of Bactria" with Ham. From Bactria, colonies were sent into China, which Kircher regarded as the end of the earth in that it represented the last inhabitable climate of the world.

We now see the seventeenth-century reductionist principle come madly into play. Kircher stated that Ham had a son named Nimrod – *Genesis* 10: 6–8 treats Nimrod as Ham's grandson – and Nimrod had a counselor named Mercurius (i.e. Hermes) Trismegistus whom Kircher called the "first inventor of the hieroglyphs". (Kircher designated Fu Hsi as the first inventor of the "characters" [of the *I ching*?], as distinct from the "hieroglyphs".) What convinced Kircher of the truth of the reduction to a single linguistic origin was the similarity between the Chinese characters and Egyptian hieroglyphs. Kircher felt that this similarity was confirmed by two sources: the form of the characters and the Chinese chronologies

Given the lack of material available, Kircher could have done only the most superficial of reading in the historical works of China. For information, he most likely depended on a missionary source such as Boym or Martini. As to the linguistic analysis, Kircher relied on only the barest of information to draw his conclusions which, nevertheless, were highly respected by his contemporaries. Even if many of Kircher's views strike us today as preposterous, we find alongside these statements some of the first accurate information on China presented to European readers.

---

45 See Boym's bibliography in Pfister, pp. 273–276 & Sommervogel, II, 70–73.
46 Kircher, *China illustrata*, p. 226.
47 Kircher, *China illustrata*, pp. 225–226.

It becomes quite clear when Kircher was drawing upon knowledgeable information from Boym or another Jesuit on the Chinese language. Kircher's estimates of a necessary knowledge of 10,000 characters for fluency and 80,000 for learned status were, at least in the second case, high, but not ridiculously so. For example, the 38-volume *Chung-wen ta-tzu-tien* (Encyclopedic dictionary of the Chinese language) (Taipei, 1962–1968), which is a translation of T. Murohashi's *Dai Kanwa Jiten*, lists 49,905 individual characters. When Kircher stated that Chinese characters contained no letters or syllables and did not follow any alphabetical arrangement, he was giving solid description. If he overexaggerated the equation between a character and a word, he correctly spoke of the lack of declinations and conjugations. If he underevaluated the role of grammatical arrangement of the characters, he accurately described the great achievement of a Chinese who mastered a large number of characters and of the public recognition which devolved upon such an achievement.

Kircher compared the ancient Chinese characters to the Egyptian hieroglyphic manner of pictorially representing things drawn from the world. He spoke of the use of serpents, vipers and dragons to represent fire; birds to represent air; fish to represent things of the water; flowers, leaves and branches to represent things of the earth and vegetative beings; and points and circles to represent stars[48]. Kircher was aware of an evolutionary element in Chinese, which he believed was similar to that of the Egyptian hieroglyphs. He was aware that the contemporary Chinese characters simplified the pictorial representations, but he believed that these simplified lines retained an identifiable resemblance to their original pictorial forms. He demonstrated this with a list of five characters with their contemporary as well as so-called "ancient" forms. These characters were *chuan* (seal-script), *tzu* (character), *huang* (lord; emperor), *wen* (writing) and *chiang* (river). While the presented etymologies seem questionable, they appear at least possible, in contrast to some of the fantastic etymologies which followed.

In spite of Kircher's lack of strong creative tendencies, he was no mere imitator. We see this in the application to Chinese characters of a linguistic theory developed from his attempt to decipher Egyptian hieroglyphs. In her study of the Hermetic tradition, Frances Yates presents Kircher as one of several enthusiastic seventeenth-century perpetuators of Renaissance religious Hermeticism which continued after its intellectual undermining by Isaac Casaubon. Casaubon had shown in his *De rebus sacris et ecclesiasticis exercitationes XVI* (London 1614) that the Hermetic writings were not authored by an ancient Egyptian priest, but dated rather from post-Christian times[49]. Like Robert Fludd (1574–1637) in England, Kircher ignored the findings of Casaubon and continued to believe that Hermes Trismegistus had authored the works attri-

---

48 Kircher, *China illustrata*, pp. 226–227.
49 Frances A. Yates, *Giordano Bruno and the Hermetic Tradition*, pp. 398–423.

buted to him. In the vein of the Hermetic tradition, Kircher believed that the Egyptian hieroglyphs were symbols containing secret truths about God and the world. According to Ms. Yates, Kircher was a Hermetist-Cabalist, but was cautious about practicing the magic associated with these traditions. The Jesuit in Kircher abjured diabolical magic, but the historian and archeologist in him led Kircher to practice a type of natural magic[50]. For Kircher, Egypt and the Egyptian cross stood in a direct line of development to Christianity.

Kircher had been interested in Egyptian script since the 1630s and his *Oedipus Aegyptiacus* (1652) and *Lingua aegyptiaca restituta* (1664) appeared before *China illustrata*. The understanding of Egyptian hieroglyphic writing died with the growth of early Christianity in the Mediterranean area. Consequently, Kircher's attempt to decipher the hieroglyphs dealt with an esoteric language. He began his investigation of Egyptian script by examining the Coptic language, which he assumed had evolved from the hieroglyphs. From the point of view of contemporary understanding of Egyptian hieroglyphic writing, this assumption was correct. Also correct was Kircher's belief that the hieroglyphs recorded phonetic values.

However, with the exception of one character, Kircher failed to decipher the Egyptian hieroglyphs, in part, because of his ungrounded belief that the hieroglyphs corresponded phonetically to an alphabet. But more essentially, he failed because he was preoccupied with a tradition dating from Horapollon, a Greek Egyptian of the fifth century, which stressed a deeper symbolical significance in the hieroglyphs. Consequently, Kircher was led incorrectly to focus on this symbolical significance and to regard the phonetic significance of the hieroglyphs as less essential to decipherment. The Egyptian hieroglyphic script was not deciphered until the early nineteenth century, after the Rosetta Stone had been discovered in Egypt in 1799[51].

Kircher maintained that the descent of the Chinese characters from the Egyptian hieroglyphs was reflected not in the shape of the characters, but in the use of images from the natural world to express their meaning. Here we see the symbolic emphasis surfacing. Kircher hypothesized sixteen types of Chinese characters, classified according to origin. He explained each of these types with a Chinese sentence, each of which contained five characters, except for the fourteenth which contained seven characters. In presenting these Chinese sentences, he attempted to give the ancient form of the characters, the modern form, romanization and translation. He used a romanization which was developed by missionaries of that time for a Latin alphabet and pronunciation. Kircher's characters are sometimes illegible and occasionally the romanizations and translations do not agree with the characters[52]. His presentation is of great

50 Yates, *Giordano Bruno and the Hermetic Tradition*, pp. 421–422.
51 E. Iverson, *The Myth of Egypt and its Hieroglyphs* (Copenhagen, 1961) pp. 137f.
52 In the following treatment of Kircher's analysis of Chinese script in *China illustrata*,

fascination to anyone interested in the mixture of truth and fiction by which China was perceived by Europeans in the seventeenth century. Kircher's — or Boym's or Cheng's? — analysis is filled with fantastic, often absurd etymological hypotheses. And yet, they clearly contain enough factual elements to prevent us from dismissing the author as a charlatan-interpreter of China.

The first of the sixteen types of characters was said by Kircher to be derived from snakes and dragons[53]. He spoke of "the book of [snakes and] dragons of Fu Hsi" (*Fu Hsi she lung shu*). Kircher accurately reflected Chinese legendary history by referring to Fu Hsi — traditionally dated 2953–2838 B.C. — as the "first inventor" of the characters, of which Kircher claimed that a hundred characters were derived from the living forms of snakes and dragons. Kircher also referred to a "book of dragons which dealt with mathematics and astrology", by which he probably meant the *I ching*, whose original text was regarded by some as the oldest Chinese written work extant. In traditional Chinese history, Fu Hsi was regarded as the inventor of the eight trigrams, which represented the first graphic representations of meaning in China. These eight trigrams were expanded to form the 64 hexagrams around which the *I ching* was based. So we see that while Kircher mangled the details, he was drawing from a true aspect of Chinese legendary culture.

Kircher's second type of Chinese character was said to be derived from agriculture. (The second through fourth of Kircher's types of Chinese characters are illustrated in plate 8.) He continued to draw from Chinese legendary culture when he spoke of "the writings on agriculture which Shen Nung wrote" (*Ch'uan* [?] *shu Shen Nung tso*)[54]. Here, as elsewhere, monumentality rather than meticulousness seems predominant in Kircher's scholarship of the curious: the skillful presentation of masses of exotic detail is more important than simple clarity of the examples. Yet he accurately conveyed the legendary significance traditionally ascribed to Shen Nung (traditionally dated 2828–2698 B.C.). The third type of character which Kircher hypothesized was produced from a variety of birds. He expressed it in the Chinese phrase "the book of the phoenix which Shao Hao wrote" (*Feng shu Shao Hao tso.*) Feng was the male phoenix, which traditionally symbolized the Chinese monarchy. Shao Hao was also a legendary ruler said to have reigned from 2598–2514 B.C. .

The remaining Chinese phrases used by Kircher are more difficult to decipher. Kircher claimed that the fourth type of character was derived from shell-fish

---

pp. 147- 151, I have corrected certain characters. In addition, I have standardized and corrected his romanizations, and converted them to Wade-Giles romanization. The inclusion of Kircher's original characters and romanizations, though of possible interest to students of seventeenth-century comparative languages, would place an unnecessary burden on the general reader. Essentially, I have viewed my task as an interpretive one.

53 Kircher, *China illustrata*, p. 228.
54 Kircher, *China illustrata*, pp. 228–229.

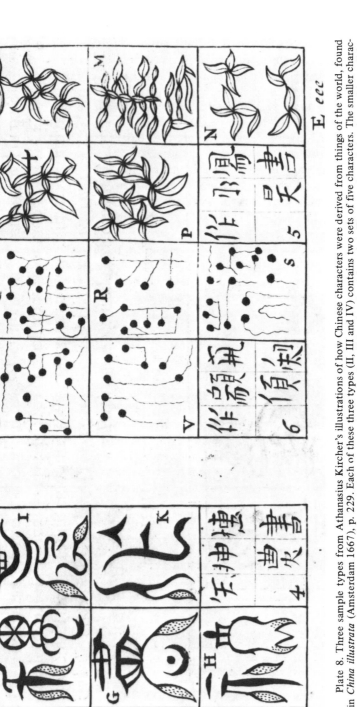

Plate 8. Three sample types from Athanasius Kircher's illustrations of how Chinese characters were derived from things of the world, found in *China illustrata* (Amsterdam 1667), p. 229. Each of these three types (II, III and IV) contains two sets of five characters. The smaller characters, which are grouped together in a single block, represent the standard traditional script (*chen-shu*). These are intended to be read in traditional Chinese style from top to bottom and from right to left. But these small characters are crudely drawn and sometimes extremely difficult to decipher. The larger characters, of which there is one to each box, represent hypothesized reconstructions of the original forms of the Chinese characters. They result from merging certain fantastic etymological forms found in popular Chinese literature which were probably supplied by Fr. Boym and blended by Fr. Kircher with his theories on the hieroglyphic origin of Chinese characters. The hieroglyphic characters labelled F, G, H, I, K, represent *Ch'uam shu shen Nung Wang* (The writings on agriculture of King Shen Nung). The hieroglyphic characters labelled L, M, N, O, P represent *Feng shu Shao Hao tso* (The book of the phoenix that Shao Hao wrote). The characters Q, R, S, T, V represent *Li* (?)

and small worms. Kircher's Chinese phrase referred to King Chuan Hsü. According to Chinese legendary history, Chuan Hsü was the grandson of Huang Ti (the Yellow Emperor) and was said to have assisted King Shao Hao before he himself ascended the throne. In terms of sequence, Kircher placed Chuan Hsü after Shao Hao and claimed that Chuan Hsü wrote a work dealing with these shell-fish and small worm forms. According to Kircher, the fifth type of character was derived from the roots of herbs, but the Chinese phrase is difficult to translate. It includes a reference to *huang-ti*, a title for emperor technically in use only since the historical reign of Ch'in Shih Huang-ti (r. 246–210 B.C.). More significantly, the phrase includes a second reference to the character *chuan*, the highly pictographic seal-script.

Mr. Szcześniak, a student of Boym's work, believes the etymologies in *China illustrata* to be seal-script characters drawn by Boym[55]. But even if supplied by Boym and over-interpreted by Kircher, the use of etymologies to trace characters back to their ancient forms was not a European imposition. Etymology has been a highly cultivated discipline among the Chinese, documentable by the ancient dictionary, the *Shuo-wen chieh-tzu* (A.D. 100). Of the four traditional styles of Chinese characters — seal-script, official/legal script, running-grass script and standard script (see plate 1), the seal-script most clearly preserves the pictographic basis of the characters. But since the seal-script was developed as a decorative script long after the historical origin of Chinese writing, it would constitute poor evidence of genetic development. Furthermore, the ancient forms found in *China illustrata* are even more literally pictographic than seal-script and appear to be hypothetical reconstructions.

The Danish scholar Knud Lundbaek has discovered that similarly fantastic Chinese characters are found in the manuscript of *Confucius Sinarum philosophus* preserved in the Bibliothèque Nationale Paris[56]. These characters were omitted from the published work and Mr. Lundbaek explains this omission by referring to a marginal comment found in the manuscript. This marginalia stated that it was not necessary to print these characters because they had already appeared in *China illustrata*! Lundbaek theorizes that these fantastic characters belonged to street-vendor rather than scholarly literature and that the Jesuits obtained them in an informal manner. He supports this theory with evidence that such fantastic etymologies are still available for purchase from bookvendors in Taipei. Boym's limited experience with the Chinese language and the youthful inexperience of his Chinese assistant, Cheng, would tend to

55 Szcześniak, "The writings of Michael Boym," pp. 496–498.

56 See the manuscript of *Confucius Sinarum philosophus* in the Bibliothèque nationale Paris, Fonds latin 6277. A sheet of the *Confucius Sinarum philosophus* manuscript containing the fanciful Chinese characters is reproduced and discussed in Knud Lundbaek, "Kinesiske fantasitegn," *Danmark Kina* 67 (April-May 1981): 10–12 & in Knud Lundbaek, "Imaginary ancient Chinese characters," *China Mission studies (1550–1800) bulletin* 5 (1983): 5–23.

support Lundbaek's theory. Given Boym's and Cheng's limited knowledge of the Chinese language and Kircher's voracious demands for information combined with his prolific speed in turning out books, it is not surprising that some of these etymologies appear ridiculous. Lundbaek's findings support the conclusion that these characters found in *China illustrata* were derived from "tadpole characters" (*ch'ung shu* or *k'o tou tzu*), which refer to a class of ancient Chinese script as well as to archaic and obsolete characters[57].

Although Kircher's hieroglyphic reconstructions are somewhat fantastical, the names and events mentioned were derived from Chinese legendary history and one should not dismiss the possibility that these phrases were taken from certain ancient Chinese texts. For example, Kircher referred to the "Sinensis ex Annalium" (Annals of the Chinese) as the source of the information that the first Chinese writing was written 300 years after the Noadic flood[58]. Secondly, Kircher mentioned the "Libro de Successione Regum" (Book of the succession of kings) as containing the first form of the Chinese characters and taught the method of writing these characters. But it is unclear whether Kircher was referring to specific works or whether these were merely vague references to Chinese works which he had heard described by his missionary sources.

The sixth type of character which Kircher hypothesized was derived from "the remainder [i.e. in addition to those birds referred to in the third and eighth types of characters?] of the birds". The seventh was from tortoises and mentioned King Yao, a legendary figure whose reign was traditionally dated, with resounding legendary significance, as exactly one century − 2357−2256 B.C. . The eighth type of character was derived from "birds and peacocks" and the ninth was from herbs, leafstalks and rushes. The derivation of the tenth was not explained by Kircher. The eleventh was derived from planets and stars. The derivation of the twelfth was not explained, but this type of character was said to be used in edicts, privileges and statues. Possibly this constituted a reference to one of the four traditional styles of script known as *li-shu* whose characters have a very squarish cast and were employed in writing legal and official documents. However, the characters presented in the twelfth phrase show little resemblance to this style of script. The thirteenth type of character was not explained, nor was the fourteenth type, except to say that the latter type of character signified repose, joy, knowledge, conversation, darkness and light!? The fifteenth type of character was derived from fish. Even Kircher denied an understanding of the sixteenth type, although I

57 See Samuel Couling, *The Encyclopaedia Sinica* (Shanghai, 1917) pp. 518 & 539. The tadpole characters are illustrated in James Legge, trans., *The Chinese Classics* 5 vols. (Oxford, 1893) III, 73.

58 Kircher, *China illustrata*, p. 225.

note that the Chinese phrase, which Kircher did not attempt to translate, referred to *chin-tso* (gold-inlay ornamentation).

Inserted as an interlude following this analysis of Chinese script was a brief, illustrated explanation of the method of Chinese writing in which Kircher described the use of a brush and inkstone in contrast to the European use of feather, pen and inkwell[59]. (See plate 9.) The engraving depicted the Chinese method of holding the brush at right angles. However, the scribe was portrayed with semi-European physical features, wearing a Mandarin-type robe and standing. The monkey seated on the floor, reading from a sheet of paper, represented more than exotica. The ape has a long background as a symbol in European history. Throughout the Middle Ages, the ape was seen as a *figura diaboli*, that is, a manifestation of the devil, who had devolved from the level of human beings just as man had been demoted from the level of angels by disobeying God in the Garden of Eden[60].

In the Renaissance, a new view of the ape as a symbol of arts, especially of painting and sculpture, emerged. This notion of *ars simia naturae*, that is, art as the ape of nature, was developed by Boccaccio and had been applied to the sculptures "Dying Slave" and "Rebellious Slave" in Michelangelo's project for the tomb of Pope Juilus II[61]. By the sixteenth century, this interpretation of the ape as *ars imitatio* in art had degenerated into slavish imitation, but there was one area of seventeenth- and eighteenth-century culture where the metaphysical significance of the notion of *ars simia naturae* was continued in the very specific and limited context of alchemy and the occult sciences. This area was represented by the group whom Frances Yates in her study of the Hermetic Tradition refers to as "Reactionary Hermetists"[62].

Robert Fludd of Oxford used the ape in this vein as the occultist metaphor which symbolized "Art" in the sense of every form of human knowledge, both practical and theoretical. The engraved title page of Fludd's *Utriusque cosmi historia* (1618) visually portrayed the ape at the center of the liberal arts and as a symbol of the "universal artist", i.e. the realm of the arts and sciences[63]. Kircher and Fludd are not only linked together by Ms. Yates as reactionary Hermetists, but the art historian H. W. Janson connects Kircher to Fludd's view of *ars simia naturae* via Kircher's work *Oedipus Aegyptiacus*[64]. Kircher stressed that the importance of Chinese characters lay in their derivation from the deeper and more substantial Egyptian hieroglyphs. For Kircher, the significance of this derivation lay in the fact that the Egyptian hieroglyphs used

59 Kircher, *China illustrata*, pp. 232–233.
60 Horst W. Janson, *Apes & Ape Lore in the Middle Ages and Renaissance* (London, 1952) p. 13.
61 Janson, pp. 287–300.
62 Yates, *Giordano Bruno and the Hermetic Tradition*, pp. 403–423.
63 Janson, pp. 304–307.
64 Janson, p. 322, fn. 62.

Plate 9. An illustration of the Chinese method of writing, from Athanasius Kircher, *China illustrata* (Amsterdam, 1667), p. 233. Courtesy of the Niedersächsische Landesbiblio-

images from the natural world to express their meaning. This form of *imitatio* appears to be what the presence of the little ape in Kircher's plate 9 from *China illustrata* represented. The little ape symbolized that the Chinese literatus in writing characters was really using images from the natural world.

In the section following his analysis of sixteen types of characters, Kircher treated the differences between Chinese characters and Egyptian hieroglyphs[65]. He stated that the ancient Chinese, who were related to the Egyptians as common descendants of Ham, shared with the Egyptians a great esteem for the cross. This was said to be manifested in the Chinese character for ten (*shih*) which took the form of a cross. Furthermore, Kircher added – with a dash of numerology – that ten was the universal symbol of perfection or completion. Kircher illustrated how adding one line to the bottom of the Chinese character for "ten" produced "earth" (*tu*). Another line added to the top of earth produced "king" (*wang*). Kircher claimed that adding a line to the upper right of "king", would produce "precious stone" (*yü*). (Actually, this diagonal stroke should be added to the lower right portion of the character for king.) Thus a cross appeared in each of these characters. One will recall that this particular illustration had appeared earlier, and perhaps for the first time in a European work – Fr. Semedo's *Imperio de la China*[66]. Semedo's work was the probable source of Kircher's duplication of this illustration in *China illustrata*. (See plate 10.) However, earlier in the third volume (1654) of *Oedipus Aegyptiacus*, Kircher used a variant form of this illustration in which two characters were added – *sheng* (to create; live) and *chu* (lord; master). These two characters were somewhat distortedly drawn in order to fit the symmetry of the illustration. For these additional characters, Kircher must have relied upon a source, probably a missionary, who was familiar with Chinese. It appears that this earlier illustration was borrowed by other European authors, such as Theophil Spizelius, who reproduced the characters, romanizations and translations, and John Webb, who gave only the characters and translations[67]. (See plate 11 from Spizelius.) In short, a number of seventeenth-century Europeans found this illustration convincing.

China illustrata has been interpreted by the French scholar Madeleine David as the completion of Kircher's "Egyptological" works. She claims that in this book Kircher rejected the challenge of Chinese characters to sharing the pre-

65 Kircher, *China illustrata*, pp. 233–235.

66 Semedo, *Relatione della grande monarchia della Cina* (Rome, 1643), pp. 45–46.

67 Theophil Spizelius (Spitzel), *De re literaria Sinensium commentarius* (Antwerp, 1660) pp. 55–56, reproduced the expanded illustration of the formation of Chinese characters, which he claimed to be from Kircher's *Oedipus Aegyptiacus* vol. 3 (Theatrum hieroglyphicum) (Rome, 1654) ch. 2. John Webb in his *Historical Essay Endeavoring a Probability that the Language of the Empire of China is like Primitive Language* (London, 1669) p. 174, reproduced the same expanded illustration, though both Spizelius and Webb were also aware of the Semedo work.

qui quello, che ſta più eſercitato nel Calepino. Per formare,
tutta queſta moltitudine di lettere, adoprano ſolamente noue
tratti : mà perche queſti ſoli per tanta machina non potrebbono
baſtare, andarono congiungendo figure, ò lettere perfette e ſi-
gnificatiue, l'vne con l'altre, con le quali ne formano altre di-
uerſe, e di diuerſa ſignificatione. Coſì queſta linea —— vale,
vna

vna : attrauerſata con vn altra in Croce ✠, vale dieci :
e poſtauene vn'altra per trauerſo alla punta d'abbaſſo
ſignifica Terra: e con vn'altra in cima alla punta di ſopra
vuol dire Re: aggiugnendole vn · ⊤ punto alla. parte
ſiniſtra tra le prime due punte ⊥ ſignifica Pietrapretioſa:
e ſe prima le mettono cert'altre linee, dice Perla : e queſt'vlti-
ma figura hauerà ſeco ogni lettera, che ha da ſignificare Pietra
pretioſa, ò quaſipretioſa. Come ancora ogni lettera di albero,
ha da hauer congionta ſeco quella di legno : e quella di metallo,
la figura che hauerà da ſignificare, ferro, rame, acciaio : non è
però regola infallibile.

Plate 10. An illustrated explanation of the formation of Chinese characters from Alvaro
Semedo, *Relatione della grande Monarchia della Cina* (Rome 1643), pp. 45–46. Courtesy
of the Niedersächsische Landesbibliothek Hannover.

la —— fignificat *unum, primum, &c.* cum tranfverfa vero -|- *Tfi* feu *de-cem* ; fuperaddita alia —⊥— notat

Thou vel *Terram*; rurfus alia —⩵— *Wang'* feu *Regem* indigetat ; cum

puncto —⊤— *Tö* feu *Iu Margari-tam* indicat, fitu vero ejus variato

⊤— notat *Sem,* feu *creare, vi-rere;* denique puncto fuperimpofito

⊤ *Chu* feu *Dominum* fignificat.

Huc etiam pertinent *Figura myftica,* cujufdam Sinici operis YEKING di-cti, magnique apud eos pretii, ob res arcanas inibi latentes. Illud tamen nil nifi Philofophiam myfticam *Py-thagoricæq*; per fimilem continere ju-dicat *Martinius Hift.Sin.*pag.6. multa enim in eodem reperiuntur de *Gene-ratione & corruptione,* de *fato;* de *Aftro-logia*

Plate 11. An illustrated explanation of the formation of Chinese characters from Theo-phil Spizelius, *De re literaria Sinensium* (Antwerp 1660), p. 56. Courtesy of the Nieder-sächsische Landesbibliothek Hannover.

eminent linguistic status of the Egyptian hieroglyphs which he had established in his previous works. In response to the similarities between the two languages often cited by seventeenth-century contemporaries, Kircher conceded that the figurative origin of the Chinese characters gave them a basic similarity to the hieroglyphs. But the hieroglyphs were more removed from daily life than the characters and this greater distance from mundane affairs enabled them to better treat exalted subject matter[68]. Such an argument is perfectly consistent with the Hermetic emphasis on the mystery required of higher forms of knowledge. Kircher believed that the Egyptian hieroglyphs contained a level of mystery deeper than their Chinese counterparts. Just as the word for sun depicted solar matter of the sensible world, it also represented an "archetype" of the Neoplatonic intelligible world. Chinese characters were said to include only the signification of the words and to lack this deeper referent to the intelligible world. Kircher concluded that the Chinese had developed a written language which had reached a clear level of communication, but lacked the more subtle features of the ancient hieroglyphs.

In a typically "curious" display of detail to support his claims, Kircher presented the composite analysis of four characters. In the first, he took "gate" (*men*) plus "heart" (*hsin*) to yield "affliction" (*men*). Kircher's second example presented the character for "man" (*jen*) plus "king" (*wang*) combining to make "complete" (*ch'uan*) by a reasoning which claimed that a king was a most complete man. Again, however, Kircher has erred in that the upper element of *ch'uan* is not *jen*, but *ju* which has the completely different meaning of "entering".

In the third example, Kircher claimed that the word for "a man enamoured of someone" (*luan*) was composed by the combination of three characters which separately meant "woman" (*nü*), "thread" (*tzu*) and "word" (*yen*): just as one is adorned by cords and threads, so the heart is spiritually adorned by words. *Luan* has the sense of physical beauty, though it is applied more to the sense of catamite than to women attracting and alluring men. Kircher's fourth and final example was "brightness" (*ming*) which is composed of the character for "sun" (*jih*) and the character for "moon" (*yüeh*). Only Kircher's incorrect drawing of the sun marred this example. An examination of these same characters in the third column of the Nestorian Tablet inscription appearing in *China illustrata* indicates that the writer of those characters — Boym or Cheng — was the probable source of Kircher's error. The inscription's calligraphy is not incorrect, but does contain an ambiguity which someone not familiar with Chinese, such as Kircher, might misinterpret.

At the end of this section on the Chinese language, Kircher demonstrated his awareness of the tonal and dialectal aspects of Chinese. If he oversimplified the

---

68 Madeleine David, *Le débat sur les écritures et l'hiéroglyphe aux XVIIe et XVIIIe siècles* (Paris, 1965) pp. 55–56.

etymological formation and structure of the characters, he did not underestimate the difficulties of learning Chinese. He noted that multiple pronunciations of the same character enormously complicated the task of mastering the language. He also noted that while "*Mandarine*" was common throughout China, it was most commonly spoken in Peking and Nanking, the administrative centers of China. He compared the Mandarin dialect to Castilian in Spain and Tuscan in Italy. Kircher was aware that while the Japanese, Koreans, Cochinese (South Vietnamese) and Tonkinese (North Vietnamese) all employed Chinese characters in their writing, their pronunciation differed to such an extent that they were unable to carry on a conversation with one another. Consequently, Kircher conveyed the crucial distinction in China between mastering the spoken and written languages.

Kircher demonstrated his understanding of the tonal qualities of Chinese by referring to Fr. Pantoja's theory of expressing the five tones through six musical tones. (It is not clear why six notes were needed to express five tones.) Kircher accepted the enduring fiction that Chinese had no polysyllables, which, as we have noted, is true only of the classical language (*wen-yen*), not of the vernacular language and literature (*pai-hua*). Kircher inserted the curious observation, doubtless gleaned from a missionary rumor, that the Chinese admired the Europeans in their fluency in Latin. Furthermore, Kircher implied that Chinese was less capable of effective communication than Latin, which is patently indemonstrable. Actually, as a written language of communication, Latin played a role in Europe quite similar to that of written Chinese throughout East Asia.

3. KIRCHER'S DESCRIPTION OF CHINESE RELIGIONS

Kircher revealingly entitled his discussion of Chinese religions "On the idolatry of the Chinese"[69]. To the contemporary reader, much of what Kircher said will be irritating and the tendency may be to dismiss him as intellectually crippled by his Europocentrism. But Kircher had one of the most inquisitive minds of an age which prized the "curious", that is, the unfamiliar, abstruse or speculative. It is too easy to dismiss Kircher as content with the European-Christian framework, though, as we have seen, he was often limited by it. Early in his priestly vocation, Kircher is said to have expressed the desire to become a missionary to China[70]. Kircher's superiors had other plans for him and he was a good enough Jesuit to submit. However, it is a compliment to the Jesuits and

---

69 Kircher, *China illustrata* p. 131.
70 Kircher is said to have expressed the wish to the General of the Society of Jesus in 1629 to serve Christianity in China. See the article on Kircher by Adolf Müller in the *Catholic Encyclopedia* (New York, 1907) VIII, 662.

to the Roman Catholic Church of Kircher's day that they encouraged and sponsored his investigations into fields as diverse as acoustics, musical theory, chemistry, medicine, mathematics, optics, geography, archeology, philology and philosophy. He organized a remarkable museum of natural history and was an active investigator who had himself lowered on a rope into the volcano of Mount Vesuvius. If today we can see only the superficiality in Kircher's work — which is indeed there — perhaps it is because we are so bound by the values of specialized scholarship that we are numb to the excitement which breadth of knowledge stirs. Perhaps it is first necessary to cultivate sensitivity to this Baroque ideal in learning. Perhaps only then can we begin to understand how the integrity of Kircher's fascination with China and the world blended, for better or worse, with his cultural blindness to perceiving the new and unique in China. And in the process we may perhaps see how a spirit of inquiry which was contributing to the European Scientific Revolution could be at the same time chauvinistic and insular.

Kircher's division of Chinese religions into three branches[71] might have been derived from Ricci-Trigault[72], from Martini's *Atlas*[73], or from other sources in that it was a widely held and not inaccurate description. But Kircher's use of the Chinese term *San-chiao* (Three Religions) specifically derived from the Ming period cultural climate which attempted to syncretize the Three Teachings into one. Kircher claimed that the Chinese regarded this tripartite division as universal. By this, he meant that the Chinese denied the existence of lands beyond the confines of their empire, which Kircher defined as China, Japan, Korea, Tongking and Cochinchina or wherever Chinese characters were used. Here Kircher confused the slant of the Chinese worldview with what the Chinese knew to exist. They had been aware of Europe since the time of the silk trade with the Roman Empire. Although that trade had lapsed, contact with Europe had been revived under the trans-Asian rule of the Mongols. During the thirteenth and fourteenth centuries, a number of Franciscans made journeys to China, in addition to the famous journey of Marco Polo to Kublai Khan's Chinese court in the years 1271–1295. In the early years of the Ming Dynasty and just prior to when missionaries such as Ricci came to China, the rulers had sponsored extensive naval voyages led by the eunuch admiral Cheng Ho (1371–1433), some of which reached East Africa and Aden on the Red Sea. Basically what Kircher misunderstood is that Chinese cultural chauvinism regarded China as the center, not the extent, of the world.

Kircher described the Three Religions as (1) the sect of the savants, i.e. Confucianism; (2) the sect of "Sciequia", i.e. *Shih-chia* or Sakyamuni, the historical Buddha; and (3) the sect of "Lancu", i.e. Lao-tzu or the traditional founder of Taoism. Kircher believed that these three sects corresponded to

71 Kircher, *China illustrata*, p. 131.
72 Ricci-Trigault, *Journals*, p. 94.
73 Martini, *Atlas*, p. 7.

the three different states of man and — in a pattern which recurred with distressing regularity — compared the Chinese situation to his hypothetical image of ancient Egyptian society with its three-tiered divisions into (1) priests and sages (2) scribes and (3) common people. In the following pages, Kircher argued that the sect of Confucius was composed of priests and sages and that the sect of Lao-tzu had in recent times become the religion of the common people. The parallel between Buddhism and the scribe class was not specifically developed. Kircher correctly conveyed that among the three sects, Confucianism received the greatest esteem and that this esteem was tied to a close association with the government of China. Confucius himself claimed to be basing his teaching upon a tradition which preceded him and perhaps Kircher had absorbed this notion to claim antiquity for the "savant sect". He compared the Chinese esteem of Confucius as a philosopher-prince to the esteem which the Egyptians showed toward their god of learning and magic, Thoth. He noted that the followers of Confucius' sect did not worship idols, but recognized a divinity whom they called "Regem Coelorum" (King of the Heavens), i.e., *Shang-ti*, which is more accurately translated as "Lord of Heaven".

A long quotation from *De Christiana expeditione apud Sinas* reveals a distorted application of the contents by Kircher. He was critical and unsympathetic toward Chinese religions and used this quotation to support his contention that the Chinese were idolatrous. Kircher took this quotation out of context and reversed the tone of the Ricci-Trigault passage by interjecting that the highest Chinese magistrates' sacrifice of sheep and oxen to the gods of heaven and earth was "just like Osiris and Isis of the Egyptians"[74]. This insertion was printed in the same typesetting as the Ricci-Trigault quotation and set off from the latter only by parentheses. As a result, the reader received the false impression that Ricci-Trigault had authored this phrase. Such tampering with quotations was not unique to Kircher, but was widespread in seventeenth-century literary practice. In fact, Trigault did some tampering of his own for while the Ricci-Trigault title of this chapter was "the various *false* religious sects in China" (writer's emphasis), Ricci's original title did not include the word "false"[75]. Furthermore, any such critical tone is contradicted by the strikingly sympathetic general tone toward the Chinese of this Ricci-Trigault chapter. The opening

74 Kircher, *China illustrata*, p. 132. Actually, the quotation from Ricci-Trigault consists of two separate passages which have been run together. See Ricci-Trigault, *De Christiana expeditione*, pp. 107–108. Cf. Ricci-Trigault, *Journals*, pp. 95–96. It is interesting to note that the reference to Isis in this passage in *China illustrata* is found in the Latin edition of 1667 printed by Waesberge, but is omitted from both the Latin edition of Meurs and the French edition of Waesberge.

75 Ricci-Trigault, *De Christiana expeditione*, p. 104, entitled this chapter "Variae apud Sinas falsae Religionis sectae." But Fr. d'Elia's *Fonti Ricciane*, I, 108, shows that Ricci's original title ("Di varie sette che nella Cina sono intorno alla Religione") did not contain the word "false" as a description of the Chinese sects. Perhaps the English translator, Fr. Gallagher, was consciously restoring the original content with his

lines of this chapter, which Kircher did not quote, clearly contradicted Kircher's tendency toward criticizing Chinese religions because of similarities to Western paganism. These lines state:

> Of all the pagan sects known to Europe, I know of no people who fell into fewer errors in the early ages of their antiquity than did the Chinese. From the very beginning of their history it is recorded in their writings that they recognized and worshipped one supreme being whom they called the King of Heaven, or designated by some other name indicating his rule over heaven and earth. . . . Nowhere do we read that the Chinese created monsters of vice out of this supreme being or from ministering deities, such as the Romans, the Greeks, and the Egyptians, evolved into gods or patrons of the vices[76].

Kircher further diverged from the Ricci-Trigault interpretation by following this quotation with a comparison of the Chinese sacrifices to those of the Egyptians toward Mercury on the first day of the month of Thoth. He reinforced the idolatrous emphasis by speaking of the multi-sized statues of Confucius which may be found in every Confucian temple. (See the discussion of the Confucian temples in the chapter on *Confucius Sinarum philosophus.*) In doing to, he neglected the civil and social content of the Confucian rites. For Kircher, as for many other European interpreters of China, it was sufficient to measure what he found in China essentially in terms of Old World polytheisms. This led to an overemphasis upon the external objects of reverence − in this case, the statues of Confucius. Consequently, Kircher was not sufficiently open to learning that in the Confucian context, a bow does not necessarily indicate the presence of a god. Confucius was rarely perceived by his adherents as a deity. What Kircher missed was the whole dimension of Confucian spiritual cultivation, of which the external rites were an important reflection.

The second sect of Chinese religions that Kircher delineated was associated with *Shih-chia* (Sakyamuni), the historical Buddha, Gautama Siddhartha, who lived in India ca. 563−480 B.C. . One wonders if it was a mark of the haste with which Kircher worked or merely due to a printer's error that his romanization of the name *Shih-chia* varied: "Sciequia" on one page became on the following page "Siequia"[77]. This inconsistent spelling was compounded in the French translation by F.S. Dalquie, which inconsistently spelled this name "Sciaguia" or "Sciequia"[78]! As an alternate name for Sakyamuni, Kircher gave "Omyto", which is a romanization of A-mi-to-fu, whom Kircher stated was commonly called "Amida", i.e., the Japanese pronunciation. By "Omyto", Kircher − perhaps unknowingly − was referring to the followers of Amitabha Buddha or to Pure Land Buddhism, a popular form of Buddhism which along with Ch'an (Zen) Buddhism dominated Chinese Buddhism during the Ming dynasty.

   translation of this title as "Religious sects among the Chinese" (Ricci-Trigault, *Journals*, p. 93).

76 Ricci-Trigault, *Journals*, p. 93.
77 Kircher, *China illustrata*, pp. 131 & 132.
78 Kircher, *La Chine illustrée*, pp. 176 & 177..

Kircher's greater criticism of Buddhism than of Confucianism was possibly influenced by the more critical attitude of Ricci-Trigault toward Buddhism. In any case, this pattern of criticism and sympathy toward Buddhism and Confucianism was a pervasive seventeenth-century missionary attitude, particularly among Jesuits. Kircher mollified his criticism with the observation that the Chinese were not fully to blame since "all these errors" and "all these idolatries" were introduced into China from "Indostan" (the region between the Indus and Ganges rivers)[79]. Here dwelt "persons who are offended by science", namely, the Brahmans, Persians and Bactrians. Kircher accurately captured the eastward transmission of Buddhism from India to China, though he seemed unaware that it was achieved not by the establishment of Indian colonies in China, but rather by the indirect means of Indian Buddhist missionary transmissions to central Asia and thence, by central Asian monks, to China.

Yet in spite of the harsh criticism, Kircher attributed to Buddhism something which he denied to Confucianism, namely, a "shadow" of the Christian Gospel. In all probability, he was following the views of someone more knowledgeable than himself. Martini's name was given as a source, but it is clear that Ricci-Trigault were a source as well[80]. As "proof" of this shadow of Christianity in Buddhism, Kircher cited certain unspecified Spanish missionaries who saw in the region of Peking a three-headed male idol. The Chinese explanation of this image spoke of the unity of will and desire in this image[81]. This three-in-one significance was regarded as a vestige of the Christian Trinity. According to Kircher, these Spanish sources also claimed to have seen an image of a woman carrying an infant in her arms, which was interpeted as a vestigial image of the Virgin Mary with the infant Jesus. Kircher also cited Martini's claim of vestiges of the presence of Christianity in the form of ancient crosses and images of the Virgin Mary[82]. Martini may have been confusing the Buddhist bodhisattva of compassion, Kuan-yin, with the Virgin Mary. This was a pervasive confusion which helped to ease the entry of Christianity into China. The matter of a cross was somewhat more ambiguous. There was a cross on the Nestorian Tablet, one of the few firm pieces of evidence for the earlier existence of Christianity in China, but Kircher did not cite this piece of evidence at this point. Rather, he took some of these vestiges to date from St. Thomas the Apostle – the "doubting Thomas" of the Gospels (*John* 20: 25–28) – who was said to have carried Christianity far into Asia. In this point about St. Thomas, as on much of his description of Chinese Buddhism, Kircher probably was drawing from Ricci-Trigault, although Ricci-Trigault are more tentative in their claims than is

79 Kircher, *China illustrata,* p. 132.

80 Martini, *Atlas,* p. 8 & Kircher, *China illustrata,* p. 132.

81 Kircher, *China illustrata,* p. 133. Cf. Ricci-Trigault, *De Christiana expeditione apud Sinas,* p. 111 & Ricci-Trigault, *Journals,* p. 99.

82 Kircher, *China illustrata,* p. 133.

Kircher. Unlike Kircher, Ricci-Trigault gave the source on which the claim that St. Thomas evangelized China is based, namely, the Chaldean breviary of the Malabar church[83].

Kircher concluded his description of Chinese Buddhism by claiming identity between a number of images and temples of this religious group with Egyptian counterparts. Here we have another instance of Kircher's pattern of reducing the unknown to a familiar European framework. He seemed distinctly closed to the possibility that there might have been something new in China, something which was unknown to the European experience and that Europeans might have something to learn from China. (This was the view of Leibniz and other more expansive seventeenth-century minds, though there were serious limitations even in their thinking.) It is interesting that Kircher was a Jesuit who did not share the attitude of accommodation toward China associated with most Jesuits. Like Nicholas Longobardi (1565–1655), a prominent Jesuit of the China Mission, Kircher was able to work with Jesuit proponents of accommodation, such as Martini, and to benefit from the writings of others, such as Ricci. Yet we have already seen that Kircher was able to use their material to draw non-accommodative interpretations.

The third Chinese religion which Kircher described was that of "Lanzu" (Lao-tzu), more familiarly known as Taoism, which was presented as a religion of the common people[84]. Actually, Taoism included so many different varieties that it was sometimes difficult to find a common thread uniting all of them. Parts of Taoism leaned toward the esoteric and other parts leaned toward the popular, while Kircher's description thoroughly confused the two tendencies. The Taoism associated with Lao-tzu was esoteric, spiritual and philosophical, but anti-intellectual. Kircher stated that the Taoists of China corresponded to the class of common people formerly found in Egypt[85]. Kircher's association of Taoism with the common people was not entirely false because by the mid-seventeenth century the Taoist clergy were found predominantly among the uneducated classes of China[86]. Kircher mentioned such

---

83 Ricci-Trigault, pp. 124–125 & *Journals*, p. 113.

84 Kircher, *China illustrata*, p. 133.

85 Kircher added the confusing statement that the Taoists also corresponded to the "*magis*" of Egypt. The French translator, Dalquié, elaborated this to mean that Taoism "anciently ... was the religion of the magi and sages of Egypt." (Cf. Kircher, *China illustrata*, p. 133 with *La Chine illustrée*, p. 179.) However, given Kircher's earlier claim that Confucianism corresponded to the Egyptian priests-wisemen (*Sacerdotibus videlicit Sapientibus*), Buddhism to the Egyptian scribes (*Hierogrammatistis seu hieroglyphis*) and Taoism to the Egyptian common people (*plebeis*) (*China illustrata*, p. 131), Dalquié's elaboration appears unjustified. More likely was that Kircher either mistakenly inserted the parenthetical phrase "*& Magis Aegyptiis*," which is set off by commas, or he meant something else by it other than learned individuals.

86 I find the tendency among some scholars to divide Taoism into "philosophical" and "religious" branches very unsatisfactory. It implies that "philosophical" Taoism is

diverse Taoist practices as the quest for longevity using "medicines" (i.e. the search for the elixir of immortality), exorcisms and sacrifices for rain, but for him the only common thread running through these various elements was their idolatrous nature.

Kircher concluded his account of the three sects of China by commenting that the country was filled with perhaps a thousand idols[87]. Idols were said to be found in temples, houses, fields, villages and palaces — the country was "crammed to all sides" with idols! Kircher then recapitulated his claim that the Chinese were the "true followers of the Egyptians and the faithful imitators of their superstitions". He gave proofs for his claim, though in accordance with the popular character of his work, he limited these proofs to three in number for fear that a more involved argument might become "tedious" to the reader[88]. First, the Chinese imitated the Egyptians and the Greeks in what they believed and they worshipped the same gods, with the same customs and ceremonies. Secondly, the religion or "superstitions" of the Chinese originated in Egypt. Here Kircher drew upon "several letters written in Spanish and Portuguese" (i.e. authored by Spanish and Portuguese missionaries to China) which claimed that there were Chinese temples dedicated to Mars, Venus, Fortune, Peace, to the Oreades, who were the nymphs of the mountains, and to other Egyptian and Greek gods. Thirdly, there were similarities not only between the letters and hieroglyphs of the Chinese and Egyptians, but also between the ceremonies and customs of the two lands. In short, Kircher stated that there were so many similarities between the religions of China, Egypt and Greece, that they appeared to be the same phenomena.

The circular nature of Kircher's three "proofs" need not concern us, except to point out that they largely restated his hypothesis without proving anything. Yet to Kircher's mind — the mind of one of the most prolific and influential scholars of mid-seventeenth century Europe — the evidence for his claims was strong. Part of the responsibility for Kircher's interpretations must be placed with the rigidly simplified and prejudiced minds of certain missionary interpreters. It was not only ignorance, but a refusal to learn that led certain Spanish and Portuguese missionaries — clearly not all, as we have seen from studying Frs. Semedo and Magalhaes — to reinforce Kircher's belief that the Chinese were worshipping the same gods as the Egyptians and Greeks. Yet there were other proto-sinologists in Europe, not very much younger than Kircher, who were coming to very different and far more informed conclusions, while relying largely on the same body of reports from China. Kircher seems to have understood very little of what Ricci was saying when the latter gave glimpses of another

more intellectual and less spiritual than it really is. Furthermore, the distinction does not adequately account for Taoist alchemy.

87 Kircher, *China illustrata*, p. 133.
88 Kircher, *China illustrata*, pp. 133–134.

world which had so fascinated and absorbed him. Ricci had come to know China and to be impressed with the challenge that China presented to his faith. Yet Kircher did not question Ricci's orthodoxy.

One must conclude that Kircher's fascination with China, although admirable in a certain light, was motivated by and confined to an extremely closed world-view. China was grist for the European cultural mill. Christianity was part of that mental set, but it is not Christianity which caused the narrowness. One of the most apt and fascinating demonstrations of this was found in Kircher's study of the Nestorian Monument. Here was Kircher, the Christian of the European setting, looking across years and miles to a record of a very different Christianity, a Christianity which originated with the same Asian Jew, Jesus, but which spread directly eastward to be shaped by an Asian milieu and, finally, to be absorbed into the Chinese viewpoint. All the rich mixing of church and Chinese state, of Christian with Buddhist and Taoist imagery — all the challenging, fascinating elements of this document which would have excited a more open mind simply eluded Kircher. His interest in the Nestorian Monument was limited by his Europocentric motives.

4. THE NESTORIAN MONUMENT

The archeological recovery of ancient artifacts has had a uniquely rich role in China. The antiquity of Chinese culture has combined with the dry climate of the first civilized centers of that land to yield a harvest which continues to flow through the museums of the world. In 1625 in the northwestern province of Shensi, a large stone tablet was accidentally discovered by workmen digging in the suburbs of Sian-fu (modern Sian). (See plate 12.) This was the region of the ancient T'ang capital of Ch'ang-an[89]. The tablet was just over nine feet in height, three and one-half feet in width and just under one foot in thickness. The stone consisted of a black, sub-granular oolitic limestone[90]. The text of the inscription contained approximately 1,780 characters in addition to the characters, mostly names of priests, in the margins. The text was clearly inscribed in thirty vertical columns which gave a remarkably aesthetic appearance. The tablet also contained approximately fifty words and seventy names in Syriac or Estangelo which were placed along the right, left and bottom borders. There

89 There are several accounts of the details of the discovery of the Nestorian Tablet which differ on the exact location in Hsian-fu, the exact date of recovery and the exact circumstances by which the find was made. However, all agree that the Tablet was recovered near Hsian-fu between 1623 and early 1625 and was dug out of the ground. I have chosen to present the more probable details in the text. For a description of the varying theories, see P. Y. Saeki, *The Nestorian Monument in China* (London, 1916) pp. 15–16 & 20–22.
90 Saeki, p. 12.

was some decoration, including a cross in relief, in a semi-circular area at the top of the tablet[91] .

We now know that this tablet originated with the Nestorian or Assyrian church, a Christian body born out of controversy. It spread throughout Asia and survives today in widely dispersed fragments. The church took its name from Nestorius (ca. 385–451), bishop of Constantinople. Nestorius identified with the position that the term *Theotokos* (Mother of God) should not be applied to Mary, a human, because it diminished the divinity of Jesus. Nestorius' chief opponent was Cyril (412–444), bishop of Alexandria, who believed that Nestorius' position was undermining the unity of the dual (i.e. God-man) nature of Christ. In addition, Cyril was motivated by wordly ambition to diminish the power of the rival see of Constantinople. After considerable ecclesistical maneuvering, Nestorius was defeated and exiled by the Roman emperor to the east where he and his followers established the Assyrian church, which spread throughout Asia.

According to the Nestorian Monument, a missionary named A-lo-pen introduced Nestorianism to China in 631, after which it grew with imperial support until its peak in 781, when the tablet was erected. The tablet probably was buried to avoid destruction in the great religious persecution of 845 which though primarily anti-Buddhist, also affected Nestorian Christians. The damage inflicted on the church in this persecution was so extensive that it failed to revive in China[92] . However, Nestorian Christianity was practiced by the Mongols and was again carried to China where it was witnessed in this form by Marco Polo in the thirteenth century.

The characters of the Nestorian Monument inscription appearing in Kircher's *China illustrata* were carefully reproduced within blocks and numbered according to both columns and characters[93]. The Latin translation of the inscription was

91 There is a very clear photograph of the tablet and rubbings of all characters and words appearing on the tablet in Havret, no. 7.
92 Saeki's claim that the Nestorians were absorbed by the secret society, *Chin-tan chiao*, and by the Chinese Moslems appears entirely ungrounded. See Saeki, p. 49.
93 In the copy of the Nestorian Monument inscription appearing in Kircher's *China illustrata*, the columns range from 0 (the title column) to 29. The maximal number of characters per column is 62. But because of the occasional blocks left empty – usually to designate a break in the inscription – the average is closer to 61 characters per column. The result is such that an efficient means of reference is possible by citing the column number and the character number of any given word, e.g. 17.29. Although most characters were individually numbered, there were frequent exceptions. Grammatical particles such as *chih* and *yeh* were not numbered. Binoms such as *hua-tsai* (wealth) (7.29), *so-i* (therefore) (7.9) and *t'ien-hsia* (world) (8.39) were assigned one number each and this would have been clear evidence to refute the widely held seventeenth century European belief that all Chinese words consisted of only one character. Single numbers also were assigned to names, such as T'ai-tsung Wen ([Emperor] T'ai-tsung the Accomplished) (8.39) and Su-tsung Wen-ming ([Emperor] Su-tsung the Accomplished and Enlightened) (17.43).

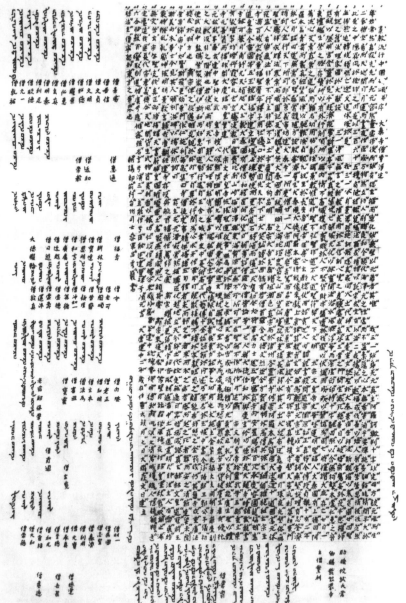

Plate 12. A reproduction of the text of the Nestorian Monument of Sian-fu, China, from Athanasius Kircher, *China illustrata* (Amsterdam, 1667). Courtesy of the Niedersächsische Landesbibliothek Hannover.

dated at Rome November 4th 1654 and was signed by three names: "P. Michael Boim. Andreas Don Sin, Sina. Matthaeus Sina."[94]. The first two are easily identified as Fr. Boym and Andreas Cheng An-to-le, who accompanied Boym from China. "Mattheus Sina" (the Chinese Matthew) was probably not, as has been claimed, an alternative name for Joseph Kuo Jo-hsi, who also was supposed to have accompanied Boym to Europe, but who, because of illness, remained in China. Pelliot believed this Matthew to have been the Chinese who accompanied Fr. Grueber on his journey from Peking through central Asia and who was in Rome during the first half of 1664 when the final transcription of the tablet for *China illustrata* was apparently made. This Matthew is said to have died in Constantinople in 1665[95]. Kircher's presentation of this inscription to European readers in a clearly printed and efficiently numbered manner was a significant scholarly contribution to European knowledge about China. Unfortunately, the level of sinological competence in Europe was not sufficiently developed to appreciate this presentation until the nineteenth century. Most later interpreters of the inscription have not made use of the column and character numbers, but a student of the Nestorian Monument still benefits by consulting the *China illustrata* presentation.

The Nestorian inscription may be divided into three sections in terms of content. The first part (columns 1.1–8.36) deals with Nestorian theology. It presents the doctrine of a personal God (A-lo-a), Creator, the Fall, the Incarnation of Christ, the Trinity and the Ascension. Although the Crucifixion of Jesus is not specifically mentioned, the symbol of the Crucifixion — the cross — was said to be carried by the Nestorians. The second part of the inscription (columns 8.35–24.20) deals with the historical arrival of the missionary A-lopen in Ch'ang-an in 635 and the growth of the "Illumined religion" (*Chingchiao*) with imperial support which continued until the year 781 when the inscription was composed. The naming of emperors and reign periods provided crucial chronological points of reference. The third part (columns 24.21–29.58) consists of eulogistic prayers in verse form.

Fr. Semedo was the first European to examine the Nestorian Monument and his account in *Imperio de la China* was one of the first published reports to reach European readers[96]. Semedo recorded that the missionaries had received several reports on the previous presence of certain Christian practices in China, such as making the sign of the Cross. One of these reports had been given to the fathers at Peking by about 1610 by a Jew who claimed that approximately 600 years before, a large number of worshippers of the Cross had lived in northern China. They were said to have acquired such a good reputation in the sciences

94 Kircher, *China illustrata*, p. 10.
95 Pfister, p. 270n, on the basis of a misreading of Kircher's *China illustrata*, makes the identification of this Matthew with Andreas Cheng An-te-lo. Pelliot makes the correction in his "Michael Boym," pp. 112–113.
96 Semedo, *Histoire universalle de la Chine*, pp. 227–240.

and military arms that the jealousy of the Chinese was aroused and the worshippers were dispersed. Others were reported as having gone underground or dissimulated Moslem or Jewish beliefs[97]. It is possible that this Jew was reporting on Mongolians who had embraced Nestorian Christianity. But neither this report nor any other on the previous existence of Christianity in China had been confirmed until the discovery of the Nestorian Monument. Consequently, Semedo was exceedingly impressed with the discovery.

Semedo claimed that the Nestorian stone was recovered in 1625 by workmen digging a foundation for a building near Sian-fu. He described the dimensions and the prominent physical characteristics of the stone. He noted that in addition to the Chinese characters, there were several foreign words in the inscription. He was unable to identify these until later when, passing through Cochin-China, he consulted with Fr. Antony Fernandez, who was familiar with the writings of the early "Christians of St. Thomas"[98]. Here Semedo was referring to the Malabar Church of southeast India, traditionally claimed to have been founded by St. Thomas the Apostle. This church had ties with the Nestorian church and at one point had used a Syriac liturgy. Fr. Fernandez identified the puzzling script on the Nestorian Monument as Syriac.

Semedo wrote that upon discovering this stone, the workmen immediately reported the find to the Chinese governor, who soon visited the site. The governor had the stone elevated on a pedestal and covered with a protective roof. Furthermore, he wished the stone to be cared for by a Buddhist monastery nearby. Semedo stated that many people visited the stone after its recovery. Some were intrigued by its antiquity and some by the novelty of its characters. When Chang Keng-yu learned of the tablet, he recognized the Christian content of the inscription and sent a copy to his friend, the Christian convert and literatus, Leon Li Chih-tsao in Hangchow. Chang had met Ricci in Peking in 1607 and possibly was himself a Christian[99]. After a month and a half, the copy of the inscription is said to have reached Li, who shared it with the Christian fathers in the region. It was through this means that Semedo first learned of the stone and consequently visited the site in Sian-fu sometime between 1625 and 1628[100].

---

97 Semedo, p. 226.

98 Semedo, p. 229.

99 Havret, no. 12, p. 38.

100 Semedo was not clear about when he visited the Nestorian Monument. He stated that "three years afterwards, which was the year 1620, several of us fathers were passing through this province [Sian-fu]." Since the time reference appears to have been the year of the discovery of the Nestorian Monument, I suspect that 1625 rather than 1620 was intended. If my suspicion is accurate, Semedo visited Sian-fu in 1628. In any case, Legge cites 1628 as the date of Semedo's visit to Sian-fu (James Legge, The Nestorian Monument of Hsi-an fu (London, 1888) p. 36). However, both Pfister, p. 144, and Dehergne, Répertoire, p. 245, state that Semedo visited Sian-fu in 1625.

News of the discovery of the tablet spread rapidly to Europe. A French translation based on a Latin version of the Nestorian Monument text by Fr. Trigault is said to have been published in 1628[101]. The Jesuit Manuel Diaz, the Younger (1574–1659) sent a Portuguese translation of the Chinese text from Macao on November 21st 1627. This was translated into Italian and published anonymously in the form of a sixteen-page pamphlet in 1631. The text was retranslated into Latin and published by Kircher in his *Prodromus Coptus sive Aegyptiacus* (1636). A rubbing of the tablet also had been received in Rome and was placed in Kircher's museum[102]. Semedo's account was first published in 1641.

The European response to the Nestorian Monument was filled with skepticism from the first reports of the tablet's recovery. The skepticism was fed by such widespread suspicion and distrust of the Jesuits that the debate over the authenticity of the tablet occupied the better part of three centuries. The prominent seventeenth-century doubters included Georg Horn, Gottlieb Spitzel (Spizelius) and Domingo Navarrete. The eighteenth-century skeptics included Mathurin de Lacroze (1661–1739) and Voltaire. In the nineteenth century, the debate became less religious and political in coloring and more academic. The chief doubters were scholars and academics, such as the Orientalist Karl Friedrich Newmann of the University of Munich, the sinologist Stanislas Julien of the Collége de France, a scholar of Arabic and Sanskrit at Yale College in the United States named Edward S. Salisbury and the scholar Ernst Renan, whose works on Semetic languages and Biblical studies were widely published.

The tide began to turn in the mid-1800s and, significantly, the non-Jesuit defenders increased in number. These included the English sinologists Alexander Wylie and James Legge and the French sinologist Jean-Pierre-Guillaume Pauthier. But the most definitive work on the subject was written by a Jesuit – Henri Havret's *Le stèle chrétienne de Si-ngan-fou* (1895–1902) in three volumes. After Fr. Havret's work, the authenticity of the Nestorian Monument was no longer seriously questioned. It was only after the intense seventeenth- and eighteenth-century anti-Jesuit pressures had receded, that an atmosphere prevailed where scholars were able to resolve the problem. Today the tablet can be found preserved in the Pei-lin (Forest of Stone Tablets) in Sian, the locale of its recovery[103].

When Kircher first published his account of the Nestorian Monument in *Prodromus Coptus sive Aegyptiacus*, far more than scholarly pressures impinged. The critics were either anti-Catholic Protestants or anti-Jesuit Roman Catholics.

Following his statement quoted above, Semedo presented a fairly detailed account of the contents of the Inscription. (See Semedo, pp. 230–239.)

101 Henri Cordier, *Bibliotheca Sinica* (Paris, 1905–1906) col. 773.
102 Kircher, *China illustrata*, p. 395.
103 I am indebted for this information to Mr. Lundbaek who in July 1982 visited the pre-servation-site of the Nestorian Monument in Sian.

Georg Horn was born in Germany in 1620, but studied in Holland and lived for a time in England where he converted to Presbyterianism. He eventually became a professor at the university of Haiderwyk and later at Leiden. In 1652 Horn published his *De originibus Americanis*. In this work he stated that the Nestorian Monument was clearly a Jesuit fraud invented to deceive the Chinese — whether the deception was for the purposes of conversion or power was not clarified, though it was probably thought to be the latter — or to sieze their treasures[104]. A second attack came from Gottlieb Spitzel (Spizelius) (1639–1691). Spitzel was an historian and preacher at Augsburg. In his *De re literaria Sinensium commentarius* (Leiden 1660), he sought to establish a connection between Chinese, Egyptian, Greek and Indian philosophic and religious conceptions of the world[105]. However, the Nestorian Monument did not fit into his conception. Spitzel said that the Chinese were silent on the Creator, with the single exception of the Nestorian Monument presented by Kircher in *Prodromus Coptus*. Spitzel attempted to banish the contradictory element by claiming that the tablet was a recent composition by some Christian Chinese doctor, presumably a reference to someone like Li Chih-tsao or Hsü Kuang-ch'i[106].

A third doubter came from within missionary ranks. Domingo Navarrete (1618–1686) was a Dominican monk who resided in China from 1658 until 1670. He returned to Madrid in 1674 and proceeded to write *Tratados historicos, politicos, ethicos, y religiosos de la monarchia de China* (Madrid 1676). Although sympathetic to the Chinese, this work was anti-Jesuit and the Society of Jesus attempted to have it suppressed[107]. The work was translated and summarized into English, French, German and Italian and became particularly popular in England. In France, the work's anti-Jesuit potential was exploited by the Jansenists. Voltaire thought Friar Navarrete a sage and Quesnay and the Physiocrats were influenced by him[108]. Navarrete doubted the authenticity of the Nestorian Monument on the grounds that the meticulously tended Chinese records and histories contained no mention of the events described on the tablet. Furthermore, he noted that the Chinese themselves questioned the tablet's authenticity[109]. Time has shown Navarrete to be mistaken on both counts. First, the events described on the tablet have been confirmed by the Chinese records and, secondly, there was little evidence of widespread Chinese

---

104 See Havret, no. 12, pp. 263–264 and G. Horn, *De originibus Americanis,* ch. 15 of the last book.
105 R. F. Merkel, "Deutsche Chinaforsche," *Archiv für Kulturgeschichte* 34 (1951): 83.
106 Spizelius, pp. 159–160.
107 See the Hakluyt Society, *The Travels and Controversies of Fray Domingo Navarrete, 1618–1686* J. S. Cummins, ed. (Cambridge, 1962).
108 See J. S. Cummins, "Fray Domingo Navarrete: a Source for Quesnay," *Bulletin of Hispanic Studies* 36 (1959): 37–50.
109 Hakluyt Society, *Travels of Navarrete,* pp. 104–105.

skepticism of the tablet's authenticity. The doubt was far more a European phenomenon which sprang from sectarian rather than scholarly grounds.

Aside from Navarrete's claim, which came later, these publicly expressed doubts appear to have been a primary motivation for Kircher's expanded treatment of the Nestorian Monument in *China illustrata* beyond that found in *Prodromus Coptus*. With the visits of knowledgeable China missionaries to Rome, Kircher's information on the stone was developed by first-hand observers, a rare luxury for a European scholar of that time. Semedo came in 1642, Boym came in 1652–1655 and Martini in 1654–1656. The section of *China illustrata* dealing with the Nestorian Monument was the first and most famous part of the book. The major contributor to this section was Boym. The latter's relatively short residence in China of less than eight years divided between south China, Macao and Tongking was insufficient to allow him to acquire the knowledge needed to translate such a difficult text as the Nestorian Monument inscription. The assistance he received is reflected in the signatures of the two Chinese at the end of the Latin translation of the inscription and mentioned by name above[110]. The ingenious tonal system which Boym used in transliterating the inscription was not his invention, but was derived from the Jesuit Lazzaro Cattaneo (1560–1640)[111]. Nevertheless, Boym seems to have been the moving force behind the translation of the Nestorian Monument. It was probably Boym who assigned numerals to the columns and characters in the inscription, delegated translation tasks to his Chinese assistants and then incorporated the results into the final whole. In short, Boym probably presented Kircher with a fairly complete manuscript for incorporation into *China illustrata*.

Kircher's "curious" style of scholarship was expansively detailed, but the details were not always carefully presented. Kircher's casualness in this regard sometimes produced confusion. In the seventeenth century, the false belief arose among Europeans that there was a facsimile tablet of the Nestorian Monument. This belief was traced by Fr. Havret to Kircher who first made such a claim in his *Prodromus coptus* and then repeated the claim in *China illustrata* even though in the same work he included a letter from Boym disproving his claim[112]! A second example of Kircher's carelessness was his contradictory

110 Kircher, *China illustrata*, p. 10.
111 Goodrich, pp. 21 & 32. Cf. Boleslaw Szcześniak in "The beginning of Chinese Lexicography in Europe with Particular Reference to the Work of Michael Boym (1612–1659)," *Journal of the American Oriental Society* 67 (1947): 163, where Szcześniak claims that the system of transliteration was Boym's invention. This claim is denied by Walter Simon, p. 169.
112 Athanasius Kircher, *Prodromus coptus sive Aegyptiacus* (Rome, 1636) p. 50 & Havret, no. 12, p. 41. Twenty years after Kircher first claimed in his *Prodromus coptus* that there existed a facsimile tablet of the Nestorian Monument, Martini repeated Kircher's claim in almost identical terms in his *Novus atlas Sinensis,* p. 44. After extended discussion with Semedo and Boym, who were in positions to clarify the misunderstanding, Kircher repeated this claim of a facsimile tablet in *China illustrata* and added as

claims for the discovery of the Nestorian Monument, namely, prior to 1581 and in 1625[113]. Yet another example of Kircher's lack of meticulousness was his inclusion in *China illustrata* of three different site locations for the discovery of the Nestorian Monument without reconciling the contradictions[114].

5. CONCLUSION

Kircher's *China illustrata* was an important part of the seventeenth-century process by which Jesuits funneled information about China back to Europe. However, the work clearly reflected some of the tensions between the Jesuit missionaries and the proto-sinologists. Because of the conflict between the China Jesuits' accommodation policy and Kircher's Hermetic outlook, the information in *China illustrata* was presented in an inconsistent mixture of theoretical elements. The broad readership of this work enabled it to play a major role in the European assimilation of an encyclopedic range of information about the geography, language, religion and even fauna of China. However, much of this information was distorted by Kircher's Hermetism which treated Chinese culture as a pale and inferior reflection of the archetypal paganism of Egypt. In his formulation of Jesuit accommodation in China, Ricci had barely mentioned the Egyptians and Greeks in the process of interpreting ancient Chinese culture as anticipating Old and New Testament truths. But the Hermetic framework entered into Jesuit accommodation soon after Ricci's time. At first it was merely implicit, as in Li Tsu-po's treatise *T'ien-hsüeh ch'uan-kai* (1664) on which Magalhaes and Buglio collaborated. But by the end of the seventeenth century, Hermetism was to become explicit in the form of Figurism.

The tensions which the Jesuits in China faced were shaped by mission strategy, but many of these tensions were essentially intellectual. The weight of the Confucian and other Chinese cultural traditions forced the Jesuits to compete on a very high intellectual level if they were to capture the minds and souls of the

support the authority of Martini, who had possibly copied the claim out of Kircher's *Prodromus coptus!* The false claim was far less excusable the second time around since Kircher included in his *China illustrata* a letter from Boym dated November 4th 1653 which clarified that the local governor had written a commemoration on the Nestorian Monument's discovery which was engraved on a stone tablet similar to that of the Nestorian Monument. (*China illustrata*, p. 8 & Havret, no. 12, p. 41). Furthermore, prior to the publication of *China illustrata*, Daniello Bartoli's *Dell' Istoria della Compagnia di Giesù. La Cina* (1663) had given a correct account. (Havret, no. 12, p. 42).

113 These contradictory claims for the discovery of the Nestorian Monument were first made in *Prodromus coptus*, pp. 50 & 71. Boym and Martini later cited the correct date of 1625 and Fr. Bartoli's *La Cina* had noted Kircher's contradiction without naming Kircher. Yet Kircher's *China illustrata* repeated the contradictory dates (*China illustrata*, pp. 5 (1625), 8 (1625) and 34 (a few years prior to 1581). Also see Havret, no. 12, p. 47.

114 *China illustrata*, pp. 5, 7, 8 & Havret, no. 12, p. 60.

Chinese literati. Kircher's *China illustrata* was shaped more by his encyclopedic curiosity about the world than by an appreciation for the unique tensions of the China Mission[115]. He lacked the deeper interest and intellectual sympathy for Chinese culture found not only among some of his confreres in China, but also among increasing numbers of European savants, many of whom participated in the search for a universal language, to which we now turn.

---

115 The current state of scholarly interest in Kircher is described by Fred Brauen, "Athanasius Kircher (1602–1680)" in the *Journal of the History of Ideas* 43 (1982): 129–134. Kircher's papers and letters are being collected, edited and published by the Internationalen Athanasius Kircher Forschungsgesellschaft e.V. of Wiesbaden and Rome.

CHAPTER VI
PROTO-SINOLOGY AND THE SEVENTEENTH-CENTURY EUROPEAN SEARCH FOR A UNIVERSAL LANGUAGE

1. INTRODUCTION

The European search for a *lingua universalis* (universal language) belongs, to a large extent, to the realm of proto-sinology. With the books based on missionary sources containing information about the Chinese and their culture, Europeans now had the ingredients for assimilating China into European culture. Some of the assimilation was done by missionaries even as they were conveying information about China. For example, Martini was not only informing Europeans of the basic facts of Chinese history, but also was adapting the European historical framework to accept it through a shift from the Vulgate to the Septuagint-based Biblical chronology. But for this information about China to be assimilated to European culture in a broader and deeper way, it would be necessary for Europeans with only pedestrian knowledge of China to be stimulated to incorporate China into their non-sinological research. This is precisely what happened in the search for a universal language.

The proto-sinological involvement of savants such as Francis Bacon, John Webb, Kircher, Andreas Müller, Christian Mentzel and Gottfried Leibniz with integrating the Chinese language into the search for a universal language confirms the degree to which China was assimilated into a primary current of seventeenth-century European intellectual history. But because these investigators were sinological amateurs with information about China inadequate to supply their sophisticated linguistic theories, much of what they concluded strikes us today as ridiculous. The difficulty of sorting out the substantive from the ludicrous is particularly apparent in one intellectual by-product of the search for a universal language, namely, the attempt focused at Berlin to develop a *Clavis Sinica* (Key to Chinese) which would simplify and expedite the learning of the Chinese language. While it is relatively easy to dismiss Müller and Mentzel as idiosyncratic mentalities, it is less easy to dismiss the intense interest in the *Clavis Sinica* by eminent and brilliant figures of the age such as Leibniz and Adam Kochanski.

2. THE BIBLICAL BACKGROUND: THE LOSS OF THE ADAMIC LANGUAGE AT BABEL

The seventeenth-century European search for a *lingua universalis* was the fruit of the cross-fertilization of Biblical tradition, a medieval idea, the sixteenth-century discovery voyages and seventeenth-century science. The European discovery of many new Asian languages conflicted with the traditional European division of languages into sacred and profane, classical and oriental, living and dead. This newfound linguistic complexity revived the Biblical conception of the proliferation of tongues at Babel[1].

Drawing from the Bible (*Genesis* 2: 19–20), many Europeans believed that God had given Adam a pure, exact and utterly simple language[2]. This language – variously referred to as the *lingua Adamica*, the *lingua humana* or the Primitive Language – was thought to have been spoken originally by all of Adam's descendants, i.e. all mankind. But somewhat later, human *hubris* led to the building of the Tower of Babel, which symbolized human competition with God (*Genesis* 11: 1–9). This act was said to have so aroused God's anger that he scattered mankind across the earth and confused their simple language into a proliferation of languages. What particularly inspired the seekers of a *lingua universalis* was the Biblical statement which began the story of Babel: "Now the whole earth had one language and few words" (Revised Standard Version). These dual characteristics of unity and simplicity became the fundamental criteria in the search for a universal language in which the Chinese language was an important model.

3. A MEDIEVAL IDEA: RAMON LULL'S *ARS COMBINATORIA*

The search for a *lingua universalis* also drew from a medieval heritage traceable to the Spanish mystic, Ramon Lull (ca. 1232–1316)[3]. Lull stood apart from the Scholastic mainstream in training and outlook, though his work reflected the Scholastic merging of spirituality with methodical intellect. He studied informally at Mallorca rather than at the cultural center of Paris and he never acquired a fluent Latin style. Consequently, he wrote in his native Catalan and became a pioneer in the use of vernacular language. This less orthodox training gave freer play to his powerful creativity and made him more open to influences from a less well-known Scholastic thinker such as Scotus Erigina, from Kabbalism and from Arabic writings. The Christian reconquest of Mallorca

1 Donald F. Lach, *Asia in the making of Europe* (Chicago, 1977) II, 3, 520–525.

2 For an extended treatment of the Adamic language, see Russell Fraser, *The language of Adam* (New York, 1977).

3 In the following biographical information, I draw from the article on Lull by R. D. F. Pring-Mill in *The dictionary of scientific biography* (New York, 1973) VIII, 547–551.

from the Moors created a unique spiritual atmosphere in which the conversion of Moslems became a key concern for Lull. Consequently, he developed an "Art of Finding Truth" for the clearly spiritual purpose of converting Moors through reason rather than through authority.

The first form of Lull's Art followed a spiritual illumination of unity revealed to him on Mount Randa, Mallorca in about 1273. In this vision, Lull saw how things could be referred to God through His divine attributes or Dignities and these became the basis of his Art. The Lullian Art was highly numerological and symbolic. The divine attributes were reduced gradually from sixteen to nine in number. In the *Ars Brevis* (1308), Lull presented his illumination in the form of a table containing the "Alphabet of the Art"[4]. This table consisted of a grid-like presentation of the six Sets (Absolute Predicates, Relative Predicates, Questions, Subjects, Virtues and Defects) arranged down the left-hand side of the table and the nine members of the Alphabet arranged across the top. Lull derived an Alphabet from his Art by assigning nine letters (*B, C, D, E, F, G, H, I* and *K*) to the nine members. The letter *A* was placed in the upper, left-hand corner of the table as representing a trinity of Essence, Unity and Perfection. The tabular juxtaposition of the six Sets and nine members of the Alphabet Yielded 54 possible combinations[5]. The Absolute Predicates (Goodness, Greatness, Eternity, Power, Knowledge, Will, Excellence, Truth and Honor) represented the divine attributes or Dignities of Lull's Art.

We are indebted to Frances Yates' meticulous investigation into a now obscure tradition for the realization that Lullism, besides being a combinatory art, was also an art of memory[6]. The art of mnemotechnics, which was of crucial importance prior to the widespread use of printing, sought to increase one's powers of memorization through the use of contemporary architecture and images. Because of his distance from the main intellectual developments

4 A photographic reproduction of this table of the "Alphabet of the Art" appears in Frances Yates' "The art of Ramon Lull," *Journal of the Warburg & Courtauld Institute* 17 (1954): figure 8a (facing p. 116).

5 The six Lullian Sets are: (1) Absolute Predicates (2) Relative Predicates (3) Questions (4) Subjects (5) Virtues and (6) Defects. The first set of B-K (Absolute Predicates) are: (B) Goodness (C) Greatness (D) Eternity (E) Power (F) Knowledge (G) Will (H) Excellence (I) Truth and (K) Honor. The second set of B-K (Relative Predicates) form groups of three and are: (B) Difference (C) Accord and (D) Opposition; (E) Beginning (F) Middle and (G) End; (H) More (I) Equal and (K) Less. The third set of B-K (Questions) are: (B) Whether? (C) Who? Which? What? (D) From What? (E) Why? (F) How Much? (G) What Kind? (H) When? (I) Where? and (K) How?. The fourth set of B-K (Subjects) are: (B) God (C) Angel (D) Heaven (E) Man (F) Imagination (G) Sensation (H) Vegetation (I) Element; First Principle and (K) Instrumentality. The fifth set of B-K (Virtues) are: (B) Justice (C) Wisdom (D) Bravery (E) Moderation (F) Faith (G) Hope (H) Charity (I) Patience and (K) Piety. The sixth set of B-K (Defects) are: (B) Avarice (C) Gluttony (D) Extravagance (E) Pride (F) Disagreeableness (G) Envy (H) Anger (I) Lying and (K) Inconstancy.

6 See Frances Yates, *The Art of memory* (London, 1966) pp. 173–198.

of Scholasticism, Lull did not draw from the classical tradition on the art of memory which traced itself to ancient Greece. Rather, he drew from the Augustinian, Platonic and Neoplatonic traditions. According to Ms. Yates, Lull's most significant contribution in the history of thought was to introduce movement into the previously static art of memory. Such Lullian devices as the revolving concentric circles or revolving triangles within circles were attempts to capture movements of the mind[7]. Lull's art of memory would later be an influence upon Leibniz in the context of his search for a universal language.

It was not the specific content of Lull's primary classification so much as the *Ars combinatoria* (Combinatory Art), or method of combining these primary elements to yield answers, which had such an enormous influence on later thinkers. In one particularly influential arrangement, the six Lullian Sets were aligned on the bodies of concentric circles of graduated sizes with a common pivot. By turning these circles to obtain differing alignments, one could mechanically determine the various possible combinations. (See plate 13.) In his novel, *Blanquerna*, Lull expressed his aim of establishing one language, one belief and one faith in the world. In spite of his pioneering work in the vernacular and his creative inclinations, Lull's proposal for a universal language took the form of universalizing the language of the Church, Latin, rather than creating a new language[8]. However, Lull probably saw the quest for a universal language as subsidiary to his Art.

Although Lull's ideas influenced such major European figures as Nicholas of Cusa (1401–1464), Pico della Mirandola (1463–1494), John Dee (1527–1608), Cornelius Agrippa (1486–1535) and Giordano Bruno (1548–1600), the historical conditions were not ripe for a Lullian influence on the quest for a universal language until the seventeenth century. The seventeenth-century vision of the world was so unlike our own, that a conscious jump is needed to see through those lost eyes. Today, we tend to see Adam's Fall in the book of *Genesis* in purely moral terms, but this is an impoverishment of an earlier view of the Bible. Athanasius Kircher's *Turris Babel* (1679) presented Adam in a deeper light. While his Fall caused a deterioration in his senses, his reason remained as pure as it had been prior to the Fall[9].

Kircher believed that this pure reason caused Adam to receive language from God in fully developed form. There was no gradual process of linguistic evolution in the Primitive Language and it was truly a universal language. The identification of the Primitive Language was a major concern of seventeenth-century scholars. Some believed that this language was Samaritan. Others believed that

7 Yates, p. 176.
8 Lull expressed this view through the character of Saint Peter in chapter 94 of his novel, *Blanquerna*. See Joaquin Carreras y Artau, *De Ramón Lull a los modernos ensayos de formación de una lengua universal* (Barcelona, 1946) pp. 7–8.
9 See Paul Cornelius, *Languages in 17th and early 18th century imaginary voyages* (Geneva, 1965) p. 7f.

it was Chaldean, Gothic, Phoenician or Chinese. However, Kircher and most seventeenth-century scholars prior to the 1670s, believed that the Primitive Language was primitive Hebrew and held that it had remained uncorrupted throughout the early history of the Jews. Noah's descendants were said to have carried this language throughout the world where it was universally propagated until the confusion of tongues at Babel. Some scholars attempted to reconstruct the Primitive Language by studying Biblical sources. A burning question concerned *when* the Hebrews had stopped using the Primitive Language and scholars pored over the Bible searching for clues. Other scholars, such as Kircher, did not believe it possible to reconstruct the primitive characters and instead proposed the creation of a new universal language.

4. CHINESE AS THE PRIMITIVE LANGUAGE

The extent to which China stimulated the seventeenth-century reading public is apparent in a little book by the Englishman John Webb entitled *An historical essay endeavoring a probability that the language of the Empire of China is the Primitive Language* (London 1669). John Webb (1611–1672) never claimed to be anything but a layman where knowledge of China was concerned. He was led to an interest in China because of the way China seemed to dovetail with the general interest of his age in Biblical concerns, and specifically in the notion of a Primitive Language. Unburdened by the enormous problems then facing students of the Chinese language, Webb could afford to be more creative. It was his creative thesis in regard to China that makes this essay so fascinating for the modern reader[10].

Webb lacked the direct missionary contacts which were so crucial to other proto-sinologists, such as Kircher. His sources were entirely written and they present a valuable barometer of influence of early works on China on the late seventeenth-century reader. Webb had a finer sense of debt to his sources than did most of his contemporaries and he carefully recorded this debt in marginal citations throughout the essay. Among those works on China most often cited were Ricci-Trigault's *De Christiana expeditione apud Sinas*, parts of which had been translated into English in 1625 in Samuel Purchas' *Pilgrims*. A second important source was Semedo's *Imperio de la China*, which was first translated into English in 1655. The third and most important source was the works of Martini. These included *De bello tartarico*, which was published in English editions in 1654 and 1655, *Novus atlas Sinensis* and *Sinicae historiae decas prima*. Finally, and also of great importance, was Kircher's *China illustrata.*

---

10 Ch'en Shou-yi recognized the fascination of Webb's work fifty years ago. See his article, "John Webb: a Forgotten Page in the Early History of Sinology in Europe," *The Chinese Social & Political Science Review* 19 (1935): 295–330.

In arguing his thesis that Chinese was the Primitive Language, Webb claimed that descendants of Noah originally migrated into India and from there into China. Stimulated by a suggestion from Martini[11] regarding the parallels between the Biblical flood and the flood said to have occurred in China during King Yao's time, Webb also claimed that Yao was identical to Noah and that the Flood was universal in extent[12]. Webb elaborated on chapter ten of *Genesis* by saying that of the three sons of Noah, the descendants of Shem peopled eastern Persia, China and the Indias; the descendants of Japheth peopled Asia Minor and Europe while the descendants of Ham peopled Babylon, Palestine, the Arabias and Africa.

Webb disagreed with Kircher's claim in *China illustrata* that China was peopled by the descendants of Ham who came out of Egypt[13]. Kircher had based his claim on the similarity between the Chinese and Egyptian written languages in their common use of hieroglyphs or picture-images rather than a phonetic alphabet. Webb regarded this as weak evidence and noted that since Kircher had also claimed hieroglyphic language for Mexico, by the same reasoning, the language of Mexico would have to be traced to Egypt. He went on to reject an implication of Kircher's claim, namely, that China was peopled after the confusion of tongues at Babel. Instead, Webb claimed, on grounds no stronger than those of Kircher, that China was peopled not by the sons of Ham, but rather by the sons of Shem and *before* Babel. At the confusion of tongues, Webb argued, not all the peoples from the east came to Babel[14]. Those remaining at home included the ancestors of the Chinese, who were thereby able to preserve the Primitive Language.

Kircher claimed[15] that Ham had moved his colonies from Egypt eastward into Persia and later into Bactria, which borders on Mogul or Industan. From here migrations took place into China. Ham's son, whom Kircher identified as Hermes Trismegistus, was said to have invented the hieroglyphs. Kircher explained the common use of hieroglyphs in Egypt and China in terms of the communication among these colonies. Differing from Kircher, Webb drew from Sir Walter Raleigh's *History of the world* (London 1614) to deny that Ham ever left Egypt. From Peter Heylin's *Cosmographia* (London 1652), Webb argued that Bactria was populated too early to have been settled by emigrants from Egypt. Webb claimed that the Chinese had a written language 500 years before Ham's descendants taught the Egyptians to write[16]. Webb further cited the Latin translation of the Jewish historian, Flavius Josephus, to the effect

---

11 Martino Martini, *Sinicae Historiae* (Munich, 1658), pp. 36–39.
12 John Webb, *An Historical Essay Endeavoring a Probability that the Language of the Empire of China is the Primitive Language* (London, 1669) pp. 61–62.
13 Webb, p. 28 & Athanasius Kircher, *China illustrata*, p. 226.
14 Webb, p. 24.
15 *China illustrata*, p. 226.
16 Webb, pp. 30–31.

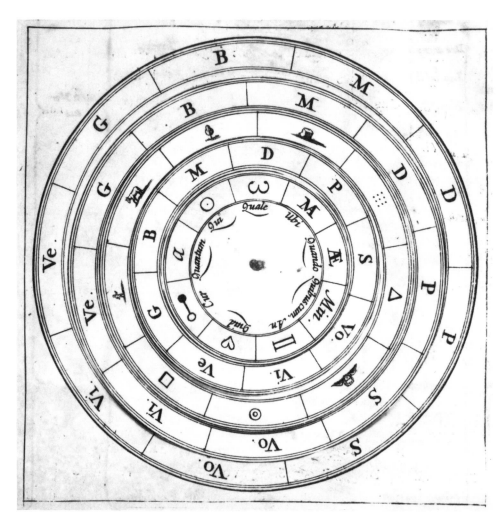

Plate 13. The Lullian diagram of six revolving, concentric circles exemplifying the Combinatorial Art, from Athanasius Kircher's *Ars magna sciendi, sive combinatoria* (Amsterdam, 1669) p. 173. Courtesy of the Niedersächsische Landesbibliothek Hannover.

TABULA *Alphabetorum Artis nostræ.*

Columna prima. *Alphabetum primum Erotematicum.*	Columna secunda. *Alphabetum principiorum absolutorum.*		Columna tertia. *Alphabetum principiorum respectivorum.*		Columna quarta. *Alphabetum principiorum universalium.*	
1. An.	1. B.	Bonitas.	1. ☰	Differentia.	1. △	Deus.
2. Quid.	2. M.	Magnitudo.	2. ♡	Concordantia.	2.	Angelus.
3. Cur.	3. D.	Duratio.	3. ●○	Contrarietas.	3. ◎	Cœlum.
4. Quantum.	4. P.	Potentia.	4. α	Principium.	4. □	Elementa.
5. Qui.	5. S.	Sapientia.	5. ☉	Medium.	5.	Homo.
6. Quale.	6. Vo.	Voluntas.	6. ♋	Finis.	6.	Animalia.
7. Ubi.	7. Vi.	Virtus.	7. M	Majoritas.	7.	Plantæ.
8. Quando.	8. Ve.	Veritas.	8. Æ	Æqualitas.	8. ⬠	Mineralia & omnia mixta.
9. Quibuscum.	9. G.	Gloria.	9. Mi.	Minoritas.	9. ⦂⦂⦂	Materialia; Instrumentalia.

Nam

Plate 14. A table of alphabets of the Lullian Art, as modified by Athanasius Kircher in *Ars magna sciendi, sive combinatoria* (Amsterdam 1669) p. 24. Courtesy of the Niedersächsische Landesbibliothek Hannover.

that it was Shem, not Ham, whose descendants inhabited Asia from the Euphrates River to the Indian Ocean. Kircher had tried to reduce all the various non-Judeo-Christian religions to a small number of pagan forms which originated in the West, usually Egypt and Greece. It was this line of reasoning that led Kircher to equate Ham with Zoroaster. However, Webb argued that since Ham never left Egypt, Kircher's claim for the identification of Ham and Zoroaster was unfounded.

In regard to dating the origin of the Chinese language, Webb drew from Semedo, Raleigh, Martini's *Atlas* and Isaac Vossius' *Dissertatio de vera aetate mundi* (Hagae-Comitis 1659) to argue for high antiquity of origin at 3000 B.C.[17] Webb claimed that the Chinese had developed their language before the Flood rather than three centuries after the Flood, as Kircher had claimed[18]. Following Martini's *Sinicae historiae*, Webb argued that Fu Hsi invented the Chinese characters in order to replace knots[19]. Both Martini and Webb appear to have been unfamiliar with the Chinese legendary claim that the eight trigrams were originally graphic representations of numerical quantity which displaced reckoning by knots in the early development of mathematics in China. Webb reproduced Martini's claim that another type of Chinese writing, namely, the ten stem and twelve branch components in the sexagenary or sixty-year Cycle of Cathay, preceded Fu Hsi's invention[20]. However, Chinese tradition normally gave Fu Hsi's invention priority.

Webb's illustrated explication of the formation of Chinese characters used the illustration of six characters, probably from Kircher's *Oedipus Aegyptiacus*, which was discussed in the preceding chapter. (See plates 10 and 11.) Webb accepted Kircher's explanation of the simplification process which took place in Chinese characters in their evolution from ancient to modern forms[21]. (Kircher noted that the earlier forms were so ancient that one could scarcely find a contemporary Chinese who could explain them.) But since Webb was arguing that contemporary Chinese was the Primitive Language, he was obliged to claim that the Chinese language had not changed. So in the face of considerable seventeenth-century evidence to the contrary, and in a manner reminiscent of the tradition of ridiculous precision in dating Biblical events, Webb made the astonishing claim that the Chinese characters were simplified to their present forms exactly 234 years after the Flood! Furthermore, Webb added that Kircher's analysis had proved that the simplified characters carried the same essential content as their unsimplified forms. Although Webb noted that there were different estimates of when the characters were invented, for his purpose

17 Webb, pp. 175–176.
18 *China illustrata*, p. 225.
19 Martini, *Sinicae historiae*, p. 12 & Webb, p. 171.
20 Martini, *Sinicae historiae*, p. 7 & Webb, p. 172.
21 Webb, p. 157 & Kircher, pp. 228–232.

it was enough to maintain that they were invented prior to the confusion of tongues at Babel.

The criteria by which the seventeenth century tested proposed candidates for the Primitive Language derived from the unity and simplicity mentioned in *Genesis* 11:1. The criteria included antiquity, simplicity, generality, modesty of expression, vitality and brevity[22]. Webb's argument for simplicity was somewhat convoluted in view of his need to confront the enormous estimates of the total numbers of Chinese characters. He noted that Semedo and Martini had estimated 60,000, Ricci-Trigault 70,000 or 80,000, Kircher 80,000 and Jean Nieuhoff 120,000[23]. All of these estimates, except for Neuhoff's, were within the range of possibility. Webb noted that the well-informed Trigault stated that no one knew all of the characters. Webb claimed — not unjustifiably — that knowledge of 8,000 or 10,000 sufficed for literacy and that unknown characters were easily handled by a dictionary, in the same manner as unknown Latin words[24]. The comparison to Latin is unsatisfactory because Webb was arguing that Chinese was *the* Primitive Language and therefore of ultimate simplicity. When scholars later followed Kircher's view that it was impossible to recover the Primitive Language and that the effort should be concentrated on creating an artificial universal language, the Biblical criteria of unity and simplicity would remain key components.

5. THE WIDESPREAD BELIEF IN REAL CHARACTERS

Underlying the search for a universal language lay the widespread linguistic premise that it was possible to discover Real Characters or symbols and sounds whose representation of things and notions was natural or "real" rather than conventional. In other words, the representation in the word would be based upon discovering the nature of things rather than on human invention. This proposal was found in the writings of Francis Bacon (1561–1625) who was one of the first in the seventeenth century to propose a universal language. The close association of the search for a universal language with major figures of the emerging Scientific Revolution such as Bacon, members of the London Royal

---

22 See Ch'en Shou-yi's discussion of these six criteria in terms of Webb's theory on the Chinese language, pp. 320–323.

23 Earlier in his work (p. 56), Webb identified Jean Nieuhoff as a Dutchman who had authored *The late embassage of the Oriental Company of the United Provinces of the Netherlands to the emperor of China,* which Webb cited frequently. Webb's estimate of 120,000 Chinese characters (p. 173) is said to come from another work authored by Nieuhoff entitled *History of Persia.*

24 Webb, p. 173.

Society and continental figures like Leibniz established the solid intellectual credentials of the search.

Bacon's dissatisfaction with existing European languages led him to call for the development of a new universal language. In his call, Bacon referred to the Chinese language as a model. Though his reference to Chinese was brief, it was very influential on mid-seventeenth-century formulators of universal language schemes such as George Dalgarno and John Wilkins. In the *Advancement of learning* (London 1605), Bacon wrote:

> it is the use of China, and the kingdoms of the High Levant, to write in characters real, which express neither letters nor words in gross, but things or notions; insomuch as countries and provinces, which understand not one another's language, can nevertheless read one another's writings, because the characters are accepted more generally than the languages do extend[25].

Bacon acquired this information on the Chinese language quite early though he treated the information as being widely known. One possible printed source was Juan Gonzalez de Mendozas' *Historia de las cosas, ritos y costumbres, del gran Reyno de la China* (Rome 1585; revised 1586)[26]. Mendoza (1545–1618), a Spanish Augustinian, was sent in 1580 by way of Mexico to China, carrying a letter to the Chinese emperor from Philip II of Spain. He encountered difficulties in Mexico, however, and was forced to return to Europe. He never actually visited China, but while in Mexico obtained materials dealing with China from Spanish missionaries based in the Philippines. Later in Rome, he used these materials to write his *Historia*, the first European work to provide detailed information on China. The book was a great success and, before the end of the century, it had been published in Italian, French, English, Latin, German and Dutch editions. In a brief section dealing with the Chinese language, Mendoza clearly stated that although many different languages were spoken throughout China, the inhabitants were able to understand one another through the written language. This, he explained, was because the same written form or character was used to express a meaning, although the character may have different pronunciations[27].

---

25 Francis Bacon, *The advancement of learning and New Atlantis*. Arthur Johnston, ed. (Oxford, 1974) book 2, XVI. 2, p. 131. In this and other works where multiple editions are found, section subdivisions are noted in order to facilitate cross-referencing.

26 Robert Streit, *Bibliotheca missionum* (Rome, 1928) IV, 531–534. The editor, Arthur Johnston, in *The advancement of learning*, p. 131n, states that Bacon received his information on the Chinese language from Joseph de Acosto's *Moral history of the East and West Indies* (1604), book 6, ch. 5, but it is likely that the ultimate European source was Mendoza's *Historia*.

27 Juan Gonzáles de Mendoza, *Historia de las cosas, ritos y costumbres, del gran Reyno de la China* (Antwerp, 1596) part 1, book 3, ch. 13, pp. 91–92.

Bacon distinguished two kinds of Real Characters. The ancient Egyptian hieroglyphs and the gestures of the deaf and dumb represented an actual relationship between the sign and the thing whereas with Chinese characters, the relationship was arbitrarily chosen by man[28]. Bacon was skeptical of the practical utility of such a language, however, because of the cumbersomely large number of Real Characters required[29]. The tendency toward identifying grammar with language was a characteristic common to Bacon and other seventeenth-century seekers of a universal language. Language was regarded as essentially logical and expressive elements were slighted.

The European discovery voyages of the sixteenth century had opened contact with unknown lands and created practical linguistic problems for traders and missionaries. The discovery of different languages gave a tremendous stimulus to the quest and served as the standard model of comparison for universal language proposals of the seventeenth century[30]. In 1615, Ricci-Trigault reported in *De Christiana expeditione apud Sinas* that Chinese script was understood by the Chinese, Japanese, Koreans, Cochinese (South Vietnamese) and Leuchian islanders (Taiwanese) even though each of them spoke distinct languages[31]. Certain Europeans believed that this universality of the Chinese script must be connected with the Chinese characters' ability to represent things and therefore to be Real Characters. Consequently, the European conception of the Chinese language came to exert a powerful influence on the European search for a universal language.

6. KIRCHER'S PIVOTAL ROLE IN BLENDING THE COMBINATORY ART, THE CHINESE LANGUAGE AND THE SEARCH FOR A UNIVERSAL LANGUAGE

Fr. Kircher's prominent position in seventeenth-century intellectual life stems from a prolific output of books which dealt with key concerns of that period, including Hermetism and the search for a universal language. But whereas the spirit animating the Hermetic tradition was esoteric and mysterious, the spirit of the search for a universal language was associated with the openness of the approach found in the new scientific societes. In his own work, Kircher was able to combine investigation into the symbolical hieroglyphs with the search for a non-figurative universal language called the Polygraphia[32]. While

28 Bacon, *The advancement of learning*, p. 131 and Cornelius, p. 31.
29 Francis Bacon, *De argumentis scientarum* (Spedding edition) p. 562.
30 Jonathan Cohen, "On the project of a universal language," *Mind* 63 (1954): 51.
31 Ricci-Trigault, *De Christiana expeditione apud Sinas* (ch. 1; 5) p. 27.
32 Medeleine David, *Le débat sur les écritures et l'hiéroglyphe aux XVIIe et XVIIIe siècles*, p. 51. It is perhaps worth noting Kircher's inspirational link to Baconianism. The academic patron of Kircher's youth, the famous French savant Peirese (d. 1637), was one of the most avid followers of Bacon on the continent. See David, pp. 44–45.

the language of the hieroglyphs, according to Kircher's interpretation, was built upon mystery and symbolism, the language of his Polygraphia attempted to banish mystery and symbols. The work in which Kircher attempted to bridge the divergent tendencies of the hieroglyphs and the Polygraphia was his *Ars magna sciendi, sive combinatoria* (The great Art of knowing, or Combinations) (1669). In this work, Kircher used the system of Lull to develop a non-alphabetic language which embraced metaphysics, theology and law and attempted to blend hieroglyphic and polygraphic communication[33].

Ars magna sciendi was a typically Kircherian monumental work of 500 pages in large folio size. In it Kircher made certain minor modifications to Lull's Art by rearranging the order of the Defects and of the Subjects (God, Angel, Heaven, Element, Man, Animal, Plant, Mineral and Material) with which Lull had created a hierarchical order extending from divine to lower forms. Building upon his criticism of Lull's repeated usage of the letters *B* through *K* as being confusing, Kircher substituted symbolic forms for the first four sets[34]. (Kircher's presentation of the first four sets is found in plate 14.) However, his *Ars magna* was basically an elaboration of Lull's principles and included the various Lullian diagrams, including a reproduction of the combinatory figure with revolving concentric circles which — through the ingenuity of the printer — actually revolved[35]! (See plate 13.) Kircher faithfully reproduced the Lullian spirit by applying the Great Art to every known body of knowledge, including theology, physics, medicine and law.

Several years before the publication of his *Ars magna*, Kircher had conceived of applying Lull's Combinatory Art to the search for a universal language. In the Leibniz archives there is a manuscript in Leibniz' hand entitled "Reductio linguarum ad unum", which Leibniz claimed was based on a "new invention for the reduction of all languages to one" by Kircher[36]. Leibniz described Kircher's proposal as dated October 17th 1660 at Rome and consisting of nine folio-sized sheets in length, each sheet containing six columns or fifty-four columns in all. Each column was said to contain thirty subject names. The numbers — 9 x 6 = 54 — paralleled the Lullian six sets of nine members each yielding fifty-four. The similarity was confirmed when Leibniz recorded the Lullianlike elements with Kircher's symbolism. But gone in Leibniz' manuscript was the geometrical feature of gridlike or circular arrangements. Instead, we seem to have a *spatial* combinatory principle giving way to a more conceptually *mathematical* principle. Leibniz had arranged all fifty-four elements in a single

33 David, pp. 52–53.

34 Athanasius Kircher, *Ars magna sciendi, sive combinatoriae* (Amsterdam, 1669) p. 467. Also cf. Louis Couturat, *La logique de Leibniz d'apres des documents inédits* (Paris, 1901) p. 542 and Kircher, *Ars magna sciendi*, p. 24.

35 Kircher, *Ars magna sciendi*, p. 173.

36 Leibniz-Handschriften (LH) V, I, 1^r-2^v. The manuscript is partially reproduced in *Opuscles et fragments inédits de Leibniz* Edited by Louis Couturat. (Paris, 1903) pp. 536–537.

series beginning with God. The list begins with seven of the Lullian Subjects, after which the entries become less identifiable.

At Rome in 1663, Kircher published his major attempt at developing a universal language – *Polygraphia nova et universalis ex combinatoria arte detecta* (A new and universal writing in many languages revealed by the Combinatory Art). The preface was entitled "Linguarum omnium ad unam reductio" and probably was a development of the proposal in Kircher's manuscript of October 17th 1660 cited by Leibniz. In this work, Kircher substituted numerical for symbolical notations, though the numbers were used merely categorically rather than mathematically. The work was organized through a "pentagloss", that is, a list of basic words with equivalents in five European languages – Latin, Italian, French, Spanish and German. This pentagloss appeared in two basic forms[37]. In the first form, each word was arranged alphabetically with a roman and arabic numeral designation, e.g. XII. 35, which referred to its position in the second form of the pentagloss. The second form grouped together the five linguistic equivalents in meaning and arranged these alphabetically according to their Latin equivalent. Each page of this form of the pentagloss was assigned a roman numeral and each entry was designated by an arabic numeral. (There were 33 roman numerals with the number of arabic numerals ranging between 32 and 40 per page, yielding a total of approximately 1,200 entries.) This constituted a numerical system of cross-referencing the two pentaglosses which would, in theory, allow one to translate any text given in one of these five languages[38]. The enormous demands of memorizing such lists rendered Kircher's universal language scheme impractical. Nevertheless, in response to a letter brimming with questions from the young Leibniz in 1670, Kircher spoke of publishing yet another work on deriving a universal language from the roots of the primary languages[39].

Lull did not propose the creation of a new universal language, but he provided a method which later scholars used for this end. Similarly, Kircher did

---

37 Athanasius Kircher, *Polygraphia nova et universalis ex combinatoria arte detecta* (Rome, 1663) pp. 18–44 & 47–48. See George E. McCracken, "Athanasius Kircher's universal polygraphy," *Isis* 39 (1948): 218–219. Mr. McCracken interprets Kircher's Polygraphia as basically a one-part code which exhibits some of the characteristics of a two-part code. McCracken argues that while Kircher's Polygraphia failed as a universal language, it made a significant contribution to cryptography.

38 Kircher's *Polygraphia* also contained an "Epistoliographia Pentaglossa" which was a series of phrases and proper nouns, such as locations and personal names, useful in writing letters. They were arranged on a basis similar to the first pentagloss, but with letters of the Latin alphabet, instead of arabic numerals, used to designate the individual entries.

39 Kircher to Leibniz, June 23rd 1670, Rome. Leibniz-Briefwechsel 473, sheet 1^r-1^v. Leibniz' letter to Kircher of May 16th 1670 along with Kircher's reply of June 23rd 1670 are published in an article by Paul Friedländer, "Athanasius Kircher und Leibniz," *Academia romana di archeologia, Rome . . . Rendiconti* 13 (1937): 229–247.

not exalt the Chinese language as a model for a universal language as did Bacon, nor say that it contained Real Characters as did both Bacon and Leibniz nor claim it as the Primitive Language as did John Webb. But Kircher disseminated information about the Chinese language from which other Europeans drew precisely these conclusions[40]. Clearly, Kircher was influenced by seventeenth-century intellectual forces and the convergence of his interests in both universal language schemes and in Chinese was no coincidence. Here we have a fascinating instance of the way intellectual forces interlock in their development. Remove one of the links — in this case Kircher — and the historical chain becomes incomplete and perhaps never would have developed. Kircher acted the part of the historical link in joining the Lullian Combinatory Art, the search for a universal language and the Chinese language for certain thinkers who followed him and who, on the basis of his information, postulated new connections between these three separate elements.

Kircher's interest in hieroglyphic and universal languages led him quite logically to an interest in Chinese and to the composition of *China illustrata*, through which he became a major influence in the dissemination of information on China. The final chapter of this work was devoted to the Chinese written script and here Kircher claimed that although the "hieroglyphic characters of the Chinese" were neither as ancient nor as deep in hidden meaning as the Egyptian hieroglyphs, they were composed in the same manner as the Egyptian hieroglyphs, that is, out of "things of the world" from things which were visible to them or from "diverse natural things"[41]. (See plate 8.) According to Kircher, the Chinese language had no letters of an alphabet, no syllables, no declinations and no conjugations. Each character was a complete word. So although Kircher spoke of the great difficulties of mastering Chinese and held that the analysis into Real Characters could be applied only to pre-simplified characters, many European readers were struck by the apparent grammatical simplicity of Chinese and its one-to-one relationship between a word and a real thing. Consequently, Kircher's explanation reinforced their belief that the Chinese language contained Real Characters.

7. THE UNIVERSAL LANGUAGE SCHEMES OF GEORGE DALGARNO AND JOHN WILKINS

It is not possible to trace a single line of development in the seventeenth-century search for a universal language because the number and variety of such

---

40 Cornelius, pp. 73–75, reads too much into Kircher's explanation of the Chinese language. No doubt others drew from Kircher to regard Chinese as a model for a universal language, but Kircher was much more negative about the universal potential for Chinese than were others.

41 Kircher, *China illustrata*, pp. 226–228.

schemes proliferated soon after the 1620s. On the Continent, the missionary and trade concerns were major stimuli while in England, anti-Roman Catholic — and therefore anti-Latin language — forces were at work. In addition to Bacon, Descartes in 1629 proposed a mathematical basis for reducing and clarifying language into an incisive tool which could be quickly mastered[42]. Many of the consequent language schemes tended to follow either the Baconian or Cartesian models[43].

Some of the many formulators of universal language schemes and the approximate dates of their formulations were: Herman Hugo (1617), William Bedell (1633), Gerhard Vossius (1635), Marin Mersenne (ca. 1636), Jan Amos Comenius (1646), Francis Lodwick (1647), an anonymous Spaniard (1653), Thomas Urquhart (1653), Seth Ward (1654), Cave Beck (1657), Brian Walton (1657), Johann J. Becher (1661), George Dalgarno (1661), Edward Somerset (1663), John Wilkins (1668), Leibniz (ca. 1679) and Gaspar Schott (1687).

The schemes of George Dalgarno and John Wilkins were particularly significant in tracing the search for a "philosophical language" or a language whose terms reflected not merely words, but the nature of the things which they represented. In 1661, the Scotsman Dalgarno published his *Ars signorum, vulgo character universalis et lingua philosophica* (The art of signs, by which I set forth a universal character and a philosophical language)[44]. The building blocks or "Alphabet of this Philosophical Language" comprised twenty letters, each of which signified a fundamental notion[45]. Dalgarno used these letters to compose his artificial philosophical language on the basis of an order which would indicate genus, species and specific differences. Additional vowels were inserted to facilitate pronunciation, and word-endings were added to designate inflectional or other grammatical necessities.

As an example from Dalgarno's philosophical language, we may consider the word *SA VA*. The initial *S* referred to the genus 'universal happening', *A* referred to the species 'being, thing' and together *SA* yielded 'cause'. *V* was a numerical prefix and followed by *A* (being, thing) signified the prime or first number. Taken as a whole, *SA VA* yielded 'first cause' or 'God'. In a second example, *KOs*, *K* signified the genus 'political event', *O* signified 'body' and *s* was merely a grammatical element. The result was 'judicial body'. Clearly, one saw how

42 Descartes' letter to Mersenne of 20 November 1629 in *Oeuvres de Descartes*. Charles Adam & Paul Tannery, eds. (Paris, 1897) I, 78–82.

43 Johathan Cohen attempts to distinguish between those who followed the respective Baconian and Cartesian lines of development in the search for a universal language in his article, "On the project of a universal character," *Mind* 63 (1954): 52–59.

44 A copy of George Dalgarno's *Ars signorum, vulgo character universalis et lingua philosophica* (London, 1661) with Leibniz' marginalia is found in the Bibliotheca Regia Hannoverana collection. Portions of Dalgarno's work are reproduced with explanations in Couturat, *La logique*, pp. 544–548 & Cornelius, pp. 80–89.

45 This "alphabet" is bound on the 11th page (unnumbered) of Dalgarno's prefatory material.

these words were intended to convey philosophical descriptions of their re-
ferents. Dalgarno's word order was intended to correlate as closely as possible
with mental processes. In his development of words on a composite basis, he
was greatly influenced by the explanations of the Chinese language which claimed
that the structure of a Chinese character could be analyzed in terms of the
things to which the characters referred. He believed that Real Characters were
in use by the Chinese and Egyptians prior to the use of vocal characters[46].

A work which closely followed and attempted to improve upon that of
Dalgarno was John Wilkins' *Essay toward a Real Character and Philosophical
Language* (London 1688)[47]. Wilkins formulated a philosophical language scheme
based upon the logical system of classification of 40 genera. These were subdivided into 6 genera of greatest generality and 36 genera ("Predicates") of lesser
generality subdivided into the categories of Substance, Quantity, Quality, Action
and Relation. Each of these categories was further subdivided into peculiar
differences and species[48]. Wilkins spoke of how certain elements of Chinese
Characters were based upon real things, and he drew examples of this from
Semedo's *Imperio de la China* (1642). Specifically, he described how the character for "precious stone" [*yü*] was combined with other elements to yield the
words for "gems and pearls, etc". [*chen* (gem), *chu* (pearl)]. Likewise, he
described how the "letter" for wood [*mu*] formed part of the characters of
specific trees [e.g. *sung* (pine; evergreen), *pei* (cypress; cedar)] and how the
particle for metal [*chin*] composed part of the characters for iron, cooper, steel,
etc. [*t'ieh* (iron), *t'ung* (copper), *kang* (steel)]. However, Wilkins also took note
of Semedo's claim that there was no constant principle in deriving Chinese
characters from real things. Consequently, he disagreed with the claim of Golius
that Chinese characters were constructed by art or with a conscious "general
Theory of Philosophy"[49]. While Wilkins' scheme had little impact upon seventeenth-century intellectual life as a universal language, its logical criterion of
simplicity influenced the development of a simpler English prose style in eighteenth-century England[50].

---

46 Dalgarno, p. 2.
47 The copy of Wilkins' *Essay* originally possessed by the Bibliotheca Regia Hannoverana
   is lost. A useful abstract, apparently written by an editor, appears in an 1802 edition
   of Wilkins' works, *The mathematical and philosophical works of the Right Rev. John
   Wilkins* (reprinted London, 1707) pp. 247–260. Illustrations and discussion of Wilkins' *Essay* are found in Couturat, *La logique*, pp. 548–552.
48 Clark Emery, "John Wilkins' universal language," *Isis* 38 (1948): 176–179.
49 See John Wilkins, *Essay toward a Real Character and philosophical language* (London,
   1668) pp. 10 & 452 & Alvaro Semedo, *Histoire universalle de la Chine* (Lyon, 1667)
   pp. 51–52. Other sources of information on China used by Wilkins were Ricci-Trigault,
   De Christiana expeditione apud Sinas, pp. 25–28 & Spizelius, *De re literaria Sinensium*, pp. 53–58.
50 Emery, "John Wilkins' universal language," pp. 184–185. Also see Stimson, "Dr
   Wilkins and the Royal Society," p. 562.

Both the systems of Dalgarno and Wilkins shared the Aristotelianlike attempt to reduce all known elements to classification by genus, species and specific differences, though they differed in the number and content of these classifications. For example, Dalgarno listed twenty genera while Wilkins listed forty. This reflected their presumption that the world was completely classifiable. Both emphasized the logical potential of language. They accepted as fact the ability of mankind to agree upon such classifications, that is, they believed in the potential of a single language to be universally accepted. They firmly believed in the human ability to determine what was natural, and it was from this perspective that Wilkins declared that the writing of oriental languages from right to left was as unnatural as writing with the light on the wrong side[51]! Our contemporary doubts about many of these assumptions may help to explain why so few of us today are seriously searching for a universal language.

8. LEIBNIZ' SEARCH FOR A UNIVERSAL CHARACTERISTIC

Leibniz was aware of the attempts of Dalgarno and Wilkins to find a universal character and philosophical language and of Descartes' proposal for a philosophical language[52]. Leibniz was also deeply familiar with the work of Ramon Lull in the areas of combinatory method and the art of memory. Frances Yates' study of history of the art of memory has shown that the seventeenth-century seekers of Real Characters and a universal language were drawing from memory treatises. Ms. Yates treats Leibniz as the outstanding example of the survival of the art of memory and of Lullist influences in the seventeenth century and she explains the role of this influence in terms of his Universal Characteristic[53].

Although Kircher had attempted to apply an art of combinations to the formulation of a universal language, he had not sought to create a philosophical language. Consequently, it was in Leibniz that we see a number of threads of the seventeenth-century search for a universal language converging. It was Leibniz who proposed that a philosophical language would not only ease communication and do away with many disputes through its greater precision, but that such a language could find truth in a manner akin to mathematics and geometry.

---

51 Wilkins, *Mathematical and Philosophical Works*, p. 254.
52 Regarding Leibniz' familiarity with the Dalgarno and Wilkins sehemes, see Couturat, *La logique*, pp. 544–552. Among the Leibniz-Handschriften is a copy of part of Descartes' letter to Mersenne which contains Descartes' proposal for a philosophical language. The copy is in a secretary's hand with sections of the letter bracketed by Leibniz. This copy has been published by Couturat in *Opuscles et fragments inédites de Leibniz*, pp. 27–28.
53 Yates, *The Art of Memory*, pp. 378–388.

Leibniz' attempt to find a Universal Characteristic dated from early in his career when his ideas of a calculus were linked with his notions of language. Leibniz demonstrated the clear connection between the two by his use of the term *"Combinatoriam Characteristicam"* (Combinatorial Characteristic) in a letter of 1675 to Henry Oldenburg, one of the secretaries of the Royal Society in London[54]. In regard to this reference, Leroy Loemker postulates that there was a transition in Leibniz' philosophical development dating from 1666 when Leibniz wrote *Ars Combinatoria*[55], to the *Ars Characteristica* of 1678 and later[56]. The Universal Characteristic was tied to Leibniz' attempt to reduce all knowledge to a relatively few simple ideas which he referred to as an "alphabet of human thought". This alphabet could then be assigned symbols or numbers and manipulated in a way similar to arithmetic or geometry to attain new truths.

Leibniz expressed this plan in 1679 in the following words:

> If we had some exact *language* (like the one called Adamitic by some) or at least a kind of *truly philosophic writing,* in which the ideas were reduced to a kind of *alphabet of human thought,* then all that follows rationally from what is given could be found by a *kind of calculus,* just as arithmetical or geometrical problems are solved.
>
> Such a language would amount to a *Cabala* of mystic vocables or to the *Arithmetic* of Pythagorean numbers or to the *Characteristic* language of magi, that is, of the wise.
>
> I suspected something of such a great discovery when I was still a boy, and I inserted a description of it in the little book on the Combinatory Art which I published in my adolescence.
>
> I can demonstrate with geometrical rigor that such a language is possible, indeed that its foundation can be easily laid within a few years by a number of cooperating scholars[57].

Leibniz, too, shared the belief in the possibility of discovering Real Characters, though he developed his own reasons for believing this. For Leibniz, Real Characters were written, drawn or engraved signs which signified not words, letters of syllables, but things and ideas[58]. He believed that some characters — such as those of chemistry, astronomy, and the Chinese and Egyptian languages — were limited to representing ideas, and did not extend to reasoning or to the discovery of knowledge and therefore were not suitable for his Universal Charac-

---

54 *Leibnizens mathematische Schriften.* Carl I. Gerhardt, ed. (Berlin and Halle, 1849–1863) I, 86.

55 Leibniz, "Ars Combinatoria," in *Die philosophischen Schriften von G. W. Leibniz.* Carl I. Gerhardt, ed. (Berlin 1875–1890) VI, 27–104.

56 See Leibniz, *Philosophical Papers and Letters.* Leroy E. Loemker, ed. & tr. (Reidel, Holland, 1969) p. 166. The role of the *Ars Characteristica* in Leibniz' dual rational and empirical approach to language is explored by Albert Heinekamp in "Ars characteristica und natürliche Sprache bei Leibniz," *Tijdschrift voor Filosofie* 34 (1972): 446–488.

57 Leibniz, "Scientia Generalis. Characteristica," in Gerhardt, *Philosophischen Schriften* VII, 198–199, translated by Paul and Anne Martin Schrecker in Leibniz, *Monadology and other Philosophical Essays* (Indianapolis, 1965) p. 12.

58 Gerhardt, *Philosophischen Schriften,* VII, 204 and Couturat, *La logique,* p. 81.

teristic. Leibniz noted that prior to that time, only arithmetical and algebraic notations had served to facilitate reasoning[59]. Much later, Leibniz raised his evaluation of Chinese to regard the characters as confirmation of the fact that marks other than words — by which he meant essentially the Indo-European and Semitic languages — could be used to construct a Universal Characteristic[60].

Leibniz's belief in Real Characters was consonant with his principles of Pre-Established Harmony and Sufficient Reason. The Pre-Established Harmony guaranteed that every thought in the metaphysical realm had a corresponding element in the physical realm. For Leibniz, this harmony between the soul, which acted freely according to the rules of final causes, and the body, which acted mechanically according to the rules of efficient causes, was the result of the way in which God created the world[61]. Following from this correspondence between the abstract and sensate realms, Leibniz believed that thinking had a corresponding manifestation in letters and sounds[62]. It was this correspondence between the realm of thought and the realm of letters and sounds that led Leibniz to conclude both that a Primitive Language had existed and that a new universal language could be constructed.

Continuing in the vein of seeing truth and falsehood as the function of God's creation of the nature of things, Leibniz derived his Principle of Sufficient Reason that all true propositions were analytic. By this, he meant that in every true proposition, the predicate (P) was contained within the subject (S) in such a way that through analysis, the predicate could be reduced to the subject (S=P). For Leibniz, this analysis consisted, firstly, of determining the list of properties of the substance which was the subject of a proposition and, secondly, seeing whether the properties contained in the predicate were included within or were derivative from the list of subject properties[63]. For example, if the list of subject properties was determined to be XYZ and X and Z were included within the predicate, then this proposition would be true. However, not all true propositions would be included in Leibniz' Universal Characteristic. Leibniz distinguished between two kinds of truths. The first kind was *contingent truths*, which were truths of fact, the opposite of which was possible and whose demonstration required an infinite analysis which only God could do. Some sample contingent truths are "Napoleon lost the Battle of Waterloo", which is drawn from history, or "He looks sick", which is drawn from observation and induction. The second kind of truth was *necessary truths* or truths of reason, the

59 Gerhardt, *Philosophischen Schriften*, VII, 205.

60 Leibniz, *Nouveaux essais sur l'entendement humain*, in *Leibniz: Sämtliche Schriften und Briefe* (Berlin, 1923–) VI; 6, 398.

61 See Leibniz' fifth letter to Sammuel Clarke, response to pars. 31 & 32, in Gerhardt, *Philosophischen Schriften*, VII, 412.

62 Leibniz, *Nouveaux essais*, VI; 6, 77.

63 Nicholas Rescher, *The Philosophy of Leibniz* (Englewood Cliffs, New Jersey, 1967) p. 23.

opposite of which was impossible and whose demonstration involved a finite analysis (at least some of which are) within the range of human ability[64]. A sample necessary truth is the Pythagorean Theorem in geometry: $h^2 = a^2 + b^2$ (The square of the length of the hypotenuse or longest side of a right triangle is equal to the sum of the squares of the lengths of the other two sides of the triangle.). This is known not from history, observation or induction, but from deduction. Leibniz' Universal Characteristic was limited to truths of a necessary nature.

Leibniz believed that there had been one or more primitive languages which had perfectly captured the relationship between the thought and the thing. However, he felt that such languages had long since deteriorated. Leibniz followed the suggestion of Gropius Becanus who in 1580 had published a book containing a theory that German was more primitive than Hebrew[65]. Leibniz accepted Gropius' view in a display of German nationalism surprising to those more familiar with his widely heralded cosmopolitanism[66].

Leibniz did not merely synthesize the various seventeenth-century intellectual threads. He transformed them as well. Lull's Art was based on a mechanical principle of combinations. For example, in Lull's diagram of six concentric circles (see plate 13), each circle contained nine concepts and the total number of combinations obtainable by turning the various circles was 531,441. Leibniz discarded the diagram, however, and applied a mathematical principle of combinations involving six sets of nine concepts each. Computing every possible combination of the entries, Leibniz concluded that there were 17,804,320, 388,674,561 possibilities[67]!

In the same year that he was enunciating his proposal for a Universal Characteristic, Leibniz wrote a letter, dated April (?) 1679, to Duke Johann Friedrich[68] in which he merged the threads of Lull's Art, Kircher's *Polygraphia*, Chinese characters and his invention of *Nombres Charactéristiques* (Characteristic Numbers). The latter was another name for the logical calculus of which Leibniz developed three distinct systems in the years 1679, 1686 and 1690, respectively[69]. This letter centered about Leibniz' request for 1,200 crowns to establish an "endowment for teaching this art" of the Characteristic Numbers. In presenting his invention, Leibniz berated Kircher's *Polygraphia*, with which the Duke was apparently familiar, as a mere trifle and quite removed from Leibniz' scheme. He compared his invention favorably to the Combinatory Art of Ramon Lull and stated that his system had "infinite advantages" over Lull's Art.

---

64 Leibniz, *Monadology* §33–38.
65 Leibniz, *Nouveaux essais*, VI; 6, 285.
66 See Daniel P. Walker, "Leibniz and Language," *Journal of the Warburg and Courtauld Institutes* 35 (1972): 300–304.
67 Couturat, *La logique*, p. 37.
68 Leibniz, *Sämtliche Schriften und Briefe*, I; 2, 167–169.
69 Couturat, *La logique*, p. 323.

Leibniz claimed that his invention of Characteristic Numbers was so completely rational that it could serve as a "judge of controversies, an interpreter of notions, a scale for probabilities, a compass which will guide us on the ocean of experience, an inventory of things, a catalogue of things, a microscope for minute examination of present things, a telescope for determining remote elements, a general calculus, a simple magic, a non-chimerical Kabbala, a script which each individual will read in his own language"[70]. These claims appear ridiculously exaggerated, but two factors should be kept in mind. First, since Leibniz was attempting to convince the Duke to support his proposal with a considerable sum of money, the description of his invention was intended to be persuasive rather than objective. Leibniz' correspondence contained abundant evidence that he was capable of being a good deal more objective about his own projects than he was here. Secondly, the benefits of Leibniz' calculus have been very impressive, though much more confined in scope than his claims. The inventors' claims should be treated seriously because the matrix of his thinking which gave rise to the invention is important. When Leibniz developed the calculus, he was clearly thinking in a matrix with wide application. He saw profound intellectual connections which are no longer apparent and for this reason, they are significant.

Leibniz' claim that his invention constituted a language which could be learned in a few weeks time and circulated throughout the world reflected an ideal to which many of the seventeenth-century universal language schemes aspired. Leibniz' reference to the missionaries and to the Chinese made it clear that he wished the missionaries, particularly the Jesuits, to circulate his Characteristic Numbers in China. He stated to the Duke that his invention should be presented to the Congregation de Propaganda Fide, the leading Roman Catholic missionary administrative body, because it would facilitate the introduction of Christianity into foreign lands. Leibniz based this belief on the assumption that Christianity was "sovereignly reasonable" and inseparable from the intellectual substance of European civilization, such as the Euclidean elements. Leibniz believed that the Chinese were particularly amenable to such an approach which appealed to intellectual persuasion. It is interesting to note that Ricci and many Jesuits in China held similar views about the implicitly rational and logical features of Christianity. These shared accommodative assumptions were doubtless at the base of the intellectual affinity between Leibniz and the Jesuits of the China Mission.

In his manuscript of 1679 on a Universal Characteristic, Leibniz had perceived Chinese characters as basically alien to the thinking of his Characteristic Numbers. He spoke of a similarity between the Chinese characters and Egyptian hieroglyphs. In effect, he appeared to be accepting the claims of Kircher and others as to the similarities between the Chinese and Egyptian scripts and to

70 Leibniz, *Sämtliche Schriften und Briefe*, I; 2, 168.

be rejecting Chinese as a model for his universal language. Yet Leibniz never lost interest in the Chinese language and twenty years later, when he received additional information from Fr. Bouvet on the structure of Chinese characters, he distinguished the Chinese from the Egyptian script and raised his assessment of the philosophical relevance of the Chinese characters to his Universal Characteristic.

In a letter to Walter von Tschirnhaus of 1678, Leibniz clarified how his Universal Characteristic and its art of combinations differed from mathematical computation[71]. While algebra was "the science of forms of similarity and dissimilarity", Leibniz stated that cryptography was part of the art which this latter science forms, though the problem was not in compounding so much as in analyzing compounds. Finally, with a significance for his belief in the possibility of a "key to Chinese", Leibniz likened a root in algebra to a key of cryptographic deciphering. Consequently, Leibniz went on to state that this art of combinations expressed situation, not magnitude and by using it, our thoughts could be "pictured . . . , fixed, abridged and ordered". It would lead us into the interior of things in the manner of a "mechanical thread" with which we can analyze any idea into its constituent elements. Leibniz likened this thread to "Ariadne's thread", a reference to Greek mythology[72]. Finally, in reference to applying the art of combinations to universal language, Leibniz stated that "a spoken or written language can also be developed with its aid which can be learned in a few days and will be adequate to express everything that occurs in everyday practice, and of astonishing value in criticism and discovery, after the model of numerical characters".

Leibniz was unable to achieve his aim of applying the art of combinations to the development of a universal language. Although he had enormous success with his mathematical discoveries, his Principle of Sufficient Reason was demonstrable only in regard to truths of reason. In regard to truths of fact, Leibniz' insistence that the infinite analysis necessary for demonstration could be performed only by God is something which must be accepted without proof, which skeptics are unwilling to do. Consequently, Leibniz was unable to achieve an alternate aim that extended his universal language proposal to pervade his philosophy as a whole, namely, a purely deductive system of knowledge[73].

Toward the end of his life, Leibniz expressed a feeling that time was running out for him and spoke of a need to turn the problem over to younger men. Nevertheless, the continuous development that his notion of a universal language

---

71 Leibniz, *Philosophical Papers and Letters*, Loemker, tr., pp. 192–194.
72 According to Greek mythology, Ariadne was the daughter of King Minos II of Crete, who placed Theseus in the notorious Labyrinth where he was to be devoured by the Minotaur. Ariadne fell in love with Theseus and gave him a clue in the form of a thread which enabled him to find his way out of the Labyrinth.
73 See Allison Coudert, "Some Theories of a Natural Language," *Studia Leibnitiana* Sonderheft 7 (1978): 108–109.

had undergone over the years was reflected in his letter of January 10th 1714 to Nicholas Remond, adviser to the Duke of Orléans. Leibniz stated:

... if I were younger or had talented young men to help me, I should still hope to create a kind of universal symbolistic (*spécieuse générale*) in which all truths of reason would be reduced to a kind of calculus. At the same time this could be a kind of universal language or writing, though infinitely different from all such languages which have thus far been proposed, for the characters and the words themselves would give directions to reason, and the errors – except those of fact – would be only mistakes in calculation. It would be very difficult to form or invent this language or characteristic but very easy to learn it without any dictionaries. When we lack sufficient data to arrive at certainty in our truths, it would also serve to estimate degrees of probability and to see what is needed to provide this certainty. Such an estimate would be most important for the problems of life and for practical considerations, where our errors in estimating probabilities often amount to more than a half . . .[74].

Leibniz' application of combinatory art to the development of a universal language was paralleled by a lifelong interest in China. One of the earliest manifestations of this interest was in the Chinese language and its significance in his quest for a universal language[75]. Leibniz was not alone in this interest. As we have noted, at this time in Europe the intellectual currents striving for a universal language found the Chinese written language a particularly fertile field. Much of this fertility was the result of mixing fact with fancy. The antiquity of the Chinese language and its effectiveness as a form of written communication between speakers of different languages was generally accurate. However, the European understanding of the structure and historical development of Chinese was of such scanty dimensions that European imaginations filled in the gaps in actual knowledge.

This filling-in consisted of a projection of model status upon the Chinese script. For example, the strong historical consciousness of the Chinese stressed the continuity of their language through an emphasis upon etymological studies. The most elementary of these revealed a pictographic or ideographic principle at work in the structure of the characters. However, as the Chinese language developed, these pictographic and ideographic processes were increasingly overlaid with phonetic processes with the result that by the seventeenth century, most Chinese characters contained phonetic as well as pictographic-ideographic elements.

74 Leibniz, *Philosophical Papers and Letters*, Loemker, trans., p. 654.
75 Rita Widmaier, "Die Rolle der chinesischen Schrift in Leibniz' Zeichentheorie," *Studia Leibnitiana* 13 (2) (1981): 278–298 and the expanded version of this paper *Die Rolle der chinesischen Schrift in Leibniz' Zeichentheorie*. Studia Leibnitiana Supplementa 24. (Wiesbaden, 1983).

9. ANDREAS MÜLLER'S *CLAVIS SINICA*

Because of the "curious" and naive intellectual atmosphere in seventeenth-century Europe, when the sinological novice, Andreas Müller of Berlin, announced in 1674 that he had discovered a "Key" to mastering the Chinese language which he would reveal upon payment of a premium — half in advance into escrow, half on delivery — there was a ready-made audience. The story behind Müller's *Clavis Sinica* (Key to the Chinese language) is surely one of the more obfuscatingly fascinating tales of scholarship of this age.

The idea of such a Key was firmly fixed by Müller as striking him on November 18th 1667[76]. After testing his Key for several years, Müller presented his proposal to his patron, the Great Elector, Friedrich Wilhelm on February 14th 1674 and soon afterwards the proposal was published in the form of a four-page pamphlet entitled *"Propositio super clave sua Sinica"*. From this point on, the story becomes increasingly muddy. In the face of requests from scholars for further information, Müller consistently refused to divulge anything without payment of the premium[77]. In Müller's favor, one notes that delayed payment of salaries and theological controversy made his status at the Brandenburg court precarious. This was exacerbated by the difficulty of supporting his large family. It also appears that the Great Elector, although unwilling or unable to pay the premium, exerted pressure to prevent the invention from leaving his patronage. Müller's need for prepayment on the Key possibly reflected his inability to secure a publisher by any other means[78]. Furthermore, Müller held a fairly respectable reputation among other contemporary scholars and was generous in sharing his manuscripts with friends who were studying the *Koran*[79]. Nevertheless, it is very difficult to explain Müller's refusals to divulge his Key without some negative reflections on his character.

The apparent end of the Key clouded the story even more since it and other manuscripts were said to be destroyed by a discouraged Müller just before his death. We are left today with a fragment in Müller's *Monumenti Sinici* of 1672 which may throw some light on what Müller had in mind. In this work, he ap-

---

76 The most reliable account of Müller's Key is found in Eva S. Kraft, "Frühe chinesische Studien in Berlin," *Medizinhistorisches Journal* 11 (1976): 92–128. Also useful, but now somewhat superceded by the work of Frau Kraft is Donald F. Lach, "The Chinese Studies of Andreas Müller," *Journal of the American Oriental Society* 60 (1940): 564–575.

77 Some of the correspondence concerning the Key was published by Müller. See the exchanges between Müller, Kircher and Adam Adamandus Kochanski, S.J. in *De Invento Sinico Epistolae Nonnullae* (undated) pp. 2–29.

78 Frau Kraft in a private letter of 21 April 1979 states that Müller had insufficient funds to publish on his own and that he claims to have been unable to find a publisher. Therefore, she suggests that the prepayment was the only means by which he would have been able to publish the Key.

79 Kraft, private letter of 21 April 1979.

plied musical notation to explaining the pronunciation of the Chinese text of the Nestorian Monument. The fact that Müller borrowed this text from Kircher's *China illustrata* simply indicated that seventeenth-century standards of authorship and plagiarism were not what they are today.

The evidence of the responses to the idea of such a *Clavis Sinica* is more firm. Although some, including Kircher, questioned the possibility of such a Key, the numbers of those who were ready to believe in it were considerable and included Leibniz himself. Leibniz' attitude toward such a Key and its relationship to a universal language was revealed in the list of fourteen questions which he asked Johann Elsholz, a physician at the Berlin court, to convey to Müller in 1679. These were:

(1) Whether such a Key is infallible and certain as one can read our A, B, C or ciphers, or whether sometimes one needs advice, as when one practices reading hieroglyphs?

(2) Since the Chinese script, as is known, was arranged not on the word but on the thing [itself], so I wish to know whether the characters are always made according to the nature of things?

(3) Whether the whole script makes use of fixed elements or a rudimentary alphabet of which the remaining characters originate out of combinations?

(4) Whether the immaterial thing is likewise expressed out of a certain material or visible standard?

(5) Whether the Chinese script is made through art or whether, as with speech in general, it has changed through usage and developed?

(6) Whether the speech of the Chinese, as some think, is also made through art, and whether it carries a certain Key?

(7) Whether Herr Müller thereby holds that the Chinese themselves are unaware of this Key to their own script?

(8) Whether he thinks this script would be easy and useful to introduce into Europe?

(9) Whether those who made this script were aware of the nature of things and were rational?

(10) Whether the characters signify natural things such as animals, vegetables, stones, such that the characteristics of things are differentiated from one another?

(11) And consequently, if and how much one learns of the nature of the thing from the bare character?

(12) If after practicing this Key, can I understand everything written in Chinese script, no matter what the subject may be?

(13) If I had this Key, could I write something in Chinese script, and would it be comprehensible by a literate Chinese?

(14) If several different Chinese and several people somewhat skilled in this Key were given a written piece (e.g. "Our Father") to translate from word to word into Chinese, would their pieces approximately agree and in a comparison of both types with one another, could someone unfamiliar with the Chinese script nevertheless conclude that they must be essentially the same[80]?

In the second question, Leibniz revealed that he shared a common seventeenth-century European view that the Chinese characters were based upon the thing rather than the word, which really amounted to Bacon's prescription for

---

80 Leibniz, *Sämtliche Schriften und Briefe* I; 2, 491–492.

Real Characters. However, Leibniz was cautious about oversimplification and asked Müller if this representational quality extended to all Chinese characters. Leibniz required that his universal language not only represent real things and concepts, but also serve the reasoning process. Consequently, in the eleventh question, he raised the issue of whether Chinese script served reasoning by asking whether the character revealed something of the nature of the thing represented. Likewise, in the tenth question, Leibniz raised the reasoning criteria by asking whether the Chinese characters signified natural things, such as animals, vegetables and stones, in a manner which differentiated their characteristics. He revealed his mathematical and combinatorial perspective in the third question when he asked whether the Chinese script was made from fixed elements or from a rudimentary alphabet, from which the remaining characters were made through combinations.

In the fifth question, Leibniz raised the fundamental question of whether Chinese speech was made through "art" (i.e. a conscious, man-made plan) or whether the language had changed through nondeliberate usage and unconscious development. Highlighted here are some fundamental differences in the way in which language development is conceived. While philosophers have tended to stress the role of human "art" in analyzing the development of language, many students of language have tended to see a spontaneously logical and dynamic aspect in language which develops from within, as well as a number of alogical factors which can be eliminated only at the expense of expression and communication. (In the sixth question, Leibniz clearly distinguished Chinese speech from Chinese script and asked whether Chinese speech was also made through art and contained a Key.) The ninth question raised a similar issue of artifice when Leibniz asked whether those who made the Chinese script were rational and aware of the nature of things. The seventh question raised a further issue of intellectual consciousness and rationality when it asked whether contemporary Chinese were aware of this Key to their script. Finally, in the twelfth, thirteenth and fourteenth questions, Leibniz raised the issue of the efficiency of the Key, that is, how effective it was in teaching one to read and write Chinese.

10. CHRISTIAN MENTZEL'S *CLAVIS SINICA*

Though Leibniz was unsuccessful in obtaining information from Müller, his continued belief in the possibility of a *Clavis Sinica* was such that one finds him still lamenting Müller's death and the loss of his Key in a letter to Bouvet in 1705[81]. So it is not surprising that Leibniz was enthusiastic when in 1697 he received a letter from Müller's sinological successor at Berlin, Christian Mentzel (1622–1701), claiming to have discovered a *Clavis Sinica*. Though Mentzel

---

81 Leibniz to Bouvet, 18 August 1705, *Leibniz-Briefwechsel* 105, sheet 42[r].

offered to assist Leibniz in learning Chinese and to send Chinese books for this purpose, Leibniz was clearly more interested in the Key. (In contrast to Müller and Leibniz, Mentzel inclined toward a more sober conception of the ability of a *Clavis Sinica* which stressed its grammatical function.) Leibniz asked, in questions with a resounding similarity to those put to Müller twenty years earlier, whether the great number of Chinese characters could be reduced to a fixed number of roots or elementary characters and whether other characters might be formed and transformed out of these elementary characters. As with Müller, Leibniz urged Mentzel to publish his Key.

A reply to Leibniz' letter was quick in coming. Unfortunately, it was from Mentzel's son, Johann Christian, who explained that his father was too paralyzed to answer. The young Mentzel wrote that although his father was practically finished with his Key, the printing of the Chinese characters had presented insuperable difficulties and the manuscript had been placed in the Electoral library. However, the title page, dedication and preface had already been printed and he enclosed a copy for Leibniz.

The full title of Mentzel's work was "Clavis Sinica, ad Chinensium Scripturam et Pronunciationem Mandarinicam" (Key to Chinese, to Chinese writing and Mandarin pronunciation). The title page spoke of 124 tables of writing which disclosed the evolving form of the characters. It further indicated that the characters had been drawn mainly from the *Tzu-hui*. The latter was the important Ming period lexical work, in twelve parts, compiled by Mei Ying-tso (1570– 1615). By modifying the ancient *Shuo-wen chieh-tzu* dictionary and other works, Mei was the first to arrange the characters according to 214 radicals (*pu*). This had a major influence upon Ch'ing period lexicographical works, including the important *K'ang-hsi tzu-tien*, a dictionary dating from 1716[82].

In his preface, Mentzel mentioned a second Chinese dictionary, *Cheng-tzu-t'ung*. (Unlike the *Tzu-hui*, where he gave the Chinese characters twice, Mentzel gave only the romanized title "*chim, çu, tum*".) The *Cheng-tzu-t'ung* was a dictionary composed late in the Ming period by Chang Tzu-lieh (fl. 1627) and reprinted with some question of plagiarism in the Ch'ing period by Liao Wen-yen. The *Cheng-tzu-t'ien* was based on the *Tzu-hui* and circulated widely in the late Ming and early Ch'ing dynasties[83].

The *Tzu-hui's* reduction of the manifold Chinese characters to a small number of radical elements was, in Mentzel's mind, confirmation of his attempt to find a Key to Chinese. This confirmation was apparent in Mentzel's preface which stressed that on the basis of "the number of lines and the fashioned form of the points"[84] one could collect an enormous number of Chinese characters under a

---

82 Mei Ying-tso was also the first to develop a list of difficult Chinese characters. See Goodrich, pp. 1061–1062.
83 Goodrich, pp. 1062–1063.
84 *Leibniz-Briefwechsel* (Mentzel) 641, sheet 13[r].

few radical elements. Mentzel referred to "King Fu Hsi" as the oldest Chinese who formed figures from lines and points and constructed them with fixed numbers. Consequently, Mentzel explained, the "radical forms" were fundamental to the evolving character compositions. He stated that in the Chinese dictionary, *Tzu-hui*, the characters were "found in the number seventeen", by which he meant the arrangement of the 214 radicals according to the number of strokes in categories from one to seventeen strokes. They ranged from *i* (one) to *yüeh* (a tubelike instrument or flute; an ancient measure of millet).

There followed a listing of seventeen categories which described the number of radical entries found in each stroke-number category. For example, the first category was described as "the radical form, which corresponds to one line or point (i.e. one stroke), has six entries (i.e. 1st-6th radicals)". The second category was described as "the radical form, which is formed from two lines or points (i.e. two strokes), has 23 entries (i.e. 7th-29th radicals)". The categorizing continued down to the seventeenth category which was described as "the form, which corresponds to 17 lines or points (i.e. 17 strokes), has one entry (i.e. the 214th radical)". It is clear from the manner in which Mentzel treated the 17 categories that he regarded them as more than an artificial arrangement of characters for the purpose of lexical efficiency, though the latter was probably how Mei Ying-tso conceived of them and how they have been used to organize most Chinese dictionaries since 1716. Mentzel, however, saw this categorization of Chinese characters as revealing the underlying structure of the Chinese written language. He believed that these seventeen categories contained a Key which would enormously simplify the task of learning Chinese. One should note that Mentzel's involvement with Mei Ying-tso's *Tzu-hui* extended to the initiating of an ambitious Chinese-Latin lexical work entitled *"Chinensium lexicum characteristicum inscriptum çu guei"*. Although the title page was printed, the work remained largely incomplete in the manuscript form of nine large bound volumes[85].

The second part of Mentzel's preface is more difficult to comprehend. He stated that his Key applied not only to the Chinese script, but also could be used to explain Chinese pronunciation and meaning[86]. In this context he drew upon the *"Vocabulario de letra China, con la explicacion castellana"* by Francisco Diaz (Diez), a seventeenth-century Dominican missionary to China. Mentzel stated that his Key consisted of five classes based on (1) number; (2) primary and secondary radical forms; (3) Chinese pronunciation arranged according to

85 Mentzel's *"Chinensium lexicum characteristicum inscriptum çú guéi"* was preserved prior to World War II in the Sammelband Ms. Sin. 10 of the Preussischen Staatsbibliothek Berlin. See Walter Artelt, *Christian Mentzel, Leibartz der Grossen Kurfürsten, Botaniker und Sinologe* (Leipzig, 1940) pp. 27–28 and table xxi (photograph of the title page) and table xxii (photograph of the first page of text).

86 *Leibniz-Briefwechsel* 641, sheet 13[v].

the Spanish pronunciation, apparently following Diaz' dictionary; (4) a specific grammar; and (5) four paradigms.

It is probable that Mentzel's conception of a *Clavis Sinica* was more modest than that of Müller. Mentzel probably viewed his *Clavis Sinica* as standing somewhere between, on one hand, a device for radically simplifying the translating of Chinese and, on the other hand, a Chinese grammar. One notes that the meaning of the term *Clavis Sinica* evolved in consequent years toward that of a grammar and it was used with that meaning as late as 1814 in the title of a book on Chinese grammar[88]. At any rate, Frau Kraft believes that Mentzel's work was probably based upon a grammar composed by Martini[89]. According to the eighteenth-century sinologist Gottlieb Siegfried Bayer, the manuscript of this grammar was left with Golius by Martini during his visit to Europe in 1654–1657 and consequently came into the hands of Mentzel and later Bayer himself[90]. But according to research with these materials in Glasgow by Mr. Lundbaek, Mentzel obtained Martini's grammar from Cleyer. This claim is supported by Frau Kraft who surmised that Martini left the manuscript of his Chinese grammer with Andreas Cleyer in Batavia where it remained until Mentzel learned of its existence and obtained it from Cleyer[91].

11. BOUVET'S CONTRIBUTION TO LEIBNIZ' UNDERSTANDING OF THE CHINESE LANGUAGE

The belief in a Key to Chinese was not limited to proto-sinologists like Müller, Mentzel and Leibniz. Certain Jesuit missionaries, such as Joachim Bouvet (1656–1730), also believed in the possibility of some Key -- though they rarely used this term -- which would reveal the underlying structure of the Chinese language and thereby expedite the tedious process of learning Chinese characters. When Leibniz put the question regarding such a Key to Fr. Bouvet, the latter responded in his letter of February 28th 1698 with great sympathy and stimulation to Leibniz' questions. Bouvet wrote that the Jesuit missionary

---

87 According to Robert Streit, V, 966, Diaz' *Vocabulario* is a manuscript of 598 pages and is located in the Staatsbibliothek, Berlin. Since Streit's writing, the former Staatsbibliothek collection has been divided between the Deutsche Staatsbibliothek, East Berlin and the Staatsbibliothek Preussischer Kulturbesitz, West Berlin.

88 See Joshua Marshman's *Clavis Sinica, or Elements of Chinese Grammar. Tchoung Koue yan fa (Chung-kuo yen-fa)*. Serampore, 1814.

89 Kraft, "Frühe chinesische Studien in Berlin," p. 116.

90 Bayer, preface, pp. 70 & 88–89.

91 Kraft, "Frühe chinesische Studien in Berlin," p. 116. Cf. Cordier, *Bibliotheca Sinica*, col. 1651.

Claude Visdelou (1656–1737) had undertaken the composition of a Chinese dictionary which would answer Leibniz' questions[92]. In reference to the possibility of a Key of the type that Müller had proposed, Bouvet implied a firm belief in the possibility of making a complete analysis of the Chinese characters. He stated that this analysis would reveal the similarity between the Chinese characters and the Egyptian hieroglyphs, and demonstrate that both were part of the language in use by savants before the Flood. (It is unclear whether Bouvet identified this prediluvian language with the Primitive Language.)

In his letter to Leibniz of November 4th 1701, Bouvet spoke further of an "analysis of the characters which [Leibniz] desires"[93]. Further along in this letter, Bouvet wrote that Leibniz' belief in a "connection" among the Chinese characters was sound and that this connection gave a basis for understanding the characters and for retaining them in the memory, i.e. exactly the intention of Müller's Key! Furthermore, Bouvet stated that if dictionaries were based on this connection, then the mastery of Chinese would be rendered far less tedious and prohibitive to so many people. Bouvet noted, in a definite advance upon Mentzel's knowledge, that the Chinese dictionaries did use a method of organizing characters according to radicals, but they limited this organization to the number of strokes rather than to a more significant arrangement[94]. In effect, Bouvet reflected the more sophisticated awareness that the arrangement of characters by stroke-count was probably a lexical rather than analytical device.

At the conclusion of his letter of November 4th 1701, Bouvet analyzed "some of the hieroglyphs which have been used for over 4,500 years by the philosophers of the Orient in order to denote the Supreme Being"[95]. On the basis of Bouvet's information about Chinese characters, Leibniz began to perceive the characters as being less literal or pictographic representatives of things and more philosophical. In his letter to Bouvet which has been tentatively dated 1703, Leibniz reversed his previous acceptance of similarities between Chinese and Egyptian script by saying:

I have been reluctant to believe that [the hieroglyphs of Egypt] have had some agreement with [the characters] of the Chinese because it seems to me that the Egyptian characters are of a very popular sort and have a great deal of resemblance to perceptible things such as animals, etc. and consequently with allegories. Instead, the Chinese characters are perhaps more philosophical and might seem to have been based more on intellectual con-

92 Leibniz-Briefwechsel 105, sheet 10^r.
93 Leibniz, *Leibnitii opera omnia* Ludovici Dutens, ed. 6 vols. (Geneva, 1768) IV, 160.
94 Dutens, IV, 162.
95 Dutens, IV, 162–164. Because the Dutens edition deleted the Chinese characters and diacritical marks and contained at least one error in transposing Bouvet's Chinese romanizations, it is important that the student of this letter of November 4th 1701 consult the original manuscript of this portion of Bouvet's letter in *Leibniz-Briefwechsel* 105, sheets 26^r-26^v. Bouvet's analysis of the Chinese "hieroglyphs" found in this letter is discussed in this author's *Leibniz and Confucianism: the Search for Accord* (Honolulu, 1977) pp. 53–58.

siderations such as number, order and relations, so that there are only detached traits which support any resemblance to some type of material form[96].

Leibniz went on to say that while some claimed that the Chinese represented colonies of the Egyptians — Kircher had claimed this in *China illustrata*[97] — Leibniz saw little proof to support this. In terms of profundity and depth, Leibniz reversed the priority of Egyptian hieroglyphs over Chinese characters which Kircher had assigned.

Stimulated by Leibniz' explanation of his binary system of mathematics, Bouvet wrote to Leibniz on November 4th 1701 explaining how he perceived a merging of mathematics and language in the ancient Chinese system of writing. Bouvet stated:

> I am not at all surprised at the Characteristic plan that you are proposing for representing thoughts so that the same characters serve all together for calculating and for demonstrating in reasoning, etc. . For this genre of writing seems to contain the true idea of the ancient hieroglyphs and of the Kabbala of the Hebrews as well as the characters of Fu Hsi who is regarded by the Chinese as the first inventor of letters or hieroglyphs of this nation, in the formation of which one commonly says that he used the 64 combinations of his system of whole and broken lines . . .[98].

Bouvet claimed that Fu Hsi's system of ancient Chinese writing was — "if one believes the Chinese chronology", which Bouvet did — over 4,600 years old and therefore the oldest written monument on earth. According to Bouvet, Fu Hsi had intended his numerically-based system of language to "teach to posterity by means of this system the causes and true principles of the production of the universe and of all the parts which compose it"[99]. Bouvet enclosed a copy of the "Natural Order" (*Hsien-t'ien tzu-hsü*) diagram of the hexagrams whose arrangement — if one allows the divided line to represent 0 and the whole line to represent 1 — corresponded to Leibniz' binary progression[100]. (See plate 20.)

Clearly, Leibniz had found a kindred spirit in Bouvet. More importantly, Bouvet had supplied him with an historical instance of a numerically-based language — said to be the oldest in the world — which showed an astounding similarity to Leibniz' own attempts to develop a mathematically-based language. As Leibniz studied this supposedly ancient Chinese diagram that Bouvet sent him, his belief

96 *Leibniz-Briefwechsel* 105, sheet 34[r].
97 Kircher, *China illustrata*, p. 226.
98 Dutens, IV, 154–155.
99 Dutens, IV, 158.
100 For a detailed description of the similarities between Leibniz' binary system of mathematics and the Natural Order (*Hsien-t'ien tzu-hsü*) diagram, see this author's *Leibniz and Confucianism*, pp. 49–52. Cf. the presentation of this diagram in Hans J. Zacher, *Die Hauptschriften zur Dyadik von G. W. Leibniz* (Frankfurt am Main, 1973) p. 86f.

that it confirmed his own work grew[101]. While the Natural Order of the hexa-grams accorded with a binary progression, there were other arrangements of the hexagrams which did not. Furthermore, the more usual Chinese manner of counting the lines of the diagrams was from the bottom up rather than from the top down, as Leibniz did. Leibniz himself was aware of the contradition between the hexagram order in the diagram Bouvet sent him and certain *kua* (diagrams) found in *Confucius Sinarum philosophus* (1687). Consequently, in a postscript to his letter of 1703, he asked Bouvet for clarification of this discrepancy[102].

In his letter to Bouvet of 1704, Leibniz showed himself clearly stimulated by the significance of these "lined characters of Fu Hsi"[103]. He spoke of acquiring increasing insights into how the figures might be apprehended by means of the "perfection of the science of numbers". But he also spoke of having meditated on certain philosophic elements in the figures which he viewed in the Euclidean manner of calculating universal species from a small number of axioms. He was particularly struck by the potential for precision, which was all too often lacking in philosophy[104]. Finally, Leibniz clearly indicated that he was thinking in terms of parallels to his own system by referring to monads or Simple Substances and the Pre-Established Harmony.

It seems quite likely that this information on the Chinese language from Bou-vet contributed to Leibniz' reference to the Chinese language in the *Nouveaux essais*. There, Leibniz spoke of Chinese as "artificial, that is, invented all at once by some capable man [i.e. Fu Hsi?] in order to establish communication be-tween a number of different nations which inhabited that large country which we call China, although this language would be altered today through long us-age"[105]. Though Leibniz attributed this view of the Chinese language to Golius, the conjunction of the composition of the *Nouveaux essais* (1703–1705) with the Bouvet correspondence, make the ultimate source of Leibniz' claim likely to have been Bouvet.

101 The Natural Order diagram of the hexagrams was not as ancient as Bouvet had as-sumed. Beginning in Bouvet's own time, Chinese scholars began tracing this diagram to the early Sung dynasty (ca. A.D. 960) rather than to 4600 B.C.. See this author's *Leibniz and Confucianism*, pp. 64–65.

102 Leibniz specifically referred to the trigrams (three-lined figures) in *Confucius Sinarum philosophus*, p. xlii, rather than to the arrangement of the hexagrams (six-lined figures) on p. xliv. Leibniz-Briefwechsel 105, sheet 35^r.

103 Leibniz-Briefwechsel 105, sheet 36^r.

104 Leibniz-Briefwechsel 105, sheet 36^r-36^v.

105 Leibniz, *Nouveaux essais*, (book III, ch. 1: "On words or language in general") VI; 6, 274.

12. CONCLUSION

The seventeenth-century European search for a universal language reveals some of the complex interplay between the forces which were shaping the European assimilation of information about China. These forces included the Biblical conceptions of language, the medieval legacy of Lull's combinatorial art and the creative intellectual currents of the Scientific Revolution. The sixteenth-century discovery voyages had stimulated European minds with the tremendous variety of foreign languages and cultures, but it was the works of seventeenth-century accommodative missionaries such as Ricci-Trigault, Semedo, Martini and (via Kircher) Boym who provided most of the detailed information on the Chinese language. The supplying of Europe with information about China appears not to have been a major part of the original formulation of Jesuit accommodation in China, but appears rather to have developed gradually out of practical needs. These involved, first, the need of Jesuit procurators to stimulate European interest and support for the China Mission and, later in the seventeenth century, the need to cultivate and rally European support for the Jesuit position in the Rites Controversy. But from an historical perspective, the European assimilation of information about China stimulated proto-sinologists to think in exciting (and often faulty) ways about languages. The blending which took place with the European search for a universal language transcended exotica to represent an example of assimilation of information from China into a main stream of seventeenth-century European culture.

CHAPTER VII
THE GERMAN PROTO-SINOLOGISTS' SEARCH FOR A
CLAVIS SINICA

1. THE GREAT ELECTOR FRIEDRICH WILHELM'S
INTEREST IN SINOLOGY

The story of the German assimilation of Chinese culture in the late seventeenth century was one of earthly visions of profit and a scholarship where dreams predominated. Friedrich Wilhelm (r. 1640–1688), the Elector of Brandenburg – known more familiarly as the Great Elector – laid the cornerstone of the modern Brandenburg-Prussian state in his attempts to consolidate his inherited and acquired territories. What he inherited were territories ravaged by the Thirty Years War (1618–1648), but what he bequeathed to his son was a state with centralized administration and finances, and a small, but remarkably efficient army.

Friedrich Wilhem's early residence in Holland and study at the University of Leiden had impressed him with the Dutch methods of maritime and commercial success and forged lifelong ties to Holland. When the Elector opened war- and plague-decimated Berlin of the 1660s to enterprising individuals, we find him greeting the Dutchman, Gijsel van Lier, a former official of the Dutch East India Company and a European relatively knowledgeable about Asia[1]. It was probably no coincidence to Van Lier's arrival that the Elector was looking for ways to free his realm from dependence on the Dutch in foreign trade and Van Lier encouraged the Elector to found an East India trading company.

But Friedrich Wilhelm faced the perennial problem of small states – he simply did not have the resources to carry out the founding of an East India company alone. Looking for assistance, he turned first to Emperor Leopold I of Vienna. The Emperor, however, tended not only to dominate things, but also offended the Elector's Protestant scruples by drawing the Spanish into the plan. The Elector dropped the plan of collaboration in 1661 and did not take it up again until 1683 when the Hapsburgs were too heavily involved in a war with the Turks to take interest. In his second attempt at finding support, the Elector encouraged British Protestants with naval skills who were disgruntled with Restoration England to emigrate to Brandenburg, but the numbers recruited were disappointing. A Brandenburg East India Company – Vereingte Ost India Compagnie – actually functioned between the years 1682 and 1732, but its activities did not extend beyond East Africa.

---

1 Kraft, "Frühe chinesische Studien in Berlin," p. 96.

Friedrich Wilhelm's maritime aspirations had their intellectual manifestations. With the possibility of profits to be reaped, the Elector was interested in learning about China and thus became a sponsor of some of the earliest sinological research in Germany. The purchase of Van Lier's Chinese books helped to provide the nucleus of what eventually became a notable East Asian collection in Berlin. For a city such as Berlin with neither academy nor university, the importance of a library was critical. The Electoral library was shaped by the Elector's interests, which were crucial to its survival. The initial phase of the building of the East Asian collection and the sinological research produced as a by-product were primarily the fruits of two men — Andreas Müller and Christian Mentzel. This phase began with the appointment of Müller as provost of the Nicholaikirche in 1667 and ended with Mentzel's death in 1701. During these nearly 33 years, Berlin was a center of proto-sinological research whose primary defect — the absence of a developed knowledge of the Chinese language — fated it to remain an amateur effort.

Nevertheless, Müller and Mentzel left a remarkable sinological legacy which has not received its due attention. This legacy was carefully studied by one of the most eminent European sinologists of the eighteenth century, Gottfried Siegfried Bayer (1694—1738). Before being called to the newly established St. Petersburg academy in 1726, the Königsberg-born Bayer made more than one trip to Berlin to copy books and manuscripts from the Chinese collection there[2]. Contemporary assessments of sinological resources in European libraries have been shaped by the curious neglect by the great French and British sinologists of the nineteenth and early twentieth centuries of Chinese collections north of the Alps and east of the Rhine. Rome and Paris were regarded as the fundamental centers of sinological research. Consequently, it may be somewhat surprising to read Julius Klaproth in 1822 referring to the Berlin collection as "not only a very useful apparatus for the study of the Chinese language, but also one more complete for Manchu than any other European library, with the exception of Paris, possesses"[3].

2. ANDREAS MÜLLER'S ACADEMIC BACKGROUND

Andreas Müller (1630—1694) was born in Greifenhagen in Pomerania, in present-day Poland. He was the son of a merchant and member of the landed

2 Siegfried Bayer's *Museum Sinicum* contains a number of comments, many of which are critical, on the sinological efforts of Müller and Mentzel. Bayer's work is the subject of a forthcoming monograph by Knud Lundbaek entitled *T. S. Bayer (1694—1738): Pioneer Sinologist.*

3 Julius Klaproth, *Verzeichniss der chinesischen und mandschuischen Bücher und Handschriften der königlichen Bibliothek zu Berlin* (Paris, 1822) p. vii.

gentry[4]. In 1649 Müller entered the university at Rostock to study Middle Eastern languages and theology. In 1653 he became the rector of the town school in Königsberg/Neumark and in 1655 was referred to as "prefect" at Treptow/Tollensee. He visited the orientalist Golius in Amsterdam in 1656[5]. In 1657 he undertook further studies at the university in Greifswald[6]. In 1658 Müller and a friend, Martinus Murray (Mourey), registered at Leiden and in 1659, Müller presented a second disputation to the philosophy faculty at Rostock.

In 1660 Müller was appointed *dozent* at Rostock, but did not appear to assume his post. Instead, he may have gone to England to visit Edmund Castell, professor of Arabic at Cambridge, and Brian Walton, bishop of Chester and a scholar associated with the seventeenth-century search for a universal language. The details of this trip remain obscure, but it is clear that any stay in England would have been brief since Müller returned to Stettin for his marriage in 1661 and to the birth of a son in 1662[7]. In 1664 Müller undertook a *Probepredigt* (test preaching) at Bernau near Berlin. His excellent sermons and his reputation in Oriental learning brought him to the attention of Friedrich Wilhelm and led to Müller's appointment in 1667 as provost of the Nicolaikirche in Berlin.

Müller's provostship in Berlin was beset by difficulties from the start. He arrived during the concluding phase of a religious controversy. In an attempt to reduce the strife between the dominant Lutherans and members of the Reformed Church, of which the Elector was an orthodox member, the latter put

4 The more recent accounts of Müller's life include: Donald F. Lach, "Chinese studies of Andreas Müller," *Journal of the American Oriental Society* 60 (1945): 564–575; Hans Wehr, "Andreas Müller," *Pommersche Lebensbilder* (Cologne) 4 (1966): 21–35; & Kraft, "Frühe chinesische Studien in Berlin." However, the Lach and Kraft accounts contradict one another on several points. In response to a query, Frau Kraft clarified in a private letter of 7 September 1978 and in conversation in August of 1979 where she believes both the Lach and Wehr accounts are in error. Her claims are based upon research which has superceded the work of Mr. Lach. Reference to the discrepancies will follow at appropriate points below.

5 Eva S. Kraft, "Die chinesische Büchersammlung des Grossen Kurfürsten," in *China und Europa Ausstellungskatalog* (Berlin, 1973) p. 20.

6 Both Lach "Chinese studies of Andreas Müller," p. 564 and Wehr, p. 21, claim that Müller studied at Wittenberg, but Frau Kraft clarifies in her letter of 7 September 1978 that this was another and younger Andreas Müller.

7 Mr. Lach claims that Müller remained in England for ten years where he lived in Castell's home and collaborated with him in the creation of a dictionary, whose manuscript was lost in the London fire of 1666. However, the scholar Bülow has noted that this ten year stay in England is erroneous – Müller was back in his homeland in 1661. See Bülow's article on Müller in *Allgemeine deutsche Biographie* (Leipzig, 1885) XXII, 513. A scholar of Müller's work has privately suggested to me that Lach's misunderstanding may have arisen from a misreading of Müller's dedication to Castell in *Disquisitio geographica et historica de Chataja* (A geographical and historical disquisition on Cathay) (1671). Here Müller states that his friend Murray was in London for ten years and this may have been misinterpreted by Lach to apply to Müller himself.

forth a toleration edict which he demanded that all churchmen sign. While other Lutheran pastors had resisted the Elector's edict, Müller signed. This exacerbated his relations with other Lutherans, who consistently opposed Müller's appointment and work, but it apparently pleased the Elector, for later Müller was charged with the expansion of the Elector's East Asian library. In 1675 he automatically succeeded to an advisorship on the Elector's council. He remained active at the Elector's court until a theological controversy, of which more will be said below, led to his leaving Berlin in 1685. Müller spent the last nine years of his life largely isolated at Stettin and died there in a house which still stands today[8].

Müller was a student of a wide range of European and Asian languages. His study of Hebrew dated from his university days. He was able to read as well as to write, on a limited degree, Turkish, Persian and Syrian. He appears to have had a deeper knowledge of Arabic. Other miscellaneous languages in which he had limited degrees of knowledge were Aramaic, Samaritan, Armenian, Coptic, Russian, Hungarian and modern Greek. His knowledge of Chinese lies under a question mark which we shall try to clarify. Müller's duties as provost involved him with the schools, the poor and the church. These duties, along with the special requests of the Elector, made Müller hard-pressed to find time for sinological studies[9].

3. MÜLLER'S INVENTION OF THE *CLAVIS SINICA*

Müller dated the beginning of his "invention" (i.e. the *Clavis Sinica*) from November 18th 1667[10]. He tested and developed his Key over the next six years and then in February of 1674 presented his invention to the Elector with a printed proposal. The proposal reflected the earthly needs and demands to which scholars are so often bound. Simply put, Müller was asking for money and for a commitment of half in advance. The Elector's interest was aroused, but not enough to pay. Yet he appears to have wanted to keep the project within his jurisdiction and lent Müller the use of his title to refer to the Key as the "Brandenburg Invention".

With the Elector's blessings, Müller's announcement of his Key was republished in April bearing its prestigious new title, describing the invention and soliciting financial contributors. In this situation, Friedrich Wilhelm showed a first sign of

8 Wehr, pp. 33–34, states that Müller's house stands at Grosser Domstrasse 27, on the corner of Grosser Domstrasse and Grosser Ritterstrasse.

9 Kraft, "Frühe chinesischen Studien in Berlin," pp. 100–101 & 103. Mr. Lach in his "Chinese studies of Andreas Müller," p. 565, credits Müller with a bit more leisure time for sinological studies than does Frau Kraft.

10 In 1686 or soon thereafter, Müller composed a brief chronology of events surrounding the *Clavis Sinica* which was later published in 1697 (?).

the equivocation which would mark his dealings with Müller's Key. The Elector's interest was significant and somewhat proprietary. When the Orientalist Hiob Jobus Ludolf (1624–1704) expressed a willingness to pay a premium of one-thousand thalers for Müller to teach Ludolf's fourteen year-old son his *Clavis Sinica*, the Elector blocked the transaction. According to Müller's claim in the "Chronolista Clavis", it was insisted in 1681 that the Key be composed under the Elector's auspices. But the Elector's interest was not strong enough to commit cash, which was no doubt scarce at Brandenburg, nor later forcefully to defend Müller's Key against charges or heresy. In the assessment of why the Key was never published, the Elector was not without responsibility.

The full title of Müller's published announcement of his Key was "*Propositio super Clave sua Sinica, quam autor Inventum Brandenburgicum cognominare constituit*" (A proposal on his Chinese Key, which the author has decided to name the Brandenburg Invention)[11]. The "Propositio" was a mere four-page pamphlet which stimulated a reaction in the scholarly world out of all proportion to its substance and makes it a prime document for the student of academic advertising. The "Propositio" consisted of 26 numbered statements and began by warning its readers against inventors who do precisely what Müller was himself later accused of doing, namely, "Many [inventors] also have promised a golden mountain, promised in vain, and one aptly quotes the verse: 'if the promiser blows his own trumpet a lot, he will perform poorly' ". Müller anticipated the reader's skepticism in claiming for his Key "a method, in which everyone can read, what is written in Chinese in spite of the well-known fact that [Chinese] deals with an immense number of characters".

Müller went on to claim a wide number of people who would benefit from his Key, including the Chinese themselves (!) for it would provide them with an extensive lexicon. He claimed that the Key would be useful for the neighbors of China, such as the Japanese, Koreans, Tonkinese, Cochinese, Siamese, Cambodians, Burmese and Laotians, all of whom Müller claimed wrote with Chinese characters, but spoke in a different tongue. (Müller erred in including the Siamese, Cambodians, Burmese and Laotians in this list.) Closer to Europe, Müller claimed that his method would be helpful to official envoys, missionaries, traders, travelers and physicians. Finally, he claimed that his Key would be useful to the spread of Christianity, to learning the Chinese sciences and to the development of a universal written language.

To emphasize the extreme difficulty of learning to read Chinese, Müller drew from Ricci-Trigault's *De Christiana expeditione apud Sinas,* Martini's *Sinicae historiae decas prima* and an unspecified work — probably *Divers voyages et missions* (Paris 1653) — by Alexander de Rhodes, S.J. (1591–1660). Müller was

---

11 I am indebted to Frau Kraft for sending me a copy of this now rare "Propositio," whose original is found in the Österreich Nationalbibliothek, Vienna. A manuscript of the "Propositio" is also held by the Österreich Nationalbibliothek.

much intrigued by the claim of the proto-sinologist Spitzel in *De re literaria Sinensium* that Chinese was constructed with neither art nor standard. (Spitzel was a complete amateur in sinology and had derived this claim from the works of the more informed Fr. Martini.) It was clearly this claim of a lack of structural order in Chinese that had attracted Müller. Faced with a strange and difficult language, certain early missionaries failed to perceive the structural elements in the Chinese language. Müller's scholarly instincts saw their error, though he underestimated the task to such an extent that he erred in the other direction. It is in this later vein of excess that one should interpret Müller's claim that his method could make Chinese characters easier to read than any other script.

Yet after rousing the reader's interest, Müller declared that the "secret" of his method had not yet been prepared for distribution. He would go no farther with its preparation until a prince, state or scholarly society recompensed him. He promised that after half of the agreed-upon amount was paid into an escrow account, he would then proceed with the preparation of the Key. By refusing to complete the Key before payment, Müller declared that he would prevent his secret from falling into unauthorized hands after his death. This claim is instructive. Though apparently ungenerous, it was consistent with Müller's later destruction of the Key just prior to his death. It is not necessary to speculate that he was distracted by illness and burned the Key accidentally or that his realization of the Key's failure to live up to his claims led him to burn the Key in order to save his reputation. If we are to believe Müller's own words, then he destroyed his Key because of a rigid and unforgiving character. As we shall see, there are other patterns in Müller's life which reinforce this conclusion.

Müller himself felt that his Key was largely complete for he estimated that after payment of the agreed-upon sum, he would need only a half-year or less in order to prepare the Key for distribution. With the completed result, he claimed that he would be able to teach even women and boys within a few days' instruction to translate a Chinese book or sheet of Chinese writing into common European tongues. Müller was so confident of his method that he proposed that a date be established for a test reading and examination to follow his period of instruction of specified students in the Key. He proposed that after the test reading – he assumed satisfactory results – the balance of the payment should be paid, as well as the prepayment in the escrow account transferred, to him and the Key would then be handed over to the purchasers.

Anticipating criticisms of his proposal, Müller stated that he had published his conditions not in order to make a profit, but that he might not be slandered later for refusing to release his Key. This pattern of anticipating criticisms with defensive explanations betrayed a streak of extreme sensitivity in Müller. (A less charitable interpretation might claim that this pattern of behavior betrayed the guilty conscience of a scholarly imposter, but I think there are justifiable grounds for rejecting the more negative viewpoint.) Finally, for the reader who wished to have further information on his aims, Müller referred him to page ten and following of *Monumenti Sinici . . . lectio.*

Why was Müller so anxious to obtain a firm commitment of renumeration for his Key? Aside from the more obvious answers of greed and fraud, several factors should be noted. The Elector presided over a poor land and his financial situation frequently was precarious. Müller and others associated with the Brandenburg court felt this in the frequent delay of their salaries. Secondly, Müller seemed to have accumulated considerable expense in his composition of a wooden typeset of Chinese characters. Default on printing or other debts was a serious crime in Müller's day and he would have been well aware of the experience of his English colleague, Edmund Castell, in debtor's prison[12]. Finally, Müller's demand for prepayment also may have sprung from an impeccably scholarly motive – the wish to publish his findings. It may be that prepayment was the only way that Müller was able to secure a printer.

Müller's typographia was perhaps the first largescale composition of a Chinese printing-type in Europe and its difficulty should not be underestimated. Fr. Couplet, the editor of *Confucius Sinarum philosophus*, had to forego his original plan of including the Chinese text because of the difficulties of composing the Chinese type[13]. In 1684 Müller presented his Chinese typographia to the Electoral library as a gift. Unlike many Chinese books and manuscripts in that collection, the typographia has survived the ravages of war and may be found today in the Deutsche Staatsbibliothek, East Berlin, stored in what appears to be the identical wooden chest in which Müller presented the typographia to the library[14]! The typographia consists of small wooden blocks on each of which is engraved one Chinese character. Each block is numbered and there are a total of 3,284 blocks[15].

12 Lach, "Chinese studies of Andreas Müller," p. 567.
13 Bayer, I, 65.
14 Through the kind cooperation of the staff of the Asien-Afrika-Abteilung of the Deutsche Staatsbibliothek, East Berlin, I was able to examine Müller's Chinese typographia in August of 1979. According to the staff, the typographia had been publicly displayed in an exhibition at the library in 1969.
15 The size of the woodblocks in Müller's Chinese typographia vary slightly, but a typical size is 2.4 cm. (width) by 2.4 cm. (length) by 2.7 cm. (depth). The chest consists of ten flat drawers, two of which have the blocks arranged in twelve groups of 40 blocks each, plus one group of 20 blocks. Some of these groupings appear to reflect certain rough similarities of character forms in which the squarish aspect has been emphasized. However, it may be that these quadratic shapes with their angular lines are essentially only reflective of the technique of wood carving. (When carved by Chinese artisans in wood or stone, the characters also take on a more quadratic and angular shape than when drawn with a brush.) In short, no clearly identifiable pattern of organization was apparent to this writer's eyes and one must not assume that the woodblocks are necessarily arranged in an order reflective of Müller's *Clavis Sinica*.
    The other eight drawers of this chest containing Müller's Chinese typographia include various woodblocks in scattered array. Some of the blocks are in various states of completion and reveal how the blocks were cut from strips of wood and the characters first inscribed with a pencil and then carved. The drawers also contain various

Müller mentioned no specific amount of recompense in his "Propositio". In his "Chronologia Clavis", he recorded that "1,000 *Kaiserthaler*" were promised in 1676, but retracted. Possibly he was referring to the promise made by the Elector which was of paper value only[17]. In 1678 Müller recorded that another individual — possibly Herr Ludolf in the offer cited earlier — was prepared to pay "1,000 *Joachimthaler*". It may have been that the 1,000 thalers consisted of the first payment only, since a total figure of 2,000 thalers appeared in later references. According to the "Chronolista Clavis", just before leaving Berlin in February 1685 and in what could hardly have been the best circumstances for asking, Müller made a somewhat desperate, departing request to the Elector for 2,000 thalers for the Key, but was rejected. This was a considerable, but by no means extravagantly large amount. By means of comparison, in 1678, Leibniz on behalf of Duke Johann Friedrich of Hannover, negotiated the purchase of the 3,600 volume library of the deceased scholar, Martin Fogel of Hamburg, for the cost of 2,000 *Reichsthaler*. One-thousand thalers were paid on delivery with the balance due within one year's time[18]. One also notes that when Müller bought a house in Stettin in 1685, he paid 510 thalers[19].

4. MÜLLER-KIRCHER CORRESPONDENCE ON THE *CLAVIS SINICA*

At the time of the publication of the "Propositio", the European intellectual climate was ripe for the invention of a *Clavis Sinica*. It had created a ready-made body of believers whereas a different climate, such as the twentieth century, would have created instant skeptics. Logically, the notion of a "key"

printed samples of the blocks, the printed form of which is crude by contemporary standards, but superior to the characters found in Kircher's *China illustrata*. Also in the chest is a hand-written statement dated "*etwa* 1936" and possibly authored by the German sinologist, Otto Franke (1863–1946). Other than identifying the typographia as a gift from Müller, the statement claims that the circumstances of the production of this typographia are unknown. It also claims that the wood blocks were probably intended for use in a *Schrifttafel* (table of script). Finally, the drawers of this chest contain miscellaneous pieces of wood carved with characters of a much smaller size in vertical columns plus some carved samples of script which appears to be Arabic. Among these smaller Chinese characters is a quotation from the *Chung yung* 2.2 and a row of characters demonstrating structural similarities. Both of these samples of smaller Chinese characters as well as the above-mentioned sample of Arabic script derive from Athanasius Kircher's letter to Müller of December 28th 1674. Müller had Kircher's examples of script made into wood type in order to include them in the publication of his correspondence with Kircher, which is discussed later in this chapter.

16 Andreas Müller, *De invento Sinico epistolae nonnullae* (Berlin?, undated) pp. 4, 6 & 7.
17 Kraft, "Frühe chinesische Studien in Berlin," p. 103.
18 Kurt Müller & Gisela Krönert, *Leben und Werk von G. W. Leibniz, eine Chronik* (Frankfurt am Main, 1969) p. 53.
19 Wehr, p. 33.

which could simplify the learning of a language such as Chinese, defied practical experience and, in particular, the reports on the difficulty of learning Chinese sent back by the missionaries in China. However, the belief in the possibility of a universal language was quite strong. Whether one could rediscover the Primitive Language of the Bible or whether one constructed a new universal language, all languages were widely believed to be based on certain fundamental principles which, once discerned, could be applied to any language. Consequently, Müller's announcement was not received with as much skepticism as would seem appropriate today.

Yet skeptics were not entirely lacking and some were cynical. After Müller's death, the more sinologically-learned Siegfried Bayer criticized the errors and defects in Müller's Key. Bayer accused Müller of being duped by the wild ideas of Kircher who was clever enough to "teach fish to sing, not to say human beings"[20]. But Bayer's harsh remark came long after the publication of the "Propositio". In the years immediately following the appearance of Müller's announcement of the Key, he received a number of letters and inquiries. He published some of the letters in *De invento Sinico epistolae nonnullae . . .* (undated) in what was more of an attempt to publicize than to explain the Key.

Included in this collection was an exchange with the far more eminent, but also novice sinologist, Kircher. Fr. Kircher's knowledge had been sobered by personal contact with missionaries who had learned Chinese in its native context. Consequently, when Müller sent the announcement of his "Propositio" to Kircher in 1674, the latter responded with a letter expressing amazement and disbelief at such a proposal[21]. Kircher's incredulity was based upon his awareness of the enormous difficulty of mastering Chinese — a language which Kircher called the most difficult in the world. Kircher referred to Prospero Intorcetta's *Sinarum scientia politico-moralis* (1667–1669) which contained a translation of the brief Chinese classic, *Chung yung*. (It is possible that Kircher had personally discussed this translation with Fr. Intorcetta during the latter's visit as Jesuit procurator to Rome in 1671.) Kircher spoke of learning through long experience that a single voiced Chinese word had many meanings and he stressed the necessity of learning from the living voice of a teacher which Kircher, unlike Müller in remote Brandenburg, had experienced in the form of returned China missionaries and their Chinese traveling companions. This lack of actual contact with an experienced Chinese speaker was perhaps Kircher's most telling criticism and the criticism which Müller made the greatest effort to rebut.

---

20 Bayer, I, 38. For this translation from Bayer's *Museum Sinicum,* I am indebted to Knud Lundbaek, whose recent research on Bayer will appear in the forthcoming *T.S. Bayer (1694–1738): Pioneer Sinologist.* Cf. Lach, "The Chinese studies of Andreas Müller," p. 568.

21 See Kircher's letter to Müller dated December 28th 1674 in Müller, *De invento Sinico,* pp. 2–8.

Kircher spoke of a Chinese dictionary in his possession composed by Fr. Intorcetta and the Jesuit missionaries in which 80,000 Chinese characters were analyzed into eight different classes of characters and reduced to 5,000 characters, which constituted a very usefully sized dictionary. Kircher referred to a Chinese dictionary called the "Ocean" and which was said to contain 6,000 characters. It seems to have been some sort of model – of size and/or organizing principle – for the Jesuit father's dictionary. The "Ocean" dictionary was possibly a reference to an obscure Chinese dictionary called the *Hai-p'ien*, a copy of which is preserved in the Vatican library. This copy of the *Hai-p'ien* consists of several thousand pages of Chinese wood-block type which have been rebound into two European-style volumes. The first volume contains a six-page preface in running-grass style script which is not clearly signed, but dated ca. 1623[22]. The complete title of the work is *Ching-kai [chün] Hai-jo T'ang hsien-sheng chiao-ting hai-p'ien t'ung-huai* (The revised Ocean-volume collection finely inscribed by Mr. Hai-jo T'ang)[23].

In regard to the content of the *Hai-p'ien*, there are two introductory *chüan*, the first of which deals primarily with the pronunciation and tones of characters and the second of which deals with the pronunciation of difficult characters from classicial literature. The main corpus of the *Hai-p'ien*, which consists of twenty *chüan,* is a dictionary organized according to radicals in a manner similar, but not identical to the manner found in the *P'ien-hai* or, in its more complete title, *Hsiang-chiao p'ien-hai* (A detailed comparative volume of oceanlike dimensions), a copy of which is also found in the Biblioteca Vaticana. There is a rather ironic possibility that the copy of the *Hai-p'ien* which Müller used is the copy now found in the Biblioteca Vaticana. This possibility derives from the fact that the German sinologist Klaproth, who worked with the Berlin collection, sold a copy of the *Hai-p'ien* to Antonio Montucci, an Italian sinologist. Montucci inserted into the *Hai-p'ien* the copy of Klaproth's formal bill of sale which lists "Un dictionnaire Chinois intitule [Chinese characters] Hai-pien en 12 cahiers" and is dated May 12th 1812. How Klaproth might have acquired the rights of sale of a valuable 200-year old Chinese dictionary from the Berlin

22 In the preface to this *Hai-p'ien* (Borgia Cinese 262–263), the T'ien-ch'i reign date (1621–1627) is clearly marked, but the designation for the year is less clear and is tentatively identified by this writer as *kuei-hai* (i.e. 1623).

23 This so-called Mr. Hai-jo T'ang (Hai Jo-t'ang? T'ang Hai-jo?) has not been identified by this author, though I note that Hai-jo is the *hao* (penname) of the Ch'ing dynasty figure Li Ch'ang-hsiang of Yen prefecture of Chekiang province. It may be significant that the *P'ien-hai* dictionary, which is somewhat similar to the *Hai-p'ien* and also found in the Vatican collection (Borgia Cinese 255) and discussed in the text, is said by the Biblioteca Vaticana cataloguers to be composed by a Chinese with the same surname, namely "Li Täng." On the other hand, the *P'ien-hai* is also said to be a re-edition dated 1608, which is somewhat prior to the Ch'ing dynasty (1644–1911) with which Li Ch'ang-hsiang was associated. Also, the preface of the *Hai-p'ien* dated it as a late Ming, not Ch'ing, period compilation.

library is an interesting question which this writer must leave to others to answer[24].

Kircher goes on to say that in the Jesuit-produced Chinese dictionary, the characters were arranged in the margins in a manner which demonstrated the underlying structural similarity between the various groupings. He gave the example of five characters all pronounced *"wei"* with a falling (i.e. fourth) tone[25]. These are as follows: (1) wei[a] (name of a river in northern China) (2) wei[b] (fire; bright light) (3) wei[c] (restless heart) (4) wei[d] (a saying) and (5) wei[e] (hedgehog). Kircher's explanations and interpretations were roughly accurate, though sometimes erroneous as in referring to the third example as *"cor quietum"* (quiet heart) when it seems to have meant the opposite. However, Kircher failed to recognize that the underlying similarity here contained in the right-hand side of each character was phonetic rather than semantic. The Jesuit missionaries were doubtless aware of this, but Kircher's lesser experience with the language led him into pitfalls. These pitfalls were exactly what he was warning Müller about!

Kircher then proceeded to give Müller examples of three characters, each of which he analyzed into two semantic elements each. In the first example, he broke down *hsin* (faith; belief) into *jen* (man) and *yen* (word). Next, he noted that Chinese equivalents were monosyllabic, but illustrated how one character might have several pronunciations and meanings. He used a character pronounced variously as *lo, yao, liao* and *yüeh*, all of which were in a falling tone. Kircher appears to have erred in transliterating the fourth pronunciation, but most standard Chinese dictionaries today list only three pronunciations for this particular character and one must consult a comprehensive dictionary such as the *Chung-wen ta-tzu-tien* to find all four plus a fifth *(luo)* pronunciation. Consequently, one would judge that Kircher's source of information on Chinese pronunciation was reasonably comprehensive.

After enumerating some of the difficulties of the Chinese language, Kircher stated — in the elaborately polite style of seventeenth-century correspondence — that it was inconceivable to him how Müller, who lacked both the ability to write in Chinese and the experience of hearing Chinese spoken, could have developed such a key. Kircher inserted one exception into his conviction of

---

24 One notes that the copy of the *Hai-p'ien* dictionary at Berlin was examined by Siegfried Bayer, who mentions this work in his *Museum Sinicum* (St. Petersburg, 1730), preface, p. 142. The same or another copy of the *Hai-p'ien* is described by the French sinologist, Etienne Fourmont, in his *Meditationes et grammatica Sinica* (Paris [?], 1737) pp. 124–126. Finally, one notes the existence of the Chinese work, *P'ien-hai lei-pien*, a dictionary in twenty *chüan* and attributed to the early Ming scholar, Sung Lien (1310–1381) and the late Ming scholar, T'u Lung (1542–1605). The Ssu-k'u catalog lists the work, but denies the attributed authorship. See Goodrich, p. 1230.

25 The wooden typeset of these five characters is found in the chest with Müller's Chinese typographia at the Deutsche Staatsbibliothek, East Berlin.

Müller's inability to develop such a key, namely, that Müller could not do it *unless* he possessed some sort of "artifice" (*artificium*). Whether Kircher intended this exception to be rhetorical or literal, it was an exception which Müller would grasp to justify his ability to produce such an invention.

Kircher was fascinated by Müller's claim to have invented a method which greatly simplified and expedited the learning of Chinese or other languages such that even young schoolboys and uneducated women could learn to write Chinese in a short time. To this end, Kircher referred to the Lullian-inspired *combinatoriae artis* (art of combination) and recommended his work, *Polygraphia nova et universalis ex combinatoria arte detecta* (1663) as a model. Kircher noted, with pedantic astonishment, that Müller had not yet read the *Polygraphia*, though it had been published for "fifteen years". (Actually, it had been published 11–12 years prior to the writing of his letter.) Kircher proposed that Müller insert the Chinese characters into such a polygraphia and demonstrated how it may be done with the example of a Chinese phrase, transliteration and Latin translation.

This phrase was taken from the Chinese Classic, the *Chung yung* 2.2: "*Chüntzu chih chung-yung yeh. Chün-tzu erh shih chung, hsiao-jen chih Chung-yung yeh. Hsiao* [here Kircher's characters leave off]". This phrase translates as: "The superior man's embodying the course of the Mean is because he is a superior man, and so always maintains the Mean. The mean man's acting contrary to the course of the Mean is because he is a mean [man and has no caution]"[26]. Kircher's Latin translation of this passage reflected a less subtle treatment: "the perfected man has the mean and because of it, is perfected. For that reason, he always holds to the mean. However the evil [man] has a mean, but one which is evil. That [mean] he does not fear to transgress, etc."[27].

On June 23rd 1670 Kircher wrote in a letter to Leibniz that he was engaged in the attempt to derive a universal language from the "roots of the primary languages" by which he meant the languages most widely in use at that time[28].

26 James Legge translation, *The Chinese classics* (Oxford, 1893) I, 386. The wooden type setting of these characters from the *Chung yung* is found with Müller's Chinese typographia at the Deutsche Staatsbibliothek, East Berlin.

27 It is quite possible, even probable, that Kircher drew this phrase and rendering from the translation of the *Chung yung* by Fr. Intorcetta, which he had mentioned earlier in his letter. One notes that the *Chung yung* translation in *Confucius Sinarum philosophus*, which incorporated and improved Intorcetta's translation, differed somewhat and was clearly an improvement upon the translation which Kircher used. For example, Kircher used *malus* [*vir*] (evil man) to translate *hsiao-jen*, while the Couplet-edited work was far closer to the mark with *improbus* [*vir*] (inferior man). (Philippe Couplet, *et al, Confucius Sinarum philosophus* (Paris, 1687) p. 42) However, this sort of refinement is what characterized a long period of revision of earlier translations prior to the publication of *Confucius Sinarum philosophus*.

28 Kircher to Leibniz, 23 June 1670, *Leibniz-Briefwechsel* 473, sheet 1^r-1^v, transcribed in Paul Friedländer, "Athansius Kircher und Leibniz," p. 233.

Kircher clarified in a letter of December 28th 1674 to Müller that the idea of this Polygraphia was not to reveal a formal conception of languages, but to offer a skillful basic method for translation[29]. In his response to this letter, Müller revealed a concern aimed more at practical utility than at intellectual truth[30]. For Müller, this probably reflected his mental inclination as well as the demands of life in the lean atmosphere at Brandenburg.

Finally, Kircher concluded his letter by referring to the Nestorian Monument. He wrote that he would send a copy of his *China illustrata* so that Müller could read through the history, translation and commentary on the Nestorian Monument contained in it. Apparently Kircher had not seen Müller's *Monumenti Sinici . . . lectio seu phrasis, versio seu metaphrasis, translatio seu paraphrasis* which was published at Berlin in 1672, and did not realize that most of its contents had been lifted from his own *China illustrata! Monumenti Sinici . . . lectio* is a brief work divided into three vertical columns of (1) transliteration of the Chinese text (2) transliteration converted into musical notation and (3) a translation. The transliteration and translation were word-for-word duplications of *China illustrata* and Müller's sole contribution was to add the musical notation. But all of this was clarified on the title page where Müller gave Kircher's work due credit. So in a sense, it was not plagiarism. On the other hand, Kircher's recommendation in 1674 that Müller read *China illustrata* implies that Kircher's permission had not been received for such a borrowing nor was he even sent a copy of the text upon publication – two acts which in the twentieth century have become standard literary practices.

Müller replied to Kircher's letter on January 27th 1675. He had just read Kircher's *Polygraphia*, but felt it to be aimed at something quite different from his *Clavis Sinica*. Müller noted that he had spent some years engaged in the study of Chinese and felt that his lack of a Chinese-speaking teacher was overcome by an "artifice" – to use the word which Kircher first introduced. Müller revealed his preoccupation with receiving a financial commitment prior to publication by bemoaning the loss of all the potential rewards as well as the expenses already incurred if his project were not published.

Kircher made seven points in order to dissuade Müller from proceeding with his Key. In rebuttal to Kircher's warning about the multitude and variety of Chinese characters, Müller stated that such a fact delighted rather than troubled him! Müller's rebuttals to Kircher's other points were not much more responsive and one is left with the impression of a man with a superficial understanding of the Chinese language. Only such superficiality would justify the confidence that he displayed in his Key. A less sympathetic interpretation would

29 Müller to Kircher, January 27th 1675 in Müller, *De invento Sinico*, pp. 6–7.
30 Müller, *De invento Sinico*, p. 11.

be that Müller's mind was not so much superficial as it was unscrupulous. Although one cannot rule out the latter, Müller's generally decent scholarly and moral reputation in areas apart from the Key would tend to make more of a case for superficiality. Furthermore, Müller's superficial understanding of the structure of language was not unique to his age. The seventeenth century was pervaded by overemphasis on the grammatical and logical aspects of language and de-emphasis of other elements, such as expression and spontaneous impetus in the development of language. These emphases constituted some of the premises on which the search for a universal language were conducted.

In response to Kircher, Müller revealed his belief in the possibility of separating the Chinese script from the spoken language. He believed that the characters could be spoken with a European pronunciation and that tones could be disregarded for the purposes of learning to write Chinese. For the same reasons, Müller argued that a Chinese-speaking teacher was not necessary in order to learn to read Chinese. Müller was an Orientalist who had achieved a certain degree of proficiency in Hebrew and Arabic. At that time, it was typical of European scholars to approach these Middle Eastern languages purely as literary tongues, without the need of studying in a native environment where the language was spoken. The antiquity and evolution of the Hebrew tongue readily lent itself to this approach. Müller seems to have extended this same approach to the study of Chinese, but the absence of an established tradition of European sinology and the uniqueness and difficulty of Chinese made this approach far more difficult to apply than to other Oriental languages. Furthermore, the presence in Europe of returned and intellectually oriented missionaries, such as the Jesuits, doomed Müller's type of sinology. Müller simply could not compete with the greater knowledge of the Jesuits. This was clearly seen in the example of Kircher, whose linguistic talents appear to have been no greater than Müller's, but whose contact with the China missionaries enabled him to have had a far more sophisticated appreciation of the Chinese language.

Müller clarified in his response to Kircher that he had obtained a copy of *China illustrata* at the time of its appearance in 1667 and had read it numerous times. Indeed, he stated that he had edited its contents in composing certain books. (The latter would include Müller's *Monumenti Sinici . . . lectio*, which is discussed below.) Müller also indicated familiarity with Kircher's *Oedipus Aegyptiacus* (1652). He claimed to have read many Chinese manuscripts and printed books and, as the librarian of one of the largest Chinese collections in seventeenth-century Europe, outside of Rome, this was probably true. Müller addressed some questions to Kircher regarding the *Hai-p'ien* and asked if there was a copy of this dictionary in the Vatican library. Müller stated that some years ago he received a Chinese dictionary from the Oxford library, but he did

31 Müller, *De invento Sinico*, pp. 9–13.

not clarify the contents of this dictionary nor its relationship to the Ocean dictionary.

Kircher's response of May 28th 1675[32] demonstrated some of the exasperated impatience that emerged in most of Müller's correspondents over the Key. In effect, Kircher stated that it was time for Müller to reveal his invention. Müller responded promptly on July 3rd[33] with resentment over Kircher's implication that his invention consisted of "false chimeras". But it is hard to see how contemporaries could have judged otherwise in the face of Müller's repeated refusal to exhibit even samples of his Key. Clearly, as Leibniz would later point out, any prospective buyer of such an expensive commodity deserved a sample. However, since Müller had discontinued serious work on the Key pending payment of the premium and since – according to the "Propositio" – he would need a half-year or less to finish the Key, one possible reason for the lack of samples was the Müller did not yet possess them! He was understandably reluctant to offer samples from an incomplete theory though he felt quite justified in accepting a financial commitment toward the revelation of a complete theory. Müller's sin here was not so much a niggardly refusal to part with samples as it was ungrounded enthusiasm and claims made for an incomplete and untested theory.

5. THE MÜLLER-KOCHANSKI CORRESPONDENCE ON THE *CLAVIS SINICA*

Further light on the response of contemporary scholars to the Key is seen in Müller's correspondence with the Jesuit Adam Adamandus Kochanski, then a professor at Olomouc (Olmüty), Mähren, Czechoslovakia, which Müller published in his *De invento*. Fr. Kochanski first wrote to Müller on March 13th (23rd) 1675. He noted that after a copy of the "Propositio" recently came into his hands, he corresponded with several scholars, particularly in Rome, Florence, Padua and several cities in Germany. Kochanski stated that he found a skepticism in regard to the possibility of such an invention and a general belief that the *Clavis Sinica* was a hoax. But he was curious enough to write to Müller for clarification, particularly since he noted that the Key was not available through the booksellers. Perhaps Kochanski sensed Müller's preoccupation with money for he hinted at the profit which such a shortened method of teaching Chinese writing would reap at the court of Florence.

Along with this letter, Kochanski composed a list of questions on the Key which he asked Müller to answer simply in the affirmative or negative. Unlike Kircher, Kochanski appeared completely inexperienced with Chinese, but gave signs of being a scholar of European and certain Middle Eastern languages.

---

32 Müller, *De invento Sinico*, pp. 13–16.
33 Müller, *De invento Sinico*, pp. 16–17.

Consequently, Kochanski asked whether two or three days of study would be the period of time involved in using Müller's Key to learn Chinese. He also asked whether the Key could be extended to learning the script of Greece, Egypt, Dalmatia-Albania and Armenia — possibly the linguistic areas in which Kochanski was working. He asked whether the Key would suffice to teach Chinese without the help of a Chinese teacher and whether the memory was able to retain the understanding of the Chinese characters acquired after such a short period of study. He further asked whether the Key conveyed a complete Chinese grammar and vocabulary. He asked to what extent the Chinese sounds compared to Latin and whether the Key taught the language of the educated Chinese. Finally, Kochanski appeared to question Müller's demand for a financial commitment by asking whether the cost was in proportion to the labor and costs expended.

Müller replied promptly on March 23rd 1675 with responses to each of Kochanski's questions, though he refused to say anything which touched on the Key itself and reiterated that he would release the Key only when the publicly stipulated conditions had been met[34]. Consequently, Müller's responses gave only indirect information on the Key. He stated that three days of study was too short and spoke of the need for eight days or even a month. He implied that three days might be sufficient to learn to pronounce, but not to understand Chinese. Müller stated that the Key was neither a grammar nor a dictionary, but a dictionary of sound that the Mandarins spoke. This remark is puzzling since three months earlier in responding to Kircher's insistence on the need for a Chinese-speaking teacher, Müller stressed that his Key taught the reading rather than the speaking of Chinese. Yet since Müller chose to publish both letters in the same volume, he probably did not think them contradictory. In regard to the payment, Müller stated that he would not ask for this if he were not deficient in funds needed to buy worthy specimens. Clearly, the composition and printing of a Chinese text in Berlin in the late seventeenth century was a major project and one cannot dismiss the fact that a considerable amount of capital had to be expended for Chinese type before printing could proceed.

Kochanski wrote again to Müller on April 20th 1675[35] and included a list of questions on the nature of Chinese characters. Müller's response was prompt but brief. He refused to answer any questions until an agreement for payment was concluded. While Müller's reaction appears extremely ungenerous, it was completely consistent with the terms he set forth in the "Propositio" and of which Kochanski was well aware. However, Müller was candid enough to admit that he did not know the answer to a question which Kochanski asked concerning the composition of the Chinese characters *chi* (good fortune) and *chao* (day; sun)[36].

34 Müller, *De invento Sinico*, pp. 21–23.
35 Müller, *De invento Sinico*, pp. 24–27.
36 Müller, *De invento Sinico*, pp. 26–27.

(Kochanski appears to have extracted these characters from the Chinese text of the Nestorian Monument found in Kircher's *China illustrata*[37]).

Kochanski's request for more information was the typical — and understandable — response of the scholarly community to Müller's announcement of his Key. In the proceedings of the meeting of March 19th 1674 of the Royal Society of London, it is recorded that Mr. Oldenburg read an undated letter from Müller. This letter contained "an offer of an anonymous person, of furnishing a key of the Chinese language, for a recompense; and that key to be learned with great ease and expedition; even by ordinary capacities"[38]. We immediately recognize that the "anonymous person" was Müller himself and that he had apparently had Johann Sigismund Elsholz of the Brandenburg court play the role of middleman in writing this letter, possibly because of the indecorum of introducing his own invention. The response of the Royal Society to Müller's announcement of a Key to Chinese was one of curious interest, an impeccably scholarly response, and Müller was requested to send the Society a "specimen of his performance by means of his invention". Not surprisingly, the specimen was not forthcoming and we read in the Society proceedings of 1681–1682 that another letter had been received from Berlin in which Dr. Elsholtz [Elsholz] claimed that Müller was "ready still" to give a specimen of his Key and that *consideratis considerandis* (after extensive consideration), "he would impart his knowledge in that and other curiosities"[39]. The reference to "other curiosities" was a characteristically Baroque turn of phrase, geared to evoke approval from the seventeenth-century "curious" ployhistors, but frowned upon by twentieth-century specialists. Yet contemporary specialists generally respect the scholarly atmosphere of the seventeenth-century Royal Society and it is worth noting that the Society took Müller's claim to a *Clavis Sinica* seriously enough to ask for more information. Such an inquiry should help us to take our intellectual bearings in evaluating Müller's work.

6. THE MÜLLER-LEIBNIZ CORRESPONDENCE ON THE *CLAVIS SINICA*

Among those who were willing to believe in the possibility of a *Clavis Sinica* was Leibniz and his interest was such that he initiated an indirect correspondence with Müller. The stimulus for this correspondence seems to have come through Leibniz' duties as adviser and librarian to the court of Hanover. Leibniz had a brief exchange of several letters in 1671 with the Oriental collector

---

37 The characters *chi* and *chao* appear in column 28, number 31 and in column 29, number 59, respectively, of the Nestorian Monument inscription in Kircher, *China illustrata*, fold-out inserted between pp. 12 & 13.

38 *Letters relating to the affairs of the Royal Society 1663–1675* (London, 1757) III, 131. I am indebted to Frau Kraft for bringing this citation to my attention.

39 *Letters . . . of the Royal Society* IV, 123.

at Hamburg, Martin Fogel. After Fogel died, Leibniz traveled to Hamburg where in 1678 he negotiated the acquisition of Fogel's 3,600-volume library for Duke Johann Friedrich of Hanover[40]. One finds in the Leibniz-Müller correspondence file in Hanover a letter from Müller to Fogel dated October 7th 1675. It appears that this letter came, along with Fogel's books, to Hanover and possibly through it, Leibniz learned of Müller's Chinese studies. (Müller's letter dealt mainly with China, and specifically mentioned Frs. Kircher and Intorcetta).

At any rate, on January 29th (February 8th) 1679 Johann Sigismund Elsholz (d. 1688), a physician to the Elector, wrote to Leibniz and listed Müller's works. (Although this listing was probably in response to Leibniz' request, there was no record of any preceding Leibniz correspondence with Elsholz). Elsholz' letter to Leibniz of April 5th (15th) 1679 spoke of sending a copy of Müller's *Hebdomas observationum de rebus Sinicis* (Berlin 1672). In his letter of June 24th (July 4th) 1679, Leibniz expressed understanding of Müller's wish to keep his Key concealed until the financial situation improved and he suggested that Müller seek another patron. Yet Leibniz' curiosity was so great that he could not resist asking fourteen questions about the Key (translated and discussed in the preceding chapter). Leibniz never received answers to his questions and Elsholz, perhaps because of embarrassment over Müller's lack of response, forwarded Müller's indirect replies of June 2nd and July 7th 1679 to Leibniz[41]. In these letters, Müller wrote what must have been for him a tiresome repetition of his terms. He stated that he preferred not to discuss the Key since he had already done so extensively. Indeed, we should see Müller's correspondence over the Key with Kircher, Kochanski and the Royal Society as representative of a much more extensive correspondence that Müller conducted. On the other hand, the tone of Müller's "Propositio" was so enticing, that one could hardly fault Leibniz for inquiring. Müller refused to answer any more questions about his Key on the grounds that to do so would leave him unable to complete his other work. He stated, with some exasperation, that no money had been forthcoming for his Key and he claimed that it was impossible to release any bits of information on the Key without revealing the whole thing.

Leibniz was furious with Müller's response. Among the Leibniz correspondence preserved at Hanover, one finds two drafts of a letter to Elsholz dated August 5th 1679. One draft breaks off in the middle of the second page. The other draft is a complete four-page letter[42]. The incomplete draft reflects Leibniz' shock at the coarseness of Müller's reply. In response to Müller's attempt to obtain money for his Key without releasing information, Leibniz himself resorted

---

40 Kurt Müller, *Eine Chronik*, p. 53.
41 Leibniz-Briefwechsel 666, sheet 5^r-5^v & 7^r.
42 The incomplete draft is found in Leibniz-Briefwechsel 666, sheet 15^r-15^v (copy on sheet 14^r). The completed letter is on sheet 12^r-13^v (copy on 10^r-11^v).

to the coarse example that any buyer of a horse wishes first to examine the merchandise. The prolific correspondent Leibniz was particularly piqued at Müller's refusal to reply on the grounds that he was too busy with other duties and believed that Müller could have responded without undue strain on his time. But something — whether cooler reason or political tact — prevailed on Leibniz to file this draft and send another. His other draft barely mentioned the Key and did so by sandwiching it casually between two other paragraphs. But his tone was unmistakeably cold. Leibniz spoke of surprise over the manner of Müller's reply and stated that Müller must not blame people for wishing to at least hear about what they have not yet seen.

Leibniz was a patient man and in this same letter to Müller he tried once more to obtain information about China. He asked if Müller would translate — in whole or part — and transliterate a small Chinese book, in quarto, of eighty pages which he had in his possession. Müller replied through Elsholz on August 24th (September 3rd) that Leibniz should send either the book or the title so that he might decide the value of doing such a translation. Leibniz must have done so since Müller shortly thereafter sent another reply through Elsholz, dated September 7th (17th) that he would prefer to translate another book because Fr. Intorcetta had already translated the book of Leibniz' request. The reference is to the Jesuit Prospero Intorcetta's editing of the Latin translation of the Chinese Classic, the *Chung yung* (Doctrine of the Mean). This translation, entitled *Sinarum scientia politico-moralis*, was really a group effort with half of the text published at Canton in 1667 and the other half published at Goa in 1669. The small work had been translated into French and republished as "La Science des Chinois" in 1672 in Melchisedec Thévenot's *Relations de divers voyages*[43]. Given the very limited edition of *Sinarum scientia politico-moralis*, it is likely that this translation came to Müller in Thévenot's work.

7. AN ASSESSMENT OF MÜLLER'S SCHOLARSHIP

How well did Müller know Chinese? There are widely varying estimates. Ludolf, who specialized in the Ethopian language, stated that although Müller could not read Chinese extemporaneously, he did have a detailed and thorough knowledge of the language[44]. But since Ludolf knew no Chinese, one may question his evaluation. The self-taught, but eminent sinologist Bayer strongly criticized Müller's *Monumenti Sinici ... lectio* in its treatment of the Chinese inscription from Kircher's *China illustrata*[45]. Mr. Szcześniak accused Müller — as

---

43 Melchisédech Thévenot, *Relations de divers voyages* 4 vols in folio. (Paris, 1663–1672) part IV, presented as a segment of thirteen pages among several unconsecutively numbered sections.

44 Kraft, "Frühe chinesische Studien in Berlin," p. 106.

45 Bayer, *Museum Sinicum*, pp. 35–36.

well as Mentzel — of being plagiarists who had no knowledge of the Chinese language[46]. The most knowledgeable scholar currently of Müller's sinological work, Frau Kraft, makes the guarded comment that given his lack of contact with China, Müller's efforts are worthy of mention.

On the basis of his written works dealing with China, I would judge that Müller knew a limited number of Chinese characters, but only enough to decipher an isolated character or phrase or to recognize a title. He did not know enough Chinese to translate any complete Chinese text. (Leibniz' request that he translate and transliterate a small Chinese text was certainly beyond Müller's abilities). Consequently, Müller's claims to competency in sinology are laughable by today's standards. But standards in the late seventeenth century were quite different. It is far fairer to evaluate Müller as a proto-sinologist. With no instruction in Chinese available except for that offered occasionally by visiting or returned missionaries, late seventeenth-century Europeans were forced to rely on the works of others in a way that seems plagiaristic by today's standards. However, at that time in Europe, the lack of adequate knowledge of Chinese by proto-sinologists was more a fact than a sin.

Some heavy charges of plagiarism and posing as sinological experts have been levelled at Müller and certain of his contemporaries. One critic refers to Müller and Mentzel as "unscrupulous seventeenth century savants" and part of a "pack of amateurish scholars in exotic sciences, men who hunted for ready-for-publication materials in their fields of interests"[47]. But some of these charges are heavy-

---

46 Boleslaw Szcześniak, "The writings of Michael Boym," *Monumenta Serica* 14 (1949–1955): 504 & 506–508.

47 These charges are levelled at Müller and Mentzel by Boleslaw Szczśniak. The more detailed and serious charges appear in "The writings of Michael Boym," pp. 504–508. Mr. Szcześniak also refers to Müller and Mentzel as "self-styled sinologists" who "pretended to a knowledge of the Chinese language." He further states that "their publications are practically plagiarized editions of Boym's work" and "their editions of Boym's works under their own names is a typically piratical practice in the history of plagiarism." Also see "Athanasius Kircher's *China illustrata*," *Osiris* 10 (1952): 398 & "The beginnings of Chinese lexicography in Europe," *Journal of the American Oriental Society* 67 (1947): 164–165. Two comments should be added here. First, Mr. Szcześniak's overly critical and unsympathetic treatment of Müller and Mentzel is paralleled by a tendency toward uncritically favorable treatment of Frs. Kircher and Boym. This has led Szcześniak to attribute achievements to Boym, such as the Chinese-French dictionary found in the French edition of Kircher's *China illustrata* (pp. 324–367) and the use of diacritical marks to indicate Chinese tones, which have been questioned. These attributions have been part of a tangled academic dispute. Agreeing with the view of Robert Chabrié in *Michael Boym jésuite polonais et la fin des Ming en Chine 1646–1662* (Paris, 1933) and disagreeing with Paul Pelliot in "Michael Boym," *T'oung pao* 31 (1935): 136–137, Szcześniak argued for Boym's authorship of the Chinese-French dictionary. Later, both of Szcześniak's above attributions to Boym were disputed by Walter Simon in "The attribution to Michael Boym of two early achievements of western sinology," *Asia major*, new series 7 (1959): 165–169. In short, applying Szcześniak's standard more objectively, Boym and Kircher also could be

handed and have not taken this different seventeenth-century sinological standard into account. An additional complication in assessing Müller's work in sinology is his knowledge of Middle Eastern languages. It was his study of this material that provided the genesis for his Key. Donald F. Lach makes the judgement that Müller was a respected scholar in Middle Eastern languages, but provides little documentation for this claim. What he does supply is a negative type of evidence for Müller's expertise in Middle Eastern languages, that is, he notes the lack of doubts on Müller's scholarship in the area. Mr. Lach also cites the judgment by August Müller that Müller's Persian translations were inaccurate[48].

The nature of Müller's Chinese studies was reflected in his published writings[49]. He had an interest in a great variety of Chinese subject-matter, but his research

accused of plagiarism. Secondly, while Szcześniak's accusations may be overly harsh, Müller's scholarship involved practices which by the quite different standards of the twentieth century, would be called plagiaristic.

48 Lach, "Chinese studies of Andreas Müller," pp. 568 & 574.

49 Müller's first published work on China was apparently *Disquisitio geographica et historica de Chataja* (1670), a light compilation of travel and missionary accounts on Cathay. Then came a Latin edition of Marco Polo (1671). This was followed by three short works on the Nestorian Monument. *Lectio monumenti Sinici* (1672) was a reproduction of the translation and paraphrase of the Nestorian Monument by Boym and his Chinese associates which had appeared in Kircher's *China illustrata*. Müller's contribution took the form of musical notation to accompany each Chinese character, which possibly reflected work done on his Key. (Lach, Chinese studies of Andreas Müller, p. 567). The second work on the Monument, *Historia lapidis* (1672?), contained excerpts drawn from China missionaries writing about the Nestorian Monument. These included Frs. Semedo, M. Diaz, Martini and Boym with the latter's Chinese collaborators. The third work in this trilogy, *De monumento Sinico commentarius novensilis* (1672?) consisted of extensive commentary on the Monument drawn primarily from other sources, but with some commentary by Müller, including references to his Key and the ease with which it facilitated the learning of Chinese. (Andreas Müller, *Lectio monumenti Sinici* (Berlin, 1672) p. 12).

There followed *Hebdomas observationum de rebus Sinicis* (Seven observations on Chinese things) (1674). The first observation was a short summary of important dates in Chinese history. The second was a summary account of Chinese missionaries in China from Old Testament times down to the contemporary mission. The third observation was a chronological table of Chinese rulers, less detailed than his later *Basilicon Sinense* (Chinese kings). Müller's primary sources were Martini's *Sinicae historiae* (1658) and Mendoza's *Historia del gran reyno de la China* (1596). The remaining observations were very short discussions of the plant ginseng, geographical remarks drawn from Marco Polo's history and astronomical subject matter dealing with the sequence and positioning of celestial phenomena.

Müller's *Basilicon Sinense* (1679?) drew from Martini, Mendoza, from a Persian history of China attributed by Müller to Abdallāh Jan-Umur Baidāwī and from unspecified Chinese manuscripts. This work consisted of a list of Chinese rulers from the beginning until the ascension of the K'ang-hsi emperor, erroneously dated 1666 instead of 1662. Although Fu Hsi was the first ruler to receive an ascension date (i.e. 2952 B.C.), there were other rulers listed prior to Fu Hsi in what was surely a confusion of legend with history. However, the dynasties, beginning with the legendary Hsia, followed fair-

lacked sustained concentration on any one subject and tended to be superficial. This pattern was reflected in his published works on China which were fragmentary in content and averaged considerably less than 100 small octavo pages per work. Müller's scholarship with its heavy borrowing from others was not out of step with his age. Kircher shared a diversity of interests and a derivative type of scholarship, but Kircher's work showed an inclination toward monumentality which Müller lacked[50].

ly closely the dates traditionally attributed to them and the lists of monarchs were fairly complete. Müller's *Imperii Sinensis nomenclator geographicus* (1680) consisted of 1,783 romanized Chinese place-names listed in alphabetical order with longitude and latitude readings. According to Mr. Lach, Müller's source for this list was a map brought to western Europe by Nicholas Witsen (d. 1717), the mayor of Amsterdam, on his return from Russia in 1666. See Lach, "The Chinese studies of Andreas Müller," p. 570 & Donald F. Lach, trans., *The preface to Leibniz' Novissima Sinica* (Honolulu, 1957) p. 41. Witsen's map, as improved by Adam Brand (1699) is reproduced in the German translation of Leibniz' *Novissima Sinica, das neueste von China* Heinz Günther Nesselrath & Hermann Reinbothe, trans. & eds. (Cologne, 1979) pp. 116–117.

Müller's *De Sinarum magnaeque Tartari rebus commentatio alphabetica* (An alphabetical commentary on things of the Chinese and of greater Tartary) (ca. 1680) is comparable to a contemporary introductory guidebook to a foreign culture. It contained just under one-hundred alphabetized entries. These included Chinese astronomy, the Buddha, Confucius – a lengthy entry –, Fu Hsi, snakes, *T'ien-tzu* ("Son of Heaven," i.e. the Chinese emperor), *Shang-ti* (Lord-on-high) and a number of Asian geographical entries. On the title page, Müller claimed to be drawing from Marco Polo's history of the east as well as "a great number of manuscripts." (Müller's tendency toward this kind of turgid description was typical of his age.) This reliance upon Marco Polo, who visited China during the Asianwide domination by the Mongols, may account for the general Asian, as opposed to more exclusively Chinese, focus of the entries. Müller's Near Eastern studies were reflected in his *Abdallae Beidavaei historia Sinensis* (1678). The historian George Sarton pointed out that Müller mistakenly attributed to Abdallae Baidāwī what is actually part 8 of the monumental history of the world, *Ta'rikh-i-Banākatī* (1317), by the Persian historian and poet, Banākatī. See George Sarton, *History of science* (Baltimore, 1947) III, 976–977. Also see III, 731. This section of Banākatī's history dealt with China and its was to Müller's credit that he edited in Persian and translated into Latin this text which included an important account of Chinese printing.

50 Müller's absorption with the encyclopedic type of scholarship of the seventeenth-century led him to produce an astronomical-mathematical computation of time and the calendar entitled "Opus synchronismorum." This manuscript was spared destruction at Müller's death, only to be condemned by Christian Grüneburg, professor of mathematics at Frankfurt-on-Oder, as filled with absurdities and contradictions. See Wehr, "Andreas Müller," p. 31. Müller's manuscript, "Opus synchronismorum," is preserved in the manuscript section of the Deutsche Staatsbibliothek, East Berlin.

8. THE THEOLOGICAL CONTROVERSY OVER THE *CLAVIS SINICA*

At this point in the story of the *Clavis Sinica*, theological controversy appeared. Since 1668 Müller had been suspected of Christian syncretism by the Lutherans because of his concession to sign the statement demanded by the Tolerance Edict of the Elector, a member of the Reformed Church. At the beginning of this controversy, Müller appears to have been strongly supported by the Elector. But ten years later, Müller's Chinese studies led to the revival of the controversy with Müller as the principal object of attack.

The occasion for reopening the controversy was the suspected imminent publication of Müller's *Clavis Sinica*. Elias Grebnitz (1627–1689) was a professor of logic and metaphysics at Frankfurt-on-Oder and held an essentially honorary position in the senior theological faculty of the so-called "Electoral University of Brandenburg"[51]. In 1678 Grebnitz published a treatise entitled *Unterricht von der reformirten und lutherischen Kirchen* (Instruction from the Reformed and Lutheran Churches). This treatise charged that since Chinese was a pictographic language, the publication of the Chinese word for God in Müller's *Clavis Sinica* would be a violation of the Biblical prohibition on such images. Therefore, Grebnitz argued that publication of Müller's Key should be prohibited.

Müller responded to Grebnitz' attack with the treatise *Besser Unterricht von der sineser Schrifft und Druck als etwa in Hrn. D. Eliae Grebnitzen Unterricht . . .* (Better instruction on the Chinese script and print than is in Herr Dr. Elias Grebnitz' instruction . . .)[52]. This forty-page pamphlet concentrated on rebutting three pages of Grebnitz' treatise on a point-by point basis[53]. Grebnitz had reasoned that if Chinese characters were likenesses of the thing, then the Chinese word for God would be a pictographic representation of God and therefore condemned by the Bible. To support his claim, Grebnitz cited *Deuteronomy* 4 [:15–29] and *Romans* 1 [: 19–23]. (Grebnitz also cited *Leviticus* 26: 1, *Isaiah* 40 [:18–20], *Jeremiah* 10 [:1–15] and *Habakkuk* 2: 18–19.) In this passage, Grebnitz did not cite the prohibition on graven images contained in the second of the ten Mosaic Commandments (*Exodus* 20: 14), though the other Biblical passages cited covered similar material.

Grebnitz pretended to no particular understanding of the Chinese language, yet he felt justified in writing such a treatise because of the widely accepted seventeenth-century assumption that general similarities overrode particular

---

51 See the title-page of Elias Grebnitz' *Verthädigung gegen . . . Müller* (Frankfurt-on-Oder, 1681).

52 The copy of Müller's *Besser Unterricht* found in the Bibliotheca Regia Hannoverana collection is without a date or place of publication and is appended to Grebnitz' *Verthädigung gegen . . . Müller*.

53 Elias Grebnitz, *Unterricht von der Reformirten und Lutherischen Kirche* (Frankfurt-on-Oder [?], 1678) ch. 1; pp. 32, 33 & 34.

differences both in regard to languages and to the religious beliefs of non-Christians. Müller tended to accept these same assumptions and so his response was filled with as many references to Mexican, Egyptian and other languages as to Chinese. The Bible was cited often by both Grebnitz and Müller. Müller made many references to classical Roman authors and included a number of expressions in Greek. Indeed, both Grebnitz and Müller reflected the still limited use of the German language as a vehicle of scholarly communication by switching to Latin terminology approximately one-fourth of the time, and particularly for more abstract concepts.

Of course, Müller claimed to understand the Chinese language better than Grebnitz, but he was surprisingly humble and at one point even stated: "I do not know Chinese or Egyptian really well"[54]. This was a remarkable statement for a scholar who claimed to have invented a Key to the Chinese language. Yet again, Müller's concession is more remarkable by contemporary standards which stress specialization than by standards of the seventeenth century which, reflecting the broad, polyhistor approach to knowledge, applied a number of fundamental premises to all languages and non-European cultures. Müller's cited sinological sources included four missionaries who resided in China — Frs. Grueber, Intorcetta, Martini and Trigault — all of whom, except for Grueber, had seriously studied the Chinese language. For the most part, however, Müller relied on the work of scholars who knew little Chinese and who worked from secondary materials. These included Kircher, Nieuhoff, Purchas and Spitzel.

Müller's rebuttal to Grebnitz followed basically two lines of approach. The first was that Chinese, unlike the ancient language of the Mexicans, was not pictographic and did not portray the likenesses of things[55]. Müller's second line was to argue that the Chinese had no character which signified God. Müller based this claim on two points. First, he argued that even the Japanese, who used the Chinese script, had taken the Latin *Deus* or Spanish *Dios* to designate God rather than a native Chinese term[56]. The second basis of Müller's claim was somewhat circular: he claimed that since the Chinese were heathens and since the Biblical sources of *I Thessalonians* 4: 5 and *Ephesians* 2: 12 stated that heathens did not know the Judeo-Christian God, therefore the Chinese could not have had a term for God[57].

Ironically, Müller's conclusions were far more tenable than his reasoning behind them. Modern scholars have confirmed that Chinese, in spite of pictographic elements in its origins, stopped being essentially pictographic long before the seventeenth century. On the other hand, the Chinese terms for God — *Shang-ti* and *T'ien-chu* — contained pictographic elements in their etymological origin

54 Müller, *Besser Unterricht*, p. 23.
55 Müller, *Besser Unterricht*, pp. 18, 20 & 23.
56 Müller, *Besser Unterricht*, p. 15.
57 Müller, *Besser Unterricht*, p. 20.

which complicated the issue. Müller's conclusion that the Chinese language contained no indigenous term for the monotheistic God of the Judeo-Christian tradition was one of the focal points of debate over Jesuit accommodation which was then building to its climax in the Rites Controversy. Müller's apparently scant awareness of key issues of this controversy revealed a lack of contact with China missionaries which contrasted with that of his Berlin colleague, Christian Mentzel.

Müller's limited knowledge of Chinese characters was revealed by his treatment of the Chinese terminology for God. He accepted Kircher's claim that the word *Fe* [*Fo*], for which he included the Chinese character, signified the "Chinese Jupiter" and was the Chinese word for God[58]. It was typical of Kircher to interpret Chinese religions in terms of European pagan forms. The dubiousness of such an approach is quite beside the point here as the character *Fo* did not refer to the "Chinese Jupiter", but to Buddha. The term was not used in China until the entry of Buddhism from India after the first century A.D. . Far closer to the Judeo-Christian God was the ancient Chinese term *Shang-ti* (Lord-on-high) or even the seventeenth-century merging of two ancient Chinese terms − *T'ien* (Heaven, in both a physical and deified sense) and *chu* (temporal lord) − to form *T'ien-chu* (Lord of Heaven).

Surprisingly, Müller was aware of both of these designations for God. *Shang-ti* and *T'ien-chu* appeared in his *De Sinarum magnaeque Tartari rebus Commentatio alphabetica,* a characteristically brief piece of Mülleriana of 71 pages in octavo, which Müller compiled from the diaries of Marco Polo. In this work, Müller included an entry on *Shang-ti* which he defined as "the Chinese name of God"[59]. His reference to *T'ien-chu* in this work was much briefer and cited from Mendoza as a Chinese name for God[60]. It is puzzling why Müller did not make greater reference to *Shang-ti* in his *Besser Unterricht.* It is possible that he knew only the romanized form of the term and, being unfamiliar with the Chinese characters, did not feel knowledgeable enough to argue that this term for God was not a pictographic representation for God. Indeed, since Müller argued both that the Chinese characters were not pictographic and that the Chinese had no term for God, the existence of this term *Shang-ti* tended to contradict his argument.

Unfortunately for Müller, his opponent Grebnitz was more sensitive to contradictions. In 1681 at Frankfurt-on-Oder, Grebnitz published his *Verthâdigung gegen . . . Müller* whose full inflammatory title was "A defense against

---

58 Müller, *Besser Unterricht,* p. 16.
59 Andreae Mülleri, *Commentatio alphabetica,* pp. 47−48. This 71-page alphabetized listing of important Chinese and Tartar terms was published without a date or place of publication, but probably appeared by 1680, at the latest. This date is confirmed by the fact that Müller's *Besser Unterricht* (1680?), p. 21, refers the reader to the entry on *Xang-ti* [*Shang-ti*] on page 68a of *Commentatio alphabetica.*
60 Müller, *Commentatio alphabetica,* p. 18.

the abusive treatise wherein M. Andreas Müller, Provost of Berlin, wishes to conceal his unlearned contamination of the instruction of the Reformed and Lutheran Churches under the pretext of an instruction on the Chinese script and printing". In this, Grebnitz seized upon Müller's contradiction by saying that if the great Chinese teacher, Confucius, said that *Shang-ti* was the name for God — as Müller claimed in his *Besser Unterricht*[61] — then Müller surely contradicted himself to say that the Chinese had no name for God[62].

Grebnitz further claimed, not without some justification, that Kircher's works on China — undoubtedly *China illustrata* was included here — were far more informative than Müller's works. In particular, Grebnitz noted Kircher's claim that the Nestorian Tablet contained a Chinese term for God. Grebnitz' conclusion was only half correct. He appeared unaware that the Nestorian Monument was the work of Christians in China who most certainly would have sought to avoid using a term which violated the Biblical proscription on graven images. Actually, the term for God appearing on the Nestorian Monument was "*E-lo-he*", a transliteration of the Syriac term for God. The latter was derived from Elohim, an alternate Hebrew designation, with Yahweh, for God[63]. Thus the Nestorian Christians in China seemed to have taken the view that while the Chinese language contained no indigenous equivalent for God, a Chinese transliteration would not violate the proscription on graven images.

Since Müller in 1672 had published three short works on the Nestorian Monument based upon materials that he found in Kircher's *China illustrata* and other missionary sources, he would doubtless have had some knowledge of this usage. Fr. Boym's paraphrase of the Nestorian inscription found in *China illustrata* clearly rendered the transliteration of God as "*Olò, ò yu*" which was explained as a name which in Chaldean signified "Eloha"[64]. It is possible that Müller took the use of a transliteration rather than an indigenous Chinese term in the Nestorian inscription as a basis for his conslusion that the Chinese language contained no term for God. In fact, it may have been precisely this instance which was behind Müller's claim that "certainly the Chinese know how to name God, but not with a single word and therefore not with a single character"[65]. Unfortunately, Müller marshalled very little solid evidence for his conclusions.

On the whole, Grebnitz' rebuttal was not a distinguished document. It was highly polemical and essentially an elaboration of the points made in his initial *Unterricht*. Consequently, as in so many controversies of this sort, the battle was won not by reasoning so much as by propaganda tactics. In this area, Grebnitz

---

61 Müller, *Besser Unterricht*, p. 21.
62 Grebnitz, *Verthädigung gegen . . . Müller*, p. 51.
63 The use of Elohim for God appears in the *Psalms* 42–83.
64 Kircher, *China illustrata*, p. 29. In the translation of the Nestorian inscription found in *China illustrata*, the somewhat variant transliteration of "*holooy*" is given, p. 22.
65 Müller, *Besser Unterricht*, p. 15.

clearly scored a victory when he obtained a copy of Müller's rebuttal prior to its publication and circulated his reply throughout Müller's parish[66].

Although Müller had obtained the privilege to publish his Key in 1676, this controversy so muddied the atmosphere that obstacles now appeared to publication and when the Elector's hand appeared in the obstacles, Müller dropped his opposition[67]. In later years, Müller would complain that the Grebnitz controversy was to blame for the failure to publish his Key and there is probably some truth in this. But the vacillation of the Elector surely contributed as well. The Elector seemed genuinely to have wanted the Key to be published, but refused to support Müller openly out of fear of antagonizing powerful elements in Brandenburg.

After Grebnitz' death, the controversy revived with a somewhat different theological focus and plagued Müller. The Elector apparently bent to enough pressure such that in June of 1684, he commanded that all of Müller's Chinese books were to be returned to the library[68]. Although Friedrich Wilhelm wished to keep Müller on at Berlin, he still refused to make his support public. When Müller insisted on having the matter resolved, he forced the issue and lost[69]. And so in January of 1685 Müller sought release from his post as provost[70]. Friedrich Wilhelm wished to retain Müller in his service and offered him the alternate post of librarian, but Müller was disillusioned with Berlin and sought escape to the more peaceful environment of Stettin[71]. However, Müller badly wanted to use books in the Electoral library and he proposed to the Elector that he continue in his service while residing at Stettin and be permitted to borrow books from the library against a deposit. The Elector refused[72].

So in February of 1685 Müller left Berlin with a disappointingly small pension and retired to Stettin. In November of that year, there were further negotia-

---

66 Lach, "Chinese studies of Andreas Müller," p. 573 & Kraft, "Frühe chinesische Studien in Berlin," p. 103.

67 Kraft, "Frühe chinesische Studien in Berlin," p. 104.

68 Andreas Müller, *Chronolista clavis*, pp. 985–986.

69 Private letter of Eva S. Kraft to the author, 7 September 1978.

70 Lach, "The Chinese studies of Andreas Müller," p. 573 & Kraft, "Frühe chinesische Studien in Berlin," pp. 104–105, present differing versions of Müller's termination of service in Berlin. While Mr. Lach states that the Elector dismissed Müller and then placed him in Spandau Prison, Frau Kraft presents Müller as seeking release from duties and rejecting the Elector's attempts to keep him in Berlin in another capacity. In her letter of 7 September 1978, Frau Kraft states that the man named Müller who was imprisoned at Spandau was a preacher from Magdeburg. Furthermore, she claims that Lach's cited source for his information, A. B. König, *Versuch einer historischen Schilderung der Hauptveränderungen der Religion* (Berlin, 1793) III, 25 is careless of its presentation of material. My account of Müller's departure from Berlin follows Frau Kraft.

71 Kraft, "Frühe chinesische Studien in Berlin," p. 104.

72 Kraft, private letter of 7 September 1978.

tions on the Key, but payment was not determined and Müller refused to alter the terms of his "Propositio" and return to work on the Key. Furthermore, politics continued to plague him. Müller's final years at Stettin seem to have intensified certain unpleasant personality traits. He appears always to have been an intense figure who could become completely absorbed in his work. A story, perhaps apocryphal, is said to be told by Martin Murray that Müller refused to leave his books to watch the triumphant return of Charles II to London in 1660, even though the procession passed nearby his residence[73]. There is little evidence of pleasing personality traits and a good bit of recorded detail to the contrary. For such an intensely driven scholar, the denial after 1684 of his passion for studying the Chinese books in the library at Berlin must have exacerbated his sense of frustration. In his later years at Stettin, bitterness predominated. His unhappy marriage – in 1693 he spoke of "thirty-two years of un-Christian torment" – was probably as much a reflection as cause of his bitterness. The intensity of negative feeling toward his wife is reflected in the attempt to donate his library to an institution rather than leave it to her as an inheritance[74].

9. THE END OF A DREAM: MÜLLER'S DESTRUCTION OF HIS *CLAVIS SINICA*

There has been a good bit of puzzled speculation surrounding Müller's burning of the manuscript of the *Clavis Sinica* prior to his death. It has been suggested that this destructive act was caused by periodic bouts of illness[75]. This implies that Müller did not burn the Key intentionally. But the claim that he declined to burn the manuscript of his astronomical-mathematical "Opus synchronismorum" because it had cost him too much effort implies a certain deliberateness to Müller's destructive actions. There is also the possibility that Müller's progress had not kept pace with expectations and that Müller realized that his Key would not do what he claimed for it. Given such a realization, burning the manuscript provided an escape for a discouraged and sick old man.

But if one looks closely at Müller's life, certain patterns emerge which are consistent with this destruction of the Key. Müller's character was unforgiving and rigid. This was clearly apparent in his "Propositio" and his "Chronolista Clavis". His pressing need for money apparently skewed many of his perceptions. Yet an unforgiving spirit is not necessarily a dishonest one and Müller gave signs of impeccable honesty. In spite of a number of signs to the contrary, I do not believe that Müller was an imposter. He believed in his Key and he was reinforced in this belief by savants as distinguished as Kochanski and Leibniz. Müller's Key was never disproved because it never came to the public test that he

73 Wehr, p. 31.
74 Wehr, p. 32.
75 Lach, "The Chinese studies of Andreas Müller," p. 573.

offered in his "Propositio" to conduct. Müller held a demanding post in Berlin until 1685 and afterwards pursued his wide breadth of scholarly interests. He may have been laughable as a sinologist, but not as a proto-sinologist. It is my contention that Müller did exactly what he said he would do in the "Propositio" — since the recompense for the Key was not forthcoming, he discontinued serious work on it. Therefore, Müller's Key remained a mere insight and an insufficiently tested theory. As his death approached, Müller carried out his publicly stated intention of keeping the Key from falling into unauthorized hands.

It is true that another sort of man might have relented from his stated intention, but as with so many rigid characters, Müller was also unforgiving. In his mind, he had made a reasonable and fair offer and had furthermore publicly explained his reasons. Was this not honesty to an eminent degree? But a preoccupation with what is fair and unfair is frequently the mark of an unforgiving spirit. Müller concluded his "*Chronolista Clavis*" with the defensive rationale that posterity should decide whether it was through the fault of the author or of many others that the Key did not appear. The reference to many other people as bearing the blame betrayed Müller's sense of being wronged.

Müller was not an imposter, as a great deal of the evidence implies, nor was he a victim, as he himself believed. Moreover, he was not entirely ungenerous and was known to have helped several friends with their study of the Koran by sharing his manuscripts with them[76]. But Müller had an exaggerated sense of justice and felt that his request for a financial commitment in advance of receiving the Key was fair and necessitated by the financial demands of his subsistence and publication. Had he not offered a public testing of his Key to be made prior to final payment? But the world had spurned his reasonable offer and so he carried out his clearly stated intention of destroying the Key. In Müller's mind, it was what the world justly deserved. Ironically, Müller's refusal to divulge his Key in the face of great seventeenth-century scholarly interest has made the Key much more fascinating to later scholars than had it been revealed and — doubtlessly — found lacking.

10. CHRISTIAN MENTZEL'S ACADEMIC BACKGROUND

Christian Mentzel (1622–1701) was born into a prominent family in the small town of Fürstenwalde, near Frankfurt-on-Oder[77]. He attended a *gymna-*

---

76 Private letter of Eva S. Kraft to the author, 21 April 1979.
77 In this biographical account of Mentzel, I draw from Donald F. Lach, "Contributions of China to German civilization, 1648–1740," doctoral dissertation, University of Chicago, 1941, pp. 69–70. A good bit of biographical detail is also found in the short monograph by Walter Artelt, *Christian Mentzel, Leibarzt des Grossen Kurfürsten, Botaniker und Sinologe*, pp. 4–11.

sium in Berlin and later studied medicine and natural sciences at Frankfurt-on-Oder and Königsberg. Afterwards, he began a period of traveling in which, still as a student, he visited Warsaw in 1647. In 1648 he taught anatomy and botany for a year at Danzig. In the early 1650s he visited Hamburg, Amsterdam, Leiden, the coast of France, Spain, Malta and Italy, finally settling in Padua. At that time, the university at Padua possessed the most eminent medical faculty in Europe and Mentzel obtained a degree in medicine there in 1654. He returned to Berlin and quickly established a prominent medical practice. In 1658 recognition came with his appointments as *Hofarzt* (Court physician) and to the Elector's council. In 1662 he was elevated to one of the two positions of physician-in-ordinary to Friedrich Wilhelm. Since the position of physician-in-ordinary required constant attendance upon the Elector, it was occupied by two holders in order to allow for rotation of duty.

Whether through the Elector's promotion of an East India commercial company or through his own botanical and medical concerns, Mentzel acquired an interest in China and its language. Through their common interests in botany, medicine and China, Mentzel developed valuable relationships with Andreas Cleyer (1634–1697/1698), the first physician of the Dutch East India Company (Vereenigde Ostindische Compagnie) in Batavia and with the prominent and prolific China missionary, Philippe Couplet[78]. When Andreas Müller departed from Berlin in 1685, Mentzel became the Elector's chief advisor on East Asia, although he was eight years Müller's senior and sixty-five years old at the time. Mentzel's advisorship was short-lived as the Elector died in 1688, but Mentzel continued his sinological activities in Berlin. There is little evidence of a personal relationship between Mentzel and Müller, though it is difficult to conceive of how the two could have been unacquainted while working in the same small court and living in the same small city of Berlin. It is probable that their relations were not cordial. Certainly they were very different personalities. Müller's secretiveness and unbending nature contrasted strongly with Mentzel's open and personable manner. Furthermore, Mentzel seems to have had a more humble opinion of himself as a sinologist than did Müller.

11. MENTZEL'S SINOLOGICAL STUDIES

Mentzel did not begin studying Chinese until the 1680s when he was approximately sixty years old[79]. He published only two books on China, but the

---

78 The botanical and medical nature of Mentzel's relationship to Cleyer and Couplet is discussed in Eva S. Kraft, "Christian Mentzel, Philippe Couplet, Andreas Cleyer und die chinesische Medizin," pp. 158–196. Also see Kraft, "Frühe chinesische Studien in Berlin," pp. 116–122 & Artelt, pp. 21–25.

79 In his monograph on Mentzel, Herr Artelt claims on page 25 that a letter from Thomas Hyde of Oxford, dated February 16th 1683, in response to Mentzel's questions about

content of his manuscripts, his contacts with prominent missionaries such as Couplet, and his status as a librarian of one of the finest Chinese collections of books and manuscripts at that time in Europe made him a significant proto-sinologist of the late seventeenth century. Mentzel's first published work on China was *Sylloge minutiarum latino-sinico-characteristici* (Nürmberg 1685) which appeared as a supplement to the Nurnberger *Miscellanea curiosa*. It is a humble little work of thirty-three pages divided between a discussion of language and script and containing approximately twenty-five Latin words per page with their counterparts in Chinese romanization and characters. The Chinese content was possibly derived from Boym's transliteration-translation-paraphrase of the Nestorian Monument in *China illustrata*[80]. Mentzel's discussion of language and writing probably derived from Martini, but other sources have yet to be determined[81]. The quality of this earliest sinological effort of Mentzel's is considered to be poor and to reflect a good bit of misunderstanding of the Chinese language.

Mentzel's other published work on China was *Kurtze chinesische Chronologia oder Zeit-Register aller chinesischen Kayser* (Berlin 1696), hereafter referred to as *Zeit-Register*. This book was closely tied to Mentzel's relationship with Fr. Couplet. Andreas Cleyer was the mediary in acquainting Mentzel with Couplet, between whom contact was made by 1686. There followed a correspondence in which Mentzel was the eager student asking many questions about the Chinese language and the use of a Chinese dictionary. Couplet was a knowledgeable teacher of Chinese — a rarity at that time in Europe — but he was also a some-what reluctant teacher. He repeatedly cautioned Mentzel that one could not learn to speak Chinese in Europe and that any study of tones there would be useless. The most one could expect to achieve was a limited ability to read. Couplet's efforts were limited to clarifying some characters and sending Mentzel some valuable Chinese books[82]. Although several sources claim that Couplet accepted Friedrich Wilhelm's invitation and visited Berlin sometime between late 1687 and early 1688, the attempt to find documentation of that visit has so eluded the efforts of one scholar that there is now considerable doubt as to whether such a visit ever took place[83].

the study of the Chinese language, marks the beginning of Mentzel's study of Chinese. At the time of Herr Artelt's writing, Hyde's letter was found in volume Ms. Sin. 10 of the Preussische Staatsbibliothek Berlin.

80 The famous French sinologist Jean-Pierre-Abel Rémusat (1788–1832) claims that Mentzel derived the Chinese content of *Sylloge minutiarum latino-sinico-caracteristici* from Kircher's *China illustrata*. See Rémusat, *Mélanges asiatiques* 2 vols. (Paris, 1825–1826) II, 69.

81 Kraft, "Frühe chinesische Studien in Berlin," p. 110.

82 Kraft, "Frühe chinesische Studien in Berlin," pp. 112–113.

83 Kraft, "Frühe chinesische Studien in Berlin," pp. 113–115. Further research since the date of writing this article has confirmed Frau Kraft in her judgement that Couplet's reported visit to Brandenburg never took place. This judgement is an important cor-rection in that certain scholars have not only reported this visit as a fact, but have

A good measure of Couplet's influence on Mentzel is found in the latter's *Zeit-Register*. In this work Mentzel gave a generally accurate outline of Chinese dynastic history. The work was more comprehensive than Müller's historical tables and was divided into chapters, most of which were devoted to a major dynasty. Each ruler was designated with the Chinese characters of the royal name or, in the case of the Ch'ing dynasty rulers, with reign titles. A paragraph of information, factual in nature, was devoted to each ruler. These paragraphs were condensed versions of material on each ruler found in Couplet's *Tabula chronologica monarchiae Sinicae* (Paris 1686). Mentzel also borrowed Couplet's system of marginal dating using the Chinese 60-year cycle. This traditional Chinese method of dating also had been used in Martini's *Sinicae historiae decas prima*, but ended in the latter work at 1 B.C.. By contrast, the last cycle of Mentzel's *Zeit-Register* was numbered 74 and dated A.D. 1684[84].

One significant difference between the Couplet and Mentzel chronologies was that only Mentzel's work contained Chinese characters. Although Couplet's plan for including characters in *Confucius Sinarum philosophus*, which is commonly found bound together with the *Chronologica*, was frustrated by the difficulties of preparing the typeset of so many characters in Europe, it is probable that Couplet had the characters for the *Chronologica* in manuscript form still at hand. However, whether he gave them to Mentzel is questionable since he is known to have made excuses for not satisfying Mentzel's requests for characters. Mentzel's *Zeit-Register* was not published until 1696, by which time Couplet was dead. It is interesting to speculate whether Couplet knew of Mentzel's extensive borrowings from his *Chronologica*. Given Mentzel's translation of Couplet's material into German and the different standards of plagiarism of that time, Mentzel's project *might* have been known to Couplet and even received his blessings. Certainly the many favorable references that Mentzel made in the work to Couplet would have been the sort of favorable publicity for the Jesuit China Mission that Couplet as procurator was seeking.

The *Zeit-Register* used other sources beside Couplet, particularly for the prefatory material and first chapter. On the first page of his foreword, Mentzel acknowledged the assistance of Cleyer of Batavia in obtaining Chinese materials. In the next two pages, Mentzel drew from the first section of Martini's *Sinicae historiae decas prima* to describe the first Chinese from P'an Ku to Fu Hsi[85]. This was followed by a long quotation regarding the ancient Chinese, drawn from the foreword of Couplet's *Chronologica*. On the fifth page of Mentzel's

described it in some detail! For example, Pfister, p. 309, states that Couplet was *"reçu fort honorablement par l'Électeur Fréderic-Guillaume."*

84 Whereas Couplet had ended his chronology on the 60th year of the 73rd cycle, Mentzel ended his chronology on the beginning of the 74th cycle. See Couplet, *Tabula chronologica monarchiae Sinicae* (Paris, 1686) p. 106 & Mentzel, *Kurtze chinesische Chronologia oder Zeit-Register aller chinesischen Kayser* (Berlin, 1696) p. 140.

85 Martini, *Sinicae historiae*, pp. 3–13.

foreword, one finds a confused reference to two Chinese works — *Hsiao-erh lun* (Dialogue [of Confucius] with a child) and *Hsiao hsüeh* (Learning for minors). Mentzel claimed that his chronology of rulers was derived from the *Hsiao-erh lun* and he regarded this work as identical to the *Hsiao hsüeh*, the classical work mentioned by Couplet in his preface to *Confucius Sinarum philosophus*[86]. But Couplet was referring to a completely different *Hsiao hsüeh*! The latter was a work in six *chüan* compiled by Chu Hsi as an elementary primer and didactic text geared to serve the moral training of youth. There was also said to be a more ancient text by the same name, but it was clearly the Chu Hsi text to which Couplet was referring. (This text would later be translated by the Jesuit father François Noël in his *Sinensis imperii libri classici sex* [Prague 1711].)

The *Hsiao-erh lun* referred to by Mentzel is actually only a four-page hypothetical discussion between Confucius and a precocious youth who casually encounter one another on a highway. Mentzel extended this title to refer to an entire collection of basic instruction for children. This collection belongs to the popular literature of that age which was composed in the colloquial language and intended for elementary instruction in certain Chinese schools[87]. The collection to which Mentzel refers as the *Hsiao-erh lun* appears in several forms with slightly variant titles[88]. (The first page of a late seventeenth-century edition of the *Hsiao-erh lun* preserved in Germany is found in plate 15.) However, nearly all of the versions which I have encountered contain the term *tsa-tzu* (character miscellany) which was a picture vocabulary used to teach characters to elementary students[89]. In summation, one can say that the seven vertical columns of awk-

---

86 See Couplet, *Confucius Sinarum philosophus,* Proëmialis Declaratio, p. xxi.
87 Evelyn Sakakida Rawski, *Education and popular literacy in Ch'ing China* (Ann Arbor, 1979) pp. 50–51 & 128–129.
88 Copies of collections of popular children's literature containing the *Hsiao-erh lun* are preserved at Wolfenbüttel, Weimar and Tübingen in Germany. See Walter Fuchs, *Chinesische und mandjurische Handschriften und seltene Drucke* in the series *Verzeichnis der orientalischen Handschriften in Deutschland* XII, 1 (Wiesbaden, 1966) pp. 78–79 & Tafel XIII. In addition, Knud Lundbaek has found in the library of the Hunterian Museum of the University of Glasgow two illustrated children's primers which fit Mentzel's description and contain excerpts of Chinese text from the *"Li-tai ti-wang tsung-chi"* (Chronological record of kings and emperors) which Mentzel reproduced in his *Zeit-Register.* These two works in Glasgow are entitled *Tseng-pu yü-t'ang tsa-tzu* (The revised and enlarged Jade Temple character miscellany) and *Tung-yüan tsa-tzu ta-ch'üan* (The complete collection of the Eastern character miscellany). I also note the possible similarity of the *Hsiao-erh lun* to the *Hsiao-erh yü* (Children's discourse) written by Lü Te-sheng (d. 1568). The *Hsiao-erh yü* is a primer of rhymed proverbs for girls and boys which I have been unable to examine. Lü's work has been published in several *ts'ung-shu* (collectanea) such as the *Lu-tzu i shu* by Lu K'un (1534–1616) (see Goodrich & Fang, p. 1009).
89 The copy of the collection containing the *Hsiao-erh lun* preserved in the Herzog August Bibliothek Wolfenbüttel is entitled *Wan-pao yu-hsüeh hsü-chih; ao-t'ou tsa-tzu ta-ch'üan* (Treasury of essential knowledge for children in the complete character

ward and not entirely correct Chinese characters with romanizations found in the *Zeit-Register* were drawn by Mentzel from a widely disseminated popular literature used in educating Chinese children of the late Ming and early Ch'ing. Their significance is that they represent one of the first instances of Chinese text, as opposed to isolated characters or phrases, to be printed in Europe.

Couplet also played an important role in Mentzel's gift to Emperor Leopold I of Vienna, presented in October of 1688. This gift consisted of a Chinese edition of the Four Books, said to have been in the possession of Matteo Ricci. The text was a Ming dynasty edition and without commentary[90]. Although there is no evidence that Couplet had a hand in getting this edition of the Four Books to Mentzel, he certainly would have been in a position to explain the value and significance of the text to Mentzel. The date of the gift — October 1688 — coincided with the period of contact between Couplet and Mentzel in written correspondence, if not through a personal meeting at Berlin, and it is likely that Couplet either initiated the idea of such a gift to Emperor Leopold or, at least, encouraged it.

Couplet's contribution is clearer in the second part of Mentzel's gift — a handwritten copy with Chinese characters made by Mentzel of the *Ta hsüeh* with a

miscellany of a prize-winning Hanlin scholar), Wolfenbüttel, Herzog August Bibliothek Cod. Guelf. 117,7 Extrav., sheet 352a–401b. (Cf. the description of this work in Fuchs, *Chinesische und mandjurische Handschriften*, p. 79.) In addition to the *Hsiao-erh lun,* this collection includes a list of the traditional hundred Chinese family names, a *tsa-tzu* picture vocabulary and a family handbook written by the famous Ming dynasty literary figure, Li Chih. The table of contents of the Wolfenbüttel copy of this collection includes the *"Li-tai ti-wang tsung-chi"* (Chronological record of kings and emperors), the first part of which Mentzel reproduced in his *Zeit-Register*. Unfortunately, the Wolfenbüttel copy is incomplete and lacks the text of this Chinese work.

90 See Eva S. Kraft, "Christian Mentzels chinesische Geschenke für Kaiser Leopold I," in Schloss Charlottenburg-Berlin-Preusser, Festschrift für Margarite Kühn (Munich, 1975) pp. 194–195. There is, as Frau Kraft herself notes, a slight complication to identifying this text of the Four Books as Matteo Ricci's because there was in China a Dominican named Vittorio Ricci, O.P., who was alive in 1659, 49 years after Ricci's death. See Goodrich & Fang, p. 29 and José Maria González, O.P., *Un misionero diplomático: Vida del Padre Victorrio Riccio* (Madrid, 1955). Partial copies of the Four Books with identifying inscriptions by Mentzel are preserved in libraries at Wolfenbüttel and Weimar. The copy in the Herzog August Bibliothek Wolfenbüttel Cod. Guelf. 148 Blankenburg is entitled *Cheng-tzu Ssu-shu* (Standard text of the Four Books). It was edited by Lo Ku-t'ang and printed in the bookshop of Huang T'ang-ch'i in Nanhai (Canton) in 1684. The work consists of a title page, 19 pages of prefatory material signed by Huang Ch'ien-i, and the texts of the *Ta-hsüeh* and *Chung yung* according to the editing of Chu Hsi, but with most of his commentary omitted. The *Lun-yü* and *Mencius* are missing from the Wolfenbüttel copy. The prefatory material is philological in nature and deals with variant forms of characters, arranged according to rhymes. Another incomplete copy of the Four Books with Mentzel's inscriptions is found in the Thüringischer Landesbibliothek Weimar Q 675 a-e. This copy is described in Fuchs, *Chinesische und mandjurische Handschriften*, pp. 3–4. A title page in Mentzel's Chinese calligraphy is reproduced in *Tafel* I.

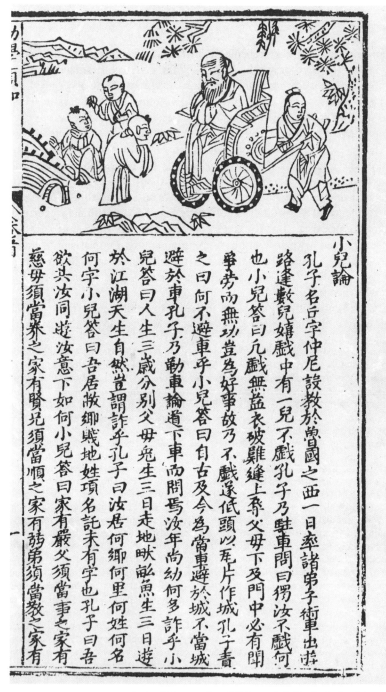

小兒論

孔子名丘字仲尼設教於魯國之西一日率諸弟子衘車出遊
路逢數兒嬉戲中有一兒不戲孔子乃駐車問曰獨汝不戲何
也小兒答曰凡戲無益衣破難縫上桑父母下及門中必有鬥
爭勞而無功豈為好事故乃不戲遂低頭以瓦片作城孔子責
之曰何不避車乎小兒答曰自古及今為當車避於城不當城
避於車孔子乃勤車論下車而問焉汝年尚幼何多詐乎小
兒答曰人生三歲分別父母兔生三日走地畎畝魚生三日遊
於江湖天生自然豈謂詐乎孔子曰汝居何鄉何里何姓何名
何宇小兒答曰吾居敝鄉賤地姓項名託未有字也孔子曰吾
欲共汝同遊汝意下如何小兒答曰家有嚴父須當事之家有
慈母須當養之家有賢兄須當順之家有弱弟須當教之家有

Plate 15. The first page of the *Hsiao-erh lun* (Dialogue [of Confucius] with a child), which opens the collection entitled *Wan-pao yao-hsüeh hsü-chih; ao-t'ou tsa-tzu ta-ch'üan* (Treasury of essential knowledge for children; the complete character miscellany of a prize-winning Hanlin scholar) 1680, preserved in the Herzog August Bibliothek, Wolfenbüttel, Cod. Guelf. 117.1 Extrav. .

character-by-character romanization and translation[91]. The text was arranged in traditional Chinese style, that is, with the words arranged in vertical columns from top to bottom and from right to left. This created a very awkward effect for a translation into a European language, but it did convey an exotic flavor, which was probably Mentzel's intention in a gift of this sort. A comparison of the first page of Mentzel's text with the first page of the *Confucius Sinarum philosophus* translation of the *Ta hsüeh*, shows an almost word-for-word duplication[92].

Mentzel's most ambitious sinological work, "Clavis Sinica", was fated, like Müller's "Clavis Sinica", never to be published. But because of Mentzel's greater openness, we know more about this Key than about Müller's invention. In this regard, it is revealing to compare the Leibniz-Mentzel correspondence with that between Leibniz and Müller. It was not Leibniz, but Mentzel who initiated the correspondence on November 22nd 1697[93]. The occasion was Mentzel's receipt of Leibniz' *Novissima Sinica* through Johann Jakob Chuno (Cuneau) (d. 1715), state secretary to the Elector. In this letter, Mentzel requested Leibniz' assistance in forwarding his *Zeit-Register* to Fr. Bouvet so that the latter might carry it to China on his return and present it to the K'ang-hsi emperor. Although expressing some regret over his physical condition — Mentzel was afflicted by a palsy condition which was gradually paralyzing his limbs — he was eager to help Leibniz or an acquaintance of his who would be willing to learn the Chinese language. He offered to send Chinese books to assist in the effort.

But what really caught Leibniz' attention was Mentzel's claim that he had developed a *Clavis Sinica* which compared favorably to that of Müller's Key. In his reply of October 15th 1698[94], Leibniz apologetically explained that it was impossible to forward Mentzel's *Zeit-Register* to China with Bouvet because the latter had already sailed. (We know that Leibniz later wrote to Bouvet about Mentzel's *Zeit-Register* from references made by Bouvet in letters to Leibniz[95]). However, Leibniz offered advice on forwarding a copy of the *Zeit-Register* to Paris where there were Jesuits in contact with China. He urged Mentzel to publish his Key and expressed the conviction — certainly based more on flattery than objective familiarity — that his Key was not inferior to that of Müller's. Furthermore, Leibniz wished to know if the enormous number of Chinese characters could be reduced to a fixed number of roots or elementary characters and whether other characters might be formed and transformed out of these. Leibniz' interest in the Key rather than in receiving the Chinese books indicated that he sought and believed in the possibility of a short-cut to learning Chinese.

91 Kraft, "Mentzel's chinesische Geschenke," p. 195.
92 Couplet, *Confucius Sinarum philosophus*, bk. 1; p. 1.
93 *Leibniz-Briefwechsel* 641, sheets 3^r-4^r & copy on sheets 1^r-2^r.
94 *Leibniz-Briefwechsel* 641, sheets 6^r-6^v & copy on sheets 5^r-5^v.
95 See Bouvet's letters to Leibniz, 28 February 1698, *Leibniz-Briefwechsel* 105, sheet 9^r & 19 September 1699, *Leibniz-Briefwechsel* 105, sheet 14^v.

His belief, in turn, reflected the widespread assumption among his contemporaries of a discernible, logical and mathematical structure to language.

A reply to Leibniz' letter was fast in coming and was dated October 25th 1698[96]. However, the reply was written not by Mentzel, but by his son, Johann Christian Mentzel, who explained that his father was too paralyzed to answer. The most significant thing about this letter concerned Mentzel's *Clavis Sinica*. On the negative side, young Mentzel noted that although his father had practically finished his Key, the printing of the Chinese characters presented enormous difficulties. (It is a puzzling and sad comment on the corporate effort of the first two Berlin sinologists that although Müller had contributed his Chinese typographia to the Electoral library as a gift in 1684, Mentzel showed no awareness of this.) Consequently, Mentzel's Key was unable to be formally presented and the manuscript was placed in the Electoral library. On the positive side, young Mentzel wrote that the title page, dedication and preface to the Key had been printed and he enclosed a copy[97]. (The contents of this prefatory material to Mentzel's "Clavis Sinica" are described in the preceding chapter.)

12. CONCLUSION

The German search for a *Clavis Sinica* as part of the seventeenth-century European assimilation of information about China showed how notions of China had penetrated the intellectual backwaters of Europe. Unlike Rome, Leiden or even Vienna where missionaries from China visited regularly, Brandenburg-Berlin rarely saw a missionary who had first-hand knowledge of the Chinese language and culture. This isolation was intensified by the fact that Berlin was a Protestant court while the China missionaries were Roman Catholic, but such isolation was typical of many small courts in Europe, whether Protestant or Catholic. What made Brandenburg-Berlin unique was the conscious attempt by the Great Elector, Friedrich Wilhelm, implemented by Müller and Mentzel, to acquire and assimilate information about China's language, geography, botany, pharmacoepia, history and literature, all of which were reflected in the collection of Chinese books at Berlin[98].

---

96 *Leibniz-Briefwechsel* 641, sheets 8ⁱ-9ᵛ.
97 *Leibniz-Briefwechsel* 641, sheets 12ʳ-13ᵛ. The standard-type dedication page of Mentzel's *Clavis Sinica* is addressed to "Friderico Tertio," i.e. the deceased (May 1688) Great Elector, Friedrich Wilhelm.
98 The Chinese library of the Great Elector and his successors was the basis for the sinological work of Müller and Mentzel. Although the earliest works of the collection are no longer extant, their titles can be reconstructed through the use of two brief catalogs which Müller printed. The first is a one-page catalog entitled "Catalogus librorum sinicorum Bibliothecae Electoralis Brandenburgicae." A copy of this now rare catalog is preserved in the Deutsche Staatsbibliothek, East Berlin and lists twenty-five titles in a collection said to total approximately 300 volumes. Though undated, this catalog is

In comparison with the eminent polymath and German-born Kircher of Rome, whose published works filled the bookstores of his day, Müller and Mentzel were obscure savants. In their assimilation of information about China, Müller and Mentzel applied a different interpretive framework than had Kircher

estimated to be pre-1683 on the grounds that the second catalog, which was printed in 1683, is indicated to be a supplement by its title: "Anderer Theil des Catalogi der Sineschen Bücher bey der Churfürstl. Brandenburgischen Bibliothec" (Cölln an der Spree, i.e. Berlin, 1683).

The date and circumstances of the first Chinese title in the Elector's library have not yet been traced, though we know that he was interested in acquiring Chinese books from 1661. (The early Chinese collection at Berlin has been the object of study by Frau Kraft in two published pieces: "Die chinesische Büchersammlung des Grossen Kurfürsten und seines Nachfolgers," in *China und Europa* (Berlin, 1973), pp. 18–25, and the concluding section of "Frühe chinesische Studien in Berlin," pp. 122–124.) The primary development of the library came during the years between 1667 and 1698 when Müller and Mentzel were active. The first major acquisition was the library of the ex-admiral Van Lier. Müller was sent to examine it in 1674 and its purchase apparently followed soon afterward. In 1680 and 1683 Chinese books as well as porcelains and other items were received from Andreas Cleyer. By 1702, the Chinese collection had expanded to approximately 400 volumes. (See Kraft, "Die chinesische Büchersammlung," pp. 22–25 & "Frühe chinesische Studien in Berlin," p. 124.

The Elector's collection of 1702 included a range of titles covering Jesuitica, dictionaries, history, philosophy, religion, literature, medicine and botany. Among the Jesuit works were two biographical works dealing with Jesus and the Christian saints – *T'ien-chu lung-sheng ch'u-hsiang ching chieh* (1637) by Fr. Giulio Aleni and *T'ien-chu sheng-chiao sheng-jen hsing shih* (1639) by Fr. Alfonso Vagnone. The collection included two apologetic works bound together – *T'ien-chu hsiang lüeh shuo fu hsiao luan pu ping ming shuo* (1619) and *K'ou tuo erh-ch'ao* (1619) – both attributed to the joint authorship of the Jesuit Juan de Rocha and two eminent literati-converts, Paul Hsü Kuang-ch'i and Michael Yang T'ing-yün. There was a very interesting small work of dialogue between a group of Chinese in Fukien province and Frs. Andreas Rudomina, Guilio Aleni and others entitled *T'ung-wen suan-fa* (1630–1640). Nearly half of the Jesuitica consisted of scientific works dealing with mathematical and astronomical matters. These included the well-known *Chi-ho yüan-pen* (1614) which was a translation of the first six books of Euclid made by Ricci and Li Chih-tsao. (Cf. Jean Claude Martzloff, "Note sur 'L'explication générale de la géométrie' *Jihe tongjie* de Mei Wending (1633–1721)," *China Mission studies (1550–1800) bulletin* 2 (1980): 3–12.) There were also books dealing with a hydraulic machine (1612) by Fr. Sabatino de Ursis and Hsü Kuang-ch'i, the reckoning of a solar eclipse with logarithm tables by Fr. Johannes Terrenz and Li Chih-tsao, a planisphere by Schall and a discussion of a solar eclipse (1669) by Verbiest. (See Kraft, "Die chinesische Büchersammlung," pp. 22–23.)

The dictionaries in the Berlin collection included the *Tzu-hui* (1615), the *Cheng Tzu-t'ung* (1662), the *Tzu hai ming chu* and the *Hai-p'ien* (ca. 1623). Of the Chinese Classics, the collection included an edition of the Four Books without commentary and portions of the *Ch'un-ch'iu* (Spring and autumn annals). There was a copy of the important historical work, the *Tzu-chih t'ung-chien* by Ssu-ma Kuang as well as a copy of a Chinese imperial edict elevating Fr. Schall and his ancestral line back to his grandparents to noble status. Of literary works, there was the famous *San-kuo-chih yen-i*

with his Hermetism. In one sense, the notion of a *Clavis Sinica* demeaned Chinese culture by assuming that there was a short-cut whereby one could in a few weeks or, at most, months acquire facility in the Chinese language. On the other hand, the belief in the possibility of finding a Key to the Chinese language was based on a belief in the commonality of languages – the Biblical confusion of tongues at Babel had a linguistic as well as historical significance. Those who studied languages felt that once this structure had been discerned – both Müller and Kircher based their claims for discernment on their primary study of Middle Eastern languages – the results could be readily applied to other languages, even to far-removed Chinese. The validity of this application was maintained in spite of the radical differences between China and Europe in terms of culture, racial type, society, fauna and religion. Kircher's *China illustrata* played upon the exotic qualities in treating China as a fascinating colony of the Egyptians. Jesuit proponents of accommodation conveyed a great deal of information about Chinese exotica to Europe, but they also emphasized the commonality and complementary features of Chinese culture, history, language and Confucian morality to that of Europe.

The widespread acceptance of a shared logical and linguistic structure between China and Europe fostered a willingness to accept the possibility of a *Clavis Sinica* among some of the most brilliant seventeenth-century European savants and proto-sinologists. This showed the extent to which information about China supplied by Jesuit missionaries had fired leading European minds with an intellectual enthusiasm which we would today regard as naive. No figure symbolized this enthusiasm more than Leibniz whose fascination with China led to an extensive correspondence with Jesuit proponents of accommodation and to his active support of their policies in the Rites Controversy[99]. Furthermore, these notions regarding China were integrated into Leibniz' philosophy where they remain as part of a lasting monument to seventeenth-century thought.

(Story of the Three Kingdoms) by Lo Kuang-chung. Geographical works were limited, but the library possessed a copy of the map of China brought back from Russia by Nicolaas Witsen. One notable non-Christian work contained in the collection was the 3-volume Buddhist work, *Tzu-pei tao-ch'ang chan fa* (1619).

Whereas Müller inclined toward history and language, Mentzel's interests in China were more medical and botanical. Consequently, we find a considerable number of books in the Berlin collection dealing with Chinese medicine. For example, there was a copy of the famous Chinese *materia medica, Pen-ts'ao kang-mu*, with copies of the first edition (1596) and the Edo-imprint (1637) of the second edition. There was also the part of the *Chih-nan pa-shih-i nan-ching* (1573) which presents the pulse teaching and diagnostics. The collection also contained Chinese works on therapeutics and anatomy.

99 Leibniz's relationship to the Jesuit policy of accommodation is discussed at some length in the author's *Leibniz & Confucianism: the search for accord*.

CHAPTER VIII

CONFUCIUS SINARUM PHILOSOPHUS AS A CULMINATION
OF RICCI'S ACCOMMODATION

1. BACKGROUND TO *CONFUCIUS SINARUM PHILOSOPHUS*

Confucius Sinarum philosophus was one of the supreme achievements of
Jesuit accommodative scholarship in China. As a translation and commentary
of three of the Confucian Four Books, it demonstrated the uniqueness of the
Jesuits among religious orders in using worldly knowledge as a mission tool.
Founded in the sixteenth century with a presentiment of the secular tendencies of later centuries, the Society of Jesus had not hesitated to embrace the
world in order to work within it. The pitfalls of this approach are perhaps only
fully appreciated by Christians themselves who were warned by Jesus that rejection of the world was a prerequisite for following him. This viewpoint is
aptly expressed in *I John* 2: 15–17 (New International Version):

> Do not love the world or anything in the world. If anyone loves the world, the love of
> the Father is not in him. For everything in the world – the cravings of sinful man, the
> lust of his eyes and the boasting of what he has and does – comes not from the Father but
> from the world. The world and its desires pass away, but the man who does the will of
> God lives forever.

Christianity has always contained a thread of distrust or even dislike of the
world as antithetical to the spiritual life. By embracing the world so fully in
order to work within it, the Jesuits laid themselves open to wordly influences
and temptations which they sometimes could not resist[2]. In working closely

---

1 Jesus repeatedly warned his followers about worldly attachments, for example, he said:
   "If anyone comes to me and does not hate his father and mother, his wife and
   children, his brothers and sisters – yes, even his own life – he cannot be my disciple.
   . . . In the same way, any of you who does not give up everything he has cannot be my
   disciple" (Luke 14: 26 & 33 [New International Version]). Jesus also said: ". . . the
   worries of this life, the deceitfulness of wealth and the desires for other things come in
   and choke the word, making it unfruitful" (*Mark* 4: 19 [NIV]). In the spirit of Jesus'
   teaching, a New Testament epistle states: ". . . don't you know that friendship with the
   world is hatred toward God? Anyone who chooses to be a friend of the world becomes an enemy of God" (*James* 4: 4 [NIV]).
2 The danger of the Jesuits becoming tainted by the world into which their vocational
   method leads them remains a problem for contemporary Jesuits, as is attested to by
   Pope John Paul II's call in September 1979 to root out "regrettable deficiencies" in
   their behavior and to return to an austere religious life "without yielding to seculariz-
   ing tendencies." (*Newsweek* December 17th 1979, p. 51)

with princes and heads of state, the Jesuits came into intimate contact with the machinations of power. This sort of power, with its tendencies toward cynicism and amorality was completely antithetical to the religious principles which the Jesuits embraced. Yet in the case of China, where the fate of the Mission frequently rested upon the political favor of the Chinese emperor, officials and eunuchs, the Jesuits were faced with difficult choices involving the use of amoral or even immoral power for the survival of the Mission.

In the seventeenth century, the Jesuits were becoming increasingly embroiled with other missionary orders in a controversy which was beginning to spread to Europe. This was the famous Rites Controversy which would lead to the Sorbonne examination and condemnation of 1700. But in the 1680s, European opinion in the controversy was in a much more malleable form than in 1700 and *Confucius Sinarum philosophus* was part of an attempt to shape that opinion. It was part of the Rites Controversy, but unlike the later works of Frs. Le Gobien and Le Comte which were the basis of the Sorbonne examination, *Confucius Sinarum philosophus* was as much informative as propagandistic and its authors were far more informed of Chinese society, culture and language than were Le Gobien and Le Comte. *Confucius Sinarum philosophus* was very far from being the work of literary hacks or gross propagandists.

Both in terms of its composition and content, *Confucius Sinarum philosophus* represented a continuation of the accommodation formula of Fr. Ricci. But even as this work was being published in Paris in 1687, the recently arrived French Jesuits in China were altering Ricci's accommodation formula in response to changed cultural and political realities there. First of all, the ascent of the Manchus and their Ch'ing dynasty in 1644 coincided with the receding of the cultural syncretism of the late Ming — an atmosphere viewed by many Chinese as contributing to the dynastic decline of the Ming. Whereas Ricci had been able in such a fluid cultural environment to forge a viable Confucian-Christian synthesis, the Ch'ing dynasty ushered in a rigidifying of cultural lines in which the purity and orthodoxy of Confucianism were again reasserted. Secondly, the Chinese scholar-officials whom Ricci had so deeply cultivated and learned from in forging his synthesis were now in retreat as a disillusioned and conquered class and in voluntary retirement as Ming Loyalists. The new power structure, to which the Jesuits were ever attuned, was at the Manchu court in Peking and centered on the occupant of the throne. By contrast, Ricci had worked in China at the time of perhaps the greatest imperial recluse of Chinese history — the Wan-li emperor. The accommodation formulas of Ricci and Bouvet shared certain fundamental features, such as the belief that Chinese antiquity had worshipped a monotheistic deity, the rejection of Neo-Confucianism as a distortion of the original philosophy of China and the ultimate aim of converting the ruling classes of China. But Ricci's method worked through contemporary Chinese literati while Bouvet's method largely ignored the literati to work through the Manchu emperor. This helps to explain the differences between Ricci and Bouvet in their respective selection of different Chinese Classics to emphasize. Ricci had chosen to concentrate on the Four Books — the focus of *Confucius Sinarum philosophus* — because it was the key to both the scholar-officials' morality and their class ladder of official examination success. Bouvet, on the other hand, rarely mentioned the Four Books or even Confucius, but concentrated on what he thought was the oldest of the Chinese Classics — the *I ching*. For Bouvet, the *I ching* was both an intellectual key to linking China with Europe and a political key to receiving the favor of the Manchu throne. He believed that parallels could be found which established the intellectual grounds of similarity between the ancient Chinese philosophy and Christianity. Practically speaking, Bouvet believed that the Jesuits could reinforce this theoretical similarity by being in the technological service of the emperor. This plan was historically played out in Bouvet's relationship with the K'ang-hsi emperor, though because of restrictions by his superiors, the plan was not openly disseminated.

In *Confucius Sinarum philosophus*, Jesuit accommodation used the spiritual ambiguity of the ancient Chinese and early Confucian tradition to forge a sympathetic treatment of the Confucian literati culture. This, in turn, was crucial to the selection of Confucius and these particular Classics for transla-tion. Given the times and the pioneering nature of the effort, the translations were surprisingly accurate, in spite of the pronounced tendency to interpret Confucian concepts in terms of natural religion and the monotheistic God of the Judeo-Christian tradition. Because of the remarkable continuity of tradi-tional Chinese culture, those choices for emphasis in *Confucius Sinarum philoso-phus* reflected the historical as well as contemporary culture. On the other hand, those aspects of Chinese culture which the Jesuits perceived as less complemen-tary to the aims of the Christian Mission, such as Taoism and Buddhism, were treated in a highly superficial and biased manner. As it stands, *Confucius Sinarum philosophus* presented Chinese culture from the scholar-official perspective. The fact that this was the politically and culturally dominant viewpoint of that time in China gives this work more value as an historical document than had it been selected solely in terms of its amenability to Christianity.

2. THE GROUP EFFORT OF PRODUCING *CONFUCIUS SINARUM PHILOSOPHUS*

Confucius Sinarum philosophus was a group effort involving at least seven-teen known European Jesuits who participated in the China Mission and several Chinese co-workers. The translation of three of the Four Books which it con-tained was a cumulative effort dating from the time of Ricci and perhaps even from the time of the Jesuit Michele Ruggieri (1543—1607)[3]. We know that

---

3 Fr. Ruggieri's partial translation of the *Ta hsüeh* is discussed in the article by Knud Lundbaek entitled "The first translation from a Confucian Classic in Europe," *China*

during Ricci's time, the Four Books were used as Chinese language primers for newly arrived Jesuits. Ricci-Trigault's *De Christiana expeditione apud Sinas* contained a reference to a paraphrase of the Four Books, *"Tetrabiblion Sinense de moribus"*, which Ricci made in the context of teaching Chinese to the newly arrived Jesuit Francesco de Petris (1562–1593) from December 1591 until November 1593 at Shaochou[4]. No copy of this manuscript has been found and some scholars have concluded that the work has been lost[5]. But it is more probable that Ricci's paraphrase was an incomplete and working manuscript which continued to be used by the newly arrived Jesuits learning Chinese. In the process, the manuscript was handed down and improved by later Jesuits so that *Confucius Sinarum philosophus* represented a later stage in the manuscript's evolution[6].

The first published fruit of this extended group translation project appeared in 1662 at the mission center at Chienchang in Kiangsi province. This brief work was entitled *Sapientia Sinica* (Wisdom from China) and included a two-page biography of Confucius, a 14-page translation of the *Ta hsüeh* — of which the title *Sapientia Sinica* was an approximate translation — and the first five parts of the *Lun yü* (Analects)[7]. The translation of the *Ta hsüeh* is attributed to Inácio da Costa (1603–1666), a Portuguese Jesuit who had been in China since 1634 and who had a knowledge of Chinese sufficient to author several books in Chinese on theological topics[8]. The translator(s) of the *Lun yü* sections is uncertain. The editor of *Sapientia Sinica* was Prosper Intorcetta (1625–1696), a Sicilian Jesuit who had been in China only since 1659 and consequently in 1662 would not yet have been capable of difficult translation work. However, Fr. Intorcetta took a sustained interest in translating the Confucian Four Books

---

Mission studies (1550–1800) bulletin 1 (1979): 2–11. Also see David E. Mungello, "The seventeenth-century Jesuit translation-project of the Confucian Four Books,": in *East meets West: the Jesuits in China (1582–1773)*, forthcoming.

4 Ricci-Trigault, *De Christiana expeditione apud Sinas* (ch. 4; 3) p. 344. The source of the information on the circumstances under which Ricci composed his translation of the Four Books is Fr. d'Elia's *Fonti Ricciane* II, 33. Also see *Fonti Ricciane* I, 330. In addition, Pfister, p. 41, states that Ricci made a paraphrase of the Four Books in 1593.

5 As one example, Otto Franke believed that Ricci's translation of the Four Books was lost. See. O. Franke, "Das chinesische Geistleben im 16. Jahrhundert und die Anfange der Jesuiten-Mission," *Orientalistische Literaturzeitung* 41 (8–9) (August-September 1938): 480.

6 Several years after coming to this conclusion on the Ricci manuscript, I found this confirmed by Fr. d'Elia who speaks of the great probability that Ricci's manuscript-translation of the Four Books became the primary basis and nucleus of *Confucius Sinarum philosophus*. See d'Elia, *Fonti Ricciane*, II, 33.

7 Cordier, *Bibliotheca Sinica*, col. 1386 & Streit, V, 695.

8 Sommervogel, IV, 641 & Streit, V, 850.

and is said to have composed a paraphrase of the Four Books entitled *"Lucu-bratio de tetrabiblio Confucii Sinice Su Xu dicto"*[9].

Intorcetta occupied an important role in the translation of the *Chung yung* (Doctrine of the Golden Mean), published partially at Canton in 1667 and partially at Goa in 1669. It was entitled *Sinarum scientia politico-moralis* (The politico-moral knowledge of the Chinese) and included a short preface by Intorcetta, a 54-page Chinese-Latin translation of the *Chung yung* and an eight-page biography of Confucius which differed from that found in *Sapientia Sinica*. The dual publication sites are probably accounted for by Intorcetta's appointment as procurator of the Jesuit mission to China and his trip to Rome in this capacity which occupied the years 1669–1674. It appears that the publication of *Sinarum scientia politico-moralis* was part of the publicity effort required of a Jesuit procurator sent to Europe aimed at securing recruits and contributions, but it was also much more. This campaign was conducted within the context of Ricci's accommodation whose Confucian-Christian synthesis represented a formula for the intellectual assimilation of China by Europeans. A European-language translation of the Four Books with their supreme importance to Chinese culture and society admirably suited this program.

Intorcetta left China carrying a largely complete translation. Like Fr. Couplet, who followed twelve years later, Intorcetta was charged with the editorial task of seeing a manuscript-translation of the Four Books through publication. The Jesuit publicity effort received a boost in 1672 at Paris when Melchisedec Thévenot chose to publish a French translation of *Sinarum scientia politico-moralis* in his famous collection of travel literature[10]. In Thévenot's reedition, the translation of the *Chung yung* and life of Confucius received a far greater exposure to readers than in the limited Canton-Goa edition.

The effort of translating the Four Books had engaged a number of other Jesuits of which no less than seventeen were listed in the opening pages of *Sinarum scientia politico-moralis* alone[11]. Intorcetta was listed as the author. Four Jesuit moderators were listed as giving formal approval: da Costa; Jacques le Faure (le Favre) (1613–1675) of France; Matias da Maia (Maya) (1616–1667) of Portugal; and Feliciano Pacheco (1622–1687) of Portugal. Twelve Jesuits were listed as having reviewed the work: Antonio de Gouvea (1592–1677) of Portugal; Pietro Canevari (Canevare) (1596–1675) of Genoa; Francesco Brancati (Brancato) (1607–1671) of Sicily; Giovanni Francesco de Ferrariis (Ferrari) (1609–1671) of Piedmont; Humbert Augery (1618–1673) of France; Adrien Grelon (Greslon) (1618–1696) of France; Jacques Motel (1619–1692)

---

9 Sommervogel, IV, 643, claims as his source of information a *Mémoire* manuscript by a Fr. Gabiani, S.J.. According to Pfister, p. 328, Fr. Southwell in *Bibliotheca scriptorum Soc. Jesu* (Rome, 1676) claims that Fr. Intorcetta's paraphrase of the Four Books was deposited at Rome.
10 Intorcetta, "La science des Chinois," in Thévenot, *Relations* IV (Sondert. 1), 1–24; reprinted in Thévenot, *Relations* (Paris, 1696) II, 349–374.

of France; Giandomenico Gabiani (1623–1694) of Piedmont; Manuel Jorge (George) (1621–1677) of Portugal; Philippe Couplet (1622–1693) of Belgium; François de Rougement (1624–1676) of Belgium; and Christian Herdtrich (Herdtricht) (1625–1684) of Austria.

This list of participants in the compilation of *Confucius Sinarum philosophus* coincided with the Jesuits who were expelled to Canton in September of 1665 as part of the anti-Christian movement led by Yang Kuang-hsien[12]. However, since Fr. da Costa died on May 11th 1666 and since not all the Jesuits on this list appear to have arrived in Canton by that time — Frs. de Ferrariis and le Faure may have arrived as late at 1668[13] — it seems likely that the participation of these Jesuits consisted of long-term study and discussion of the translations and commentary on the Four Books rather than any concentrated period of consideration. This approach would have been consistent with the gradual evolution of the translation of the Four Books which had been under way since the days of Ruggieri and Ricci. At any rate, the Canton phase of the compilation of *Confucius Sinarum philosophus* would have ended by 1671 when most of the exiled missionaries were able to leave their exile in Canton for a return to mainland China or elsewhere.

Most of the names in this list of contributors to *Confucius Sinarum philosophus* are not well known for their accomplishments in the mastery of Chinese culture. However, including da Costa and Intorcetta, ten out of seventeen of these Jesuits mastered Chinese sufficiently to have authored at least one literary work in Chinese, usually on a theological subject[14]. According to Couplet, Fr. Herdtrich composed a large Chinese-Latin dictionary entitled *Wen tzu k'ao* which was sent to the press, but nothing is known of this work[15]. Fr. de Gouvea has been credited with authoring only one work in Chinese — a catechism in colloquial style. This style was frowned upon by the classically-minded Chinese literati and was quite unlike the difficult literary style in which de Gouvea's predecessor, Ricci, composed — with considerable help from literati friends. However, de Gouvea is also credited with writing a history of China which required a considerable immersion in Chinese literature[16]. Frs. Brancati, Couplet and de Rougemont each wrote several treatises in Chinese on theological subjects[17]. De Rougemont studied Chinese-Manchu history as well and Couplet

11 Cordier, *Bibliotheca Sinica,* col. 1387.

12 Dehergne, *Répertoire,* p. 347.

13 Dehergne, *Répertoire,* pp. 71 & 147.

14 My information is drawn from the biographical and bibliographical entries on these Jesuits in Pfister. As there are lacunae in Pfister, it is possible that one or several of the remaining seven Jesuits also authored some short treatises in Chinese which have not yet been credited to their names.

15 Pfister, p. 366.

16 Sommervogel, III, 1637.

17 Pfister, pp. 228–230, 310–313 & 335–336.

participated in the compilation of a Chinese dictionary which was left at Paris[18]. In short, while the participants of this translation effort did not belong to the first rank of Jesuits learned in Chinese language and culture, they represented a highly respectable body of students. Furthermore, the intellectual standards of European Jesuits in the seventeenth century were very high and the China Mission received its share of this talent.

3. FR. COUPLET, EDITOR OF *CONFUCIUS SINARUM PHILOSOPHUS*

The key individual in the group effort of producing *Confucius Sinarum philosophus* was Philippe Couplet, a Fleming born in Mecheln (Malines) in 1622 or 1623[19]. Unlike Ricci or Martini or many other Jesuits of that time who came from aristocratic or eminent families, Couplet's origins were obscure. He was ordained in November 1654 at Brussels with another future China missionary and contributor to *Confucius Sinarum philosophus*, François de Rougemont. Couplet and Rougemont together decided in 1654 to apply for service in the China Mission. They embarked in 1656 from Lisbon as part of a group of eight Jesuits under the direction of Fr. Boym, who had just completed his return voyage to Europe to seek aid at Rome for the Ming pretender. Boym died on August 22nd 1659 near the border between Tonking and Kwangsi province, but Couplet had apparently become separated from Boym at some earlier point and was possibly already in Macao[20].

During his time in China, Couplet was extremely active in evangelistic work in the provinces of Kiangsi, Hukwang, Chekiang and especially Chiangnan[21].

18 Pfister, p. 312.
19 While most accounts, following Couplet's own novitiate autobiography, list his birth date as May 31st 1622, Fr. C. F. Waldeck in "Le Père Philippe Couplet, Malinos, S.J.," *Analectes pour servir a l'histoire ecclésiastique de la Belgique* 9 (1872): 5–6, claims that Couplet's birth date was May 31st 1623 and argues that the often-cited birth date of May 31st 1623 is a mistake. For the period of Couplet's life between his birth and departure for China, I rely on Waldeck, pp. 6–8. After his novitiate, Couplet studied philosophy for two years at Louvain (1642–1644), after which he taught rudimentary subject matter at Antwerp until 1646. Couplet traveled to Spain in 1647 and taught humanities and rhetoric at Kortrijk (Courtrai) in 1648 and 1649. In 1652 he began his theological training at Louvain.
20 Couplet's signature appears on a letter dated December 23rd 1659 at Macao. The letter was written by Fr. Rougemont and cosigned by Frs. Couplet, Dorville and Verbiest. See Henri Bosmans, S.J., "Lettres inédites de François Rougemont," *Analectes pour servir l'histoire ecclésiastique de la Belgique* 39 (1913): 30–33.
21 Couplet worked at Sungchiang, Shanghai, Chiating, Suchou, Chenchiang, Huaian and the island of Ch'ungming. In 1664, the anti-Christian movement led from Peking by the scholar-official Yang Kuang-hsien broke out and extended throughout China. Couplet was sent to Peking from which in September of 1655 most of the missionaries were expelled to Canton (Dehergne, *Répertoire,* p. 347). With the abating of the per-

During this time, Couplet met and formed a close association with Hsü Kantiti (Candida) (1607–1680), a granddaughter of Hsü Kuang-ch'i and a devout Christian. Under Madam Hsü's patronage, Couplet was able to build a number of churches in Chiangnan province[22]. We have only the barest details of what must have been twenty extremely active years for him. He undoubtedly had considerable contact with literati as he mastered Chinese sufficiently to compose at least seven short works in Chinese. Their subject matter was typical proselytizing material aimed at the Chinese, and included *Pai wen ta* (A catechism of 100 questions and answers) published at Peking in 1675, *Ssu mo chen lun* (The true doctrine of the four final aims) also published at Peking in 1675 and *Chou-sui sheng-jen hsing lüeh* (A very condensed lives of the saints for each day of the year) which is undated.

Couplet's talents melded with the aims of the Society of Jesus to produce one of the outstanding missionaries of the seventeenth century. He lacked the intellectual powers of Ricci or Schall, but like Trigault, Semedo, Martini, Boym, Grueber and Intorcetta before him and Grimaldi after him, Couplet possessed organizational talents which led his superiors to select him for the difficult role of procurator to Europe[23]. The procurator's tasks involved arousing public interest in the mission through visits to eminent persons, the cultivation of contacts with scholars, and publications. The procurator's success in obtaining new recruits, financial support and favorable papal rulings was something on which the Jesuit missionaries desperately depended and only those Jesuits deemed most capable were selected for the task. After being appointed procurator in 1680, Couplet departed from Macao in December 1681. A layover in Batavia early in 1682 allowed him to make the personal acquaintance of Andreas Cleyer (1634–1697/98), the German-born physician of the Dutch East India Company[24]. A common interest in Chinese medicine had led to the first known

secution, Couplet returned to Chiangnan province in 1671 and was particularly successful in winning converts and building churches after 1677 on Ch'ungming island.

22 Couplet wrote a work honoring Candida Hsü entitled *Historia nobilis feminae Candidae Hiu christianae Sinicae* which was translated and published in French (1688), Spanish (1691) and Flemish (1694). (See Pfister, p. 310.) In addition to Candida Hsü, other prominent Chinese ladies who contributed greatly to the development of the Christian church in mid-seventeenth-century China were the wife of the eminent Chinese official, T'ung Kuo-ch'i (d. 1684), who was known in Europe as Lady Agathe, and the daughter of the Christian scholar-official, Yang T'ing-yün (1557–1627), known as Lady Agnès.

23 Bouvet was sent to Europe at the command of the K'ang-hsi emperor rather than of his Jesuit superiors, though certainly he had their consent. Consequently, though Bouvet was charged with many of the tasks of a procurator, he lacked the formal title of one.

24 Waldeck, p. 29, states that Couplet was forced to land in Batavia because of a storm and that this layover was a great disappointment to his plans. However, one wonders if Couplet did not actively seek to make Cleyers' acquaintance.

contact between Couplet and Cleyer by mail through the Dutch trade mission to Canton in 1669[25].

Couplet reached Holland in October 1682 with his young Chinese companion, Michael Shen Fu-tsung, and received a triumphal homecoming in Mecheln where he visited his aged father[26]. At Rome, Couplet sought authorization for missionaries in China to celebrate the mass in Chinese. He dispensed the golden chalice and ornaments made from the jewelry contributed by the female converts of the town of Sungchiang and by Madame Hsü. In his audience with Pope Alexander VII, Couplet presented over 400 volumes of works in Chinese composed by missionaries[27]. A letter inserted into the *Mercure Galant* of September 1684 stated that on the fifteenth of that month, Fr. Couplet and a traveling companion were introduced to Louis XIV at Versailles and attended a royal dinner on the following day. The introduction to the King was arranged by Fr. de La Chaise, Jesuit confessor to the throne, who described Couplet's companion as an object of great royal attention, clothed in green silk and deep blue brocade adorned with Chinese dragons and eating with chopsticks at a royal dinner[28]. Clearly, the rage for chinoiserie was fostered at Versailles. Several days later, Couplet and the Chinese visited the St. Louis House where they displayed a number of portraits on silk cloth, including one of Confucius with a long black moustache. Couplet and his Chinese companion were a much-talked-about attraction in Parisian society and this was soon to produce practical consequences.

The Marquis de Louvois, who had recently succeeded Colbert in administering the Académie des Sciences, had a list of thirty-five questions about China composed and sent to Couplet for answers[29]. The questions covered a broad range of interests. These included the Chinese histories, sciences, plants, beverages, birds, domestic animals, weaponry, army, festivals, textiles, porcelains, transportation, architecture, mines, women, slavery, legal and penal system, religions,

25 Kraft, "Mentzel, Couplet, Cleyer und die chinesische Medizin," p. 179. However, contact between Couplet and Cleyer probably preceded 1669 because Rougemont in his letter of November 5th 1670 from Canton shows that the Jesuit fathers had found in Herr Cleyer a secure middleman for conveying mail to and from Europe (Bosmans, p. 43). From late January until late June 1682, Couplet and Cleyer were either located together or traveling in the same vicinity and appears to have met frequently (Kraft, "Mentzel, Couplet, Cleyer und die chinesische Medizin," p. 182).

26 Waldeck, p. 29.

27 Pfister, p. 308.

28 Letter from Fr. de la Chaize to Fr. de Noyellez, December 29th 1684, in Chantelauze, *Le Père de la Chaize* (Paris, 1859) p. 53.

29 The questions about China which the Marquis de Louvois (François-Michel le Tellier) sent to Couplet are reproduced in Virgile Pinot, ed., *Documents inédits relatifs a la connaissance de la Chine en France de 1685 a 1740* (Paris, 1932) pp. 7–9. Also see Virgile Pinot, *La Chine et la formation de l'esprit philosophique en France (1640–1740)* (Paris, 1932; reprinted Geneva, 1971) p. 44.

the Great Wall, ports, imperial revenue, climate, geography and – one wonders with what anti-Portuguese strategic motive – the condition of Macao and if it occupied the mainland. These questions reflected the broad range of interest in China held by one of the most eminent scholarly bodies of that time in Europe. This list of questions, which presumably Couplet answered and returned to the Académie, represented one of the contributing links in the chain of events which culminated in the French missionary expedition to China under the auspices of the Académie and the patronage of King Louis XIV.

The evidence that the Jesuits had conceived of and initiated this mission is found partly in Ferdinand Verbiest's invitation to visit China which Couplet delivered to Jean de Fontaney (1643–1710). Fr. Verbiest was a Belgian like Couplet and from 1664 until 1688 served as president of the Chinese Bureau of Astronomy in Peking[30]. Couplet, during the course of his extended stay in Paris, was able to meet with Fr. Fontaney several times and these meetings were instrumental in the formation of the important French mission of 1685. Under the banner of science, the Jesuit aim of mission and Louis XIV's aim of extending French influence at the expense of Portugal's missionary monopoly were merged. Five French Jesuits – Frs. Bouvet, Gerbillon, Le Comte, Tachard and Visdelou – trained in mathematics and astronomy were selected, organized and led by Fontaney. Couplet was still in Paris to witness the formation and departure of this group early in 1685 from Brest on board *l'Oyseau*.

In the effort of promoting the China Mission, Couplet entered into correspondence with a number of European savants interested in China, including Mentzel. The latter appears to have secured for Couplet an invitation to visit the Great Elector's court in Brandenburg but this visit – as noted in the previous chapter – probably did not take place. Along with *Confucius Sinarum philosophus*, Couplet occupied himself with producing several publications. His biography of Madam Hsü in Latin was translated into the French *Histoire d'une dame chrétienne de Chine, Candide Hiu* by Fr. d'Orleans and published at Paris in 1688. Other translations followed. Couplet wrote several pieces on the Chinese rites question which were later found among the papers of the French sinologist, Jean-Pierre-Guillaume Pauthier (1801–1873)[31].

Couplet was at Paris until mid-December of 1687, after which he traveled to England, Portugal and Spain where he resided at Madrid during 1689 and 1690[32]. He was forced to delay his return to China for several years because of disagreements between the King of Portugal and Rome. Although the Portuguese empire was in decline, the king was able to exert considerable pressure to retain his jurisdiction over the Church in Asia (*padroado*) through his control of the key

30 Pfister, p. 308 & Dehergne, *Répertoire*, p. 307.
31 Pfister, pp. 310–312.
32 See Kraft, "Frühe chinesische Studien in Berlin," p. 114 & Couplet's letter from Madrid in Rome in Archivum Romanum Societatis Jesu, Rome, Jap/Sin 164.

ports of Lisbon, Goa and Macao on the missionary route to China. Until the issue was resolved, the king refused to grant missionaries exit permits from Lisbon. Finally, an agreement was reached which allowed Couplet with several companions to embark from Lisbon early in 1692. But Couplet, like Boym, never returned to China. As his ship neared Goa, it encountered a severe storm which shook loose a heavy chest, inflicting a fatal wound to Couplet's head. He died on the following day – May 16th 1693[33].

4. AN OUTLINE OF *CONFUCIUS SINARUM PHILOSOPHUS*

Confucius Sinarum philosophus sive scientia Sinensis latine exposita was published in a folio-edition of 412 pages plus illustrations at Paris in 1687. It was printed by Daniel Horthemels and was bound with Couplet's *Tabula chronologica monarchiae Sinicae* in 126 pages. Four names appeared on the title page in this order: Frs. Intorcetta, Herdtrich, Rougemont and Couplet. Not only does the overlap of translators connect this work with *Sapientia Sinica* and *Sinarum scientia politico-moralis*, but the sustained duration of the project is shown by the fact that Rougemont had died in 1676 and Herdtrich in 1684. Consequently, the names of these four Jesuits appear to represent a list of only the primary contributors. Between the time of Ruggieri and Ricci (the first Jesuits to begin translating the Four Books) and Herdtricht (the last Jesuit to arrive in China – at Macao in 1660 – who was specifically tied to the translation effort) there were, according to Pfister, 116 other Jesuits participating in the China Mission. As noted above, in addition to Herdricht, sixteen of these 116 were listed as contributors to *Sinarum scientia politico-moralis*. How many of the other 100 may have contributed is difficult to discern, particularly as the translation appears to have evolved through its usage as a literary Chinese primer for the Jesuits. It appears that much as a contemporary scholar might develop his translation of a work through using it as a teaching device and thereby receive contributions from his students, so did the Jesuits develop their translations of the Four Books. The Jesuits of one student generation successively became the teachers of the next generation of Jesuits and there seems to have been a text of translations which was improved and passed on in this manner and published in several editions, including *Confucius Sinarum philosophus.*

The continual process of modification in the translation is apparent in a comparison of the opening line of the *Ta hsüeh* in *Sapientia Sinica* with that found in *Confucius Sinarum philosophus. "Ta-hsüeh chih tao tsai ming ming te"* in *Sapientia Sinica* was rendered: "The *purpose of the learning of great* men *consists in illuminating spiritual power* by means of virtue, that one may receive from heaven, certainly a rational soul, so that this may be returned to its original

---

33 Pfister, pp. 309–310 & Dehergne, *Répertoire*, p. 67. Also see Waldeck, p. 30.

clarity, as the animal appetites have beclouded [them]"[34]. (The italics in the translation was used by Intorcetta to indicate classical text, as opposed to commentary.) The refinements and elaborations of this passage are apparent in the rendering of this same passage in *Confucius Sinarum philosophus*: "Moreover, the ³purpose of the ²learning of ¹great men ⁴consists in ⁵refining or improving the ⁶rational ⁷nature, that one may receive from heaven, so that certainly this, as if a most transparent mirror, by means of wiping away a blemish of deformed appetites, may be returned to its pristine purity"[35]. (The numerical superscripts used by Couplet signified the characters of the classical text as opposed to commentary.) An important change in the translation is the alteration of "illuminating spiritual power by means of virtue" to "refining or improving the rational nature". However, this was not necessarily an improvement upon the translation of *ming-te*, which most modern translators render as "illuminated virtue". If the *Sapientia Sinica* translation was overspiritualized, then the *Confucius Sinarum philosophus* rendering was overrationalized, perhaps in order to allow it to meld more fully with the Jesuits' interpretation of the Chinese Classics in terms of natural religion.

The collaborative translation effort of the Jesuits did not end with *Confucius Sinarum philosophus*. It is highly probable that the Jesuit François Noël (1651–1729) used the *Confucius Sinarum philosophus* translations as the basis of his expanded translations of the Chinese Classics in *Sinensis imperii libri classici sex* published at Prague in 1711[36]. This work included the three Classics in *Confucius Sinarum philosophus* as well as the *Mencius*, a translation of which had been promised to the reader on the last page of the Couplet-edited work[37]. In addition to the Four Books, Fr. Noel published translations of two short works of near classical status among Confucians – *Hsiao-ching* (Book of filial piety) and *Hsiao hsüeh* (Learning for minors). A comparison of *Confucius Sinarum philosophus* with Noël's translations shows the same sort of development and refinement which took place between the translations of the *Ta hsüeh* in *Sapientia Sinica* and in *Confucius Sinarum philosophus*. It is probable that had those engaged in the translation effort of the Chinese Classics not been members of the same religious order, the translations would never have attained their

34 Ignacio a Costa & Prospero Intorcetta, *Sapientia Sinica* (Ch'ien-ch'ang, 1662) p. 1: "*Magnorum virorum sciendi institutum constitit in illuminando virtutibus spiritualem potentiam à coelo inditam, nempe Animam, ut haec redice possit ad originale claritatem, quam appetitus animales obicubilaverant.*"

35 Couplet, *Confucius*, bk. 1, p. 1: "¹*Magnum adeoque virorum Principum,* ²*sciendi* ³*institutum* ⁴*consistit in* ⁵*expoliendo, seu excolendo* ⁶*rationalem* ⁷*naturam à coelo inditam; ut scilicet haec, ceu limpidissimum spaeculum, abstersis pravorum appetitum maculis, ad pristinam claritem suam redire possit.*"

36 See David E. Mungello, "The first complete translation of the Confucian Four Books in the West," in *International Symposium on Chinese-Western Cultural Interchange* (Taipei, 1983) pp. 515–541.

degree of proficiency. Furthermore, without the combined force of the Jesuit order behind this translation effort, it is unlikely that there would have been translations of all Four Books into a European language by 1711.

Confucius Sinarum philosophus was dedicated by Couplet to "Louis the Great", i.e. King Louis XIV of France. The dedication was partly a reward for the king's sponsorship of the mission of 1685 led by Fontaney and partly a ploy to elicit further support. With Jesuits such as La Chaise and, later, Michel Le Tellier serving as confessors to the French king, the Jesuits were in a strong position to wage such a campaign, though their very position of strength would be a source of antagonism to their opponents. In this regard, we can note the reaction of one seventeenth-century reader to Couplet's dedication. The copy of *Confucius Sinarum philosophus* currently found in the Bibliotheca Regia Hannoverana collection was owned by Gerhard Wolter Molanus (d. 1722), an abbot of the Lutheran monastery in Loccum and a long-time acquaintance of Leibniz. But Molanus was less sympathetic to the Jesuits than was Leibniz and, following Couplet's name at the end of his dedication to Louis XIV, Molanus inscribed *"adulator mendacissimus"* (most mendacious sycophant)! Apart from amateur sinologists like Mentzel, it appears that not all Protestant Germans were as impressed by Couplet as were Catholic Frenchmen.

Following the dedication, *Confucius Sinarum philosophus* opened with a 106-page Proëmialis Declaratio (Introductory exposition) which was signed, but apparently not entirely written, by Couplet. An examination of the manuscript of the work in the Bibliothèque Nationale Paris by Mr. Lundbaek has revealed two different styles of handwriting in the introduction, the second of which probably belonged to Couplet[38]. The Proëmialis Declaratio constituted the interpretive core of the whole work. It was followed by an eight-page biography of Confucius with the only portrait-type engraving in *Confucius Sinarum philosophus*, which was, fittingly, reserved for the Chinese sage, as conceived by a European artist[39]. (See plate 16 and the discussion of this engraving in the next section of this chapter.)

The next portion of *Confucius Sinarum philosophus* contained the translations of the *Ta hsüeh, Chung yung* and *Lun yü*. The entire section of translations was entitled "Scientiae Sinicae" (Learning of the Chinese) with the respective Classics designated as books one, two and three and occupying 39, 69 and 180 pages, respectively[40]. The *Tabula chronologica monarchiae Sinicae* followed

37 Couplet, *Confucius,* bk. 3, p. 159.
38 For more information on Mr. Lundbaek's examination of the manuscript of *Confucius Sinarum philosophus* held at the Bibliothèque Nationale Paris (Fonds Latin 6277, 2 vols.), see his article, "The Image of Neo-Confucianism in *Confucius Sinarum Philosophus,*" *Journal of the History of Ideas* 44 (1983): 19–30.
39 Couplet, *Confucius,* p. cxvi.
40 The pagination of *Confucius Sinarum philosophus* is not consecutive. The *Ta hsüeh* and *Chung yung* occupy 108 consecutive pages as books 1 & 2, respectively, while

and since it lacked any reference to a printer, it was probably also printed by Daniel Horthemels, but was dated 1686 or one year prior to the publication of the larger work to which it was appended. Finally, there followed a map by Couplet of the fifteen provinces and 155 major cities of China with markings of nearly 200 churches founded by Jesuits[41]. Following the map was a four-page synopsis of demographic, geographic and related statistics, signed by Couplet and on the final page a "Privilege du Roy", dated at Paris in 1687.

5. THE CONTENT OF THE PROËMIALIS DECLARATIO

The full title of the Proëmialis Declaratio informed the reader that it would discuss the origin and scope of *Confucius Sinarum philosophus* as well as Chinese books and their interpretations, indigenous Chinese religious "sects" and philosophies. At the outset, the work stated that the Jesuits' intention in writing *Confucius Sinarum philosophus* was not to serve the "amusement and curiosity of those who live in Europe", but to serve as a useful tool to those missionaries carrying the Christian Gospel to China and elsewhere. This aim fit well into the use of the translations as a literary Chinese primer in order to equip Jesuits for work in the China Mission, but it was somewhat at odds with publicly promoting and distributing the work among the laity in Europe. Therefore, one cannot help wondering to what extent this statement was included for obligatory reasons, that is, to establish missionary bona fides and to attempt to silence in advance those more narrowly focused European Christians who were hostile to missionaries pursuing "curious" interests as well as proselytizing aims. The Jesuits, in particular, with their wide-ranging intellectual pursuits were subject to attack from those who feared more secular interests.

In order to evaluate the Jesuit disclaimers of appealing to "curious" interests in *Confucius Sinarum philosophus*, it is important to recognize the powerful threat posed by seventeenth-century forces which were hostile to mixing religious missions with secular interests. It is clear that the Jesuits *were* attempting to stimulate imaginations and rouse European interest in China as a "curious land". By presenting a massive folio volume which reflected the skillful handling of extensive details about an exotic and remote philosophy, the Jesuits were seeking to arouse support for the sustenance and expansion of Jesuit activities in China. In the attempt to achieve their ultimate religious ends of spreading the Faith, the Jesuits were quite willing to appeal to secular interests and simultaneously deny that they were doing so. Critics who insist on more precise lines

the *Lun yü* occupies book 3 and consists of a first part with pages numbered 1–21 and the second through tenth parts numbered pages 1–159.

41 For a reproduction and discussion of the background of Couplet's map of China, see Boleslaw Szcześniak, "The Seventeenth Century Maps of China: an Inquiry into the Compilations of European Cartographers," *Imago Mundi* 13 (1956): 131–133.

being drawn between right and wrong will today, as did critics in the seventeenth century, find the Jesuit approach questionable and will be unimpressed by the fact that it achieved some spectacular successes in China.

The discussion of the Chinese Classics in the Proëmialis Declaratio was highly critical of the *Neoterici Interpretes* (Modern Interpreters), by which was meant mainly the Sung Neo-Confucians, for distorting the earlier corpus of Confucianism[42]. The Jesuit authors accepted the Neoterics' categorization of the classical literature into the Five Classics and Four Books, although prior to this recategorization by Neo-Confucians in the late 1100s, these texts had been part of the Thirteen Classics[43].

Two of the Four Books − the *Ta hsüeh* and *Chung yung* − were originally chapters in a larger Classic, *Li chi* (Book of rites), and were not established as separate works until the time of the Sung dynasty Neo-Confucians[44]. The author and even the date of the composition of the *Ta hsüeh* are uncertain. According to Chu Hsi, the *Ta hsüeh* was composed by Confucius' disciple, Tseng Tzu (505–436 B.C.). However, a near-contemporary of Chu Hsi, Wang Po, attributed the work to Confucius' grandson, Tzu Ssu (492–431). More recently, the work has been dated as late as 200 B.C., although there seems to be a lack of evidence for any firm attribution[45]. Chu Hsi's authority in seventeenth-century China was such that his view on the authorship of the *Ta hsüeh* was widely accepted. Of particular importance, Tseng Tzu's authorship was accepted by Chang Chü-cheng, whose commentary on the Four Books was followed closely by the Jesuits in their translations in *Confucius Sinarum philosophus*. There is also uncertainty surrounding the author of the *Chung yung*. In his biography of Confucius in the *Shih chi* (Historical records), Ssu-ma Ch'ien attributed the *Chung yung* to Confucius' grandson, Tzu Ssu. But because of inconsistencies in style and thinking, the work may constitute a merging of different works by several authors over a period of time even as late as the early Han dynasty (i.e.

---

42 Couplet, *Confucius*, p. xxxv.

43 The Thirteen Classics include the *Shih ching* (Book of odes), *Shu ching* (Book of documents), *Li chi* (Book of rites), *I ching* (Book of changes), *Ch'un-ch'iu kung-yang ch'uan* (Kung-yang commentary on the spring and autumn annals), *Ch'un-ch'iu ku-liang ch'uan* (Ku-liang commentary on the spring and autumn annals), *Ch'un-ch'iu tso-ch'uan* (Tso commentary on the spring and autumn annals), *I li* (Ceremonies and rituals), *Chou li* (Rituals of Chou), *Lun yü* (Analects), *Meng-tzu* (Mencius), *Hsiao ching* (Book of filial piety), *Erh ya* (a dictionary).

44 The *Ta hsüeh* and *Chung yung* constituted chapters 39 and 29, respectively, of the *Li chi*. See Fung Yu-lan, *History*, I, 361–377.

45 See Chu Hsi, *Ssu-shu chi-chu* (reprinted Taipei, 1969) Chung yung section, p. 1a & Fung, *History* I, 362. In regard to the dating of the *Ta hsüeh*, see Wing-tsit Chan, *A source book in Chinese philosophy* (Princeton, 1963) p. 85n.

ca. 200 B.C.)[46]. The Jesuits contended that the *Chung yung* was the work of Confucius, but was edited by his grandson, Tzu Ssu[47]. In this contention, the compilers of *Confucius Sinarum philosophus* accurately reflected the traditional emphasis on transmission of the *Tao* received from the ancients rather than on creative discovery of the *Tao* by contemporary search.

The *Ta hsüeh* and *Chung yung*, along with two other Classics — the *Lun yü* and *Mencius* — were grouped by Chu Hsi into the category of the Four Books when he wrote new commentaries on them during the late twelfth century[48]. The Four Books, along with the Five Classics, became firmly entrenched as the basis of the literati examination curriculum from ca. 1415[49]. These categories of the Classics were largely accepted by the Jesuits as the original Classical corpus which they were attempting to isolate from later Neo-Confucian accretions. Consequently, it appears that Couplet and his fellow Jesuits lacked an informed historical perspective in their understanding of the Confucian Classics. The Jesuits' rejection of the Neo-Confucian interpreters of the Classics undoubtedly stemmed from that position first formulated by Ricci.

The rejection of modern interpretations of the Classics in order to return to the original meaning of the Classics is an ingrained aspect of the Confucian tradition. In adopting this position, which Ricci and other Jesuits in part absorbed from their association with Chinese literati, the Jesuits anticipated the intellectual rejection of the Neo-Confucian interpreters which became quite pronounced in eighteenth-century China. In sum, one can say that a rejection of the Neo-Confucian interpretations of the Chinese Classics was quite possible for solid scholarly reasons. The Jesuits developed some of these reasons on their own. But not all of the Jesuits' reasons for adopting this position were of this objective category and some can only be characterized as unabashedly serving the aims of their missionary enterprise.

The Jesuits were clearly impressed by the extensiveness of Chinese books and writings. In an attempt to discern the oldest and most significant of Chinese works, they noted the complicating factor of the burning of books which took place in 213 B.C.. Because of the extensive destruction and the horror which the event aroused in the minds of most intellectuals like the Jesuits, the authors regarded the event as unique in world history. The *Proëmialis Declaratio* claimed

---

46 Wang Po argued that the present *Chung yung* was formed by the merging of the *Chung yung* text of Tzu Ssu with a work entitled *Chung yung shuo* (Explanations of the doctrine of the Mean) in the Han dynasty by Tai Sheng, who reduced the *Li chi* to its final form of 46 chapters. See Fung, *History* I, 370–371 & 417. Cf. Chan, *Source book*, p. 97n.

47 Couplet, *Confucius,* bk. 2, p. 40.

48 For a discussion of Chu Hsi's recategorization of the Classics into the Four Books, see Wing-tsit Chan, "Chu Hsi's completion of Neo-Confucianism," pp. 81–87.

49 For background information, see James T. C. Liu, "How did Neo-Confucianism become a state orthodoxy?" *Philosophy East & West* 23 (1973): 483–505.

that the book burning of Ch'in Shih Huang-ti was far worse than other book burnings known in world history, including the destruction of the famous library at Alexandria in the anti-pagan campaign of the Christian Roman Emperor Theodosius the Great (r. 379–395)[50].

The Jesuit authors placed the *quinque volumina* (Five Classics) and the *Tetrabiblion* (Four Books) among the oldest Chinese books. They ranked each of the Five Classics on the basis of their respective importance or significance and assigned first place to the *Shu ching* (Book of documents or history). One of their reasons for this claim was that this work dealt with the three "greatest rulers" of China who were Yao, Shun and Yü and from whom the Hsia family of the first traditional dynasty was thought to have descended. But the Jesuits did not claim chronological precedence for the *Shu ching*. Rather, they noted that the *I ching* was the most ancient of the Five Classics "if you accept the Commentaries" of the Chinese[51]. Yet the compilers of *Confucius Sinarum philosophus* did not accept all of the Chinese commentaries. Not only was skepticism expressed over whether these commentaries should be accepted, but the *I ching* itself was criticized as being obscure and enigmatical. At any rate, these Jesuit compilers assigned the *I ching* the position of third place in importance or significance among the Five Classics[52]. (On the basis of degree of archaic language, contemporary scholars regard the *I ching* and the *Shih ching* (Book of odes) as the most prominent candidates for highest antiquity, but the question is surely not easily resolved.)

Although the authorship of the *I ching* was attributed to the so-called founder of China, Fu Hsi, one finds the Jesuits treating Fu Hsi in a different way than they treated the legendary figures Yao, Shun and Yü. Whereas Yao was assigned the traditional date of 2357 B.C., Fu Hsi was assigned no date[53]. This omission may be a sign that the Jesuits did not accept Fu Hsi as an historical figure in the way that they accepted Yao, Shun and Yü, but rather regarded him essentially as a legendary figure. If the historical status of Fu Hsi was cast into doubt, perhaps the most ancient status of the *I ching*, which Fu Hsi was said to have written, was also cast into doubt. There was another reason why the compilers of *Confucius Sinarum philosophus* were critical of the *I ching*. This work was regarded by them, somewhat inaccurately, as the fount of Neo-Confucianism, a philosophy whose atheistic and materialistic tendencies were felt by most missionaries to completely eliminate it as a complementary element to Christianity.

---

50 Couplet, *Confucius*, p. xv.
51 Couplet, *Confucius*, p. xviii.
52 Couplet, *Confucius*, p. xxxviii.
53 Couplet repeated this dating of Yao as 2357 B.C. in his *Tabula chronologica*, p. 3, and although the ultimate source of this dating was Chinese, Couplet may have derived the early part of his chronology from Chinese sources indirectly through Martini's *Sinicae historiae decas prima*, p. 24, where one finds a dating of 2357 B.C. for Yao.

The Jesuits reproduced the Chinese portrayal of Yao, Shun and Yü as being moral and able rulers and cited Shun specifically as honoring "*Shang ti*, Supreme Emperor of the heavens"[54]. Yü was credited with dispersing the waters of the Flood — presumably in the Yellow River region — and establishing boundaries between the new provinces in a manner harmonious with celestial forces. The Jesuits described the *Shu ching* as containing a record of the second imperial family or dynasty called the Shang or Yin. They accepted traditional chronology as fact rather than legend when they cited the founder of this house as Ch'eng T'ang who established the Shang dynasty in exactly 1776 B.C.. The second Classic to be discussed was the *Shih ching*[55] and the third was, as noted above, the *I ching* which was described as obscure and enigmatical[56]. The *Ch'un-ch'iu* (Spring and Autumn annals) and the *Li chi* (Book of rites) were presented as the fourth and fifth Classics[57].

The authors of the *Proëmialis Declaratio* described the Four Books as secondary to, but following closely in authority, the Five Classics and noted that all nine works were the basis of study for whomever aspired to literary degrees[58]. The Jesuits attempted to isolate the original corpus of ancient Chinese knowledge in these books by cutting through the layers of later interpretive accretions to reach the "pure simplicity of the golden age" in China[59]. The next section in *Confucius Sinarum philosophus* was devoted to defining some of the later forces which distorted the ancients' philosophy. Aside from mentioning some philosophy-religions associated with Lao Tzu (Taoism), Yang Chu (a school of egoism), Mo Ti (a school of universal love) and Buddhism, all of which were regarded as heterodoxies in the traditional Confucian perspective, the Jesuits were very specific in citing one focal point of this distortive influence. This point was traced to the philosophy developed by the *Neoterici Interpretes* (Modern Interpreters) and of which the ancient Chinese sages were completely unaware. The Jesuits placed the Neoterics in the Sung dynasty beginning in 960 A.D. among the ranks of those most learned and prolific literati who developed a new philosophy based "not only on the interpretations of the five books of the Classics and the Chronicles [*Shih-lu* (Veritable records)?], but also on the commentaries of these Interpreters of Confucius and certainly of Mencius and others, and their own efforts; and many copious explanatory discourses"[60]. The Sung Neo-Confucian identity of the Jesuits' reference is confirmed with their citation of Chu Hsi and the Ch'eng brothers — Ch'eng Hao (Ming-tao,

54 Couplet, *Confucius*, p. xvi.
55 Couplet, *Confucius*, p. xvij.
56 Couplet, *Confucius*, p. xviij.
57 Couplet, *Confucius*, p. xix.
58 Couplet, Confucius, p. xx. Cf. Miyazaki, *China's examination hell*, pp. 14–17.
59 Couplet, *Confucius*, p. xx.
60 Couplet, *Confucius*, p. xxxv.

1032–1085) and Ch'eng I (I-ch'uan, 1033–1107) — as the most eminent of these Neoterics[61].

The *Proëmialis Declaratio* noted that the philosophy of the Neoterics was consolidated in the Ming dynasty during the reign of the Yung-lo emperor (r. 1403–1424) who gathered together some 400 scholars to compile a work of extensive explanation on the Five Classics (*Wu-ching ta-ch'üan*, 1415), an explanatory work on the Four Books (*Ssu-shu ta-ch'üan*, 1414) and a collection of quotations from the Sung masters entitled *Hsing-li ta-ch'üan* (1415) whose title the Jesuits translated as "the collection on Nature or on natural Philosophy"[62]. The Jesuits noted that these Ming compilations closely followed the interpretations of Chu Hsi and the Ch'eng brothers — as well as certain other Sung Neo-Confucians such as Chou Tun-i and Chang Tsai. More debatably, the Jesuit authors remarked that the interpretations of these Ming compilations were a distortion of ancient Chinese philosophy. This was the substance of the position which the Jesuits were attempting to argue.

In the next section of the *Proëmialis Declaratio*, the Jesuits traced the source of the Neoterics' new philosophy to the *I ching* whose primary author, Fu Hsi, was said to have left behind an explanation whose incomprehensibility was "comparable to the ancient Gordian knot"[63]. Here the Jesuits fell upon ground which was not merely contentious, but also exaggerated. It is true that the *I ching* was an important stimulus upon the cosmologies of the early Sung Neo-Confucians, but among the main Sung Neo-Confucians, namely, Chu Hsi and the Ch'eng brothers, the *I ching* was not a primary philosophical influence. Chu Hsi himself regarded the work as filled more with divinatory than philosophical significance. So whatever the exact degree of its influence, the *I ching* was not the "fount" of Sung Neo-Confucianism, as the Jesuits claimed in their title to this section of *Confucius Sinarum philosophus*. Actually, the Sung Neo-Confucians believed themselves to be engaged in an enterprise absolutely antithetical to the Jesuits' interpretation. The Jesuits agreed with the Sung Neo-Confucians that after Mencius' time, the true meaning of the ancient philosophy or the "transmission of the Tao" (*Tao-t'ung*) lapsed[64]. But in direct contrast to the Jesuits' interpretation, the Neo-Confucians saw themselves as reviving the transmission of the Tao and re-establishing the true lost meaning of the Classics!

Part II of the *Proëmialis Declaratio* cited the example of Ricci to show how the testimony of ancient authorities could be used to refute the Neoterics[65]. It is quite probable that the authors were referring to Ricci's work in *T'ien-chu shih-i* (The true meaning of the Lord-of-Heaven) (1603) which attempted such

---

61 Couplet, *Confucius*, pp. xxxv-xxxvi.
62 Couplet, *Confucius*, pp. xxxvi-xxxvii.
63 Couplet, *Confucius*, p. xxxviii.
64 Couplet, *Confucius*, p. xxxvi & lv. Cf. Chan, "Chu Hsi's completion of Neo-Confucianism," p. 75f.
65 Couplet, *Confucius*, p. liiij.

a rebuttal. The Jesuit authors were quite familiar with this work and later described how it developed through Ricci's twenty years of painstaking examination of ancient books and discussions with learned Chinese[66]. According to the Jesuit authors, Ricci dared to voice his criticism of contemporary literati in the court at Peking[67]. There Ricci claimed that contemporary explanations of ancient books were ornate and florid in style and lacked substance and agreement with action or deeds. The *Proëmialis Declaratio*, following Ricci, argued that the ancient Chinese had professed a belief in God whom they designated variously as *T'ien-chu* or *Shang-ti*. The Jesuits believed that these beliefs faded with the destruction of the ancient Chinese books, but survived in vestigial form in fragments of old texts.

The Jesuits explained the Chinese anti-Christian campaign of "1615" (Persecution of 1617?) not as an opposition to Christian doctrine and practices per se, but as a defensive reaction to the threat which Christianity posed to Chinese teachings such as those of Buddhists, Taoists and certain contemporary literati (i.e. adherents of Ch'eng-Chu Neo-Confucianism)[68]. According to the *Proëmialis Declaratio* description, Christian missionaries were suspected of inciting rebellion and of teaching a false and depraved religion. In the face of this opposition, the authors claimed that the Jesuits were sustained by the emperor — a sustenance fully in harmony with the Jesuit approach. The Chinese emperors — no reference was made to any discontinuity caused by the Chinese Ming dynasty being replaced by the Manchu Ch'ing dynasty in 1644 — permitted the Jesuits to reside at the imperial court in Peking and practice their faith. The authors noted an important mark of imperial favor when on July 12th 1675 the K'ang-hsi emperor visited the Jesuit temple in Peking and honored the Jesuits by inscribing the words *"ching t'ien"* (revere Heaven). They interpreted this phrase to be consonant with Christianity, but this interpretation would become an issue in the Rites Controversy.

The writers of the *Proëmialis Declaratio* claimed that the Neo-Confucians established their system on a material philosophy at whose basis — drawing from the *Hsing-li ta-ch'üan* — was the primary concept of *T'ai-chi*[69]. However, the Jesuits noted that even Chu Hsi conceded that neither Fu Hsi, King Wen nor the Duke of Chou ever used this term. The Jesuits noted that the term *T'ai-chi* was found in the third appendix to the *I ching*, which was added by Confucius, and stated: "Change contains a great axis or pivot [*T'ai-chi*]. This produced two power-virtues, namely, completion and incompletion [i.e. *yang* and *yin*] as heaven and earth. The two power-virtues produced the four images; the four

---

66 Couplet, *Confucius*, p. cvij.
67 Couplet, *Confucius*, p. cviij.
68 Couplet, *Confucius*, pp. cxj-cxij.
69 Couplet, *Confucius*, p. lv.
70 Couplet, *Confucius*, p. lv. Cf. the translation of this passage from the third appendix to the *I ching* in Fung Yu-lan, *History*, I, 384.

images produced the eight hanging figures [i.e. the *pa kua* or eight trigrams] "[70].
The Jesuits argued that since this passage was merely part of an appendix and
since the term *T'ai-chi* did not appear in the text proper of any of the Five
Classics or Four Books, then the cosmological basis of Neo-Confucianism was
not firmly based on the ancient Classics.

In describing some of the extensive discussion that the Neo-Confucians
devoted to *T'ai-chi*, the *Proëmialis Declaratio* noted that they bestowed upon
the term a spiritual mysteriousness which transcended the human mode of
thinking. *T'ai-chi* was likened to a great terminal or pole, a master axle of a
carriage, the root of a tree, a pivot of things and a foundation[71]. The Neo-
Confucians were said to firmly rebut any implication that *T'ai-chi* was merely
imaginary and so rejected any associations with the Buddhist sense of void and
emptiness (*hsü*) or of the Taoist nothingness (*wu*). *T'ai-chi* was both quiescent
and moving; it produced *yang* and *yin*, which were described in some detail by
the Jesuits and likened to perpetual systolic and diastolic motion, to day and
night, to summer and winter[72].

The *Proëmialis Declaratio* authors linked *T'ai-chi* to *li*, the most fundamental
term in Sung Neo-Confucianism. They said that the Neo-Confucians understood
T'ai-chi to be "prime matter" and *li* to be "a certain true reason or constituent
form of things" and regarded *li* as another name for *T'ai-chi*[73]. This was much
too forced an identity between *T'ai-chi* and *li*. Furthermore, *T'ai-chi* was only
prime matter to the extent that it was the source of cosmological process. But
the concept transcended the limitations of matter, particularly in terms of
energy. It is interesting to note that the Jesuit Niccolò Longobardi's treatise on
Chinese religion written in the 1620s also traced his criticism of the materialist
root of Neo-Confucian philosophy to the concepts *li* and *T'ai-chi*. But Fr.
Longobardi defined *li* somewhat differently from Couplet as "infinite prime
matter . . . from which the *T'ai-chi* emanated"[74]. Longobardi had traced Neo-
Confucian atheism to a source in materialist philosophy. Couplet followed a
similar, though not identical, line of argument by saying that intricate and
confused disputes over *li* and *T'ai-chi* by the Neoterics led in an atheistic direction to the point where all supernatural origin was excluded[75].

In an attempt to combat the Sung Neo-Confucian interpretation of the
Classics, the Jesuits rejected the authoritative commentary on the Four Books

71 Cf. the references to the *T'ai-chi* found in Ricci (Li), *T'ien-chu shih-i* bk. 1, pp. 15a–b,
    17b, 18b & 19b.
72 Couplet, *Confucius*, p. lvj. This passage led the Jesuits into a discussion of a 29,600
    year cycle which might have been a mistaken reference to the 129,600 year cycle
    developed by the somewhat peripheral Sung Neo-Confucian, Shao Yung (1011–1077).
73 Couplet, *Confucius*, p. lvij.
74 Nichola Longobardi, *Traité sur quelques points de la réligion des chinois* (Paris, 1701)
    §5: 7 in Kortholt, p. 202 & Dutens, p. 110.
75 Couplet, *Confucius*, p. lvij.

by Chu Hsi and turned to a commentary by Chang Chü-cheng (1525–1582)[76]. The title of Chang's commentary was not specified in *Confucius Sinarum philosophus*, but is *Ssu-shu chih-chieh* (Colloquial commentary on the Four Books). The Jesuit authors described Chang as a native of Chiangling in Hukuang province who devotedly served the Wan-li emperor for ten years as tutor, teacher and prime minister. Following his death, Chang was said to have received posthumous honors which were soon retracted in an official degrading. The process, however, stopped short of the destruction of his literary works when the Wan-li emperor decided that "the Books did not sin"[77]. The Jesuits were well aware of the esteem in which Chang's name and works were held in mid-seventeenth century China. The *Proëmialis Declaratio* stated that the Jesuits were attracted to Chang's commentary on the Four Books because of his abilities as an interpreter of ancient works and because his style was both content-filled and lucid. Furthermore, the authors claimed that Chang's commentaries received widespread usage and high praise from contemporary Chinese.

Some of the Jesuits' remarks on Chang Chü-cheng's commentary strike the contemporary sinologist as surprising. First of all, Chang is not well known as an important literary figure, but rather as a practical man of action whose historical significance derived from his political power and influence. Secondly, Chang's commentary on the Four Books, *Ssu-shu chih-chieh*, is barely touched upon in recent scholarly work done on Chang[78]. This is not to say that the Jesuit author's comments were incorrect as an assessment of seventeenth-century Chinese culture. There is some evidence that Chang's works were taken up by the Ming Loyalists who were prominent at the time when the Jesuits were working on the translations found in *Confucius Sinarum philosophus*. Chang was preoccupied with the dynastic decline of the Ming dynasty, which he perceived in a number of signs of his age, and devoted himself to arresting that decline. Somewhat subjectively, he developed a philosophy of history, deeply influenced by his reading of the *I ching*, whereby a reversal of dynastic decline

---

76 As far as I am aware, the first scholar to identify "Cham Colai" [Chang Ko-lao] as Chang Chü-cheng was the Jesuit Henri Bernard-Maitre in his *Sagesse chinoisie et philosophie chrétienne* (Paris & Leiden, 1935) p. 131.

77 Couplet, *Confucius*, p. cxiv.

78 See Robert Crawford, "Chang Chü-cheng's Confucian Legalism," *Self & society in Ming thought* Wm. Theodore de Bary, ed. (New York, 1970) pp. 367–413. Also see the entry on Chang by Mr. Crawford & L. Carrington Goodrich in Goodrich & Fang, pp. 53–60. There is no mention of Chang's commentary on the Four Books in Ray Huang's extensive treatment of Chang in his highly acclaimed *1587, a year of no significance* (New Heaven, 1981). An attempt to rectify past neglect of Chang's commentary on the Four Books is found in complementary articles by Knud Lundbaek and this writer in the *China Mission studies (1550–1800) bulletin* 3 (1981): 2–11 & 12–22.

seemed possible[79]. This he took to be his chief objective during his term as prime minister. Chang's preoccupation with the *I ching* appears to have escaped the notice of Jesuits working on the translations of the Four Books. Unlike Fr. Bouvet later, these earlier Jesuits found the *I ching* filled with superstitious elements and were generally critical of this Classic.

Chang's commentaries on the Four Books were published in at least five editions, four of which appeared during the early years of the Ch'ing dynasty. The work was first presented to the Wan-li emperor in 1573, but it could have been printed as late as 1584[80]. While all of these editions contained a short four-page introduction by Chang dated 1573, the 1651 edition bore an elaborate title page with the alternate title *"Chang Ko-lao chih-chieh"* (The true explanation of the Statesminister Chang). This is the title that the Jesuits appear to have cited in *Confucius Sinarum philosophus*. The 1651 edition also contains a preface dated 1651 by Wu Wei-yeh (*hao*: Hui-ts'un) (1609–1672), a native of T'ai-tsang in Chiangsu province who obtained his *chin-shih* degree in 1631 and served in the Hanlin Academy[81]. Wu was an eminent poet, landscape painter and scholar-official as well as a Ming Loyalist.

The next edition of Chang's commentaries on the Four Books contained a preface by Chu Feng-t'ai dated 1672. The following edition of Chang's commentaries bore the alternate title of *Ssu-shu chi-chu ch'an wei chih-chieh* (A detailed and enlightening true explanation of collected commentary on the Four Books) and contained a preface dated 1677 by Hsü Ch'ien-hsüeh (1631–1694), a native of K'un-shan in Chiangsu province, a chin-shih degree-holder (1670) and a member of the Hanlin Academy[82]. The 1677 and 1683 editions of Chang's commentary differed from the editions of 1651 and 1672 in that they included Chu Hsi's commentary.

We know from a reference in Fr. Magalhaes' *Nouvelle relation de la Chine* that the Jesuits in China were familiar at least by 1668 with the commentaries

79 Crawford, "Chang's Confucian Legalism," pp. 373–375 & 403–404. In his research, Mr. Lundbaek has discovered a commentary on the *I ching* by Chang Chü-cheng in the Bibliothèque Nationale Paris.

80 The first edition of Chang Chü-cheng's *Ssu-shu chih-chieh* is dated 1573 in the U.S. Library of Congress' *Kuo-hui t'u-shu-kuan-ts'ang Chung-kuo shan-pen shu-lu* (A descriptive catalog of rare Chinese books in the Library of Congress), compiled by Wang Chung-min and edited by T. L. Yuan. Washington, D.C., 1957, I, 46. However, an unsigned letter of November 19th 1981 to Mr. Lundbaek from the Chung-kuo Kuo-chia T'u-shu-kuan (National Library of China) of Peking stated that although the *Ssu-shu chih-chieh* was presented to the Wan-li emperor in 1573, it is difficult to state exactly when it was printed. For reasons of style of wood-block characters and honorary titles used in referring to Chang, the author(s) of the letter estimated the date of printing of the commentary to have been sometime between 1574 and 1584.

81 T'an Cheng-pi, ed., *Chung-kuo wen-hsüeh-chia ta-tz'u-tien* 2 vols. (Shanghai, 1934; reprinted Taipei, 1974) pp. 1289–1290 (no. 5103).

82 T'an Cheng-pi, ed., p. 1374 (no. 5418).

on the Four Books of both Chang Chü-cheng and Chu Hsi[83]. These editions of
Chang's commentaries appeared in China at a time when the Jesuits were actively engaged in translating the Four Books and it is hardly a coincidence that
copies of the 1651, 1672 and 1683 editions are found among the old collection
of the Bibliothèque Nationale Paris[84]. It is probable that these copies were
brought to Europe by a seventeenth-century China missionary, and perhaps by
Couplet.

  Why did the Jesuits use this particular commentary on the Four Books to
combat the Sung Neo-Confucian interpretation? This question is complicated
by the fact that the differences of interpretation between Chu Hsi and Chang
are not substantial. One possibility is that the simplicity of Chang's commentary
appealed to Jesuits burdened by translation difficulties. The somewhat later
learned Jesuit, Joseph Henri-Marie de Prémare (1666–1736), stated that Chang's
commentary on the Four Books was done in an "informal and simple style"[85].
A contemporary student of Chang, Robert Crawford, states that the *Ssu-shu
chih-chieh* "is, for the most part, a stylistically simplified version of Chu Hsi's
commentaries"[86]. In comparison with Chu Hsi's commentaries on the Four
Books, Chang's work consists of a simpler language and is easier to comprehend.
This greater simplicity was probably the result of Chang's attempt to compose
an explanation of the Four Books which would be suitable for the young Wan-li
emperor. At the time of Chang's presentation of his commentary in 1573, the
boy-emperor was only nine or ten years old. By no means are Chu Hsi's commentaries difficult by the standards of classical Chinese, but relative degrees of
simplicity are more important for foreign readers of a language – such as the
seventeenth-century Jesuits – than for native readers. However, there were also
slight differences of interpretation between Chu Hsi and Chang which led the
Jesuits to prefer Chang's commentaries. Mr. Crawford notes that Chang not
only simplified Chu Hsi's commentary, but disagreed with Chu Hsi's interpretation of "the highest good" (*chih-shan*) as found in the *Ta Hsüeh* and *Chung
yung*. Chang rejected Chu Hsi's "to rest in the highest good" as too stagnant
and instead proposed the meaning of not exceeding the mean[87]. Furthermore,
the thrust of Chang's philosophy was based on a rejection of the Sung Neo-

83 Magaillans, p. 102.

84 I am further indebted to Mr. Lundbaek for his discovery that these copies of Chang
   Chü-cheng's commentaries on the Four Books are in the Bibliothèque nationale Paris.
   The editions are identified as follows: Fonds chinois 2844–46 (1651), 2847–48
   (1672) and 2849 (1683). This writer has located a copy of the 1677 edition in the
   Far Eastern Library of the University of Chicago as a posthumous donation by the
   Sung historian, Edward Kracke.

85 Joseph Henry-Marie Prémare, *Notitia linguae Sinicae* (Hong Kong, 1893) p. 8.

86 Crawford, "Chang's Confucian legalism," pp. 391–392. Mr. Crawford wrote his
   doctoral dissertation on Chang Chü-cheng at the University of Washington.

87 Crawford, "Chang's Confucian legalism," p. 378.

Confucian philosophy as overly contemplative. Nevertheless, a close comparison of the Chang and Chu Hsi commentaries on the Four Books reveals that Chang agreed with Chu Hsi on most points and was often merely explaining through elaboration and simpler phrasing the interpetations written by Chu Hsi, of which more will be said below. Chang attempted to arrest the decline of the Ming dynasty by drawing from the ancients, but, of course, the attempt to return to the ancient philosophy as manifested in the Classics was common to all Confucians, including the Neo-Confucians.

6. THE BIOGRAPHY OF CONFUCIUS

In accord with the Jesuit focus on Confucius in *Confucius Sinarum philosophus*, the section of the book following the *Proëmialis Declaratio* was devoted to a short biography of Confucius — most likely translated from a Chinese source. This section opens with a striking frontal portrait of Confucius standing larger than lifesize before a structure which blends a Confucian temple and a library[88]. (See plate 16.) Although Confucius is depicted as awe-inspiring, the setting of this portrait and of the tablets would have struck the European reader as less a temple than a library whose shelves were lined with books, albeit bound in the style of Europe rather than China of the seventeenth century. A library is a fitting temple to Confucius and traditionally the Confucian temple was found in institutions of learning and examination throughout China. Furthermore, the Jesuits were doubtless aware that associating a temple with a library would dull the religious import of the temple. In the traditional Confucian temple, there was a main hall facing south wherein stood a statue of Confucius or a tablet of his spirit[89]. Surrounding the statue or tablet of Confucius were statues or tablets of four favored disciples. Along the eastern and western walls of this main hall were lined the statues or tablets of the next twelve disciples in degree of honor. Directly opposite from these twelve on the outside walls were two side galleries, each of which contained sixty-four tablets of disciples and other worthies. Finally, beyond the main hall was the hall, also facing south, dedicated to Confucius' ancestors which contained tablets of other honored disciples.

The Confucian temple portrayed in *Confucius Sinarum philosophus* is a copy of the typical Chinese temple only in general outline. Confucius is portrayed by a statue, but he also holds a tablet of his spirit. There are no separate groupings of disciples, but merely eighteen tablets, nine of which are placed along the inside eastern wall and nine along the inside western wall. Upon each tablet

88 Couplet, *Confucius*, p. cxvj.
89 In this description of a Confucian temple, I draw from Legge, *The Chinese Classics* I, 91–92 & 113n.

a disciple's name in Chinese is inscribed. With the receding perspective, the names become more difficult to read and this difficulty is compounded by the darkening of the right side of the drawing. Nevertheless, one can discern the following names along the western wall, front to back: Tseng Tzu, attributed author of the *Ta hsüeh*; Meng-tzu (Mencius) who wrote the work of the same name; Tzu Kung; Tzu Chang; Min Tzu-ch'ien; and Tzu Yü. Along the eastern wall, front to back, one can discern: Yen Hui who was Confucius' favorite disciple; Tzu Ssu who was Confucius' grandson and the attributed author of the *Chung yung*; Tzu Lu; and Tzu Yu.

Above the tablets on both sides are shelves of books reaching nearly to the ceiling. Inscribed over the front shelves of books are the Chinese and romanized names of the Five Classics, Four Books and the *Hsi tz'u*, which is the Great Appendix to the *I ching*. Other than for symmetrical reasons of having five titles on each side, it is difficult to see why the *Hsi tz'u* should have been included as it had no classical status of its own. Perhaps given some of Couplet's critical comments about the key Neo-Confucian term *T'ai-chi* being found only in this appendix, there were reasons for the authors of *Confucius Sinarum philosophus* to have separated it from the Classics and thereby to de-emphasize its importance. But such reasoning is somewhat at odds with the Jesuits placing the title of the work in such a prominent place in Confucius' temple-library. On the back wall of the temple-library are inscribed, horizontally, Chung-ni, which is Confucius' cognomen. To the right, vertically, one finds *T'ien-hsia* (the world) and to the left, vertically, *Hsien-shih* (preeminent teacher). In the table overriding the entire structure, one finds inscribed *Kuo hsüeh* with transliteration and the Latin translation "Gymnasium Imperii" (Imperial Academy). Clearly, the Jesuits thought the latter was worth translating to be certain that the European reader did not miss the academic significance of the honors to Confucius. *Kuo-hsüeh* (Imperial Academy) is an abbreviated form of the *Kuo-tzu hsüeh* or *Kuo-tzu chien*, commonly referred to as the *T'ai-hsüeh* (literally, supreme academy). The Imperial Academy was established by the first Ming dynasty emperor for the purpose of training new officials. During the Ming, it functioned as the highest academic institution in China, not only instructing students and administering examinations, but also formulating policy for state-supported local schools[90].

The caption below the engraving of Confucius in *Confucius Sinarum philosophus* speaks of the 3,000 disciples who followed Confucius during his lifetime, of whom 72 were eminent. Of these, the caption states that ten have had their names inscribed on tablets and may be viewed in the Imperial Academy (*Kuo-hsüeh*). The reference to only ten disciples in the caption is puzzling because

90 Albert Chan, S.J., *The glory and fall of the Ming dynasty* (Norman, 1982) pp. 96–97
    & Charles H. Hucker, "Governmental organization of the Ming dynasty," *Harvard Journal of Asiatic Studies* 21 (1952): 38.

there are eighteen tablets – nine to the east and nine to the west – in the engraving. The contradiction is probably explained by the lack of coordination between the engraver and editor(s).

Although the engraving of Confucius has a distinctly Chinese flavor, its form was borrowed from a fairly common genre in seventeenth-century European portraiture. This genre was used especially for portraying famous men and women such as scholars, artists, collectors, bibliophiles or scientists. In its usual form, this genre presented the individual standing in front of a backdrop-like picture of a room containing the sitter's collection of objects. Although the sitter in the foreground and the room in the background are consistent in perspective, the scale differs. The sitter, in this case Confucius, stands on a ledge separate from the vast hall behind him. The centering of the pediment and the arch over his head reinforces the revered status of the sitter in the manner that a niche enshrines a statue. In making the above observations, the art historian, T. Kaori Kitao places this portrait of Confucius in a tradition of portraiture, of which a very late example historically is Charles Wilson Peale's *Artist in his Museum* (1822) (see plate 17)[91]. Although in Peale's painting, there is more continuity between the hall in the background and the figure in the foreground than is the case in the portrait of Confucius from *Confucius Sinarum philosophus*, still, the hall is treated as a separate compositional entity in the portrait.

An important change in the Confucian temples had taken place just prior to the arrival of the Jesuit missionaries in China. Since the reign of the T'ang emperor T'ai-tsung (r. 627–649), the temples had been turned into national halls of fame. To the tablets of Confucius and his original seventy-two disciples were added the names of twenty-two scholars who, though not all immediate disciples of Confucius, were all of orthodox Confucian coloring[92]. In consequent years the Confucian temple became crowded with historical figures elevated to the status and honors of deities. This expansion continued until the Ming period when the Confucian temple underwent a number of reforms. The first reforms were made by the dynastic founder, the Hung-wu emperor in 1370, who in his attempt to establish Confucian orthodoxy was influenced by the rationalist outlook of Chu Hsi and other Neo-Confucians. In an effort to diminish these deities while elevating Confucius, the Hung-wu emperor ordered that all the titles of these deities be removed from the temple, except for that of Confucius[93]. The reforms continued until their culmination in 1530. The final set of reforms was based upon a memorial submitted to the Chia-ching emperor by the scholar-official Chang Tsung. Chang's proposals were grounded on the historical records of the Chou dynasty and on the attempt to more accurately

91 Private correspondence of T. Korai Kitao to the author, dated January 8th 1982.
92 John K. Shryock, *The origin and development of the state cult of Confucius* (New York, 1932) pp. 135–136.
93 Shryock, p. 185.

Plate 16. Confucius depicted in the so-called "*Kuo Hsüeh*" (Imperial Academy), from Philippe Couplet et al, *Confucius Sinarum philosophus* (Paris 1687) p. cxvi. Courtesy of the Niedersächsische Landesbibliothek Hannover.

Plate 17. Charles Wilson Peale's *The Artist in his Museum* (1822). Oil on Canvas. Courtesy of the Pennsylvania Academy of the Fine Arts (Philadelphia), Joseph And Sarah Harrison Collection.

reproduce these conditions. This meant a diminishing of the explicitly religious elements of the Confucian honors. He argued, for example, that the images should be replaced with tablets — Confucius had spoken against the use of images — and the building itself should no longer be called a *miao* (temple), but a *tien* (hall). Also, Chang proposed removing from Confucius the title of *wang* (king) — whose use Confucius himself would have opposed as a usurpation of the lawful authority of the Chou — and substituting the more pedagogically oriented title of "Master K'ung, the Most Elevated Sage and Teacher of Highest Antiquity" (*chih sheng-hsien shih K'ung-tzu*). The proposed reforms provoked a flurry of controversy among scholar-officials, but such opposition only made the Chia-cheng emperor more determined to support Chang's memorial. The reforms were enacted and the temple images were ordered to be destroyed and replaced by wooden tablets[94]. The effect of these reforms was to shift the thrust of the Confucian rites away from religious honors and toward civil and social honors.

This engraving in *Confucius Sinarum philosophus* reflected the reformed condition of the Confucian temples which the Jesuits would have found upon their arrival in China after 1580. Tablets (*shen-wei* or *p'ai-wei*) rather than images of Confucian disciples line the side walls in the illustration. However, the image of Confucius holding a tablet appears to be inconsistent with the reforms of 1530 which replaced images with tablets. Yet over the years there appears to have been at least one exception to this prohibition of Confucius' image, as well as variations on the number and order of the disciples' tablets. For example, Samuel Couling noted the presence of an image of Confucius ca. 1900 in the Confucian temple at the Sage's hometown of Ch'ü-fu[95]. Given the tendency of Jesuit proponents of accommodation to argue that the Confucian rites were civil and social rather than religious in nature, it would have strengthened the Jesuits' argument if the image of Confucius with its idolatrous connotations could have been omitted. Therefore, the image of Confucius was included probably because it represented what the Jesuits saw in China.

The visual emphasis on the academic aspect of the Confucian temple and Confucius' role as a teacher was reinforced by the conclusion of the biography of Confucius in *Confucius Sinarum philosophus*[96]. This conclusion argued that Confucius' role as a teacher of the Chinese people confirmed Christian truth in the way that the Greek poets influenced the Athenians. The probable reference here was to *Acts* 17: 22–27 in which St. Paul noted that the altar in Athens inscribed by the Greek (poets?) "to an unknown god" anticipated the coming preaching of the Christian God. (One wonders if the Jesuit authors consciously regarded St. Paul's claim as a confirmation of Hermetism.) The Jesuit authors

94 Shryock, pp. 189–190 & 237.
95 Samuel Couling, *The encyclopedia Sinica* (Shanghai, 1917) p. 127.
96 Couplet, *Confucius*, p. cxxiv.

stated that the Jesuits in China commended and praised Confucius to a moderate degree — surely an understatement for any Jesuit following Ricci's accommodative framework to make! Indeed, the authors asked how Europeans could disdain and condemn a doctrine (i.e. Confucius' teaching) which so harmoniously blended life with morality. In sum, it was made quite clear early in *Confucius Sinarum philosophus* that the Jesuits saw Confucius' teaching as a cornerstone to their enterprise in China.

7. THE TRANSLATION OF THE *TA HSÜEH*

The common ground between Confucianism and Christianity in terms of the dynamics of moral and spiritual cultivation contributed to a relatively accurate treatment of spiritual cultivation in *Confucius Sinarum philosophus*. On the other hand, significant theological and doctrinal differences were apparent in the translation of conceptual terms. For example, the Chinese term *chün-tzu* was the keystone of a philosophy emphasizing moral and spiritual cultivation, learning and serving the people. Those who excelled in these areas were intended to form a social elite. The *Confucius Sinarum philosophus* translation accurately captured this sense of social mobility and recognition in rendering *chün-tzu* most often as *Princeps* (preeminent man) in *Ta hsüeh* 3.4, 9.1 and 10.3[97]. Also, the alternate rendering of *probus vir* (superior or virtuous man) in *Ta hsüeh* 6.2 captured the sense of moral cultivation, as did the rendering *perfectus vir* (perfected man) captured the sense of spiritual cultivation which was also found in *Ta hsüeh* 6.2[98]. Finally, the rendering of *chün-tzu* as *probus Rex* (virtuous king) in *Ta hsüeh* 9.4 and 10.6 connected this moral cultivation to serving the people[99].

The sense of moral and spiritual cultivation contained in the terms *hsiu-shen* (self-cultivation) is absolutely fundamental to Confucianism. This sense was adequately captured in *Confucius Sinarum philosophus* when *hsiu-shen* was translated as "to properly harmonize one's body or person" in *Ta hsüeh* 7.1 and 8.1[100]. But the translation of the important term *jen* was distorted by a

---

97 Couplet, *Confucius*, pp. 10–11, 18 & 27. As noted previously, the arabic numeration for the pages of *Confucius Sinarum philosophus* is not continuous, but is broken into pp. 1–108 for the *Ta hsüeh* and *Chung yung* and pp. 1–21; 1–159 for the *Lun yü*. In that most of the references in this work are to the *Ta hsüeh* and *Chung yung* sections, I cite those passages without further specification (e.g. Couplet, *Confucius*, pp. 10–11), but I specifically note the *Lun yü* segment and whether part 1 or 2 whenever citing pages from the latter (e.g., Couplet, *Confucius, Lun yü*; part 1, p. 3).

98 Couplet, *Confucius*, p. 14.

99 Couplet, *Confucius*, pp. 20 & 28.

100 Couplet, *Confucius*, pp. 15 & 16. Also see *Ta hsüeh*, preface, 1.5 in Couplet, *Confucius*, p. 5.

specifically Christian preoccupation. Instead of the Chinese intended sense of "humanity", the Jesuits rendered this term as "piety and mercy" (*pietate & clementia*) in *Ta hsüeh* 9.4[101]. Also, the important term *i* (righteousness) was rendered with a distinctly Christian slant as "faithfulness" (*fidelitatem*)[102]. *Hsin* (heart-mind) was rendered with a slightly overly rational slant as *animus* (the rational principle in man) in *Ta hsüeh* 1.4, 1.5 and 7.2[103].

The Jesuits' rendering of the opening lines of the *Ta hsüeh* reflected their integration of text with commentary. As noted previously, the parts of the translation based directly on the text, as opposed to the commentary, were indicated by the use of numerical superscripts which corresponded to the Chinese characters. Certain Chinese grammatical particles — such as the genitive indicator *chih* — were omitted from the numeration. *Confucius Sinarum philosophus* rendered these opening lines as follows

Moreover, the [3]purpose of [2]learning of [1]great men [4]consists in [5]refining or improving a [6]rational [7]nature that I may draw down from heaven, so that certainly, as a most transparent mirror, by means of wiping away a blemish of deformed appetites, may be returned to its pristine clarity. [The learning of great men] [8]consists next in [9]renewing or reviving the [10]people, certainly by means of one's own example and exhortation. [The learning of great men] [11]consists next in [12]standing firm, or persevering in the [13]greatest [14]good by which I understand that the interpreters wished all the greatest actions to be in conformity with right reason[104].

In an italicized commentary immediately following this passage, the *Confucius Sinarum philosophus* authors took their position in a long-standing controversy over whether two characters (*hsin min*) meant "renewing/reviving the people" or "loving the people". The pronunciation of *hsin* with the meaning of "renewing" or "reviving" had first been suggested by Ch'eng I and was accepted by the commentaries of Chu Hsi, Chang Chü-cheng and Wang Fu-chih. But other commentators, such as the Ming Neo-Confucian Wang Yang-ming and, in more recent times, Ch'ien Mu and James Legge, have argued that the earlier pronunciation of *ch'in* with its meaning of "loving" should be used[105]. The Jesuits, who

101 Couplet, *Confucius*, p. 20.

102 *Ta hsüeh* 10.21 in Couplet, *Confucius*, p. 35.

103 Couplet, *Confucius*, pp. 4, 5 & 16.

104 Couplet, *Confucius*, p. 1. The Latin text reads as follows: [1]*Magnum adeoque virorum Principum,* [2]*sciendi* [3]*institutm* [4]*consistit in* [5]*expoliendo, seu excolendo* [6]*rationalem* [7]*naturam a coelo inditam; ut scilicet haec, ceu limpidissimum speculum, abstersis pravorum appetituum maculis, ad pristinam claritatem suam redire possit.* [8]*Consistit deinde in* [9]*renovando seu reparando* [10]*populum, suo ipsius scilicet exemplo & adhortatione.* [11]*Consistit demum in* [12]*sistendo firmiter, seu perseverando* [13]*in summo* [14]*bono: per quod hic Interpretes intelligi volunt summam actionum omnium cum recta ratione conformitatem.*

105 Chu Hsi, *Ssu-shu chi-chu* (reprinted Taipei, 1969), *Ta hsüeh*, p. la; Chang Chü-cheng, *Ssu-shu chih-chieh* (1651 edition) *Ta hsüeh*, p. la; Wang Fu-chih, *Tu ssu-shu ta-ch'üan-shuo* (1665?; reprinted Peking, 1975) preface, p. 2; Ch'ien Mu, *Ssu-shu shih-i* (Taipei, 1978) p. 330; & Legge, *Chinese Classics* I, 356n.

claimed to be drawing from a text of uncorrupted authority, rejected the Sung Neo-Confucian interpretation, although they used it in their translation, and argued that "loving the people" was the correct meaning. They clarified in their commentary that this character was nowhere pronounced *hsin*, signifying "newness," but instead was pronounced *ch'in*, signifying "to love one's parents and kinsmen (neighbors)". The Jesuits also noted that the translation "loving" carried a meaning far closer to Christianity than did "renewing". Moreover, loving the people through setting an admirable model of behavior for the people was also quite true to the spirit of Confucianism.

Less acceptable in the Jesuits' translation of the opening passage of the *Ta hsüeh* was their rendering of *ming-te* as "rational nature" (*rationalem naturam*) rather than as the Chinese intended sense of "illuminated virtue"[106]. This European slant was continued in *Ta hsüeh* 1.1 when *ko ming-te* was translated "to refine his natural reason" (*expolire suam naturam rationalem*) rather than in the sense of being able to illumine one's virtue or to exemplify a clear character[107]. Consequently, *Confucius Sinarum philosophus* altered a fundamental statement of moral and spiritual cultivation into something overly intellectual. The Jesuits were not merely groping for a translation. That they had a good sense of the Chinese meaning was clear from their translation of the sentence "*Ko ming chün te*" in *Ta hsüeh* 1.3 as "He was able (certainly King Yao) to refine or to cultivate this great and sublime gift or sublime virtue, that is, rational nature"[108]. The term "sublime virtue" (*sublimen virtutem*), which is very close to "illustrious virtue", was used here as the translation and "rational nature" was used as the explication.

The Jesuits' rejection of Chu Hsi's interpretations was most emphatic when theological matters were involved. For example, in treating the spiritually significant passage 19.6 of the *Chung yung*, the Jesuits explicitly rejected the interpretation of the "atheistic-political interpreter/contriver Chu Hsi" (*Chuhi commentator Atheopoliticus*). Chu Hsi had argued that a reference to the "divinity of earth" (*numen terrae; hou-tu*) was meant to have been included in this passage as a complementary spiritual force to *Shang-ti* (Lord-of-Heaven), but had been omitted for the sake of conciseness[109]. In attempting to establish the monotheistic authority of *Shang-ti* as the object of veneration in ancient Chinese texts, the Jesuits rejected Chu Hsi's claim that the "divinity of earth"

106 The phrase "*ming ming te*" is translated by Legge, *Chinese Classics* I, 356, as "to illustrate illustrious virtue"; by Derk Bodde in Fung, *History* I, 362, as "to exemplify illustrious virtue"; and by Wing-tsit Chan, *Source book*, p. 86, as "manifesting clear character."

107 Couplet, *Confucius*, p. 6.

108 Couplet, *Confucius*, p. 7.

109 Couplet, *Confucius*, p. 59 & Chu Hsi, *Ssu-shu chi-chu, Chung yung*, p. 14b. The Jesuits had been aware of the significance of the *Chung yung* 19.6 passage since the beginning of the seventeenth century. Ricci discussed it in his *T'ien-chu shih-i*, p. 20a.

was implied in this passage to complement *Shang-ti* as the polytheistic gods of earth and heaven, respectively. It is interesting to note that in the nineteenth century, the accommodative European interpreter and Christian missionary James Legge would translate *hou-tu* as "Sovereign Earth" and see no obstacle in interpreting this *Chung yung* passage in terms of the divine forces of heaven and earth as manifestations of the same single deity[110].

Even though the Jesuits may have disputed many points of Chu Hsi's philosophy and interpretation of the Classics, their translations in *Confucius Sinarum philosophus* indicated not only that they were familiar with Chu Hsi's commentary, but also that they sometimes borrowed from Chu Hsi's interpretations[111]. The *Proëmialis Declaratio* explained that the Jesuits preferred the commentary of Chang Chü-cheng to that of Chu Hsi because of its differences in interpreting the Classics. However, these differences are far less significant than the *Proëmialis Declaratio* implied. (We are speaking here only of the commentary per se and not of the implications which Chu Hsi and his Neo-Confucian followers drew from his commentary.) For example, in their explanation of *Ta hsüeh* 4, the Jesuits referred twice to refining one's rational nature and included a direct quotation from Chang's commentary. But when one compares this quotation from Chang with Chu's commentary, one finds a similar content[112].

Another instance where the Jesuits exaggerated the differences between the commentaries of Chu and Chang was in chapter 4 of the *Ta hsüeh*. Commentators prior to Chu Hsi had treated this chapter as identical to *Lun yü* 12.13 where Confucius spoke of preventing litigation as preferable to court proceedings. In this light, ancient commentators interpreted this passage in the *Ta hsüeh* as the conclusion of the chapter on making one's thoughts sincere[113]. Chu Hsi's commentary changed this by interpreting the passage to mean that "illumination of illumined virtue" is the beginning (*pen*) from which a result (*mo*) follows. Chang's commentary followed the reasoning of Chu rather than the older commentators and referred to the illuminating of illumined virtue as the be-

110 Legge, *Chinese Classics*, I, 404.

111 Jesuit familiarity with Chu Hsi's commentary on the Four Books is confirmed repeatedly. For example, in the Jesuits' explanation of the *Ta hsüeh* 4, they refer twice to refining one's rational nature (Couplet, *Confucius*, p. 12). The Chinese characters corresponding to this phrase are found in Chu Hsi's commentary on this passage: *kai wo chih ming te chi ming* (see Chu Hsi, *Ssu-shu chi-chu*, p. 5b). Likewise, in explaining *Ta hsüeh* 5.2, the Jesuits state: "This repetition is seen (so the interpreters note) as redundant . . ." (Couplet, *Confucius*, p. 13). Chu Hsi's commentary quotes one of the Ch'eng brothers making just such a claim (Chu Hsi, *Ssu-shu chi-chu*, *Ta hsüeh*, p. 5b). Also, on the subject of more general borrowing of the Jesuit compilers from Chu Hsi and Neo-Confucianism, see Knud Lundbaek, "The image of Neo-Confucianism in *Confucius Sinarum philosophus*," pp. 29–30.

112 Couplet, *Confucius*, p. 12; Chang, *Ssu-shu chih-chieh* (1677), *Ta hsüeh*, p. 13a; & Chu Hsi, *Ssu-shu chi-chu*, *Ta hsüeh*, p. 5b.

113 Legge, *Chinese classics* I, 364n.

ginning (*pen*) and renewing the people as the result (*mo*). In translating the relevant portions of Chang's commentary, the Jesuits appear to have accepted the reasoning not only of Chang, but of Chu as well. The Jesuits apparently first encountered Chang Chü-cheng's *Ssu-shu chih-chieh* in one of its earlier editions — possibly that of 1651 — in which Chu Hsi's commentary was not included. Its absence reinforced the Jesuit perception of differences between the commentaries of Chang and Chu. However, the late seventeenth-century Chinese intellectual climate was changing and the 1677 and 1683 editions of Chang's commentary included the commentary of Chu Hsi. The way in which Chang's and Chu's commentaries were published together indicated that the Chinese editors of the late seventeenth century viewed the two commentaries as being more complementary than contradictory. Viewed in this light, the Jesuit authors of the Proëmialis Declaratio were at odds with these later Chinese editors.

If the interpretations found in the commentary on the Four Books by Chang did not significantly differ from those of Chu, why then did the Jesuits make such an issue over the differences[114]? Most seventeenth-century Jesuit proponents of accommodation agreed with Ricci's judgment that Sung Neo-Confucianism was tainted with atheism and philosophic materialism. Chang's criticism of Sung Neo-Confucians such as Chu Hsi had focused on their tendency to be more concerned with the metaphysical than with the practical implications of ethics. Clearly, this sort of criticism fit well into Jesuit accommodative plans which stressed excluding most metaphysical and spiritual elements of Confucianism while emphasizing its moral, as well as social, elements in a Confucian-Christian synthesis. Furthermore, Chang's background strongly appealed to the Jesuit preference for working through politically and socially prominent figures.

In terms of Chang's commentary on the Four Books itself, there were two features which made it especially attractive to the Jesuits. First of all, it was written in a simple and colloquial style. Chang had written his commentary in a style geared to communicating with a boy — the young Wan-li emperor — and the Jesuits, struggling with the difficult literary language of the Chinese, found Chang's commentary extremely readable. Secondly, Chang's commentary provided an alternative interpretation to Chu Hsi's commentary on the all-important Classics — the Four Books. Although the Jesuits exaggerated the degree of differences between the commentaries of Chang and Chu, Chang's name was less tainted by atheistic and materialistic elements which were alien to the Confucian-Christian synthesis that the Jesuits were attempting to forge. By relying on Chang's work, the Jesuits could better minimize the presence of those

114 The differences between the commentaries on the Four Books of Chu Hsi and Chang Chü-cheng as well as the reasons why the Jesuits preferred Chang's commentary are discussed in greater detail by the author in his article "The Jesuits' use of Chang Chü-cheng's commentary in their translation of the Confucian Four Books (1687)."

alien elements in their translation of the Four Books and yet still follow what was accepted by the Chinese as an orthodox Confucian commentary.

Although the *Ta hsüeh* and *Chung yung* were favorite texts of Neo-Confucians because of their emphasis on spiritual cultivation and metaphysical implications, these texts and the Four Books as a whole make extremely minimal reference to the important Sung Neo-Confucian metaphysical terms — *ch'i* (material force), *li* (principle) and *T'ai-chi* (Supreme Ultimate). Since these terms were part of the atheistic materialism which the Jesuits perceived in the Neo-Confucian writings, their absence from the Four Books made these Classics ideal for the Jesuits to emphasize in their program of accommodation. Chang's commentary proved an admirable alternative for the Jesuits in just this respect. The specific instructional needs of the boy-emperor reinforced Chang's own disinclination toward Sung Neo-Confucian metaphysics. This led Chang to write a commentary which minimized metaphysical discussion even below the already brief, though suggestive, metaphysical treatment in Chu Hsi's commentary. Chu's concise comments implied and tied into a much larger metaphysical and — according to the seventeenth-century Jesuits — anti-Christian system. But Chang's commentary tied into a more classical form of Confucianism which the Jesuits felt was more amenable to their Confucian-Christian synthesis.

One of the few passages in the Four Books where Chu Hsi's commentary does use the primal pair of Sung Neo-Confucian metaphysics — *li* and *ch'i* — is in *Chung yung* 1.1. Here is it useful to compare the commentarial treatments of Chu and Chang. Whereas Chu defined *hsing* (inherent nature) as *li*, Chang avoided any such isolated equation and instead defined *li* in the context of its connection with *ch'i*, that is, *ch'i* was what completed the physical form of a thing while *li* was the arranging which completed the inherent nature of something[115]. But since Chu also defined *ch'i* and *li* in the context of taking physical form and arranging things, respectively, Chang's difference in treatment was not a complete break with Chu, but rather a shift of emphasis. Chang attempted to reduce the significance of *li* by reducing its incidence in his commentary to only one occurrence whereas Chu used *li* three times. Chang reinforced this shift by moving away from metaphysical discussion to a more classical Confucian emphasis on the four primary Confucian virtues — Humanity (*Jen*), Righteousness (*I*), Ritual (*Li*) and Wisdom (*Chih*). Also, the classical Confucian term *Tao* (Way) was referred to eleven times while Chu's commentary referred to *Tao* only three times. But since Chang's commentary appeared to be following and elaborating upon the commentary of Chu Hsi, one could not go beyond saying that the difference between the two was merely one of emphasis. This difference in emphasis rather than of radical breaks of interpretation had been a perennial pattern of the Confucian tradition. It was a pattern to which the Jesuits could not be entirely sensitive because of the anti-Neo-Confucian agenda

---

115 Chu Hsi, *Ssu-shu chi-chu, Chung yung*, p. 1b & Chang, *Ssu-shu chih-chieh* (1677), *Chung yung*, pp 1b–2a.

of accommodation established by Ricci and continued by the compilers of *Confucius Sinarum philosophus*.

The evidence is clear that the Jesuits did project Christian ideas and missionary concerns into their translation and interpretation of the Four Books. But after conceding this not very surprising point, one should add that the Jesuit interpretations were usually reasonable elaborations on the Chinese text. This point may become clearer through a contrasting example. *Ta hsüeh* 2.1 speaks of King T'ang, legendary founder of the Shang dynasty, having a bathing tub inscribed with the words "if you can renovate yourself one day, then do so every day and keep doing so daily". The Jesuits in *Confucius Sinarum philosophus* followed Chang's commentary in stressing the renewal aspect of regular washing which returned the washer to a pristine purity and cleanliness and compared this symbolic washing to the root or basis of renewing the people[116]. But in 1664, a bolder Christian missionary by the name of Antonio Caballero a Santa Maria (Antoine de Sainte-Marie), a Franciscan, wrote in a Chinese treatise, *T'ien Ju yin* (Christianity and Confucianism compared), that King T'ang's daily renovation through cleansing was consonant with the rite of baptism in which the sacramental outward sign of washing the body (*hsing*) implied an inward cleansing of the soul (*shen*) or original sin through the presence of God's Grace[117]. The Jesuits usually stopped short of this degree of overloading their translations.

8. TRANSLATION OF THE *CHUNG YUNG*

The *Confucius Sinarum philosophus* interpretation of the *Chung yung* (Doctrine of the Mean) was more rationalized than that of the *Ta hsüeh*. In the *Chung yung* 1.4, the cardinal concept of the Mean (*chung*) was presented as smoothly melding with what was rational and through "right reason" ordering the passions. *Ho* was not translated merely as "harmony", but as *ratione concentus* (rationality of harmony) and *rationi consentanea* (agreeable reason)[118]. Such an interpretation which set off the emotions against reason was a distinctly European interpretation and far too sharply defined for the Chinese sense. The Mean which the *Chung yung* teaches is both natural and rational and the harmony which the Mean advocates is more appropriately conceived as the goal of our natural potential rather than the subjection of uncontrollable passions to

116 Couplet, Confucius, p. 7 & Chang, *Ssu-chu chih-chieh* (1651), *Ta hsüeh*, p. 7b–8a.
117 Antonio Caballero a Santa Maria (Li An-tang), *T'ien Ju yin* (1664) in Wu Hsiang-hsiang (ed.), *T'ien-chu-chiao tung-ch'uan wen-hsien hsü-pien* 3 vols. (Taipei, 1966) II, 996–997 (pp. 2b–3a). Also see the author's "Sinological Torque: the influence of cultural preoccupations on seventeenth-century missionary interpretations of Confucianism," *Philosophy East & West* 28 (1978): 129.
118 Couplet, *Confucius*, p. 41.

the reasoning mind. This overprojection of rationality into the *Chung yung* was confirmed by the Jesuit interpretation of the opening passage of the *Chung yung* 1.1 which the Jesuits translated as:

> That which is placed into man by Heaven (*t'ien ming*) is called the rational nature (*hsing*). Because this is fashioned by means of nature and imitates it, it is called a rule (*tao*) or is said to be in harmony with reason. Repetition to the point of diligently practicing this rule (*hsiu tao*) and one's own regulating of it is called education (*chiao*) or the learning of virtue[119].

A translation of this passage closer to the Chinese sense would be:

> That which is mandated by Heaven is called one's inherent nature. Fulfilling one's inherent nature is called the *Tao* (the way). Cultivating the *Tao* is called philosophy/religion.

The rationality which the Jesuits projected into the Confucian text was derived not from Chang Chü-cheng's commentary, but from seventeenth-century Christian theology. The Jesuits tended to be more intellectual than mystical and this influenced their interpretation of Confucianism. If their interpretation of Confucianism was overly rational, a Christian today might regard their interpretation of Christianity as overly rational as well. The synthesis of St. Thomas Acquinas and other Scholastics had created an absolute resonance between rationality and spirituality in Christianity which began to fracture in the late seventeenth century. Today as in earlier times, Christians do not view their religion in terms as much rational as efficacious to their spiritual needs. Consequently, one finds Western students of Confucianism more able today than in the seventeenth century to appreciate the moral and spiritual cultivation present in Confucianism.

The Jesuit use of *regula* as a translation of *Tao* had connotations which were more geometrical than natural. The sense of *regula* as rule, pattern, model or example derived not from an organic image, but from the mechanical sense of a straight piece of wood used as a ruler. The Chinese sense of *Tao* was clearly organic, as in the sense of a path following natural contours through a forest, rather than a mechanical ruler. The harmony associated with *Tao* involved a comprehensive harmony with nature and society, as well as with reason, rather than a harmony focusing primarily on reason. Likewise, *hsing* for the Chinese meant "inherent nature" in the organic sense rather than the Jesuits' "rational nature". *Hsiu tao* meant not merely repetition and diligently practicing a rational rule, but had a much more inclusive sense of cultivating the *Tao*. That the Jesuits were neither unaware nor unsympathetic to the Confucian concern with education as moral cultivation rather than narrow intellectuality was

---

119 Couplet, Confucius, p. 40. The Latin text reads: *Id quod à caelo est homini inditum dicitur natura rationalis: quod huic conformatur natura & eam consequitur, dicitur regula, seu consentaneum rationi, restaurare quoad exercitium hanc regulam se suaque per eam moderando, dicitur institutio, seu disciplina virtutum.*

shown in their translation of *chiao* as "the learning of virtue". Further signs of the Jesuits' rationalizing of the *Chung yung* was found in their translation of *Tao* as *regula rationis* (rule of reason) and as *regula & lege naturali* (rule and natural law)[120].

A notion fundamental to the *Chung yung* and to Confucianism as a whole is the *chün-tzu* which is most commonly translated into English as "superior man"[121]. The *chün-tzu* is the key which joins the Confucian notions of learning, moral-spiritual cultivation and social mobility. All elements focus on the *chün-tze* who through personal growth and achievement, rather than through inheritance, achieves a superior status in society. The Jesuit translation of *chün-tzu* as *perfectus vir* (perfected man) accurately captured this sense of moral and spiritual cultivation contained in fulfilling the potential of one's inherent nature. Confucius' frequently cited contrast between the *chün-tzu* and *hsiao-jen* was expressed by the Jesuits in their translation of *Chung yung* 2.1: "the perfected man (*chün-tzu*) holds to the Mean always and everywhere; the inferior man (*hsiao-jen*) truly transgresses the Mean through excess or defect"[122]. The Jesuits translated *hsiao-jen* as *improbus* (*vir*) meaning "not according to the standard; inferior or poor quality". In *Chung yung* 2.2, the perfected man and inferior man were defined in terms of their conformance to the Mean. The Jesuits explained that the actions of the perfected man were characterized by caution and vigilance while the inferior man lacked fear and shame and acted wantonly[123].

The religious preoccupation of the Jesuits led them to interpret the concluding passage of the *Chung yung* (33.6) as supporting a Chinese belief in the existence of a supreme divinity[124]. They also saw in this passage the basis of the Chinese belief in the immortality of the soul. The Jesuits based their interpretation on two key phrases. The first was *ming te* which they rendered as *clarissimam & purissimam virtutem* (brightest and purest virtue), a phrase also found in the opening passage of the *Ta hsüeh*. The Jesuit argument was somewhat convoluted. It claimed that *te* (virtue) of the phrase *ming te* was explained by its association with *hsing* (inherent nature). The Jesuits argued that since the two terms *te* and *hsing* were able to be linked together in a phrase

120 *Chung yung* 13.1 & 13.3 in Couplet, Confucius, pp. 47 & 48, respectively.
121 Tu Wei-ming's rendering of *chün-tzu* as "profound person" in *Centrality and commonality: an essay on Chung-yung* (Honolulu, 1976) is more an interpretation aimed at infusing the concept with contemporary relevance than a translation of the historical sense of the term.
122 Couplet, *Confucius*, p. 42.
123 The Jesuit interpretation of this passage followed the commentary of Chang Chü-cheng, but also agreed with Chu Hsi's commentary in that the Chang and Chu commentaries are nearly identical. See Chang, *Ssu-shu chih-chieh* (1677), *Chung yung*, p. 6b & Chu, *Ssu-shu chi-chu, Chung yung*, p. 3b.
124 Couplet, *Confucius*, pp. 93–94.

— literally, the phrase appeared as *hsing chih te yeh* (the power-virtue of inherent nature) in *Chung yung* 25.3 — therefore the meaning of *ming te* (brightest
and purest virtue) could be associated with *hsing* (inherent nature). Since *Chung
yung* 1.1 stated that *hsing* (inherent nature) was bestowed by Heaven, the Jesuits
felt justified in arguing that *ming te* also was bestowed by Heaven. This explains
why they interpreted the reference to *ming te* in *Ta hsüeh* 1.1 as "a rational
nature that I draw down from heaven"[125]. Consequently, the Jesuits interpreted
ming te to be "that portion of rationality given to man from heaven"[126]. The
second key phrase which the Jesuits drew from the concluding passage of the
Chung yung (33.6) in order to argue for the Chinese belief in the existence of a
supreme deity also appears in ode 235 of the *Shih ching*. It is: *shang t'ien chih
tsai*. The Jesuits translated this phrases as "something of supreme heaven far
removed from human sensation"[127] and compares with a contemporary rendering: "*the operations of Heaven* have neither sound nor smell"[128]. The Jesuits'
use of these phrases to prove that the Chinese believed in a supreme deity
constitutes a weak argument and it is worth noting that the nineteenth-century
missionary and translator of the Classics, James Legge, made no such interpretation in his commentary on this passage[129].

A religious preoccupation also was apparent in the Jesuits' translation of
sheng-jen as *sanctus* (saint; holy man) in *Chung yung* 12.2 and 17.1 rather than
as "sage" or "wise man". The translation of "saint" made the concept overly
religious and too narrow for the Chinese context. It is true that the sage was the
embodiment of a wisdom essentially moral. But by means of the amateur ideal
— as opposed to the specialist ideal — which Chinese scholar-officials embraced,
this essentially moral wisdom carried over into leadership in all areas of Chinese
learning and society. Admittedly, translating *sheng-jen* as "saint" rather than
"sage" made the term more intellectually amenable to Christianity, but any
gain in the direction of intellectual accommodation was surely cancelled by the
negative reaction of certain European Christians less willing to diminish the
spiritual divide between pagan and Christian which they perceived as separating
China and Europe[130]. Some of these reactions are explored in the next section.

---

125 Couplet, *Confucius*, p. 1.

126 Couplet, *Confucius*, p. 94.

127 Couplet, *Confucius*, p. 94.

128 Chan, *Source book*, p. 113. Cf. the translation of *Shih ching* III.i. stanza 7 in Legge,
    Chinese classics, I, 433.

129 Legge, *Chinese classics*, I, 433n.

130 The issue of how the Jesuits were to translate certain Chinese terms is not merely
    of historical interest, but raises questions of approach in ecumenical relations today,
    such as to what extent ecumenical relations should be limited to the realm of social
    cooperation versus being extended to spiritual doctrine and practice.

9. THE EUROPEAN REACTION TO *CONFUCIUS SINARUM PHILOSOPHUS*

On January 26th 1687, the Jesuit Daniel Papebroch, editor of the *Acta Sanctorum*, sent news to Leibniz of a forthcoming Latin translation of Confucius' works and other Chinese books[131]. Fr. Papebroch identified the author as Fr. Phillipe Couplet, a procurator of the China Mission, who was said to be preparing the edition under the orders of Louis XIV. While the Jesuits officially associated the French monarch with the production of *Confucius Sinarum philosophus*, it is unlikely that the association was as crucial to the publication of the work as Papebroch implied. The effort behind this work was such that it would have been published in Europe eventually, regardless of Louis XIV's patronage. What the Jesuits sought from the powerful French monarch was substantial support of the China Mission and, to this end, it may have suited their effort to state on the title page that *Confucius Sinarum philosophus* was being prepared under the monarch's command — *jussu Ludovici Magni* (by order of Louis the Great). The dedication of the work to the French king certainly reinforced this impression.

Papebroch also told Leibniz that Couplet was engaged in a search for a key to writing Chinese characters. Leibniz, in a letter probably written in February 1687, responded that he hoped Couplet would produce a bi-lingual Chinese-Latin edition which would help explain the structure of the Chinese characters and reveal a *Clavis Sinica*[132]. Papebroch replied on April 1st saying that Couplet was due to complete his publication of the translation of the Confucian books in mid-April. He noted that the Parisian translation would deal with the moral philosophy of Confucius and produce specimens of the Chinese text. Although Couplet's intention of including Chinese characters was frustrated by technical difficulties, the signs of the intention are still visible in the text of the *Ta hsüeh* and in part one (pages 1–29) of the *Lun yü* translations. In fact, this numerical superscript probably accounts for the separate pagination of the first part of the *Lun yü* and would indicate that the intention to publish the characters continued until very late in the publication process.

In a letter of December 9th (19th) 1687 to the Langdrave, Ernst von Hessen-Rheinfels, Leibniz revealed that his long-awaited hope of seeing a copy of "Confucius Prince des Philosophes Chinois" (i.e. *Confucius Sinarum philosophus*) was realized through the bookdealer, Johann David Zunner (d. 1704) of Frankfurt-am-Main. Leibniz commented on the work as follows:

The work was not made by Confucius himself, but was compiled by his disciples and gathered in part from his own words. This philosopher surpasses in age almost all that we have of the Greek philosophers and there are often excellent thoughts and maxims. He

---

131 Gottfried Wilhelm Leibniz, *Sämtliche Schriften und Briefe* in six series (Darmstadt, Leipzig & Berlin, 1923–) I; 4, 612.
132 Leibniz, *Sämtliche Schriften* I; 4, 622.

usually employs similes. For example, he says that one learns only through seeing in the winter which trees protect their greenery. Likewise, all men might appear similar in times of calm and of happiness, but it is during danger and disorder that one perceives the men of valor and merit[133].

The simile of evergreens in winter symbolizing men whose good character is revealed only in times of adversity is found in the *Lun yü* 9.27. The *Lun yü* text itself referred only to the pine and cypress being the last to lose their leaves, but the simile was explained in Chu Hsi's commentary. A Mr. Fan (Fan-*shih*) was quoted by Chu Hsi as saying that the superior man and mean man are indistinguishable in times of peace, but the good qualities of the superior man became revealed in times of flux. A Mr. Shih (Shih-*shih*) was further quoted by Chu Hsi to the effect that the loyalty of the scholar-gentleman is revealed only in times of chaos[134]. Probably following the commentary of Chang Chü-cheng, the Jesuits inserted a similar interpretation into the *Confucius Sinarum philosophus* text: the wise and stupid, although indistinguishable in tranquil times, are revealed — like the lingering leaves on the pines and cypresses in winter — in times of turbulence[135]. Leibniz was paraphrasing this portion of the Jesuits' translation in his comments to the Landgrave.

Leibniz' response to *Confucius Sinarum philosophus* was favorable, but measured in its praise. One wonders why he chose this particular passage from the work to cite in his letter to the Landgrave. It appears that he skimmed rather quickly through Couplet's Proëmialis Declaratio and focused on the *Lun yü* and the *Tabula chronologica*. Leibniz stated that the appended Chinese chronology was a substantial work and he believed that Europeans would be compelled to accept the chronology of the "70 interpreters of the Hebrew Text" (i.e. the Septuagint) because of its revelations that the earliest Chinese, such as Fu Hsi and Huang-ti (the Yellow Emperor), predated the Biblical Flood.

These comments were made in 1687 and prior to Leibniz' deeper involvement with China which began with his meeting the Jesuit Claudio Filippo Grimaldi in Rome in 1689. We know from later correspondence with Fr. Bouvet, that Leibniz at some point looked rather carefully at the diagrams of the *I ching* in the Proëmialis Declaratio. In a letter to Bouvet of 1703 (?), he mentioned a discrepancy between the diagrams in *Confucius Sinarum philosophus* [i.e. the *Hou-t'ien tzu-hsü* (Empirical Hexagram Order; literally, Posterior to Heaven Order)] and the diagrams of the *I ching* which Bouvet had sent him[136]. (Compare plates 19 & 20.) But why did Leibniz not cite *Confucius Sinarum philosophus* more fully in his work on China and particularly in his "*Discours*

133 Leibniz, *Sämtliche Schriften* I; 5, 26.
134 Chu, *Ssu-shu chi-chu, Lun yü*, pp. 8a–b.
135 Couplet, *Confucius, Lun yü*, p. 59. I was unable to compare Chang's commentary because at this point I lacked access to the *Lun yü* portion of Chang's work.
136 *Leibniz-Briefwechsel* 105, sheet 35[r]. See chapter six (Proto-Sinology and the Seventeenth-century European Search for a Universal Language).

sur la theologie naturelle des Chinois" of 1716? In seeking an answer, perhaps we should not overlook simple explanations. Leibniz had purchased and apparently quickly scanned a copy of the Jesuit work in the year of its publication. But the copy of *Confucius Sinarum philosophus* found in the old Hannover collection today is inscribed with the name of Gerhard Molanus, the long-time acquaintance of Leibniz. Did Leibniz perhaps lend or give his personal copy of this work to another reader and then lack it for later reference? Was he perhaps too polemically involved in the Chinese Rites Controversy or too weary – he died within the year of completing his discourse on the Chinese – to make the effort of doing a more substantive comparison?

The impact of *Confucius Sinarum philosophus* upon the learned European world was reflected in the appearance of reviews, beginning shortly after publication, in the *Basnage histoire de ouvrages des sçavans* (Rotterdam) (September 1687), *Journal des sçavans* (January 5th 1688), *Bibliotheque universalle et historique* (Amsterdam) (1688) and *Acta eruditorum* (Leipzig) (1688). The review in the *Journal des sçavans* was an unsigned piece by Pierre-Sylvain Régis[137]. In keeping with the digestlike nature of the *Journal*, this review was more descriptive than evaluative, but conveyed a generally favorable impression of the Jesuit work. Not surprisingly, we find that the reviewer's perception of China – one stage farther removed from the original Chinese context – contained additional distortions. For example, the reviewer made no reference to the fundamental Confucian conception of *chün-tzu* (perfected man). Without the perfected men of each generation, the Confucian philosophy could not be viable. Confucianism is not the teaching of one great founder-sage who taught once-and-for-all an eternal message. Confucius was not merely employing Chinese modesty when he denied that he was a creator and insisted that he was merely a transmitter of the past. The *Tao* is a vital and fluid force which flows through time. One generation can pass it to the next generation, but this next generation can allow the *Tao* to lapse through immorality, neglect or simply lack of interest. Confucius kept insisting that he had not created his teaching, but had received it from sages of Chinese antiquity. His overriding concern was that human contact with the *Tao* as a guide to our lives not be allowed to lapse.

When a philosophical and religious teaching begins to fade as a vital force, the process of discipling becomes more rotelike and the mouthing of words which have lost meaning becomes more pronounced. In China where the Confucian tradition had been flowing for some 2,000 years by the time the Jesuits arrived, the fading of vitality was a recurring event which required periodical revivals, variations of which were constantly in motion. In the seventeenth

---

137 *Journal des savants* 15 (5 January 1688): 167–180. The identification of the author of this review of *Confucius Sinarum philosophus* as Pierre-Sylvain Régis is made by Bernier in *Journal des savants* 15 (7 June 1688): 39. Also see Pinot, pp. 375–376.

century, China was a mix of Confucians mouthing empty words and Confucians drawing vitality from their tradition. But throughout China there ran the common denominator of a reverence for Confucius and this was reproduced by the Jesuits in *Confucius Sinarum philosophus.* The Jesuit intention was to de-emphasize Confucius' pagan edges while emphasizing the commonality of his teaching with Christianity.

The Jesuit attempt to create such an impression succeeded admirably with the *Journal des sçavans* reviewer. The review portrayed Confucius as a teacher of moral principles vaguely like those of Christianity and lacking only knowledge of Revelation through Jesus Christ. The reviewer cited Fr. Couplet as claiming that the Chinese have so much respect for the memory of Confucius that for over 2,000 years, only his disciples have been admitted into public office[138]. Yet this was surely an exaggerated claim since it did not take into account the four centuries in China between the fall of the Han dynasty (A.D. 220) and the rise of the T'ang dynasty (618) when Confucianism was merely one of several competing philosophies. The reviewer claimed that the Jesuits had found nothing opposed to natural law in "the philosophy of the Chinese", but surely this was an oversimplification of the Jesuit viewpoint, since it did not account for the often-stated Jesuit criticisms of Neo-Confucianism[139]. The reviewer followed the Jesuit lead in treating the important Confucian virtue of *Jen* (Humanity; Benevolence) as closely comparable to Christian love. The reviewer stated:

> I do not see in regard to the present theme, that the charity of the Chinese would be different from that of the Christians; so much is it true that God has spread in the souls of the infidels the same lights which lead us to virtue which, insofar as the exterior of action is concerned, they are not at all different from Christian virtues[141].

This statement indicated the success of the Jesuit effort in having a reader accept their portrayal of the Chinese – or at least the Chinese literati – as very much like Europeans themselves. Viewed in this light, *Confucius Sinarum philosophus* succeeded in reducing the conceptual wall dividing Europeans from the Chinese, though events of the Chinese Rites Controversy would later so permeate the European conception of China, that the achievement of this Jesuit work was set back by a flood of anger and accusations.

Also in 1688 there appeared a long review of 69 pages in the *Bibliotheque universalle et historique* of Amsterdam by the eminent Protestant savant Jean Le Clerc[142]. This review contained extensive translations in French of passages from each of the three Confucian Classics found in *Confucius Sinarum philo-*

138 *Journal des savants* 15: 171.
139 *Journal des savants* 15: 168.
140 *Journal des savants* 15: 174–175.
141 *Journal des savants* 15: 176.
142 The review of *Confucius Sinarum philosophus* by Jean Leclerc is dated December of
    1687, but was not published until 1688. See *Bibliotheque universalle et historique*

sophus. Although implicitly favorable, particularly in his length of treatment, M. Le Clerc was a bit more critical than was the *Journal des sçavans* reviewer, M. Régis. Le Clerc was aware that a Jesuit translation of the *Chung yung* had previously been published in Thévenot's *Relations de divers voyages*, though he listed the edition as 1682 rather than the earliest edition of 1672. Furthermore, Le Clerc read the Jesuit work more carefully and perceptively than Regis and perceived Confucius' role as a transmitter rather than a "primary author"[143]. Le Clerc noted that according to Fr. Intorcetta and the Jesuits, the veneration that the Chinese — common people as well as savants — have for Confucius was similar to that rendered to deceased parents. This veneration was so great that Le Clerc felt "the reverend Jesuit fathers will have a great deal of effort persuading Europeans that the excessive veneration of the Chinese for this philosopher [Confucius] is a purely civil respect and that they do not render him divine honors"[144]. The distinction which Le Clerc made between civil and religious honors would become one of the primary points of contention in Rites Controversy debate and is discussed in the last chapter of this work.

Le Clerc also noted that the "excessive honor" which the ancient Chinese rendered to their deceased parents mentioned in *Confucius Sinarum philosophus*[145] would be difficult to justify, particularly as Couplet admitted that the respect which the ancient Chinese had for their ancestors had degenerated into superstition in modern times[146]. However, he noted Couplet's claim that the Chinese Classics revealed such honors to have been purely civil and that divine Province raised up Confucius' effort to "preserve the purity of the divine cult and of morality, he was innocently used to achieve its corruption"[148]. In regard to conceptions of the divinity, Le Clerc referred to the Chinese worship of *Shang-ti* as "Sovereign Master"[149] and noted that Couplet "takes a long time to prove that [the Chinese] understand nothing else by *T'ien* than the true God, but he does not believe himself obliged to report his reasons, since there is nothing more ordinary in all languages than giving the name of Heaven to the Divinity . . ."[150].

Le Clerc repeated numerous untrue and biased statements that Couplet made about Buddhism. For example, the historical Sakyamuni Buddha was said to have been regarded by St. Francis Xavier as an "incarnate demon and

(Amsterdam) 7 (1688): 387–455. The identification of the author of this review as M. Leclerc is made in Pinot, p. 152.
143 *Bibliotheque* 7: 400. Also see p. 394.
144 *Bibliotheque* 7: 401.
145 Couplet, *Confucius*, p. 84.
146 *Bibliotheque* 7: 401.
147 *Bibliotheque* 7: 395 & 397.
148 *Bibliotheque* 7: 409.
149 *Bibliotheque* 7: 394.
150 *Bibliotheque* 7: 395 & Couplet, *Confucius*, p. 395.

ingendered from an incubus". Furthermore, the Buddha was claimed to have said: "I am the only one whom people should worship in Heaven and on earth"[151]. The Jesuits' understanding of Buddhism was so meagre that they failed to see that such a statement contradicted what the Buddha originally taught. He never "taught men to regard him as a God". Further Christian distortion is found in the attempt to imply that the supposed dream of the Emperor Ming in A.D. 65 about a holy man in the west was really about Jesus and that if the Emperor's expedition in search of this holy man had continued farther west, instead of stopping in India, they would have realized the true Christian identity of the dream's personage, rather than returning to China with a statue of the Buddha. Le Clerc's indiscriminating evaluation of the Jesuit treatment of Buddhism was revealed in his echoing of the widely held belief among Europeans that the philosophy of the Indians and Chinese was not very different from the system of the Spinozists[153]!

Le Clerc concluded his review on a critical note when he questioned the validity of Kircher's *China illustrata* report on the discovery of the Nestorian Monument in 1625[154]. His doubt, springing from a somewhat insular line of reasoning, questioned how the Chinese histories, which were so detailed in their reporting of even minor events, could fail to mention "such a great event" as the occurrence of Christianity in China. (The student of Chinese history knows that the answer to Le Clerc's question is that the arrival of Nestorian Christianity was a relatively minor event in the T'ang dynasty when foreign embassies from the west arrived in the capital on a fairly regular basis.) After impugning Fr. Kircher's veracity for allowing an imaginary monument to be reported as real, Le Clerc claimed that Couplet's presentation of the *Tabula Chronologica* represented a selection of extracts from various Chinese annals rather than a complete translation. Coming on the heels of Le Clerc's criticism of Kircher for fabrication, the implied criticism was that Couplet had distorted the picture of Chinese history through a calculated selection. However, one must hasten to add that compared with the acidic and polemical tone of criticism which marked post-1700 European debate on Jesuit writings about China, Le Clerc's criticisms were gentlemanly indeed.

10. DELAYED CRITICAL REACTIONS TO *CONFUCIUS SINARUM PHILOSOPHUS* FOSTERED BY THE RITES CONTROVERSY

In the last decade of the seventeenth century, the growing contention between the very different missionary programs of the Jesuits and the Société des

151 *Bibliotheque* 7:402–403.
152 *Bibliotheque* 7:410. Emperor Ming's dream and this expedition are discussed in the first chapter.
153 *Bibliotheque* 7:407.
154 *Bibliotheque* 7:454–455.

Missions Étrangères of Paris began to dominate the shaping of the China-image in Europe. This contention occurred not only on the European front in Paris with the Sorbonne examination of 1700 and with the Missions Étrangères' publication of the anti-accommodation treatises by Frs. Longobardi and Sainte-Marie (Caballero) in 1701. In China, this opposition carried all the way to the throne through the mission of the Papal legate Carlo Tommaso Maillard de Tournon (1668–1710). The Tournon legation is one of the saddest chapters in the history of Christianity in China because it is a story of great damage done to the Mission not by outsiders, but by European Christians themselves[155]. However, it is a story which lies beyond the chronological parameters of this work.

We shall consider one critique of *Confucius Sinarum philosophus* published after 1700 because of the light it throws upon the composition of the 1687 work. In the *Acta eruditorum* of 1713 there appeared an intemperate and polemical notice on *Confucius Sinarum philosophus* by V. C. Aymon (Aymonio)[156]. M. Aymon claimed to have come into possession of the manuscript of the Jesuit work and he argued that his discovery proved that the Jesuits had published barely one-third of the entire work. He contended that while *Confucius Sinarum philosophus* contained 274 pages of large type – actually the translations alone constituted 288 pages – an unedited printing of the entire manuscript would have produced 950 pages in small type or two folio volumes of 500 pages each.

Aymon claimed not only that the Jesuits distorted the philosophy of Confucius by deleting two-thirds of the text, but that they falsified the remaining material by superimposing glosses whose interpretation distorted the original Chinese meaning. For example, Aymon cited the opening passage from the *Ta hsüeh*: "the purpose of the learning of great men consists in refining the rational nature". To this passage in the original text, Aymon claimed that the Jesuits superimposed the gloss: "that I may draw down from heaven, so that certainly this, as if a most transparent mirror, by means of wiping away a blemish of deformed appetites, may be returned to its pristine clarity". Aymon stated that through this gloss, the Jesuits interpreted "the rational soul to descend from heaven, the true light to be obfuscated by means of these original sins" whereas he declared – accurately – that the Chinese text made no such claim and that Confucius and his disciples were silent on such matters[157].

155 The story of the De Tournon legation is told in some detail in Antonio Sisto Rosso, *Apostolic legations to China in the eighteenth century* (South Pasadena, 1948) pp. 157–186 & in Francis A. Rouleau, S.I., "Maillard de Tournon, Papal legate at the Court of Peking," *Archivum Historicum Societatis Iesu* 31 (1962): 264–323. The latter article was revised, but not yet republished by Fr. Rouleau prior to his death.
156 *Acta eruditorum* (1713): 46–48.
157 *Acta eruditorum* (1713): 47.

Unfortunately, Aymon's *"exposé"* of the Jesuit distortion through commentarial glosses did some distorting of its own and ignorance of Chinese literature was probably a contributing cause. The numerical superscripts in this portion of *Confucius Sinarum philosophus* distinguished the translation from the commentary, though one must concede that in most parts of the Jesuit work, there were no numerical superscripts to make such a distinction. Aymon was justified in criticizing the Jesuit gloss as inaccurate or even a distortion of the original meaning, but glosses are always open to such criticism and there was nothing underhanded about putting forth an interpretation by using a commentary. Glossing the Classical texts was a firmly established literary tradition in China. The Jesuits were well aware of this tradition, but Aymon, without the experience of working with Chinese texts, apparently was not.

Defenders as well as critics of Jesuit accommodation had begun by the end of the seventeenth century to absorb a highly polemical tone into their writings and by 1713, Aymon was merely engaging in the standard give-and-take. But from the point of view of evaluating *Confucius Sinarum philosophus*, the primary flaw in Aymon's notice was his assumption that the translators and editor of the work shared this polemicized atmosphere. In fact, between the 1590s and 1687, the years when the translations and interpretations of *Confucius Sinarum philosophus* were in preparation, the atmosphere was far more open and objective than later. Consequently, the compilers of *Confucius Sinarum philosophus* felt less obliged to defend Jesuit accommodation than they would have had they worked after 1700.

The French scholar Virgile Pinot has examined the charge of Aymon and others that the Jesuits deleted and recast the material of *Confucius Sinarum philosophus* into a form more conducive to securing papal approval for the Jesuit accommodation formula and for discrediting the approach of non-Jesuit missionaries in China[158]. Others, such as David Clément and d'Uffenbach, echoed this criticism, but examination shows that they all lead back to the same source[159]. This source turns out to be a somewhat omnipresent figure on the early eighteenth-century Parisian intellectual scene by the name of Artus de Lionne (1655–1713), bishop of Rosalie. Bishop de Lionne was one of the early associates of the Société des Missions Étrangères, and worked with Maigrot in Fukien province. Between 1689 and his departure for Rome in 1702, De Lionne was active in southern China. During this time he became a rabid opponent of the Jesuits and afterwards returned to Paris to throw himself into

158 Pinot, *La Chine*, p. 152. Apparently Pinot saw only the first of two parts of the manuscript. Mr. Lundbaek has recently examined the manuscript and is one of the few scholars to be in a position to speak knowledgeably on the subject. See Knud Lundbaek, "The image of Neo-Confucianism in *Confucius Sinarum philosophus*," *Journal of the history of ideas* 44 (1983): 20–21.

159 David Clément, *Bibliothèque curieuse, historique et critique* VII, 265f & d'Uffenbach, *Merkwürdige Reisen* III, 481.

the Rites Controversy[160]. M. Pinot's contribution to clarifying this controversy has been to locate in the Bibliothèque Nationale Paris and examine the manuscript which Aymon referred to in his notice of 1713. This manuscript contains part of the preface by Couplet, the translations of the *Ta hsüeh, Chung yung* and the first part of the *Lun yü*[161]. At the end of the manuscript, Pinot discovered a handwritten note signed by Aymon which said that he had received the manuscript on October 15th 1706 from Artus de Lionne on the condition that Aymon publish the manuscript in its entirety in order to rectify the Jesuits' editorial mutilation of it.

But when Pinot compared this manuscript with the published text of *Confucius Sinarum philosophus*, he found Aymon's charges of over-editing and conscious distortion much exaggerated. Pinot did discover deleted portions, but he was more dispassionate in his explanation of them. To his mind, they represented deletions of repetitions material and therefore editorial corrections rather than mutilations[162]. But Pinot did concede that the Jesuits drew unjustified conclusions about the Chinese from the given materials. For example, he criticized Couplet for concluding from the ancient Chinese knowledge of a first principle that the Chinese possessed a knowledge of a divine intelligence[163]. He criticized Couplet for postulating a general belief of the Chinese in the immortality of the soul from a mere gloss on King Wen standing at the side of the Supreme Being[164]. He criticized the Jesuits for interpreting the spirits, which the ancient Chinese revered, as intelligences, that is, immaterial beings[165]. Finally, Pinot criticized the Jesuits for suppressing the miraculous elements in Chinese history such as the legend of the "dragon-knight of Fu Hsi" or of "the tortoise which at the time of Yao and Yü appeared, bearing hieroglyphs". (Pinot's reference here appears somewhat confused: the *I ching* appendix speaks of a dragon emerging out of the river bearing the trigrams on its back and is referred to as the *Ho-t'u Lo-shu* (Diagram of the Yellow River and book of the Lo River)[166].)

Shortly after the appearance of Pinot's work, the Jesuit Alexander Brou responded in two articles defending the seventeenth-century Jesuits against the

160 For a discussion of Artus de Lionne and his crucial role in Nicholas de Malebranche's composition of a treatise on Chinese philosophy, see the author's "Malebranche and Chinese philosophy," *Journal of the history of ideas* 41 (1980): 551–578.
161 Pinot, *La Chine,* pp. 152–153.
162 Pinot, *La Chine,* p. 153.
163 Pinot, La Chine, p. 154.
164 Pinot, La Chine, p. 155, drawing from sheet 224 of the manuscript of *Confucius Sinarum philosophus* preserved in the Bibliothèque Nationale Paris. Actually, the source of the passage in which King Wen is described as standing at the side of the Supreme Being is not the *Lun yü,* as Pinot claims, but the *Shih ching* (Book of odes) III, 1, i, 1 in the Legge translation.
165 Pinot, *La Chine,* p. 156.
166 Pinot, *La Chine,* p. 157.

charge that they furnished incomplete, false and tendentious documentation on China[167]. While conceding that Pinot had correctly noted changes in the manuscript of *Confucius Sinarum philosophus*, Fr. Brou argued that the changes should be viewed less as superimpositions made by a far-removed editor, and more as corrections made by one of the authors, namely, Couplet[168]. Nevertheless, Brou concedes that these changes in the manuscript were influenced by contemporary controversy over the Chinese rites[169].

There is another argument against De Lionne's and Aymon's accusations, at least in regard to the translations of the Chinese Classics. Pinot apparently did not read Chinese and so was unable to compare the *Confucius Sinarum philosophus* translations with the Chinese text. But in my comparison of the two, I have not found a single phrase of Chinese text — as opposed to commentary — omitted from the Jesuit translations. Furthermore, it is my judgment that while one may fault the Jesuits for allowing their missionary preoccupations to affect their translations, the distortion was nearly always of a relatively mild nature.

One basis of these accusations against the Jesuits may have arisen from the Jesuits' interweaving of commentary with the text. Although the Jesuit commentarial reinterpretation of the Classical texts was fully within the Confucian tradition of reinterpretation aimed at recapturing the original and true meaning of the Classics, European readers were unfamiliar with this tradition. The Chinese editions of the Classics usually clearly distinguished the text from the commentary through the use of differently sized characters and, in any case, the Chinese readership was quite familiar with the Classical text. By contrast, *Confucius Sinarum philosophus* readers were presented with a translation which, aside from a few sections which used numerical superscripts to distinguish the Classical text, merged the text with commentary in an indiscernible manner. It is probable that De Lionne's and Aymon's criticism of Jesuit deletions were based on the detection of commentary which they mistakenly assumed to be Classical text. Given the polemicized climate of the time, they were in no mood to seek a sympathetic or even objective explanation of the Jesuits' actions.

I must differ with a judgment of Pinot's regarding *Confucius Sinarum philosophus* and the Chinese Rites Controversy in Europe. Pinot claims that although the *Proëmialis Declaratio* of 1687 said essentially everything that Fr. Le Comte was to say in his *Nouveaux memoires sur l'etat présent de la Chine* (1696), Le

---

167 See Alexander Brou, S.J., "De certains conflits entre missionaires au XVIIe siècle (a propos d'un livre récent)," *Revue d'histoire des missions* 11 (1934): 187–202 & "Les Jésuites sinologues de Pékin et leurs éditeurs de Paris," *Revue d'histoire des missions* 11 (1934): 551–566.
168 Brou, "Les Jésuites sinologues de Pékin," p. 554.
169 Brou, "Les Jésuites sinologues de Pékin," pp. 551–552.

Comte's work was condemned by the Sorbonne in 1700 while *Confucius Sinarum philosophus* was not because of a change in the theological climate in France. One concedes that the earlier Jesuit work preceded Le Comte in diminishing the traditionally favored status of the Jews through giving the Chinese a chronological priority over Mosaic Judaism. Furthermore, the *Proëmialis Declaratio* argued that God had blessed the virtues of the Chinese with rewards, such as God's supposed blessing of Emperor Ti-Kao's (r. 1436–1400 B.C.) many sacrifices to *Shang-ti* and requests for a healing of his infertile wife with the birth of a son[170]. Certainly there was an intensification of the Rites Controversy between 1687 and 1697 which fueled the Sorbonne's examination of Le Comte's book in 1700. However, in terms of their respective scholarship and erudition, the two books are hardly comparable. The *Nouveaux memoires* was written by a missionary who had little working knowledge of the Chinese language and a rather short exposure of three and one-half years to Chinese culture. By contrast, *Confucius Sinarum philosophus* was a pioneering effort in translating Chinese Classical texts made by a group effort of Jesuits whose total years of individual experience in China must be counted in decades. Couplet himself, whose return to China was cut short by death in 1693, had spent twelve and one-half years in China at the time of the editing of *Confucius Sinarum philosophus*. The other known Jesuit contributors and their number of years in China were as follows: de Costa (32 years), Intorcetta (17), Le Faure (19), Maia (21), Pacheco (30), Gouvea (41), Canevari (45), Brancati (35), De Ferrariis (31), Augery (17), Grelon (25), Motel (25), Gabiani (25), Jorge (26), Rougemont (18) and Herdtrich (21). In the short period of time between the works of Couplet and Le Comte, the tone of the accommodation effort in Europe underwent dramatic changes. Le Comte wrote his work for a more exclusively polemical purpose than had the compilers of *Confucius Sinarum philosophus* and the differing natures of the two works helped to shape their different receptions. *Confucius Sinarum philosophus* was scholarly both in tone and dimensions and consequently was read by a more scholarly audience. Le Comte's work was written to maximize exposure and debating points and therefore was read and responded to in that popular and polemical spirit.

11. CONCLUSION

Confucius Sinarum philosophus represented a watershed in the seventeenth-century Jesuit accommodation of China. Not only was it a culmination of Ricci's formula of accommodation, but it was also one of the last instances in the period 1600–1700 in which the most advanced Jesuit thinking on accommodation was fully presented to the European public. While momentous dynas-

---

170 Couplet, *Confucius*, p. lxxviij.

tic changes in China were dictating a modification in Ricci's original formula, the Rites Controversy in Europe was further polarizing a fundamental difference of approach among missionaries in China between proponents and opponents of accommodation. This basic difference in approach had divided China missionaries and had isolated even a few dissenting Jesuits such as Frs. Longobardi and Visdelou from the dominant accommodative outlook of Jesuit missionaries[171]. These differences produced rivalries which impeded the momentum of the China Mission. By the end of the century, these missiological differences were extending to larger conflicts in Europe, such as between Jesuits and their spiritual rivals, the Jansenists, who established a missionary base with the Société des Missions Étrangères of Paris. This escalation and broadening of the debate on missionary methods produced an atmosphere in which serious scholarship on China was increasingly sacrificed for polemical debate. After 1687, the most advanced thinking on Jesuit accommodation, as in the case of Fr. Bouvet's

171 Frs. Longobardi and Visdelou were among the most knowledgeable Jesuit dissenters to the policy of accommodation and the periods of their respective work in China show that such dissent was expressed throughout the seventeenth century. Niccolò Longobardi (Lung Hua-min, 1565–1655) developed a viewpoint on mission methodology which differed from Ricci's accommodation. When he succeeded Ricci as head of the Jesuit mission in China, he began airing these views more openly and thereby helped to initiate the Chinese Rites Controversy. Around 1623, Longobardi wrote a treatise in Latin which remained in manuscript until it was carried back to Europe by the Franciscan Antonio Caballero a Santa Maria (Antoine de Sainte-Marie) and was translated into Spanish and published by Friar Domingo Navarrete in his *Tratados* (Madrid, 1676–1679) pp. 245–289. Longobardi's work was later translated into French by the Société des Missions Étrangères and published as *Traité sur quelques points de la réligion des Chinois* (Paris, 1701). In this form, the treatise had a significant influence upon Leibniz and became an important document in the Rites Controversy. This treatise is discussed in detail in the author's *Leibniz & Confucianism*, pp. 26–29 & 69–116. Also see Wing-tsit Chan, "The study of Chu Hsi in the West," *Journal of Asian studies* 35 (1976): 559–560.
Claude de Visdelou (Liu Ying Sheng-wen, 1656–1737) was one of the talented Jesuits chosen by Fr. Fontaney to be a part of the first French mission to China of 1685. In China, Fr. Visdelou was praised by his confreres for his knowledge of the Chinese language. (Bouvet spoke in a letter to Leibniz of September 19th 1699 of Visdelou composing a Chinese dictionary which would help to answer some of Leibniz' questions about a *Clavis Sinica*.) Visdelou's growing dissent from the Jesuit policy of accommodation led him to support the abortive mission of the Papal legate, Cardinal de Tournon. Visdelou's association with Tournon forced him to leave China in June 1709 and he went to India where he remained for 28 years at Pondicherry. He lived first with the Mission Étrangères and finally with the Capuchins from 1726 until his death late in 1737. Although he received Papal letters, he was forbidden to return to France. He continued to write on the Chinese Classics, including the *I ching*, on Chinese philosophy, including Taoism, on Chinese history and on the Chinese ancestral rites. For a list of his works, see K. F. Neumann, "Claude Visdelou und das Verzeichniss seiner Werke," *Zeitschrift der Deutschen Morgenländische Gesellschaft* 4 (1850): 225–242.

Figurist theories, was no longer able to be fully and publicly presented to European readers. But while the most advanced thinking received only incomplete exposure, there was an increase of Jesuit-authored treatises on accommodation which presented both previous ideas and fragments of new ideas on accommodation, but in a more polemical and popular tone. To these belong the famous treatises of Frs. Le Comte and Le Gobien. As a result, *Confucius Sinarum philosophus* represents a culmination of the public dissemination of Jesuit scholarship on China in the seventeenth century.

CHAPTER IX

THE EVOLUTION OF JESUIT ACCOMMODATION IN
THE FIGURISM OF BOUVET

1. FR. BOUVET'S MODIFICATION OF RICCI'S ACCOMMODATION

Although most seventeenth-century Jesuits of the China Mission were associated with a sympathetic and accommodative attitude toward China, not all expressions of this attitude involved Confucius and the scholar-official ideal. There was an evolution in Jesuit accommodation made in response to changes which had occurred in China during the course of the century. These changes were concentrated in the Chinese political and cultural climate and in the position and status of Jesuits in China. A leading role in this evolution of Jesuit accommodation was played by Joachim Bouvet (1656–1730).

Fr. Bouvet was born at Mans or Conlie (Sarthe) in France as the younger son of a counselor to the regional court of Mans[1]. In 1673 he entered the Society of Jesus where his mathematical and scholarly talents led to his selection as part of the first group of French Jesuits sent to China. The ability of this group to travel to Peking directly after arriving in China in 1688 shows how far things had advanced in the century since Ricci had first attempted to reside in the capital. For Ricci, it had taken 18 years of struggle to establish a Jesuit residence in Peking. Of the five new arrivals, Bouvet and Gerbillon were ordered to remain in Peking while the others were sent into the provinces. In 1693–1699, Bouvet returned to Europe. But apart from this and short trips in the Emperor's service, including a trip to Canton in 1706 as imperial envoy on the Chinese rites question[2], Bouvet spent the remaining 37 years of his life in Peking working at the imperial court. His proximity to the Emperor gave him a perspective quite different from those Jesuits living in the Chinese provinces. Bouvet saw China through Manchu imperial eyes. His imperial ties restricted his cultivation of close associations with scholar-officials and so he was cut off from the sort of literati guidance which was so crucial to the work of Ricci and other Jesuits. After the ascent of the Manchus in 1644, the Jesuits failed to convert more literati of the stature of Li Chih-tsao (d. 1630) and Hsü Kuang-ch'i (d. 1633). Consequently, during the first half of the seventeenth century, the most creative of the Jesuit proponents of accommodation worked

---

1 Cordier, *Bibliotheca Sinica* II, 1056.
2 Dehergne, *Répertoire*, p. 34.

closely with and depended upon literati located primarily in south China. But in the second half of the century, the most creative advocates of accommodation worked increasingly at the Peking court under imperial patronage and protection.

The K'ang-hsi emperor appeared to have been quite pleased with the French missionaries for he requested Bouvet to return to Europe as his representative in order to thank Louis XIV and to procure more Jesuits of similar caliber[3]. Bouvet departed from Canton in October 1693, but did not reach France until March 1697. There were a number of features of Bouvet's European trip which set it off from the return trips of Frs. Trigault (1613–1622), Semedo (1636–1644), Martini (1650–1659), Boym (1651–1658), Grueber (1661–1680), Intorcetta (1669–1674), Couplet (1682–1692) and Grimaldi (1686–1694). First of all, Bouvet stayed only one year and appears to have confined his visit to France. Unlike his Jesuit predecessors, Bouvet did not make a trip to Rome, thus indicating the emergence of nationalist influence (Chinese and French) at the expense of Papal influence in the China Mission. Also, growing criticism of Jesuit accommodation from Rome probably contributed to his avoidance of the Papal City during his visit. Secondly, Bouvet lacked a Chinese traveling companion. These differences probably reflected the fact that Bouvet was making this trip as a representative of the K'ang-hsi emperor rather than as an official Jesuit procurator. Yet surely Bouvet's European trip had the blessing of his immediate French superior, Fr. Fontaney, even if not his official Jesuit superiors, and during his time in Europe, Bouvet fulfilled many of the tasks of a procurator. In fact, he followed the pattern which had proved so successful previously in building support for the China Mission and in recruiting talented and committed missionaries.

Like Couplet, Bouvet brought a number of Chinese books to Europe. But reflecting a shift in patronage, 300 of these volumes went not to Rome, but to Paris where they were offered to Louis XIV as a gift from the K'ang-hsi emperor and thereby fulfilled one of the original aims of the French mission of 1685[4]. Apparently pleased, the French king authorized funding for a second mission to China. In order to facilitate their passage, Bouvet arranged for a businessman, Jean Jourdan Groussay, to underwrite the costs of a ship carrying both glassware and Jesuit recruits to China[5]. Bouvet departed from La Rochelle in

---

3 Pfister, p. 434; Dehergne, *Répertoire,* p. 34; & Witek, *Controversial ideas in China and Europe,* p. 86.

4 Pfister, p. 434, states that Bouvet presented Louis XIV with "49 magnificently printed volumns from Peking." Other scholars appear to have accepted this statement from Pfister, e.g. Fang Hao, *Chung-kuo T'ien-chu-chiao shih-jen wu ch'uan* 3 vols. (Hong Kong, 1970) II, 279. However, Bouvet himself stated in a letter to Leibniz of October 18th 1697 that he brought 300 Chinese volumes to the library of the French king. See *Leibniz-Briefwechsel* 105, sheet 2[v].

5 Bouvet's preparations for sending this second group of French Jesuits to China are briefly discussed in Witek, *Controversial ideas in China and Europe,* pp. 86–87 who

March of 1698 aboard the *Amphitrite* with eight Jesuit recruits, who included the talented Frs. Parennin, Prémare and Regis. He reached China in March 1699.

While in Europe, Bouvet combined the traditional task of publishing materials favorable to the China Mission with the new task of representing the K'ang-hsi emperor. One of the results was the *Portrait historique de l'Empereur de la Chine* (Paris 1697). Bouvet's *Portrait* was a modest little work whose significance must be measured more in terms of the shift it signaled in Jesuit accommodation than in the extent of its influence in Europe. Although it was republished six times (La Haye 1699, London 1699, Utrecht 1699, Hannover (?) 1699, Utrecht 1710 and Padua 1710) and, in the process, translated into English, Dutch, Latin and Italian, there are few signs of its impact in the literature of that time. Its 264 pages belie its length. It was published in small duodecimo dimensions, had large typeface and lacked a single chapter division. As a portrait of a contemporary ruler, today's reader might be just as skeptical as were the sprinkling of reviewers in Bouvet's time, although for different reasons. Today, one might regard the portrait as too favorable to be real, whereas readers at the end of the seventeenth century tended to regard it as a calculated Jesuit exaggeration. Bouvet himself is said to have later had second thoughts about the degree to which he had idealized the K'ang-hsi emperor in the Portrait[6].

The dedication of this portrait of the K'ang-hsi emperor to Louis XIV revealed a fascinating aspect of Bouvet's dual commitment. He is one of the few men in history whose two earthly masters have been the rulers of the most powerful lands of the East and West. Here was a man of God who served the emperor of China and who returned bearing gifts to honor his European master, the king of France. Technological advancements since then have not lessened the uniqueness of Bouvet's position. If anything, the idea of such a dual allegiance — actually a triple allegiance if one includes his Heavenly master — seems less possible today than it was in Bouvet's time.

Bouvet's portrait was made of the K'ang-hsi emperor when the latter was 44 years of age and in the thirty-sixth year of his reign. It was the peak in the life

draws from a "Résponse" by Foucquet preserved in the Bibliothèque nationale Paris. Mss. fr. 25670, 8. For details of the voyage of the French Jesuits, see the account written by Fr. Prémare in Giovanni Gherardini, *Relation de voyage fait à Chine sur le vaisseau l'Amphrite, en l'année 1698* (Paris, 1700).

6 Fr. Rouleau claimed that when Bouvet returned to Peking in 1699, he was "shocked" to discover the degree to which the Emperor had dashed his high hopes for Christian conversion by patronizing Buddhism. According to Fr. Rouleau, Bouvet's reassessment of his earlier optimism was part of a mission-wide readjustment to more sober expectations of success among Jesuits in China. See Francis A. Rouleau S.I., "Maillard de Tournon, Papal Legate at the Court of Peking," *Archivum Historicum Societatis Iesu* 31 (1962): 270n. On the European reaction to Bouvet's *Portrait*, also see Lawrence D. Kessler, *K'ang-hsi and the consolidation of Ch'ing rule, 1661–1684* (Chicago, 1976) p. 152.

of a monarch who has been acknowledged by numerous witnesses and historians to have been a remarkable ruler. If we allow ourselves to read Bouvet's portrait in this light of objective confirmation, we may be impressed in the same way as were doubtless many European readers of some 300 years ago. Bouvet wrote:

There is nothing in his person which is not worthy of the throne he occupies. He has a majestic air, a stature very well proportioned and above average, all of the traits of normal appearance, with the eyes more alive and larger than is common in his land. The nose is slightly aqualine and rounded to a point. And several marks, which the smallpox has left him, do not at all diminish the charm which shines through his person.

But in this prince the qualities of the soul stand above those of the body. . . . He has a vast amount of extraordinary talent, a firmness of spirit during all manner of ordeals, and also fitting to the formation of great enterprises by which to conduct them and bring them to a close. All his inclinations are noble and worthy of a great king. His people are unable to sufficiently admire his love for fairness and justice, his paternal fondness for his subjects, his penchant for virtue and for all that reason dictates, and the absolute control that he has over his emotions. And one is no less surprised to discover in a monarch so busy, that he has as much application to all sorts of sciences as appreciation for the fine arts[7].

This is hagiography, but it is not *merely* hagiography. the K'ang-hsi emperor was an extremely capable ruler, particularly during the midpoint of his career when this portrait was made. Allowing for slight exaggeration and adjustment of adjectives to less florid contemporary levels, what Bouvet described in the above was basically accurate. Alongside of Bouvet's description one must add the less enthusiastic appraisal of the K'ang-hsi emperor by the secular priest, Matteo Ripa (1682–1745), who served as a painter and engraver in the Chinese court from 1710 to 1723[8]. Fr. Ripa credited the Emperor with an interest in learning, but felt that he vastly overrated his own achievements in music and mathematics. However, Ripa's criticisms must be gauged against the fact that he did not reach Peking until 1710[9]. Bouvet's glowing appraisal in the *Portrait* was drawn from his experience with the K'ang-hsi emperor between 1688 and 1693, nearly 20 years before Ripa first observed the Emperor. By the time Ripa arrived, the Emperor was an aging man whose enthusiasm for Western learning had dimmed. Also, Ripa's lack of first-rate intellectual powers caused the Emperor to have a more distant relationship with him than he had with the more brilliant missionaries, such as Verbiest and Bouvet. Finally, Ripa's

---

7 Joachim Bouvet, *Portrait historique de l'empereur de la Chine* (Paris, 1697) pp. 11–13.

8 Matteo Rippa, *Storia della fondazione della Congregazione e del Collegio de'Cinesi* 3 vols. (Naples, 1789). This work was later abridged and translated into English by Fortunato Prandi as the *Memoirs of Father Ripa* (London, 1844) A semi-popular account of Fr. Ripa's Chinese activities appears in Nigel Cameron, *Barbarians and mandarins, thirteen centuries of Western travelers in China* (Chicago, 1976) pp. 263–275 & 284–287.

9 Fang Hao, II, 344.

portrayal of the K'ang-hsi emperor should be used with caution because of discrepancies between the manuscripts and published versions[10].

As the *Portrait* progresses, one finds a favoritism to the Emperor which does injustice to the other elements of Chinese civilization. Bouvet presented the "mandarins" or scholar-officials as a relatively unreliable group who were in constant need of imperial supervision. According to Bouvet, the government of China was "perfectly monarchical" not because of the independent contributions of the scholar-officials, but because they were being so well supervised by the Emperor. Bouvet wrote: "the vigilance of the emperor is such that it is difficult for the most hidden faults to long escape his detection" and "the least fault which [the scholar-officials] make in the matter of government, suffices in order to remove them from office, if it comes to the attention of the Emperor. But if someone is accused of being bribed with money, the Emperor is inexorable on the matter, without regard to whom it may be"[11]. Such remarks were exaggerated on several counts. First of all, Ch'ing China was a vast area whose estimated population of between 150 and 200 million made close personal surveillance by the monarch extremely difficult. Secondly, official bribes were a commonly practiced method in China of raising inadequate official salaries to adequate levels. Although the K'ang-hsi emperor was himself impeccably honest, an historical study has shown that in the matter of anti-corruption policies, the K'ang-hsi emperor's imperial predecessor and successor were both more vigorous campaigners against corruption[12]. Whereas the Shun-chih emperor (1644–1660) enthusiastically fought corruption as the dynastic founder who was well aware of the corruption of the preceding Ming dynasty, the K'ang-hsi emperor's attitudes toward corruption were more lenient. The latter reigned during a time of great prosperity and possibly he felt that the surcharges and customary fees (*lou-k'uei*) which were added to the tax burden and associated with bribes aided officials coping with inflation while not significantly hurting either the people's livelihood or state security. It was the Yung-cheng emperor (1723–1735) who temporarily solved the problem by converting the surcharges and customary fees to part of the official salary.

Bouvet painted a picture of great instability and continuous fluctuations in the tenure of office of both high and low ranking scholar-officials. Here he surely overprojected the Peking perspective for his observations would have applied mainly to higher-ranking capital officials and provincial governors. But the vast majority of scholar-officials who occupied the magistracies and

---

10 Fr. Antonio Sisto Rosso has noted errors which have been made both in the process of printing the Italian original and in translating it into English. These observations are included in Walter Fuchs, "Zu Pater Ripa's Debut als chinesischer Hofmaler in das Jahr 1710," in *Tamura Hakushi shōju tōyoshi ronsō* (Kyoto, 1968) pp. 1–5.

11 Bouvet, *Portrait*, pp. 62 & 65.

12 These remarks are drawn from Adam Y. C. Lui, *Corruption in China during the early Ch'ing period 1644–1660* (Hong Kong, 1979) pp. 61–65.

district offices were too remote to come to the Emperor's attention. Barring a scandal or a severe drop in the collection of imperial tax revenues, the Emperor permitted most officials to serve out their brief terms uninterrupted. This was the usual peacetime situation during the history of imperial China. The K'ang-hsi emperor's period was atypical in that his reign began only 18 years after the beginning of the Manchu overlordship in China. The early period of the Ch'ing dynasty was marked by the widespread refusal to participate in government by Chinese scholar-officials loyal to the Ming dynasty. But by Bouvet's time, a half-century had elapsed since the onset of Manchu rule and the resistance of the Ming Loyalists was receding.

The starting point of Bouvet's accommodation toward China was the excellence of her government. But Bouvet was not like other European interpreters such as Couplet and, later, Enlightenment thinkers who saw this excellence in terms of the philosophy of Confucius and its contemporary exemplars — the scholar-officials[13]. Bouvet based his case on the excellence of the Chinese system of monarchical government and particularly on its manifestation in the K'ang-hsi emperor. His *Portrait* did not mention Confucius, nor did it refer to his contemporary followers in a very favorable light. The second basis of Bouvet's accommodation emerged more gradually and derived from his study of the Chinese Classics. Confucianism drew its foundations from these Classics, but it was not the specifically Confucian aspect of these texts which interested Bouvet. What Bouvet focused on were the most ancient parts of the Classics, particularly those which he believed to foreshadow Christ's Revelation.

The Jesuits of Bouvet's time had succeeded in achieving an official status and proximity to the ruling powers of China which Ricci had merely dreamt about. Such contacts with the throne had been severely impeded during Ricci's time by a monarch whose reclusive tendencies marked him as one of the great imperial eccentrics in Chinese history. During the years 1589–1615, the Wan-li emperor suspended all public audiences and from 1593 to 1615 met with the Grand Secretary only five times[14]! Lacking direct ties to the throne, Ricci cultivated the scholar-officials through social and intellectual relationships which brought him into intimate contact with the syncretic culture of the late Ming. This was the context in which Ricci developed his policy of accommodation.

By Ricci's time, China's cultural atmosphere was no longer syncretic. The searching appraisals made by Chinese literati over the loss of the Ming dynasty indicted the eclectic attitudes of late Ming scholars and the finger of blame was

13 Eighteenth-century English admiration for Confucianism is treated by Edmund Leites in "Confucianism in eighteenth-century England: natural morality and social reform," *Philosophy East & West* 28 (1978): 143–159.

14 Goodrich, I, 326–327.

often pointed at the school of Wang Yang-ming, sometimes referred to as Ming Neo-Confucianism or the Lu-Wang School in order to distinguish it from Sung Neo-Confucianism or the Ch'eng-Chu School. Early Ch'ing literati specifically attacked the highly introspective philosophizing of the school of Wang Yang-ming which had proliferated in the late Ming into a variety of speculative philosophies and unrestrained wild Ch'anism. Most early Ch'ing appraisals felt that the Ming philosophers had strayed too far from the true Confucian *Tao* and that it was now time to return to Confucian fundamentals[15]. The Manchu rulers reinforced and focused this movement back to more objective studies in statecraft and research on classical literature. The return to orthodoxy was reflected in the K'ang-hsi emperor's order of 1715 for Li Kuang-ti to re-edit the *Chu-tzu ta-ch'üan* (Collected works of Chu Hsi) and to compile an abridgement of the Sung Neo-Confucian anthology, the *Hsing-li ta-ch'üan* (Great compendium of natural and moral philosophy). Although not all early Ch'ing thinkers sought a return to the Sung Neo-Confucian philosophy, it was expedient for the new rulers in China to legitimize their imperial status by embracing Sung Neo-Confucianism as the most orthodox form of Confucianism then available. Consequently, in the late seventeenth century, the lines of orthodoxy began narrowing far beyond what they had been at the time of Ricci. These changes in both the situation of the Jesuits and in the cultural climate required that Ricci's accommodation program be modified to fit these new realities.

Ricci had built his accommodation upon the Confucian tradition because of the dual grounds of its commanding position in Chinese culture and its amenability to Christianity. But practically every seventeenth-century Jesuit of the China Mission rejected the prominent Sung Neo-Confucian manifestation of the Confucian tradition on the grounds that its apparently materialistic and atheistic outlook was antithetical to Christianity. (Early in the eighteenth century, Jesuits such as Prémare and Noël would begin to reconcile Sung Neo-Confucianism with Christianity, but this shift lies beyond the confines of this study[16].) The greater openness of late Ming culture allowed Ricci to forge a

---

15 Some of the most famous literary figures of late seventeenth-century China who reflect this general shift in cultural direction from Ming to Ch'ing include Huang Tsung-hsi (1610–1695), Ku Yen-wu (1613–1682), Wang Fu-chih (1619–1672) and Yen Yüan (1635–1704). The revival of Sung Neo-Confucianism – the so-called "return to Ch'eng-Chu" movement – has in the recent past been treated as a fairly uncreative movement, e.g. see Carson Chang, *The development of Neo-Confucian thought* 2 vols. (New York, 1962) II, 317–336 & Wing-tsit Chan, *Historical charts of Chinese philosophy* (New Haven, 1955) 15th page (chart 6). However, more recently a shift in thinking has occurred and a more creative aspect to the early Ch'ing dynasty Ch'eng-Chu revival has been discerned. See Wing-tsit Chan, "The *Hsing-li ching-i* and the Ch'eng-Chu school of the seventeenth century."

16 See the author's "The reconciliation of Neo-Confucianism with Christianity in the writings of Joseph de Prémare, S.J.," *Philosophy East & West* 26 (1976): 389–410 and "The first complete translation of the Confucian Four Books in the West."

form of Confucianism other than Sung Neo-Confucianism. But when the culturally acceptable forms of the Confucian tradition had by the late seventeenth
century and particularly at the Manchu court contracted much closer to the
interpretations of the Sung Neo-Confucians, Bouvet was forced to look elsewhere for an accommodative base. Since Bouvet was less dependent on the
scholar-officials than Ricci had been, it was less necessary for him to appeal to
them in his modification of Ricci's program of accommodation. The con-
stituency which Bouvet had to satisfy was located on and about the Chinese
throne. Since the early Manchu emperors honored and respected the tradition
of the ancient sage-emperors of China, which the Confucian tradition also
claimed as its spiritual ancestry, it is not surprising that Bouvet sought elements in this ancient sage-wisdom which were amenable to Christianity and
which could serve as a new basis for a modified Chinese-Christian synthesis.
So although Bouvet modified the content of Ricci's accommodation, the new
components which Bouvet used continued to satisfy Ricci's dual criteria of
having a commanding position in Chinese culture and an amenability to Christianity.

2. HERMETISM AND BOUVET'S FIGURISM

The tradition of Christian apologetics called *prisca theologia* (Ancient Theology) or Hermetism maintained that certain pagan writings contained vestiges
of the true religion and dated itself to the early Church Fathers, including
Lactantius (ca. 240–320), Clement of Alexandria (ca. 150–215) and Eusebius
(ca. 260–340)[17]. By 1650, a list of the Ancient Theologians included: Adam,
Ennoch, Abraham, Zoroaster, Moses, Hermes Trismegistus, the Brahmans,
Druids, David, Orpheus, Pythagoras, Plato and the Sybils. By 1700 the list had
grown to include Fu Hsi. The most influential texts of the Ancient Theologians
were attributed to Orpheus and Hermes Trismegistus. Except for the Asclepius
dialogue of the *Hermetica* (or *Corpus Hermeticum*), the fragments which pieced
together the *Hermetica* and the *Orphica* were not known in western Europe
until they became part of the Platonic revival initiated in Italy by Marsilio Ficino's Latin translations of Plato (1484) and Plotinus (1490). The sixteenth
century widely accepted Ficino's interpretation of Platonism as a religious
philosophy as well as the Neoplatonic view of Platonism which drew from a
highly mystical and magical environment. There was a strongly magical element which led Ficino, Giovanni Pico della Mirandola (1463–1494) and Giordano Bruno (1548–1600) into conflict with orthodox Christianity.

The Renaissance revivers of the Ancient Theology were able to be more
favorable towards the pagans than the early Church Fathers had been. While

17 See Daniel P. Walker, *The Ancient Theology* (London, 1972).

the latter had been in direct competition with these rival religious forms, by the time of the Renaissance, these paganisms had become mere vestiges barely relating to practicing beliefs. The Renaissance authors attempted to integrate Platonism and Neoplatonism into Christianity. They saw similarities between Christianity and these pagan writings in the areas of monotheism, the immortality of the soul, rewards and punishments in an afterlife, the ascetic devaluation of the body in relationship to the soul, the Trinity and creation *ex nihilo*. The pre-Christian foreshadowing of Christ's Revelation could be seen from two differing perspectives. Either the emphasis was upon the Jewish tradition which influenced a pagan group or the emphasis tended to favor a more purely pagan foreshadowing which was usually confirmed by Jewish tradition. The focal point of the Jewish influence upon paganism was usually Egypt and the medium was Moses whose teachings were said to be preserved in Egyptian culture.

The problem with all this was that by the middle of the seventeenth century, historical criticism had proved the major Ancient Theologies to have been mis-dated. They were in fact post- rather than pre-Christian in origin. Isaac Casaubon (1559–1614) first redated the *Hermetica* in 1614 and doubt was cast on the antiquity of the *Orphica* by ca. 1649[18]. Yet the Ancient Theology continued to survive. It survived in England – in the very country where Casaubon had researched and published his redating – in the form of the Platonic revival associated with the Cambridge Platonists. It survived in the writings of Pierre-Daniel Huet (1630–1721) and Athanasius Kircher. And it survived in certain French Jesuits associated with the China Mission who included Bouvet, Prémare, Jean-Alexis de Gollet (1664–1741) and Jean-François Foucquet (1665–1741)[19]. Peripherally identified with this outlook were the Jesuits Jean-Simon Bayard (1662–1725), Jean Noëlas (1669–1740) and François Noël[20].

---

18 Isaac Casaubon's redating of the Hermetic texts was done in his *De rebus sacris et ecclesiasticus exercitationes XVI* (London, 1614). For a discussion of this redating, see Frances Yates, *The Hermetic teachings of Giordano Bruno* (London, 1964) pp. 398–403 & Walker, *The Ancient Theology*, p. 195.

19 For a general view of Figurism, see Arnold H. Rowbotham, "The Jesuit Figurists and eighteenth century religious thought," *Journal of the history of ideas* 17 (1956): 471–485. Mr. Walker devotes a chapter to the Figurists from the viewpoint of Hermetism in his *The Ancient Theology*, pp. 194–230. Figurism is treated briefly is John W. Witek, "Jean-François Foucquet: un controversiste Jésuite en Chine et en Europe," in *Acts du colloque international de sinologie, Chantilly, 1974* (Paris, 1976) pp. 115–135. The same subject is treated more extensively in Fr. Witek's *Controversial ideas in China and in Europe: a biography of Jean-François Foucquet*. Prémare's Figurism is briefly treated by the author in "The reconciliation of Neo-Confucianism with Christianity in the writings of Joseph de Prémare, S.J.," pp. 391–392. Bouvet's Figurist views as expressed in the Leibniz-Bouvet correspondence are treated in the author's *Leibniz & Confucianism*, pp. 39–68.

20 Dehergne, *Répertoire*, pp. 28 & 186, associates Frs. Bayard and Noëlas with Figurism. Pfister, p. 416, suggests that Noël was a Figurist. On Noël's relationship to the Fi-

There were several names given to these Jesuits who applied the Ancient Theology to China. Kilian Stumpf (1673–1720), who was both a Jesuit and critic of this group, referred to them as "Kinisticae", that is, *ching*-ists, after the fact that they focused on the *ching* or ancient Chinese Classics[21]. In the eighteenth century the Jesuit missionary Joseph-Marie Amiot used the name "Ykingnistes" (*I ching*-ists) to refer to the group of Jesuit missionaries who regarded the *I ching* as a prophetic book which contained the mysteries of Christianity[22]. Another name applied to this group was "symbolists", after the fact that its adherents interpreted the ancient Chinese texts symbolically or figuratively rather than historically[23]. But the term most commonly applied to this group is "Figurists".

The term "Figurism" is somewhat misleading in that it implies a greater unity to the views of the Jesuits associated with it than was actually the case. As with so many labels in history, the name appears to have been coined by critics of the viewpoint. Perhaps the first recorded instance of the term is found in a letter from Fréret to Fr. Prémare dated December 1732[24]. In this letter, Fréret was responding to critical remarks made by Prémare in regard to Antoine Gaubil's *Histoire de l'Astronomie chinoisie* (1729)[25]. Fr. Gaubil was a frequent correspondent of Fréret's, from whom the latter gained much of his knowledge of China. Much of Fréret's letter to Prémare referred to questions of Chinese chronology in which Fréret supported Gaubil's more conservative claims for the antiquity of the Chinese. In the course of this discussion, Fréret claimed to recognize in the writings received from Prémare — at least one of which was anonymous — a *"figurisme"* whose harmful effects in Europe he associated with Fr. Fouçquet. Fréret asked Prémare, somewhat rhetorically, if it were possible that solid intellects would allow themselves to become tainted by this malady (i.e. Figurism) and that it would become widespread enough to infect

gurists, see the author's "The first complete translation of the Confucian Four Books in the West," pp. 525–526.

21 Kilian Stumpf, S.J., *"De controversia libri y kim seu contra sententias Kinisticas,"* Archivum Romanum Societatis Jesu, Jap.Sin. 176, 422–426 (original Latin text and German translation) are published as an appendix in Claudia von Collani, *Die Figuristen in der Chinamission* (Frankfurt am Main, 1981) pp. 81–108. Also see Sebald Reil, *Kilian Stumpf 1655–1720, ein Würzburger Jesuit am Kaiserhof zu Peking* (Münster Westfalen, 1978) pp. 160–164.

22 Joseph-Marie Amiot, "L'antiquité des Chinois prouvée par les Monuments," in *Mémoires concernant l'histoire, les sciences, les arts, les moeurs, et les usages . . . des Chinois par les Missionaires de Pekin.* vols. 1–17 (Paris, 1776–1814) vol. II (1777).

23 Johannes Beckmann, "Die katholischen Missionare und der Taoismus," *Neue Zeitschrift für Missionswissenschaft* 26 (Beckenried, 1970): 7, fn. 37.

24 Pinot, *Documents inédits,* p. 45.

25 Fr. Gaubil's work constituted part of a multi-volumed work entitled *Observations mathematiques, astronomiques, géographiques, chronologiques et physiques, tirées*

the two ends of the earth (i.e. Europe and China) and antagonize the relations between Jesuits and Jansenists. It seems probable that Fréret was using the term "Figurism" in a pejorative sense, though it is not certain that Fréret coined the term. The fact that Fréret mentioned Frs. Gollet, Fouçquet and Prémare together in this letter and repeated these names along with that of Bouvet in a letter dated September 20th 1733 indicated a perception of affinity in the views of these four Jesuits in regard to the Ancient Theology, at least by their opponents[26].

In general, the Figurists argued the if one were able to trace far enough back in the history of any culture, one could find the point at which it diverged from the primary Judeo-Christian tradition. The fact that this theory was widely applied is shown by the French Jesuit Jean-François Lafitau (1681–1746) who utilized this theory in regard to the North American indians[27]. The Figurists felt that Chinese civilization offered a unique situation for the study of this divergence from the Judeo-Christian tradition because of its remarkably accurate historical records, which the Figurists sometimes even suggested excelled the Biblical record[28]. The Figurists applied themselves assiduously to the study of ancient Chinese texts with the aim of interpreting them not as literal historical records, but as symbolical works which contained the deepest mysteries of Christianity[29]. The Figurists argued that Chinese was a hieroglyphic script whose characters contained these secret Christian truths.

The Figurists as a whole suffered from excessive enthusiasm for their ideas. For example, Bouvet's belief that *all* Christian mysteries were revealed in the Chinese Classics offended those Jesuits and other Christians who accepted the traditional Judeo-Christian assignment of priority to the Israelites. Furthermore, while Jesuits such as Martini and Couplet had demonstrated the reliability of ancient Chinese chronologies and the validity of the ancient Chinese Classics, they interpreted these works historically rather than in the symbolical manner of the Figurists. The Figurists identified traditional Chinese history with world history. Shem and his descendants brought God's law to East Asia, but there, as elsewhere, human evil over a period of time had corrupted the revelation[30].

The Figurist views of these respective Jesuits were, in fact, a great deal more diverse than the label would indicate. They became mixed with the controversy

des anciens livres chinois . . . par les Pères de la Compagnie de Jésus, edited and published by Et. Souciet, S.J. in Paris, 1929.

26 Pinot, Documents inédits, p. 50.
27 Between 1711 and 1717, Fr. Lafitau lived in North America and upon his return to France, expressed his Figurist views in a book called Moeurs des Sauvages américains comparées aux moeurs des premiers temps which appeared in 1724. See Colani, Die Figuristen, pp. 37–39.
28 Collani, Die Figuristen, pp. 20–21.
29 Pinot, La Chine, pp. 347 & 350f.
30 Collani, Die Figuristen, p. 23.

over the Chinese rites and peaked on a public and polemical level in 1700 at the
noisy Sorbonne examination of Le Comte's *Nouveaux mémoires sur l'état présent de la Chine* (1696) and Le Gobien's *Histoire de l'Edit de l'Empereur de la
Chine en faveur de la religion Chretienne* (1698). Even before 1700, the Jesuits
in China had been restricted to points of physics and mathematics in discussing
the *I ching* with the K'ang-hsi emperor. Furthermore, any writings on Figurism
were required to be in Latin rather than Chinese[31]. After the Sorbonne condemnation, the Jesuit superiors appear to have demanded greater caution in the
presentation of extreme accommodation viewpoints in regard to China, such as
Figurism. These demands may help to explain the sudden silence on Bouvet's
part in the Leibniz-Bouvet correspondence, a silence which Leibniz found both
puzzling and frustrating[32]. But the ideas associated with Figurism were too
alive to be suppressed. They continued to develop privately and to be communicated through correspondence, which in the early eighteenth century was
a powerful means of communication. Manuscripts continued to be written,
although their publication was delayed by 150 years or more[33].

Two variable factors in historical evaluation are external influence and
individual creativity. Creativity is particularly variable because creative thinkers
will sometimes think creatively merely to spite the weight of the past. Consequently, the claim that the French Jesuits of the China Mission were believers
in a tradition of Hermetism which had been repudiated by historical criticism
neglects the creativity factor. This is because at least two, and possibly more,
of the Figurists were extremely creative thinkers, namely, Bouvet and Prémare.
When Bouvet argued that there were certain elements of ancient Chinese culture which anticipated Christian truths, he was referring to elements which
were only partly repetitive of traditional notions of Hermetism. What was
novel in Bouvet's ideas stemmed from applying these traditional ideas to the
context of China. A look at Bouvet's correspondence with Leibniz will reveal
some of these new elements.

31 The Superior General of the French Mission, François-Xavier Dentrecolles had prescribed that in speaking to the Emperor about the *I ching,* the Jesuits were to avoid any
reference to an allegorical, sacred sense and limit themselves to points of physics and
mathematics. See Witek, *Controversial ideas in China and Europe,* pp. 176 & 237.
32 See Mungello, *Leibniz & Confucianism,* p. 40.
33 As examples of the extended delay in the publication of Figurist texts, one notes that
Prémare wrote his monumental *"Selecta quaedam vestigia praecipuorum Christianae
Relligionis dogmatum ex antiquis Sinarum libris eruta"* between 1712 and 1725, but
it was not published until a French translation of it appeared in 1878. Also Prémare
composed his *"Lettre sur le monotheisme des Chinois"* in 1728, but it was not published until 1861. These two works are discussed further in footnote 84 below.

3. THE TRANSMISSION OF BOUVET'S FIGURIST THEORIES TO EUROPE
THROUGH LEIBNIZ

The Jesuit Antoine Verjus (1632–1706) of Paris was responsible for putting Bouvet and Leibniz in touch with one another. Fr. Verjus was a close associate of François la Chaise (d. 1709), Jesuit confessor to Louis XIV. Just as there were procurators sent from the China Mission field to Europe, so too were there European-based procurators who served the Mission. It was in his role first as procurator of the missions in India and China (proc. miss. orient.) from 1678 to 1702 and then as procurator of the province of France (proc. Provinciae) in 1705–1706 that Verjus was in close communication with the French Jesuits of China[34]. Apparently after having been told about Leibniz by Christophe Brosseau (d. 1717), Verjus made his first direct contact[35]. This consisted of sending Leibniz ca. October 1692 in care of the Hanoverian diplomat A. Ballati (Balati) a packet of letters from Jesuits in China[36]. This packet contained physical and mathematical observations of the Jesuit missionaries[37]. Verjus appears also to have sent Leibniz prior to 1695 some additional letters from Jesuit missionaries in China[38]. It is quite likely that one of these various missionary letters was either written by or at least referred to Bouvet. If not, it is certain that Leibniz heard of Bouvet by 1695 because Verjus mentioned him by name in his letter to Leibniz of March 30th of that year[39]. In this context, Verjus cited Bouvet, along with Frs. Gerbillon and Visdelou, as supplying information on the languages of East Asia.

In his letter to Leibniz dated at Fontainebleau on October 18th 1697, Verjus began by saying that Bouvet had asked him to deliver a small book which had been presented to Louis XIV, namely, the *Portrait historique de l'Empereur de la Chine*[40]. Bouvet wrote a letter to Leibniz on the same day from Fontainebleau, which was apparently enclosed with Verjus' letter[41]. It was clearly Bou-

34 Dehergne, *Répertoire*, p. 317.
35 See Leibniz' letter to Christophe Brosseau, 18 (28) November 1692 in Leibniz, *Sämtliche Schriften* I; 8, 544.
36 Müller, *Eine Chronik*, p. 119.
37 See Leibniz' letter to the Landgrave Ernst, of Hessen-Rheinfels, mid-November 1692 in Leibniz, *Sämtliche Schriften* 1; 8, 187.
38 The evidence for this claim is in the first correspondence between Fr. Verjus and Leibniz, dated at Paris on March 30th 1695. In this letter, Verjus assumed that Leibniz has received some of the letters written by Jesuits in China ca. 1689–1690 and conveyed with the help of the Muscovites. (*Leibniz-Briefwechsel* 954, shett 2^v) However, Verjus' assumption may have been misplaced, since Leibniz in his letter of July 5th 1695 speaks of just recently receiving letters from the fathers in China returned by the Muscovites. (*Leibniz-Briefwechsel* 954, sheet 16^r)
39 *Leibniz-Briefwechsel* 954, sheet 4^r.
40 *Leibniz-Briefwechsel* 954, sheets 18^r-18^v.
41 *Leibniz-Briefwechsel* 105, sheets 1^r-2^v.

vet's first letter to Leibniz and was friendly and filled with apparently sincere flattery. Bouvet stated that he had thought of writing to Leibniz several times since his return to Europe. Whether his intention preceded his reading of Leibniz' *Novissima Sinica* (1697) is not clear, but Bouvet noted that he received this book through a "Mr. Gigues, doctor of the Sorbonne", with whom he doubts that Leibniz was acquainted. Bouvet wrote that he had read and re-read Leibniz' work with pleasure. Even allowing for the standard measure of flattery for that time, this remark surely must have seemed a compliment coming from someone with Bouvet's knowledge of China. Bouvet went on to state that he was sending a copy of his *Portrait*. The brief letter concluded with reference to the K'ang-hsi emperor's edict of toleration for Christianity (1692) and to the Chinese books that he had brought to King Louis. The tone of Bouvet's letter clearly invited further contact. Leibniz responded on December 2nd 1697 with a long letter to Verjus and an even longer letter to Bouvet which he asked Verjus to deliver[42].

Bouvet first presented his Figurist views to Leibniz in his letter of February 28th 1698, written from La Rochelle just before departing on his return voyage to China. The accommodation of *Confucius Sinarum philosophus* had emphasized Confucius and the Classics most closely associated with his name, i.e. the Four Books. By contrast, Bouvet's accommodation avoided dealing with Confucius by concentrating on the period of Chinese history prior to Confucius' time, that is, prior to 551 B.C.. The focus of Bouvet's concern was on the *I ching*. While the *I ching* had been incorporated into Confucianism as one of the Five Classics, the original corpus of this work was possibly the oldest Chinese text extant. If one sorts out the layers of later commentarial accretions, some of which became incorporated into the text, it is possible to treat the *I ching* as a pre-Confucian text. This is what Bouvet sought to do. One problem with this is that the oldest body of the text is so archaic and cryptic, that it is extremely difficult to comprehend without an interpretive commentary. What Bouvet was doing was really writing a new commentary. He looked upon his role as that of restoring the original and lost meaning to the text, a perspective which has been shared by most other Chinese commentators on the *I ching*. In brief, Bouvet reinterpreted the *I ching*, but he did so, at least in part, within a traditional Chinese pattern of reinterpretation.

If one can for the moment lay aside what has since been repudiated of Bouvet's ideas and try to read them from the perspective of an intelligent, educated seventeenth-century European with proto-sinological interests, what Bouvet wrote in this letter must have been extremely exciting. In fact, it still makes for intellectually exciting reading. Fu Hsi's name was associated with the invention of the whole and broken horizontal line units. As single-lined units, they may be treated as *yang* and *yin*. If expanded to double-lined units,

---

42 *Leibniz-Briefwechsel* 954, sheets 20^r-21^v and *Leibniz-Briefwechsel* 105, sheets 4^r-7^v.

they yield 4 possible permutations and combinations, i.e. ═ ══ ══ ══ . If expanded to triple-lined units, they yield 8 possible permutations and combinations which are referred to as the 8 trigrams (*pa kua*), i.e.☰ ☱ ☲ ☳ ☴ ☵ ☶ ☷.If these horizontal lines are expanded to 6-lined units or hexagrams, they yield 64 possible permutations and combinations. (As Bouvet noted in his letter to Leibniz, these diagrams were presented in Couplet's preface to *Confucius Sinarum philosophus*[43]. See plate 19) Although Fu Hsi's name had traditionally been more associated with the 8 trigrams than with the 64 hexagrams, Bouvet identified him with both.

In response to all the European speculation over finding a *Clavis Sinica*, Bouvet believed these diagrams revealed that Fu Hsi found a key not only to the Chinese language, but a "true key" to all knowledge. He wrote that Fu Hsi's diagrams "represent in a very simple and natural manner the principles of all the sciences"[44]. Bouvet noted that although the Chinese no longer understood the original significance of these diagrams, they revered them enormously. By re-establishing the original meaning of these *I ching* diagrams, one not only re-establishes the principles of true philosophy of the ancient Chinese and re-shapes the understanding of this nation to that of the true God, but one also "re-establishes the natural method which one should follow in all sciences"[45]. Although Bouvet was not explicit, the clear implication was that the last result, unlike the first two, would benefit not only China, but the whole world. For Bouvet, the philosophy of ancient China was the philosophy of the universal ancients, the forefathers of all mankind. What was so exciting about these diagrams was that they were vestiges of these ancients and so they allow us to look into the creations of humans whose minds were clearer than ours and whose lights of reason were purer than ours[46]. Consequently, Bouvet clarified at the outset that he was not bringing the revelation of true knowledge merely to the Chinese, but to Europeans as well.

In response to Leibniz' questions about finding a key to Chinese of the sort that Andreas Müller sought, Bouvet revealed that he too was a believer in the notion of a Primitive Language or, as he expressed it, "the writing utilized by savants before the Flood"[47]. Bouvet believed that it would be possible eventually to make a complete analysis of the Chinese characters and to reduce them to certain common denominators with the Egyptian hieroglyphs and so reveal the pre-diluvian universal language.

Bouvet gave a more detailed presentation of his Figurist views in a letter dated at Peking on November 8th 1700 and sent to Fr. Le Gobien at Paris with

43 *Leibniz-Briefwechsel* 105, sheet 10^v & Couplet, *Confucius*, pp. xl-xliv.
44 *Leibniz-Briefwechsel* 105, sheet 10^v.
45 *Leibniz-Briefwechsel* 105, sheet 11^r.
46 *Leibniz-Briefwechsel* 105, 11^r.
47 *Leibniz-Briefwechsel* 105, sheet 10^r.

the request that it be forwarded to Leibniz[48]. In this letter, Bouvet spoke of the *I ching* not only as the oldest written work of China, but also as the oldest written work in the world. Bouvet realized that a number of fellow missionaries regarded the *I ching* as filled with superstition and baseless foundations. In his view, the problem lay in the commentaries on the *I ching* which contained "many errors and a type of purely superstitious divination"[49]. Yet one could still perceive in these accretions "precious vestiges from the remains of the most ancient and excellent philosophy taught by the first patriarchs of the world to their descendants, and afterwards corrupted and almost completely obscured by the passage of time"[50].

Bouvet explained that the contemporary Chinese believed their ancestors of three or four thousand years before, i.e. ca. 2300–1300 B.C., to have possessed fields of knowledge such as arithmetic, music, astronomy-astrology and medicine to a supreme degree and that they still attempted to recover this knowledge. For Bouvet, the "Prince of Philosophers", i.e. Fu Hsi, developed the 64 hexagrams with their 384 constituent whole and broken lines, and these elements contained the principles of all these sciences[51]. Bouvet went on to say that he was basing his statement not only on the *I ching*, but on a general consensus of Chinese down through the ages and confirmed with marvelous agreement in many different Chinese books. Then Bouvet dropped one of those ideas which made Figurist views so extreme to so many Europeans: Fu Hsi was not the forefather merely of the Chinese, but of all mankind! Bouvet added: "The shape of the system of Fu Hsi was like a universal symbol, invented by some extraordinary genius of antiquity, like Hermes Trismegistus, in order to represent to the eyes the most abstract principles of all the sciences"[52].

In Bouvet's view, the commentaries on Fu Hsi's system written during the past 3,0000 years (since ca. 1300 B.C.) had only obscured and confused the original meaning. He specifically included Confucius as one of these misled commentators. Bouvet must have been aware that the Chou dynasty was traditionally dated from 1122 B.C. and that the founders of the Chou — King Wen and the Duke of Chou — were associated with certain interpretations of the *I ching*. Confucius built his philosophy on the founders of the Chou. Consequently, it appears that Bouvet was taking issue with the commentarial tradition on the *I ching* which dated from the origin of the Chou dynasty. It was only by laying aside this entire commentarial tradition and examining Fu Hsi's diagram mathematically that Bouvet claimed to have discovered Fu Hsi's universal nature and how his system embraced all fields of knowledge[53].

48 Kortholt, III, 5–14 or Dutens, IV, 146–151.
49 Kortholt, III, 6 or Dutens, IV, 147.
50 Kortholt, III, 7 or Dutens, IV, 147.
51 Kortholt, III, 7 or Dutens, IV, 147.
52 Kortholt, III, 8 or Dutens, IV, 147–148.
53 Kortholt, III, 8–9 or Dutens, IV, 148.

Bouvet revealed a mystical mathematical vision by which Fu Hsi's diagrams were seen as a numerological metaphysic (*métaphysique numéraire*) or general method of knowledge for reducing all things to the quantitative elements of number, weight and measure. According to Bouvet, the method of Fu Hsi's diagrams followed rules of three sorts of numerical progressions, as well as the rules of proportion and geometry and laws of statics. The result made rational the works of the Creator[54]. At this point, Bouvet stood before a chasm of heterodoxy.

The dividing line between the humanly knowable and unknowable in relationships to God is, in Christianity, a border zone characterized by the Mysteries. It is in the nature of a wall to attract climbers. Down through history, eyes have drifted toward that wall. Some have resisted its pull and others have attempted to climb it. To those who identify with rebels and define values essentially in individual terms, that divide will appear oppressive and crippling of human freedom and individual development. To others, some of whom have caught glimpses of the beyond, the divide is not only a good, but a necessary restraint on human *hubris*. One's response to what Bouvet and the Figurists and to other thinkers affected by the Ancient Theology such as Marcilio Ficino, Pico della Mirandola and Giordano Bruno were doing will tend to follow how one perceives this divide. To those champions of the individual, Bouvet's boldness may be applauded. To the orthodox believers, Bouvet's acts may be seen as warning signals of growing human pride.

Bouvet explained his mystical mathematical vision by saying that it consisted of a double set of numbers (i.e. represented by whole and broken lines?) in a geometrical plane and solid. They were joined together by means of all the consonances of music and by means of a perpetual harmony corresponding precisely with the 64 hexagrams and 384 whole and broken lines of the "figure"[55]. These numbers represented the periods (of creation?) with all the harmony of celestial movements. In addition, they represented all the principles needed to explain the natures and properties of things, the cause of their generation and corruption. Then in an extremely Pythagorean manner which joined number with music, Bouvet stated that these numbers would furnish the basis to recover the lost music of both China and the Greeks. Bouvet's reference to the music of China, lost fifteen or sixteen centuries before, referred to the loss of the ancient Chinese Classical text on music. Confucius, whose view of music was widely accepted in China, regarded music as having an important relationship to human morality. But Confucius did not posit the mathematical association with music of the Pythagoreans.

---

54 Kortholt, III, 9 or Dutens, IV, 148.

55 Based on the hexagram figure which Bouvet later sent to Leibniz, one can probably identify this figure with the *Hsien-t'ien tzu-hsü* hexagram order portrayed in illustration 20.

Bouvet explained this lost music — he appeared not to distinguish between the ancient music of China and Greece — to contain three systems or scales which were the diatonic, chromatic and enharmonic[56]. The diatonic scale consisted of five whole tones and two semi-tones and is represented today by the white keys on a piano. The chromatic scale, which in modified form has become the prevalent scale in the twentieth century, employed half-tones to yield an octave with twelve tones. The enharmonic scale was obscure and Bouvet noted that it was unknown in his own day. Possibly it referred to the scale of ancient Greek musical theory which used quarter-tones.

Bouvet identified the numbers of the system of Fu Hsi with those of Plato and suggested a possible accord with the numerical system of the ancient Hebrews. Bouvet argued that if Fu Hsi's numerical system agreed with the numbers of the Sabbath (7?) and of the jubilee (50) years of the Hebrews as well as with the mysterious numbers of the ancient Kabbala — he excluded the modern Kabbala as being filled with superstitions and errors — then the importance of Fu Hsi's system would be confirmed.

Bouvet's distinction between the "ancient" and "modern" Kabbala is a bit confusing. The term "Kabbala", which itself means "tradition", is generally treated as a medieval movement[57]. Perhaps the earliest Kabbalistic treatise is the twelfth century Provençal work, *Bahir* (Brightness), which incorporated the Jewish creation mysticism of *Sefer Yetsirah* (The book of formation) and suggested that God created the world out of 32 mysterious paths of wisdom, that is, the ten basic numbers and 22 letters of the Hebrew alphabet. The ten basic numbers, called *Sefiroth*, implied that the denary (10) system was primary to the structure of the universe. If by "ancient" and "modern", Bouvet did not mean medieval and post-1450, respectively, then it is unlikely that he was referring to what we presently know as the Kabbala and was probably referring to ancient Hebrew philosophy. On the other hand, Bouvet was not unique to his age in making a distinction between the true Kabbala and a popular Kabbala of later and fallacious origins. Leibniz, for example, referred to this distinction in a manuscript (ca. 1689) dealing with the General Characteristic[58]. Clearly, Bouvet betrayed a hesitancy and lack of knowledge toward the Kabbala. For him, the ancient Hebrew philosophy was the philosophy "of Moses and of the ancient patriarchs, who received their doctrine by means of a revelation from the Creator"[59].

56 Kortholt, III, 9–10 or Dutens, IV, 148–149.
57 I draw here from Joseph L. Blau, *The story of Jewish philosophy* (New York, 1962) pp. 89–121.
58 See Leibniz, *Leibniz: philosophical papers & letters* Leroy E. Loemker, trs. & ed. (Dordrecht, Holland, 1969) p. 221.
59 Kortholt, III, 11 or Dutens, IV, 149.

Bouvet applied his theory to practical mission problems by saying that those missionaries like the opponent of Jesuit accommodation, Maigrot of the Missions Étrangères, who focused on the study of Chinese books dated after the time of Confucius, were misguided. These later books all reflected an age which had, for the most part, lost the principles of Fu Hsi's philosophy or, as Bouvet put it, "almost lost the distinct knowledge of the true God and of the genuine cult of which their first fathers used to honor"[60]. Consequently, Bouvet argued that these misguided missionaries, by seeing only part of the whole of Chinese history, falsely concluded that Chinese culture had always been superstitious and atheistic. Bouvet suggested that a small work drawing the connection between the "true philosophy" of ancient China and the "true religion" of contemporary Christianity would be pleasing to the K'ang-hsi emperor and, if passed on by the emperor to the "savants of the imperial college", i.e. Hanlin academicians, would soon become an intellectual current spread throughout China[61]. Such was Jesuit conversion from the top down!

Bouvet's response to Leibniz' explanation of his binary system was made in his letter of November 4th 1701[62]. Bouvet indicated at the beginning of this letter that he had previously heard of Leibniz's binary system from certain friends. One of these friends was most probably the Jesuit and China missionary Claudio Filippo Grimaldi (1638–1712) to whom Leibniz had communicated his binary system in a letter of December 20th 1696[63]. But the direct stimulus for Bouvet's enthusiastic response was Leibniz' letter of February 15th 1701 which contained an extensive description of Leibniz' binary system[64]. Bouvet's letter reflected an intense stimulation which had come from his discovery that an eminent European savant had independently developed a mathematical system which confirmed his Figurist views. Bouvet was truly excited over this "marvelous similarity" that Leibniz' dyadic and his own views had with the true philosophy of ancient China[65]. Bouvet saw a particular link in this forgotten ancient philosophy between the science of numbers and "physics or the science which teaches the principles and causes of generation and of corruption of all things"[66].

60 Kortholt, III, 12 or Dutens, IV, 149.
61 Kortholt, III, 13–14 or Dutens, IV, 150–151.
62 *Leibniz-Briefwechsel* 105, sheets 21^r-29. This letter has been edited by Ludovici Dutens and published with deletions from sheets 21^r and 24^r-24^v. See Dutens IV, 152–168.
63 *Leibniz-Briefwechsel* 330, sheets 15^r-18^r.
64 *Leibniz-Briefwechsel* 728, sheets 94^r-96^v. For reasons unknown to this author, Leibniz' letter to Bouvet of 15 February 1701 is not filed with the Leibniz-Bouvet correspondence, but with the correspondence file of Leibniz and François Pinsson des Riolles.
65 *Leibniz-Briefwechsel* 105, sheet 21^v & Dutens, IV, 152.
66 *Leibniz-Briefwechsel* 105, sheet 21^v & Dutens, IV, 152.

Bouvet was particularly impressed by the fact that Leibniz' "numerical calculus" reduced the generation of numbers and the production of things to a common mathematical basis and used the same analogy to explain both. Bouvet believed that this reproduced the state of knowledge in ancient China where he believed all knowledge was based on a system similar to Leibniz' numerical table of progression used in explaining his binary mathematics. Leibniz' dyadic was based on using two units instead of the usual ten units found in the denary or decimal system. Instead of using 0, 1, 2, 3, 4, 5, 6, 7, 8, 9, Leibniz used only 0 and 1. In terms of equivalents, the denary 0 equaled 0 in the binary system, the denary 1 equaled 1 in the binary system, but since there are only two units in the binary system, these elements must be repeated. Consequently, the denary 2 = 10 in the binary system, the denary 3 = 11 in the binary system, 4 = 100, 5 = 101, 6 = 110, 7= 111, 8 = 1000, 9 = 1001, 10 = 1010, 32 = 100000, 62 = 111110 and 63 = 111111. While the binary system on first sight appears much more cumbersome than the denary system, the number of units in each system is equally arbitrary and for certain usages, e.g. computers, the binary system is more efficient because of the greater simplicity of its basic components.

Fu Hsi's diagrams also contained only two basic components: the broken and whole lines. Consequently, if one lets the broken line ‐ ‐ represent 0 and the whole line — represent 1 and if one also counts the lines of the diagrams from the top down, it yields remarkable similarities to Leibniz' dyadic. For example, the trigram ☰ would yield 000, ☱ = 001, ☲ = 010, ☳ = 011, ☴ = 101, ☵ = 110, ☷ = 111. Although the above is not a commonly found order with the trigrams, the *Hsien-t'ien tzu-hsü* (literally: Prior to Heaven Order) or Natural Order of Hexagrams is such that both the circular and square arrangements of the hexagrams yield a perfect correspondence to a binary system. The copy of the Natural Order of Hexagrams that Bouvet sent to Leibniz with his letter of November 4th 1701 is found in plate 20[67]. Of course, there are other orders of the *I ching* diagrams to which the correspondence does not apply. Furthermore, the traditional Chinese manner of reading such a diagram was from the bottom up rather than from the top down. Such a reversal of the order of counting lines would complicate, but not invalidate the correspondence in principle. Withal, the correspondences between the hexagrams and the dyadic were remarkable and neither Bouvet nor Leibniz was in a frame of mind to disregard them as coincidental.

The role of theory, and even of mysticism, frequently outruns that of experiment in the work of natural scientists. Johannis Kepler (1571–1630), to name one of the more prominent examples of this type, was a dreamer whose

---

67 The similarities between Leibniz' binary system and the hexagrams in the context of the Leibniz-Bouvet correspondence is treated in greater detail by the author in *Leibniz & Confucianism*, pp. 39–68.

mathematics was inextricably mixed in his mind with astrology. Kepler reflected the Pythagorean number mysticism which was such an important part of the development of the seventeenth century Scientific Revolution. This number mysticism sought to reduce mathematically the multiplicity of external phenomena to a simple equation which was not only universal in its application, but beautiful to behold. Bouvet reflected this same Pythagorean impulse when, after extensive meditation on the lines of the diagrams devoted to unraveling their mystery, believed he had "caught a glimpse of the economy, beauty and extensiveness of this science"[68].

Bouvet merged his attempt to recover the understanding of nature and of all knowledge possessed by the ancient patriarchs with Leibniz' plan for a Universal Characteristic, i.e. an exact language consisting of characteristic symbols which correspond to concepts and which may be used in the way that arithmetical signs serve for numbers and algebraic signs for abstract qualities. Bouvet regarded Leibniz' notion of a Universal Characteristic as embracing the idea of ancient hieroglyphs, of the Kabbala of the Hebrews and the characters of Fu Hsi[69]. All of these are languages. (Bouvet explained that the Chinese regarded Fu Hsi as the inventor of the Chinese language.) Although Leibniz believed in the historical possibility of a Primitive Language, the ancient Kabbala and Pythagorean arithmetic, he regarded the search for a Universal Characteristic more as an invention for the present rather than a rediscovery from the past[70]. But Bouvet's thought patterns were very oriented toward antiquity and consequently he spoke to Leibniz of "the shortest means of reestablishing this ancient characteristic"[71]. Bouvet's reconstruction of Fu Hsi's system combined the Pythagorean-Platonic tendency toward mathematics with the Aristotelian-Thomistic tendency toward classification. Bouvet linked the "double geometrical progression" of the 64 hexagrams with the genealogical unfolding by genera and species, working from the universal down to the particular[72]. Bouvet likened the tracing out of the divisions and subdivisions to going from the trunk to the branches of a genealogical tree. The point, the simplest sign imaginable, was used to symbolize unity as well as the first principle and transcendent being, i.e. God.

Two genera immediately arise from the first principle — perfection and imperfection or what is complete and incomplete or the faultless and defective. These are represented by Bouvet with two dots and three dots, respectively, or by a whole and broken line, respectively. Thus a whole line represents the

68 *Leibniz-Briefwechsel* 105, sheet 22^I or Dutens, IV, 154.
69 *Leibniz-Briefwechsel* 105, sheet 22^r or Dutens, IV, 154–155.
70 See "On the Universal Science: Characteristic," in Leibniz, *Monadology and other philosophical essays* Paul & Anne Schrecker, trs. (New York, 1965) p. 12.
71 *Leibniz-Briefwechsel* 105, sheet 22^v or Dutens, IV, 155.
72 *Leibniz-Briefwechsel* 105, sheet 22^v or Dutens, IV, 155.

universal genus of things or perfect (i.e. complete) ideas. Following the "double geometrical progression", just as 1 produced 2, now 2 will produce 4. In this case, 2 superior genera produce 4 subordinate genera; 4 will in turn produce 8 further subordinate genera. Bouvet applied the abstract progression to the concrete example of color. Light and darkness are seen as the two universal principles. Light in its most intense degree will produce the genus white, in a less intense degree it will produce yellow. Darkness or shadow in its most intense degree will produce black and in a less intense degree, blue. Thus, white, yellow, blue and black are presented as the "four elementary colors"[73]. Although their manifestation will yield a qualitative difference, the more fundamental cause of this difference is reducible to differing degrees of itensity, that is, quantitative differences.Following the geometrical progression, the 4 elementary colors will alternate and transform into 8 colors.

Eight is the number of the trigrams and these are the most fundamental figures of Fu Hsi's diagrams which, according to Bouvet, the Chinese have regarded as the foundation of their sciences. The fourth degree of generation will yield 16 quadragrams (i.e. diagrams consisting of 4 lines, each of which is either whole or broken, and will yield 16 possible permutations and combinations). The 5th degree will yield 32 pentagrams and the 6th degree will yield 64 hexagrams (i.e. a diagram consisting of 6 lines, each of which is either whole or broken, and will yield 64 possible permutations and combinations). At each level of generation, the difference between it and the previous level is, most fundamentally, a difference of degree. Bouvet explained the absence of 4-lined and 5-lined diagrams in the *I ching* by suggesting that a jump is made from the 8 trigrams to the 64 hexagrams because of the finer mathematical quality of 8 being multiplied by itself. Bouvet pointed out that, besides color, the system may be applied to the analysis of other qualities such as temperature and humidity such that a precise analysis emerges[74]. In the context of the material in his letter of November 4th 1701 to Leibniz, Bouvet argued that Fu Hsi was not Chinese and was never in China. Rather he was said to be the same figure who had been reported in other ancient and eastern cultures as Zoroaster, Mercurius [Hermes] Trismegistus and Ennoch[75]. Clearly then, Bouvet revealed himself to be a believer in Hermes Trismegistus and the Ancient Theology nearly a century after its textual foundations had been shaken.

When in 1768 Ludovicus Dutens published three of Bouvet's letters to Leibniz, he deleted three parts of Bouvet's letter of November 4th 1701. The most significant deletion involved one and one-half folio-sized manuscript pages

73 *Leibniz-Briefwechsel* 105, sheet 22^v or Dutens, IV, 156.
74 *Leibniz-Briefwechsel* 105, sheet 23^r or Dutens, IV, 157.
75 *Leibniz-Briefwechsel* 105, sheets 23^r-23^v or Dutens, IV, 158.

Antiquiſſi-
mus Sinarum
liber.

Habent Sinæ librum YE KING dictum, qui totus in his figuris explicandis eſt; magni apud eos pretij ob res arcanas, quas illic la-tére ſibi perſuadent. Mihi quædam philoſophia myſtica videtur eſſe Pythagoricæque perſimilis, etſi multis ſeculis prior; quippe quæ ini-tium habuit à F o H I o, de quo dicemus infrà. Multa ſunt in eo libro de generatione & corruptione, de fato, de aſtrologià judiciarià, de quibuſdam principijs naturalibus. Sed ea jejunè diſputantur & exi-

Plate 18. One of the earliest depictions of the 64 hexagrams of the Chinese classic, the *I ching*, to be published in Europe, from Martino Martini's *Sinicae Historiae decas prima* (Munich, 1658) p. 6. Courtesy of the Niedersächsische Landesbibliothek Hannover.

Tabula sexaginta quatuor Figurarum,
seu Liber mutationum *Ye kim* dictus.

1. Cælum. / Cælum.	2. Terra. / Terra.	3. Aqua. / Tonitrua.	4. Montes. / Aqua.	5. Aqua. / Cælum.	6. Cælum. / Aqua.	7. Terra. / Aqua.	8. Aqua. / Terra.
9. Venti. / Cælum.	10. Cælum. / Aquæ m.	11. Terra. / Cælum.	12. Cælum. / Terra.	13. Cælum. / Ignis.	14. Ignis. / Cælum.	15. Terra. / Montes.	16. Tonitrua. / Terra.
17. Aquæ m. / Tonitrua.	18. Montes. / Venti.	19. Terra. / Aquæ m.	20. Venti. / Terra.	21. Ignis. / Tonitrua.	22. Montes. / Ignis.	23. Montes. / Terra.	24. Terra. / Tonitrua.
25. Cælum. / Tonitrua.	26. Montes. / Cælum.	27. Montes. / Tonitrua.	28. Aquæ m. / Venti.	29. Aqua. / Aqua.	30. Ignis. / Ignis.	31. Aquæ m. / Montes.	32. Tonitrua. / Venti.
33. Cælum. / Montes.	34. Tonitrua. / Cælum.	35. Ignis. / Terra.	36. Terra. / Ignis.	37. Venti. / Ignis.	38. Ignis. / Aquæ m.	39. Aqua. / Montes.	40. Tonitrua. / Aqua.
41. Montes. / Aquæ m.	42. Venti. / Tonitrua.	43. Aquæ m. / Cælum.	44. Cælum. / Venti.	45. Aquæ m. / Terra.	46. Terra. / Venti.	47. Aquæ m. / Aqua.	48. Aqua. / Venti.
49. Aquæ m. / Ignis.	50. Ignis. / Venti.	51. Tonitrua. / Tonitrua.	52. Montes. / Montes.	53. Venti. / Montes.	54. Tonitrua. / Aquæ m.	55. Tonitrua. / Ignis.	56. Ignis. / Montes.
57. Venti. / Venti.	58. Aquæ m. / Aquæ m.	59. Venti. / Aqua.	60. Aqua. / Aquæ m.	61. Venti. / Aquæ m.	62. Tonitrua. / Montes.	63. Aqua. / Ignis.	64. Ignis. / Aqua.

Has

Plate 19. The Empirical Hexagram Order (*Hou-t'ien tzu-hsü*), a table of 64 hexagrams from the *I ching,* found in *Confucius Sinarum philosophus* (Paris, 1687), p. xliv. Courtesy of the Niedersächsische Landesbibliothek Hannover.

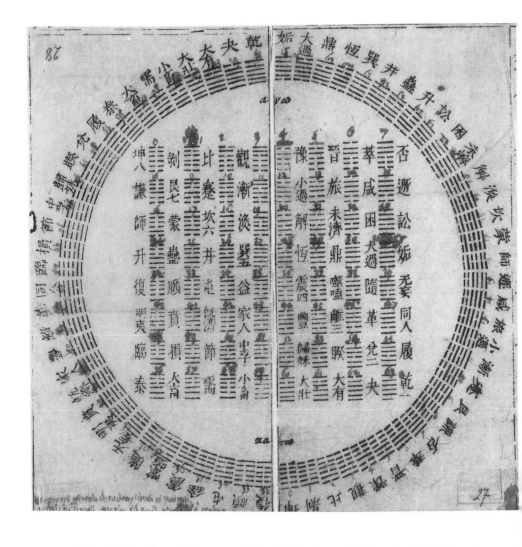

Plate 20. The Natural Hexagramm Order (*Hsien-t'ien tzu-hsü*), enclosed with Bouvet's letter to Leibniz of 4 November 1701 (Leibniz Briefwechsel 105, sheets 27–28). Courtesy of the Leibniz-Archiv, Niedersächsische Landesbibliothek Hannover.

which contained some very radical Figurist views[76]. In this deleted passage, Bouvet claimed that the ancient Chinese had a knowledge of God as the Creator and Principle of all natural things and of the mystery of the Trinity. Furthermore, Bouvet wrote that it could be confirmed by numerous passages from their ancient books that they also had a knowledge of sin, of the punishment of rebellious angels, of the longevity of the Patriarchs, of the corruption of human nature by sin (i.e. Adam's fall from grace), of the Flood, of the future Incarnation of Jesus Christ, and of Salvation. In short, Bouvet stated that the ancient Chinese had a very complete understanding of the Divinity. These editorial deletions possibly represented a tempering of Leibniz' correspondence by Dutens for the anti-Jesuit element of the reading public of 1768, which was only five years before the suppression of the Society of Jesus in 1773.

Interestingly enough, Christian Kortholt had omitted this letter entirely in his publication of Leibniz materials in 1738. However, Kortholt did publish Bouvet's letter to Leibniz of November 8th 1702 which began with a somewhat vaguer and slightly less radical presentation of Bouvet's Figurism[77]. Dutens reprinted this letter of November 8th 1702 from Kortholt's edition without deleting the opening passage on Figurism[78]. In this letter, Bouvet spoke of new discoveries[79]. He stated that his further study of the ancient Chinese texts had revealed an easy and natural path leading the spirit of the Chinese not only to an understanding of the Creator and of natural religion, but also to "Jesus Christ, [the Creator's] unique son and to those truths of the greatest difficulty in Christianity"[80]. More specifically, Bouvet claimed that almost the whole of the true religion was contained in the Chinese Classical books: the mysteries of the Incarnation of the Word, of the life and death of the Savior and of Jesus' ministry were contained in a prophetic manner.

Bouvet claimed that there were two sources of this ancient Chinese repository of sacred knowledge: (1) the hieroglyphic significance of the Chinese characters and (2) the contents of the Classics. Bouvet believed that both sources derived from an anterior source which predated the Chinese[81]. These vestiges existed in a contemporary Chinese form because the Chinese had been more careful than other nations in preserving them. (Such a view definitely diminished the uniqueness of the Jews and it was just such a view that fanned the flames of the

---

76 *Leibniz-Briefwechsel* 105, sheets 24^r-24^v. The other principal deletions of Bouvet's letter made by Dutens are from sheet 21^r (paragraphs 1–3) and sheet 26^v (the last eleven lines).

77 Kortholt, III, 16–18.

78 Dutens, IV, 165–166.

79 The manuscript of Bouvet's letter to Leibniz of November 8th 1702 appears to be lost. There remains only the published version in Kortholt, III, 15–22 or Dutens IV, 165–168.

80 Kortholt, III, 16 or Dutens, IV, 165.

Rites Controversy.) Bouvet felt that the Chinese treatment of the chronological period between Fu Hsi and Confucius had become filled with myths and fictions. These, like the myths of the ancient Greeks, should be subjected to interpretation — in this case drawing from the spirit of the original heritage and a hieroglyphic analysis of the characters[82]. Bouvet was aware that a great deal more study of the Classics and characters was needed to confirm his ideas. He proposed an extensive project for doing so and doubtless sought to interest Leibniz in participating. He clearly succeeded in arousing Leibniz' interest, as the latter indicated in his letters of 1703 (?), 1704, 1705, 1706 (?) and 1707. But after his letter of November 8th 1702, there was a curious lapse in Bouvet's letters although Bouvet remained active in China until his death there in 1730. It is probable that Jesuit attempts to discourage further public discussion of Rites Controversy reached China as well and this is one possible explanation of Bouvet's silence.

We have gone slightly beyond the year 1700 in treating Bouvet's Figurism because the correspondence between Bouvet and Leibniz during 1701 and 1702 represents the culmination of ideas which were developed essentially in the seventeenth century. After his last letter to Leibniz in 1702, Bouvet continued to labor over his Figurist theories with the encouragement of the K'ang-hsi emperor[83]. Yet in spite of sustained study of the *I ching*, Bouvet produced no works of substance in his later years[84].

81 Kortholt, III, 17 or Dutens, IV, 166.

82 Kortholt, III, 18 or Dutens IV, 166—167.

83 With the encouragement of the K'ang-hsi emperor, Bouvet was able to devote much of his time to studying the ancient Chinese texts, particularly the *I ching*, and refining his ideas on Hermetism as it applied to China. When in 1711, the Emperor generously asked Bouvet if there was a talented Jesuit in the provinces who might assist Bouvet in his research on the *I ching*, Bouvet answered with the name of Jean-François Foucquet, who was then called by imperial decree from Kiangsi province to the capital in a matter of months. See Witek, "Jean-François Foucquet," p. 123 and *Controversial ideas in China and in Europe,* p. 143f. Until 1720 when Fr. Foucquet was recalled to Europe, he remained at the palace working with Bouvet on the *I ching.* See Fang Hao, II, 281. Some of the fruits of Bouvet's and Foucquet's study of the *I ching* which they presented to the K'ang-hsi emperor are contained in a document in Chinese in ten segments, only two of which are dated (1713 & 1716) in the Biblioteca Vaticana, Borgia Cinese 439. This document has been reprinted in Fang Hao, II, 281—286.

84 Through this research effort, Bouvet was able to present the K'ang-hsi emperor with his *I-ching tsung-chih* (A summary interpretation of the book of changes). See Fang Hao, II, 282—283. As with Bouvet's work, *Ku-chin ching-t'ien-chien* (1706), there seem to be both Chinese and Latin texts of this work. The Latin text is entitled *"Idea generalis doctrinae libri Ye kim,"* whose rather instructive subtitle is *"brevis expositio totius Systematis philosophiae hieroglyphicae, in antiquissimis Sinarum libris contentae."* The manuscript is only 6 1/2 pages in length and is signed by Bouvet. It is found in the Bibliotheque nationale Paris, Fonds fr. no. 17.239. But in comparison with his younger fellow Figurist, Fr. Prémare, Bouvet's literary production was unprolific and disappointing to those interested in studying the results of his research.

In contrast to our knowledge of the extensive reliance of the Jesuits upon the commentary of Chang Chü-cheng in translating the Four Books for *Confucius Sinarum philosophus*, to date, little evidence has been uncovered that Bouvet was substantially influenced by the work of Chinese scholars on the *I ching*[85]. Instead, the influence of Bouvet's European background and particularly Hermetism appears to have been far more significant. And yet, Fr. Witek recently discovered a point of contact between Bouvet and Chinese scholarship. Bouvet's theories on the *I ching* were conveyed to the Grand Secretary Li Kuang-ti (1642–1718) by the K'ang-hsi emperor and Li responded sympathetically in a memorial dated August 10th 1712 which Bouvet read and cited[86]. In spite of repeated claims by the Jesuits in *Confucius Sinarum philosophus* that they were drawing upon a Chinese commentary, it was not until recently that this commentary was identified[87]. Bouvet claimed that he was drawing upon ancient

The most substantive Figurist work was produced by Joseph Henry-Marie de Prémare and entitled "*Selecta quaedam vestigia praeciporum Christianae Relligionis dogmatum, ex antiquis Sinarum libris eruta*" (Selected vestiges of certain preeminent Christian religious dogmas extracted from ancient books of the Chinese). This manuscript was completed by Fr. Prémare in Canton in 1724, but the Rites Controversy delayed its publication until 1878 in Paris. The monumental task of translation and editing this work of several hundred pages was done by A. Bonnetty and Paul Perny and published as *Vestiges des principaux dogmes chrétiens tirés des anciens livres chinois*. A much more modest work by Prémare, but with important Figurist implications is his *Lettre sur le monotheisme des Chinois,* composed at Canton in 1728, but not published until 1862 in Paris when the manuscript was discovered in the then Bibliothèque Imperiale of Paris and edited by Jean Pierre Guillaume Pauthier. The latter work is treated by this writer in the article "The reconciliation of Neo-Confucianism with Christianity in the writings of Joseph de Prémare, S.J. ."

The bibliographies of Bouvet's works found in Pfister and Sommervogel appear incomplete and not all of the works listed there had been recovered at the time of their composition of these bibliographies, e.g. the manuscript of Bouvet's small Chinese-French dictionary (Pfister, p. 438). A Chinese title not listed in either Pfister or Sommervogel is *T'ien-hsüeh pen-wen* (Basic writings on the Heavenly Teaching, i.e. Christianity). See Hsü Tsung-tse, *Ming-ch'ing chien Yeh-su-hui shih-i chu t'i-yao,* p. 399. A more recent bibliography of Bouvet's works may be found in Janette C. Gatty's *Voiage de Siam du Père Bouvet* (Leiden, 1963). Mme. Gatty also lists Bouvet's works with comments in her essay "Les recherches de Joachim Bouvet (1656–1730)" in *Colloque international de sinologie, Chantilly, 1974* (Paris, 1976).

85 See the author's *Leibniz & Confucianism,* pp. 62–65.

86 See Witek, *Controversial ideas in China and Europe,* pp. 204–206. In regard to the relationship between the Jesuits Bouvet and Foucquet and the Chinese studies on the *I ching* then being produced by Hu Wei (1633–1714) and Li Kuang-ti, compare Fr. Witek's *Controversial ideas in China and Europe,* pp. 172–173 with the author's *Leibniz & Confucianism,* pp. 62–65.

87 For more information on the Jesuits' use of Chang Chü-cheng's commentary on the Four Books in compiling *Confucius Sinarum philosophus,* see the complementary articles by Knud Lundbaek and this author in the *China Mission studies (1550–1800) bulletin* 3 (1981): 2–22.

Chinese sources and in spite of the lack of evidence, it would be premature to conclude at this point in our understanding that Bouvet did not rely upon Chinese commentarial sources.

CHAPTER X

PROPAGANDIZERS AND CRITICS OF JESUIT ACCOMMODATION

1. THE BACKGROUND TO FR. LE COMTE'S *NOUVEAUX MÉMOIRES SUR L'ETAT PRÉSENT DE LA CHINE*

After the anti-Christian persecution of 1664–1668 and the recall of most of the Jesuits from exile in Canton in 1671, the leading Jesuit, Ferdinand Verbiest (1623–1688) was struck by the rich harvests which awaited the Mission in China, could they but find the right missionaries[1]. Fr. Verbiest expressed these thoughts in several letters to Europe, one of which is said to have impressed Louis XIV. Besides, the French king saw a means of increasing the influence of France while breaking the shaky Portuguese monopoly of ecclesiastical patronage. He and his advisers saw that the most effective political means of achieving this would be to capitalize on the scientific interests of the age, which were manifested in the widely publicized activities of the Académie des Sciences. For King Louis, the Académie could serve ably as a vehicle for science, God and France. Consequently, he ordered the mission organized in what was one of the earliest uses of a scientific and religious mission for the political interests of a modern nation-state.

The Jesuits were requested to supply six of their number with appropriate scientific skills for this purpose. The Jesuit Jean de Fontaney (1643–1710) had distinguished himself as a teacher of mathematics and astronomy at the Collège Louis le Grand and by publishing several pieces on astronomical subjects in the widely read *Journal des sçavans* and *Mémoires de l'académie des sciences*[2]. Fr. Fontaney was assigned the task of finding other skilled young Jesuits and under his leadership the following missionaries were enrolled: Bouvet, Jean-François Gerbillon, (1647–1707), Louis-Daniel Le Comte (1655–1728), Guy Tachard (1648–1712) and Claude de Visdelou (1656–1737). All were members of the Collège Louis le Grand and therefore had a special identification with the French king. Prior to departing, Fontaney and three other Jesuits were admitted to the Académie des Sciences and were equipped with instruments to

---

1 Pfister, pp. 420–423.

2 In describing the origin and preparation of the first French mission to China, I rely upon Gatty, *Voiage*, p. 14, and Fr. Witek's account in his *Controversial ideas in China and Europe*, pp. 23–39, to expand and correct information found in Pfister, pp. 420–424 & 431–432 and in the article on Bouvet by Henry M. Brock in the *Catholic encyclopedia* (New York, 1907) II, 723.

be used in collecting astronomical and geographical information[3]. The group departed on the *Oyseau* from Brest in March 1685. The voyage was long and included a complicated stopover at Siam where Fr. Tachard remained. The group — now reduced to five in number — continued on and first touched Chinese territory at Ningpo in July of 1687. Nearly three years after their departure from Europe, they arrived in Peking on February 7th 1688, ten days after the death of the man who had helped to inspire their mission — Verbiest.

In their assignments, Bouvet and Gerbillon were ordered to remain at the court in Peking while Fontaney went to Nanking. Fr. Le Comte was sent first to Kiangchow in Shansi province with Visdelou. After a few months, he proceeded on alone to Sian in Shensi province where he worked as a proselytizer for two years[4]. Soon afterward, national rivalry surfaced at Macao and the Portuguese attempted to sabotage the French missions by intercepting money and books sent from France. The French missions outside of Peking consequently became so impoverished that they were abandoned and in 1690 Fontaney, accompanied by Le Comte, sought redress in Canton. Le Comte was assigned the task of returning to France to inform their superiors of the situation[5]. He departed at the end of 1691, after having been in China for only three and one-half years. Le Comte told his story in France and Rome and then returned to France where he became confessor to the Duchess of Bordeaux. He never returned to China, but was to become one of the prime figures in that phase of the Chinese Rites Controversy which climaxed at Paris in 1700.

Fr. Le Comte entered this controversy publicly with the publication of his *Nouveaux mémoires sur l'etat présent de la Chine* at Paris in 1696 in two volumes. It was unfortunate, though perhaps inevitable, given the polemical nature of the controversy, that the two works most intensely involved in the Rites Controversy debate at this period in France were Le Comte's *Nouveaux mémoires* and Charles Le Gobien's *Histoire de l'edit de la Chine en faveur de la religion chrestienne* (Paris, 1698). Fr. Le Gobien had never been to China and Le Comte's mere three and one-half years there were insufficient preparation for the role of a prime spokesman for Jesuit accommodation.

It is doubtful that Le Comte was literate in Chinese or had first-hand acquaintance with Chinese literature. His work in Shensi does not seem to have given him the opportunities for study and association with literati that it gave to others who worked in the provinces. This situation was shaped by the short period of time he was there, but Le Comte's intellectual character also played a role. He appears to have been far less intellectually distinguished than the other Jesuits of the first French China mission. It is true that the value of his astronom-

3 I am indebted to Fr. Witek for pointing out this information as found in Institut de France, *Index biographique des membres et correspondants de l'Académie des Sciences (1666–1697)* (Paris, 1968) pp. 206–207.
4 Pfister, pp. 440–441 & Dehergne, *Répertoire*, pp. 146–147.

ical observations made on the journey to China and later in China has been recognized. For example, Mr. Needham states that the best drawings of six of the astronomical instruments with which Verbiest outfitted the Peking observatory in 1669–1674 are to be found in Le Comte's *Nouveaux mémoires*[6]. Le Comte also sketched a map of the river systems between Nanking and Canton as well as a road guide from Ningpo to Peking and from Peking to Chiang-chou[7]. But his written works did not compare with the scientific treatises of Fontaney and Gerbillon nor with the sinological competency of Visdelou nor with the creative pieces by Bouvet. Le Comte's limited list of written works were popular and polemical in tone and centered primarily around the Rites Controversy[8]. Le Comte's major work, *Nouveaux mémoires*, reflected this popular tone. It was organized in the manner so favored by his age, namely, long letters addressed to apparently prominent persons. The letters emphasized travel literature, such as the journey from Sian to Peking and the climate and geography of China, and contained a brief treatment of the Chinese government, history, culture, language, religions and the Christian mission in China.

Although the *Nouveaux mémoires* was a two-volume work of over 500 pages per volume, the octavo size and large typeface reduced it to popular dimensions. Its untechnical tone and interesting illustrations reinforced this "bestseller" character. But contrary to what certain anti Jesuits believed, the work was *not* filled with falsehoods and was more sophisticated in its treatment of Chinese culture than were most works published fifty years earlier in Europe. The problem was that this should have been one of the *last* works on which to base a serious debate over Jesuit accommodation in China. Neither its popular tone nor the limited experience of the author in China allowed it the deeper treatment which Rites Controversy issues demanded. This situation was not merely Le Comte's fault. It was the result of an intellectual climate which had become so exacerbated by theological and political controversy that source materials were chosen with an eye to triumph rather than truth. Four years passed after the publication of Le Comte's *Nouveaux mémoires* before it was brought before the Sorbonne faculty for examination. By that time, the work had gone through at least ten editions and had been translated into English, German and Italian[9]. And — as with best-sellers today — public censure did not hurt the work's popularity as two more editions were published at Paris in the following year.

5 Pfister, pp. 428 & 449 and Witek, *Controversial ideas*, p. 68n.
6 Louis Le Comte, *Nouveaux mémoires sur l'état présent de la Chine* 2 vols. (Paris, 1696) I, 143–147; Pfister, p. 440; & Needham, III, 451n.
7 Nesselrath & Reinbothe, *Das Neueste von China*, p. 50.
8 Sommervogel, II, 1356–1362 & Pfister, pp. 441–443.
9 Sommervogel, II, 1356–1357.

2. THE THEOLOGICAL CONTROVERSY OVER *NOUVEAUX MÉMOIRES*

The climax of the Paris phase of the Rites Controversy was set when Fr. Brisacier, head of the Société des Missions Étrangères, retracted his approbation of Michel Le Tellier's *Defense des nouveaux Chrétiens* (Paris, 1696). The Jesuit Le Tellier was an extremely controversial figure. As confessor to Louis XIV, he represented a strongly political thread in this story. Critics of the Jesuits had always been extremely suspicious and jealous of the Jesuit access to power through proximity to the throne. This was a pattern of access reproduced in more or less successful fashion in France, China and many other lands where Jesuits were to be found. In the last years of Louix XIV's rule, Fr. Le Tellier was thought by many to exert a sinister influence. Consequently, he symbolized the most hated of Jesuit practices.

With Fr. Brisacier's retraction of the approbation went an open letter to the Pope from the superior and directors of the Missions Étrangères dated April 20th 1700 at Brussels, whose title referred to "les idolâtries et la superstitions chinoises". Charges and countercharges followed[10]. Why did it take four years for a book as widely read as Le Comte's to be brought before the Sorbonne faculty? The Jesuits suggested that it was because of political expedience on their opponents' part[11]. Although the Jesuits' behavior in this controversy was not exemplary, there is some evidence to support their explanation for the delay and it is indeed true that they were in a weakened position at the French court in 1700[12]. As someone sent back to Europe charged with the task of aiding the material needs of the French mission, Le Comte was doubtless interested in presenting the missionaries' task in the most favorable light. As propaganda for the mission, *Nouveaux mémoires* succeeded admirably and it may have been this very success that helped make it a target. Given its unsophisticated presentation of theological complexities surrounding the Chinese rites issues, it is not surprising that anti-Jesuits found it an admirable weapon to turn against their foes.

The Sorbonne theologians were Jansenist in sympathy and therefore were far more reluctant to accept the notion of saved pagans than were the Jesuits.

---

10 See *Journal des savants* 28 (1700): 767–774; Rowbotham, *Missionary & Mandarin*, pp. 141–147; and Walker, *The Ancient Theology*, pp. 196–205.

11 Malcolm Hay has written a book in which he describes anti-Jesuit forces of the late seventeenth century and early eighteenth century located in the Propaganda in Rome and among the Jansenists and Missions Étrangères in France. Mr. Hay's polemical approach to the subject matter complicates any objective evaluation of his presentation and conclusions. See Malcolm Hay, *Failure in the Far East* (London, 1956).

12 Walker, *The Ancient Theology*, p. 202, draws upon the Sorbonne scholar, Noël Varet, whose dairylike account of the Sorbonne examination, *Journal d'un Docteur de Sorbonne*, supports the view that political expediency determined the timing of the examination of Le Comte's work.

The Jesuits tended to believe that all men could be saved and therefore saw the mission of the Church in terms of bringing all mankind into the Church. But as Augustinians, the Jansenists believed that God's grace was bestowed more on some men than on others. Consequently, they denied the possibility of salvation for all mankind. The clear protagonist of the Jesuits in the Sorbonne examination was the Société des Missions Étrangères which had interlocking ties with the theological faculty of the Sorbonne. The letter of April 20th 1700 from the Missions Étrangères to the Pope impeached six propositions extracted from Le Comte's *Nouveaux mémoires* and from Le Gobien's *Histoire de l'édit de l'empereur de la Chine*. The similarity of these propositions to the five propositions eventually censured was no coincidence. On July 1st 1700, M. Salomon Prioux, a doctor in theology of the Sorbonne faculty and one of the directors of the Missions Étrangères, impeached Le Comte's *Nouveaux mémoires*, Le Gobien's *Histoire* and the anonymous *Letre sur les ceremonies de la Chine* and declared that these works contained propositions which should be censured[13]. A group of eight deputies of the Sorbonne faculty examined the impeached books and extracted several propositions which they reduced to five in number and to which they added qualifications[14]. Consequently, on August 2nd, M. Boileau, the senior member of the deputies, presented their report to the faculty.

Although most of the Sorbonne faculty favored the proceedings, there seems to have been a significant minority in opposition. This opposition was expressed by M. du Mas who argued that since the letter of April 20th to the Pope was still awaiting a reply, the faculty should abstain from dealing with the matter. This objection was rejected. The five propositions were ordered to be printed and circulated to the faculty and the beginning date of the proceedings was set for August 17th.

Except for the third proposition, which is a summary, the five propositions represent a fairly close quotation from the original sources. The five impeached propositions were as follows[15]:

(1) The people of China preserved for almost two-thousand years [i.e. ca. 2000 B.C. – A.D. 1] a knowledge of the true God, and honored him in a manner which can serve as an example and as instruction even to Christians[16].

---

13 *Journal des savants* 28: 768. The *Letre sur les ceremonies de la Chine* is said to have been printed at Liege in 1700 by Daniel Memnal. This is possibly identical to the work, *Lettre a Monsieur ** touchant les honneurs que les Chinois rendent au Philosophe Confucius & à leurs Ancètres*, identified only by the date of publication, 1700. A copy of this work is found in the Bibliotheca Regia Hannoverana collection.

14 *Journal des savants* 28: 769.

15 *Journal des savants* 28: 770–772.

16 Le Comte, II, 141.

(2) If Judea had the advantage of consecrating (a temple to God) richer and more magnificent, sanctified even by means of the presence and by means of the prayers of the Redeemer, is this not a glorious piety to China, of having sacrificed to the Creator in the oldest temple of the universe[17].

(3) That the purity of the morality, the holiness of manners and customs, the faith, the interior and exterior cult of the true God, the prayers, the sacrifices, of the saints, of men inspired by God, of miracles, the spirit of Religion, the purest charity which is perfection and the character of Religion, and, if I dare to say, said the author, the Spirit of God was preserved formerly among the Chinese during more than two-thousand years.

(4) Be that as it may in the wise distribution of grace that divine Providence has made among the nations of the earth, China has nothing to complain of, since there is no nation that He has more constantly favored[18].

(5) Moreover, it is not necessary that his majesty (Chinese) regard the Christian religion as a foreign religion, since it was the same in its principles and in its fundamental points that the ancient religion, of which the sages and first emperors of China professed, worshipping the same God as the Christians worshipped and recognizing as well as them the Lord of Heaven and of the earth[19].

The Sorbonne deliberations on these propositions extended over two months and involved thirty meetings at which 160 academics expressed their opinions. The proceedings were concluded on October 17th with 114 voting in favor of censure and 46 opposed. Separate judgements were made of each of the propositions with all five being declared "false and rash"[20]. Aside from the third proposition, which was in any case a questionable summary of the views of Le Comte and Le Gobien, the first proposition received the harshest condemnation as "false, rash, scandalous, erroneous, injurious to the holy Christian religion". On October 18th, the censure was confirmed and − in a judicial procedure which approached mockery − the accused were finally allowed to present an explanation. This was done by Fr. Le Gobien, whose protests of the nullity of such a censure were, of course, without effect, though one suspects that it served both sides to have a statement from Le Gobien in the record.

As far as the Sorbonne examination went, Jesuit defeat was inevitable from the very point at which they failed to prevent the examination from taking place. Given the proclivity of the Sorbonne theology at that time, both the ascerbic Abbé Boileau and the panel were predisposed against the Jesuits. Most of the proceedings, which were conducted in a highly acrimonious atmosphere, centered about the chronological claim made by Le Comte that the Chinese had known and revered God for 2,000 years prior to the birth of Christ in a manner worthy of emulation by Christians[21]. Le Comte's claim, in addition to raising some very old and deep controversies over the relationship of pagans to Christian

---

17   Le Comte, II, 134−136, 141 & 146.
18   Le Comte, II, 147−148.
19   Charles Le Gobien, *Histoire de l'edit de l'empereur de la Chine, en faveur de la Religion Chrestienne* (Paris, 1698) pp. 104−105.
20   *Journal des savants* 28: 773.
21   Le Comte, II, 134−135.

salvation, also raised some important historical issues which had been under discussion in Europe since the publication of Martini's *Sinicae historiae decas prima*.

In his first volume, Le Comte echoed some of the claims of Martini on the high antiquity of the Chinese. He noted that Chinese history extended farther back in time than all profane histories[22]. (The traditional distinction between sacred and profane history was made on the basis of whether the sources were Biblical or non-Biblical.) Furthermore, Le Comte echoed a Jesuit judgment predating Martini's *Sinicae historiae decas prima* that the chronology derived from the Vulgate was insufficient to harmonize with Chinese chronology. Consequently, a Septuagint-based chronology was needed. Le Comte also shared with Martini some of the skepticism toward certain parts of Chinese chronology. Whereas Martini's skepticism had focused on Chinese fables, Le Comte doubted the validity of Chinese "popular history" which claimed a chronological span of 40,000 years. However, Le Comte felt that the 4,000 year chronology presented by the Chinese "savants" had been so generally accepted by Chinese scholars and was so firmly supported by tradition that he found it not open to questioning[23]. Furthermore, Le Comte noted that the ancient Chinese had recorded eclipses which their calculations were insufficiently exact to compute and therefore must have been made through direct observation[24].

Drawing from the chronology of the Chinese savants, Le Comte spoke of 22 royal families, i.e. dynasties, and 236 emperors[25]. Although Le Comte's limited experience in China made it highly unlikely that he was drawing directly from a Chinese source, it is difficult to pinpoint a European source since he did not cite his sources. The chronology presented in Martini's *Sinicae historiae decas prima* was incomplete and stopped at the birth of Christ which was nearly two-thirds of the way through the entire Chinese chronology. Couplet had published a complete chronology in his *Tabula chronologia monarchiae Sinicae* (1686), but Couplet's early dates were in close accord with those of Martini. Furthermore, there are unaccountable discrepancies between the chronologies of Couplet and Le Comte and the possibility is quite strong that Le Comte relied upon an additional source on Chinese history[26].

22 Le Comte, I, 254.
23 Le Comte, I, 254–255.
24 Le Comte, I, 257.
25 Le Comte, I, 255.
26 The title page of Couplet's *Tabula chronologia monarchiae Sinicae* claimed to go from 2952 BC to AD 1683, although Couplet omitted Fu Hsi and Shen Nung from the formal chronology and began in 2697 BC with Huang-ti (the Yellow Emperor). Couplet began the first dynasty with the Hsia and continued down to the Ch'ing, which totaled 22 dynasties and in that respect corresponded with Le Comte's account. But Couplet listed 234 emperors, excluding the pre-Hsia legendary emperors, while Le Comte referred to 236 emperors. Since the number of 22 dynasties was a commonly accepted figure, it was quite possible that Le Comte was drawing from a source other

Le Comte spoke of "several doctors" who had demonstrated that Chinese history included 500 or 600 years more than 4,000[27]. He argued that even if one rejected the claims of these doctors, the antiquity of China would be only slightly diminished. Martini's *Sinicae historiae decas prima* dated the beginning of Chinese history from 2952 B.C., which at the time of Le Comte's writing about 1696 would have amounted to 4,648 years. Couplet's *Tabula chronologica* was somewhat equivocal on whether to follow Martini in beginning Chinese history with Fu Hsi at 2952 B.C. or with Huang-ti (the Yellow Emperor) at 2697 B.C., but inclined toward the latter[28]. It is probable that the debate among Chinese scholars, to which Le Comte referred, involved the historical validity of the legends dealing with such figures as P'an Ku, Fu Hsi and Sheng Nung.

Le Comte regarded it as probable that the children and grandchildren of Noah spread into Asia and penetrated into the present-day region of Shansi and Shensi provinces. He referred to these provinces as the "most westerly" part of China which was accurate not in a general geopolitical sense, but in the sense of the northwesterly home of ethnic and cultural Chinese prior to the nineteenth century. Le Comte selected this area not only because of its westerly proximity, but also because of his awareness that this region was part of the Yellow River basin in which Chinese civilization originated. It also happened to be the region where he worked as a missionary for two years.

In 1664 the short treatise *T'ien-hsüeh ch'uan-kai* (Summary of the spread of the Heavenly Teaching) had added to Ricci's accommodation the radical proposal that the Chinese were blood descendants of Biblical figures. While Ricci had merely said that the Chinese were eminently virtuous pagans whose morality had been achieved through natural religion, Li Tsu-po with the aid of the Jesuits Buglio and Magalhaes had argued that the Chinese were direct descendants of the Biblical Adam. The reaction of Yang Kuang-hsien and many Chinese literati to this sort of argument was extremely hostile. Nevertheless the idea of a common descent of Chinese and Europeans had been aired. Shortly thereafter, in 1667, Kircher argued in *China illustrata*, under the influence of Hermetism and reports of returned Jesuits from China, that the Chinese were descendants of the Biblical Ham, that is, one of Noah's three sons who had

than Couplet. The possibility of another source for Le Comte's chronology is strengthened when one compares the total years of the reigns given for legendary Chinese emperors. Le Comte listed Fu Hsi, Shen Nung, Huang-ti and Yao with 150, 140, 111 and 168 years, respectively (Le Comte, I, 256). In contrast, Couplet's attribution of reign years was in close accord with Martini's *Sinicae historiae decas prima* which assigned these same legendary rulers 115, 140, 100 and 99 years. (See Martini, *Sinicae historiae decas prima*, pp. 11, 13, 14, 20, 24 & 30 and Couplet, *Tabula chronologica*, pp. 1, 3 & 106.)

27 Le Comte, I, 255–256.

28 See Couplet, *Tabula chronologica*, pp. iii-xi, 1 & 106.

migrated out of Egypt. After being stimulated by reading Martini's claim of a Noadic-type flood in China, John Webb argued in 1669 that the Chinese also were descended from Noah whose Chinese name was the legendary Yao. Finally, the Figurists were to develop with a passion the accommodative notion of a common lineal and spiritual descent of the Chinese and Europeans, though most of their claims remained in the form of private correspondence, such as between Bouvet and Leibniz, or in unpublished manuscripts. Consequently, from the point of view of the development of Jesuit accommodation, Le Comte's claim that the Chinese were descendants of the Biblical patriarch Noah was neither new nor as radical as it had been when first presented thirty years previously.

For seventeenth-century Europeans who regarded the Bible as the source not only of spiritual truth, but of worldly truth as well, a place had to be found for the Chinese in the Bible. This was the crucial accommodative significance of treating the Chinese as descended from Noah. However, for the Jesuits' mission it was not enough that they merely be blood descendants. They must also be shown to be spiritual descendants of Noah and participants in the Covenant with the monotheistic God. Therefore, Le Comte argued that the Chinese were adherents of the ancient religion through descent from Noah's line[29]. Having witnessed the power of the Creator at the time of the Flood, these descendants in turn were said to have inspired the belief in God among their descendants.

According to Le Comte, the Chinese possessed the knowledge of God for almost 2,000 years, under the reigns of 24 emperors[30]. In another passage he stated that this knowledge of the true God lasted until several centuries after King K'ang (r. 1078–1058 B.C.) and probably lasted for a long time after Confucius (551–479?). But the Chinese knowledge of God was said by Le Comte to have suffered a gradual degeneration from its original purity[31]. Morals became corrupted and idolatry appeared. Le Comte regarded the entry of Buddhism into China as a milestone in accelerating this degeneration. He claimed that there were no idols or statues to be found among the Chinese prior to the entry of the "God Fo", i.e. the Buddha. Admittedly, the entry of Buddhism into China fostered the development of religious statuary, but images of local vegetative and tutelary gods had existed prior to this time.

The claim that these vestiges represented the presence of the true religion in ancient China permitted Le Comte to offer a fresh perspective on the unfolding of knowledge of God in world history. He wrote that most Europeans believed that China and India has been "buried in the darkness of idolatry" since the birth of Christ while Greece, part of Africa and almost all of Europe had possessed the true faith. Yet in the 2,000 years preceding the birth of

29 Le Comte, II, 133–134.
30 Le Comte, II, 136.
31 Le Comte, II, 148.

Christ, Le Comte claimed that it was China which had "knowledge of the true God and practiced the purest maxims of morality, while Europe and almost all the rest of the world lived in error and corruption"[32].

This was a very shocking claim to many Europeans, but the escalating Rites Controversy debate apparently exacerbated the shock. Only thirteen years earlier in 1687 the Jesuits had published the somewhat milder claim in *Confucius Sinarum philosophus* that the ancient Chinese had worshipped "*Shang-ti, Supreme Ruler of the heavens*"[33]. To this earlier claim reviewers gave few signs of being shocked at all. What made Le Comte's viewpoint shocking in 1700 was not simply because he said that the Chinese possessed knowledge of the true God, but that the Chinese were said to possess this knowledge to such a degree that they could serve as a model for Europeans! The Sorbonne debate of 1700 centered around the issue of emulation as phrased quite explicitly by Le Comte: "[the Chinese] people had preserved for nearly 2,000 years the knowledge of the true God, and had honored Him in a manner which can serve as an example and as instruction even to Christians"[34]. When one got down to fundamental self-conceptions in the seventeenth-century outlook, European Christians regarded themselves as the chosen people in the new Covenant with God since the Jews' rejection of Jesus' messiahship. For such people to admire the secular achievements of the Chinese was one thing. But the notion that the Chinese, whom everyone conceded to be pagans in their present form, were worthy of model emulation in the spiritual realm by such chosen people appeared to many Europeans to be so patently false that it merited condemnation.

There were other statements by Le Comte which were almost as shocking and which were debated at the Sorbonne, though, again, these statements had been expressed in a milder and more scholarly context in *Confucius Sinarum philosophus*. One was Le Comte's that the Chinese "had sacrificed to the Creator in the oldest temple in the Universe"[35]. It is doubtful that Le Comte had a specific Chinese temple in mind, but was probably merely referring to the early date at which Chinese sacrifices to God took place in *a* temple. Another statement was the claim that in God's distribution of grace to the world, China had not been slighted. On the contrary, Le Comte argued, there was no nation which had been more constantly favored by God[36]. This, of course, played havoc with the traditional European conception of the Old Testament in which the Jews were the people chosen by God for his Covenant.

32 Le Comte, II, 146–147.
33 Couplet, *Confucius,* pp. xvi-xxxv.
34 Le Comte, II, 141.
35 Le Comte, II, 135. *Confucius Sinarum philosophus* spoke of the ancient Chinese worshipping *Shang-ti* through ritual and sacrifice on pp. xvi & xxxv. Also see pp. 59–60.
36 Le Comte, II, 148.

In his emphasis upon God's favor to the Chinese, Le Comte was engaged in geographically expanding the European conception of God's grace. The long-established tendency toward viewing themselves as the primary body of worshippers of God and followers of Christ's Revelation had fostered a provincial outlook among Europeans which they mistook for a universal perspective. Largely cut off from developments to the east of Europe, their ignorance assumed the force of wisdom. And yet it is clear that the Christian Gospel not only came out of Asia, but continued to survive in Asia in such forms as the Nestorian (Assyrian) church. The Jesuits interpreted the Bible as a spiritual guide to completing God's work in the world rather than as a book which told a story of salvation whose geographical and cultural limits had already been reached. Consequently, they saw China as part of God's plan for salvation. Le Comte was reflecting this view when he stressed the universality of God's gifts. For Le Comte, God made no unjust preference in the distribution of his gifts. He linkened the appearance of God's grace to the sun which "rises and falls successively in different parts of the world, according to if the peoples are engaging in good or evil practices"[37]. Le Comte's statement reflected the debate over how God's grace affected human salvation.

The classical positions on grace were defined in the controversy between St. Augustine (354–430) and Pelagius, the English theologian who taught in Rome during the late fourth and fifth centuries, and their differences derived from opposing views of human nature. In Augustine's view, man's inherent nature was so sinful that grace was crucial for choosing good. Pelagius saw man's inherent nature as God-given and the means through which one could choose good. For these choices, Pelagius said that grace was not necessary, but merely a means of facilitating God's commands.

The polemics of the controversy led Augustine to stress grace to such an extent that human freedom of choice was restricted by predestination. Even after the condemnation of Pelagianism as heretical in 416, a correction of this de-emphasis of free will was sought. Consequently, the controversy continued throughout the Middle Ages and into the modern era. In the Reformation, Protestants tended to follow Augustine to the point of explicitly teaching predestination. An attempted compromise between the positions of Augustine and Pelagius called "semi-Pelagianism" accepted the notion of original sin, but rejected complete depravity. It stressed the free choice of the will and consequently rejected predestination. It accepted the fundamental necessity of grace while rejecting the notion of irresistible grace which limited man's freedom of choice.

The Jesuits tended toward a semi-Pelagian position on grace, while the Jansenists favored Augustinianism. Consequently, Le Comte's reference to God's bestowal of grace in accordance with the good or evil practices of a given people would be opposed by the Jansenists. For the latter, grace was bestowed regard-

37 Le Comte, II, 147.

less of human merit. Since grace tended for Jansenists to be irresistible, the Chinese demonstrated that they had not been the recipients of grace by not having converted to Christianity. Furthermore, if God had chosen to withhold his grace from the Chinese, then human effort in the form of missions would be of highly questionable value. The Jesuits, on the other hand, laid greater stress on free will and the fact that the Chinese had chosen to worship one God and to practice a pure morality in their antiquity. They believed that God had intended the Chinese to be included in salvation and so emphasized the China Mission.

Predestinationist views led the Jansenists to reject the Chinese as condemned by God because of the absence of signs of grace in the form of specifically Christian worship and morality. But 'conversely, the Jansenists' belief in an elect led to severe demands upon themselves. If the presence of God's grace was signaled by spiritual purity and moral living, then they felt compelled to demonstrate these in their lives. This uncompromising austerity of Jansenist spirituality was symbolized by the community of nuns at Port-Royal-des-Champs and its close association with prominent intellectuals like Antoine Arnauld (1613–1694) and Blaise Pascal (1623–1662). The resistance of the Port-Royal community to ecclesiastical persecution was peaking at the time of the Sorbonne examination and later from 1709 to 1713. Following their refusal to submit to Papal decrees, the nuns of Port-Royal were dispersed, the buildings destroyed and the site desecrated. Such a committed group found the tendency of the Jesuits to compromise in God's name incomprehensible and repulsive.

3. LE COMTE ON THE CHINESE LANGUAGE

Le Comte's treatment of the Chinese language is very revealing. The subject of Chinese script apparently was still a subject of great interest in Europe, and Le Comte felt obliged to address it. Gone, however, were the references to a Primitive Language, *lingua universalis* and *Clavis Sinica* that had so animated the treatments of Kircher, Müller, Mentzel and Webb. Did these omissions represent a shifting of interests of the age or did it reflect the different inclinations of Le Comte's mind? Although the general seventeenth-century ardor in the search for a Primitive Language was cooling, powerful and creative mentalities such as Bouvet and Leibniz were at the very time pursuing the possibilities of a universal language in regard to Chinese. The fact is that Le Comte's treatment was of a mundane quality. It was this very quality which helped make him such an effective popularizer but which doomed him as a spokesman for as complex an issue as Jesuit accommodation.

Le Comte's treatment of Chinese writing was more sophisticated than his proto-sinological predecessors — Kircher, Müller, Mentzel and Webb. He recognized that while the basic structural unit of the Chinese script was the "hieroglyph", he also noted that there were elements such as sound, odor, feelings and passions for which no images were appropriate and required the invention of a character on a non-pictorial basis[38]. Furthermore, Le Comte showed a practical awareness of the complexity and difficulty of the Chinese characters. On the other hand, he lacked an appreciation for the positive elements of Chinese script. He showed no sensitivity toward the aesthetic aspects of Chinese calligraphy and its connection with painting. He noted, but could not explain, why poor calligraphy — unlike in France — had never been a mark of nobility among the Chinese. To Le Comte, good calligraphy was a requirement of literati achievement, but he could not explain why this was so[39]. When he expressed the Chinese admiration for the alphabet of the European languages, Le Comte implied that it would be preferable if the Chinese system of writing were based on the European model and, in so doing, foreshadowed several generations of early and mid-twentieth century Chinese language reformers[40].

There is a very revealing passage in Le Comte's description of Chinese which reads like the diary of a frustrated language student. He spoke of the disgust that the study of Chinese characters aroused in the Chinese. The need of "taking into one's head the frightful multitude of characters" was a "very heavy cross that one is obliged to carry during his whole life"[41]. Le Comte found no consoling elements in the study of these characters which compared to the benefits of studying European sciences. He felt that the demands of learning the enormous number of Chinese characters had been "the source of ignorance of the Chinese" in that the literati had no time left for the pursuit of other knowledge. Furthermore, he stated that they did not regret this, but regarded the ability to read as a sufficient mark of learning[42].

One cannot deny that the difficulty of mastering Chinese characters was a problem. The early twentieth-century Chinese language reformers amply echoed Le Comte's criticisms on this point. To the Western student of the Chinese classical language, Le Comte's complaints will sound familiar. But he seems not to have achieved that breakthrough which leads to appreciation. One must not begrudge Le Comte the sympathy he deserves. Much of his three and one-half years in China was spent traveling between Ningpo, Peking, Shansi, Shensi and Canton. His less than two-year residence in Shansi and Shensi provinces could not have been sufficient to get beyond the early frustrations of language study.

38 Le Comte, I, 382–383.
39 Le Comte, I, 387–388.
40 Le Comte, I, 381–382. In regard to Chinese language reform, Bernhard Karlgren in
   Philology and ancient China (Oslo, 1926) p. 152, proposed that Chinese ideography
   be replaced with phonetic writing. For an opposing viewpoint, see Herrlee Glessner
   Creel, "On the nature of Chinese ideography," *T'oung pao* 32 (1936): 85–166.
41 Le Comte, I, 384.
42 Le Comte, I, 384.

On the other hand, Le Comte wrote the *Nouveaux mémoires* as an authority on China. If there had not been other missionaries who had achieved break-throughs in the language and an understanding and appreciation which he lacked, then perhaps his book would have been more justified. As it was, Le Comte was writing a book defending an accommodation approach toward China while he lacked the understanding of those, such as Ricci or Magalhaes or Bouvet, who were able to make creative contributions to the effort. For Le Comte, accommodation was primarily a mission strategy. It was much less a framework for the meeting of cultures because he lacked the intellectual un-derstanding and sympathy for China which characterized most Jesuit propo-nents of accommodation. When Le Comte praised China for having been favored in antiquity, he was speaking not so much from an understanding or apprecia-tion of China's past as from a conviction of the soundness of accommodation policy. Significant fragments of China's antiquity were revealed through the oldest Classical texts, but Le Comte showed little awareness of their contents. His *Nouveaux mémoires* shows that his expertise on China consisted essentially of observations on contemporary Chinese geography, dress, customs and culture. Yet it was contemporary Chinese culture which was, according to Le Comte's expression of accommodation, most guilty of idolatry and therefore most ex-cluded from the accommodation formula.

We catch a revealing insight into Le Comte's views on accommodation when he described his frustration over the study of Chinese characters:

> In China, in order not to become discouraged, it is necessary to seek motives more exalted than natural fancy. And we are pleased to think that this study, as rude and as unfruitful as it may appear, is not sterile because this is a very sure means of making known Jesus Christ.
>
> It is by means of the latter that one obtains a hearing from the savants, that one in-sinuates oneself into their spirits, and that one prepares them for the great truths of the Christian religion[43].

In short, one studied the Chinese language and culture merely in order to secure the success of the Mission. There was no appreciation for Chinese culture per se.

Had Le Comte's attitudes been shared by all Jesuits in the China Mission, then the subject could be concluded here. But it was quite clear that for a num-ber of Jesuits — because of initial disposition and long exposure to Chinese culture — their underlying attitudes toward China were quite different from those of Le Comte. China had changed some of these Jesuits. These changes made them considerably less Europocentric in their expression of Christianity and brought them to the brink of heterodoxy. The changes which took place in them made them less comprehensible to their European brethren to the extent that charges of heresy would occasionally be raised, as was the case with the Figurists. Le Comte was not one of their number and the great irony of the late seventeenth-century portion of the Rites Controversy was that a Jesuit who neither fully appreciated nor understood the accommodation program became the spokesman for accommodation in Europe.

4. FR. LE GOBIEN'S *HISTOIRE DE L'ÉDIT DE L'EMPEREUR DE LA CHINE*

Charles Le Gobien was born at St. Malo, Britanny in 1653 and entered the Society of Jesus just before his eighteenth birthday. He taught grammar, humanities and philosophy in Jesuit schools at Tours and Alençon and acquired an interest in the China Mission. French participation in the China Mission required that there be administrative personnel in France. Though Fr. Le Gobien never visited China, he possessed qualities which led his superiors to appoint him to succeed Fr. Verjus in 1706 as procurator in France[44].

Le Gobien's publications dated from 1697 and related almost exclusively to his involvement with China. His talents were not scholarly so much as editorial. Like Le Comte, he excelled in popularizing the scholarship of others rather than being a creative source. Consequently, he was ideally suited to the office of a procurator in France which served as a clearing-house for correspondence, reports and written works from French missionaries in China. It was Le Gobien who determined which of these pieces should be publicly circulated and in what form. Since his task was not entirely unlike a modern public relations representative, his work involved a selection process aimed at materials which would cast the French Jesuits in China in a light most favorable to Europeans. It was Le Gobien who was in a position to foster a correspondence between Jesuits and eminent Europeans by acting as a go-between, as he did in the case of Leibniz and Bouvet[45].

Le Gobien's editorial talents were crucial in his editing of the first eight volumes of the *Lettres édifiantes et curieuses écrites des missions etrangères*, which were published in 34 volumes from 1702 until 1776[46]. Intended as a propaganda tool for the foreign missions, the letters from Jesuits in China were selected on the basis of their interest and informative quality. The propaganda emphasis later became more apparent when the Jesuit Jean-Baptiste Du Halde succeeded Le Gobien as editor of the *Lettres édifiantes* in 1708. Catering to the French reading public's desire for a culture-idol, Fr. Du Halde extensively edited the Jesuit reports to remove material unsympathetic to either the Chinese or the Jesuits. The editing reached such a degree that several Jesuit missionaries in China complained. But Du Halde had judged his reading public correctly and was consequently honored by Voltaire who placed him on the list of great men of his time[47]!

43 Le Comte, I, 384–385.
44 Sommervogel, III, 1512–1515; *Catholic encyclopedia* IX, 132–133; & *New Catholic encyclopedia* VIII, 618.
45 Fr. Le Gobien acted as a middleman in forwarding Bouvet's letter of November 8th 1700 to Leibniz. See the author's *Leibniz & Confucianism*, p. 46.
46 Sommervogel, III, 1514.
47 See A Brou, "Les jésuites sinologues de Pékin et leur editeurs de Paris," pp. 556–566; Witek, *Controversial ideas*, p. 323n; Rowbotham, *Missionary & Mandarin*, pp.

Le Gobien's role as editor and popularizer were revealingly evident in his small but controversial work, *Histoire de l'édit de l'empereur de la Chine en faveur de la religion chrestienne* (Paris 1698). Although this work never equalled Le Comte's *Nouveaux mémoires* in popularity, it was reprinted in the year of its appearance, along with Le Comte's book. It appeared in a second edition at Paris in 1700 and was translated into Italian (1699), German (1699) and Dutch (1710)[48]. Because of the distinguished service by the Jesuits Gerbillon and Pereira in negotiations with the Russians at Nerchinsk, the K'ang-hsi emperor was persuaded to issue in 1692 an edict which gave increased legal sanction to Christianity in China[49]. Le Gobien drew from reports surrounding the remarkable success of the Jesuits in obtaining this decree. He surveyed the events leading up to the decree of 1692 by beginning with the Chinese persecution against the Christians of 1617–1621 centered at Nanking and led by Shen Ch'üeh (d. 1624) and the persecution beginning in 1664 led by Yang Kuang-hsien[50].

The second part of Le Gobien's *Histoire de l'édit* consisted of an explanation of the Chinese rites to Confucius and to the dead[51]. The polemical treatment of the subject-matter diminished the value of these two sections as objective reflections of the European conception of China of that period, though these sections were important to the debate which shaped that conception. Of greater value is the less polemical presentation in the preface of the four main religious sects of the Chinese. The preface consisted of 16 un-numbered pages. Although

255–257; & C. R. Boxer, "Some aspects of Western historical writing on the Far East, 1500–1800" in E. G. Pulleyblank & W. G. Beasley, eds., *Historians of China and Japan* (London, 1961) pp. 312–315.

48 Sommervogel, III, 689 & 1512–1513, cites the Italian and Dutch translations of Le Comte's *Nouveaux mémoires*, but does not note the German translation, a copy of which may be found in the Bibliotheca Regia Hannoverana collection. It is entitled *Das heutigen Sina dritter Teil, oder historischer Bericht des Edictes, welches der letzte regierende Kayser in Sina der christlichen Religion zum besten ergehen lassen* (Frankfurt & Leipzig, 1699).

49 The K'ang-hsi emperor's edict ot toleration has been translated into English in Rowbotham, *Missionary & Mandarin*, p. 110. Also see Latourette, *History*, pp. 126–127. The significance of this edict is discussed in a paper by John W. Witek, S.J., "Understanding the Chinese: a comparison of Matteo Ricci and the early French Jesuits," in *East meets West: the Jesuits in China (1582–1773)*, forthcoming.

50 For the anti-Christian persecution of 1617–1621, see E. Zürcher, "The first Anti-Christian movement in China," *Acta Orientalia Neederlandica* (1971):188–195; George H. C. Wong, "The Anti-Christian movement in China: the late Ming and early Ch'ing," *Tsing Hua journal of Chinese studies* new series 3. I (1962): 187–222; & John D. Young, "The early Confucian attack on Christianity: Yang Kuang-hsien and his *Pu-te-i*," *Journal of the Chinese University of Hong Kong* 3 (1975): 155–186.

51 Discounting prefatory material in Le Gobien's work, which appears on un-numbered pages, the history of the Toleration Edict occupies pages 1–216 of the small work in duodecimo, while the explanation of Chinese rites occupies pages 217–322.

Le Gobien included no quotations or references to specific sources, the relatively sophisticated content confirms that he drew from informed missionary sources.

Le Gobien categorized the four religious sects of China as: (1) vestigial worship of *"Seigneur du Ciel"* (Lord of Heaven) or *Shang-ti*; (2) the school of philosophers associated with *"La Raison"* (*li*, principle), i.e. Sung Neo-Confucianism; (3) the religion of the Brahmans, i.e. Buddhism; and (4) the religion of the Bonzes, i.e. Taoism. Le Gobien's division between the first two sects was consistent with the Jesuit accommodation formulated by Ricci, continued by Couplet and modified by Bouvet. Le Gobien defined the first sect as animated primarily by reverence for the ancients rather than by religious piety. This group was said to have kept alive the ancient Chinese belief in a "superior spirit" which was eternal and all-powerful and which the Chinese forefathers referred to as "Lord of Heaven" (*Shang-ti*)[52]. Le Gobien stated that the number of worshippers of this sect was very small, but included the Emperor as its head. According to Le Gobien, the Emperor himself had declared that his temple sacrifices were offered to this Lord of Heaven and not to the minor deities which the people worshipped. The inclusion of the Emperor in the first sect reflected the political sensitivity of the French Jesuits and the attempt to build their policy of accommodation upon imperial favor.

The second sect was that of the "true philosophers," i.e. modern literati[53]. Le Gobien claimed that although this sect was smaller in numbers than the Buddhist and Taoist sects, it was the dominant sect. This was apparently a reference to the political as well as cultural influence which the scholar-officials exerted. Le Gobien went on to identify this sect of modern literati with the philosophy of nature of Chou Lien-hsi (Chou Tun-i) (1017–1073) and Shao K'ang-chieh (Shao Yung) (1011–1077). His references to the Diagram of the Supreme Ultimate (*T'ai-chi t'u-shuo*) and *li* (principle) make it clear that Le Gobien meant the Neo-Confucianism which originated in the Sung dynasty with the reinterpretation of the Classics by the Ch'eng brothers and Chu Hsi. Le Gobien never used the terms "Neo-Confucianism" or "Confucianism", but then, neither did the Chinese. These labels were clarifying distinctions invented by Europeans in the eighteenth century and Le Gobien's designation, "the school of philosophers", was probably much truer to the traditional Chinese description of the school of Confucius — *Ju-hsüeh* (School of scholars)[54]. In a pattern duplicating that of Bouvet, Le Gobien did not

---

52 Le Gobien, preface 1st page.

53 Le Gobien, preface, 2nd page.

54 Possibly the first to use the term *"néo-confucéens"* was the China missionary and learned Jesuit, Jean-Joseph-Marie Amiot (Ch'ien Te-ming, 1718–1793) in volume 2 (1777) of *Mémoires concernant l'histoire . . . des Chinois, par les missionnaires de Pékin.* See Lundbaek, "Notes sur l'image du néo-confucianisme dans la littérature européenne du XIIIe siècle a la fin du XIXe siècle," in *Actes du IIIe colloque international de Sinologie de Chantilly* (Paris, 1983) pp. 131–176.

mention Confucius, the founding figure of Confucianism. Part of the reason for this omission lay in the seventeenth-century evolution of Jesuit accommodation policy described in the preceding pages.

Another reason why Le Gobien did not mention Confucius stems from the continuity of Chinese tradition in which Confucius was seen as a transmitter rather than a founder. Where outsiders tend to see breaks in this tradition, Chinese see variations within a general continuity. Ricci did not create the difference between the religious beliefs of ancient Chinese and modern literati, but he did *sharpen* the distinction for accommodative purposes. By rejecting a modern form of Confucianism (i.e. Neo-Confucianism) as a distortion of the ancients, Ricci avoided having to defend contemporary Chinese who were not Neo-Confucians from charges of atheism and idolatry. Moreover, since one of the time-honored forms of the Confucian tradition was to reject modern interpretation in order to seek the true meaning of the ancient culture as embodied in the Classics, Ricci was not simply imposing an alien form upon his interpretation of the Classics. In Ricci's formulation of Jesuit accommodation, that part of Confucianism which preserved the most ancient culture was given a very special position and received far more sympathy than those elements of modern Confucianism, Buddhism and Taoism. This special status of ancient Confucianism was reflected in Le Gobien's first religious sect. As a group which preserved a vestige of China's reverence for a monotheistic God, this group confirmed the Jesuit claim of a natural religion in ancient China. But the small size of its membership reflected that most Chinese had departed from the worship of the monotheistic God into idolatry.

Le Gobien's description of Neo-Confucianism gave a misleading emphasis to the theories of Chou Tun-i and Shao Yung. Both were seminal thinkers whose firm identities as founders of Neo-Confucianism were established only after their deaths. Shao Yung's Neo-Confucian credentials are debatable in that his interests were essentially numerological rather than social and moral. On the other hand, Shao emphasized the basic Confucian work, the *I ching*, and based his philosophy on the same cosmological unfolding from *T'ai-chi*, as had other early Neo-Confucians. Like Shao Yung, Chou Tun-i showed marked Taoist influence and his famous diagram of the *T'ai-chi* probably came from a Taoist source. This did not mean that Shao and Chou rejected the Confucian tradition, but it did show that in eleventh-century China, the distinctions between Confucianism and Taoism had become blurred. The revival of Confucianism in the late eleventh and in the twelfth centuries resharpened the distinction between the two schools. It established a firm sense of Confucian orthodoxy by establishing a link between themselves and antiquity in the form of the "transmission of the *Tao*" (*Tao-t'ung*), a link which had been lost for over a thousand years.

What Shao Yung and Chou Tun-i did supply to the synthesis of Chu Hsi were significant portions of the latter's physical theory and cosmology. Chu

Hsi built his system on this cosmology and so it was fundamental. But by itself, the cosmology explained very little of the whole system. Yet this is exactly how Le Gobien attempted to explain Neo-Confucianism. Out of the six pages of explanation, five pages were devoted to the numerological and cosmological theories of Shao Yung and Chou Tun-i while less than one page was used to explain the ethical system, which Le Gobien conceded, "seems a good deal more reasonable" than their other theories[55].

The explanation why Le Gobien used this approach may be found in the needs of Jesuit accommodation of the late seventeenth century. Since this outlook was based upon reconciling vestigial elements of ancient China with Christianity and rejecting modern Chinese culture as atheistic and idolatrous, it is understandable that the Jesuits would not seek reconcilable spiritual elements in the modern teaching of Neo-Confucianism. The morality of Neo-Confucianism was treated by Le Gobien as rigidly secular and without a spiritual foundation. For Le Gobien's missionary sources, the absence of a single, clearly definable God amounted to the same thing as the presence of a number of deities. What eluded Le Gobien's sources was the highly important tradition of spiritual cultivation in Confucianism.

Le Gobien's outlook differed from that of Ricci who fully concurred with the viewpoint of the prominent Chinese scholar-official and Christian convert, Hsü Kuang-ch'i. This approach used typically Chinese mind-catching formulas, such as *Pu Ju i Fo* (complete Confucianism and displace Buddhism) or *Pu Ju ch'üeh Fo* (complement Confucianism and eliminate Buddhism). Underlying these formulas was the belief in the fundamental complementarity of Confucianism and Christianity. While Ricci thought that much of Neo-Confucianism was atheistic, he nevertheless believed that the living representatives of the Confucian tradition — the scholar-officials — held in their Confucianism elements complementary enough to form a Confucian-Christian amalgam. Consequently, Ricci cultivated this group intensely and identified with them.

The seventeenth-century evolution of Jesuit accommodation had produced certain modifications in Ricci's program while maintaining Ricci's basic strategy for a Chinese-Christian synthesis. Some, such as Bouvet, appear to have believed that the antiquity of the Chinese was reconcilable with Christianity, but that most of the Confucian philosophy of the modern literati was irreconcilable. It appears that Bouvet sought not to complement or "complete" modern Confucianism, but to substitute in its place an older and purer form of the Chinese tradition found in the *I ching*. It is clear from Le Gobien's description of Neo-Confucianism that his China interpreters were far closer to the thinking of Bouvet than of Ricci. In fact, it is quite probable that one of Le Gobien's sources of information on Chinese religions was Bouvet since the latter visited

---

55 Le Gobien, preface, 7th page.

Paris in the year preceding Le Gobien's publication of his history of the Chinese toleration edict.

Le Gobien wrote that the Neo-Confucians saw in nature nothing more than nature itself, that is, they saw no transcendent guiding force such as God[56]. In nature, they perceived a principle of motion and rest which they called "*la Raison*" or *li*. This Reason created order and caused all change in the universe. According to Le Gobien, the Chinese compared the universe to a large building in which nature, i.e. *li*, was the summit or pinnacle. In the same way that a pinnacle "joins and supports all the parts which compose the roof of the structure, likewise does nature unite and preserve all the parts of the universe"[57]. In a footnote, Le Gobien added that the Neo-Confucians also called nature *T'ai-chi*, which signified a "large pinnacle" and which was taken from one of the canonical books. Le Gobien claimed that Chou Tun-i further defined nature with the phrase "*wu-chi erh t'ai-chi*" which he translated as "*le grand faite, qui est sans faite*" (the great pinnacle which is without a pinnacle).

The ultimate source of Le Gobien's explanation was clearly Chou's "Explication of the *T'ai-chi* diagram" (*T'ai-chi t'u-shuo*). However, it was not Chou, but Chu Hsi who compared *li* (principle) as a fundamental element of the universe to *T'ai-chi*. Chou's "Explication" made no reference to *li*. The use of the terms *le sommet* (summit) and *le baite* (pinnacle) to translate *T'ai-chi* was a fairly accurate rendering of the Chinese meaning. Le Gobien's reference to the pinnacle of a building was a reference to the Chinese meaning of a ridgepole as a crucial structural unit in a roof. Clearly, Le Gobien's sources drew upon Chu Hsi's explication of Chou Tun-i's philosophy of the *T'ai-chi*. This is confirmed by Le Gobien's reference to a "canonical book" as a source for the term *T'ai-chi*, which was a probable reference to the *Hsing-li ta-ch'üan* (Great collection of natural and moral philosophy) (1415). Although the term *T'ai-chi* was almost totally absent from the standard Confucian Classics — it does appear in the Great Appendix (*Hsi tzu*) to the *I ching* —, it was prominent in the *Hsing-li ta-ch'üan*, a Ming dynasty collection of excerpts from Sung Neo-Confucian philosophers which had acquired tremendous authority by the time of the Ch'ing dynasty.

In Neo-Confucian philosophy, *T'ai-chi* has a metaphysical significance of Supreme Ultimate or Supreme Pole as the phrase "*wu-chi erh t'ai-chi*" represents a much-discussed metaphysical paradox in Chinese philosophy. For example, the phrase might be translated as "under the circumstances of their being *wu-chi* (maximization of nothingness), there is *T'ai-chi* (maximization of everything)"[58]. Le Gobien was not unaware of the metaphysical significance attributed to this

---

56 Le Gobien, preface, 2nd page.

57 Le Gobien, preface, 2nd page.

58 The *T'ai-chi* diagram and this interpretation appears in the author's *Leibniz & Confucianism*, pp. 94–97.

statement, but he believed that the Chinese literati had over-interpreted the phrase. He believed that Chou Tun-i meant only to say that "nature is a principle which depends on no other principle" whereas the literati extended the significance to mean "the first principle has neither form nor shape"[59].

What Le Gobien missed was the very strong sense of a tradition in Neo-Confucianism. Neo-Confucians believed that Truth, or *Tao* as they referred to it, had been possessed by the ancients and was transmitted to Confucius and his disciples, but had then lapsed after Mencius (371–289). The Sung philosophers perceived themselves as reviving the "transmission of the *Tao*" (*Tao-t'ung*). Since Chu Hsi's synthesis and interpretations of Chou's diagram were seen essentially as recapturing the lost Truth of the ancients, Neo-Confucians would not have viewed it as a *new* teaching, as did Le Gobien.

While Le Gobien's presentation of Neo-Confucianism cannot be described as sympathetic, it was a great deal less critical than his description of Chinese Buddhism. In contrast to the six pages devoted to Neo-Confucianism, Le Gobien gave a mere three pages to Buddhism and one of these pages was filled primarily with Neo-Confucian criticism of Buddhism. It appears that Le Gobien's source had absorbed the literati's negative interpretation of Buddhism, which contained a highly pro-Neo-Confucian bias. Le Gobien stated that the Buddhist "Priests" revered "the God *Fo* [i.e. Buddha], his law and the books which contain their particular rules"[60]. However, from the viewpoint of Buddhism, there is more than one Buddha (enlightened one) – there is the historical Buddha, Sakyamuni or Gautama; the future Buddha, Maitreya; and the Buddha who presides over the Western Paradise, Amitabha Buddha. In fact, the Buddhas may be viewed as potentially infinite in number. Le Gobien's reference was probably to the historical Buddha, Sakyamuni, but doctrinally speaking, neither Sakyamuni Buddha nor any other Buddha has been regarded as a god. However, the popular practice of Buddhism has blurred this point and given the impression of worshipping Buddha as a god. This was particularly true of the Pure Land sect of Amitabha Buddha which was quite prominent in the sixteenth and seventeenth centuries when the Christian missionaries entered China.

In spite of the misleading reference to the Buddha as a god, it appears that Le Gobien was accurately describing the threefold objects of Buddhist reverence. In Buddhist terminology, these objects are called the "*Tripitaka*" (literally, three baskets; three canons) and refers to the Buddha, the *Dharma* (doctrinal Truth) and the *Sangha* (body of followers). Le Gobien was unable to explain the Buddhist philosophy of nature because he claimed that he had not yet been instructed by the Neo-Confucians on this subject[61]! However, the Neo-Confucians apparently did inform him, indirectly through other missionaries, of

59 Le Gobien, preface, 3rd page.
60 Le Gobien, preface, 8th page.
61 Le Gobien, preface, 8th page.

their great opposition to the Buddhist view of the world as an illusion or dream. Furthermore, Le Gobien made a vague reference to emptiness, which was the fundamental Buddhist doctrine of *sunyata*. On the other hand, the Buddhists were said to agree with the Neo-Confucians in saying that the world existed in continually revolving cycles of creation and destruction. (Actually, the Neo-Confucians probably borrowed this view from Taoism or Buddhism.) According to Le Gobien, the Buddhist period at 134,004,006,000 years – the Buddhists referred to it as a *kalpa* – was "a great deal longer and no less bizarre and chimerical" than the Neo-Confucian cycle[62].

Le Gobien's presentation of Taoism – "the religion of the bonzes" – was only slightly less critical than that of Buddhism[63]. He stated that this sect originated in China and its priests referred to themselves as *Tao-tzu* or "doctors of the Law". Perhaps in an attempt to help the European reader to assimilate these Chinese teachings, Le Gobien likened the Taoists to Epicureans, whereas previously he had compared the Buddhists to extreme Stoics. He saw the Taoists as considerably less extreme than the Buddhists in that they limited themselves to removing only the stronger desires and passions rather than all desires. He saw their goal as peace and tranquility.

Le Gobien seems to have been unaware of the eremitic tendency of the Taoists and treated them as if they were as publicly and socially oriented as the Confucians. For example, he wrote that the Taoists believed the sage should sacrifice his repose to the public good[64]. But the basic Taoist texts, the *Lao-tzu* and *Chuang-tzu*, were critical of the public efforts of the Confucians and espoused a *laissez-faire* approach toward government. In its origins and throughout its later history, one dominant strain of Taoism clearly represented a retreat from society into nature, though there was little indication of this in Le Gobien's presentation. Le Gobien also erred in saying that the bonzes did not permit themselves to marry and to raise families.

Although Taoism was very diverse in its manifestations and included celibate monks, the importance of sexual practices to the quest for immortality belied Le Gobien's statement. The doctrine of balancing *yin* and *yang* forces led aging men to seek sexual intercourse with young virgins in order to counter their overbalance of *yang* with *yin* forces and so extend their lifespan. It is true that older men sometimes retired from family responsibilities to pursue the *Tao* – and the quest for immortality was obviously of greatest interest to the older generations – but most did so only after fulfilling their familial responsibilities of providing descendants for the family line. On the other hand, while Taoist sexual techniques were still practiced in the seventeenth century, the deeper understanding of them was becoming increasingly confined to smaller and more

62 Le Gobien, preface, 9th page.
63 Le Gobien, preface, 11th page.
64 Le Gobien, preface, 12th page.

secret circles[65]. The strict censorship introduced by the Manchus further constricted dissemination of information on the Art of the Bedchamber and helps to explain Le Gobien's lack of full understanding.

Le Gobien was aware of the Taoist quest for "the secret of becoming immortal" and he correctly referred to the Chinese term *shen-hsien* for immortals[66]. He spoke of the Taoist quest as being based on the belief that art could supplement nature. Le Gobien had some awareness of the diversity of quests in Taoism. He referred to the "hundred different recipes taken from chemistry" and to the "regimen of life" which corresponded to one's age, humors and temperament[67]. But he stated that the Taoists prized, above all, the meditation which was based on circulating an element in the body. (Le Gobien appears to have been unaware of the distinction between cultivating the "external pill" of Taoist alchemy and the "inner pill" of Taoist meditation.) He dismissed Taoist meditation as a blindness fostered by the human desire for immortality. If the "ridiculous manner" of the way the "bonzes" — a term normally reserved for Buddhist monks, but here applied to Taoists — explained their meditation did not undeceive one, then Le Gobien was sure that the ineffectiveness of the meditation would confirm the baselessness of their claims[68]. Le Gobien summarized his discussion of Taoism by speaking of "the love of life which is so profoundly rooted in our hearts" and how we blindly follow anything which promises more life "because we never cease to desire it"[69].

The Jesuits' tunnel-vision in regard to the role of Buddhism in the China Mission prevented them from recognizing that this religion was founded on the suffering caused by the insatiable human craving for life. In its tendency to counter the attraction of life by proposing Nirvana, which is the cessation of craving and a goal antithetical to life, Buddhism revealed much more affinity to Christianity than did Taoism, whose quest was centered on prolonging life. In fact, Buddhism has probably developed more insights into the phenomenon of craving than any other religion. Here in Le Gobien's preface from the end of the seventeenth century, we have an example of how the accommodative outlook begun by Ricci at the beginning of the century continued to shape Jesuit interpretations of China. Ricci had first perceived and later Jesuits had accepted that Buddhism was the primary religious opponent of Christianity in China because it was Buddhism with which Christianity was most directly in competition. Both religions appealed to a transcendent and anti-wordly impulse in the human spirit and both were much more uncompromising on matters such as celibacy and material possessions than were Confucianism and Taoism.

---

65 R. H. Van Gulik, *Sexual life in ancient China* (Leiden, 1961) p. 285f.
66 Le Gobien, preface, 12th-13th pages.
67 Le Gobien, preface, 13th page.
68 Le Gobien, preface, 13th-14th pages.
69 Le Gobien, preface, 14th page.

Le Gobien stated that out of the Taoists there emerged yet another teaching which claimed that the three sects differed only in appearance and fundamentally represented the same teaching[70]. This was a reference to Ming syncretism, which was more a cultural movement than a distinct teaching. Le Gobien identified this syncretic group by one of its Chinese names, *San-chiao*, which he rendered as "the three sects amount to the same thing"[71]. He explained that the three sects referred to Neo-Confucianism, Buddhism and Taoism. But the exponents of Ming syncretism, such as Lin Chao-en (1517–1598), thought of the syncretism in terms of the entire traditions of Confucianism, Buddhism and Taoism. Lin was not atypical of such thinkers when he focused on the founders of the three religions – Confucius, Sakyamuni Buddha and Lao Tzu[72].

In regard to morality, Le Gobien saw considerable doctrinal differences between the three religions. But he conceded a tendency for them to agree in practice, which he explained was due to their shared tendencies toward defective doctrine[73]. For Le Gobien, Taoism and Buddhism – he omitted Neo-Confucianism – served as "two poisoned sources" to inundate and corrupt the spirit and morals of the people of China. Their poisonous streams included "magicians, enchanters and professional crooks"[74]. It was true that in seventeenth-century China these disreputable types bloated the ranks of Buddhist and Taoist monks and priests, and the Confucian literati were disdainful of the manner in which these types played upon human superstition. The course of accommodation set by Ricci had led the Jesuits to absorb these critical attitudes from the literati.

Finally, Le Gobien made the puzzling reference to a small number of Chinese who, inspired by a "spark of reason", opposed the teachings of the Neo-Confucians. But since they were only "half-atheists who combat idolatry by an impiety yet grander", they succeeded only in becoming drawn into the current of idolatry[75]. Who this small group of Chinese might have been is unclear, though the late Ming was a very creative period for Chinese philosophy and fostered many splinter groups, such as that led by Li Chih, of which this was possibly one.

In concluding his preface, Le Gobien noted that "human reason obscured by passion has never had enough force to entirely destroy error. As Jesus Christ is the only means which leads to the truth and which gives the way, there is only his all-powerful grace" to help those people blinded by iniquity. To a con-

---

70 Le Gobien, preface, 14th page.
71 Le Gobien, preface, 14h page. More specifically, Le Gobien refers to this sect as "*San-Kiao coiici yi*," of which I regard the third word to be a mistaken or unintelligible romanization of *ho*, as in *San-chiao ho-i*.
72 Goodrich & Fang, pp. 912–915.
73 Le Gobien, preface, 15th page.
74 Le Gobien, preface, 15th page.
75 Le Gobien, preface, 15th-16th pages.

temporary reader, such words certainly do not sound very flattering to the Chinese and yet, this book, along with Le Comte's *Nouveaux mémoires,* provoked the Sorbonne commission into condemning them as overly favorable to the Chinese.

CONCLUSION

The most important sources shaping the seventeenth-century European assimilation of information about China were the published writings of the Jesuit missionaries. These were highly informative works interwoven with generally sympathetic attitudes toward the Chinese and their civilization, though as the century progressed, these works grew more defensive and polemical in tone in response to attacks on Jesuit accommodation.

Some of these Jesuit works were popularly oriented general accounts of Chinese society and culture, such as Ricci-Trigault's *De Christiana expeditione apud Sinas* (1615), Semedo's *Imperio de la China* (1642) and Magalhaes-Bernou's *Nouvelle relation de la Chine* (1690). Others were scholarly works aimed at a more circumscribed audience, such as Martini's *Novus atlas Sinensis* (1655) and *Sinicae historiae decas prima* (1658). Some works, such as Martini's *De bello tartarico in Sinis historia* (1655), were hastily ground-out pieces aimed at capitalizing on public interest in a current event. Others, such as the group translation of the Confucian Four Books, *Confucius Sinarum philosophus* (1687), had been in progress since the beginning of the century. While most of these books were written by highly informed Jesuits, the intensification of the Rites Controversy at the end of the century caused the content of these works to suffer by fostering propaganda pieces aimed at a more blatant promotion of the Jesuit position on accommodation. Such were *Nouveaux mémoires sur l'etat présent de la Chine* (1696) by Le Comte and *Histoire de l'edit de l'empereur de la Chine* (1698) by Le Gobien who was the procurator in France and a Jesuit who had never set foot in China.

While the Jesuit missionary authors of works under consideration reflected that blend of respect and admiration for Chinese society and culture which was characteristic of accommodation policy, the European proto-sinologists had a somewhat different outlook toward China. The dominant seventeenth-century European intellectual style of encyclopedic interests was clearly apparent in the fascination with China. Kircher was an intellectual prototype of his age in blending a vast range of interests with amateur boldness of investigation, and his *China illustrata* most eminently symbolized China as the object of "curious" (i.e. painstaking, detailed and skillful) investigation. Viewed in this light, Kircher's Hermetism may be seen as the product of a restless and encyclopedic mind in an intense state of fascination with unknown and exotic elements of the world — whether of ancient Egypt or far-distant China. While Kircher's Hermetism may have been relatively unique, his "curious" interest in China was a motivating force shared by most of the proto-sinologists who studied the Jesuit works on China and who went on to develop their own, often bizarre theories.

One of the most significant areas of the seventeenth-century European assimilation of information about China was historical chronology. Europeans of this time were very chronologically minded in interpreting the Bible and so the appearance on the scene of a traditional Chinese chronology which seemed to antedate Biblical chronology caused a great stir among Christian savants. Although Jesuits working in China had been aware of this conflict between the traditional Chinese chronology and the Vulgate-based Biblical chronology since early in the century, it was Martini's *Sinicae historiae decas prima* which clearly revealed the contradiction to European scholars. Martini's work was very persuasive in convincing Europeans of the validity of the traditional Chinese chronology. He expressed the Jesuit preference for supplanting the extremely literal chronology which had become associated with the Vulgate with the slightly more ancient and flexible Septuagint-based chronology. But he left many questions unanswered about possible historical connections between Chinese and European civilizations. His work helped to stimulate many European savants to consider these issues and to attempt to accommodate European notions of Biblical history with traditional Chinese history. One of the most striking of these attempts at adaptation was John Webb's identification of the Biblical patriarch Noah with the Chinese patriarch Yao.

A second significant area of proto-sinological concern was in the assimilation of the Chinese language. Seventeenth-century Europeans were preoccupied with language — they investigated its nature, believed in its endless ability to resolve human difficulties, and made outrageous claims for its logical structure. Ricci emphasized the practical side of language in the construction of the Jesuit formula of accommodation. Fluency in the Chinese spoken and literary language was to be required of each Jesuit missionary. But it is clear that Ricci's legacy was not merely pragmatic. Semedo's and Magalhaes' fascination with the structure and phonetic qualities of the Chinese language shows that the study of Chinese for practical reasons had a theoretical carryover among missionaries. Meanwhile, the European search for a universal language was fostering an intense interest in the Chinese language as a possible candidate for *lingua universalis* status. The interest among savants was so widespread and intense that it was impossible to limit the discussion to the known features of the Chinese language.

Not only were there not enough knowledgeable returned missionaries from China to supply accurate information, but the European imagination had been so fired by predisposing theoretical notions about the Chinese language, that it proved impossible to ground these theories fully in known facts. In the overheated minds of Müller and Mentzel, the pictographic and radical-etymological structure of Chinese readily lent itself to the classifatory rage of their age and led them to claim that they separately had devised "keys" which would simplify the learning of the language. All of this was done on the basis of incomplete and inadequate knowledge of Chinese. But even the accurate information that was available from China missionaries such as Martini and Boym was grist for the Hermetic mill of the eminent Kircher. For Kircher, this information about the Chinese language served to confirm his theory that the Chinese language, culture and even its religious forms had all originated in Egypt. Like the degenerated Chinese religious forms, the Chinese characters were said by Kircher to have devolved from the Egyptian hieroglyphs.

Jesuit missionaries in China continued to pursue both practical and theoretical lines in studying the Chinese language. The fruits of the practical line of development are apparent in the seventeenth-century Jesuit translation-project of the Confucian Four Books. Beginning with Ricci's paraphrase of these Classics, the Jesuits continued to refine and extend their translations whose published results appeared in 1662, 1667–1669, 1687 and 1711. The contrast between the practical and theoretical lines of development in the study of the Chinese language is apparent in the differing work of Couplet and Bouvet. Couplet's practical talents as an editor enabled him to bring to completion the culmination of Ricci's accommodation plan in *Confucius Sinarum philosophus* (1687). Although the long introduction to this work contained a great deal of theoretical development of the Confucian-Christian synthesis at the expense of Sung Neo-Confucianism, there was very little theoretical interest in the Chinese language. By contrast, Bouvet, a primary figure in adapting Jesuit accommodation to the changing circumstances in late seventeenth-century China, was preoccupied with the theoretical component of the Chinese language.

Bouvet not only grounded his Figurist ideas partly upon his theories of the nature of the Chinese characters, but he also used Hermetism to interpret the Chinese characters, however, in a very different way from Kircher. Whereas the proto-sinologist Kircher had treated Chinese characters as derivative from and as lesser forms of Egyptian hieroglyphs, the Jesuit missionary Bouvet argued that the ancient Chinese characters of Fu Hsi and the *I ching* had numerological and representative simplicity and clarity which made them not only candidates for Primitive Language status which seventeenth-century Europeans sought to recover, but also contained the deepest mysteries of Christianity, in some aspects even antedating Biblical Revelation. In short, Bouvet argued that Fu Hsi had been not merely a Chinese patriarch, but a universal lawgiver whose numerical system of the *I ching* diagrams comprehended all human knowledge. Therefore Bouvet argued that Fu Hsi's teachings should be accommodated within the most fundamental notions of European Christianity. While Bouvet's work was severely restricted in its public dissemination, it nevertheless provided a last fanning of the flames of the European search for a universal language from China and it worked to do this through the eminent and brilliant Leibniz. Unlike Müller and Mentzel who might be dismissed as limited mentalities and historical curiosities, Leibniz was an intellectual giant. The enormous intellectual stimulation which Leibniz received from his contact with Bouvet shows the tremendous fascination which the Chinese language and its implications for human knowledge continued to inspire among learned Europeans at the end of the seventeenth century.

The victory of the anti-Jesuit forces in the Sorbonne censure of 1700 was followed-up by other attacks on Jesuit accommodation. These attacks were so effective that Rome eventually ruled against the Jesuit interpretation of the Chinese rites in the Papal bulls *Ex illa die* (1715) and *Ex quo singulari* (1742). However, it is important to realize that only part of Jesuit accommodation was formally repudiated, namely, the mission strategy. While the China Mission had made significant progress in converting Chinese to Christianity, it had by no means been completely successful. With the eighteenth-century condemnations from Rome, the direction of mission strategy was radically altered from the framework initially formulated by Ricci. Attempts to convert the Chinese through the molding of a Confucian-Christian synthesis or through the proposed, but unrealized, modification in the form of the *I ching*-ist-Christian synthesis no longer set the tone of mission policy in China. The failure of Ricci's Jesuit successors to adapt the Confucian-Christian synthesis to later circumstances demands viewing the seventeenth-century China Mission in an evolving historical context. It is my emphasis on this evolving context which distinguishes my approach from that found in Jacques Gernet's *Chine et Christianisme* (1982). Although we often deal with similar material, M. Gernet's tendency to treat the Chinese cultural context in terms of more constant philosophical and theological categories leads him to some very different conclusions, including a greater criticism of Ricci[1].

There is another aspect of Jesuit accommodation, in addition to mission strategy, which was less vulnerable to formal condemnation. Ricci's initial plan involved a formula for the meeting of Chinese and European cultures which went beyond mission strategy. If the Confucian-Christian and *I ching*-ist-Christian syntheses never realized their full potential as mission strategies, it does not necessarily follow that the notion of a synthesis as an intellectual framework for the assimilation of knowledge between China and Europe was also rejected. The task of intellectual assimilation required a degree of parity between the two cultures. Jesuit accommodation policy had attempted to establish some

---

1 Another difference which distinguishes my treatment of the seventeenth-century Sino-European cultural encounter from that of M. Gernet, at least where it overlaps in subject matter, is in regard to the choice of sources for reconstructing the European side of the encounter. (Gernet's attempt to reconstruct the Chinese side of this encounter transcends the scope of my work.) But in regard to the European side, I believe that M. Gernet's over-reliance upon French-language sources distorts his picture. Had he used some of the major Latin sources, such as Martini's *Sinicae historiae decas prima* and Couplet's *Confucius Sinarum philosophus* – no Latin-language work appears in his list of sources – he could have reconstructed a fuller picture of the evolution of the European side of this encounter and perhaps had a more sympathetic understanding of certain Jesuits.

degree of parity by showing that the Chinese possessed many affinities with
Christianity. Chinese culture was integrated into Biblical experience through
its history (the postulation of common experiences such as in identifying Yao's
flood with the Noadic flood and the general reconciliation of traditional Chinese
chronology with Septuagint chronology), through its language (dispersion of
Tongues at Babel and of structural elements common to Chinese and European
languages) and through its people [common descent of Chinese and Europeans
via Biblical figures Adam, Noah (Yao) and Ham]. Jesuit accommodation also
worked among the Chinese to integrate the European experience into traditional
Chinese culture, though with limited success. When the Chinese studied European
learning, it was primarily for utilitarian reasons.

Intellectual assimilation of one culture by another is not done in a vacuum
and this integration of Chinese culture into Biblical experience had deep-seated
influences in European thinking about the "curious land" China which were not
eradicated by Papal rulings. The contributions of Jesuit accommodation went
into the flow of history through its influence on the proto-sinologists. What the
proto-sinologists began in the seventeenth century with amateur enthusiasm,
"curious" investigation and inadequate knowledge of China was carried on in the
eighteenth and later centuries by sinologists with an evergrowing seriousness,
focus and expertise. Viewed in this light, Jesuit accommodation constituted
the foundation of modern sinology and, viewed in this light, Ricci's formula was
enveloped rather than rejected by history.

A NOTE EXPLAINING THE DUAL DATING OF CERTAIN LETTERS

The dual dating of certain letters in this work, e.g. March 13th (23rd) 1675, reflects the differences in the dual calendrical system — the Julian and Gregorian — then employed in Europe. In the sixteenth century, papal authorities, out of a concern over the growing discrepancy between the calendrical accuracy of feast days and their actual celebration, acted to correct this discrepancy. The discrepancy was the result of the accumulated difference between the Julian calendar year, in use since the mid-first century, of 365.25 days and the correct yearly value of 365.242199 days. This resulted in a Papal bull of 1572 by Pope Gregory XIII directing the Jesuit astronomer Christopher Clavius (1537—1612) to draw up a new calendar. This new formulation, known as the Gregorian calendar, was promulgated by Papal bull in 1582 and involved an omission of ten calendar days between October 4th and October 15th. However, in spite of the greater accuracy of the new calendar, religious divisions between the Roman Catholic, Eastern Orthodox and Protestant churches impeded the calendar's adoption. The Protestant lands were particularly slow and not until 1699—1700 did Denmark, the Dutch and German Protestant states adopt the Gregorian calendar. England and Sweden did not adopt it until 1752 and 1753, respectively. Consequently, references to letters written from these Protestant lands prior to the time of adoption of the Gregorian calendar frequently contain two dates: the originally assigned (Julian calendar) dating and, in parenthesis, the corrected (Gregorian calendar) dating.

GLOSSARY OF CHINESE TERMS

Ai Ti 哀帝

A-lo-a 阿羅訶

A-lo-pen 阿羅本

A-mi-ta-fo 阿彌陀佛

An Wen-ssu 安文思

Cheng An-te-lo 鄭安德助

Chang Ch'eng 張誠

Chang Chü-cheng 張居正

Chang Hsien-chung 張獻忠

Chang ko-lao chih-chieh 張閣老
直解

Chang Ma-no Chung-ch'un
張瑪諾仲春

Chang Tai 張代

Chang T'ing-yü 張廷玉

Chang Tsung 張聰

Chang Tzu-lieh 張自烈

chao 朝

Chen 沈

Chenchiang 鎮江

chen-shu 眞書

Chen Hsü 顓頊

Cheng Ho 鄭和

Cheng-tzu ssu-shu 正字四書

Cheng-tzu-t'ung 正字通

chi 吉

chi 雞

Chi Liu-chi'i 計六奇

Chi-nien Li Ma-t'ou lai Hua ssu-pai
chou-nien Chung-Hsi wen-hua chiao-
liu kuo-chi hsüeh-shu hui-i 紀念
利瑪竇來華四百週年
中西文化交流國際學
術會議

chia 家

chia 嫁

Chia-shen ch'uan-hsin lu 甲申
傳信錄

chiang 江

Chiang Yu-jen 蔣友仁

Chiangling 江陸

chiao 教

chiao-shu 楷書

Chiao Lien 焦璉

Chiating 嘉定

Chieh 桀

Ch'ien Hsing 錢熙

chien-tan 鍊丹

chih 之

chih 智

Chih-nan pa-shih-i nan-ching 指南
八十一難經

Chih sheng hsien shih K'ung-tz'u 至聖
先師孔子

Chi-ho yüan-pen 幾何原本

chih-shan 至善

chin 金

Chin Ssu-piao 金四表

chin-tso 金錯

Chin-tai Ou-chou Han-hsüeh chia te
hsien-chü Ma-erh-ti-ni 近代歐
洲漢學家的先驱马
尔莘尼

Chin-tan-chiao 金丹教

ching t'ien 敬天

Ching-chiao 景教

Ching-kai [chün] Hai-jo T'ang hsien-
sheng chiao-ting hai-p'ien t'ung-huai
精亥鐫海若湯先生校
訂海篇統滙

Chiu yu pien 逑友篇

Chou 紂

Chou-sui sheng-jen hsing lüeh 週歲
聖人行略

Chou Lien-hsi (Tun-i) 周濂溪
(敦頤)

chu 主

chu 柱

Chu Feng-t'ai 朱鳳台

Chu Shao-pen 朱紹本

Chu Ssu-pen 朱思本

Chu Ts'u-hsüan (Tang-ting) 朱慈烜
(當定)

Chu Yu-lang 朱由榔

Chu Yu-chien 朱由檢

Chu Yü-chien 朱聿鍵

Chu-tzu ta-ch'üan 朱子大全

chuan 篆

chuan-shu 篆書

Chung-kuo nei-luan wai-huo li-shih
ts'ung-shu 中國內亂外禍
歷史叢書

Chung-kuo T'ien-chu-chiao shih-jen
wu ch'uan 中國天主教史
人物傳

Chung-kuo wen-hsüeh-chai ta-tz'a-tien
中國文學家大辭典

Chung-kuo yen-fa 中國言法

Chung-ni 仲尼

Chung-wen ta-tzu-tien 中文大辭
典

Chung yung shuo 中庸說

chün-tzu 君子

Ch'ao-hsing-hsüeh yao 超性學要

Ch'eng Chi-li 成際理

Ch'eng T'ang 成湯

ch'i 氣

Ch'ien Mu 錢穆

Ch'ien k'un t'i i 乾坤體義

Ch'ien Te-ming 錢德明

ch'in min 親民

Ch'ingming 崇明

ch'i-tan 契丹

ch'üan 全

Ch'uan shu Shen Nung tso 傳書 神農作

Ch'un-ch'iu 春秋

Ch'ung-chen 崇禎

ch'ung-shu 蟲書

Ch'ü Ju-k'uei (T'ai-su) 瞿汝夔 (太素)

En Li-ko 恩理格

Fang Hao 方豪

Fan-shih 范氏

Feng Mu-kang 馬慕岡

Feng shu Shao Hao tso 鳳書小 昊作

Fo 佛

Fu Fan-chi 傅汎際

Fu Hsi she lung shu 伏羲蛇龍 書

Fu Sheng-tse 傅聖澤

Fu-huo lan 復活論

Hai-p'ien 海篇

ho 和

Ho Ta-hua 何大化

ho-shang 和尚

Ho-t'u lo-shu 河圖洛書

Hou-t'ien tzu-hsü 後天次序

hou-tu 后土

Hsi tzu 擊辭

Hsiang-chiao p'ien-hai 詳校篇海

Hsiao erh lun 小兒論

Hsiao hsüeh 小學

Hsiao-erh yü 小兒語

Hsichangan chieh 西長安街

Hsieh Wu-lu 謝務祿

Hsi-ho ch'üan-chi 西河全集

hsien-ju 先儒

Hsien-shih 先師

Hsien-t'ien tzu-hsü 先天次序

hsin 信

hsin min 新民

hsing 性

hsing 形

hsing chih te yeh 性之德也

Hsing-li ching-i 性理精義

Hsing ming chia 形名家

Hsing-li ta-ch'üan 性理全大全

hsiu-shen 修身

hsiu-tao 修道

hsü 虛

Hsü Jih-sheng 徐日昇

Hsü Kantita 徐甘弟大

Hsü Tsung-tse 徐宗澤

hsüan yeh 宣夜

hua-tsai 貨財

Huaian 淮安

Huang Ch'ien-i 黃遷逸

Huang T'ang-ch'i 黃棠溪

huang-ti 皇帝

Hui-Shih 惠施

Hung Jo-han 洪若翰

Hung Tu-chen 洪度貝

Hu Wei 胡渭

I 義

I ching 易經

I-ching tsung-chih 易經總旨

I ssu-shu ta-ch'üan shuo 譯四書大全說

Jen 仁

Jen-min jih-pao 人民日報

jih 日

Jihe Tongjie [Chi-ho t'ung-chieh] 幾何通解

ju 入

ju 如

Ju-hsüeh 儒學

Kai wo chih ming te chi ming 蓋我之明德旣明

Kao I-chih 高一志

ko ming chün te 克明峻德

ko ming te 克明德

Ku-chin ching-t'ien-chien 古今敬天鑑

kua 卦

kuan hua 官話

Kuang yü t'u 廣輿圖

Kuei-hai 癸亥

Kuo Chu-ching 郭居静

Kuo-hui t'u-shu-kuan-ts'ang Chung-kuo shan-pen shu lun 國會圖書舘藏中國善本書錄

Kuo Jo-hsi 郭若習

Kuo Na-chüeh 郭納爵

Kuo-tzu chien 國子監

Kuo-hsüeh 國學

Kuo-tzu hsüeh 國子學

k'ang 炕

K'ang-hsi tzu-tien 康熙字典

K'ang Wang 康王

k'o tou tzu 科斗字; 蝌蚪字

k'ou tuo jih-ch'ao 口鐸日抄

k'un-shan 崑山

Lao-tzu 老子

li 里

li 理

li 禮

Li An-tang 利安當

Li chi 禮記

Li Chih 李贄

Li Ch'ang-hsiang 李昌泉

Li Fang-hsi 李方西

Li Lei-ssu 利類思

Li Kuang-ti 李光地

Li Ma-ti 利瑪竇

Li Ma-t'ou 利瑪竇
Li Ming 李明
Li-tai ti-li-chih-chang t'u 歷代地理指掌圖
Li Tzu-ch'eng 李自成
Li Tsu-po (tzu Jan-chen) 李祖白 (然真)
li-shu 隸書
Li-tai ti-wang tsung-chi 歷代帝王總紀
lin 林
Lin Chao-en 林兆恩
Lin Jin Shui 林金水
ling 鈴   ling 令
ling-hun 靈魂
Lishi yanjiu [Li-shih yen-chiu] 历史研究
Liu pang 劉邦
Liu Ti-wo 劉迪我
Liu Ying Sheng-wen 劉應聲開
Lo 羅
Lo Hung-hsien 羅洪先
Lo Ku-t'ang 樂古堂
lou-k'uei 陋規
Lu Jih-man 魚日滿
Lu K'un 呂坤
Lu Shih-chiang 呂實強
Lu Te-ming 陸德明
Lu-tzu i shu 呂子遺書

luan 孿
Lun yü 論語
Lung Hua-min 龍華民
Lung-wu 隆武
Lü Te-sheng 呂得勝
Ma Kuo-hsien 馬國賢
Ma Jo-se 馬若瑟
Ma Ko-wu 穆格我
Ma Ma-li-ya 馬瑪利納
Ma T'ang 馬堂
Ma Yong [Yung] 马雍
Mao Ch'i-ling 毛奇齡
Mei Wending [Wen-ting] 梅文鼎
Mei Ying-tso 梅膺祚
men 門
men 悶悶懣
mi-ts'u 米醋
miao 廟
Min Ming-wo 閔明我
Min Tsu-ch'ien 閔子騫
ming 明
Ming-Ch'ieng chien Yeh-su-hui shih-i chu t'i-yao 明清間耶穌會士譯著提要
ming-te 明德
mo 末
Mo ching 脈經
mu 木
Mu Ti-wo 穆迪我

Nanchihli 南直隸

nei-tan 內丹

niao 鳥

ni-ku 尼姑

Nieh Chung-ch'ien 聶仲遷

Nieh Shih-tsung 聶石宗

nyu 女

pa-ku 八股

pa-kua 八卦

Pai wen ta 百問答

pen 本

Pen-ts'ao kang-mu 本草綱目

Pi Chia 畢嘉

Pien che 辯者

Po Chin 白晉

Po Nai-hsin 白乃心

Po Ying-li 柏應理

pu 部

Pu Chih-yüan 卜致遠

Pu Ju ch'üeh Fo 補儒卻佛

Pu Ju i Fo 補儒易佛

Pu te i 不得已

Pu te i pien 不得已辨

p'ai wei 牌位

P'an Kuo-kuang 潘國光

P'ang T'ien-shou 龐天壽

P'i-hsieh-lun 闢邪論

P'ien-hai lei-pien 篇海類編

Saeki 佐伯好郎

San-chiao i-ho (ho-i) 三教一合 (合一)

San-kuo-chih yen-i 三教志演義

San-tsai 三才

Shan-hai yü-ti ch'üan-t'u 山海輿地全圖

Shao Hao 少昊

Shang-ti 上帝

shang t'ien chih tsai 上天之載

Shao K'ang-chieh (Yung) 邵康節 (雍)

shen 神

Shen Ch'üeh 沈淮

Shen Fu-tsung 沈福宗

Shen Nung 神農

shen wei 神位

shih 十

Shih-chia 釋迦

Shih ching 詩經

Shih Huang-ti 始皇帝

shih-lu 史錄

Shih-shih 謝氏

shu 恕

Shu ching 書經

Shui-tien 水殿

Shun 舜

Shuo-wen chieh-tzu 說文解字

Ssu mo chen lun 四末眞論

Ssu-shu shih-i 四書釋義

ssu-t'i 四體

Ssu-shu chi-chu 四書集注

Ssu-shu chih-chieh 四書直解

Su Ju-wang 蘇如望

Su Shih 蘇軾

Suchou 蘇州

Sung Lien 宗濂

Sungchiang 松江, 肅宗文明

Su-tsung wen-ming 肅宗文明

Ta hsüeh chih tao tsai ming ming te
大學之道在明明德

T'ai-hsüeh 太學

Tai Sheng 戴聖

T'an Cheng-pi 譚正璧

T'an Ch'ien 談遷

Tao-t'ung 道統

Ti Chang 帝摯

tien 殿

Ti K'u Kao 帝嚳高

Ti-t'u tsung-yao 地圖綜要

ting 丁

Tungchangan chieh 東長安街

Tseng-pu yü-t'ang tsa-tzu 增補玉
堂雜字

Tseng-tzu 曾子

Tseng Te-chao 曾德照

Tung-yüan tsa-tzu ta-ch'üan 東園

雜字大全

tzu 糸

Tzu-chih t'ung-chien 資製通鑑

Tzu-hui 字彙

Tzu-pei tao-ch'ang chan-fa 慈悲
道場懺法

Tzu Chang 于長

Tzu hai 辭海

Tzu hai ming chu 字海明珠

tzu k'ao 字考

Tzu Kung 子貢

Tzu Lu 子路

Tzu Ssu 子思

Tzu Yu 子遊

T'ai-chi t'u-shuo 太極圖説

T'ai-ts'ang 太倉

T'ai-tsung wen 太宗文

T'ang 湯

T'ang Jo-wang 湯若望

T'ien Jo-wang

T'ien Ju yin 天儒印

T'ienanmen 天安門

T'ien-ch'i 天格

T'ien-chu hsiang lüeh shuo fu hsiao
luan pu ping ming shuo 天主像
略説附鶏鸞不並鳴説

T'ien-chu lung-sheng ch'u-hsiang ching
chieh 天主隆生出像經
解

T'ien-chu sheng-chiao sheng-jen
hsing-shih 天主聖教聖人
行實
T'ien-chu shih-i 天主實義
T'ien-chu-chiao sheng yüeh-yen
天主教聖約言
T'ien-chu-chiao tung-ch'uan wen-hsien
hsü-pien 天主教東傳文
獻續編
T'ien-hsüeh ch'uan-kai 天學傳
概
T'ien-hsüeh pen-wen 天學本文
t'ien-kan 天干
t'ien-shen 天神
T'u Lung 屠隆
T'ung Kuo-ch'i 佟國器
T'ung-wen suan-fa 同文算法
wai-tan 外丹
Wan-pao yu-hsüeh hsü-chih: ao-t'ou
tsa-tzu ta-ch'üan 萬寶幼學須
知:鼇頭雜字大全
wang 王
Wang Feng-su 王豐肅
Wang Fu-chih 王夫之
Wang Ju-wang 汪儒望
Wang Lieh-na 王烈納
Wang Po 王柏
Wang Shuo-ko 王叔和
Wang Ya-na 王亞納

wei[a] 渭
wei[b] 熰
wei[c] 愲
wei[d] 謂
wei[e] 蝟
Wei Fang-chi 衛防濟
Wei K'uang-kuo 衛匡國
Wenchou 溫州
Wen tzu k'ao 文字考
Wu-ching 五經
Wu Erh-to 吳爾鐸
Wu Hsiang-hsiang 吳相湘
Wu-hsing 五行
Wu Hsüeh-yen 吳學儼
Wu-lun 五倫
Wu Wei-yeh (Hui-ts'un) 吳偉業
(梅村)
Wu Ti 武帝
wu-wei 無為
Yang Kuang-hsien 楊光先
Yang Ma-no 楊瑪諾
Yang Ting-yün 楊廷筠
Yao 堯
Yen 鄞
yen 言
Yen Hui 顏回
Yen Tang 顏璫
yu-chi 游擊
Yu Ming-Ch'ing chih chi Chung-

kuo chih-shih fen-tzu Fan-Chiao yen-
lun k'an Chung-Hsi wen-hua chiao-liu

由明清之際中國知識
份子反教言論看中
西文化交流

yueh 月

yueh 龠

Yung-li 永曆

yü 玉

yü 禹

BIBLIOGRAPHY

List of Works Cited

Primary Literature

Abdallae, Beidavaei. *Historia Sinensis.* Edited by Andreas Müller. Jeana, 1689.

Acta eruditorum (Leipzig).

Bacon, Francis. *The advancement of learning and the New Atlantis.* Edited by Arthur Johnston. Reprinted Oxford, 1974.

Bartoli, Daniello. *Dell'Istoria della Compagnia di Giesù. La Cina.* Rome, 1663.

Bayer, Gottlieb Siegfried. *Museum Sinicum.* 2 vols. St. Petersburg, 1730.

Bibliothèque curieuse, historique et critique.

Bibliothèque universalle et historique.

Bosmans, Henri, S.J. "Lettres inédites de François Rougemont." *Analectes pour servir l'histoire ecclésiastique de la Belgique* 39 (1913): 21–54.

Bouvet, Joachim. *Portrait historique de l'empereur de la Chine.* Paris, 1697.

Boym, Michaele. *Flora Sinensis.* Vienna, 1656.

Casaubon, Issac. *De rebus sacris et ecclesiasticus exercitationes XVI.* London, 1614.

Chang, Chü-cheng. *Ssu-shu chih-chieh.* 1573.

Chang, T'ing-yü *et al. Ming shih.* 28 vols. (326 *chüan*) compiled Peking, 1678–1739; reprinted 1974.

Ch'ien, Mu. *Ssu-shu shih-i.* Taipei, 1978.

Couplet, Philippe *et al. Confucius Sinarum philosophus.* Paris, 1687.

–. *Tabula chronologica monarchiae Sinicae.* Paris, 1686.

Dalgarno, George. *Ars signorum, vulgo character universalis et lingua philosophica.* London, 1661.

d'Elia, Pasquale, S.I. *Fonti Ricciane.* 3 vols. Rome, 1942–1949.

–. *Il mappemondo Cinese del P. Matteo Ricci.* Vatican, 1938.

Descartes, René. *Oeuvres de Descartes.* Edited by Charles Adam & Paul Tannery. Paris, 1897.

Encyclopédie ou dictionnaire raissone des sciences, des arts et des métiers. Aneufchastel, 1765.

Fourmont, Etienne. *Meditationes et grammatica Sinica.* Paris, 1737.

Galilei, Galileo. *Dialogue concerning the two chief world systems – Ptolemaic and Copernican.* Translated by Stillman Drake. Berkeley, 1953.

Gherardini, Giovanni. *Relation du voyage fait à Chine sur le vaisseau l'Amphitrite, en l'année 1698.* Paris, 1700.

Grebnitz, Elias. *Unterricht von der Reformirten und Lutherischen Kirche.* Frankfurt an der Oder (?), 1678.

–. *Verthädigung gegen den anzüglichen Tractat worinnen M. Andreas Müller ... seine ungelährte Anstechung des Unterrichts von der Reformirten und Lutherischen Kirchen unter der Decken eines Unterrichts von der chinästchen Schrift und Druck verbergen wollen.* Frankfurt an der Oder, 1681.

Journal des savants (Journal des sçavans).

Kircher, Athanasius. *Ars magna sciendi, sive combinatoriae.* Amsterdam, 1669.

–. *China monumentis qua sacris quà profanis, nec non variis naturae & artis spectaculis, aliarumque rerum memorabilium argumentis illustrata.* Amsterdam, 1667.

–. *La Chine illustrée de plusierus monuments tant sacrés que profanes, et de quantité de recherchés de la nature & de l'art.* Translated by F. S. Dalquié. Amsterdam, 1670.

–. *Oedipus Aegyptiacus.* 3 vols. Rome, 1652–1655.

–. *Prodromus Coptus sive Aegyptiacus.* Rome, 1636.

Legge, James, trans. *The Chinese Classics.* 5 vols. Oxford, 1893.

Le Comte, Louis. *Nouveaux mémoires sur l'état présent de la Chine.* 2 vols. Paris, 1696.

Le Gobien, Charles. *Histoire de l'edit de l'empereur de la Chine, en faveur Religion Chrestienne.* Paris, 1698.

Leibniz, Gottfried Wilhelm. *Discourse on the natural theology of the Chinese.* Translated & edited by Daniel J. Cook & Henry Rosemont, Jr. Honolulu, 1977.

—. *Leibnitii opera omnia.* Edited by Ludovicus Dutens. 6 vols. Geneva, 1768.

—. *Monadology and other philosophical essays.* Translated by Paul & Anne Martin Schrecker. Indianapolis, 1965.

—. *Das Neueste von China (1697). Novissima Sinica.* Translated & edited by Heinz Günther Nesselrath & Hermann Reinbothe. Bonn-Oedekoven, 1979.

—. *Opuscules et fragments inédits de Leibniz.* Edited by Louis Couturat. Paris, 1903.

—. *Philosophical papers and letters.* Edited & translated by Leroy E. Loemker. Reidel, Holland, 1969.

—. *Die philosophischen Schriften von G. W. Leibniz.* Edited by Carl Immanuel Gerhardt. 7 vols. Berlin, 1875–1890.

—. *The preface to Leibniz' Novissima Sinica.* Edited & translated by Donald F. Lach. Honolulu, 1957.

—. *Sämtliche Schriften und Briefe.* Edited by the Deutschen (formerly Preußischen) Akademie der Wissenschaften zu Berlin. In seven series. Darmstadt, Leipzig & Berlin, 1923–.

—. *Vivi illustris Godefridi Guil. Leibnitii epistolae ad diversos . . .* Edited by Christian Kortholt. 4 vols. Leipzig, 1735.

Letters relating to the affairs of the Royal Society 1663–1675. London, 1757.

*Lettre a Monsieur ** touchant les honneurs que les Chinois rendent au Philosophe & a leurs Ancêtres.* 1700.

Li, An-tang [Antonio Caballero a Santa Maria]. *T'ien Ju yin.* 1664. in *T'ien-chu-chiao tung-ch'uan wen-hsien hsü-pien.* Edited by Wu Hsiang-hsiang. 3 vols. Taipei, 1966. II, 981–1042.

Li, Ma-t'ou [Matteo Ricci]. *T'ien-chu shih-i.* 1603.

Li, Tsu-po. *T'ien-hsüeh ch'uan-kai.* in *T'ien-chu-chiao tung-ch'uan wen-hsien hsü-pien.* Edited by Wu Hsiang-hsiang. 3 vols. Taipei, 1966. II, 1043–1068.

Longobardi, Nichola. *Traité sur quelques points de la religion des Chinois.* Paris, 1701.

Magaillans [Magalhaes], Gabriel de. *A new history of China containing a description of the most considerable particulars of that vast empire.* Translated by John Quliby. London, 1688.

—. *Nouvelle relation de la Chine contenant la description des particularitez les plus considérables de ce grand empire.* Edited by Claude Bernou [Bernon]. Paris, 1690.

Martini, Martino. *De bello Tartarico historia.* Amsterdam, 1655.

—. *Histoire de la guerre des Tartares contre la Chine.* Translated by Gilbert Girault. Paris, 1654.

—. *Novus atlas Sinensis.* Amsterdam, 1655. Published as part six of Joannis Bleau's *Theatrum orbis terrarum sive novus atlas.*

—. *Sinicae historiae decas prima res a gentis origine ad Christum natum in extrema Asia.* Munich, 1658.

Mémoires concernant l'histoire, les sciences, les arts, les moeurs, les usages, etc. des Chinois, par les Missionnaries de Pékin. 17 vols. Paris, 1776–1814.

Mendoza, Joan Gonzàles de. *Historia de las cosas, ritos y costumbres, del gran Reyno de la China.* Antwerp, 1596.

Mentzel, Christian. *Kurtze chinesische Chronologia oder Zeit-Register aller chinesischen Kayser.* Berlin, 1696.

—. *Sylloge minutiarum latino-sinico-caracteristici.* Nuremburg, 1685.

Müller, Andreas. *Basilicon Sinense.* 1679 (?).

—. *Besser Unterricht von der sineser Schrift und Druck als etwa in Hrn. D. Eliae Grebnitzen Unterricht . . .* 1680 (?).

—. *Chronolista clavis.*

—. *De invento Sinico epistolae nonnullae.*

—. *De Sinarum magnaeque Tartari rebus commentatio alphabetica.* 1689.

—. *Disquisitio geographica et historica de Chataja.* 1671.

—. *Hebdomas observationum de rebus Sinicis*. Berlin, 1672.

—. *Imperii Sinensis nomenclator geographicus*. 1680.

—. *Lectio Monumenti Sinici, quod in China terris erutum*. Berlin, 1672.

—. *Propositio super clave sua Sinica, quam autor Inventum Brandenburgicum cognominare constituit*.

Navarrete, Domingo Fernandez. *Tratados historicos, politicos, ethicos, y religiosos de la Monarchia de China*. Madrid, 1676.

Noël, Francisco. *Sinensis imperii libri classici sex*. Prague, 1711.

Pinot, Virgile, ed. *Documents inédits relatifs a la connaissance de la Chine en France de 1685 à 1740*. Paris, 1932.

Prémare, Joseph Henry-Marie de. *Lettre sur le monotheisme des Chinois*. Edited by Jean Pierre Guillaume Pauthier. Paris, 1862.

—. *Notitia linguae Sinicae*. Hong Kong, 1893.

—. *Vestiges des principaux dogmes Chrétiens trés des anciens livrés chinois*. Translated by Augustin Bonnetty & Paul Perny. Paris, 1878.

Ricci, Matteo. *The catechism* (The true meaning of the Lord of Heaven). Translated with notes by Douglas Lancashire in collaboration with Peter Hu Kuo-chen, S.J. St. Louis, forthcoming. First chapter published in *China Mission Studies (1550–1800) Bulletin* 4 (1982): 1–11.

—. *China in the sixteenth century: the journals of Matthew Ricci 1583–1610*. Edited by Nicolas Trigault. Translated by Louis J. Gallagher, S.J.. New York, 1953.

—. *De Christiana expeditione apud Sinas*. Edited by Nicolas Trigault. Augsburg, 1615.

—. *Entretiens d'un lettré chinois & d'un doctor européen, sur la vrai idée de Dieu*. Translated by Ch. Jacques. in *Lettres édifiantes et curieuses* (Paris) 25 (1783).

—. *Histoire de l'expedition chrétienne au royaume de la Chine 1582–1610*. Lille, 1617; reprinted Paris, 1978.

Ripa, Matthew [Matteo Rippa]. *Memoirs of Father Ripa*. Translated by Fortunato Prandi. London, 1844.

Rippa, Matteo. *Storia della fondazione della Congregazione e del Collegio de' Cinesi*. 3 vols. Naples, 1789.

Semedo, Alvaro. *Histoire universelle de la Chine*. Lyon & Paris, 1667.

—. *Relatione della Grande Monarchia della Cina*. Rome, 1643.

Southwell [alias Ribadeneira; alias Alegambe], S.J.. *Bibliotheca scriptorum Soc. Jesu*. Rome, 1676.

Spizelius [Spitzel], Theophil. *De re literaria Sinensium commentarius*. Antwerp, 1660.

Tacchi Venturi, Pietro. *Opere storiche del P. Matteo Ricci*. 2 vols. Macerata, 1911–1913.

Thévenot, Melchisédec. *Relations de divers voyages curieux ...* 4 vols. Paris, 1663–1672; reprinted Paris, 1696.

Tizzoni, Francesco, ed.. *Compendiosa relatione della stato della Missione Cinese*. Rome, 1672.

T'ang,Li. *P'ien-hai*. 1623.

Verbiest, Ferdinand. *Correspondence de Ferdinand Verbiest (1623–1688)*. Edited by Frs. Josson & Willaert. 1938.

Wang Fu-chih. *Hsü ssu-shu ta-ch'üan-shuo*. 1665; reprinted Peking, 1975.

Webb, John. *Historical essay endeavoring a probability that the language of the Empire of China is like Primitive Language*. London, 1669.

Wilkins, John. *Essay toward a Real Character and Philosophical Language*. London, 1668.

—. *The mathematical and philosophical works of the Right Rev. John Wilkins*. Reprinted London, 1707.

Yang, Kuang-hsien. *Pu-te-i*. in *T'ien-chu-chiao tung-ch'uan wen-hsien hü-pien*. Edited by Wu Hsiang-hsiang. 3 vols. Taipei, 1966. III, 1069–1332.

Zedlar. *Großes vollständiges Universal-Lexicon aller Wissenschaften und Künste*. Leipzig & Halle, 1739.

Secondary Literature

Artelt, Walter. *Christian Mentzel, Leibarzt des Großen Kurfürsten, Botaniker und Sinologe.* Leipzig, 1940.

Baddeley, John F. "Father Matteo Ricci's Chinese world-maps, 1584–1608." *The geographical journal of the Royal Geographical Society* 53 (1919): 254–270.

Bauer, Wolfang. *China und die Hoffnung auf Glück.* Munich, 1974.

Beckmann, Johannis, S.M.B. "Die katholischen Missionare und der Taoismus vom 16. Jahrhundert bis Gegenwart." *Neue Zeitschrift für Missionswissenschaft* 26 (1970): 1–17.

Berling, Judith A. *The snycretic religion of Lin Chao-en.* New York, 1980.

Bernard, Henri, S.J. "Les adaptations chinoises d'ouvrages europeens, bibliographie chronologique." *Monumenta Serica* 10 (1945): 1–57 & 309–388 (depuis la venue des Portugais à Canton jusqu'à la Mission française de Pékin 1514–1688); 19 (1960): 349–383 (depuis la fondation de la Mission française de Pékin jusqu'à la mort de l'empereur K'ien-long 1689–1799).

–. "Les etapes de la cartographie scientifique pour la Chine et les pays voisins depuis le XVIe jusqu'à la fin du XVIIIe siècle." *Monumenta Serica* 1 (1936): 428–477.

–. [Bernard-Maitre]. "Ferdinand Verbiest, continuateur de l'oeuvre scientifique d'Adam Schall." *Monumenta Serica* 5 (1940): 103–140.

–. *Sagesse chinoisie et philosophie chrétienne.* Paris & Leiden, 1935.

Billiter, Jean-François. *Li Zhi philosophe maudit (1527–1602).* Geneva, 1979.

Blau, Joseph L. *The story of Jewish philosophy.* New York, 1962.

Blumenberg, Hans. *Der prozeß der theoretischen Neugierde.* Frankfurt am Main, 1980.

Boas, Marie. *The scientific renaissance 1450–1630.* New York, 1962.

Boxer, C. R. "Some aspects of Western historical writing on the Far East, 1500–1800." in *Historians of China & Japan.* Edited by E. G. Pulleyblank & W. G. Beasley. London, 1961.

Brauen, Fred. "Athanasius Kircher (1602–1680)." *Journal of the history of ideas* 43 (1982): 129–134.

Brou, Alexander, S.J. "De certains conflits entre missionnaires au XVIIe siècle." *Revue d'histoire des missions* 11 (1934): 187–202.

–. "Les jésuites sinologues de Pékin et leurs éditeurs de Paris." *Revue d'histoire des missions* 11 (1934): 551–566.

Brown, Lloyd A. *The story of maps.* Boston, 1949.

Cameron, Nigel. *Barbarians and Mandarins.* Tokyo, 1970.

Carreras y Artau, Joaquin. *De Ramón Lull a los modernos ensayos de formación de una lengua universal.* Barcelona, 1946.

Carter, Thomas Francis. *The invention of printing in China and its spread westward.* New York, 1925.

Catholic encyclopedia. vols 2 & 9. New York, 1907.

Chabrié, Robert. *Michael Boym jésuite polonais et la fin des Ming en Chine 1646–1662.* Paris, 1933.

Chan, Albert. *The glory and fall of the Ming dynasty.* Norman, Oklahoma, 1982.

Chan, Hok-lam. *Li Chih 1527–1602 in contemporary Chinese historiography.* White Plains, New York, 1980. Published simultaneously as vol. 13, no. 1–2 of *Chinese studies in history.*

Chan, Wing-tsit. "Chu Hsi's completion of Neo-Confucianism." in Francoise Aubin, ed. . *Étues Song – Sung studies.* In memoriam Etienne Balazs. series II, no. 1, Paris, 1973. pp. 59–90.

–. *Historical charts of Chinese philosophy.* New Haven, 1955.

—. "The *Hsing-li ching-i* and the Ch'eng-Chu school of the seventeenth century." in *The unfolding of Neo-Confucianism*. Edited by Wm. Theodore de Bary. New York, 1975.

—. *A source book in Chinese philosophy*. Princeton, 1963.

Chan, Wing-tsit. "The study of Chu Hsi in the West." *Journal of Asian studies* 35 (1976): 555–577.

Chang, Carson. *The development of Neo-Confucian thought*. 2 vols. New York, 1962.

Ch'en, Kenneth K. S. *Buddhism in China*. Princeton, 1964.

Ch'en Shou-yi. "John Webb: a forgotten page in the early history of sinology in Europe." *The Chinese social & political science review* 19 (1935): 295–330.

—. "Ming-mo Ch'ing-ch'u Yeh-su-hui shih ti Ju-chiao-kuan chi ch'i fan-ying." *Kuo hsüeh chi k'an* 5 (2) (1935): 1–64.

Ching, Julia. *Confucianism & Christianity*. Tokyo, 1977.

—. "Truth and ideology: the Confucian Way (Tao) and its Transmission (Tao-t'ung)." *Journal of the history of ideas* 35 (1974): 371–388.

Cippola, Carlo. *Before the Industrial Revolution: European society and economy, 1000–1700*. 2nd edition. New York, 1980.

Cohen, Paul A. *China and Christianity: the missionary movement and the growth of Chinese antiforeignism, 1860–1870*. Cambridge, Massachusetts, 1963.

Cohen, Jonathan. "On the project of a universal language." *Mind* 63 (1954): 49–63.

Collani, Claudia von. *Die Figuristen in der Chinamission*. Frankfurt am Main, 1981.

Cordier, Henri. *Bibliotheca Sinica*. 5 vols. Paris, 1904–1922.

Cornelius, Paul. *Languages in seventeenth- and eighteenth-century imaginary voyages*. Geneva, 1965.

Corradini, Piero. "Actuality and modernity of Matteo Ricci, a man of the Renaissance in the framework of cultural relations between East and West." in *International Symposium on Chinese-Western Cultural Interchange*. Taipei, 1983. pp. 173–180.

Couling, Samuel. *The encyclopedia Sinica*. Shanghai, 1917.

Coudert, Allison. "Some theories of a natural language." *Studia Leibnitiana* Sonderheft 7. (1978): 56–118.

Couturat, Louis. *La logique de Leibniz*. Paris, 1901.

Crawford, Robert. "Chang Chü-cheng's Confucian Legalism." in *Self & society in Ming thought*. Edited by Wm. Theodore de Bary. New York, 1970.

Creel, Herrlee Glessner. "On the nature of Chinese ideography." *T'oung pao* 32 (1936): 85–166.

—. "Was Confucius agnostic?" *T'oung pao* 29 (1932): 55–99.

Cummins, J. S. "Fray Domingo Navarrete: a source for Quesnay." *Bulletin of Hispanic studies* 36 (1959): 37–50.

—, ed. *The travels and controversies of Fray Domingo Navarrete, 1618–1686*. Published by the Hakluyt Society. Cambridge, 1962.

—. "Two missionary methods in China: mendicants and Jesuits." *Archivo Ibero-Americano* 38 (149–152) (1978): 33–108.

David, Madeleine. *La débat sur les écritures et l'hiéroglyphe aux XVIIe et XVIIIe siècles*. Paris, 1965.

de Bary, Wm. Theodore. "Individualism and humanitarianism." in *Self and society in Ming thought*. New York, 1970. pp. 145–245.

Dehergne, Joseph, S.J. *Répertoire des Jésuites de Chine de 1552 à 1800*. Rome, 1973.

d'Elia, Pasquale, S.I. "Further notes on Matteo Ricci's *De amicitia*." *Monumenta Serica* 15 (1956): 356–377.

—. "The spread of Galileo's discoveries in the Far East (1610–1640)." *East & West* (Rome) 1 (1950): 156–163.

de Rialle, Girard. "Une mission chinoise à Venise au XVIIe siècle." *T'oung pao* 1 (1890): 99–117.

Duyvendak, J. J. L. "Early Chinese studies in Holland." *T'oung pao* 32 (1936): 293–344.

Elvin, Mark. *The pattern of the Chinese past*. Stanford, 1973.

Emery, Clark. "John Wilkins' Universal Language." *Isis* 38 (1948): 174–185.

Fang, Hao. *Chung-kuo T'ien-chu-chiao shih jen-wu ch'uan*. 3 vols. Hong Kong, 1970.

—. "Notes on Matteo Ricci's *De amicitia.*" *Monumenta Serica* 14 (1949–1955): 574–583.

Finegan, Jack. *Handbook of Biblical chronology*. Princeton, 1964.

Franke, Otto. "Das chinesische Geistesleben im 16. Jahrhundert und die Anfänge der Jesuiten-Mission." *Orientalistische Literaturzeitung* 41 (8–9): (August-September 1938): 473–484.

—. "Li Tschi und Matteo Ricci." *Abhandlungen der preußischen Akademie der Wissenschaften* (Berlin) (1937) Philosophisch-historische Klasse nr. 10,pp. 1–62.

Friedländer, Paul. "Athanasius Kircher und Leibniz." *Academia romana di archeologia, Roma . . . Rendiconti* 13 (1937): 229–247.

Frühsorge, Gotthardt. *Der politische Körper. Zum Begriff des Politischen im 17. Jahrhundert und in den Romanen Christian Weises*. Stuttgart, 1974.

Fuchs, Walter. *Chinesische und mandjurische Handschriften und seltene Drucke* in the series Verzeichnis der Orientalischen Handschriften in Deutschland, XII, 1. Wiesbaden, 1966.

—. *The "Mongol Atlas" of China by Chu Ssu-pen and the Kuang-yü-t'u*. Monumenta Serica monograph VIII. Peking, 1946.

—. "Zu Pater Ripa's Debut als chinesischer Hofmaler in das Jahr 1710." in *Tamura hakushi shōju tōyōshi ronsō*. Kyoto, 1968. pp. 1–5.

Fung [Feng], Yu-lan. *A history of Chinese philosophy*. Translated by Derk Bodde. 2 vols. Princeton, 1953.

Gatty, Janette C. "Les recherches de Joachim Bouvet (1656–1730)." in *Acts du Colloque international de sinologie, Chantilly, 1974*. Paris, 1976.

—. *Voiage de Siam du Pére Bouvet*. Leiden, 1963.

Gernet, Jacques. *Chine et christianisme. Action et réaction*. Paris, 1982.

—. "Philosophie chinoise et Christianisme de la fin du XVIe au milieu du XVIIe siècle." in *Actes du colloque international de sinologie, Chantilly, 1974*. Paris, 1976. pp. 13–25.

—. "La politique de conversion de Matteo Ricci et l'evolution de le vie politique et intellectuelle en Chine aux environs de 1600." in *Sviluppi scientifici, prospettive religiose, movimenti rivoluzionare in Cina*. Florence, 1975.

—. "A propos des contacts entre la Chine et l'Europe aus XVIIe et XVIIIe siècles." *Acta Asiatica* (Tokyo) 23 (1972): 78–92.

—. "Sur les different versions du premier catechisme en Chinois de 1584." in *Studia Sino-Mongolica* (Wiesbaden). Festschrift for Herbert Franke. 25 (1979): 407–416.

Giles, Lionel. "Translations from the Chinese map of Father Ricci." *The geographical journal of the Royal Geographical Society* 52 (1918): 367–385.

Gillespie, Charles C., ed. *Dictionary of scientific biography*. New York, 1973.

Goodrich, L. Carrington. "China's first knowledge of the Americas." *Geographical review* 28 (1938): 400–411.

— & Fang, Chaoying, eds. *Dictionary of Ming biography, 1368–1644*. 2 vols. New York, 1976.

Goubert, Pierre. *Louis XIV and twenty million Frenchmen*. Translated by Anne Carter. New York, 1972.

Granet, Marcel. *La pensée chinoise*. Paris, 1934.

Haeger, John Winthrop. "The intellectual context of Neo-Confucian syncretism." *Journal of Asian studies* 31 (1972): 499–513.

Han Yu-shan. *Elements of Chinese historiography*. Hollywood, 1955.

Hay, Malcolm. *Failure in the Far East*. London, 1956.

Harris, George L. "The mission of Matteo Ricci, S.J. ." *Monumenta Serica* 25 (1966): 1–167.

Havret, Henri S.J. *La stèle chrétienne de Si-ngan-fou.* Variétés Sinologiques no. 7, 12 & 20. T'ou-sè-wè, 1895–1902.

Heawood, E. "The relationships of the Ricci maps." *The geographical journal of the Royal Geographical Society* 53 (1919): 271–276.

Heinekamp, Albert. "Ars characteristica und natürliche Sprache bei Leibniz." *Tijdschrift voor Filosofie* 34 (1972): 446–488.

Ho, Ping-t'i. *Studies on the population of China, 1368–1953.* Cambridge, Massachusetts, 1959.

Hsü, Tsung-tse. *Ming-Ch'ing chien Yeh-su-hui shih-i ch'ü t'i-yao.* Taipei, 1958.

Huang, Ray. *1587, a year of no significance.* New Haven, 1981.

Hucker, Charles H. "Governmental organization in the Ming dynasty." *Harvard journal of Asiatic studies* 21 (1952): 1–66.

Hudson, G. F. *Europe and China: a survey of their relations from the earliest times to 1800.* Boston, 1961.

Hummel, Arthur, ed. *Eminent Chinese of the Ch'ing period (1644–1912).* Washington, D.C., 1943.

Iverson, E. *The myth of Egypt and its hieroglyphs.* Copenhagen, 1961.

Janson, Horst W. *Apes and ape lore in the Middle Ages and Renaissance.* London, 1952.

Karlgren, Bernhard. *Philology and ancient China.* Oslo, 1926.

Kearney, Hugh. *Science and change 1500–1700.* New York, 1971.

Kessler, Lawrence D. *K'ang-hsi and the consolidation of Ch'ing rule, 1661–1684.* Chicago, 1976.

Kish, George, ed. *A source book in geography.* Cambridge, Massachusetts, 1978.

Klaproh, Julius. *Verzeichniß der chinesischen und mandschuischen Bücher und Handschriften der königlichen Bibliothek zu Berlin.* Paris, 1822.

König, A. B. *Versuch einer historischen Schilderung der Hauptveränderungen der Religion.* Berlin, 1793.

Kraft, Eva S. "Christian Mentzel, Philippe Couplet, Andreas Cleyer und die chinesische Medizin." in *Festschrift für Wolf Haenisde.* Marburg, 1975.

–. "Christian Mentzels chinesische Geschenk für Kaiser Leopold I." in *Schloß Charlottenburg-Berlin-Preußer, Festschrift für Margarite Kühn.* Munich, 1975.

–. "Die chinesische Büchersammlung des Großen Kurfürsten." in *China und Europa Ausstellungskatalog.* Berlin, 1973.

–. "Frühe chinesische Studien in Berlin." *Medizinhistorisches Journal* 11 (1976): 92–128.

Labhardt, André. "Curiositas. Notes sur l'histoire d'un mot et d'une notion." *Museum Helveticum* 17 (1969): 206–224.

Lach, Donald F. *Asia in the making of Europe.* 5 vols in progress. Chicago, 1965–.

–. "The Chinese studies of Andreas Müller." *Journal of the American Oriental Society* 60 (1940): 564–575.

–. "Contributions of China to German civilization, 1648–1740." Doctoral dissertation, University of Chicago, 1941.

Lamalle, Edmond, S.I. "La propagande du P. Nicolas Trigault en faveur des missions de Chine (1616)." *Archivum historicum Societatis Iesu* 9 (1940): 49–120.

Legge, James. *The Nestorian Monument of Hsi-an-fu.* London, 1888.

Latourette, Kenneth Scott. *A history of Christian missions in China.* London, 1929.

Leites, Edmund. "Confucianism in eighteenth-century England: natural morality and social reform." *Philosophy East & West* 28 (1978): 143–159.

Levenson, Joseph R. *Confucian China and its modern fate.* 3 vols. Berkeley, 1958–1965.

Lin Jin Shui, "Li Ma-t'ou tsai Chung-kuo huo-tung yü ying-hsiang," *Lishi yangjiu* 1 (1983).

Liu, James T. C. "How did Neo-Confucianism become a state orthodoxy?" *Philosophy East & West* 23 (1973): 483–505.

—. "What can be done with China?" *China notes* 12 (spring 1979): 65–67.

Lohmeier, Dieter. "Vom Nutzbarkeit der frembden Reysen. Rechtfertigungen des Reisens in Zeitalter der Entdeckungen." in *Trier Beitrage* 1979, Sonderheft 3, pp. 3–8.

Lu, Shih-chiang. "Yu Ming-Ch'ing chih chi Chung-kuo chih-shih fen-tzu Fan-Chiao yen-lun k'an Chung-Hsi wen-hua chiao-liu." in *International Symposium on Chinese-Western Cultural Interchange*. Taipei, 1983. pp. 407–430. Reprinted in *China Mission studies (1550–1800) bulletin* 6 (1984): 1–42.

Lui, Adam Y. C. *Corruption in China during the early Ch'ing period 1644–1660*. Hong Kong, 1979.

Lundbaek, Knud. "Chief Grand Secretary Chang Chü-cheng & the early China Jesuits." *China Mission studies (1550–1800) bulletin* 3 (1981): 2–11.

—. "The first translation from a Confucian Classic in Europe." *China Mission studies (1550–1800) bulletin* 1 (1979): 1–11.

—. "The image of Neo-Confucianism in *Confucius Sinarum philosophus*." *Journal of the history of ideas* 44 (1983): 19–30.

—. "Imaginary ancient Chinese characters." *China Mission studies (1550–1800) bulletin* 5 (1983): 5–23.

—. "Kinesiske fantasitegn." *Denmark Kina* 67 (April-May 1981): 10–12.

—. "Notes sur l'image du néo-confucianisme dans la littérature européene du XVIIe a la fin du XIXe siècle." in *Acts du IIIe colloque international de sinologie de Chantilly*. Paris, 1983. pp. 131–176.

—. *T. S. Bayer (1694–1738) — pioneer sinologist*. forthcoming.

Ma, Yong. "Chin-tai Ou-chou Han-hsüeh-chia te hsien-ch'ü Ma-erh-ti-ni." *Lishi yanjiu* 6 (1980): 153–168.

Marrou, Henri-Irénée. *Saint Augustin et la fin de la culture antique*. Paris, 1938.

McCracken, George E. "Athanasius Kircher's universal polygraphy." *Isis* 39 (1948): 215–228.

Melis, Giorgio. "Chinese philosophy and Classics in the works of Martino Martini, S.J. (1614–1661)." in *International Symposium on Chinese-Western Cultural Interchange*. Taipei, 1983. pp. 473–513.

Merkel, R. F. "Deutsche Chinaforscher." *Archiv für Kulturgeschichte* 34 (1951): 81–106.

Miyazaki, Ichisada. *China's examination hell*. Translated by Conrad Schirokauer. New Haven, 1981.

Moule, A. C. "The first arrival of the Jesuits at the capital of China." *The new China review* 4 (1922): 450–456.

Müller, Kurt & Gisela Krönert. *Leben und Werk von G. W. Leibniz, eine Chronik*. Frankfurt am Main, 1969.

Mungello, David E. "The first complete translation of the Confucian Four Books in the West." in *International Symposium on Chinese-Western Cultural Interchange*. Taipei, 1983. pp. 515–541.

—. "The Jesuits' use of Chang Chü-cheng's Commentary in their translation of the Confucian Four Books (1687)." *China Mission studies (1550–1800) bulletin* 3 (1981): 12–22.

—. *Leibniz & Confucianism: the search for accord*. Honolulu, 1977.

—. "Malebranche and Chinese philosophy." *Journal of the history of ideas* 41 (1980): 551–578.

—. "Die Quellen für das Chinabild Leibnizens." *Studia Leibnitiana* 14 (1982): 233–243.

—. "The Reconciliation of Neo-Confucianism with Christianity in the writings of Joseph de Prémare, S.J. ." *Philosophy East & West* 26 (1976): 389–410.

—. "The seventeenth-century Jesuit translation-project of the Confucian Four Books." in *East meets West: the Jesuits in China (1582–1773)*. forthcoming.

—. "Die Schrift T'ien-hsüeh ch'uan-kai als eine Zwischenformulierung der jesuitischen

Anpassungsmethode im 17. Jahrhundert." *China Mission studies (1550–1800) bulletin* 4 (1982): 24–39.

–. "Sinological torque: the influence of cultural preoccupations on seventeenth-century missionary interpretations of Confucianism." *Philosophy East & West* 28 (1978): 123–141.

Needham, Joseph. *Science and civilisation in China.* 7 vols. in progress. Cambridge, 1954–.

Neill, Stephen. *A history of Christian missions.* Harmondsworth, Middlesex, England, 1964.

Neumann, K. F. "Claude Visdelou und das Verzeichniss seiner Werke." *Zeitschrift der Deutschen Morgenländischen Gesellschaft* 4 (1850): 225–242.

New Catholic encyclopedia. vol. 8. Washington, D.C., 1967.

Ornstein, Martha. *The role of scientific societies in the seventeenth century.* Chicago, 1928.

Parker, E. H. "Letters from a Chinese empress and a Chinese eunuch to the Pope in the year 1650." *Contemporary review* (January 1912): 79–83.

Pelliot, Paul. "Inventaire sommaire des manuscrits et imprimés chinois de la Bibliothèque Vaticane." 1922.

–. "Michel Boym." *T'oung pao* 31 (1935): 95–151.

Peterson, Willard J. "From interest to indifference: Fang I-chih and Western learning." *Ch'ing-shih wen-t'i* (1976): 60–80.

–. "Fang I-chih: Western learning and the 'Investigation of Things.' " in *The unfolding of Neo-Confucianism.* Edited by Wm. Theodore de Bary. New York, 1975. pp. 369–411.

–. "Western natural philosophy published in late Ming China." *Proceedings of the American Philosophical Society* 117 (1973): 295–322.

Pfister, Louis [Aloys], S.J. *Notices biographiques et bibliographiques sur les Jésuites de l'ancienne mission de Chine, 1552–1773.* 2 vols. Shanghai, 1932–1934.

Pih, Irene. *Le Père Gabriel de Magalhaes un Jesuite portugais en Chine au XVIIe siècle.* Paris, 1979.

Pinot, Virgile. *La Chine et la formation de l'esprit philosophique en France (1640–1740).* Paris, 1932.

Rawski, Evelyn Sakakida. *Education and popular literacy in Ch'ing China.* Ann Arbor, 1979.

Reichwein, Adolf. *China and Europe: intellectual and artistic contacts in eighteenth-century Europe.* Translated by J. C. Powell. London, 1925.

Reil, Sebald. *Kilian Stumpf 1655–1720, ein Würzburger Jesuit am Kaiserhof zu Peking.* Münster Westfalen, 1978.

Reinhard, Wolfgang. "Gelenkter Kulturwandel im siebzehnten Jahrhundert. Akkulturation in den Jesuitenmissionen als universalhistorisches Problem." *Historische Zeitschrift* 223 (1976): 529–590.

–. *Geschichte der europäischen Expansion.* vol. I: die alte Welt bis 1818. Stuttgart, 1983.

Rémusat, Jean-Pierre-Abel. *Mélanges asiatiques.* 2 vols. Paris, 1825–1826.

Rescher, Nicholas. *The philosophy of Leibniz.* Englewood Cliffs, New Jersey, 1967.

Richthofen, Ferdinand Freiherr von. *China. Ergebnisse eigener Reisen.* 5 vols. Berlin, 1877.

Rosso, Antonio Sisto. *Apostolic legations to China of the eighteenth century.* South Pasadena, 1948.

Rouleau, Francis A., S.I. "Maillard de Tournon, Papal Legate at the Court of Peking." *Archivum historicum Societatis Iesu* 31 (1962): 264–323.

–. "The first Chinese priest of the Society of Jesus, Emmanuel de Siqueira (1633–1673) Cheng Ma-no Wei-hsin." *Archivum historicum Societatis Iesu* 28 (1959): 3–50.

Rowbotham, Arnold H. "The Jesuit Figurists and eighteenth century religious thought." *Journal of the history of ideas* 17 (1956): 471–485.

–. *Missionary and Mandarin: the Jesuits at the Court of China.* Berkeley, 1942.

Rule, Paul A. "The Confucian interpretation of the Jesuits." *Papers on Far Eastern history* (Canberra) 6 (1972): 1–61.

Saeki, P. Y. *The Nestorian Monument in China.* London, 1916.

Santillana, Giorgio de. *The crime of Galileo.* Chicago, 1955.

Sarton, George. *History of science.* Baltimore, 1947. vol. 3.

Schofield, Robert E. "Histories of scientific societies: needs and opportunities for research." *History of science* (Cambridge) 2 (1963): 70–83.

Schott, Wilhelm. *Verzeichniss der chinesischen und Mandschu-Tungusischen Bücher und Handschriften der Königlichen Bibliothek zu Berlin.* Berlin, 1840.

Shryock, John K. *The origin and development of the state cult of Confucius.* New York, 1932.

Shumaker, Wayne. *The occult sciences in the Renaissance: a study in intellectual patterns.* Berkeley, 1972.

Simon, Walter. "The attribution to Michael Boym of two early achievements of Western sinology." *Asia major* new series 7 (1959): 165–169.

Sivin, Nathan. "Copernicus in China." *Studia Copernicana* 6 (1973): 63–122.

Sommervogel, Carlos, S.J. *Bibliothèque de la Compagnie de Jésus.* 12 vols. Brussels & Paris, 1890–1932.

Spence, Jonathan D. & John D. Wills, Jr. *From Ming to Ch'ing: conquest, region and continuity in seventeenth-century China.* New Haven, 1979.

Stimson, Dorothy. "Dr. Wilkins and the Royal Society." *The journal of modern history* 3 (1931): 539–563.

Streit, Robert, O.M.I. *Bibliotheca Missionum.* vols V & VII. Rome, 1929–1931.

Szcześniak, Boleslaw. "Athanasius Kircher's *China illustrata.*" *Osiris* 10 (1952): 385–411.

–. "The beginnings of Chinese lexicography in Europe with particular reference to the work of Michael Boym (1612–1659)." *Journal of the American Oriental Society* 67 (1947): 160–165.

–. "Matteo Ricci's maps of China." *Imago mundi* (Leiden) 11 (1954): 126–136.

–. "The seventeenth century maps of China: an inquiry into the compilations of European cartographers." *Imago mundi* (Leiden) 13 (1956): 116–136.

–. "The writings of Michael Boym." *Monumenta Serica* 14 (1949–1955): 481–538.

T'an, Cheng-pi, ed. *Chung-kuo wen-hsüeh-chia ta-tz'u-tien.* 2 vols. Shanghai, 1934; reprinted Taipei, 1974.

Treadgold, Donald W. *The West in Russia and China.* vol. 2: China 1582–1949. Cambridge, 1973.

Tu, Wei-ming. *Centrality and commonality: an essay on Chung-yung.* Honolulu, 1976.

–. "Reconstructing the Confucian tradition." *Journal of Asian studies* 33 (1974): 441–454.

Übelhör, Monika. "Geistesströmungen der späten Ming-Zeit, die das Wirken der Jesuiten in China begünstigten." *Saeculum* 23 (1972): 172–185.

–. "Hsü Kuang-ch'i (1562–1633) und seine Einstellung zum Christentum." *Oriens Extremus* 14–15 (1967–1968): 191–257 & 16 (1969): 41–76.

U.S. Library of Congress. *Kuo-hui t'u-shu-kuan-ts'ang Chung-kuo shan-pen shu-lu* (A descriptive catalog of rare Chinese books in the Library of Congress). Compiled by Wang Chung-min. Edited by T. L. Yuan. 2 vols. Washington, D.C., 1957.

Van Kley, Edwin J. "An alternate muse: the Manchu conquest of China in the literature of seventeenth-century northern Europe." *European studies review* 6 (1976): 21–43.

–. "Europe's 'discovery' of China and the writing of world history." *American historical review* 76 (1971): 358–385.

–. "News from China: seventeenth-century European notices of the Manchu conquest." *Journal of modern history* 45 (1973): 561–582.

Verhaeren, H., C.M. *Catalogue de la bibliothèque du Pé-t'ang.* Peking, 1949; reprinted Paris, 1969.

Waldeck, C. F. "Le Père Philippe Couplet, Malinos, S.J. ." *Analectes pour servir a l'histoire ecclésiastique de la Belgique.* 9 (1872): 5–33.

Walker, Daniel P. *The Ancient Theology.* London, 1972.

–. "Leibniz and language." *Journal of the Warburg and Courtauld Institutes* 35 (1972): 294–307.

Walravens, Hartmut. "Eine Anmerkung zu Michael Boyms *Flora Sinensis* (1656) – einer wichtigen naturhistorischen Quelle." *China Mission studies (1550–1800) bulletin* 1 (1979): 16–20.

Wehr, Hans. "Andreas Müller." *Pommersche Lebensbilder* (Cologne) 4 (1966): 21–35.

Widmaier, Rita. "Die Rolle der chinesischen Schrift in Leibniz' Zeichentheorie." *Studia Leibnitiana* 13 (2) (1981): 278–298.

–. *Die Rolle der chinesischen Schrift in Leibniz' Zeichentheorie.* Studia Leibnitiana Supplementa vol. 24. Wiesbaden, 1983.

Wiener, Philip P. "Leibniz's project of a public exhibition of scientific inventions." in Philip P. Wiener & Aaron Noland, eds. . *Roots of scientific thought.* New York, 1957. pp. 460–468.

Wills, John E., Jr. *Pepper, guns and parleys: the Dutch East India Company and China, 1662–1681.* Cambridge, Massachusetts, 1974.

–. "Some Dutch sources on the Jesuit China mission, 1662–1687." *Archivum historicum Societatis Iesu,* forthcoming.

Witek, John W. *Controversial ideas in China and in Europe: a biography of Jean-François Foucquet, S.J. (1665–1741).* Rome, 1982.

–. "Jean-François Foucquet: un controversiste Jesuite en Chine et en Europe." in *Acts du colloque international de sinologie, Chantilly, 1974.* Paris, 1976. pp. 115–135.

Wittkower, Rudolf. *Art & architecture in Italy 1600 to 1750.* Harmondsworth, Middlesex, England, 1958.

Wong, George H. C. "The anti-Christian movement in China: the late Ming and early Ch'ing." *Tsing Hua journal of Chinese studies* new series 3. 1 (1962): 187–222.

Yates, Frances. *The art of memory.* London, 1966.

–. The Art of Ramon Lull." *Journal of the Warburg & Courtauld Institutes* 17 (1954): 115–173.

–. *Giordano Bruno and the Hermetic tradition.* New York, 1964.

Young, John D. *Confucianism and Christianity: the first encounter.* Hong Kong, 1983.

–. "The early Confucian attack on Christianity: Yang Kuang-hsien and his *Pu-te-i.*" Journal of the Chinese University of Hong Kong 3 (1975): 155–186.

–. "Original Confucianism versus Neo-Confucianism in Matteo Ricci's Chinese writings." in *International Congress of Orientalists (29th).* Paris, 1973.

Zacher, Hans J. *Die Hauptschriften zur Dyadik von G. W. Leibniz.* Frankfurt am Main, 1973.

Zürcher, E. *The Buddhist conquest of China.* Leiden, 1959.

–. "The first anti-Christian movement in China." in P. W. Pestman, ed. *Acta Orientalia Neederlandica: Proceedings of the Congress of the Dutch Oriental Society held in Leiden on the occasion of its fiftieth anniversary.* Leiden, 1971. pp. 188–195.

INDEX

Abacus: 86

Académie des Sciences, Paris: founding of, 32, 34; Leibniz encountered, 33; interest in practical affairs, 36; questions about China from, 255–256; Louis XIV capitalized on, 329

Accademie dei Lincei, Rome: 32

Accademia del Cimento, Florence: 32

Acquaviva, Fr. Claude (Jesuit General): 46, 47

Acquinas, St. Thomas: 284

Acta eruditorum: 289, 293

Acta Sanctorum: 43, 287

Adam: Primitive Language of, 16, 34, 175; Biblical teachings carried to China by descendants of, 93, 105; as patriarch of Chinese, 94; as an Ancient Theologian, 307; fall from grace of, 325; Chinese as direct descendants of, 336; used to assimilate China with Biblical experience, 358

Adamitic language: 192

Advancement of learning (Bacon): 184

Agathe, Lady (Mrs. T'ung Kuo-ch'i): 254n

Aggression of Chinese: 66–67

Agnès, Lady (daughter of Yang T'ing-yün): 254n

Akademie der Wissenschaften, Berlin: 32, 34

Alchemy: 70–72, 351

Alexander VI (Pope): 24

Alexander VII (Pope): 109, 140, 255

Alexander von Humboldt-Stiftung (AvH): 21, 22

Alexandria library destruction: 263

Algebra: 86

A-lo-pen: 165, 167

Alphabet of human thought: 192. See also Universal Characteristic.

Alphabet of the Art: 176

Amateur: 37; sinologists, 77; versus specialist ideal, 286

Amiot, Fr. Joseph-Marie (Ch'ien Te-ming): 309, 345n

Amphitrite: 302

Analects. See *Lun yü*

Ancestors: rites to, 64; of Confucius, 271

Ancient Chinese: 64, 346, 349

Ancient sage-emperors: 307

Ancient Theology *(prisca theologia):* 137, 307–310; thinkers affected by, 316; Bouvet as believer in, 321; See also Hermetism and Figurism

Ancients: 13n, 30, 84; as possessing the *Tao*, 345

Andreae Don Sin: 134n

Annales veteris et Novi Testamenti (Ussher): 125

Anti-accommodation: 14–15, 293

Anti-Christian movement: of Yang Kuang-hsien, 93, 252, 253n; persecution of 1615 (1617?), 266

Anti-Confucianism: 56, 84

Anti-Jesuits: use of Le Comte's *Nouveaux mémoires*, 332; victory of, 357

Antiquity: 30, 63; of China, 336, 342

Ape: as *figura diaboli,* 151; *ars simia natura,* 151–153

Ariadne's thread: 196

Aristotelianism: as creative froce, 25; Jesuits as leaders in breaking away from, 28; criticized by Bacon, 32; Padua as vital center of, 40; universal language schemes' classification similar to, 191

Aristotelian-Ptolemaic worldview: 26–27, 66

Aristotelian-Thomistic classification: 320

Aristotle: as a pagan philosopher, 57; logic of, 58

Arnauld, Antoine: 340

Ars brevis (Lull): 176

Ars Characteristica: 192

Ars Combinatoria (Combinatory Art) of R. Lull: search for a universal language drew upon, 35; as historically influential, 177; used by Kircher, 180, 186, 219; Leibniz on, 192, 194, 196, 197; as shaping European assimilation of China, 207. See also Lullian Art

ward the *Clavis Sinica,* 198; interest in sinology, 208–209; learned of Müller, 210; poverty of Brandenburg, 214; interest in Müller's *Clavis Sinica,* 215; physician to, 225; toleration edict of, 230; opposition to publication of *Clavis Sinica,* 234; Mentzel's service of, 237; invitation to Couplet, 238; promoted Chinese collection, 244

Friendship: theme of Martini & Ricci, 109–110

Fu Hsi: compared to Hermes Trismegistus, 31; invented Chinese characters, 78, 144, 147, 182, 202, 205, 320; invented moral & speculative sciences of China, 83; descendant of Adam, 93–94; founder of China, 103; Martini dated history from, 124, 126; reign dated form 2952 B.C., 127; inventor of the trigrams & hexagrams, 128–129; omitted from Chinese chronology, 131; lined figures of, 206, 313, 314, 319, 321; as one of first Chinese, 239; as author of *I ching,* 265; never referred to *T'ai-chi,* 266; as predating Biblical Flood, 288; dragon-knight of, 295; as an Ancient Theologian, 307; as "Prince of Philosophers", 315; created a numerological metaphysic, 316; numerical system of compared to Plato, 317; philosophy of as lost, 318, fictional historical treatment of period of, 326; omitted from Couplet's chronology, 335n; Martini began Chinese history with, 336; as universal lawgiver, 356

Fu-huo-lun (Magalhaes): 95

Furtado, Fr. Francisco (Fu Fan-chi): 92

Gabiani, Fr. Giandomenico (Pi Chia): 252, 297

Galen: school of medicine of, 40; doctrine of homours of, 41

Galileo: 35

Gaubil, Fr. Antoine (Sung Chün-yung): 309

Gautama. See Buddha, Sakyamuni

Genesis: 76, 144, 175, 177, 179, 183

Gentry: 82

Geography: of Middle Kingdom, 16

German nationalism: 194

Gerbillon, Fr. Jean-François (Chang Ch'eng): in first French mission to China, 256,

329; ordered to reside in Peking, 300, 330; supplied information of languages of East Asia, 312; scientific treatises of, 331; in negotiations at Nerchinsk, 344

Gernet, Jacques: 66, 357

Goa: 251, 257

God: ancients as maintaining contact with, 30; Primitive Language given to Adam by, 34; placed above family in Christianity unlike in Confucianism, 45; ancient Chinese worshipped 63, 91, 248; of Old Testament, 74; the highest good as interpreted trough *Ta-hsüeh,* 102; Egyptian hieroglyphs as containing secret truths about, 146; in Leibniz' arrangement, 187; as first cause, 189; created the world, 193; Bouvet on ancient Chinese Supreme Being, 204; Chinese word for, 230–233, as influencing interpretation of Confucianism, 249; anticipated by "unknown god", 276; Chinese belief in, 285–286; King Wen standing at side of, 295; as Creator, 325; Chinese knowledge of, 337–338; absence of in Neo-Confucianism, 347, 348; Buddha as a, 349

Golden Rule: 63

Golius (Gool), Jacobus: met Martini, 108; composed appendix to *Novus atlas Sinensis,* 116; claimed that Chinese characters were constructed by art, 190, 206; Martini's grammar allegedly left with, 203; Müller visited, 210

Gollet, Fr. Jean-Alexis (Kuo Chung-ch'uan): 308, 310

Gospel: 161

Gouvea, Fr. Antonio de (Ho Ta-hua): 251–252, 297

Grace: 17, 325, 333, 338–340, 352

Granet, Marcel: 129

Great Appendix *(Hsi tzu):* 129, 272, 348

Great Elector. See Friedrich Wilhelm

Great learning. See *Ta hsüeh*

Grebnitz, Elias: 230–234

Greece: religions of, 163

Gregorian calendar: 359

Gregory XIII (Pope): 359

Grelon (Greslon), Fr. Adrien (Nieh Chung-ch'ien): 251, 297

Grimaldi, Fr. Claudio Filippo (Min Ming-wo): returned to Europe as procurator 254, 301; met Leibniz, 288

ERRATA

p. 14, l. 3: which referred to — something remarkable that required

p. 20, l. 31: which with

p. 42, l. 34: 1770 1700

p. 46, n. 6, ll. 1–2 et passim: Li Ma-t'ou Li Ma-tou

p. 46, n. 6, l. 5: Wu Wang Su-i (composer) and Tsai Yang-nien (illustrator)

p. 46, n. 6, l. 7: *Lishi yangjiu* *Lishi yanjiu*

p. 103, ll. 30–31: chronology from the reign of Huang-ti (the Yellow Emperor) in 2697 B.C. history from the time of Fu Hsi in 2952 B.C.

p. 107, l. 1: Chu Yü chien Chu Yu-chien

p. 108, l. 27: (Antwerp 1655) (Munich 1658)

p. 124, l. 9: 1962 1692

p. 132, table: sole ruler first ruler

p. 140, l. 20: Gratz Graz

p. 144, ll. 23–24: Nimrod — *Genesis* 10: 6–8 treats Nimrod as Ham's grandson — and Nimrod Nesraim, i.e. Mizraim (Egypt), and Nesraim

p. 146, l. 9: 1664 1643

p. 148, plate 8, l. 8: *Ch'uan shu shen Nung Wang* *Ch'uan shu Shen Nung Wang*

p. 150, ll. 11–12: "Sinensis ex Annalium" "Sinensis Annalium"

p. 161, ll. 8–9: "persons who are offended by science" "persons who pride themselves on their science" *(les personnes qui se piquoient de science)*

p. 161, n. 79, add: & Kircher, *La Chine illustrée,* pp. 177–178.

p. 165, l. 13: Roman emperor Byzantine emperor

p. 169, l. 22: Ernst Renan Ernest Renan

p. 169, l. 23: Semetic Semitic

p. 175, l. 30: Scotus Erigina Scotus Erigena

p. 185, n. 32, l. 3: Peirese Peiresc

p. 195, l. 26: Congregation Congregatio

p. 204, n. 95, l. 5, middle, add: (A copy of the letter is also preserved in the Bibliothèque Nationale Paris, MS. fr. 17 240, ff. 75–88.)

p. 208, l. 29: Vereingte Vereinigte

p. 219, l. 9: *combinatoriae artis* *combinatoria ars*

p. 230, l. 30: *Exodus* 20: 14 *Exodus* 20: 4

p. 241, n. 89, l. 2: 117,7 — 117,1

p. 247, l. 15: forever — forever[1].

p. 250, n. 5, l. 2: Geistleben — Geistesleben

p. 253, n. 19, l. 5: 1623 — 1622

p. 262, l. 28: extensivenese — extensiveness

p. 293, ll. 14–15: Aymonio — Aymonius

p. 298, n. 171, l. 8: remained in manuscript until it was carried back to Europe — was transmitted to the Propaganda in Rome (along with a copy given to Navarrete)

p. 300, l. 13: 1688 — 1687

p. 302, n. 5, l. 4: *l'Amphrite* — *l'Amphitrite*

p. 305, l. 36: Ricci's time — Bouvet's time

p. 309, l. 2: Stumpf (1673– — Stumpf (1655–

p. 309, l. 15: Perhaps the first recorded instance — One of the first recorded instances

p. 326, ll. 21–22: Bouvet produced no works of substance in his later years — Bouvet's works written after 1700 were suppressed because of the Rites Controversy

p. 326, n. 84, ll. 9–10: Bouvet's literary production was unprolific and disappointing — Bouvet's literary works have been less accessible

p. 330, ll.18–19: three and one-half years — four and one-half years

p. 330, l. 30: Le Comte's mere three and one-half years — Le Comte's mere four and one-half years

p. 341, ll. 31–32: his three and one-half years in China — his four and one-half years in China

p. 370, l. 19: *Vivi illustris* — *Viri illustris*

p. 375, l. 51: *Lishi yangjiu* — *Lishi yanjiu*

p. 404, l. 1: Trigault, Fr. Nicolas (Chin Ssu-piao) — Trigault, Fr. Nicolas (Chin Ni-ko (*tzu* Ssu-piao))